AF651311

The Encyclopedia of Dream Interpretation

From bees to tarantulas, from robberies to gold, interpret the world of the subconscious mind and unfold the path that lies ahead.

The Encyclopedia of Dream Interpretation

Eili Goldberg

New Age Books

ISBN: 978-81-7822-348-3

First Indian Edition: Delhi, 2010

First published by Astrolog Publishing House Ltd. 2003

Published by
NEW AGE BOOKS
A-44 Naraina Industrial Area, Phase-I
New Delhi (India)-110 028
Email: nab@vsnl.in
Website: www.newagebooksindia.com

For Sale in Indian Subcontinent Only

Printed in India
at Swan Press
B-71 Naraina Indl. Area, Phase-II, New Delhi-110 028

PUBLISHER'S NOTE

The publishers present here an exemplary collection of interpretations from the subconscious world. Whilst many of us awaken, perturbed by images created by the impulses of our mind, a rare few as Eili Goldberg have mastered an exit to this chaos. The author gives the highest cliff or the deepest trench the most fragrant flowers or the most poisonous scorpions, a simple definition that directly relates to our life and environment. It is our strong belief that the same will help many more who render this dictionary, a faithful reading. The Publishers take this opportunity to thank Shri Rajeev Jain for obtaining this masterpiece from Frankfurt Book Fair. The Index has been compiled by Mrs. Kusum Lata. Warm thanks are also extended for the cooperation and encouragement from CEO, Mrs. Jyotsna Khandelwal.

Editor
New Age Books

CONTENTS

PREFACE

The Encyclopedia of Dream Interpretation is the fruit of six year's hard labour, during which the author went through some eighty different dictionaries of dream interpretation in various languages. These volumes included dictionaries from Ancient Egypt, Greece and Rome, the Middle Ages in Europe and the Far East, and modern dictionaries that began to appear as a result of the influence of Freud and Jung.

As opposed to many dictionaries of dreams in which the interpretation is give in a word or brief sentence, the author has delved into and expanded on the various interpretations. If you dreamed about a butterfly, you can look up "butterfly" and find a broad interpretation of butterflies in general, and additional interpretations of a butterfly that is flying, being pursued or resting, several butterflies, and so on. If you dreamed about a chain, you will find interpretations for an open chain, a gold chain, a valuable chain, a thick chain, and so on. Every entry is elaborated upon in many secondary entries.

Wherever the word "dreamer" appears in the dictionary, it refers to either a male or a female. For the sake of brevity, the dreamer has been referred to as "he" unless a woman is specifically addressed

A

Abandonment

It is important to know who is doing the abandoning in the dream. If it is the dreamer himself, it attests to a certain disappointment that he will experience soon and that will cause him to change his opinions about a topic that was considered stable up till now. It is very possible that a problem in his personal relationship is liable to crop up suddenly, and will turn out to be more complex than it appeared on the surface. Alternatively, a simple argument at work will develop into an exhausting power struggle. This will cause the dreamer to reassess his situation. Chances are that he will decide to leave, whether it is because of a personal struggle or because of something in the field of his occupation. If another figure appears in the dream and abandons the dreamer, it is a hint at a painful departure and separation. It is also possible that the dreamer feels anxiety and fear about that close person because he is so afraid that the latter will leave. A pleasant conversation will help clarify the uncertainty.

Abbey

If a young woman dreams that she enters an abbey, the dream predicts that she will succumb to a serious illness. If the abbey in the dream is dilapidated and in ruins, it attests to the fact that the dreamer can expect his plans to fail and his hopes to crash.

If the dreamer wishes to enter an abbey, but finds a priest barring his way, it means that the dreamer will be spared humiliation and shame at the hands of his enemies.

Abdomen

In general, a dream that features a person's abdomen does not augur well. A dream about an abdomen usually indicates great expectations. If a person sees a hollow and shrunken abdomen in his dream, it means that he will be hounded and betrayed by treacherous friends. Conversely, if the abdomen in the dream is swollen, the dreamer is about to face difficulties, but will eventually overcome them. If the dreamer sees a bleeding abdomen in his dream, it is a warning dream: some kind of disaster will befall his family.

Abhorrence

A dream about abhorring someone indicates that the dreamer's feeling of loathing for that person is entirely justified. If the dreamer himself is abhorred by other people, he will no longer feel kindly toward them – his altruistic feelings will soon become egoistic. If a woman dreams that her lover abhors her, the dream warns her that she has chosen the wrong man and should rectify the situation as quickly as possible.

Abode

In general, dreams about an abode have negative

A B C D E F G H I J K L M N O P Q R S T U V W X Y Z

connotations. If a person dreams that he does not have an abode, he is about to experience bad luck in financial matters. If he wanders around looking for his abode, but does not find it, it means that he has lost his faith in other people's integrity. A dream about a change of abode implies that the dreamer will receive urgent tidings and will have to depart on a journey. If a young woman dreams that she leaves her abode, it means that she is the object of vicious gossip and slander.

Abroad

A dream about a visit abroad is a positive dream that foretells and enjoyable trip to a foreign country in the company of other people in the near future.

Abscess

If a person dreams that he is suffering from an abscess, he can expect enormous problems and vicissitudes in the near future. To add insult to injury, he will have to comfort other people in their hour of need.

Absence

If a person dreams that a friend of his is absent, it brings him the good news that he will soon be rid of one of his adversaries.

Abundance

A dream about abundance attests to the dreamer's achievement-oriented nature. It is a kind of warning dream according to which the infinitely ambitious dreamer, on his way to realizing his dream of becoming wealthy, must not forget the people around him who love him. A dream about abundance indicates that the dreamer can definitely look forward to great abundance in his life; he will possess a great deal of money and property. However, despite his aspiration to succeed, and his almost unrestrained ambition for achievements and positions of power, he will only be successful as a result of hard work. The dream warns against neglecting his primary obligations in life, such as his home and family, on the path to success. Moreover, there is a hint that he should refrain from accomplishing his goals at any cost, and that he should carefully weigh up the price his loved ones will pay for his obsession.

Abuse

In general, a dream about abuse is a negative dream. If the dreamer himself abuses someone, it is a warning dream about financial losses. If the dreamer is abused by someone else, his enemies will make him suffer and will harm him. If someone directs verbal abuse at a young woman, it means that someone is jealous of her. If she herself dreams that she uses abusive language to other people, her friends will reject her because of the way she treated them

Abyss

If a person dreams about falling into an abyss and surviving, it is a warning dream against loaning money to a friend. The dream implies that the dreamer will not see his money again, since the friend has no possibility or desire to return the money he borrowed.

If the dreamer looks down into the abyss in the dream, it

is a sign that he is in danger and may not be aware of it at all. The dream serves to clarify to the dreamer that he must take immediate steps in order to prevent the danger he is in. If he acts spontaneously and without delay, the danger will most likely pass.

If a person dreams that he rescues a hiker from an abyss into which he has fallen, the dream predicts that very soon the dreamer will enjoy fame and honor. He will be held in high regard by the people around him because of an extremely daring action or deed. The dreamer will find his new status very much to his liking, and he will enjoy other people's adulation.

Academy

A dream about an academy generally attests to the dreamer's lack of initiative and drive. If he visits an academy, he will realize that he has missed many opportunities in life because of his indifferent and apathetic nature, and he will be filled with regret. If he dreams that he is a member of an academy, it indicates that he is incapable of applying his theoretical knowledge in the practical realm. If he returns to an academy in a dream, it means that impossible demands are being made on him.

Acceptance

If a person dreams that the person he loves accepts his offer of marriage, he will enjoy a life of married bliss. If a businessman dreams that he clinches a deal, it means that things are looking up for him: after a period of losses and failure, he will enjoy some success.

Accident

The meaning of a dream like this changes in accordance with the type of accident that occurs in the dream:

If a person dreams that he is involved in a hit-and-run accident, he can expect to be fined for smuggling something through customs. Therefore, if he has not yet reached the point of actually breaking the law, the dream tells him that it is not worth his while to do so and that he should stop himself before it is too late.

A dream about a multiple collision is a sign that the dreamer can expect losses in the financial realm and that he has to prepare himself as soon as possible if he wants to prevent the expected deterioration in the situation.

If a person dreams that he is the cause of an accident, the dreams contains a hint that he is in mortal danger. He should go for a general checkup in order to ensure that he is not coming down with some disease, and at the same time, he should be wide awake on the roads and in any other place where his life could be in danger.

If a person dreams that one of the members of his family is involved in an accident, most likely some family member is about to sue for compensation.

If an accident involving a public transportation vehicle occurs, the dream implies that the dreamer can soon expect to make the acquaintance of a very powerful and positive person. The latter will make him aware of the positive side of his own personality, will get him to contribute to the community and will bring out the good sides in him.

If a person dreams that he is involved in an accident at sea, he can expect a disappointment in a love affair. The dreamer had high hopes for a life together with the partner

A B C D E F G H I J K L M N O P Q R S T U V W X Y Z

at his side, but the latter has apparently let him down, and his/her intentions are different than those of the dreamer.

If an accident occurs in the air – in an airplane, a helicopter, a parachute, and so on – the dreamer must refrain from taking business risks in the near future. He must adopt an aggressive attitude in anything to do with business, otherwise he will find himself exploited by various elements that know how to identify other people's weaknesses and exploit them.

If a person dreams that he is involved in a train crash, the dream warns him about his exaggerated self-confidence, which is liable to be a stumbling-block in his path. The dream implies that the dreamer must be on the alert and exercise extreme caution in financial matters and deals connected with his work.

If the accident in the dream occurs in a distant town or an unfamiliar place, it is a hint at the dreamer's love life. It will not go well, and he can expect disappointments.

If the dreamer is married, his marriage is just about on the rocks, and a process of estrangement from his partner is going to begin. However, if the dreamer has this dream before his relationship has fallen apart totally, there is still a chance of reviving it, and it is not too late to save it.

Accordion

A dream in which the dreamer himself is playing an accordion means that marriage in the offing. The dreamer is about to make a long-time relationship official. Apparently, he debated whether to actually do so or not in the past. The dream hints at the correct direction. If the dreamer is not in a relationship, it is on the horizon, and it will be serious.

A dream in which only the sound of an accordion is heard is a sign that a series of expectations the dreamer was nurturing will prove to be a bitter disappointment. The truth will explode in his face and the dreamer will discover that he was laboring under an illusion.

If a person dreams that he hears an accordion being played with wrong notes, or that he himself plays wrong notes, it is a sign that a disease is incubating in his body. He must have himself checked to find out what the disease is as quickly as possible and treat it. If everything is fine, and the dreamer knows for certain that he is not about to contract a physical disease, the dream hints that mental depression is liable to afflict him. His poor mental state will continue for a limited length of time, and the dreamer will snap out of it relatively quickly.

If a young woman dreams that she is playing an accordion, the dream predicts happiness and triumph in love. It will not come easily, however, but agonizingly, and will entail emotions of pain and sorrow. Ultimately, love will make up for those emotions, but she will not be able to avoid experiencing them if she wants to obtain her heart's desire.

If a dreamer hears a well-known and well-loved song played on the accordion in his dream, it is a hint of a good period in the offing, full of joy and happiness. Joyous events will take place in the near future, and the dreamer will play an important part in them.

A dream that features a gypsy or a street musician standing and playing the accordion is a warning dream: the dreamer must stay away from soothsayers and charlatans of various kinds, and not believe people who pose as seers of the occult and mystics.

A B C D E F G H I J K L M N O P Q R S T U V W X Y Z

Accountant / Accounts (bills)

If a person dreams about an accountant, it means that he has financial problems. If he has a conversation with an accountant, the dream indicates that the dreamer is yearning to improve his standard of living. If a person dreams that he has to pay his accounts, the dream warns him that he is in a dangerous situation. However, if he pays them, a dispute in which he is involved will finally be settled.

Accusation

A dream about an accusation is a clear hint that the dreamer is about to find himself in the center of a row, get into trouble, and be the victim of strife or extortion.

If a person dreams that he has been accused, the dream implies a huge row that is liable to break out in the near future, but it will only cause the dreamer minor damage. He will even emerge from this row fortified, and the people around him will accord him greater respect than before.

If a person sees himself heaping accusations on someone else in a dream, it also means that there is a danger of a row breaking out soon in which the dreamer will be involved, but a dream like this implies a quarrel between the dreamer and his professional partners. If the person does not work with partners, the row will probably involve his family. It is advisable to prevent the row at its very onset and relate to the dream as a warning.

Aches

If a person dreams that he has aches in various parts of

his body, it means that he is not acting with enough initiative and determination, and other people are stealing his ideas and profiting from them. If his heart aches in a dream, it means that he will be devastated by his partner's indifferent attitude toward him. A dream about a backache warns the dreamer of an impending illness. A headache in a dream indicates the fact that the dreamer is in a state of distress because of worries. If the dreamer's jaws ache in a dream, it means that he has an illness that is undermining his general state of health and causing him financial troubles.

Acid

If a person sees himself drinking acid in a dream, it means that he is plagued by profound anxiety. When a dream features toxic acids, it means that the dreamer has found out that people are betraying him.

Acorns

If a dream features whole acorns, it means that the dreamer will be successful in both love and business, and can look forward to good things in life. However, If he sees rotten or broken acorns in his dream, he must brace himself for hardships and disappointments.

Acquaintance

If a young woman dreams that she has many acquaintances, it means that she is very popular with the opposite sex. However, if she dreams that she hardly has any acquaintances, her success with men will be negligible.

If a person dreams of holding an amicable conversation with an acquaintance, things will go smoothly for him at work and at home. If an acquaintance of the dreamer behaves in a belligerent or abusive way toward him, the dream hints that the dreamer is about to be shamed and embarrassed. If the dreamer is ashamed at meeting a particular acquaintance in a dream, it means that a deep dark secret is about to be revealed.

Acquittal

A dream about an acquittal usually augurs well. If the dreamer is on trial for a crime and is acquitted, it means that he is about to come into possession of some property – even though this may involve a legal dispute beforehand. If the dreamer sees other people being acquitted, it means that he has good friends who will make his life happy.

Acrobat

A dream that features an acrobat is a warning dream: it warns the dreamer that he has a dangerous adversary that he is completely unaware of.

If the dreamer sees an acrobat falling from the tightrope or trapeze, it means that someone has been plotting against him, but has failed. If a person dreams that he himself is an acrobat, it means that he is in need of encouragement and reinforcement from the people around him.

Actor / Actress

If a person sees an actor in his dream, it attests to a lack of inner integrity and to the fact that the dreamer feels that he is not acting according to the dictates of his heart. This may sometimes be cause by his desire to fit in with the rules of the game of the society he is in.

The dream may also imply that the person feels that a plot is being devised around him, and people are pretending to support him while actually conspiring against him. The dream should be seen as a kind of warning sign against the people around him who want to hurt him.

A dream about an actor or actress sometimes attests to the dreamer's haughtiness or to his fierce desire to occupy a higher status than the one he has reached. Conceit and the desire to lord it over others stem from some kind of deprivation, and he should sift through his past carefully in order to find the source.

Adam and Eve

A dream that features the biblical Adam and Eve wearing only a fig leaf, as is customary to depict them in the classic manner, implies that the dreamer is in a work environment in which the people around him tend to "steal" ideas from him. Things that he thinks of first, his original ideas, are taken from him and presented as if they were somebody else's ideas. The dreamer is not always aware that this is the situation, and the dream tells him about things that are emerging from his subconscious.

If the dreamer sees himself in the role of "Adam" in the dream, the dream implies that he can expect unusual, exciting and noisy experiences in everything to do with the personal domain. The dreamer is about to undergo pleasurable physical experiences of a kind he did not know existed until now. Even if he thinks that he is very experienced sexually, he still has a lot to learn. He will discover that what he thought to be sensual and sexual experiences up till now were nothing compared to what he is about to experience. (Remember – the dreamer may well be a female!)

If the dreamer sees himself in the role of "Eve" in the dream, the dream prophesies that guilt feelings and a bad conscience will cause the dreamer (generally speaking, a female) to make mistakes that she will regret later on. The dream implies that it is worthwhile looking at things from as objective a point of view as possible before setting out to do things that are liable to turn out to be mistakes (and again, the dreamer may well be a female).

If the dreamer sees Adam and Eve in their Garden of Eden outfits (that is, naked), and their nudity is the focal point of the "scene," the dream hints that an act of treachery and deceit is liable to end in an unexpected surprise. If the dreamer is scheming to cheat on his partner, for instance, or if he is already doing so, the dream implies that he can expect surprises in that connection that will not necessarily be pleasant for him.

Adder

In most cases, a dream about an adder does not augur well.

If a person dreams about an adder, the dream refers to the fact that his friends will suffer misfortunes and he will suffer losses. If a young woman dreams about an adder, it means that she is in jeopardy from a person who is betraying her. However, if she sees the adder slithering away in her dream, it means that she will triumph over the treacherous person.

Adding up figures

Adding up figures incorrectly and reaching a wrong sum in a dream is a sign that the dreamer must be careful of swindlers with whom he is about to enter into negotiations. They are liable to trip him up. He must be on the alert in order to be sure that they are not swindling him. If the dreamer is not sure that he can do this alone, he is advised to consult with a professional and entrust the difficult decisions to him so that the dreamer does not make mistakes that are liable to cost him dearly.

He should leave any commercial negotiations to a professional, but at the same time remain alert to the risk of falling victim to an act of fraud.

Admiration

If the dreamer is accorded admiration in a dream, the dream hints that he will be accepted and liked by colleagues whom he has overtaken in rank.

Adoption

If a dream features the dreamer's adopted child or adoptive parent, it indicates that he is about to enjoy enormous financial profits thanks to strangers' schemes. If a person dreams that he adopts a child, it means that he will make some kind of mistake when he moves to a new home.

Adulation

If a person seeks adulation in a dream, it means that he is about to receive a position of honor that is completely unjustified and undeserved. If he accords someone else adulation in a dream, it means that he will sacrifice something he really values in order to enjoy material benefits.

Adultery

The dreamer is harboring guilt feelings either because he has actually cheated on his partner or has thought about doing so. The dream reflects unsatisfied sexuality and the desire to fulfill it versus the anxiety and fear regarding the consequences of his actions.

· A dream of this kind can sometimes express feelings of jealousy and aggression that are not directly linked to the dreamer's family. There could be a hint of a betrayal of trust at work or among close friends.

Advancement

A dream of advancement is a positive dream. If a person dreams that he is advancing, it means that he will enjoy success in the professional or romantic realm. If other people advance in his dream, it means that his friends will succeed.

Adventurer

If a person dreams that he is being taken advantage of by an adventurer, it is an indication that he is completely naive and incompetent in anything to do with managing his affairs. If a young woman dreams that she is an adventuress, she can rest assured that someone is exploiting her and ruining her reputation.

A
B
C
D
E
F
G
H
I
J
K
L
M
N
O
P
Q
R
S
T
U
V
W
X
Y
Z

Adversary

If a person sees an adversary in his dream, it means that he will succeed in fending off attacks. If he overcomes the adversary, the dream implies that he will have a narrow escape from a disaster.

Adversity

A dream about being in a situation of adversity indicates that the dreamer is about to fail and experience bad luck. If he sees other people in a situation of adversity, it is a sign that he can look forward to melancholy times and failed plans.

Advertisement

In general, a dream about advertising or advertisements does not augur well. If the dreamer advertises, it means that he will have to resort to manual labor if he wants to advance in life. If he reads advertisements in a newspaper, it means that his adversaries will get the better of him.

Advice

If the dreamer receives advice in a dream, it means that his moral integrity has increased. If he seeks legal advice, it means that his ventures and deals are not quite above board.

Advocate

If the dreamer dreams that he is advocating a cause, it means that he is honest and loyal in both his public and personal dealings.

A B C D E F G H I J K L M N O P Q R S T U V W X Y Z

Affliction

If a person dreams about suffering from some kind of affliction, it is a prophetic dream that indicates the advent of some kind of catastrophe. If he dreams about the affliction of other people, the dream implies that the dreamer will see bad luck and hardship all around him.

Affluence

A dream about affluence is a very positive dream: It indicates that the dreamer will enjoy great success in business and will establish profitable ties with rich people.

Affront

In general, a dream about an affront is a negative dream. If a person dreams about being affronted by someone, it means that he will be very upset about something and will actually cry. If a young woman has a dream in which she is affronted, it means that someone will take advantage of her and she will be placed in a compromising situation in which her interests will be jeopardized.

Afraid

If the dreamer dreams that he is feeling afraid, it is a bad sign: he will experience problems at home and losses in his business. If he dreams that other people are afraid, it means that they will not be able to come to the dreamer's assistance because they will be bogged down in their own problems.

Afternoon

If the dream of a woman features the afternoon, it is a sign that she will make friends that will last for a very long time. A dream about a dull, rain-swept afternoon implies dissatisfaction and disillusionment for the dreamer.

Age

A dream in which the dreamer sees himself as significantly older than he is in reality, or sees the people around him in this way (a lot older than they really are) warns of a disease that the dreamer, one of his family members, or someone close and dear to him is about to contract. This is also true of a dreamer who is very worried and bothered by his age in the dream. The dream hints that some kind of health problem will crop up soon. It will not be a serious problem or illness, but rather something that serves as a warning sign for the future. For instance, flu can hint that the dreamer neglects his health and must take better care of himself, or a mild heart attack can imply that the person must change his lifestyle and mend his ways in order to achieve a better quality of life that will promote longevity.

A dream in which the dreamer sees himself as younger than his actual age (which is a more common dream) implies that the dreamer is inclined to get into rows and conflicts with the people around him, and he must find a way to refrain from doing so as much as possible. The less he gets into disputes and rows with other people, the better his general feeling – both mental and physical – will be, since the dreamer is the kind of person who tends to take things to heart. Quarrels, conflicts and disputes are the type of things that directly affect the dreamer's mental and physical state, and he must learn to avoid them as much as he can.

Agony

If a person dreams about agony, the dream implies that he will experience a mixture of joy and anxiety – with the latter predominating. If the dreamer dreams that he is in agony about financial losses, it means that he is fraught with imaginary fears about matters of business or about the health of someone close to him.

Ague

If a person dreams that he is suffering from ague, it can have two meanings: the first states that a dream like this is a reference to the dreamer's poor state of health. The second indicates that the dreamer will suffer losses in business because he is not decisive enough.

If a person dreams that other people are suffering from ague, it is a warning dream: the dreamer must try to curb his arrogance, otherwise he runs the risk of offending other people.

Agreement

A dream about an agreement based on awareness predicts that soon something valuable that the dreamer holds dear to his heart will be returned to him. This is a positive dream, according to which problems the dreamer encounters will be solved quickly and worries that are plaguing him are about to disappear.

If a person dreams that he agrees to give or deliver something, it means that he is about to lose something of value. If a person dreams that he agrees to receive something, the success of a certain project he is working on, or hopes to finish, is doubtful.

If a person dreams that the agreement in the dream resulted from certain concessions, the dream predicts that he is about to have something expensive taken from him.

Air

Dreams about air do not augur well. If the person dreams about hot air, it means that he will resort to doing malevolent things as a reaction to being oppressed. If he dreams about cold air, the dream implies that he is engaging in slippery business practices and is also suffering from a lack of domestic harmony. If the air in a dream is humid, it refers to impending misfortunes that will be disastrous for the dreamer.

Air force officer

If a dream features an officer in the air force, it implies that soon the dreamer will receive an unexpected visit or that he may go on a brief trip. If a person dreams that he is an air force officer, it means that he will soon be promoted at work.

Airplane

If a person dreams about an airplane, it actually expresses his wishes to move to another place far away. This could well be because of a difficult financial situation

A B C D E F G H I J K L M N O P Q R S T U V W X Y Z

or an emotional problem linked to his relationship with his partner or with his extended family. This kind of dream attests to the fact that the dreamer must examine himself and his surroundings in order to discover what is bothering him and causing him such dissatisfaction that he is dreaming about "escaping."

Alabaster

A dream that features alabaster bodes well for the dreamer: it indicates success in marriage and in legal matters. On the other hand, if an object made of alabaster falls and breaks in a dream, it is a sign of sorrow and regret.

Alarm bell

If a person hears an alarm bell in a dream, it means that he has every reason to worry.

Albatross

A dream about an albatross implies that the dreamer is in a dilemma or in a difficult situation, and it is hard for him to decide what the correct thing is for him to do. The problem he is facing gives him no rest and bothers him a lot. Having said that, the dream indicates that although there is a serious, heavyweight problem, which sometimes stems from the necessity to determine people's fate, the dreamer will find the correct way to resolve the matter in the best way possible. He will overcome the problem, find the way to appease those involved, and finally manage to calm down and feel that he acted in the best and most correct way. He must be absolutely certain that any problem that is bothering him at the moment will be solved in the best possible way.

The aim of the dream is to put the dreamer's mind at rest and to get him to understand that the path he selects is the best one from his point of view.

Album

A dream about an album is a very auspicious dream. It means success and true friendship. If a young woman dreams about looking at photographs in an album, she will soon find herself involved with a wonderful new lover.

Alchemist

A dream about an alchemist is basically a negative dream. If a person dreams that he is an alchemist, and sees himself trying to turn base metals into gold, it means that even though his ideas are very good, he is incapable of achieving his goals. This means that he will suffer disappointments in love and in business.

Alien

Dreams about aliens can refer to strangers or beings from outer space. If a person dreams about aliens (strangers) who are amicable people, it is an indication of good things in the offing. Conversely, if the dreamer meets an unfriendly alien, he will suffer disappointment in many areas. If a person dreams about aliens (extraterrestrial beings), it refers to the fact that the dreamer will meet people who he finds extremely weird initially. However, as he gets to know them, he realizes that they will have a positive effect on his life.

Alley

An alley in a dream does not bode well. If a person sees an alley in a dream, it means that his luck is running out, and he is about to encounter problems and worries. If a young woman dreams about being in a dark alley, it is a warning dream: she must steer clear of bad company, because she is in danger of getting a very bad reputation.

Alligator

This is a particularly negative dream. The only situation involving an alligator in a dream that does not predict bad events and incidents in the dreamer's life is if the dreamer kills the alligator.

Alloy

If a person dreams about an alloy, it means that in the near future, the dreamer is going to find himself entangled in financial worries. If a woman has this dream, it means that she is going to experience sorrow and pain.

Almanac

A dream that features an almanac means that the dreamer will experience alternating periods of good and bad luck. If a person studies the signs in an almanac in a dream, it means that he is bogged down by small details and cannot see the wood for the trees.

Almonds

Eating almonds in a dream heralds a trip to a faraway

destination. The trip, whether business or pleasure, is about to change the dreamer's life dramatically: he may find the love of his life on the way; somebody he meets may cause him to change his attitude toward life; some incident may make him look at life differently. In any case, something in the dreamer's life is about to change as a result of this trip, and the dream enables him to prepare himself for it psychologically.

Alms

If a person dreams that he is giving alms to someone else, there is a hint of joy and happiness. A feeling of charity and helping others attests to the fact that the dreamer is in a good economic situation or feels that he has a lot to give others. It is a win-win situation for both giver and recipient. If the dreamer sees a situation in which he is forced by others to give alms, it is not such a good situation. It can hint at the deterioration of the financial situation of someone close, a situation that will compel the dreamer to reach into his wallet and give money that he himself needs to other people. He must be careful of and refrain from giving that will entail more and more requests.

Altar

A dream about an altar can indicate that the dreamer feels that he is a victim of circumstances. If he is the sacrificial victim lying on the altar, the message is obvious. The dreamer must muster his courage and make a rapid change in the circumstances of his life, otherwise things will snowball into an all-over disaster. If in the dream the dreamer is the one who is responsible for placing someone else on the altar to be sacrificed, he must check into how his close family and relatives feel. A dream of this type generally hints at the severe emotional distress of one of the dreamer's relatives. An early check can prevent a disaster.

Aluminum

If a person dreams about aluminum, it means that he is satisfied and content with what he has in life. On the other hand, if the aluminum in the dream is tarnished and stained, it implies that the dreamer will suffer pain and loss.

Amateur

If a person dreams that he is an amateur actor, it means that he will see the fulfillment of his hopes and expectations. If he sees himself in an amateur performance of a tragedy, it means that his hopes will be dashed.

Ambulance

A dream about an ambulance does not augur well. If a person sees an ambulance with its siren blaring in his dream, it means that bad luck is in the offing. If he sees himself being wheeled into the ambulance on a gurney and taken to the hospital, he can expect to become ill in the near future.

Ambush

A dream about an ambush is basically a negative dream. If a person dreams that he is ambushed, it means that he will find himself in a dangerous situation if he does not take the necessary precautions. If he himself is lying in ambush for someone, it means that he will do whatever is necessary to deceive, cheat and defraud his friends.

America

A dream about either of the American continents, north or south, only has significance if the dreamer is a high-ranking official. If that is the case, a dream about America does not augur well for him: he can expect problems an personal danger.

Amethyst

If a person dreams about an amethyst, it means that he will be involved in honest business practices. If he dreams about the loss of an amethyst, it means that a forthcoming marriage has been called off.

Ammonia

A dream about this chemical symbolizes the dreamer's displeasure with the conduct of one of his friends. If the friend persists in his behavior, the friendship between the two will terminate.

Amorous

If a person has a dream about being amorous, it is a warning dream: he must not indulge his personal desires and seek out the pleasures of the flesh unless he is prepared to be the object of scandal and vicious gossip as a result. The dream warns the dreamer against immoral and lascivious behavior.

A B C D E F G H I J K L M N O P Q R S T U V W X Y Z

Amputation

Dreams about amputation almost always refer to losses of some kind. If a person dreams that part of one of his limbs is amputated, it means that he can expect to sustain some minor losses in business. If he dreams that an entire limb is amputated, the dream signifies a real major business loss – one that is quite unprecedented.

If a person dreams that his leg is amputated, it means that he will lose good friends and will lead a life of domestic dissent. If he dreams that his arm is amputated, it symbolizes divorce or separation. It is also a warning dream, warning the dreamer of hypocrisy and deception. A dream that features fingers being amputated refers to financial losses caused by the dreamer's adversaries.

Amusement

If a person dreams about an amusing situation in which he is in a good mood, the dream hints that he will be blessed with good luck.

If a person dreams that he attends an amusing show, the dream implies that he can look forward to a golden opportunity to accomplish something that he has been dreaming about for a long time. Now the door is open, and he has to take advantage of this situation for his benefit.

If a person dreams that he is forced to go out in the middle of an amusing show rather than remain until the end, it means that he is liable to miss the important opportunity that has come his way – in most cases because of someone else's behavior, which had a bad effect on him.

Amusement park

If a dream features an amusement park, it means that the dreamer will soon go on vacation. If he goes on one of the rides in the amusement park, he will learn how to make the most of life.

Anchor

A dream in which the dreamer sees an anchor is a sign that all of his hopes will materialize. He must be patient, and eventually he will see his hopes materializing one by one.

An anchor in a dream, as in reality, represents security, stability and permanence. This is particularly true if the anchor is seen lying on dry land. A dream like this prophesies peace, good fortune and success.

In contrast, if the anchor is in its natural place in the dream – that is, in water – the dream warns against unpleasant things, failures, delays, frustration and disappointment.

A dream that features a ship anchored at sea, without the anchor actually being visible, hints at some kind of stability in life and at the knowledge and awareness that there is stability in life. The knowledge itself is important here. The very fact of the knowledge is what gives the dreamer peace and repose.

Anecdote

If a person relates anecdotes in his dream, it means that he has a tendency to seek out superficial, light-hearted company. This tendency emerges in his business dealings as well.

Angel

A person who dreams about an angel or angels can expect to undergo a unique spiritual experience that he has been awaiting for a long time but only now is he ready to have it. A sick person who dreams about angels will soon get well, even though his condition seems serious. There could well be a trip to a new place in which the dreamer will have a unique adventure that will greatly affect his life. There is a reasonable possibility of moving house because of a fateful meeting with a new person. If a person dreams that a troop of angels is accompanying him, he feels secure. This person feels protected, even though he may be in a difficult situation. He trusts his personal friends and work colleagues, who protect him from every possible negative development.

A dream about angels means faith in heaven's mercy. It is a sign to the dreamer that there is someone watching over him from above, and he will overcome the problems even if the period he is going through at the moment is particularly difficult. Dreams about angels also characterize people who have undergone some kind of mystical experience and are in a state of elation. In many cases, a dream about angels indicates a burst of creativity. This may be reflected in a good commercial idea or in a solution to a social or domestic problem that has been bothering the dreamer for a long time and will be solved in a flash of genius and sensitivity.

Anger

Anger appears in a dream as a warning sign. This means that if the dreamer meets a stranger and is very angry at him, he can expect a good meeting. Conversely, if a familiar person appears in a dream and he is the object of the dreamer's anger, a negative incident can be expected between the two. The dreamer may well have been holding and nursing grudges and rage in his heart for a long time. For reasons known only to him, he does not dare let them out. As a result, he loses his *joie de vivre* and feels disappointed and frustrated.

Animals

A dream in which a certain animal appears must be interpreted according to that animal (see the appropriate entry in the book). Having said that, the dreamer might see himself at a zoo, a safari park or in another place that is full of animals, and is not dreaming about a specific animal. In such a case, we must try to interpret the dream according to the personal contexts of each person, based on his life experience and memories, and decipher it by referring to insights that originate in the subconscious.

Researchers believe that a dream about animals means that the subconscious has woken up and come to life, and is sending impulses and wishes that can be interpreted according to the cultural links of the person to the animals he saw – not just according to their name, but also according to their type (birds, reptiles, fish, and so on).

If a person dreams about purchasing some kind of animal, the dream implies that in the near future, he can expect to get embroiled in complications in several areas of his life. This dream, therefore, should be taken as a warning dream. The dream hints that there could be hitches on the personal level, that is, in the dreamer's domestic or conjugal life. He must be aware of interpersonal tensions and of the relations with a person close to him, with the people around him and mainly with the ones who are closest to him (children, if there are, or parents). The complications are liable to cause problems in anything to do with income: job, business, the IRS, bad bets or investments, and so on.

If a person dreams about selling animals, the dream implies that he will not have the joy of seeing success in something for which he hoped and prayed in the near future; it will be postponed. Nevertheless, he must not lose hope, since this does not mean that success will not come – only that things will happen in the longer run, and he must be patient. Only patience and a calm state of mind together with inner calmness will help the dreamer get through the expected interim period until he sees the light at the end of the tunnel.

Animal young

A dream that features animal young hints at a developed maternal or paternal instinct. Whether the dreamer has experienced maternity or paternity, the dream hints at a longing for children, that is, for offspring. The dreamer wants to give of himself, and feels a need to give vent to the emotion of compassion and love within him.

Some people differentiate between a dream in which the young of wild animals appear and a dream featuring the young of domestic animals.

The young of wild animals symbolize problems the dreamer encounters along the path to what he perceives as happiness – establishing a family and having children.

Despite his heart's great longing to fulfill his desires for a family and children, there is a certain obstacle in his path that prevents him from fulfilling his wishes.

A dream that features the young of domestic animals also hints at the dreamer's very powerful desire to establish a family and have children, but it indicates the dreamer's childish character that stands in the way of his happiness. The dreamer is not mature enough to establish a family, and he cannot yet become a parent and assume the enormous responsibility involved in this role. Having said that, even in this case, the dream indicates that the essence of happiness, according to the dreamer, lies in establishing a family, and especially in raising children.

Ankle

A dream that features the dreamer's ankle is a sign of success. It also means that the dreamer's problems will be solved. If a person dreams about his partner's ankle, it means that one of the couple is being unfaithful.

Annoy

If a person is annoyed with or by someone else in a dream, it means that he has enemies. If he dreams that he is expressing his annoyance or anger, the dream means that he will have a happy and successful life.

Antelope

A dream that features an antelope indicates that the dreamer will accomplish his goals if he makes a huge effort.

A B C D E F G H I J K L M N O P Q R S T U V W X Y Z

Antenna

If a person sees an antenna in a dream, it means that he is uncertain or curious about the other person in a relationship. If he puts up an antenna in a dream, it means that the person about whom he is uncertain will soon provide him with the answers.

Antibiotics

A dream about antibiotics is a warning dream. It warns the dreamer that he is about to succumb to some kind of illness. However, if he seeks medical help immediately, he will be able to tone down the virulence of the disease and ensure that it is brief.

Ant/s

Predictably, a dream about an ant usually attests to difficulties the dreamer is experiencing in his workplace, in earning a living, and in his career.

A dream that features a single ant implies that the dreamer has to change his ways and habits in everything to do with matters of work and career: he will have to work harder in order to achieve what he wants, but ultimately, the investment will pay off, and he will earn a promotion and enjoy financial prosperity and a life of ease.

If the dreamer sees more than one ant, it implies that he can expect a very difficult period at work and in everything linked to his career. Things will not progress as quickly and efficiently as he had expected. He will go through a period fraught with obstacles and difficulties that will cause him endless frustration. Hassles at work will turn out to be strengthening, and the dreamer will eventually emerge from them stronger, with renewed energy for a new start.

Anvil

A dream that features anvil means that the work the dreamer undertakes will bring its rewards. If the dreamer is a farmer, the dream implies that his crops will be particularly abundant. Generally speaking, if anvil appears in a dream, it means that the dreamer will be successful if he works hard.

If a dream features broken anvil, it means that the dreamer has thrown away an opportunity.

Anxiety

If a dreamer feels anxiety in a dream, it can have two meanings: if the anxiety does not concern anything too important, it means that the dreamer will finally enjoy success after going through a negative phase. If, on the other hand, his anxiety concerns something of major importance, he must brace himself for something really disastrous in the near future.

Ape

A dream about an ape or apes does not augur well. If a person dreams about apes, it is a sign of humiliation as well as the ill health of a good friend of his. If he sees a small ape clinging to a tree in a dream, it warns him of falling victim to deception and treachery.

Apparel

There are many interpretations of a dream about apparel. These depend on the color, style, type and condition of the particular item of apparel.

If a dream features high-quality but unfashionable apparel, it means that the dreamer will be lucky, but is reactionary in his ideas. If a person dreams about white apparel, it is generally a sign of sadness. The exception to this is if a girl or a young woman has this dream. Black apparel in a dream implies arguments, losses in business, and disloyal friends. Green apparel is a sign of prosperity and happiness. Yellow apparel in a dream means that the dreamer is about to come into a substantial sum of money and will enjoy life. Yellow fabric means good luck. Blue apparel in a dream is a symbol of success and the loyalty of friends.

Apparition

If a person sees an apparition in a dream, it is a warning to him that disaster is about to strike. The disaster concerns people and property. The dream warns him to take particular care of his family.

Appetite

A dream about an appetite reflects an especially lively urge – in most cases, a voracious sexual drive – but it can also reflect other urges.

The greater the appetite for a food item in a dream, the more this attests to an especially voracious sexual appetite. If a person is longing to assuage his hunger or quench his thirst in a dream, it is an expression of his highly developed sex drive.

If a person dreams that he is eating ravenously in order to assuage a fierce hunger, and he is in the company of another person who is also eating until he is sated, the latter may be the object of the dreamer's lust; the dreamer wants to make love with him/her. The greater the hunger in the dream, the more desperately the dreamer wants to have intercourse with that person.

The dream may be a recurring dream: if a person sees himself time after time in a dream, attacked by a fierce hunger that he is unable to satiate and assuage, it is reasonable to assume that this reflects his poor financial situation. Sometimes a dream like this indicates extravagance and the inability to control profligate expenditure.

Apple

In general, a dream about an apple is auspicious, and predicts a tranquil and happy life and a rosy future. Having said that, a dream like this is interpreted in different ways, according to the appearance of the apple in the dream:

If a person dreams about a ripe, sweet apple, it is a sign that he can expect a good and sweet life devoid of worry and rich in content.

A dream in which the apple tastes sour is a sign that the dreamer is liable to find himself in the middle of a big row or dispute that will be difficult to settle, or in some other difficult and dangerous situation. The dreamer will be wise to avoid conflicts. A sour apple in a dream also serves as a hint that the dreamer is liable to fail in an important task, or suffer a bitter disappointment from something he anticipated eagerly but did not meet his expectations.

If the apple in the dream is green, the dream serves as a warning against health problems stemming from weak nerves or excessive nervousness. The dreamer must be careful to avoid rows or disputes that are liable to have a bad effect on his heart or blood pressure.

An apple lying on the ground next to the tree from which it fell in a dream is a sign of great joy and of a life of merriment and amusements. The dreamer will have many happy experiences in his life. This does not refer to sublime happiness or other sublime experiences, but rather to joy in its simplest, basic and primal form. The ability to be happy will bring other good things later on, such as peace of mind, patience and so on.

If a person dreams about taking a bite from an apple, it is impossible to ignore the similarity to the story of Adam and Eve in the Bible. In this case, the dream attests to the fact that the dreamer cannot resist temptation. It is difficult for him to say "no", even when he knows it's the right thing to do.

His inability to resist temptation is liable to get him into situations he does not want to be in. If the dreamer remains steadfastly opposed to things that he finds particularly bewitching, he can avoid plunging to depths that he has never known the likes of in his life.

Apprentice

If a person dreams that he is an apprentice, it means that he will have to struggle very hard if he wants to gain status among his colleagues.

Apricot

A dream about an apricot is a prophetic dream according to which the dreamer can expect a good life in almost every sphere and on every level. He will earn a respectable living and his economic situation will be solid. His health will be good and he need not expect to come down with any serious diseases. In general, his situation will be more than satisfactory. Having said that, he will have difficulty in one area of his life, and the path leading to it will not be simple: the romantic realm. He can expect difficulties in this area, and the way to accomplish this objective will not be straightforward. The dreamer will experience disappointments, setbacks and mental anguish.

Despite the difficulties, after he finds a suitable partner, his married and family life will be good and will complete the rosy picture that he can expect in the future.

April

A dream about the month of April is a positive dream, symbolizing happiness and prosperity. If a person dreams that the weather during April is bad, it means that there will be a brief bout of bad luck that will soon pass.

Apron

If a young woman dreams about an apron, the dream has moral implications. She must watch her behavior if she values her reputation.

Arch

A dream that features an arch implies that the way for

the dreamer to gain recognition and wealth is through hard work. If a person sees a fallen arch in a dream, it is a sign of bad luck and disappointments.

Archbishop

This is not a particularly positive dream. If a person sees an archbishop in his dream, it means that he will have to struggle with many obstacles along the road to success.

Architect

If a dream features an architect drawing up plans, it implies that the dreamer's business will undergo changes. These may not be positive changes, however. If a woman dreams about an architect, the dream predicts that she will be disappointed in her quest to find a suitable husband.

Arm

If a dream features a healthy, well-formed and shapely arm or arms, it means that success will come to the dreamer from an unexpected source. Its arrival will be a surprise, since there will be no prior warning or hint that it is on the threshold.

A sick and weak arm in a dream is a sign of a great disappointment that the dreamer is about to suffer. He is about to go through a period filled with frustrations, depression, and feelings of having missed out. All of these emotions may also affect his physical state.

Hairy arms in a dream attest to the fact that the dreamer has a high threshold of endurance and a lot of mental fortitude. He can go through unbearably difficult experiences and still move forward without anyone sensing that he has been through anything difficult. From the physical point of view, too, he is very strong, and is known to be someone who does not tend to get ill and take to his bed.

If a person sees injured arms in his dream, he can expect a lengthy period of sadness, a period filled with melancholy and a bad feeling of gloom in life.

Aroma

If a sweet aroma features in the dream of a young woman, it means that she can look forward to receiving a lovely surprise or gift.

Arrest

If a person sees a respectable-looking stranger being arrested in a dream, it means that he is very keen to make changes in his life, but does not have the courage to do so. If the stranger resists arrest, the dreamer will succeed in effecting the desired changes.

Arrow

In general, seeing an arrow in a dream has a positive meaning. It predicts that the dreamer will enjoy all kinds of entertainment, trips, and festivities.

If a dreamer sees a bow and arrow in his dream, it means that he will take advantage of someone else's inability to do something. An old or broken arrow in a dream is a sign of bad luck in love or business.

A B C D E F G H I J K L M N O P Q R S T U V W X Y Z

Art gallery

A dream about an art gallery does not augur well as far as domestic life is concerned. The dreamer is pretending to be content with his present situation, but deep down he is longing for a change.

Artichoke

A dream about an artichoke predicts a period that will bring a great deal of embarrassment. The dreamer can expect to go through some kind of experience that is liable to cause him great embarrassment that he will find difficult to shrug off. The dream is giving him advance notice of what he can expect, so that he may be able to accept things differently and brace himself psychologically. Ultimately, the less importance he attributes to the experience, the sooner he can extricate himself from the embarrassing situation he has landed in.

If the dreamer eats an artichoke in his dream, this implies his inability to communicate with his life partner. This lack of communication is reflected in every area of life, and the purpose of the dream is to "shake" the dreamer and make him think twice about the nature of the relationship. The basic lack of understanding between the dreamer and his partner brings him to the point of outbursts and states of mind that are not like him at all. He is tense and nervous. However, he can easily alter the situation so that his life will look completely different.

Article

If a person dreams that an article that vilifies him is

published in a newspaper, it implies a possible betrayal on the part of close friends. In contrast, a positive article attests to the fact that the dreamer can expect success and public recognition. He may get into the political scene or some other area. In any event, the dream can expect to receive waves of adulation and admiration from a large group of people.

Artist

A dream about an artist does not necessarily attest to the dreamer's creative ability. Sometimes the opposite is true, and the dream must be interpreted as a recommendation that the dreamer develop his talents in other fields that are better suited to him, and that his creative development will actually come to the fore in more scientific and earthly fields.

In most cases, a dream like this refers to a mysterious affair in the past that is soon to be revealed, and will undermine the solid foundations of the dreamer's world. The affair is linked to fraud, deception or a lie, and will be revealed suddenly in all its glory. This scam is about to expose several layers of the dreamer's life, and will reveal the "nakedness" of some of those around him. People in whom he trusted blindly will be shown up as liars who have been defrauding him for years and allowing him to believe in a mendacious reality.

Ascending

A dream about ascending some kind of slope is interpreted in two ways, according to the context of the dream: if the dreamer succeeds in making the ascent without sliding back or stumbling, things in his life will run smoothly. However, if he stumbles and slides back, he will have to cope with many obstacles in his path.

Asceticism

If a person dreams about asceticism, it means that in real life he is liable to champion a variety of really strange ideas. People who do not know him will find this quaint and interesting, but the people who do know him well will consider his ideas odious.

Ashes

A dream about ashes is an extremely negative dream, since it symbolizes only problems, sadness, losses and failure.

Asia

A dream about the continent of Asia is indicative of change, but this does not necessarily mean an improvement in financial status.

Asp

If a person dreams about this poisonous snake, it is a very bad sign. If a woman dreams about an asp, it implies the loss of her good reputation. If a man has this dream, it refers to vicious conspiracies against him. For lovers, the dream means angry quarrels.

Asparagus

The appearance of an asparagus in a dream attests powerfully to the dreamer's excellent powers of judgment: He must not rely on others and their advice, but only on his own ability to judge. The decisions he takes are wise and correct, and he must be calm and believe that his choices are better than anything other people propose. If he continues listening to himself only and is not tempted to listen to other people's advice, he will succeed in whatever he does. The dreamer is an individualistic and autodidactic type. He loves learning about various things by himself and achieving his goals on his own. Sometimes this deters the people around him, since his lack of cooperation with others is occasionally interpreted as haughtiness, but the dream attests to the fact that the dreamer is taking the only correct path, and that he must continue relying only on himself.

Ass

A dream that features an ass means that the dreamer will suffer annoying incidents and delays. If a person dreams that he is chased by an ass, it means that he will be the butt of ridicule and the object of gossip. If an ass brays in a dream, it implies bad or unwelcome tidings.

Assassin / Assassination

If a person dreams that he is assassinated, the dream implies that he will fail to overcome his problems. If he sees someone else being assassinated in a dream, especially if there is a great deal of blood, it means that there is trouble in store for the dreamer.

Any dream that features an assassin implies that the dreamer has hidden enemies who are conspiring to harm him.

Assistance

If a person dreams that he offers someone else assistance, it implies that his attempts to advance in life will be successful. If the dreamer is offered assistance, the dream implies that he has good, loyal friends, and he will live in comfort and ease.

Astral plane / Astral self

A dream about the astral plane attests to the fact that the dreamer's plans and efforts will meet with success and recognition.

If, however, the dreamer sees his astral self, it is a very bad sign.

Astrologer / Astronomer

The appearance of a "stargazer" in a dream implies that the dreamer's thoughts all look forward – toward the future. He is the kind of person who does not look back nostalgically, and if it were up to him, he would not go back to any point in his past. This is not because the past was so bad for him, but because the future is beckoning him much more.

The dreamer is a person who is bursting with plans and full of ideas, who wants to discover marvelous realms, whether this entails actual journeys or investigation and research at home, by surfing the Internet and so on.

If a rich man dreams this dream, it actually means that he is facing bankruptcy. He will lose his fortune, which he amassed with great toil, and he will go back to square one. He will have to work very hard to restore it to its former glory. Having said that, he is not a person who sinks into despair easily, so he will know how to pick up the pieces and carry on.

If a poor man dreams this dream, it implies that soon there will be a death in the family. A close person, whom the dreamer knows well, is about to die. In most cases, the cause of death will be old age.

A dream in which the person sees himself visiting an astrologer in order to have his future predicted hints at spiritual enlightenment that the person is about to cxperience. He will gain insights previously unknown to him and will change his world-view diametrically. Things he previously considcred extremely important will appear worthless, while the spiritual and mystical world will fill his life. He will also change his immediate surroundings and will prefer to be in touch with people who are close to him from the spiritual point of view. As a result, he will lose his former friends, since they will not be able to understand what has come over him, and will distance themselves from him.

Asylum

A dream about an asylum is basically a negative dream that is indicative of illness and bad luck. Only if the dreamer makes a huge effort will he be able to overcomc these negative things.

Atlas

If a person dreams that he is consulting an atlas, the dream implies that he will not institute any changes or take trips without carefully considering all of the implications.

Atomic bomb

If a person sees the mushroom cloud that results from the explosion of an atomic bomb in a dream, he should prepare himself psychologically to face something really terrible that is about to happen to him and his family.

If the atomic bomb appears in the dream in the context of a nuclear war, it implies that the dreamer is nursing a great deal of anger, and this is liable to erupt in a very destructive manner.

Atonement

A dream about atonement is a positive dream. If a person has this dream, it means that his relations with his friends. If he is involved in a relationship, it means that he will enjoy positive things with his partner. If he is involved in business, he will be successful.

However, if a person dreams that other people are atoning for the bad things he has done, it means that the dreamer or his close friends are about to suffer humiliation.

Attic

A dream about an attic attests to the fact that the dreamer's hopes can never be fulfilled. If a person dreams about sleeping in an attic, it means that he is very dissatisfied with his job.

Attire

A dream about attire has different meanings according to the content. If a person dreams that he is wearing a special ethnic outfit, there is a hint of an essential change in his way of life. Dreams of this kind generally attest to the desire for a change that is about to take place, a kind of prophecy or premonition that the dreamer is already feeling, even before the event itself occurs. There is a high probability that the dreamer will be successful in some kind of deal or gamble or that he will receive a large and unexpected sum of money. If a person dreams that he empties out his closet and buys a lot of new clothes, he can expect new things to happen in his emotional life, too. A new player is about to enter his love life.

White clothing in a dream is an especially good sign that attests to the fact that the dreamer sees himself as a pure and virtuous person and as someone who is blessed with the spiritual qualities of wisdom and the ability to counsel and help others.

Black clothes can indicate a brief period of hardship for the dreamer.

If a person dreams that he is in a store or a large warehouse and is deliberating about the appropriate clothes to buy, it attests to changes that can be expected in his lifestyle. The dramatic change in his appearance may be necessitated by advancement at work or a new job.

Attorney

Attorneys in dreams symbolize serious disputes about material things. If a person dreams about an attorney, it means that he is being threatened by the accusations of his adversaries. If a person is defended by an attorney in his dream, it implies that his friends will come to his aid, but they will actually do more harm than good.

Auction

A dream about an auction is interpreted according to whether a man or a woman dreams it. If a man dreams about an auction, it is a sign that his business will thrive. If a woman dreams about an auction, it means that she will be rich and enjoy a life of affluence.

August

If a person dreams about the month of August, it implies that business deals he hoped to clinch will fall through, and he and his partner will have misunderstandings in their relationship. If a young woman dreams that she will get married in August, it is a warning dream: she will have sorrow early on in her marriage.

Aunt

If a woman dreams about an aunt, she has done something that will engender severe criticism. However, if the aunt in the dream is smiling, everything will calm down and get back to normal.

Aura / Halo

An aura that is seen around a person in a dream attests to the dreamer's spiritual enlightenment, to the return to spiritual-religious sources, to a spiritual quest or to a special experience that the dreamer has undergone or is about to undergo. The latter could be a seance, meditation and so on, which has a special influence on his life.

If a person sees himself in a dream with a halo around his head, it is a warning dream, implying that someone is about to replace him, is threatening his status, and covets his position or what he represents. The dreamer must be on guard, since inattention is liable to cost him dearly later on.

A halo around the dreamer's head is also interpreted as the ability to provide assistance and healing to the ailments of body and mind. The dream may hint at the dreamer's healing abilities of which he is not in the least aware. He may be blessed with healing powers, and may be capable of developing his healing ability by means of touch and intensifying the powerful energies inside him that are begging to be used, even if he is not aware of them in the slightest. The dream brings these unknown abilities up from the dreamer's subconscious, and he can certainly develop and use them for his own benefit and for the benefit of those around him.

If a person sees another person with a halo around his head, it is a sign that the second person is the object of the dreamer's envy. The dreamer must find out the reason why this is coming to the fore in a dream as well as the source of the jealousy that is liable to ruin his life.

Author

If a person dreams about an anxiety-ridden author, it mean that he is worried about his own or someone else's literary output. If he is an author, and he dreams that his manuscript has been rejected, the opposite is true: it may take time, but eventually it will be accepted for publication.

A
B
C
D
E
F
G
H
I
J
K
L
M
N
O
P
Q
R
S
T
U
V
W
X
Y
Z

Automobile

If a person dreams about an automobile, it attests to the fact that even though things are going well for him, he is restless and discontent. The dream warns him that this can result in dire consequences. If the dream involves an automobile that breaks down on the road, the dreamer will not achieve the pleasure he anticipated.

A dream in which the dreamer is almost run over by an automobile implies that he should keep out of his rival's way.

Autumn / Fall

A dream about the autumn is a positive dream, especially if a woman has it. If a woman dreams about the autumn, it implies that she will receive a substantial amount of property thanks to the efforts of other people. If she dreams about getting married in the autumn, it bodes well for the marriage.

Avalanche

Contrary to what one might think, if a person is caught in an avalanche in a dream, it means that he can look forward to good things in life. If he sees other people caught in an avalanche, the dream implies that he really wants to move to another place.

Avenue

A dream that features an avenue of trees symbolizes ideal love. However, if the dream features an avenue of trees that are shedding their leaves, it implies a difficult life that is fraught with obstacles and problems.

Avocado

An avocado in a dream – whether it is a ripe fruit that is ready to be eaten or a fruit that is still hanging on the tree – implies that the dreamer will soon experience a considerable improvement in his financial status and will enjoy substantial luxury. The dream hints at a change that will result from a new workplace, a new home, a promotion in the present workplace, or a good business investment that yields positive results. Economic prosperity goes hand in hand with social blooming, and the dreamer will be accorded respect by those around him. His status will improve beyond recognition, and he may even reach the point of being famous. People will seek him out because of his status, and he can expect to be invited to festive events, official openings, and so on. If the dreamer is not accustomed to that kind of thing, the dream contains a hint of a real "revolution" that is going to occur in his life in the near future.

Awake

If a person dreams that he is awake, it means that he is about to undergo weird experiences that will make him feel very bad.

Ax

A dream that features an ax that is blurred and cannot be seen in all its details implies that soon the dreamer will receive a sum of money that he did not have to work for. It could be an inheritance, but it is more likely that he will win money from gambling, and not necessarily in casinos. It

A B C D E F G H I J K L M N O P Q R S T U V W X Y Z

could be money from a lottery. While this money will bring him great prosperity and wealth, the dream hints that the dreamer must know how to deal with it wisely and prudently. If not, he will quickly lose everything he received – a case of "easy come, easy go." He should not blow this opportunity. He should relate to the advance knowledge provided by the dream in order to be ready for it when the time comes, and not lose his head when the win materializes.

If a person sees himself in a dream with an ax being wielded above him, the dream implies that he will be able to extricate himself from any mess. Even if it looks as if there is no way out, everything will turn out fine in the end.

An ax with a sharp blade in a dream means that the dreamer's life is beginning to progress. Even if the situation looks as if it is stagnant, in the end a way out of the mess will be found. If the dreamer is in some kind of danger, he will eventually get out of the situation stronger and with the upper hand. He will control and direct the situation and will know how to maneuver in order to get out unscathed and even strengthened.

An ax with a blunt blade in a dream hints that a change is in progress at the dreamer's workplace, and things are moving in low gear at the moment – perhaps too low, and not according to the desired rate. However, this is a transient period, and it will pass quickly. The dreamer may feel that he is marching on the spot, is not moving in any direction, and is becoming "rusty," but he will only feel this way for a short time. If he is a businessman, there will be a slowdown in business in the immediate future. This may be cause by a general recession; however, it may not be linked to the situation in the economy at all, but rather to the dreamer's specific business. In a case like this, too, the dreamer must know that the situation is only temporary, and that it will soon pass.

A dream that features an ax that looks as if it is flawed hints at disappointment. The dreamer, who is eagerly looking forward to progress in some area, is liable to suffer a bitter disappointment. His feeling of defeat will be severe, and he may even feel cheated, but he must relate to it as another good lesson in life, and take advantage of the situation to learn from it and grow in new directions.

B

Baby carriage

This is a positive dream. If a person dreams about a baby carriage, it means that he has good friends who care about him and enjoy preparing nice surprises for him.

Bachelor

If a man dreams about being a bachelor, it is a warning dream, telling him that he should not seek the company of women. If a married person dreams about being a bachelor, it indicates that he wants to cheat on his spouse.

Back

If a person sees a bare back in a dream, it is a warning against giving advice or lending other people money. If someone else turns his back on the dreamer and walks away, it is a sign of that person's jealousy and intent to harm the dreamer. A dream that features the dreamer's own back does not bode well.

Back door

If the dreamer sees himself entering and leaving through the back door, it attests to the fact that he is in desperate need of change in his life. It is not a very good sign if he dreams that another person is leaving through the back door, since it indicates that a financial loss is in the offing. The dream basically warns him against entering a business partnership.

Backgammon

If a person dreams about playing a game of backgammon, it means that he will not be treated very hospitably during a visit. However, things will improve, and gradually he will make friends. If he dreams about losing a game of backgammon, it means that he will not be lucky in love or money matters.

Bacon

A dream that features bacon that is not fresh attests to the fact that the dreamer is not seeing things very clearly and is plagued by anxiety. If a person dreams that he is eating bacon and is managing to keep his hands clean, it is a good sign.

Badger

Dreams about various types of rodents, such as a badger (as well as moles, rats and mice of various types) that live under the surface of the earth and feed on roots, insects or worms, indicate the dreamer's suspicious nature. He is afraid that someone will steal his thunder and of the possibility that someone else will enjoy his success instead of him. In this dream, the dreamer expresses his fear that somebody will steal the fruits of his success and will wear laurels that do not belong to him (at the dreamer's expense). This fear and worry attest to the dreamer's basic lack of self-confidence in his ability to express his talents and display them outwardly to the world. Even if he is certain that he is talented and gifted with unique abilities, what bothers him and comes to the fore in the dream is his inability to be given credit for his accomplishments from the people around him. He is not sure that he knows how to act in order to get them to acknowledge his abilities, and is afraid that because of this "defect," someone else will ultimately reap the success that was supposed to be his.

Bag

A dream that features a bag – whether it is a large traveling bag or a woman's handbag – almost always augurs well.

If the dream features an especially beautiful bag, it means that the dreamer will enjoy abundance in all areas of life – financial and material as well as emotional. He will be loved, people will lavish warmth on him, and there will always be happiness in his home.

A bag or a purse in a dream indicates that good news is about to reach the dreamer. It will influence the course of his life. The turning point will be positive; it will bring new opportunities and it will refresh his life. For this reason, he should be happy with the news that is in the offing.

If a worn-out or empty bag is seen in a dream, it is a sign that extreme behavior on the part of the dreamer is liable to ruin a good opportunity.

Baggage / Luggage

A dream about baggage indicates that the dreamer is worried. If he carries his own baggage, it means that he is bogged down in his own worries to the point that he does not acknowledge other people's worries. If a person loses his luggage in a dream, it implies that he will become embroiled in a bad business venture or in domestic strife.

Bagpipes

If a dream features a person playing the bagpipes crudely and angrily, it is not a good sign.

Bail

A dream about bail does not bode well. It indicates that the dreamer will encounter unexpected hassles and will be involved in accidents and relationships that do not work out.

Bailiff

A dream about a bailiff means that the dreamer is making every effort to advance in life, but unfortunately does not have the intellectual capacity to do so.

Baker

In contrast to the usual association of an abundance of cakes, breads and other baked goods, and the implications thereof, a baker who appears in a dream is mainly an indication of the dreamer's fears. It is usual (especially in Europe and the U.S.) to attribute this dream to a person who has gone through a trauma because of something he was forced to do. This does not necessarily refer to rape, but rather to acts such as extortion, threats to his safety if he reveals something – a secret and so on. This trauma is with him constantly, and for the dreamer, it is the kind of secret that cannot be revealed. Keeping the secret makes him an especially vulnerable and perpetually fearful person.

In rare instances, a dream about a baker can imply that friends of the dreamer will soon make him various offers. These can be good offers, but are equally liable to be offers that set him up for failure. He must therefore be very cautious in his dealings in the near future, and examine every offer made to him by a friend very carefully. He must use his discretion and not be afraid to doubt his friend's intentions. He must try to discern what the true motives behind these offers are.

If a woman dreams about baking, it is a warning dream: she can expect a life of poverty, too many children, and ill health.

A dream about a bakery is a warning dream, warning the dreamer to be on the lookout for pitfalls if he is making a career change.

Balcony

In most cases, a balcony in a dream appears in different contexts, each with a different interpretation. In general, a dream about a balcony implies that a vacation is in the offing. The dreamer needs a break to calm down from everything around him and to get a bit of repose and tranquillity in his life. If a dream features people standing on a balcony, it contains a hint of a party or some other festivity that will take place in the near future.

If the dreamer sees himself standing on the balcony alone, it implies that there are difficulties in his life that he has to cope with, and that he must try to overcome them.

Having said that, the dreamer should know that these difficulties are temporary, and that even though initially they seem annoying and problematic, he will ultimately be able to cope with them and overcome them easily.

If a person dreams about an animal on the balcony, he can soon expect a quarrel with the people around him. Alternatively, he will have to suffer a loss of some kind concerning money and property, not life. If a cockroach is seen on the balcony in the dream, it is a warning against becoming involved in a criminal matter. If a mouse appears on the balcony, there are people who want to quarrel with the dreamer. They are looking for a pretext for starting a row with him so that they can ostracize him.

Bald

There is nothing positive about a dream about baldness. If a dream features a bald man, the dreamer is warned that he should be on the alert for swindlers. If a woman dreams that her hair is falling out and she is going bald, it indicates that she will have to support herself. If she dreams about a bald man, she should not accept the next proposal of marriage that comes along.

If a bald woman appears in a man's dream, it informs him that he will have a nagging, shrill and petulant wife.

Ball

If a person dreams that he is playing a team game, it means that he is busy extending the social circle to which he belongs. Dreams about a ball can also indicate that good news will come by phone or mail, or that there is a positive trend toward expanding the family. If a person dreams that

A B C D E F G H I J K L M N O P Q R S T U V W X Y Z

he is watching a ball game but not participating in it, he feels distanced from the social point of view and perhaps even isolated. This could be a new family situation that has developed or something that has been going on for a long time. If this happens at work, it is a good opportunity to reassess the situation and act accordingly.

Ball (dance)

A dream about a ball prophesies that the dreamer will make new acquaintances. Even if he is not in the habit of socializing with people and taking part in functions, in one way or another he will meet someone who will become his close friend.

A dream in which the dreamer sees himself leaping about on the dance floor is a sign that he can soon expect happy days with a great deal of love and joy.

If a man dreams about a ball where many young girls are in evidence, it is a sign that he is about to lose a lot of money, and as a result will lose his power and influence.

If a woman dreams that she is dancing with a man at a ball, it is a sign that her secret is about to be revealed in public.

A dream in which a woman sees herself dancing with her husband is a sign that she is about to be highly successful in various areas of her life, especially in things concerning matters of the heart and love.

If an unmarried woman dreams that she is dancing with a married man at a ball, it is a sign that in real life, she is the object of superfluous gossip. She should behave judiciously in order to avoid talk that is only liable to complicate things and serve as an obstacle.

If an unmarried woman dreams that she is dancing with her boyfriend at a ball, it is a sign that she is incubating an illness that will soon erupt. She must be doubly cautious about and alert to her state of health.

If a widow dreams about dancing with a married man, it is a sign that the man in question is about to get divorced.

If the dream features young girls dancing at a ball, it is a sign that the dreamer can expect to receive a great deal of money. The source of the money is not necessarily the fruit of the dreamer's hard work. It could be money from an inheritance, from a lottery, or from some kind of win.

If a person dreams about a professional dancer dancing at a ball, it is a warning sign for him, warning him against obstacles that are difficult to see or anticipate. The dream warns of these obstacles and alerts the dreamer to be careful in his conduct.

If a person dreams that he is watching a dance contest that is being held at a ball, it is a sign that he will soon experience great happiness. This feeling will come as a result of some kind of dramatic incident in which he will be involved.

If a person dreams that he is watching a ball where nobody is dancing, he can expect to receive an inheritance in the near future.

If the dreamer dreams that he is outside of the circle of dancers at a ball, it is a sign that he can soon expect to become involved in a romantic liaison. It will go well, and the dreamer will find himself in a happy relationship.

A B C D E F G H I J K L M N O P Q R S T U V W X Y Z

Ballet

Ballets and various types of ballet dancing are supposed to inspire pleasure, tranquillity, serenity and beauty. In the case of a dream about ballet, the opposite is true in almost everything. A dream like this predicts bad things in the offing for the dreamer, mainly in anything to do with interpersonal relations. Jealousy, envy, treachery, meanness of spirit, quarrels and injustice – all these will be the dreamer's lot, and they will encourage the failure of his relations with people. Actually, it's all in the dreamer's hands; he is the one who will ultimately determine the direction in which things will move, but he must take into account that "the forces of blackness" and evil feature in the picture. In order to cause things to turn around in positive directions, he must make an effort. If he does not "interfere" and simply lets things happen by themselves, he is liable to find himself in the center of a fierce conflict, surrounded by uncomfortable relationships, rows, angers and many negative energies.

Balloon

A balloon in a dream has several meanings:

A large balloon that is inflated to the maximum so that even the tiniest jab will burst it is a sign that what seems to the dreamer to be solid friendship with his friends is nothing but tenuous friendship that can be burst by the tiniest "jab." This friendship is false, and he is well advised to check out the intentions of the people who call themselves "his close friends."

A large but not a huge balloon is a sign that the dreamer can realize aspirations and wishes and make his heart's desires come true.

A small balloon – or several small balloons in a dream, especially if they are used in a game – means that the dreamer is about to face problems, disappointments, worries and anxiety. He is about to enter a period of stress from the psychological point of view, and this will compel him to be strong and not to break. He must face serious challenges that will ultimately fortify him, and his ability to control his life will be greater.

Ballpoint pen

A dream that features a ballpoint pen indicates that the dreamer will soon write a letter to a long-lost friend.

Banana

The appearance of a banana or of bananas in a dream refers to a lack of self-satisfaction resulting from not fulfilling one's potential. The dreamer knows that he can achieve much more in life than he has done, and he lives in a feeling of constant frustration at the fact that his talents do not come to the fore. Several factors are responsible for his inability to achieve more – some of them objective and some of them a result of his personality structure and character. One way or another, he has to implement a drastic change in his life in order to succeed in achieving what he sees right in front of him as a coveted goal that he wants to accomplish.

A peeled banana in a dream means that the dreamer is about to find himself "peeled" of his clothes. An embarrassing situation will cause him to be at the center of an affair that is linked to the loss of his clothes.

If a person dreams that he is eating a banana, the dream

hints that he is suffering from a minor health problem such as a cold or a cough. He must take care of himself, even though it does not seem to be anything serious. If he does not, the minor health problem is liable to deteriorate into a more serious problem.

If a person dreams about a woman eating a banana, this is an erotic symbol that attests to an unsuccessful attempt at infidelity.

Bandage

One interpretation of a dream about a bandage states that the dreamer can expect to sustain a mild injury, or that he has already been injured and is bandaged, and he is dreaming about his appearance.

According to another interpretation, a bandage in a dream attests to the fact that the dreamer has good friends who worry about him and come to his aid in times of trouble.

The dream implies that the dreamer can trust his friends completely and be certain that when push comes to shove, his friends will be there for him and will be loyal to him. His friends will not let him down, and he can rest assured that he is in a supportive environment.

Banishment

A dream about banishment does not augur well. If a person dreams that he is banished, it means that he is haunted and pursued by evil, and can expect to die young. If a person dreams about banishing a child, the dream warns of treacherous business partners as well as death.

Banister

If a person dreams that he leans on a banister that breaks upon contact with his hand, it is advisable for him to watch out for disasters or accidents. This is not an easy period, and he must go through it as cautiously as possible. People with whom the dreamer is involved in business are liable to disappoint him even though they do not have any bad intentions. A person who dreams about going down the stairs in a high building while leaning on the banister will find himself in a difficult situation, but he will receive support from unexpected quarters. This refers to friends, family or strangers who will mobilize to help him.

Banjo

A dream about a banjo is indicative of fun, amusement and entertainment.

Bank

A dream in which a bank building or structure is seen attests to financial difficulties or problems in business. Even if the dreamer does not see any problem on the horizon at the moment, he will encounter difficulties like those very soon, and he should plan for them in time. This is especially true for a dream featuring a bank clerk, or worse still, the bank manager. A dream like this predicts bankruptcy in business, problems at work to the point of dismissal, serious losses or a severe financial downfall.

If, on the other hand, a person dreams that he owns a bank or is a bank manager, the dream hints at early retirement from work as a result of financial abundance.

A B C D E F G H I J K L M N O P Q R S T U V W X Y Z

The person will enjoy prosperity and satisfaction in everything to do with material matters, so much so that he will no longer find it necessary to work for money, and will be able to retire to enjoy his hobbies at a relatively young age.

If a person dreams about depositing money in the bank, or alternatively, if he sees money bills in the bank, the dream predicts financial improvement and stability in everything to do with financial matters. The dreamer will succeed in business and will make good profits. Even if he decides to invest in securities or in savings plans, these will yield respectable dividends.

A dream in which a person sees himself withdrawing money from the bank predicts a decrease in business profits or a drop in financial status.

A dream in which a person sees himself preventing a bank robbery is a sign that the dreamer is about to earn great honor, and that the people in his immediate surroundings will hold his actions and abilities in high esteem.

If a person dreams that he is present at a bank robbery as no more than a spectator and as a witness to what occurred, it is a sign that a plot is being devised against him right under his nose. One of the people around him, in whom the dreamer trusts absolutely – either a family member or someone else close to him – is betraying that trust and is trying to deceive the dreamer or lead him astray.

Bankrupt

A dream about bankruptcy is a warning dream. The dreamer will go through a crisis in business and his intellectual capacities will deteriorate. He should not speculate or gamble.

Banner

If a person sees a banner floating in a clear sky, it means that his country has just scored a military victory over its enemies. However, should he see a tattered banner, it means the opposite: his country has been defeated and humiliated.

Banquet / Feast

If a person dreams about a banquet in which many people are participating, it predicts that the dreamer will quarrel with his partner. If the dreamer is single, the dream predicts that he will get married soon – but there is no guarantee that the marriage will last.

Baptism

A dream about baptism has nothing to do with the religious ritual. In fact, if a person dreams about baptism, it means that he needs to tone down the way he taunts and scoffs at his friends and show a bit of strength of character. If he dreams that he is undergoing baptism, it means that he will stoop to anything, no matter how degrading, to win public acclaim.

Bar counter

If a person sees himself sitting at a bar counter in a dream, the dream attests to a hidden hope for a better future as well as the dreamer's lack of confidence.

If the dreamer sees himself leaning on the bar counter,

with the weight of his body inclined forward, the dream hints that the dreamer can expect advancement in life. This may mean anything to do with business and work, but advancement can be expressed in different areas: the birth of a new child, good results on a certain exam, a great improvement in his relationship with his spouse, and so on.

If a person sees himself sitting at the bar, drinking alone, it is a sign that there is someone who is pretending to be his friend but actually seeks to harm him and undermine him.

If the dreamer sees himself surrounded with friends at a bar, the dream hints at the fact that the patience and forbearance displayed by the dreamer will ultimately pay off. In order to accomplish the objective he set himself, he has to muster great mental fortitude, but he will ultimately come out on top.

If a person sees his friends drinking in a bar in a dream while he is not present, it is a sign that in reality he is far more important to his friends than he thinks. He sees himself as a marginal figure in the society in which he lives, but in fact he serves as an important and central figure, even though it always seems to him that he is worth "less" than in reality.

If a woman dreams this dream, and she sees herself sitting alone at the bar, there is a hint that she can expect not only financial success, but overall success in all the domains that are considered to be "male." She will do well in the "male" domain and will notch up respectable achievements as a result of her talents, mainly thanks to her exceptional ability to survive.

Barbecue

A dream about a barbecue indicates that the dreamer is suffering from extreme emotional pressure but is not making any effort to alleviate things or change the situation.

Barefoot

A person who dreams of strolling barefoot on the beach is on his way to success right now. Although difficulties can be expected, the future looks really rosy.

If the dreamer is wearing fancy clothes, it means that he is afraid of financial losses that are liable to leave him destitute, naked and barefoot. If the dreamer is a vagabond, barefoot and devoid of all possessions, it means that his fears are unbearable.

If the dreamer arrives at a party or fancy occasion barefoot and everyone looks at him in astonishment, it means that he has a secret that he is afraid to reveal publicly. He goes to great lengths to hide the secret, even though if he were to let others in on it, he would discover that there are many others in his situation and he has no reason to be ashamed.

Barking

If a person dreams that dogs are chasing him and barking, he must watch out. An unpleasant surprise will come from an unexpected quarter. There could be a huge family row that is liable to cause a break in relations or the dismantling of a business partnership. There could also be problems in the business realm. This is the time to scrutinize the paperwork regarding everything to do with banks and bookkeeping.

Barley

A dream that features fields of barely is a very positive dream, since it predicts great success of the dreamer. All of his wishes and desires will be realized. On the other hand, a dream about rotting barley implies loss.

Barn

If a dream features a barn that is packed with grain and corn, with well-fed, sleek cattle around it, it is a wonderful dream of prosperity and ease. The opposite is true if a person sees an empty barn in a dream: it warns of poverty.

Barometer

If a person sees a barometer in a dream, it means that there will be an upward trend and positive changes in his business affairs. If his dream features a broken barometer, it means that a series of undesirable and unanticipated events will take place in his professional life.

Baseball

If a person sees himself playing baseball in a dream, it means that his wishes will come true, he is easily pleased, and he enjoys great popularity with his comrades. If a young woman dreams that she is playing baseball, it will be a lot of fun, but she will not get anything more permanent or solid out of it.

Basin

This is a very good dream for a woman: If a woman dreams that she is washing herself in a basin, it attests to the fact that she will enjoy true friendship and will advance in life thanks to her feminine charms.

Basket

A basket in a dream implies good things, abundance, gifts and joy. This is even truer if the basket in the dream is full. A full basket promises success, prosperity and wealth, both on the financial and business level and on the social and personal level.

If a person dreams that he is carrying a full basket on his back, he feels that solutions to various situations in his life have been imposed on him rather than in agreement with his opinion. Inside himself, he feels the residues of these actions, and has not accepted this fact.

If a dream features a woman carrying a basket on her shoulders or on her back, it is a sign that the dreamer can expect health problems. The dreamer may be suffering from problems that have not yet manifested themselves outwardly, and he should be checked up in order to diagnose the problem as soon as possible. Such a dream also serves as a warning dream against various spells. This is not the time to consult with coffee readers or various people who bring back love by using spells. These types of magic must be avoided.

If a person dreams that he is carrying a particularly heavy basket, it is a sign that he is working very hard in his everyday life, and he feels that the burden weighs heavily on him. Sometimes he feels like a workhorse. He should take some time off, reorganize, and amass renewed energy.

A B C D E F G H I J K L M N O P Q R S T U V W X Y Z

Bass voice

If a person dreams that he has a bass voice, it means that one of his employees has been defrauding him. Hearing a bass voice in a dream does not bode well for lovers, since it predicts rows and arguments.

Basting

If a person sees himself basting meat in a dream, it means that he will sabotage his own chances of accomplishing his goals through his own egoism and stupidity.

Bat

If a dream features a bat that is not flying, it implies wisdom in most cases. The bat should be linked to the subject or object of the dream, and in general the appearance of the bat attests to the feeling of esteem and respect the dreamer has for the object of the dream, since he attributes qualities of wisdom and intelligence to him.

If a dream features a flying bat, it is a warning dream. It is a sign that bad, generally unreliable, news is in the offing, and the dreamer must check it out carefully. The dream hints at the negative atmosphere that will descend upon the dreamer along with awful feelings of sadness, grief, pain, anxiety and worry.

If a white bat appears in a dream (this is rare), the dream hints at potential disasters such as deaths, natural disasters and other calamities, whose results will be appalling.

Bath

A dream in which the dreamer sees himself taking a bath is a sign of prosperous business and of the fact that deals made by the dreamer will be successful and profitable.

If a person dreams about taking a bath together with other people, it is a sign that he is about to find himself at the epicenter of a scandal that will stick with him for a long time. The dreamer is liable to get into trouble because of simple, even stupid, things he did and could most certainly have avoided doing. A dream like this also attests to the fact that the friends around him do not demonstrate loyalty toward him and are liable to turn their backs on him when he needs them most. (This could happen exactly when he is in the middle of the scandal.)

A dream in which the bath-water looks murky attests to the fact that other people have conspired against the dreamer and are scheming against him. He is about to cope with difficulties whose dimensions he cannot measure, so it would be a good idea for him to prepare himself emotionally for a difficult period.

A dream in which the bath-water is boiling is a sign that the dreamer is unable to withstand his evil, diabolical urges and succumbs to them without a struggle. He does not have a strong character; it is easy to convince him to do things that he knows can in fact harm him, but he does not have the strength to resist. Even if his conscience tells him otherwise, he tends to seek immediate gratification and physical pleasures, and is unable to delay gratification.

A dream about a bath containing blocks of ice and icy water attests to the fact that the person succeeds in overcoming many obstacles in his path and in accomplishing his coveted goal. He does not shy away from dealing with difficult and unpleasant situations, and knows that only obstinacy, pertinacity and hard work will ultimately lead him successfully to the objective he set himself.

If the bath in the dream is cold (not icy), the dreamer is at a crossroads in his life. The future is cloudy and vague, and the dreamer does not know which road he should take and how he should act in order to fulfill his potential. He should let time tell. The answers to the questions at hand will appear later on.

If a person dreams about making love in the bath, the dream predicts a new love in the offing. Even if the dreamer is in a good relationship and everything looks fine, things will change in the near future, and a new love will burst into his life.

A dream in which the dreamer sees himself remaining in the bath for an especially long time attests to the fact that he has a penchant for a life of partying and entertainment, and is insatiable. Ultimately, the dreamer will find himself addicted – if not to the actual partying, to something related to it, such as alcohol, drugs, sex, and so on. The dream is a kind of warning against continuing this lifestyle when subconsciously, the dreamer knows that it is not doing him any good, and that he must begin to control it.

Bathing

If a person dreams about bathing in an icy river, sorrow is in the offing because of an illness or disaster that will afflict his family. Bathing in warm water (a sauna or a heated pool) is a good sign. Taking a bubble-bath in a fancy bathtub symbolizes unexpected financial success that will take the dreamer by surprise.

Bathroom

If a person dreams about a bathroom, it means that he is inclined to seek out empty and frivolous fun and amusement.

Batter

A dream about batter for pancakes or a cake means that the dreamer has luck in love. Moreover, he will inherit a place to live.

Battle

If a person witnesses a battle in a dream, it means that he will have to contend with difficulties, but eventually he will emerge victorious. If a dream features a defeat in battle, it implies that the dreamer will bear the brunt of other people's failed business ventures.

Bay

A dream about a bay or a lagoon that leads to the sea or ocean reflects the dreamer's desire for a breakthrough. This could refer to the professional arena; equally, there may be room for change in the dreamer's private life. If the water is turbulent, it means that he is in for some tough times when setting new plans in motion, and this will require courage and persistence on his part. In contrast, if the water is clear and calm, and the dreamer is going to swim, he can expect to succeed. If he is attacked by some creature in the water, he must shelve his plans at this stage, irrespective of the advice of experts or friends. The waiting period will turn out to be worthwhile.

Bay tree

A dream about a bay tree augurs very well: the person who has this dream will really enjoy his leisure time.

Bayonet

If a person dreams about a bayonet, it means that his enemies will capture him, and the only way he will be able to escape is if he gets hold of the bayonet in the dream.

Beaches

A beach (or beaches) in a dream indicates a longing for freedom, for a lack of borders, for hedonism, for trips, for journeys, for getting rid of a burden, for pampering and for recreation. The dream in fact indicates the desire for the repose, tranquillity and rest that the dreamer is sadly lacking. Life might be stressing the dreamer out and he wants to escape to a place where there are no obligations. He may be suffering from some other hardship that is troubling him, such as his marriage or another framework in which he feels a commitment from which he wants to free himself or take time out. In most cases, a dream about beaches occurs when the dreamer feels that he is in a situation in which it is not clear which path he must choose and what the best thing is for him to do. A dream about a beach or beaches also has a sexual connotation. Some people interpret it as indicating a longing to have sex and the absence of a relationship. The dreamer is yearning for physical pleasures that are sorely lacking in his life, and this is one of the expressions of his longing for sensuous lovemaking, full of passion and sexual thrills.

Beacon

If a dream features a shining beacon, it is a good omen for the sick, for people in distress and for seamen. A shining beacon is also a good sign for anything to do with business affairs. However, if the beacon goes out, it means that the dreamer's good luck will run out.

Beads

The meaning of a dream that features beads states that the dreamer will come to the notice of important people. If he counts beads in a dream, it is a sign of joy and happiness. If the beads are scattered all over in the dream, it means that the people who know the dreamer will think less highly of him than they did before.

Beans

A dream about beans is not a positive dream. If a person eats beans in a dream, it means that one of his good friends will fall ill or be plagued with problems and vicissitudes. If the person cultivates beans in his dream, it indicates that children will become ill.

A dream about dried beans indicates the dreamer's growing disillusionment with the state of the world. Some people interpret dried beans as indicating the advent of epidemics.

A
B
C
D
E
F
G
H
I
J
K
L
M
N
O
P
Q
R
S
T
U
V
W
X
Y
Z

Bear

A bear in a dream has various interpretations. A bear that is not connected to a particular deed or sight that is especially linked to the dream may imply two principal things:

The dreamer is expected to get into an argument or a conflict with someone who is known to be his enemy and wants to harm him. This is liable to lead to a real quarrel, so it is a kind of warning dream that alerts the dreamer to a possible future development. Anyway, the dreamer must be aware of what's awaiting him around the corner, and that is why he is liable to fall into a trap or encounter failure in a place where it was difficult for him to foresee it.

A bear that is not connected to anything specific can also indicate that things will not come to the dreamer easily. In order to reach his goal or fulfill his expectations and wishes, he will have to toil hard and invest in hard, back-breaking work. While he can expect difficult periods, if he persists, he will ultimately achieve the success he so longs and hopes for.

In contrast, if a person dreams about a bear in a cage, he can expect to enjoy success, but it may not necessarily result from hard work or toil. The success will come soon, even if the dreamer is not expecting it at this time at all.

The appearance of a bear or bears in a circus or in some kind of performance where they have to entertain an audience is a hint that the person is setting himself up for mockery and ridicule, and people are gossiping about him behind his back. He appears ridiculous, grotesque and contemptible in the eyes of other people. Despite his attempt to ignore the fact that this is how the people around him perceive him, he subconsciously knows that he must change his ways if he wants to change his image in the eyes of society. The dream reminds him that even if in his everyday life he does not come across blatant manifestations of contempt for him, the people around him are making fun of him behind his back.

If a person sees several bears in his dream and not just one, the meaning of the dream is similar: he is being gossiped about behind his back. Here the meaning is mainly that because of the lack of information concerning the dreamer's situation, rumors are flying, even if they do not have a firm basis in fact. People are slandering and transmitting incorrect information about the dreamer.

A dream about killing or overpowering a bear is a sign that the dreamer will enjoy a great deal of happiness, respect and success in the future, especially in the material realm. However, along with material success, there will be social success, with honor for the dreamer in tow. His economic basis will accord him a firm social standing, and as far as it can be seen, his social environment will change beyond recognition. Even if his status changes 180 degrees, as the dream prophesies, the dreamer must always remember where he came from, and what his roots are.

Dressing up as a bear in a dream implies that unpleasant news is in the offing. The dreamer will have to deal with bad news and be prepared to cope with it psychologically. The bad news will arrive unexpectedly, and is liable to change things so radically that the dreamer's entire world will be torn apart. If he is mentally strong, he will not let the things that will happen darken his world. Standing firm against the trouble will ensure the possibility of quickly overcoming the difficult events and getting back to normal.

A **B** C D E F G H I J K L M N O P Q R S T U V W X Y Z

Beard

A dream in which the dreamer sees a person with a full beard implies that he has great chances for success in almost all domains.

If a person with a sparse beard appears in a dream, it is a sign that the dreamer is about to lose a dear friend. This can happen because of the death of a friend or because of his sudden disappearance from the dreamer's world as a result of a breach in communication or the friend's desire to break off his relations with the dreamer.

If a married woman dreams about a man with a beard, it implies that she wants to leave her husband. Even if she is not aware of this in her everyday life, and continues to play the role of the faithful wife and the devoted and loving mother, deep in her heart she is yearning for the day when she will be released from all this and can really live as she wants to live.

If a pregnant woman dreams about a man with a beard, it is a prophetic dream that predicts that the dreamer's wish to give birth to a son is about to be fulfilled.

If a young girl dreams about a man with a beard, the dream prophesies that she will indeed marry the man of her choice. A dream like this generally occurs in problematic situations, when the marriage is not certain and there is a stumbling-block preventing the girl from marrying easily. This could take the form of objections on the part of his or her parents or the hesitance of the intended bridegroom.

If a person sees someone he does not know shaving off his beard in a dream, the dream prophesies a loss of money – as if the dreamer were having his assets "shaved off." In contrast, if the dreamer knows the person who is shaving, the dream hints at the dreamer's exaggerated self-confidence and his over-inflated self-esteem to the point of displaying contempt for others. He must be careful, otherwise his behavior will backfire on him.

The color of a beard in a dream is of particular importance:

A white beard attests to the dreamer's steadfast opinions and to the fact that he is a person of strong opinions from which it is difficult to budge him. Moreover, he gives the impression of someone who knows what he is talking about when he gets into an argument or an exchange in which he displays his knowledge to other people. Furthermore, a dream like this attests to prosperity, creativity and an ability to earn a good living and amass a great deal of money.

A black beard attests to the dreamer's success in business and his hedonism. His guiding motto is "eat, drink and be merry, for tomorrow…" He is a sharp person and is known for his great wisdom, so he succeeds in business.

A red beard implies that people are gossiping behind the dreamer's back, and that even if he thinks he has many friends, it turns out that not all of them are concerned for his well-being. This gossip has been provoked by some recent action of his.

A gray beard implies that the dreamer can expect a loss from his securities. The implication only involves investments of this type. If a person who does not have investments like these has this dream, it means that he must look after his health.

Beating

If a dreamer is beaten in a dream, it means that domestic strife and rows are in the offing. If he dreams that he beats a child in a dream, the dream serves to point out to the dreamer that he has a vile tendency to exploit other people mercilessly – particularly if they are weaker than he is.

Beauty

A dream about beauty in any form is a very positive dream. If a person sees a beautiful woman in a dream, he can look forward to a life of enjoyment and financial ease. If he dreams about a beautiful child, he can anticipate a good relationship with his partner.

Beauty parlor / Barbershop

A dream about a visit to a beauty parlor or barbershop can have many meanings. Coloring the hair or having a haircut (for both men and women) very likely attests to a fierce desire for change. One of the couple may feel tired, deceived or disappointed with the relationship and wants to alter his/her external appearance drastically in order to change, improve or annoy. If the husband likes long hair and the wife goes to the beauty salon and cuts her hair, this may indicate that she is rebelling against him and his desires. She may have found an easy way of telling him that she no longer takes his opinion into consideration. (One shouldn't generalize, of course, since in certain cases there are other reasons for this behavior.) In any event, a dream of this kind can also indicate the dreamer's sincere desire for changing and improving his external appearance. It is necessary to cut to the chase and examine the dream on the backdrop of the situation in reality. Not every visit to a beauty parlor or barbershop and change of image is necessarily a reason for a domestic row. If the results are satisfactory, the only thing left to do is to give a compliment.

Beaver

If a person sees a beaver in a dream, it implies that if he works diligently and with forbearance, he will achieve a very reasonable standard of living. If he kills a beaver in order to obtain its fur, the dream warns him of cheating innocent people and behaving unjustly and improperly toward them.

Bed

A dream about a bed can attest to problems in the marital and emotional sphere. A person who dreams that he buys a bed is in fact preparing himself for a new love affair. A person who sells a bed (in reality as well as in a dream) is detaching himself from an old love. The dreamer may not be ready to open his heart once more to a relationship of any kind. A bed upon which there are piles of objects attests to the fact that the dreamer is not sure about his sexuality and relationship. The topic requires profound examination.

Bedbugs

This is a very negative dream, since bedbugs in a dream symbolize disease, embroilments and often death. If a person sees a swarm of bedbugs, it foretells a death.

A B C D E F G H I J K L M N O P Q R S T U V W X Y Z

Bedfellow

If a person dreams that he cannot stand his bedfellow, it means that there is someone who is doing everything in his power to make the dreamer's life unbearable. If the person dreams that he finds a strange bedfellow in his bed, the dream implies that he will burden everyone around him with his own misery and problems.

Bed linen / Sheets

If the bed linen in a dream is clean, it means that the dreamer will soon receive good news from far away. If the bed linen in the dream is soiled, he can expect to suffer financial losses or health problems.

Bedroom

A dream about a bedroom is generally connected to sex and eroticism. Another interpretation of a bedroom in a dream is a positive turning-point in life.

Bedwetting

If a person dreams that he wets his bed, it implies some kind of disease or catastrophe that will throw his life into disarray. If a mother dreams that her child wets its bed, the dream indicates that she is fraught with the most extreme anxiety. This dream also implies that sick people will take a long time to recover from their illnesses.

Beef

The interpretation of beef in a dream varies according to the type of beef that appears:

If a person sees or eats cooked beef in a dream, it is a prediction of unbearable suffering and a really gruesome death.

If he sees raw, bloody beef in a dream, the dream warns of malignant tumors, and tells the dreamer to be on the lookout for any wounds or blemishes.

If he sees beef that is well-cooked and served, the dreamer will enjoy harmonious relations in business and love.

Beehive

The appearance of a beehive in a dream always attests to a happy event that is soon going to occur in the framework of the immediate family. A beehive symbolizes the center of life and activity, diligence, cooperation and happiness. It may refer to a happy event like a birth, an engagement or a wedding. This is the time for the dreamer and his family to reexamine existing relationships.

Beeper

If a person hears a beeper in his dream, it is a sign of an imminent crisis. If he dreams that he is using a beeper, it implies that someone close to the dreamer is soon going to become a burden, requiring constant care and attention.

Beer

If a dream features beer, it means that disappointment is in the offing. If a person sees people drinking beer at a bar, it means that there are people who are plotting to undermine his hopes.

Bees

The appearance of bees in a dream indicates various possibilities. The character of the dream changes according to the way in which the bees appear:

A general dream about bees hints at abundance and advancement in life, and points especially at good things that are about to occur in the dreamer's family life: festivities, happy events, and so on. A dream about bees also attests to the fact that the dreamer has good friends who would go through fire and water for him. The dreamer knows that he has people to depend on in times of trouble, and he is given a great deal of support by his friends for anything he does.

If a person sees swarms of bees in his dream, his success in life will be as great.

A dream about a bee sting or bee stings is a sign that the dreamer is placing his trust in a person who is completely untrustworthy. Not only can the dreamer expect that person to scheme against him, but other betrayals may be lying in wait for him. He must be cautious and plan for every unexpected blow that is liable to come like a stab in the back. A dream like this hints at a great disappointment and a momentary loss of control.

Chasing bees away in a dream: If a person dreams that he sees a lot of bees and he flaps his hands at them in order to chase them away, it is a prophetic dream that hints that a fire is liable to break out in his home. He must make very sure to enforce safety regulations so that a fire does not actually break out in his home.

If wealthy people dream about bees: If a rich man dreams about bees, the dream implies that eventually, from all the honey and the sting, he will remain with only the sting. He must be careful of spurious deals and of the temptation to make a fast buck. It would be preferable for him not to take shortcuts that lead nowhere, but rather to go the long, hard way that eventually leads safely to the goal.

If a poor man dreams about bees, the dream hints at the opposite: From all thc honey and the sting, he will remain with an abundance of honey. The dream does not necessarily refer to financial abundance, but rather at "honey" in the form of a good and happy life that will be reflected mainly in his family life. Even if the dreamer has many children and no financial resources, the "honey" will appear in other ways, such as through the great love between the children and between the parents, mutual support and great self-confidence in his inner abilities.

Beet

Dreams about beets augur well. A dream that features a lush beet field implies that the dreamer's country will enjoy peace. If a person dreams about eating beets in the company of other people, the beets indicate that good news is on the way.

Beetle

Despite the immediate associations the beetle evokes in us (such as the common "dung" beetle), it was considered to be a sacred symbol in ancient cultures. For this reason, a dream about a beetle is accorded particular importancc, hinting at the fact that the drcamer is not an ordinary person like evcryone else around him: he is destined for greatness. He may become very famous in the near future because of his life's work or because of a special activity in which he is a participant or that he initiated or carried out. He may also not be aware of the fact that he is creating something special that will be discovered by the media one day – possibly as a result of coincidental publicity. The dream implies that the dreamer will be widely recognized for something in which he is involved in and which will bring him a great deal of honor and prestige. The fame following the discovery will arrive suddenly, and the dreamer will have no way of "preparing himself" for it. For this reason, he must relate to the dream as an advance signal.

A dream about a beetle – not necessarily the common "dung" beetle, but rather any beetle – can also imply that the dreamer is surrounded by malicious gossip that is being spread by someone who wishes him ill. In general, the envious person is spreading lies because he cannot stomach the dreamer's success or the wholeness of his life. This vicious gossip will eventually die down, since the people around the dreamer known him well and are aware of his deeds and personality. The dreamer can discard this worry.

If a person dreams about a ladybird – a small red beetle with black dots – the meaning of the dream is similar but more specific. The dream implies that the dreamer is facing a special opportunity for success, and he must take advantage of it and not let it slip through his fingers. The dream hints at a window of opportunity that will soon open up in front of the dreamer. There is no guarantee that it will ever recur. The dreamer must identify the once-in-a-lifetime nature of the situation and be able to exploit the moment for his own benefit. He must not be complacent; he should be alert, since this opportunity is on the doorstep.

Beggar

If a person dreams about himself dressed like a beggar, his present situation is not good but will soon change. A win of a large sum of money or an inheritance will surprise him and his family. If a person dreams that the members of his family are beggars, his dream indicates that he is very anxious about the situation and is worried about his family's welfare. The situation is likely to change very soon.

Beheading

If a person dreams about being beheaded, it is a very negative dream that predicts total failure in some kind of enterprise or a terrible defeat in the near future. If the person sees others being beheaded in a dream, with blood spurting out copiously, it portends violence, exile and death.

Bell

If a person hears a bell ringing in a dream, he can be sure that it predicts the arrival of bad tidings regarding a distant relative: this could be death.

Belladonna

A dream about belladonna signifies that if a person makes the correct moves in business, he will enjoy financial success. However, if a woman dreams about belladonna, it means that she will have to fight other rivals for the man she has her eye on.

If a person dreams that he takes belladonna, the dream

implies that he is not acquitting his duties, and that he will experience devastating unhappiness.

Bellman

If a person sees a bellman in his dream, he will have good luck and will be able to settle any disputes he may have in an amicable manner. If the bellman looks sad, the dream predicts that there is some kind of sad event in the offing.

Bellows

If a dream features bellows, it means that the dreamer will not have an easy time at all. However, he will gradually overcome his difficulties and poverty by means of hard work and an energetic attitude. If he sees a bellows in a dream, it means that friends who are far away miss him. If he can hear a bellows in his dream, he will become familiar with occult practices.

Belly

If a person sees a healthy belly in a dream, it means that he is suffering from irrational desires. If the belly in his dream is swollen, the dream predicts illness.

Belt

A dream in which the dreamer sees himself wearing a belt or measuring his waist – with decorative intentions – is a sign that the dreamer can expect treats and pleasures linked to pleasant company, trips, physical pleasure and hedonism for its own sake.

A belt that appears randomly in a dream implies that a sum of money that was supposed to reach the dreamer a long time ago will arrive soon. This could be money owing to him that was supposed to be repaid but has not yet been repaid, but it may come from savings and freeing up other money such as a pension fund or the like.

A dream about a belt whose purpose is utilitarian symbolizes completely disinterested love that is coming the dreamer's way. That love will be innocent and will give him solace from the extreme hardship that has been his lot until now. The dream predicts a good period that will soothe and heal the pains of the past.

If a particularly worn-out belt appears in a dream, it is a sign that the dreamer must watch out for stingy friends and that he should not trust them. The dream warns him that this kind of relationship will end in great disappointment.

A leather belt in a dream implies a financial achievement of the dreamer that will happen because of parsimonious behavior. Even though this is generally a bad trait, in this instance it is thanks to the dreamer's penny-pinching conduct in a particular financial deal that he will gain handsome profits and notch up respectable achievements. His extreme thrift has benefited him greatly this time.

If a tight belt features in a dream, it is a sign of extravagance. The dreamer has gotten into a situation in which his expenses were much higher than he expected and what he can afford.

Bench

If a person sees himself sitting on a bench in a dream, it warns him not to confide in anyone. If he sees other people sitting on a bench, it is a good sign: he will enjoy happy reunions and reconciliation with long-lost friends.

Bequest

A dream about a bequest is a positive dream. If a person dreams about a bequest, it means that he will derive pleasure from tasks and duties well done. It also means that he will have healthy children.

Bereavement

This dream has a symbolic rather than a literal meaning. If a person dreams about the death of a child, it implies that his plans will be foiled unexpectedly, and rather than enjoying success, he will suffer the humiliation of failure.

Betting

If a person dreams that he is placing bets on races, it is a warning dream: he must exercise great caution when undertaking new ventures. This is because his adversaries are lying in wait to entrap him and get him entangled in a mass of complications and problems.

If the dreamer sees himself placing his bets in a casino, it means that someone is about to extort money from him.

Beverages

Intoxicating beverages in a dream are a sign that someone is trying to defraud the dreamer and that he is liable to fall into the trap. He must be careful of people who are plotting against him.

If a person dreams about thirst, a lack of water and an

inability to drink, the dream implies that he will suffer from poverty and deprivation all his life because this is his fate.

If a dream features a murky beverage, it means that the dreamer's good friends are liable to turn their backs on him, and he will find himself isolated. He has to muster psychological forces for this struggle.

If the beverage in the dream is warm, it is a sign that the dreamer's friends are loyal to him, are prepared to through fire and water for him, and will help him in difficult times.

A dream about a beverage that looks like clear spring water is a sign of a speedy recovery from a serious illness the dreamer will have to cope with. It can also mean that great happiness can be expected in his family, bringing him and his family joy and a feeling of unity and shared destiny.

If a person dreams about drinking blood, the dream hints that happiness and joy are in store for him.

If the cup from which the dreamer drinks in the dream is clean, it is a sign that he will find immediate employment. If he is unemployed or a student who is looking for work in his field of study, the dreamer can be absolutely sure that he will find work soon. If, in contrast, the dreamer is a person who is already working and is not looking for a job, the dream must be interpreted as a hint that he is about to receive a promotion or a raise or both.

A dream that features mineral water as a beverage implies that the dreamer can expect to become involved in a romantic liaison in the near future.

If the dreamer sees himself drinking from a jar, it is a sign that he enjoys his circle of acquaintances and that the people around him believe in him. He can rely on them.

If the dreamer sees another person sipping from his drink in the dream, it is a sign that great sorrow is in the offing for him.

A dream in which the dreamer sees himself sipping a sweet beverage with his partner is a sign that many people will love and admire him.

If a person dreams that he becomes intoxicated as a result of drinking a sweet beverage, the dream hints at great wealth for the dreamer as a result of the support of his friends and acquaintances.

Bible

If a person dreams about the Bible, it means that there are innocent pleasures in store for him. If he scoffs at the Bible, it means that he is about to succumb to the immoral temptations offered by one of his friends.

Bicycle

Riding a bicycle in a dream implies haste on the one hand and the dreamer's willingness to help someone in distress on the other.

If the dreamer sees himself riding a bicycle, especially downhill, the dream indicates that the pace of the dreamer's life is too fast. He must slow down and arrange his actions judiciously. Sometimes, the mistakes he makes stem from the fact that he does not stop to think about whether what he is doing is good for him. If the slope is especially steep, the dream warns of an accident and danger – a traffic accident or some other kind of accident. The danger is real and is liable to cost the dreamer his life. It is a warning dream to which the dreamer must pay attention; he must not scoff at it.

If the dreamer sees himself riding uphill, the dream brings good tidings: he can anticipate economic, social and domestic success, and his future looks rosier than ever.

A dream about a new bicycle attests to the fact that the dreamer is endowed with powerful ambition and with a fierce desire to prove himself and succeed in life.

A dream about an old bicycle attests to the fact that the dreamer is going through a period of transition. He is in the process of moving from an old apartment to a new one, from one country to another, from one job to another, from a particular occupation to a completely different field, from one relationship to another, and so on. In one or more areas of his life, the dreamer is not in a clear-cut position, but a dream about an old bicycle generally attests to the fact that the forthcoming period in the dreamer's life will be good, and that the future will be rosier than before. In any event, he can expect a better period than the preceding one and an improvement in his lot in life up till now.

If the dreamer sees himself falling off a bicycle in a dream, it means that the dream is warning him of an economic crash. He is about to lose money or property or some kind of capital.

Bier

A dream about a bier does not augur well. If a person dreams about a bier, it predicts huge losses and a deterioration in the state of health of one of his relatives. If he sees a flower-strewn bier in a church, he can be sure that he will have an unhappy marriage.

Bigamy

If a man dreams about bigamy, it attests to the fact that his potency is failing him and he is losing his cerebral powers. If a woman dreams about bigamy, she risks losing her good reputation unless she behaves with tremendous discretion.

Billiards

When a billiard table appears in a dream, with or without are people playing billiards on it, it is a warning dream. It warns mainly of people who seek to harm the dreamer, and hints that problems are in the offing. The problems will be caused principally by people with whom the dreamer is in contact, and not by objective difficulties. The dreamer will find it difficult to make contact with people whose actions are likely to affect his economic situation. He must be tolerant and adaptable. If he stands up for his principles and is too stubborn, he is liable to lose.

Bills

A dream in which a person sees himself paying bills is a sign that he is about to come into a large sum of money. Whether it is money from a win or profits from a big business transaction, the dreamer is exempt from any money worries. Soon, all his money-related problems will be solved, and he will be able to breathe freely.

If the dreamer sees himself receiving a bill for payment, the dream does not augur well. It attests to the fact that someone is conspiring against him and seeks to harm him. This person does not sit with his arms folded, but rather works toward paying the dreamer back for something he did that was not to the person's liking. The dreamer may soon be served a summons to appear in court or will be "punished" somehow for something he did. This could take the form of vicious gossip or some other way of spreading malicious rumors about the dreamer.

Billy-goat

A billy-goat in a dream symbolizes Satan, demons, or an evil spirit.

Binoculars – See Eyeglasses.

Birds

A dream about birds is interpreted in different ways, in accordance with the context in which the birds appear and the dreamer's situation:

Birds flying in a dream are a sign that the dreamer will enjoy a life of ease, prosperity and wealth. Success will shine on him, and he may make handsome profits in business or from investments that yield excellent dividends. This meaning is ascribed to the dream if it is dreamed by an ordinary person who is neither rich nor poor. The meaning of the dream is the opposite if it is dreamed by a wealthy person who is used to living in conditions of financial ease. In such a case, the dream actually implies that the rich person will be stripped of some of his assets, and is liable to lose his entire fortune in the near future. His economic status, just like his social status, will plummet.

If a person dreams about a bird of prey, the dream means that the dreamer can expect good luck in gambling, lotteries or investments (such as stocks and so on). The consequences of this good luck include a rise in standard of living, a chance to achieve things that previously seemed to be attainable only in dreams, and the accomplishment of goals that are now achievable. Some people attribute a dream that features birds of prey to possible difficulties in

A B C D E F G H I J K L M N O P Q R S T U V W X Y Z

the near future. Despite the problems that will crop up, the dreamer will most likely cope with the difficulties and solve them within a short time. In other words, even if he encounters a difficult and problematic period, he must know that it is only temporary.

An injured or sick bird in a dream is a sign of problems in the family that will evoke feelings of frustration, anxiety and insecurity in the dreamer. The dreamer will suffer from a material or psychological wound caused by a member of his family. The wound will torment the dreamer and cause him great disappointment.

A killed bird in a dream hints at a lack of success in various areas, mainly those connected with money matters. The dreamer will suffer from economic problems that will influence every aspect of his life. He can expect to experience a chain reaction, since his inability to stand his ground economically will harm his family and social life. His depressed mental condition will make his return to work difficult, and only the latter can restore his economic security.

A dream in which birds are deliberately exterminated hints that the dreamer can expect to go through a period of cruelty that will cause him great suffering. Even if this period is brief, its effects will be felt for a long time after it has ended. (People suffering from shell-shock have reported a dream of this kind.) Memories and experiences from the difficult period will accompany the dreamer for a long time and will not let up.

A dream that features a bird in a cage actually hints at a very happy period that the dreamer will go through all of a sudden (a big love will come onto the scene unexpectedly, he will come into a large some of money, etc.). The good surprise will change the course of the person's life, and it will never go back to what it was.

A dream that features birds in a tree serves as a symbol of love, warmth, tranquillity and calm that will be the dreamer's lot in anything concerning his family life and his marriage. Life will flow smoothly, and the dreamer's personal "nest" will be padded with love and happiness.

A dream about birds that approach the dreamer fearlessly or about birds that feed from the dreamer's hand implies that good and happy things are about to happen to the dreamer, even though he does not think about or imagine them at all. This refers mainly to advancement at work, such as a higher rank, a raise in salary and so on.

A dream in which birds are fighting is a sign that there will soon be a row between the dreamer and one of his good friends. The differences of opinion will be expressed in a threatening and unpleasant way, and the argument is liable to be bitter. As a result of the incident, the dreamer may lose one of his best and closest friends.

Birds mating in a dream is a joyful sign that hints that the dreamer will enjoy happiness and good luck in his love life. He will find a mate who will complement him, his sex life will be good and fulfilling, and he will derive satisfaction from his excellent relationship with his partner.

If a dream features a bird that is obviously black in color, it is a hint that soon the dreamer can expect to receive unusual news, some kind of surprise, something that he is not expecting at all. The dream does not indicate the nature of the news, but rather implies that it will arrive soon.

A dream in which a bird appears on the background of dazzling sunshine is a sign that in the near future, the dreamer will be satisfied with the situation he is in. Matters concerning his job or his family may reach an even keel and give him satisfaction.

A dream that features a bird flying in the dark is a sign of bad luck that will plague the dreamer: plans he devised will not be implemented or will be implemented in the wrong way, investments he made will not yield the desired results, and so on. Having said that, the bad luck will last for a short time only, and he will recover from it quickly and without any serious "scars."

Chirping birds in a dream are a sign of the joy and happiness the dreamer will enjoy. A dream like this also symbolizes the dreamer's optimistic attitude toward life. Even during difficult and stressful periods, he always looks at the full half of the glass. This attitude always makes him feel happy and satisfied with his lot.

Bird's nest

The meaning of a bird's nest in a dream changes in accordance with the situation in which the bird's nest appeared in the dream – empty or with nestlings or eggs.

An abandoned nest in a dream means that nothing that is linked to the dreamer's future looks good. The dreamer must prepare for a difficult period that will strengthen him in life and cause a change in his view of the world. Ultimately, difficult experiences like the ones he can expect to go through will cause him to appreciate everything he achieves in life more.

A dream that features a nest with eggs implies that the dreamer will have a rosy future filled with good luck. The world will shine on the dreamer and he will not have to toil too hard to accomplish his goals. He will see the fruits of all his actions and will enjoy prosperity and success, both on the economic and on the social planes. He will be fortunate in business (and if he is lucky, in his work) and will be held in high esteem by all the people around him.

A dream that features a nest in which there are nestlings implies that the dreamer will be clever enough to strike good deals in all his affairs. If the dreamer of this dream is self-employed and owns a business, the investments he makes will yield good dividends, and he will earn more and more money.

A person who does not have a great deal of capital will also see good results in every financial investment he makes both in investments in saving plans or shares, and in "investments" in a game of chance or gambling – from a game in a casino to the investment of not particularly large sums of money in games of chance that will engender impressive success.

Birth

A dream about a birth hint at great joy and a new beginning. Perhaps the birth of a baby in the family is in the offing. There may be other changes, such as moving to a new home or buying a car.

Birth (of animals)

A dream about animals being born is a warning dream: the dreamer has enemies who are conspiring against him behind his back. However, he will get the better of them and will manage to achieve his goals.

A B C D E F G H I J K L M N O P Q R S T U V W X Y Z

Birthday

If the dreamer is a young person, a birthday warns of crooked dealings and poverty. If an old person dreams about a birthday, he can expect to suffer from problems and solitude.

However, if a person has a dream about birthday gifts, it is a good dream that predicts pleasant surprises, advancement and fulfilled potential.

Biscuit – See Cookie

Bishop

If the person who dreams about a bishop is an author or a teacher, his mind will be tortured by the intricacies of the material he works with. If the dreamer is a tradesman, the dream warns him that if he persists in getting involved in illogical transactions, he is going to lose a great deal of money. If any other person sees a bishop in a dream, hard labor is in store for him – in addition, he will have a fever and will suffer from chills. If the dreamer admires a bishop in real life, and the latter gives him his approval, the dreamer will be successful.

Bite

This is not a positive dream. If a person dreams about biting something, it means that he wants to turn back the clock and undo something that cannot be undone. In addition, one of his adversaries will make him suffer.

Blackberries

A dream about blackberries carries a warning: the dreamer must be on the ball when it comes to anything to do with changes in his financial status. The dream warns of a financial downfall and of material losses. The dreamer might find himself involved in some kind of crisis that will cause him to lose a portion of his assets. He must keep away from anything that can engender his financial ruin, such as investments that he did not check out thoroughly, gambles of various kinds, and so on. Having said that, the dream only warns of a drop in economic status; this need not necessarily be accompanied by a deterioration in any other sphere of life, such as a change in his social status, his family status, or the like.

Blackout

If a person dreams about an electrical blackout, it means that he will forget something very important.

Black person

If a person finds himself in a room full of people and immediately notices a black person among them, he can expect good and surprising news.

If the dreamer sees himself as another person's black servant, he may have a year of particularly hard work ahead of him.

A woman who dreams that she is in love with a black man expresses her desire for a different relationship than the one she is in at the moment.

A B C D E F G H I J K L M N O P Q R S T U V W X Y Z

Blacksmith

A dream about a blacksmith has several meanings. On the one hand, a blacksmith constitutes a symbol of the link between the conscious and the unconscious worlds. The dreamer is advised to examine himself or avail himself of professional help in order to discover whether he has any "dark secrets" from the past that he does not remember clearly and that are affecting his present-day life. On the other hand, a less mystical meaning of a dream about a blacksmith represents the dreamer's feeling of power. Traditionally, a blacksmith is a strong person who succeeds in subduing the strongest metal, shaping and molding it according to his wishes. The dreamer may not really be conscious of his inner strengths, but he is capable of using them to attain very significant achievements in the future. If he does in fact succeed in focusing on his precise desires, he will surprise himself and those around him with his rapid and impressive achievements.

Bladder

A dream about a bladder is a warning dream: the dreamer must on no account neglect any health problems, because this could lead to problems in business.

Blame

If a person dreams that he is being blamed for something, the dream implies that he will soon get into some kind of dispute. If the dreamer himself is blaming someone else, it means that he is about to quarrel with his associates.

Blanket

A dream about a blanket generally indicates changes for the better that the dreamer can look forward to in his life: a positive turning point in his status at work or in business; a move to a better home; a salary raise or an improvement in his financial situation; and an improvement in his quality of life.

As ridiculous as it sounds, the appearance of the blanket is what determines the meaning of the dream. The thicker the blanket, and the more colorful and beautiful the design on it is, the better the dreamer's luck will be.

A dream in which a person covers himself with a blanket is a sign of his desire to flee from reality. Having said that, the dreamer must know that reality will pursue him and he cannot avoid dealing with things.

If a person covers himself and someone else (usually his partner) with a blanket, his dream predicts that help will come from an unexpected or unknown quarter. Even if the dreamer does not expect any difficulties at the moment, he is liable to get into a difficult situation from which he will quickly be able to extricate himself thanks to this help.

If a dreamer sees other people asleep under a blanket, the dream implies that he is liable to be tempted to commit a misdemeanor. A friend will convince him to participate in an illegal activity, and he is liable to be drawn into it out of curiosity or the desire to get something out of it. This could cost him dearly, so he is advised to be cautious and refuse any such proposal. He should heed the dream's message and adopt it.

A B C D E F G H I J K L M N O P Q R S T U V W X Y Z

Blasphemy

If a person witnesses blasphemy in a dream, or blasphemes, it is a warning that he has false friends who can do him a great deal of damage.

Blaze

If a person dreams about a blaze or roaring flames, it symbolizes pent-up rage that is finally released. If a blaze is extinguished in a dream, the dreamer can expect to receive good tidings in the near future.

Bleating

If a person hears the sound of animals bleating in a dream, he can soon expect to have new cares and responsibilities. These will not necessarily be negative ones. He will have to display generosity.

Bleeding

A dream about bleeding is a warning dream: the dreamer should have a checkup in order to preempt or identify health problems.

Blind

If a person dreams that he is blind, it is a very negative dream that indicates that he will soon plummet from wealth to poverty. If other people appear blind in his dream, he can expect to be called upon to help someone who needs his assistance.

Blindfold

A person who dreams that his eyes are blindfolded is expressing his feeling of dissatisfaction, loss of control and sense that there are many things that are hidden from him, despite all of his efforts to see straightforwardly.

The person who dreams that his eyes are blindfolded is not satisfied and has to take action to change this situation quickly, whether it involves changing his workplace or moving house. Perhaps somebody has set a trap for him or is concealing information from him. The disappointment can be temporary on condition that the dreamer takes action to clarify the situation thoroughly.

Blind Man's Buff

A dream about the children's game of Blind Man's Buff is a warning dream: The dreamer is on the verge of doing something that will cause him humiliation and financial loss.

Blindness

Blindness in a dream generally indicates infidelity or a mild illness that the dreamer is about to contract. If a person dreams that he himself is blind, it is a dream with a clear message: the dreamer is blind to everything that is linked to his love life, and is about to be led astray by misrepresentation.

His intended partner does not really feel great love for him. He must open his eyes and look at reality and be able to internalize what is so difficult for him to admit: that the love he thinks he is receiving is not genuine. He made the

A B C D E F G H I J K L M N O P Q R S T U V W X Y Z

wrong choice. Having said that, it's not too late to fix it.

If a person dreams that he is leading a blind person and showing him the way, the dream implies that the dreamer is placing his trust in someone who is not worthy of it and who is deceiving him.

He must not be taken in by sweet talk, but must rather examine things and see the extent to which they can actually tried and tested.

Blood

In general, if blood appears in a dream, no matter in what context, it is a warning dream. In most cases, the dream warns of rows with people close to the dreamer, of differences of opinions, of quarrels with the dreamer's partner, of a difficult period of anger and outbursts as a result of the slightest provocation, especially at the workplace, and of unnecessary irritation and **....?** that the dreamer will later regret, but it may be too late.

If a person sees blood flowing from a wound in a dream, it implies that he is going to suffer from diseases and worries, or that they are knocking at the door. He must prepare himself properly and not become unduly stressed. Keeping his cool will mitigate the situation and lead to a rapid improvement.

If a person who is involved in a romantic relationship dreams about blood, the dream implies that this relationship is not successful and that the dreamer must end it, since he is in some kind of danger.

If the blood that is seen in the dream is the dreamer's blood, the dream implies that the dreamer is involved in a love affair that will only lead to disappointment, disillusionment, despair, worries and an overall bad feeling.

If the person sees other people's blood in the dream, and it is clear to him that it is not his own blood, the dream attests to his ruthless nature. He will do anything to accomplish his goal and get what he wants, including trampling on his good friends without the slightest hesitation. The dream warns of "elbowing one's way" unnecessarily and of despicable behavior that cannot be forgiven.

If a person sees blood flooding the place in which the dream is taking place, the dream warns him against a dangerous occupation he is thinking of engaging in or is already engaged in. The dream also warns of an accident that is liable to have very bad consequences. The dreamer must calculate his actions wisely and carefully, be responsible and act logically, since not only is his life at stake, but also the lives of people who are connected to him, and he should behave more cautiously.

If a person dreams of having a blood test, the dream warns of a terrible embroilment from which he will have no chance of extricating himself. The embroilment will only get worse until there is no way out of the situation. It is better to adopt the attitude of "a stitch in time saves nine" and get out now while it is still possible.

Bloodstone

This is not a particularly good omen for the success of the dreamer's relationships.

Blossom

A dream that features one blossom or several blossoms opening indicates that the dreamer can expect to receive good news. This could be economic blooming, or success in the business or personal realm.

A blooming blossom that wilts soon afterwards implies disappointment in the romantic realm. What started with a bang will go out with a whimper. The dreamer will awaken from his initial enthusiasm after he gets to know the object of his love better.

Blows

Dreams that feature blows of any kind serve as an expression of the dreamer's feelings of anger. Whether the dreamer participates in a fistfight or whether he is the victim of an assault, the dream actually refers to a feeling of emptiness, frustration and cumulative anger. If the dreamer does not examine it and change it, there is no doubt that there will be a crisis in personal or work relations.

The dream implies the dreamer's lack of peace of mind. The dreamer may be involved in a real brawl or in a verbal argument in the workplace or within the family framework. The dispute will quickly ignite, and those involved will not realize that they are being dragged into a situation that will be difficult to resolve or to predict its outcome. Recommendation: Be careful of delicate situations.

Blushing

If a woman dreams about blushing, she will be embarrassed and tormented by unjustified accusations. If she sees other people blush in a dream, it means that her friends do not approve of her behavior in the least.

Boa constrictor

If a person dreams about a boa constrictor, it means that there are problems and misfortunes in the offing. However, if he manages to kill the snake, it is a good sign.

Board

There are different interpretations for dreams about boards. A dream about a teacher who is standing next to the board and explaining something means that the dreamer is in need of professional help and counseling. In his heart, he longs to return to his schooldays, when he could address every problem to his teacher for clarification.

A person who dreams that he himself is standing next to the board and writing on it is going through a period of hard work that irks him more than he is prepared to admit to other people. However, it is important to mention that the effort is worthwhile, and if he persists, he will gain recognition, remuneration, power and influence.

A dream about the Ouija board used in seances generally serves as a warning to the dreamer. A work-related or a personal problem is bothering the dreamer. He is prepared to consult with and listen to anyone at all in order to ease his bad feeling.

Consulting with people who are involved in the world of mysticism is liable to do more harm than good since the dreamer may succumb to temptation and follow undesirable directions. Contradictory information is liable to cause him confusion and will not help him reach a decision. The dreamer must take a break and weigh up the moves that will be good for him in the future.

Boarding house

A dream about a boarding house implies that the dreamer will become badly embroiled in problems in business. It also indicates that he will move house.

Boasting

If a person dreams that he boasts to a rival, it implies that he will use unfair means to beat him. If the person hears someone else boasting in a dream, it means that the dreamer is about to do something impulsive that will cause tremendous trouble for his friends. He will pay dearly for this action.

Boat

A boat in a dream heralds changes in life and the ability to accomplish missions successfully.

A dream in which the dreamer sees himself sailing in stormy waters is a sign that soon the dreamer will receive bad news that will cause him great disappointment. On the other hand, however, some people interpret such a dream as predicting great and long-lasting joy.

A dream about sailing in calm waters is a sign of the changes that can be expected in life. In most cases, these changes refer to the dreamer's residence – a change of address and moving from a small home to a large one. However, the expected changes in his life will also take place in other areas, such as work, financial status and so on.

If a person dreams that there is a hole in the boat he is sailing in and water is threatening to seep in, the dream warns of a secret being leaked. When secrets are not kept efficiently, they are liable to be revealed in public.

Rowing a boat in a dream is a sign of success in business and in everything to do with money matters. Correct and important decisions will yield positive results that will be manifested in financial profit.

A dream about a lifeboat is a prophetic dream. A stranger will come to the dreamer's aid in his hour of distress and need. Even if the dreamer has close friends, salvation will come from an unexpected quarter – from a stranger – in time of trouble.

A rubber dinghy in a dream does not augur well. It prophesies despair in matters of the heart as well as a financial loss that will be significant in the dreamer's life and will affect his future.

If a person dreams about a security boat (such as a navy vessel or a boat in the service of the coast guard), he feels that the authorities are sticking their noses into his affairs and are not giving him any peace. There may be an unresolved matter on the agenda, and the bureaucratic mess is bothering the dreamer.

A dream in which the dreamer sees himself smuggling someone in a boat is a sign that he is about to receive money from a spurious source. This is liable to be a stumbling-block for him and may well trip him up. He should examine every deal he gets into very carefully and ascertain what the source of the money he receives from it is.

If a person sees himself sailing in a boat with a lover, it is a sign that his love is in danger.

If the dreamer sees a sailor in the boat, he can expect to notch up a financial achievement, and his situation is about to improve beyond recognition.

If an empty boat is seen sailing in mid-ocean, it is a sign that a friend or an associate of the dreamer is in danger.

An inverted boat in a dream implies that soon the dreamer will receive very important news that will have an enormous effect on his future.

Bobbin

A dream about a bobbin implies that the dreamer will be entrusted with an important project. He will be in deep trouble if the project is not completed.

Bog

A dream that features a bog symbolizes unbearably oppressive worries and burdens. Moreover, it is a sign that the dreamer is liable to become ill.

Boiler

If a person dreams about a boiler that does not work, it implies disappointment and mismanagement. If he dreams that he is checking on a boiler, the dream warns of disease and loss.

Boiling

If a woman dreams about a pot that is boiling, it is a good omen that hints at congenial social obligations. If a dreamer sees a boiling kettle, he can be sure that his problems are over and he can look forward to a good phase in life.

Boils

If a person sees a pus-filled, bleeding boil in his dream, it is a warning that bad things are going to happen in the immediate future – for instance, he is going to discover that one of his best friends is not a friend at all. If the dreamer has a boil on his forehead in the dream, it means that someone close to him is soon going to become ill.

Boisterousness

A dream about the dreamer's wildness and unrestrained behavior, his lack of limits, frameworks or conditions, is interpreted as implying that the dreamer is about to lose his shirt. He is facing a difficult financial period, and even bankruptcy is possible. He must reduce his expenditure, plan his actions judiciously and take steps for "recovery" so as not to allow the situation to deteriorate to such an extent that there is no way back. The boisterousness in the dream reflects the dreamer's irresponsibility in everyday life in anything to do with money and economic measures. If the dreamer is single, and it is only his life that depends on his rash conduct, so be it. However, if the dreamer is a family man with children, and other people's lives depend on him, he has to stop squandering his money and curb himself financially sooner rather than later.

Bolts

The appearance of bolts in a dream does not augur well: it means that the dreamer will encounter almost insurmountable obstacles along his path. If he sees old or broken bolts in his dream, it means that he can expect to fail.

A B C D E F G H I J K L M N O P Q R S T U V W X Y Z

Bombshell

A dream about a bombshell is a negative dream: it is an indication of disputes and legal litigation.

Bones

If a person sees his bones protruding from his flesh in a dream, it implies that he is going to fall victim to the treachery of other people. If a dream features a pile of bones, it predicts famine and other very negative things.

Bonnet

If a person dreams about a bonnet, it is a sign of slander and gossip. If a dream features a black bonnet, it means that the dreamer's friends of the opposite sex cannot be trusted.

Book

A book that appears in a dream attests to prosperity and growth on the horizon that will result from studying.

If the dreamer sees a torn, worn-out book in his dream, it is a sign that ancient wisdom is about to direct him along his path in life. He will encounter the ancient theory or wisdom that will guide him, and will give him powers and strengths to carry on.

If a person dreams about looking at a row of books (on a shelf, for example), the dream attests to the fact that studies bring the dreamer joy and happiness, and that his career will be a success story.

A dream in which the dreamer repairs a torn book is a sign that he will achieve illumination in life, and will always be happy with his lot.

If a stained book appears in a dream, the dreamer can expect problems in business. Because of these problems, he will be sad, and things will be bad and difficult for him.

If a person dreams that there are pages torn out of the book, the dream implies that he has made a serious mistake in judgment. He did not weigh up all the aspects that were presented to him, and by so doing has done a certain person a great injustice.

If a person sees himself leafing through a book in a dream, the dream implies that he is looking for solutions to difficult situations and is trying hard to solve various problems that are linked to a trial that will take place in the near future.

Bookcase

A dream that features a bookcase implies that the dreamer's whole life – professional and domestic – will revolve around learning. If the bookcase in the dream is empty, it means that he is unable to earn a living.

Bookstore

If a person dreams about a bookstore, it means that his regular job is disrupted by his literary aspirations.

Boots

A person who dreams about boots that are too tight for him is in a tight and uncomfortable position, worse than he thinks and admits to himself and others. High or military boots can attest to a long journey to distant lands where a lot of walking is required. The dream serves as a kind of mental preparation for the adventures and difficulties the dreamer can expect. Boots that are stuck in mud imply difficult situations that the dreamer is liable to get himself into in the future if he does not display great caution. High shoes or fancy boots indicate a possible rise in social status or even a marriage because of an unexpected meeting.

Borrowing

A dream in which the dreamer borrows from someone else means that he has financial problems. If someone else borrows from the dreamer, the dream implies that the dreamer's friends will come to his aid in times of need. If a person dreams that he spends money he has borrowed, it means that he has been dishonest, and this will be discovered. As a result, he will lose a good friend.

Bosom

A dream about a full, white bosom is a sign of good luck. If the bosom in the dream is wizened and speckled, the dreamer can expect a disappointment in love. If the bosom sustains an injury in the dream, the dream warns of problems. If a woman's lover is peeking at her bosom surreptitiously through her transparent clothing in a dream, she will be negatively influenced by someone.

Boss – See Manager

Bottles

If a bottle is filled with a clear liquid in a dream, it is a good sign that predicts luck in love. Empty bottles in a dream are an indication that the dreamer has gotten himself into a difficult situation from which he will only be able to extricate himself if he uses his wits.

If a dream features a broken bottle of wine, it refers to excessive sexual lust. Bottles of whisky in a dream mean that the dreamer is very careful with his finances, and invests his money wisely and profitably.

Bothering – See Pestering

Bottom

A person who dreams that he is caught with his pants down must be careful during the present time and in the immediate future. He must not make deals that could result in disaster. If a person dreams that he is caught in the middle of a bowel movement, the dream expresses the dreamer's feeling of humiliation. Perhaps the infidelity of his partner has been made public knowledge, or an undesirable situation has occurred at work.

Bouquet

If a dream features a bouquet of flowers, it means that the dreamer feels that his abilities and talents are not sufficiently recognized.

Bow and arrow

A dream that features a bow and arrow means that the dreamer is fully aware of his abilities and has a healthy amount of self-esteem. He trusts and relies on himself and has great faith in his powers of judgment.

A
B
C
D
E
F
G
H
I
J
K
L
M
N
O
P
Q
R
S
T
U
V
W
X
Y
Z

Bowl

A dream about a full bowl means that disputes or disagreements with a partner are in the offing. A dream about an empty bowl, however, signifies serenity, peace and quiet.

Bowling

If a person dreams about bowling, the dream predicts that he will become involved in a scandal that will be injurious to his reputation, financial situation and social position. If he sees other people bowling in his dream, it implies that he will lose his job because he prefers superficial, frivolous people.

Box

A person who dreams about an empty box can expect disappointment, and a person who dreams about a full box should try to remember its contents (food, jewelry, money bills). Whatever is in the box is the object of the dreamer's desire and yearning. He must make every effort to be alert, and success will be assured.

Bracelet

If a person dreams that he is wearing a bracelet on his wrist, it means that he can expect to get married soon. If he loses a bracelet in a dream, he is about to experience a series of problems and maddening losses. If he finds a bracelet in a dream, it means that he will soon be given some property.

Brain

If a person sees his own brain in a dream, it means that his surroundings will affect him adversely, and he will become an unpleasant person. If he sees animal brains in a dream, it is a sign of mental illness. A dream that features brains being eaten means that the dreamer will enjoy wealth and knowledge.

Brakes

Malfunctioning brakes in a car hint that there is something preventing the dreamer from advancing. There could be someone who is purposely getting in his way and trying to trip him up. This refers mainly to the business or work area. Malfunctioning brakes that causes a car to slip backward means that the dreamer has already crossed the red line – at least from the point of view of his inner feeling – and is no longer in control of the situation. In order to restore his feeling of control of his life and get rid of his helplessness, the dreamer must examine himself thoroughly and find out who his friends are and who his enemies are. The moment he decides on a line of action, he will feel better and there will be a significant improvement in the situation.

Brambles

The appearance of brambles in a dream is negative, since it refers to the unsuccessful outcomes of lawsuits as well as to illness in the dreamer's family. If the dreamer is caught in brambles in a dream, it indicates that he is involved in a bitter rivalry or in domestic strife.

Branch

A dream that features lush green branches covered with leaves implies profound friendships. If the branches in the dream are withered and dry, it means that the dreamer will receive sad tidings about friends and relatives who are far away.

Brandy

A dream about brandy indicates that the dreamer will achieve social status and wealth. However, because he is not very refined in his behavior and habits, he will not be able to form friendships with the people he most wants to be with.

Brass

A dream about brass implies that even though the dreamer will advance to the highest rungs of the professional ladder, he will be plagued by fears of a downfall.

Braying

If a person hears an ass bray in a dream, it is a sign of bad news. The bray of a donkey in a dream is equally negative: it means that the dreamer will be publicly humiliated by a revolting person. If the dreamer hears sad braying far in the distance, it means that he will inherit from someone close to him.

Bread

A dream about bread implies abundance, an improvement in the economic situation and a good, economically carefree period for the dreamer. If a person dreams about a table full of food, including numerous loaves of bread, he can expect to receive a large sum of money from an unexpected quarter. That person can also expect to get a promotion at work and to improve his social standing. If a person dreams that he is hiding pieces of bread in his pockets or bag, it attests to the deep worry and fear he is feeling. The dreamer feels alone in the battle, and it seems to him that the members of his family do not understand him at all and are not considerate of him. In this situation, he feels that the entire burden is resting on his shoulders. This kind of dream indicates a lonely, tired and angry person. Recommendation: Open your heart and mouth and speak about everything that's on your mind.

Breakage

A dream about any kind of breakage is negative – it makes no different who causes the breakage. The dream refers mainly to health and domestic problems. If a dream features broken limbs, it means that the dreamer has failed and has badly mismanaged things.

Breakfast

If a person dreams about breakfast, it means that he is about to face a difficult test. He is afraid of failing.

Break-in

A dream about a break-in, thieves or burglars refers to an unpleasant event that is about to occur in the dreamer's life. A person close to him is about to betray him, undermine him, plot against him and spread rumors. This person is liable to cause a great deal of damage if he is not stopped in time. The dream makes it clear to the dreamer that this is his last chance to wake up and prevent the situation from deteriorating.

Breath

If a person encounters someone with fresh, sweet breath in a dream, it means that he will undertake profitable business ventures and will conduct himself admirably. If he dreams that someone has bad breath, however, the dream indicates problems and illness. If the dreamer loses his breath in a dream, he will encounter unexpected failure.

Brewing

In general, dreams about brewing imply that success will follow a period of anxiety. If a person dreams about brewing, it means that he will have the authorities hot on his tail for some alleged misdemeanor. However, he will ultimately be proved innocent.

Briars

If a person dreams that he is caught in briars, it means that he has been entrapped and embroiled by his enemies. If he manages to extricate himself from the briars, however, his good friends will come to his assistance. If a person sees himself walking through briars in a dream, it means that he has problems in his business as well as a lack of communication.

Brick

If a dream features bricks, it means that the dreamer has unsettled business and is going through some difficult times in his love life. If he dreams about making bricks, it means that he is not making any money.

Bride

If a person dreams about a bride, it implies virginity, immaturity and a lack of life experience. If a woman dreams about being a bride, she is about to receive an inheritance. If the dreamer kisses the bride, it means that he is making up with a friend after a quarrel. If the dreamer is kissed by the bride, the dream implies health for him and an inheritance for his partner.

Bridge

A dream about a bridge hints at opportunities in all spheres: from the social plane to the financial, health and mental planes. The dreamer will have good fortune in anything he turns to, and fate will ensure that he enjoys a great deal of success.

If a person dreams about crossing a bridge or walking over a bridge, it is a sign that he is facing a big and important turning point in his life. He is about to change jobs, move house or meet a partner with whom he will begin a new chapter in life... or all of the above. The

A B C D E F G H I J K L M N O P Q R S T U V W X Y Z

extreme change will eventually cause him to live a far better and more fulfilling life, and it can be said that the change will be for the better and will bring new meaning and content to the dreamer's life.

If a person dreams about falling off a bridge, he can expect to go through a difficult psychological period that will be accompanied by a great deal of sorrow, depression, bad mental feeling and a feeling of destruction. The dreamer will go through this period of crisis with great difficulty, but will be fortified by it and will emerge from it far stronger than he was beforehand.

According to another version, a bridge can appear in a dream in different ways, and each time the meaning of the dream will change:

If a person sees himself crossing a bridge in a dream, it is a symbol that there are a lot of opportunities in all fields along the dreamer's path. The bridge is a symbol of the fact that this is really a period in which the dreamer can bridge gaps. Possibilities of doing exactly that are open to him, and he must find the right way to make things materialize.

It is also possible that the dreamer is exaggerating the importance he attributes to the crises in his life at the moment. The dream serves as a hint that he must let go, give himself a bit of leeway, and understand that even if he is in a crisis, it is not as serious as it seems to him, and that it is about to pass.

If a dream features a bridge that is about to collapse or be pulled down, it symbolizes a period in which the opportunities along the dreamer's path are slipping through his fingers, and he is not fulfilling his potential or taking advantage of the possibilities facing him. Some people interpret a dream like this as a crisis in the financial realm

– perhaps the financial problems that are haunting the dreamer are not being solved, and perhaps the dreamer has to be more cautious in the path he chooses to follow.

If a person sees himself standing on a bridge for a long time and gazing ahead in a dream, it implies that he is bursting with ideas and initiatives that he can set in motion, and that he must make these ideas a reality and try to implement them. This is the ideal time to do so.

If the bridge in the dream is a bridge whose end the dreamer cannot see, it means that he is facing financial or property losses. He must calculate his actions wisely and not do anything hasty without careful thought and planning.

Bridle

If a person sees a bridle in a dream, it means that a complicated project in which he is involved will reach a successful conclusion and will be profitable and enjoyable. An old and worn bridle in a dream indicates that the dreamer will be overcome by insurmountable problems.

Brimstone

A dream about brimstone is a warning dream: It warns the dreamer to be more cautious and circumspect in what he does. If he is not careful in his actions, he might lose good friends.

Bronchitis

If a person dreams that he has bronchitis, it means that his plans will not materialize because someone at home is ill. He will fail to accomplish his goals.

A B C D E F G H I J K L M N O P Q R S T U V W X Y Z

Bronze

Bronze indicates uncertainty and dissatisfaction with one's fate. If a woman dreams about a bronze statue, there is no way she will marry the man she really wants. If a bronze statue moves in a dream, it implies a love affair but not marriage. If a person dreams about bronze snakes or insects, it means that he will be plagued by jealousy and destruction.

Brood

A dream about a hen with her brood of chick implies that the dreamer will have a lot of troublesome children. However, a dream about a brood can also refer to wealth.

Broom

A dream that features a broom indicates that the dreamer is involved in a process of spring-cleaning – both physical and mental. It is quite possible that he has decided to make a break, whether with his partner of many years or in business. A new broom implies a positive turning point in the foreseeable future. An old, ragged broom hints at financial difficulties.

Broth

If a person sees broth in a dream, it is an indication of loyal and caring friends who are prepared to offer the dreamer any kind of assistance, financial included. Broth in a dream also symbolizes everlasting love.

If the dreamer prepares broth in his dream, it means that he will be responsible for other people's fate.

Brothel

A dream about a brothel is not linked to immorality or lasciviousness, but rather serves as a warning to the dreamer not to be extravagant and wasteful in financial matters. If he does not mend his ways, he will fall into disgrace.

Brother / Sister

There are many interpretations for a dream about a brother or a sister, and these depend on the character traits of the dreamer's siblings. If a person dreams about a dead brother, it means that he will soon be required to offer aid in the form of money or some other type of help.

Brush

The appearance of different types of brushes in a dream implies that the dreamer has several rather pleasant and lucrative ways of earning money. If a person dreams about using a hairbrush, it means that he is mismanaging his affairs, and this will result in financial losses. If he uses a clothes brush, he can expect to have to work hard, but he will reap the fruits of his labor.

Buckle

A dream about a buckle can imply two things: the first is that the dreamer will receive many very nice invitations, and the second is that he is warned of a state of disorder in his business affairs.

A
B
C
D
E
F
G
H
I
J
K
L
M
N
O
P
Q
R
S
T
U
V
W
X
Y
Z

Buffalo

If a dream features buffaloes, it means that the dreamer has powerful but not particularly intelligent enemies whom he can outwit and overcome with ease. If a woman dreams that she kills buffaloes in her dream, it means that she will succeed in completing a complicated project, and this will engender the admiration and respect of the opposite sex.

Bugle

The appearance of a bugle in a dream is an auspicious sign. This is true of the sound of triumphant and happy bugle notes as well, since this means a great deal of happiness and harmony for the dreamer. If a person dreams that he is blowing a bugle, he will be successful in business..

Building

A building in a dream augurs well for the future. This is especially true regarding a tall building or buildings. If the building in the dream is much taller than the ones the dreamer is accustomed to seeing around him, he can expect a great deal of success in the future on several levels, but mainly in anything to do with money and romantic matters. Moreover, there may be long trips to distant places and marvelous adventures in the offing for him.

If the dreamer sees particularly low buildings in the dream, it is a hint that he is going to hit rock-bottom. The dreamer may be about to find himself in a worse state than he is in today. He is liable to need the help of close friends in order to extricate himself from the miserable situation in which he finds himself. He will not always receive help, especially because of his unpleasant behavior toward people who are close to him. Mistakes he made in the past will come back at him like a boomerang. When he desperately needs help, he must not be surprised that it is not forthcoming. In order to survive, the dreamer will be forced to do things he never imagined he would do. He is liable to feel scorned and humiliated, but he must remember that no one but himself is to blame for this wretched situation.

If the dreamer sees particularly old buildings in a dream, it is a sign that he is about to fail in certain projects in the present because of oversights in the past. Errors he made in the past stand like stumbling-blocks in the way of anything to do with his present and future achievements.

A wrecked building in a dream is a sign of an accident or disaster that is liable to befall the dreamer. He must prepare himself for it psychologically. The event is an act of fate, and there is nothing he can do to mitigate the severity of the sentence. It won't help him if he drives slower or is more alert while driving. Things have already been predetermined from "above." A wrecked building in a dream can also imply that it does not matter how much trouble and effort the dreamer invested in changing things, building new things and turning over new leaves – all his efforts will go down the drain. The cards are about to be shuffled, and he will have to start over again.

An "ordinary" building in a dream, of a reasonable height and in good condition, is a sign that the dreamer can anticipate good luck. This is the time to embark on new projects; the timing is also good for things he always wanted to set in motion but did not because of various delays. Whatever he does in the near future will be successful. Luck will shine on him, and he will hit the jackpot.

Bull

A dream about a bull attests to the dreamer's aggressiveness, particularly in anything to do with sex. The dreamer is a nervous person who sometimes cannot control the way he expresses himself. If a bull appears in a man's dream, it implies that the dreamer does not give his partner warmth and tenderness, and treats her aggressively and disrespectfully.

A bull that appears in a woman's dream attests to sexual distress. Generally, this refers to sexual deprivation, a dearth of sexual experimentation and a lack of confidence in anything to do with this topic. It bothers her, and that is the reason why it comes up in her dream. This deprivation may stem from psychological difficulties. Alternatively, it could be explained by a temporary lack of sexual activity that is taking its toll on the dreamer. The accumulation of tensions and the inability to achieve release cause her to act in a stiff and constrained manner.

Bulldog

If a person dreams that a bulldog attacks him in an unfamiliar location, the dream implies that he is about to get into trouble with the authorities because of fraudulent activities. If he sees a friendly bulldog in his dream, he will overcome his adversaries and the problems that face him and succeed.

Bullock

If a dream features a bullock, it means that the dreamer's friends will rally around him in times of trouble. Furthermore, it means that he will enjoy good health.

Bullying

A dream about bullying implies that certain people want to cause strife between the dreamer and his children. In most cases, it is people who are extremely jealous of the dreamer.

A dream about bullying can also give a hint of the loss of self-confidence as a result of the futile conversations, empty nonsense, worthless words and ridiculous gossip in which the dreamer is involved. All these are ultimately liable to cause the dreamer to lose his self-esteem.

A dream about bullying can also express the dreamer's selfishness. His egoism is liable to cause the people around him to mistrust him, and he is well advised to mend his ways.

Bunch (of flowers)

A person who dreams about a bunch of flowers uses the dream to vent his feeling of frustration at the fact that the people around him do not value him at all. He feels that even though he is making a huge effort in a certain direction and is showing them that he has special talents and suitable instincts, he is not being given the esteem he feels is his due. The feeling frustrates him, and he feels that he is working for nothing. The dream hints that his feeling is about to undergo an about-turn. Suddenly everyone will

A B C D E F G H I J K L M N O P Q R S T U V W X Y Z

value the dreamer for his efforts and his abilities, and will even express their gratitude and appreciation for what he has done. The dreamer will finally be mollified, so he must not let this feeling that his efforts were in vain bother him. Soon he will be shown appreciation for his actions.

Bundle

The appearance of a bundle in a dream is a warning dream: the dreamer will be facing a bitter disappointment in the near future.

Burden

If a person dreams that he is bearing a burden, it indicates that he is hounded by serious worries and being treated in a patently unjust way. The root of these troubles lies in a conspiracy between the dreamer's enemies and the authorities. However, despite the heavy burden of anxiety, the dreamer will overcome all of these problems and will reach the peak of success.

Burglars

If a dream features burglars, it warns the dreamer of dangerous enemies who are hell bent on eliminating him. He must take very great precautions.

Burglary

If a person dreams about a burglary or a break-in, it means that a person the dreamer has trusted blindly has proved to be unworthy of his trust. A dream about a burglary may predict various accidents.

Burial

A dream about a burial or about a funeral symbolizes a new beginning and a breakthrough, whether the deceased is the dreamer himself or someone he knows. If the dream is about the burial of a stranger, the dreamer must take precautionary measures for a few weeks, especially in anything to do with financial transactions.

Burn

The meaning of a dream in which the dreamer is burned is that a surprise is in the offing. It is very likely that this entails a sum of money or a promotion at work. If the dreamer dreams that someone else is burned, it implies the beginning of a new relationship or friendship that will develop between the dreamer and the person who was burned. In general, the dream refers to the appearance of a new, unknown person.

Burr

A dream about a prickly burr symbolizes the dreamer's struggle to free himself of a burden and move to a new environment.

Bus

If a person dreams about a bus, it implies that his progress along his path to his goals will be slow. If his dream features a crowded bus where he has to stand, it means that he has to cope with a great deal of competition.

If the dreamer gets on to the wrong bus, it means that he has chosen the wrong path in life and he should stop, take a time-out, and reevaluate his goals.

A B C D E F G H I J K L M N O P Q R S T U V W X Y Z

Butcher

If a dream features a butcher slaughtering cattle, with copious amounts of blood all over the place, it implies that there will be a long and serious illness in the dreamer's family. If the butcher is slicing meat in a dream, it signifies that somebody is analyzing the dreamer's character in fine detail and not at all to the dreamer's advantage. The dream warns the dreamer not to write letters or documents.

Butter

A dream that features butter implies disappointments in the dreamer's life as a result of a lack of concentration. The dreamer does not concentrate his efforts on one fixed thing, but rather spreads himself thinly over many things. This proves to be useless. He must place the focus on the thing he wants to achieve and direct all of his efforts in that direction. If he goes on acting as he has until now, it will be a matter of "now you have it, now you don't."

Butterfly

A dream about a butterfly is generally a positive dream that predicts good things. It is customary to link a dream about a butterfly to the dreamer's love life and marriage: he will soon find himself in a perfect relationship in which both sides give out of a sense of love and warmth. He will lavish attention on his partner and this will be reciprocated in the identical manner. If the dreamer is in a relationship, the dream implies that it will last for a long time and will be mutual from the point of view of giving.

If a dream features a flying butterfly, it refers to a

sensuous and pleasure-filled relationship in the context of the dreamer's sex life. The dreamer is a passionate person, as is his partner. He loves touch, caresses and the ability to lavish warmth and attention on the physical and sensual planes.

In contrast, if it looks as if the butterfly in the dream is being chased, the dream attests to passing happiness, especially in matters of love. The dream does not warn of a breakup, but rather of an unhappy relationship. The dreamer may be married or involved in a long-standing relationship, and the dream prophesies that happiness will not necessarily continue to thrive in his home, even if the couple decides to stay together for various reasons (children, convenience, economic situation and so on).

If a dream features several butterflies together, it is a sign of a good and rosy future for the dreamer from every point of view.

If a dream features a butterfly landing directly on the dreamer, it is a sign that all of his wishes will come true. His secret desires, wishes and passions will all be fulfilled and realized in one way or another. He must wait patiently, since these things will not happen overnight, but rather gradually, over time.

Buttermilk

If a person dreams that he is drinking buttermilk, the dream implies that he will indulge in some kind of superficial pleasure that will be followed by grief. He will perform some kind of careless action that will be detrimental to his health. A dream in which the dreamer feeds pigs with buttermilk is an extremely inauspicious sign.

A
B
C
D
E
F
G
H
I
J
K
L
M
N
O
P
Q
R
S
T
U
V
W
X
Y
Z

Button

A dream that features wooden buttons hints at success at work after a period of very hard work. Pearl buttons indicate that a trip to a surprising destination is in the offing. The trip may come as the result of an unexpected win of a sum of money.

Silver buttons imply that the dreamer is about to be surprised by a new love. Fabric-covered buttons, especially gray or black, hint at a possible health problem.

A dream that features an article of clothing from which one of the buttons is about to get lost attests to the possibility that there is a commotion or row in the dreamer's home following a financial loss as a result of a fire or a promising financial deal that went sour.

Buzzard

In general, buzzards in dreams are a sign of vicious gossip or scandal that involves the dreamer. If the dreamer approaches a buzzard and it flies away, the scandal surrounding the dreamer or his associates will die down. If a dream features a buzzard sitting on the railroad tracks, the dreamer should brace himself for an imminent accident or loss.

C

Cab – See Taxi

Cabbage

A dream about cabbage indicates the nature of the dreamer: He is a person who is considered lazy, who does not like to work too hard, and always prefers repose and idleness. Even if the dreamer's indolence and lack of desire to work hard cause him ultimately to be "left behind" in many areas of life, it makes absolutely no difference to him, and he prefers to live his life in a way that allows him idleness and repose. He is generally an indifferent person who is not inclined to get excited about things that move him or anger him. He is not an ambitious type, and he certainly isn't achievement-oriented. While his particular nature does not let him "take things to heart" or worry about life too much, it does have an effect on the formation of his life in the future. Laziness and indolence are crucial factors in his life and will not enable him to make significant progress even if he sets himself serious goals to accomplish. These character traits will always be a stumbling-block, and if he does not find some element, such as a partner, who will spur him on to do things, he will probably continue wallowing in inactivity and idleness out of choice.

Cabin

A dream that features a cabin is not positive, since it implies that the dreamer will be involved in an unsuccessful lawsuit.

Cable / Telegram

If a person sees a cable in a dream, it predicts that he will undertake to do something that is terribly dangerous. If he succeeds in bringing it off, he will be accorded honor and wealth. If a person dreams about receiving a telegram, it means that important tidings are in the offing, but people will not have anything good to say about them.

Cackling

If a person hears the sound of cackling in a dream, it symbolizes the shock of a sudden death of someone close to the dreamer. Cackling also implies illness.

Café

If a person dreams that he has been invited to drink a cup of coffee in a café, it is a sign that he must be alert, with senses honed, in order not to fall into a trap that somebody may be setting for him. Evidently, there are people around him who are out to harm him or are plotting against him. He must be aware of this and not give them an opportunity to do him harm.

If a person dreams that he is drinking coffee in a café in the company of people who are considered to be his enemies, it is a sign that he will soon come into money in a dishonest way. His economic means will increase, but this will happen as a result of the dishonest methods he employed.

Cage

A dream about a cage does not predict good things. The dreamer can expect to get in trouble with the law – such as getting a stiff fine or even a jail sentence. He could have problems with the IRS and even be sued by someone. A cage intimates that plans will not turn out well and he should devise contingency plans for every eventuality. A bird in a cage implies that rows and obstacles will arise in the family and business realms. An animal trapped in a cage attests to the fact that the dreamer is in a serious emotional state. He feels that people are conspiring against him and seeking his downfall. It is advisable to find out whether the feeling matches reality.

Cake

In most cases, a cake in a dream implies that the dreamer will enjoy good health.

If a person sees a particularly festive cake in a dream – one that is decorated with whipped cream and other festive accoutrements, such as a birthday or wedding cake –the dream implies that happy events will soon occur in the dreamer's life. He will go through an encouraging period that will bring him nothing but good things.

A wedding cake with the figures of a bride and groom on it implies that the dreamer can soon expect to become involved in some kind of romantic liaison. He is on the threshold of making a new acquaintance, which will lead to a period of love, courtship, butterflies in the stomach, beauty and harmony.

If the person dreams about baking a cake, the dream implies that a positive turning point is about to occur in his life, especially in everything to do with participating in happy events. He may be about to meet a new partner or establish an interesting contact at a large function.

A dream in which the dreamer sees himself eating cake implies that soon he will lose the love of his life. The relationship may run its course by itself, but the breakup could happen under unpleasant circumstances, such as the infidelity of his partner, or because of an accident or some other incident that will drive a wedge between the dreamer and his partner.

A dream in which the dreamer sees himself serving cake to friends implies that he is giving in to the obstacles in his life, and is not mustering enough audacity to stand up to them by himself. The dreamer must try to assume greater responsibility for his life, and cope with the obstacles it contains, even if they seem to be insurmountable.

If a woman dreams about eating her wedding cake, there is danger on the horizon. She must keep her eyes open and be alert to every change in her life, so as to grapple with the roots of the danger and be prepared for it in the days ahead.

A dream about buying a cake implies that the dreamer is very popular with his friends, receives a great deal of affection from them, and is surrounded by friends who want to be in his company.

Calendar

A dream that features a calendar attests to the fact that the dreamer is bothered by the passage of time. The dreamer has a feeling that the days are floating away and passing by like birds in the sky while he fails to do all the things he wants to do. His feeling of frustration and helplessness is liable to cause him to vent his anger on the wrong people. Rows and quarrels in the immediate family or at his workplace will cause hard feelings and nothing else for everyone involved. He must take a good look and see which things are not being dealt with properly and solve the problems one at a time.

Calf

A dream that features a calf implies that all kinds of pleasures and festivities are in the offing. Moreover, the dreamer can look forward to an increase in prosperity.

Calling by name

If a person hears himself called by name in a dream, or conversely, calls the name of someone else in a dream, he is about to enter a happy phase regarding love and marriage.

Calm

If the feeling that pervades the dream is one of calmness and happiness, it means that the dreamer's life is worthwhile and he will enjoy a long life. If the dream features a calm sea, it means that some rather shaky and uncertain enterprise will have a very successful ending. A calm ocean is a very good sign.

Calumny

A dream about calumny serves as a warning to the

dreamer against vicious gossip that is going to be very harmful to him.

Camcorder

If a person dreams about using a camcorder, it is a sign that something really important and exciting is about to occur in his life.

Camel

If a camel appears in a dream, the interpretation depends on its form:

An "ordinary" camel in a dream (with one hump) indicates that if terrible things have been said about the dreamer, if he has been the subject of malicious gossip behind his back, or if people have cursed him and cast evil spells on him, all of these negative things of which he has been the victim him will be canceled. Even spells that were actually performed will eventually be canceled.

A dream featuring a two-humped camel is a prophetic dream that implies that the dreamer can expect a good life and great success on his way to accomplishing his goals in life. The dream hints mainly at a life of wealth and comfort and at the accomplishment of the tasks the dreamer set himself, but it does not necessarily promise happiness.

A dream about riding a camel hints at overcoming obstacles. The dreamer, generally with a little help from close friends, family members and people who care about him, will be able to overcome obstacles in life and achieve a state of repose and security. Any problem or barrier that bothers him will simply disappear. Riding a camel symbolizes a difficult path paved with pitfalls and obstacles that the dreamer will have to overcome on his way to success.

Cameo brooch

The appearance of a cameo brooch in a dream does not augur well. The dreamer must brace himself for the occurrence of a sad event.

Camera

If a person sees a camera in a dream, it means that the dreamer will find himself in places that are not particularly congenial. If a woman dreams that she takes photographs with a camera, the dream indicates that she can expect a friend to let her down. Moreover, unpleasant things are going to happen in her future.

Campaign

If a person dreams about a political campaign, it implies that the dreamer wants to implement changes in conventional business practices – and this horrifies his adversaries. Despite their opposition, he will succeed in introducing the new practices.

If the dreamer sees a religious campaign condemning sin in his dream, it means that the dreamer will be asked to make a financial donate.

Camping

A dream about camping, in which the dreamer sees himself sleeping outdoors in natural surroundings, is a warning dream: the dreamer must not resign himself to an banal existence of dull routine. The dream admonishes him that he needs to take a vacation.

Canal

A dream about a canal is interpreted in accordance with the appearance of the canal in the dream:

A person who sees a clean canal in a dream can expect a tranquil life filled with satisfaction, warmth and love. He will be surrounded by family members and close friends whom he loves to be with more than anything else. His dear ones are his entire world, and being with them is the most important thing for him.

Murky, putrid and dirty water in a canal is a sign of an illness in the near future, and of health problems that will be accompanied by worries, pressure and anxiety. The dreamer may be a sensitive person, and this is liable to be manifested in a heart disease, a heart attack or an anxiety attack. It is advisable to have a checkup in order to allay all doubts.

Clear water in a canal is a sign that the dreamer's problems are about to come to an end. Worries that bothered him will stop bothering him, and peace and quiet will be restored to his life. The solutions to the hardships and worries will enable the dreamer to live a life of ease once more and free himself up for business and work.

If a person dreams about a canal with weeds in it, it is a warning dream that serves to warn the dreamer against signing a contract or clinching deals that are liable to fail or yield rotten fruit. This is liable to get him into financial trouble and a downward spiral from which there is no way out. The dream also hints that precisely in his hour of need, his friends are liable to turn their backs on him and not stand by him. He must plan his moves very wisely in order not to be totally dependent on the help of his friends and feel betrayed and rejected.

If the dreamer falls into a canal, it is a portent of what will happen in the future: The dreamer is liable to lose his social and economic status in reality, too. He may experience a drastic drop in his quality of life, and must do everything in order to prevent the fall and decline hinted at in the dream.

If a person sees himself jumping over a canal in a dream, it is a sign that in spite of the difficulties and bad experiences that he can expect to go through, he will manage to maintain his self-respect and status. People will continue respecting him, even if he gets into financial difficulties. His social status will not be jeopardized, and he will remain as popular and well-liked as ever.

Canary

A dream about a canary indicates unexpected but happy occurrences – for instance, the union of two lovers or literary success.

Cancer

In general, when a dream features cancer, it does not augur well: it warns of the end of love and business deals that come to nothing. A dream about cancer implies that someone close to the dreamer is ill. Furthermore, it implies conflicts with people he loves. The dream may be followed by a drop in business activity.

A dream about curing cancer means that the dreamer's status in the world will improve suddenly and drastically.

Candles

If candles burn steadily in a dream, it is an indication that the people surrounding the dreamer enjoy stable conditions and a firm economic basis. If a girl dreams that she is lighting a candle, it means that she is having clandestine meetings with her lover, in opposition to her parents' will. If a draft causes a candle to burn down in a dream, it is a warning: the dreamer should be aware that his enemies are disseminating malicious gossip about him. If a candle is extinguished in a dream, it warns that there will be hardship and even death among the dreamer's friends.

Candlesticks

A dream about candlesticks is always a particularly good dream: it indicates success, economic prosperity, good health and a correct lifestyle.

If the dreamer sees candlesticks on their own in a dream, it is a sign that he can expect positive opportunities and changes in life.

If a person dreams that he himself is carrying candlesticks or that he bought candlesticks in a dream, it is a prediction that the dreamer will be at the center of an important and prestigious event with symbolic significance.

A candlestick with a new candle in it means that the dreamer can expect days of joy, happiness, material wealth and social blooming. The new candle symbolizes the inner renewal of the dreamer.

Candy – See Sweets

A
B
C
D
E
F
G
H
I
J
K
L
M
N
O
P
Q
R
S
T
U
V
W
X
Y
Z

Cane

A dream that features fields of rippling cane implies that the dreamer can look forward to prosperity and advancement, while a dream that features piles of cut cane warns of impending disaster.

Canker

If canker is seen on anything in a dream, it is a sign of evil, since it predicts untrustworthy friends and death for youngsters and death and grief for the elderly. A canker on the flesh, on the contrary, predicts that the dreamer will be accorded honor in the future.

Cannibal

A dream that features a cannibal indicates that the dreamer is tortured by pressure, worry and fear. It may also indicate that the dreamer is suffering from some kind of physical ailment.

Cannibalism

A dream about cannibalism is a nit of the dreamer's tendency toward a loss of self-control and self-destruction.

Cannon

A dream that features a cannon can be a prophetic dream about the beginning of a war in which the dreamer is liable to fight in the front lines (but not necessarily in the role of an artillery soldier). A cannon in a dream symbolizes war, a struggle or a battle. The dreamer's fear of the security situation is reflected in the dream.

Having said that, a dream about a cannon can also be interpreted as a mirror of the dreamer, who feels that he possesses special powers and that he can undertake any task – both on the personal level and on the national level – and succeed.

Cannonball

If a person sees a cannonball in a dream, it means that he has hidden enemies who are plotting against him. If a young girl sees a cannonball in her dream, it implies that she will fall in love with a soldier. If a young man has this dream, he will have to fight for his country.

Canoe

If a person dreams that he is paddling a canoe in calm waters, it means that he is completely capable of running a successful business. If the water is muddy in his dream, he will suffer setbacks in business. If he sees the person he loves riding in the canoe, he can be sure that he will have a good marriage. If the water is choppy in his dream, it means that he will have to tame his spouse.

Canopy

If a person sees a canopy or sees himself under a canopy, it is a warning dream: he should know that so-called friends are doing everything in their power to exert a negative influence over him. The dreamer must look after the people he loves.

Cap

If a woman sees a cap in a dream, it is a sign that she will be invited to a party. If a dream features a prisoner's cap, it means that the dreamer is losing his courage.

Cape

A dream about a cape is interpreted according to the way in which the cape appears in the dream:

If a person sees himself wearing a cape in a dream, it indicates that the dreamer is a person who can be trusted. He is responsible and carries out the tasks he is assigned in the best way possible. This fact is well known, and his reputation as someone who can be relied on precedes him. The dreamer is a person with a strong character who is not prone to whims and knows how to bear responsibility and create a feeling of security in the people around him. Sometimes he takes numerous tasks on himself, but he will never find himself in a situation that he cannot control. Having said that, his nature sometimes causes him a feeling of distress because of the commitments he is inclined to take on himself and the attendant emotional burden.

If the dreamer sees another person wearing a cape in a dream, it is a sign that the person in question can be relied on unhesitatingly and trusted blindly. The dreamer has total belief in that person and knows that he will never turn his back on him or let him down. The dreamer accepts the authority of that person unflinchingly, and is prepared to follow him through fire and flood.

If a dream features a young girl wearing a cape, it implies that she is willing to obey another person in whose power she believes, and accepts his authority and control over her. The dream attests to her willingness to be his protégée.

Captain

If a person dreams about a captain (either of a ship or an airplane), the dream indicates the fact that the dreamer is ambitious by nature and wants to lead and rule others.

Captive

If a person dreams that he is taken captive, he should watch out for some kind of treacherous activity in his environment. If he is not vigilant, he may be injured or suffer a mishap. If the dreamer sees someone else being taken captive, the dream implies that he is joining ranks with people or organizations that are not his social equals. If a woman dreams that she is being taken captive, it means that she has a jealous husband.

Car

There can be several different meanings for a dream about a car. A dream about a traffic accident in which more than one car is involved hints at danger. The dreamer is liable to find himself in trouble – not necessarily because he has been physically injured, but rather an emotional mess. An extramarital love affair is liable to be discovered unexpectedly and cause the breakup of the permanent relationship. Embezzlement at the workplace as well as legal issues and problems are liable to be discovered. On the other hand, a dream about racing cars, for instance, hints that the dreamer is an ambitious person who is seeking a fast way to get ahead in life. To this end, he is prepared to take risks and even resort to illegal means. The dream serves as a warning sign for the dreamer not to take unnecessary risks. A dream about cars traveling along a winding road, especially between mountains and along a high cliff edge, has a similar meaning. The dreamer feels that he is in danger and is looking for a way out, sometimes by taking a risk that is liable to end in disaster. Recommendation: This is a period during which the dreamer must be careful of hasty decisions, trips abroad, and spurious financial deals.

Caravan

A caravan in a dream attests to the fact that the dreamer will soon bc going off on a journey. The dream warns him to be careful of being injured physically

Cardinal

A dream about a cardinal does not bode well. If a person sees a cardinal in a dream, it means that he can expect to be ruined so completely that he may have to leave the country. If a woman sees a cardinal in a dream, it could refer to her moral downfall. If a person encounters a cardinal in a dream, the dream may serve to warn him against imminent evil.

Cards

If a person dreams that he wins a card game, the dream predicts that he will get married soon. If he loses a card game in a dream, it means that he will have no choice but to take risks.

Carnival

A dream that features a carnival indicates that the dreamer's life will be filled with pleasurable activities in the near future. If a person sees carnival masks in a dream, it means that he is about to suffer problems at work and at home.

Carousel

If a person sees himself riding on a carousel, it attests to the fact that the dreamer feels that he is in a rut. If he sees other people on the carousel, the dream refers to his unfulfilled hopes and desires. If a carousel appears in a completely incongruous place or in the middle of nowhere, the dream predicts gloomy and bad things.

Carpenter / Carpentry

A dream about carpentry or about a carpenter indicates that soon the dreamer will find a solution to issues that are bothering him. Even if he is going through a difficult and stress-filled period, it will soon come to an end, and he will once again feel free and unfettered. The situation he is in at the moment causes him to feel as if he is not making the most of his talent nor is he taking maximal advantage of the things he could have done. However, this period is about to end. He will reach a state of mental well-being and have an opportunity to express his talents and abilities.

In most cases, a dream about carpentry also indicates boredom with the dreamer's professional life, which causes him to be indifferent to what is happening around him. The dreamer suffers from his daily routine, which is nothing but detrimental to him. It would be a good idea for him to think about changing jobs or introducing new stimuli into his professional life so that he can get up in the morning and look forward to the day ahead.

Carpenter's plane

A carpenter's plane in a dream is a very good sign of happiness and success. The dreamer will not fall into the trap of following a false love blindly. If a person sees a carpenter using his plane in a dream, it means that his plans will be implemented without a hitch.

Carpet

A dream about a carpet is generally a good dream that attests to the fact that the dreamer can look forward to ease, prosperity and a great deal of regard. However, a dream about a carpet can have different meanings, depending on the context:

If a person dreams that he is walking on a carpet, it is a sign that he loves luxury, lives a hedonistic life, and is not afraid of spending his money liberally on pleasures and treats, even if this is sometimes interpreted as pure selfishness.

If a person sees himself lying on a carpet in a dream, it is a hint that he no longer has his feet planted firmly on the ground and is losing himself in illusion. The dream may also hint that he has to avoid using hallucinatory drugs.

If a person dreams that he is cleaning carpets, his dream attests to the fact that he suffers from mental problems or from other personal problems that bother him a great deal, such as not getting on with his partner, problems with the children, and so on.

Carriage

If a person dreams that he is riding in a carriage, it means that he will contract a disease, but he will soon recover. If he dreams that he wants to purchase a carriage, the dream implies that he has to work hard, but he will eventually become very good at his job.

Carrot

A carrot that appears in a dream, whether it is in the ground or the dreamer is holding it, implies that the dreamer is incapable of standing his ground when it comes to problems he has to face, and chooses to ignore them, like an ostrich that buries its head in the sand. The dreamer feels that psychologically, he cannot cope with the difficulties in his path. Although he knows that eventually he will have to deal with the situation, he chooses not to deal with these difficult things, preferring to flee from them.

Other interpretations that are given for a dream about a carrot state that a carrot, when it appears alone in a dream, actually implies that the dreamer will enjoy prosperity in business, financial profit and abundance in the near future.

If the dreamer sees himself eating a carrot in a dream, the dream symbolizes that the dreamer will enjoy health and abundance. His state of health will improve remarkably, and this will help him advance to good positions in various fields.

If a person dreams that he is growing a carrot in his garden, the dream implies that the dreamer is sexually attracted to young girls or to women who look like girls, kind of "Lolitas." However, we must not worry. The dreamer is aware of the fact that if he realizes his fantasies, his perversion will become common knowledge, and he will be ostracized.

If an unmarried person dreams of a carrot, the dream hints that he is operating against his will or his conscience, since a certain element is forcing him to do so. Various situations may have caused this: a compulsive mother or father who is forcing him to study or work in a field he hates; an employer who is causing him to declare that he holds a certain opinion that is opposed to his original standpoint; and so on.

If a young woman dreams about a carrot, the dream means that in the near future she will face a commitment. This could be connected to work matters, but it could also be a commitment to marriage or a long-term relationship.

Cart

A cart in a dream is an indication of bad tidings concerning friends and family. If a person dreams that he is driving a cart, it means that he will enjoy success in financial affairs and other areas. If a dream features two lovers riding in a cart, it signifies that they will remain faithful to each other despite the evil designs of their enemies.

Cartridge

If a person sees a cartridge in a dream, it is a prediction of quarrels and rows. There are threatening elements in the offing. If a dream features empty cartridges, it implies that the dreamer's relationships are not constant and steady.

A B C D E F G H I J K L M N O P Q R S T U V W X Y Z

Carving

A dream about carving poultry indicates that the dreamer will not enjoy financial ease and that other people will annoy him. A dream about carving meat warns the dreamer of making bad investments: he can avoid mistakes by changing his objectives.

Cash

If a person dreams that he has plenty of cash, but in fact it is all borrowed, it attests to the fact that even though the dreamer gives the impression of being honest and above-board, he will eventually be exposed as the ruthless pursuer of mammon that he really is.

Cash box

A dream that features a cash box is a sign of very promising opportunities in the offing. However, if the cash box is empty, it means that the dreamer will not receive a great deal of money.

Cashier

This is a warning dream: the dreamer's property will be claimed by other people.

Casino

If a person dreams about a casino, he has to be particularly careful of a gamble or spurious deals proposed to him by people he does not know. There is a possibility of a big gamble in which he has a chance of winning;

however, the problem is that too many elements are involved, and he should display caution and consult with an expert in the relevant field.

Cask

If a dream features a full cask, it is a sign of prosperity and joy. If it features an empty cask, it is a sign of a barren, comfortless life.

Caster oil

If a person dreams about caster oil, it means that the dreamer may effect the downfall of a friend who has secretly been working toward his (the dreamer's) advancement.

Castle

If a person dreams about a castle, it means that he will become extremely rich and will travel extensively. If a dream features an ancient, overgrown castle, the dreamer should be careful not to become overly romantic when choosing a spouse. He is liable to make a mistake. If the dreamer sees himself leaving a castle, the dream warns that he is about to be robbed of his possessions, or worse still, the person he loves is going to die.

Cat

A dream about a cat in almost any form (except for two that will be discussed later on) has a negative meaning, with the cat generally symbolizing the people around the dreamer.

In dreams, the cat mainly hints at measures that will be taken by people who want to harm the dreamer. They will use everything the cat represents – cunning, subversion, faithlessness, treachery, hostility and so on. It is necessary to relate to a dream that features a cat as a warning dream that serves to warn against getting too close to people of whose intentions the dreamer is ignorant. It is advisable to be very cautious when establishing ties with new people, but especially to pay attention to the person to whom the dreamer reveals his secrets and whom he trusts.

A dream in which a cat attacks the dreamer means that someone in the dreamer's work environment is trying to trip him up, or alternatively, a person close to the dreamer may be doing everything in his power to cause the dreamer to lose his assets.

A dream in which the dreamer sees more than one cat (sometimes a whole pack of cats) warns the dreamer of the everyday surroundings in which he lives. The surroundings are not beneficial to the dreamer, and they may actually be hostile to him. The dreamer must be conscious of the dangers and operate accordingly.

A dream in which the dreamer fights a cat and is bruised or scratched as a result attests to the fact that there is another element or other elements threatening to cause the dreamer to stray from the straight and narrow path and follow violent or dishonest paths instead. The dreamer may even be walking a thin line between the decent world and the world of crime. He must be aware of the fact that there are people who would be thrilled to see him sink into the world of sin, and all he needs for that is one small slip.

A dream in which one or more cats are seen crossing the

dreamer's path (it doesn't matter how many there are or what size or color they are) attests to the fact that the dreamer is about to come down with a disease of some kind, and even if he has not yet noticed it, it is already in the offing, and he is already experiencing its first symptoms. He must be alert to every change in his condition, and the dream warns against ignoring it.

A dream about a pregnant cat attests to the fact that the dreamer must pay close attention to his personal objects and tools since they are in danger of being stolen: hostile elements are trying to steal the dreamer's property.

A dream about the birth of kittens can be interpreted in two extreme ways: the dream may indicate that the dreamer or his partner can expect a joyous birth, a birth that will bring a great deal of joy, light and happiness to their home and to their life together. However, if the dreamer is not in a happy relationship, and is not expecting the birth of a child, the dream may imply a breach in the relationship that will eventually result in a separation. This dream must be interpreted as expressing the dreamer's hidden desire for the birth of a child, and of the inner struggle raging in him concerning the complexity of his relations with his partner.

A dream about kittens indicates the dreamer's over-sentimentality. If the dreamer sees kittens nursing, the dream attests to an essential mental difficulty, to a loss or to profound emotional sorrow. The dream is typical of people who are going through a difficult period, who experienced profound mental difficulties, and are having a hard time getting out of the state they are in.

However unexpected and unlikely this may sound, a dream about a black cat is actually a positive dream. It has two main interpretations:

A B C D E F G H I J K L M N O P Q R S T U V W X Y Z

Good luck will shine on the dreamer. He must know that if he sees a black cat in his dream and up till now he has been embroiled in troubles, a new leaf will start now, and it will only show good results. If the dreamer takes part in any kind of gamble – from filling in the football pools or buying a lottery ticket to gambling in a casino – there is a high probability that he will be lucky, even if he is not used to gambling and taking part in games of chance. If the dreamer is not involved in anything in which there is the element of chance (that is, he does not subscribe to the lottery, doesn't fill in lottery forms and doesn't visit casinos), he will get lucky in matters of income or in a particular business investment.

A black cat that crosses the dreamer's path is also interpreted as a sign that if the dreamer is worried that he or a member of his family was about to come down with a serious disease, he can stop worrying: the dream implies that he has nothing to fear. The disease is imaginary, and its symptoms will disappear as quickly as they appeared.

The appearance of a ginger cat in a dream is far less common, but it symbolizes something positive: the dreamer will have real love and great luck in everything to do with matters of the heart. His relationship with his partner, present or future, is real, honest and completely devoid of posturing and games.

Catechism

A dream about catechism predicts that the dreamer will be offered a lucrative job, but will be reluctant to accept it because of the strings attached.

Caterpillar

A dream about a caterpillar implies that the dreamer will get himself into uncomfortable situations and surround himself with two-faced and unworthy individuals. If a person sees a caterpillar in a dream, he can expect to suffer setbacks in both his love life and his professional life.

Catfish

The appearance of a catfish in a dream implies that the dreamer will be humiliated by his enemies, but he will soon get over it because of his quick thinking.

Cathedral

If a person sees a cathedral in a dream, it indicates his jealous and possessive nature – this applies to both material and spiritual things. If the dreamer sees himself going into a cathedral, it means that there will be an improvement in his status in life.

Cattle

In general, a dream about cattle hints at the financial success the dreamer can expect. In Judaism and Islam, a dream like this is common (viz. Joseph's dream about the seven fat cows and the seven lean cows that were interpreted as seven good years and seven bad years).

The appearance of old cows in a dream means that the dreamer does not like to work hard and that he is thoroughly lazy. This is the reason why he will run into difficulties and hard times, especially from the financial point of view.

A B C D E F G H I J K L M N O P Q R S T U V W X Y Z

A dream that features a cow means that the dreamer made a good investment of some kind, and it will yield dividends and positive results.

Milking a cow in a dream attests to the fact that the dreamer can expect good luck in the near future: things will come right by themselves, he will derive satisfaction from his work, he will not have any difficulty earning a living, and he will enjoy good health, a successful marriage and a good family life. He can place his trust in his friends and in the people around him, since they will be loyal to him, and he can depend on them blindly.

Cauliflower

A dream about a cauliflower implies a good, tranquil, calm and pleasant future without mental stress and environmental pressures. Even if a person is highly strung by nature and tends to become stressed out and affect his surroundings, the dream tells him that something will enter his life and cause a complete turnabout in his character. If the dreamer tends to get stressed out because of economic problems, his money problems will be solved and he can calm down. If the dreamer tends to become stressed out mentally because of family or psychological problems, a solution will appear on the horizon to calm him down and let him reach the ideal state he has been dreaming of. Even if he has problems with his family – his children and so on – every problem that causes mental stress is about to be solved. The dream predicts that the dreamer will soon enjoy the peace of mind that everyone yearns for.

If a person who is calm by nature has this dream, it means that the future holds nothing but good things for him, and everything will work out in such a way that he will always be able to maintain his easy-going and good nature.

Cavalry

This is a very good dream, signifying distinction and advancement.

Cave

A dream about a cave reflects the fact that the dreamer has withdrawn into himself. This is a period of depression and sadness, and expresses his will to cut himself off from the world for a while. The darkness in the cave reflects the gloom and grayness of his life. The duration of the dreamer's stay in the cave refers to the degree of his depression. If he stays in the cave for several hours, it means that he is in a state of temporary and transient distress because of things that are not particularly serious. However, if he stays in the cave for weeks or months, it means that he is unable to cope with the hardships in his life right now. Events that occur in the cave also refer to the dreamer's gloomy mood and the extent of his anxiety, as well as to his inability to snap out of it and work toward improving the situation. This is the time for a vacation in order to improve the dreamer's mood and help him muster his strength.

Cedar

A dream about green, healthy cedars signify that the dreamer will be successful in an enterprise. On the other hand, if the cedars are dry and dead, it indicates that despair will be his lot.

A
B
C
D
E
F
G
H
I
J
K
L
M
N
O
P
Q
R
S
T
U
V
W
X
Y
Z

Celebration / Party

A dream about a celebration or a party is interpreted according to the nature of the dream:

If the nature of the celebration in the dream is joyful and merry, and the dreamer sees himself cheerful and happy, celebrating and enjoying himself, and he gets up in a good mood with a good taste remaining from the dream, it predicts good news in all areas of life in general. The dreamer can expect to have a good, satisfying family life and a good marriage.

If a person dreams about a celebration in which the emphasis is on music and dancing, the dream prophesies that in the near future, several important issues that were problematic for the dreamer and that he could not overcome will be resolved. These are mainly social problems or some kind of embroilment on a social basis. Some people interpret such a dream as a hint that soon the dreamer will meet a very important person or people who will be very influential in his life.

A dream in which the dreamer sees himself alone at an enjoyable party without a partner or any other of his friends or acquaintances, is a sign that a new pleasure is on his doorstep. Mostly, it is a physical pleasure (hinting at something sexual), but it could also be a spiritual pleasure like a catharsis.

If a person dreams that he is at a crowded party with a lot of other people, both familiar and alien to him, the dream implies that the dreamer can expect to experience difficulties resulting from a deterioration in his behavior. He takes up bad habits that lead him to addictions such as excessive drinking, the use of drugs, or uncontrolled eating.

The dream serves as a kind of warning against going downhill into places from which it will be very hard for him to return and lead a normal life.

If the celebration was sad, unsuccessful and not happy, the dream indicates that an enjoyable event eagerly anticipated by the dreamer will not materialize in the end. Something like a trip, going out for a good time, and so on will be canceled, and will not work out.

Celery

A dream that features celery signifies that the dreamer will know nothing but good things, and these will fill his life with joy, happiness and abundance.

Celestial signs

If a dream features celestial signs, it indicates that the dreamer will embark on unexpected journeys because of sad occurrences. These could include the end of a loving relationship, business problems, or domestic strife.

Cellar

A dream about a damp and moldy cellar attests to the dreamer's hidden fears, the origins of which he is unaware. He suffers from problems and pressures that he represses in his subconscious and has never dared to face, deal with, and bring to a resolution.

A dream about a cellar hints at fear of a loss of control and a loss of self-confidence. The dreamer is in a kind of emotional whirlpool from which he does not know how to extricate himself. He feels lost and is afraid to find himself in "dark" places from the emotional and psychological points of view.

Besides his emotional confusion, a fear of losing his property also lurks inside him, and this exacerbates the situation and brings him down even further emotionally.

In contrast, a dream that features a wine cellar indicates the exact opposite. The person is self-confident and enjoys financial abundance and stability in everything to do with business.

However, if a young woman sees a wine cellar in a dream, it is a warning about a partner with whom she is going to have a battle in the future. It hints at his penchant for gambling, something that is liable to bring her world collapsing down on her. She must check out her potential life partner very carefully in order to ascertain whether he actually does display tendencies to gamble (in any form). If he does, and she sees that there is no way to make him stop, she is advised to break off this relationship immediately, before it is too late.

Cellular phone

The appearance of a cell-phone in a dream indicates that the dreamer will soon discover the solution to a problem that has been gnawing at him. In addition, he will find that he is in greater control of his professional life.

Cement

This is a positive dream. No matter how cement appears in the dream, it implies that the dreamer's life is about to improve in various ways – especially financially.

Cemetery

Contrary to what might be expected, a general dream about a cemetery actually implies the arrival of good news and an improvement in the health of a close friend. There are several exceptions to this generalization, however:

If a run-down cemetery appears in a dream on a dull, rainy day, the dream hints at the loss of a beloved person who is very close to the dreamer. Someone the dreamer loves is about to depart from this world.

If a cemetery appears in a dream with the sun blazing in the sky on a particularly hot day, the dreamer is about to undergo an unpleasant experience. It need not necessarily be an especially difficult or traumatic one. It will simply be unpleasant, the kind of everyday occurrence that is liable to cause temporary despair, such as your car breaking down just as you are setting out for work in the morning, or the disappointment of missing the opportunity of becoming a millionaire because of one wrong number in the lottery.

If a widow dreams that she is visiting a cemetery, it is a sign that she will soon marry again. She is about to meet the person with whom she will establish a true and sincere relationship, and will eventually marry him.

Cereal / Porridge

A dream that features either cereal or porridge is a warning dream: the dreamer must be on the lookout for dangerous enemies who may be conspiring to cause his downfall.

A
B
C
D
E
F
G
H
I
J
K
L
M
N
O
P
Q
R
S
T
U
V
W
X
Y
Z

Chaff

A dream about chaff is a prediction about some kind of enterprise that has absolutely no chance of succeeding. In addition, the dreamer will be worried about an illness.

Chain

A chain of almost any shape or form in a dream predicts good news and implies that the dreamer can look forward to a good and happy love life.

A dream that features an open chain indicates that the dreamer can expect to overcome every obstacle in his life and notch up respectable achievements, high status, honor and a great deal of money.

A dream that features a golden chain is a sign of the prosperity the dreamer will enjoy. He will not have to worry about his financial situation since he can expect to live an easy, financially comfortable life.

If a person sees a very expensive chain in a dream or a member of his family is wearing it around his neck, the dream symbolizes domestic peace, a satisfying and enjoyable family life, joy and love.

If a person dreams about a woman wearing a silver or gold chain, the dream is interpreted in a special way: it is a sign that a problem that has been bothering the dreamer for a long time is about to be solved. Something that greatly preoccupied the dreamer and sometimes even gave him sleepless nights will soon be solved, liberating him from his bonds. In the near future, he can expect to go through a good period of repose and calm. The dream must stop worrying, since there is no reason for him to be tense and stressed out.

Chair

A person who dreams about a chair in which an unknown person is sitting will receive a one-time sum of money or financial dividends from someone else. If the chair is empty, it has two meanings. The first is that news will arrive from someone who has been far away for a long time and has not kept in particularly close touch up till now.

The second possible meaning is that the dreamer has aspirations for a higher position in his workplace or that his status in the family has been weakened recently. If a person dreams that he is sitting in a chair with a crown on his head, it means that a very positive development can be expected in the near future, during the course of which his social and personal status will increase incredibly. If a rocking chair appcars in a dream, it means that the dreamer is enjoying balance and tranquillity in life. If the chair becomes vacant, disappointment is in the offing.

Chair maker

If a person dreams about a chair maker, it means that something he enjoys doing is about to cause him anxiety.

Chairman

If a dream features the chairman of a public organization, it implies that the dreamer is looking for a new job that has higher status and a better salary. He will be successful in his quest. If a person sees an irascible chairman, it is a bad sign. If the dreamcr himself is a chairman in his dream, it means that he will be recognized for his kindness and even-handedness.

Chalice

If a dream features a chalice, it means that the people around the dreamer will be jealous of any pleasure or happiness he has. A broken chalice in a dream implies that much as he wants to, the dreamer will not be able to get the better of a friend.

Chalk

If a person sees himself writing on a blackboard with chalk in a dream, it is a sign of bad luck. If he holds a handful of chalk in a dream, he should brace himself for a disappointment.

Challenge

If a person accepts any kind of challenge in a dream, it means that he is prepared to take the rap in order to cover for other people.

Chamber

If a person dreams that he is in a lavishly appointed chamber, it means that he is on the verge of receiving a large and unexpected sum of money. This could be through inheritance or a good investment. If a woman has this dream, it means that a very rich man is about to ask her to marry him. However, if she dreams about a plain, modest chamber, her lifestyle will be very ordinary.

Chambermaid

If a person sees a chambermaid in a dream, it is a sign of

misfortune and indication of changes that have to be made. If a man seduces a chambermaid in a dream, he can be sure that people are going to mock and despise him for his indiscreet conduct.

Chameleon

A chameleon in a dream symbolizes deceit, capriciousness and advancement at the expense of other people.

Champion / Championship

In most cases, people dream about a championship in the context of sports matches, but a championship can also be interpreted as the success inherent in becoming the best in a particular field. If a person dreams that he is a champion, whether in sports or in other fields, the dream implies a fighting nature and a person who has great ambitions for success; almost nothing can stand in his way. He is not one of those people who give up when the going gets tough. On the contrary – he does not throw in the towel, but rather perseveres and tries to achieve what he wants at almost any price.

A person who dreams about a championship is generally a very charismatic person, and tends to be a social leader rather than a follower. It is important for him to prove himself, and there is almost nothing that stands between him and his desire to realize his ambitions.

Chandelier

If a person dreams about a chandelier, it is an indication of unexpected and unimaginable luxury and wealth. If a dream features a broken chandelier, it warns the dreamer to prepare himself for financial loss. If the dreamer sees the lights in the chandelier being turned out, he should know that the wonderful future he was sure he was going to have will be spoiled by illness and hardship.

Chapel

If a person sees a chapel in a dream, it is an indication of disagreements among the members of various social circles, of business that has not been finalized, and of disappointment. If a young person dreams about a chapel, it is a warning about making mistakes in love.

Charcoal

If a person sees unlit charcoal in a dream, it signifies wretchedness and unhappiness. On the other hand, glowing charcoal in a dream predicts that the dreamer will enjoy a large increase in his capital as well as a great deal of happiness.

Chariot

If a dream features a chariot, it means that the dreamer is on the verge of being offered excellent and lucrative opportunities. However, if he sees himself or other people falling from a chariot, it is a warning that he will be demoted from his present position.

Charity

If a person receives charity in a dream, it means that his financial status will deteriorate slightly – not too much, though. If he sees himself giving charity in a dream, it means that he will enjoy an improvement in his economic situation.

Cheated

A dream about being cheated is a warning dream: if a person dreams that he is cheated in business, it means that there are people who are envious of him and will do anything in their power to cause his downfall.

Checkers

If a person dreams about a game of checkers, it implies that he will get bogged down in difficulties. Moreover, people who do not have his interests at heart are going to become involved in his life.

Checks

If a person dreams that he tries to pay his friends with bad checks, the dream attests to the fact that nothing is too low for him – even deception and cheating – if it enables him to implement his plans. If he receives checks, it means that he will be able to pay his debts. It also means that he is about to inherit money. If a person dreams about paying checks, it means that he is about to suffer financial losses.

Cheese

A dream about hard or yellow cheese attests to the fact that the dreamer is going to be subjected to humiliation as well as feelings of disgrace, shame and disappointment. These could all result from a bad and unhealthy relationship with his partner or a serious problem in some other relationship (such as father-son, mother-daughter, and so on). A dream like this also hints at the dreamer's character: he is a stubborn person, whose stubbornness is sometimes liable to lead to situations that involve unpleasantness to the point of losing good friends who are close to him.

Chemise

If a woman dreams about a chemise, it means that she will hear vicious gossip about herself.

Cherries

A dream about cherries implies the good times and treats that lie ahead of the dreamer, as well as all the wonderful things that go with them. Even if the dreamer does not define himself as a hedonist, the dream promises him treats of the type that he would define as hedonistic. The crux of such a dream is the fulfillment of the dreamer's wishes. Whatever he has wished for in life is about to come true, whether his aspirations are modest or whether they are enormous and seem to be of the kind that can never be realized.

In the future, the dreamer will enjoy wealth, happiness in his family life and in life generally, and his wishes are about to come true in such a good way that he cannot even imagine it. A dream like this is also interpreted as a sign of luck in gambling. The dreamer can remain calm if he made some kind of high-risk investment, since the dream promises that the investment will yield excellent profits – way beyond his wildest dreams. The dreamer can also be sure of good luck in casinos or in lotteries and so on.

Cherubs

If a person sees cherubs in a dream, it is a good dream that prophesies that the dreamer's life will be filled with happiness and joy. If the cherubs in the dream look sad, however, the dreamer must be prepared for misfortune.

Chess game

A dream that features a game of chess symbolizes success in gambling. If the dreamer wants to invest in something but hesitates to do so because he thinks that it is rather a gamble, the dream reassures him and implies that the investment will pay off, since ultimately it will double or triple in value.

A game of chess in a dream also hints that a huge row with friends is in the offing. The relationship will never again be what it was in the past. The resentment and the residual anger will be so great that it will not be possible to turn the clock back; the former friends will now be enemies.

If a chessboard appears very clearly in a dream, it is a sign that soon the dreamer will have new friends after he gets through the crisis with the old ones.

Chest (Box)

A dream about a chest generally symbolizes sexuality. A dream about a chest that has been broken into and opened symbolizes lasciviousness and prostitution. The dreamer's thoughts are not pure, and he is obsessed with sex. He is driven by his urges when he should be controlling them.

Conversely, a closed chest symbolizes morality and

A B **C** D E F G H I J K L M N O P Q R S T U V W X Y Z

virginity. A person who dreams about a closed chest is a person with high moral standards. He does not succumb to his urges, and manages to control them effectively.

Another meaning of a dream about an open box: a secret that the dreamer nursed and safeguarded is about to be revealed and exposed – or perhaps it is already common knowledge. This is keeping the dreamer awake at night, and he feels confused and threatened.

A closed chest in a dream is also interpreted as a hint at economic problems that are in the offing. Deals that are being thrashed out now are liable to fail. For this reason, before signing the deal or the contract, the dreamer should make sure that he knows exactly what it is about. If the dreamer is not sure about what he is doing, he should consult with professionals and not make the decisions on his own, relying on his intuition. This is liable to have an effect on his financial future, so he is well advised to listen to the dream's message carefully.

Chest (body)

A dream about a chest generally indicates the dreamer's desire to lean on someone older such as a father or mother figure, and feel that he has backing. It is an expression of the dreamer's helplessness and of his yearning for the days in which he was dependent on others.

A hairy male chest in a dream hints at strength for a male dreamer and at a lack of strength for a female dreamer.

A shrunken and sunken chest is a sign of the dreamer's loss of health. It is a dream that warns the dreamer that if he keeps up his present lifestyle, he is liable to contract a serious disease. Moreover, a dream like this hints at the loss of love and the disappearance of a person the dreamer loved from his life.

A dream that features a chest also attests to a desire for intimate relations with a person close to the dreamer, or with a person whose image appears in the dream.

A dream about a wounded chest attests to the fact that the dreamer's good name will be ruined. He may fall victim to malicious gossip that people will tend to believe, or a mistake he makes will cause him to lose his credibility in the eyes of others.

A dream about a mother's breast is a sign of the dreamer's desire to "return to the womb." Such a dream indicates the dreamer's fierce desire for a mother figure. The dreamer longs for a dependent relationship in which he will feel that he is the one who is being led rather than the leader. He prefers his life to be arranged for him and his decisions made for him, since this will make his life easier. Having said that, he also yearns for maternal warmth to envelop and caress him and in which he can revel endlessly.

Chestnuts

If a person dreams about chestnuts, he can expect to suffer financial losses. However, this is not the case with his love life, which will thrive. If he dreams about eating chestnuts, it means that he will go through a phase of sadness of sorrow, but it will pass, and eventually lead to happiness.

Chick

If a person dreams about a chick without being especially involved with chicks – such as raising them or

A B C D E F G H I J K L M N O P Q R S T U V W X Y Z

some indirect involvement with them – it is a positive dream that hints at the arrival of good news. The dreamer can expect to receive positive information by mail, whether in the form of a letter, an email or a telegram. The good news will not only make him happy, but also everyone around him, especially his close family – his spouse, children or parents.

If the dreamer has a particular connection with chicks, whether he is a farmer who raises them, or whether he deals with them indirectly in the raising of chickens or the marketing of eggs, the meaning of the dream is different. In this case, the dream contains a warning. It implies that soon damage connected to the dreamer's occupation will occur. This could mean diseases, natural disasters or damage caused by some person or other factor that is threatening harm to the dreamer's occupation. If the dreamer has enemies, he should make careful inquiries as to what their intentions are and placate them in appropriate ways.

If a person who has no special connection with chicks dreams about a chick, the dream hints at the dreamer's character and personality and admonishes him that he is not sufficiently realistic. It warns him of succumbing to illusions. He must be more realistic, with both feet planted firmly on the ground. He must not think that he has accomplished his goals and boast about his achievements too soon, but only after he has actually accomplished them. He must rely only on solid facts, and not daydream about things he is unsure will come true, or about things that are not truly anchored in reality.

If a person dreams about a chick in a chicken run, the dream attests to the fact that the person is innocent and naïve, and these traits are liable to cause him disappointment. He must try to get to the real meaning of things and be a bit more suspicious of the people around him. Sometimes some of them are out to get him or lead him astray. If he is more alert and less naïve, and stops believing in people indiscriminately, he will be able to avoid a great deal of mental anguish.

Childbirth

If a person dreams about giving birth, it is a good omen; the birth will go well and easily and the infant will be healthy and beautiful. If an unmarried woman dreams about childbirth, however, she is about to lose her good reputation.

Children

A dream that features children is generally an optimistic dream that predicts positive events in the dreamer's life. A woman who dreams about children is generally a happy woman, at least from the point of view of family. When a man dreams about children, it means that the man is going through a relatively calm and peaceful period. He is financially secure, his domestic life is running smoothly, and no changes or earth-shattering events should be taking place in the foreseeable future. Dreams about children generally occur during periods of calm, well-being and general satisfaction with life. A dream about children playing together in a sandbox or playground implies future economic success.

Sometimes dreams about children contain hints of negative events that are expressed in less pleasant situations in the dream, for instance, a crying child hints at anger in the family. A dream about an orphaned child is liable to occur during a period of friction between parents and children, especially during adolescence.

Chiming of a clock

This is always a good dream that predicts good things. The louder the chiming in the dream, the happier the dreamer's life will be.

Chimney

Smoke that pours out of a tall chimney in a dream indicate that the dreamer is about to receive good news. This news will bring the dreamer joy and happiness and will be very significant for him. In most cases, the news concerns a transition in life or a drastic change. It may be connected with promotion at work or moving somewhere else. In any event, it will create a turning point in the dreamer's life.

A tall, stable chimney is a sign that the dreamer will succeed in the tasks he set himself and in the objectives he wanted to accomplish. His achievements will be formidable, and this will cause his self-confidence to increase.

A tumble-down, broken chimney on a dilapidated roof is a sign that the future does not hold glad tidings: the dreamer will experience troubles and worries. The difficult period he will have to go through will strengthen him, and he will learn lessons from it. Having said that, he will have to prepare himself psychologically for a period that will not be easy and that cannot be avoided.

If a person dreams that he is going through a chimney, it

means that he is about to have mystical experiences. He is a spiritual person who is drawn to the occult world, and if he continues exploring and entering this world, he can expect revelations and encounters "of the third kind."

If a person dreams that he is standing and cleaning a chimney, it is a sign that his conscience is bothering him. He is not accustomed to behaving as he behaved, and he cannot simply ignore it. He must work out what the matter is (since he is liable to repeat his behavior in other variations) and iron everything out until his conscience is clear and he can sleep peacefully.

China

If a woman dreams about setting out her china in an orderly and attractive way, it means that she will run a thriving household and stick to her budget.

China store

If a person who owns a china store dreams that the store looks empty of merchandise, he will undergo a serious drop in business and will suffer losses.

Chocolate

If a person dreams about chocolate, it implies that he provides well for his dependants. Furthermore, it means that he will enjoy his job and have a pleasant social life with his friends. A dream in which the dreamer drinks chocolate indicates that he will go through a brief period of adversity, but this will be followed by a very good phase.

A B **C** D E F G H I J K L M N O P Q R S T U V W X Y Z

Choir

If a person dreams that he is a member of a choir that sings at a particular event, it attests to his desire to belong to a group and live a harmonious life. It is a dream that characteristically occurs prior to beginning a new job or joining a group such as the army or any other such united group. A dream in which the dreamer is kicked out of a choir or in which the choir sings out of tune and arouses the ire of the conductor or the public serves as a warning sign. The dreamer must reexamine himself and those opposite him more thoroughly before taking a stand or a step that will commit him.

Choking – See Suffocation

Cholera

If a person dreams that he succumbs to cholera, it means that he is about to become ill. A dream that features a cholera epidemic that spreads all over the country indicates that there will be an outbreak of a fatal illness. Moreover, there will be a great deal of disillusionment.

Christ

A dream about the infant Jesus being worshipped is a sign of peace, happiness and knowledge. If the dreamer sees Christ in Gethsemane, it means that he is filled with nostalgia and longing for change. If a dream features Christ expelling the money-changers from the Temple, it is an indication that honesty will prevail over evil.

Christmas tree

If a person sees a Christmas tree in a dream, he can expect good things and good luck. If he dreams about taking it down, it means that the festivities will be followed immediately by a painful occurrence.

Chrysanthemum

A dream about a chrysanthemum, especially if the dreamer sees himself walking through a field of chrysanthemums, prophesies that the dreamer can soon expect to make an acquaintance that will lead him to fall in love with someone he does not yet know, and to a love affair that will sweep him into new realms. However, it is also possible that the dream only indicates the beginning of a close friendship or an acquaintance with a person who will become close to the dreamer and who will have particular significance in his life. Whether it is an acquaintance on the romantic level or simply friendship, the person whom the dreamer is about to meet will accompany the dreamer along his path for a long time. It won't be a person who suddenly bursts into the dreamer's life and disappears just as quickly, but rather a person whose acquaintance will be meaningful for the long term, the kind that will make changes in the dreamer's life.

Church

A dream about a church does not bode well. If a person sees a church in a dream, it means that he will be sadly disappointed by things he has been looking forward to for a long time. If the dreamer goes into a dark church, it means that a funeral is in the offing. He does not have much hope for a better future.

Churchyard

If a person dreams about walking in a churchyard during the winter, it means that he will have an unending and relentless struggle with poverty. This will involve living far away from his home and family. If the churchyard is seen in the spring, however, it means that the dreamer will enjoy good company. A dream that features lovers in a churchyard predicts that the lovers will never marry each other.

Churning

If a person dreams that he is churning, it means that he is going to have to perform tedious and difficult tasks. However, his reward will be success and prosperity. If a farmer dreams about churning, he can look forward to a plentiful and lucrative harvest.

Cider

If a person drinks cider in a dream, it implies that if he can resist material temptations, he will be able to amass a huge amount of money. If a person sees other people drinking cider in a dream, it means that the dreamer is easily influenced by treacherous friends.

Cigarettes

A dream about cigarettes refers to the dreamer's influential friends.

If a person dreams that someone lights a cigarette the dreamer is holding in his hand, it is a sign that he will soon require someone's help in a sudden and unexpected way. He should brace himself for "surprises" that will not always be pleasant ones.

Smoking an entire cigarette in a dream is a sign that the dreamer will soon get to realize one of the goals he has set for himself in life or one of the heartfelt wishes he really wants to fulfill.

If a dream features an ashtray filled with cigarette butts, the dreamer no longer has a future to look forward to. He can no longer hope to get far and realize the ambitions and goals he set for himself years ago and always worked toward. He must begin to resign himself to the fact that he will never succeed in realizing his fantasies and fulfilling all of his wishes, even the most realistic of them.

Cipher

A dream about a cipher means that the dreamer is interested in literary and classical topics and will become proficient in them if he studies hard.

Circle

A person who dreams about a circle is in some kind of trouble. He is looking for a way out of a situation he has gotten himself into. A dream in which a person is surrounded by a circle of people may mean that the dreamer will be seriously embarrassed in public. It could well be a business meeting in which he will find himself "trapped" in a circle and will feel as if he has no way out.

A dream in which the dreamer finds himself in a circle

A B C D E F G H I J K L M N O P Q R S T U V W X Y Z

of trees or other objects may attest to a good economic situation alongside a feeling of dissatisfaction on the personal level. A feeling of an unnecessary burden has arisen in the dreamer because of a great deal of property he has amassed – not because of his own personal initiative, but because of the pressure of someone close to him. The dreamer feels overloaded and is looking for a way to shed his obligations.

Cistern

If a person dreams about a cistern, it means that he is liable to put his friends' rights and pleasures at risk. If he dreams about drawing water from a cistern, it means that he intends to take up a hobby that is socially taboo. A dream about an empty cistern is a very bad dream, indicating a drastic switch from joy to sorrow.

City

If a person dreams that he is in a strange city, the dream attests to the fact that due to circumstances beyond his control, he has been compelled to move house or lower his standard of living.

City council

A dream about a city council predicts disputes with public bodies. The dreamer can basically forget about winning any of them – the outcome will not be in his favor.

City hall

If a person sees a city hall in his dream, it symbolizes

lawsuits and disputes. If a young woman sees a city hall in her dream, it means that her immoral conduct will cause her to lose her lover.

Clairvoyance

If a person sees his own future in a dream, it implies that he will undergo a professional switch and become involved in disputes with people who do not have his interests at heart. If a person dreams about a visit to a clairvoyant, it is a sign of bad luck in matters of business and in love.

Clams

If a person sees clams in a dream, it symbolizes dealing with an obstinate but honest person. If he eats clams in his dream, it means that he is making the most of another person's prosperity.

Claret

A dream in which the dreamer drinks claret signifies that the dreamer will be influenced by good people. If the dreamer sees broken bottles of claret, he will be negatively influenced by immoral people.

Clarinet

If a person sees a clarinet in a dream, it means that he will act frivolously – in complete contrast to his usual dignified demeanor. If he sees a broken clarinet in the dream, it implies that he will do something to displease a good friend.

Clay

A dream about clay, especially one that features a classic clay vessel (the color of terra cotta in an old-fashioned style), is a sign that the dreamer's worries are about to end. From now on, he can expect relief, especially in financially, but also prosperity and spiritual happiness. In the forthcoming period, the dreamer will have time to get involved in things he always wanted to do, but was too busy earning a living and had no time or money to realize these wishes.

If a person dreams about a broken clay vessel, it is a sign that soon he will have to do something that goes against his conscience or world-view, since he is about to be forced to do something he does not agree with, and he will have to consent to it against his will.

It is probably something to do with religious matters or honoring parents (a religious burial rather than a secular one, religious restrictions that will be imposed on him, and so on). However, despite the coercion involved, the dreamer will derive a lot of benefit from the matter, along with a great deal of happiness, since he will see the positive results and the change for the good.

Cleanliness

A dream in which the dreamer sees himself doing cleaning jobs and throwing away old things refers to his profound need for change. It could be house-cleaning or mental and emotional cleaning. The dreamer is apparently going through a period of distress. He feels that the load on his shoulders is heavy and that there are too many factors around him that are preventing him from seeing the situation clearly. There is therefore a need to clean up and throw out useless things. The actual task of classifying things serves as a separation from the past and from the burden, while getting rid of unnecessary stuff will give his soul distance and space. From now on, things will only improve.

Clergyman

If a person dreams that he sends for a clergyman to deliver a eulogy at a funeral, it means that he is involved in a futile battle against an illness and against negative influences. If a young woman dreams about marrying a clergyman, she will suffer from psychological anguish and a whole range of hardships.

Climb

A dream about a climb has several meanings. It can attest to a struggle to advance at work. This is mainly the case when the dream is about a climb to a mountain-top, which represents a new and challenging position. Climbing back up after falls means that the dreamer is a stubborn type who does not relinquish his goal easily. In such a case, his stubbornness pays off, because he is blessed with strength, fitness, courage and persistence. A dream about pillars indicates that despite difficulties at work, the management will show the dreamer appreciation, whether it is a verbal commendation or a financial reward. A dream in which the dreamer climbs and falls over and over again means that the dreamer has gotten into difficulties. His achievements are relatively few, because of various obstacles in his path stemming mainly from personal lack of ability. He is well advised to check out the reasons for the difficulties.

A
B
C
D
E
F
G
H
I
J
K
L
M
N
O
P
Q
R
S
T
U
V
W
X
Y
Z

Clock / Watch

A clock in a dream implies that with time, everything will come right. In other words, if the dreamer runs into problems that seem to have no solution, the dream implies that time will play an important part in solving them.

A clock that appears in a dream also symbolizes achievements or achievement-orientation.

If a person hears an alarm clock in a dream, there is a hint that soon the dreamer can expect to become involved in a romantic liaison that will effect a significant change in his life and will bring him great happiness, tranquillity and repose.

A dream about a large clock in the town square or in some institution such as the town hall, a church and so on, implies that the dreamer knows how to enjoy every minute and take full advantage of every hour. He is a person who seizes the day and experiences life in full. The dream implies that the dreamer feels that he knows how to make the most of life.

If a person sees a wristwatch in his dream, it is a sign that he is about to receive good news, and that he will have wealth, growth and prosperity in business.

If a person sees a grandfather clock hanging on or standing next to a wall in his home, the dream attests to the fact that he can expect a great deal of happiness in the domestic framework. His family life will be full and happy, and his children and spouse will be a source of pride and joy to him.

If the dreamer sees that the clock he owns has stopped, the dream implies that he will recover from a serious illness.

If a person sees himself watching the clock impatiently in a dream, it is a sign that although he is ambitious, and despite his abilities to "go far" and notch up highly significant achievements, he is not blessed with patience. He is impatient and looks for short cuts, so he does not always put his heart and soul into things. He strives for achievements in a short time, and this is not always possible.

Cloister

If a person sees a cloister in a dream, he will soon feel the urge to make a change in his surroundings. If a woman has this dream, it means that life's vicissitudes and grief have caused her to lead a less selfish existence.

Closet

If a person sees a full, clean closet in a dream, it indicates comfort and enjoyment. On the other hand, an empty, dirty closet is an indication of poverty and misery.

Clothing

Clothing appears in a great variety of ways in dreams, and the dreams are interpreted accordingly.

A new item of clothing in a dream is a sign that the dreamer knows how to maneuver his way successfully along his path until his goals are accomplished. He operates cleverly and sometimes slyly, if necessary, when he is focusing on the goal. Ultimately, without a doubt, he accomplishes it.

If an old or tattered piece of clothing is seen in a dream,

A B C D E F G H I J K L M N O P Q R S T U V W X Y Z

it implies that the dreamer has to employ "tricks" and stratagems taken from the past in order to succeed in accomplishing his goals. He must recall the methods he employed in the past and apply them in the present because in this way he will succeed in repeating the success he enjoyed in the past.

If a particularly venerable piece of clothing is seen in a dream, it is a sign that soon the dreamer will receive money from his family. This does not necessarily mean an inheritance, but rather a substantial sum of money from someone in his family for a reason other than inheritance (a bet or a joint venture).

If the dreamer sees himself partially naked, with only his lower torso dressed, it is a sign that he will get his wish soon, and that there is nothing that can stand in the way of his desire and ambitions.

Conversely, if the dreamer sees himself stripped completely naked in his dream, he can expect a regression in every area of life. Things will not happen at the rate he expected; on the contrary – there will be delays that are evidently caused by his state of mind. Until he faces the mental problem that is bothering him, things will remain stagnant.

If the dreamer sees himself wearing clothes that he would never dream of wearing in reality because they are too weird or daring, the dream hints at imminent surprises. Unexpected things will cause a change in the dreamer's way of life. They will bring him dizzying success, and he will enter realms he never dreamed that he would enter.

If the dreamer's clothes closet appears in a dream, and it is very crowded and overflowing with clothes, it is a sign of danger. Trouble is on the way. The dreamer must be ready for something that will happen suddenly, unexpectedly, which will have a negative effect on his life.

Clouds

If a dream features dark, massive clouds, it is a prediction of hard times and mismanagement. If rain is falling from the clouds in the dream, it means that problems and ill health are in the offing. If a person sees bright clouds with sunshine pouring through them in a dream, he will enjoy success after struggling for some time. If a dream features clouds and stars together, the dreamer can look forward to minor rewards and pleasures.

Cloven foot

A dream about a cloven foot is a warning dream: it warns the dreamer that he is threatened by some exceptional bad luck. He should eschew the company of strangers.

Clover

In most cases, clover in a dream is a sign of sure success and good fortune for the dreamer. In countries where the English culture reigns supreme, a dream that features clover is common. (Clover is a plant that consists of a formation of three or four leaves.) The division of the leaves symbolizes a crossroads in the dreamer's life. If he is not at a crossroads, he will soon have to deal with an important decision that will have a far reaching effect on his life. He will face several possible options and will have to choose one of them in order to pave his way in life. In most cases, the decision is linked to studies or work, or – conversely – to choosing a suitable mate.

If the decision concerns the romantic realm, and the dreamer is vacillating between two potential partners, the dream indicates that he should listen to his heart and take his intuition into account. He should not just make cold and rational calculations, since this decision is likely to be one of the most crucial ones of his life.

If a person sees himself in a field of clover in a dream, it implies that if he yearns for real achievements in life and wants to accomplish the goals he has set himself, he must not rely on luck. He must make an effort and work hard, and above all act wisely and industriously. Then he will accomplish his goals very easily and will be sure that he has done the right thing.

Clown

A clown in a dream is a symbol of two-faced behavior, cunning and treachery. If the dreamer himself is the clown hiding behind a mask, it implies that he presents an external image in public and in company generally and a completely different image to the members of his household and to himself. Some introspection will help the dreamer understand the reasons for this. If a dream features a clown that later turns out to be someone the dreamer knows, it is a warning. The dreamer must be more careful. He is too quick to trust people who sometimes "don masks" to disguise ulterior motives. The dreamer must therefore relate to business proposals with a certain degree of suspicion.

Club

A person who dreams that he is in a club and meets friends can expect an exciting encounter with a friend from the distant past. A dream of this type can also predict a party or a festivity that will take place in the family framework.

A person who dreams that he is not permitted to enter a club must watch his step, particularly in the social sphere. A place where he goes regularly and where he is welcome is suddenly off-limits to him. He may get in trouble because of other people's gossip or lies. In any case, caution can do no harm.

Coach

If a person dreams that he is traveling in a coach, it is a sign of financial losses. If he dreams that he is driving a coach, it means that he will move house or implement changes in his business practices.

Coals

A dream that features bright coals is a positive dream that foretells happiness and changes for the better. If the dreamer holds these coals, his happiness will know no bounds. However, if a dream features burnt-out coals, it is an indication of hardship and disappointment.

Coat

If a dream features a coat that is either worn, sold or purchased, it means that an investment the dreamer made will come through and yield excellent dividends for the dreamer. A dream in which the dreamer is wearing a coat that belongs to someone else implies that the dreamer is in need of help from that person. If a person loses a coat in a dream, it warns him to exercise caution when making any decisions in business.

Coat-of-arms

If a dreamer sees a coat-of-arms in a dream, it portends bad luck. Furthermore, it means that he will never receive a title.

Cobra

The appearance of this snake in a dream indicates that the dreamer has serious sexual problems. This is particularly true for men.

Cock crowing

If a person dreams about a cock crowing at dawn, it is a sign of good luck. If a single person has this dream, it means that he will marry soon and have a lovely home. A dream that features a cock crowing at night is a negative dream, since it presages grief and despair.

Cocktail

If a person dreams about drinking a cocktail, it implies that he is giving his friends the impression of being a serious person when in fact he prefers the company of light-hearted, pleasure-seeking superficial people. If a woman dreams that she is drinking a cocktail, it means that she leads a promiscuous and immoral life.

Cocoa

A dream about cocoa means that the dreamer has a deliberate policy of cultivating the wrong type of person in order to advance.

Coconut

A dream about a coconut is a warning dream. It warns the dreamer that people he considers his friends are actually enemies who want to shatter his expectations and dash his hopes. If a dream features dead coconut trees, it is a prediction of grief and bereavement.

Coffee

If a person dreams about coffee, it means that he is under emotional stress and is suffering from tension in his everyday life. A dream about drinking coffee warns of domestic strife and financial losses if the dreamer is married. If he is unmarried, it implies that his friends disapprove of his marriage plans.

If a person dreams that he trades in coffee, it foretells setbacks in business. If he sells coffee in a dream, he will suffer financial losses. If he purchases coffee, his financial situation will be stable.

If a young woman sees or touches coffee in a dream, she should act discreetly, otherwise she will find herself at the center of a scandal.

A dream that features ground coffee means that enemies and problems will be overcome. A dream about roasted coffee is a warning for the dreamer to exercise caution when dealing with strangers. If the coffee in a dream is green, it means that the dreamer has implacable enemies.

Coffee house

A dream about a coffee mill predicts that the dreamer will be entrapped by false friends who are in fact enemies who are conspiring against him. The dream warns him that women might try to seduce him and abscond with his property.

Coffee mill

If a person sees a coffee mill in a dream, it is a warning that some kind of danger is approaching rapidly. He can only ward it off if he is extremely alert and strong. If the dreamer hears the grinding of a coffee mill, it implies that he will have no difficulty countering the evil that people are scheming against him.

Coffin

A dream about a coffin is a negative dream, indicating bad luck for the dreamer. If a farmer dreams about a coffin, he will lose his crops; a businessman will suffer losses; young people will be bereft of people they love. If the dreamer sees his own coffin, he can expect domestic strife, sorrow, and losses in business. If he sees his own body lying in the coffin, he will be defeated in his endeavors despite his brave struggle.

Coins

If a person sees a gold coin in a dream, it means that he will go out to enjoy nature. If he sees a silver coin, it signifies bad luck in the form of domestic strife. If the coin in the dream is worn, the dreamer's day will be melancholy.

A copper coin in a dream means that the dreamer bears a heavy burden and shoulders enormous responsibility. If the coin in the dream is shiny, the dream predicts a successful romance for the dreamer.

Cold

This is a warning dream. The dreamer must watch out for enemies who are hell bent to destroy him. It also warns him to keep a watchful eye on his state of health, because it is in jeopardy.

Collar

If a person dreams that the collar around his neck is tight, it means that he is afraid of a powerful individual who is terrorizing him.

College

If a person dreams about college, it means that he will soon receive a promotion that he has long been waiting for. If he dreams that he is back in college, the dream implies that he is about to receive an award for an outstanding achievement.

Colliery or coal mine

If a person dreams about a coal mine, the dream warns that enemies are plotting the dreamer's downfall. If the dreamer has shares in the coal mine in his dream, however, it means that he need not worry about an investment in a certain venture.

A B **C** D E F G H I J K L M N O P Q R S T U V W X Y Z

Collision

If a dream features a collision, it means that the dreamer can expect a serious accident or a setback in business. If a woman dreams about a collision, it implies that she will be unable to choose between two lovers. This will place her at the center of a dispute.

Colonel

A dream in which the dreamer either sees or is a colonel means that his aspirations to achieve social or professional distinction will not be realized. If a colonel has this dream, it means that he is attempting to pull rank on the people around him.

Colors

In a dream, all the colors of the spectrum, except black, are a good sign. If the colors are bright, they symbolize security and tranquillity. White is a symbol of purity and innocence. Blue means that problems can be overcome with the help of friends. Yellow is a symbol of high expectations. Orange and gray indicate that the dreamer needs to have patience. Red predicts social events. Green implies jealousy. Brown is a sign of glad tidings. Pink heralds a surprise. Black means bad moods and depression.

Comb

A dream about a fancy comb the dreamer finds on his table or uses is a reference to an expensive gift that will arrive in the near future or that has already arrived in the last few days. The dreamer, or the recipient of the expensive gift, is not certain what to do in the new situation that has arisen. If it is a woman, the sender's action has revealed serious intentions with regard to her, while she was not thinking in that direction at all – possibly because of a big age difference. It could also be the opposite situation, in which the recipient is a man. He is surprised that a particular woman in his life, with whom he has a professional or friendly relationship, is "signaling" clearly to him that "he is worth the investment." This is the time to clarify the situation that has arisen and to lower the sender's expectations. A frank conversation with the person (the giver of the present), in which the dreamer makes it clear that there is no chance of any romantic developments, will make things much easier for the dreamer.

Combat

If a person dreams that he is in combat with someone else, it means that he is trying to steal another person's love. It also means that his business reputation will be ruined. A dream about combat symbolizes the battle to maintain an even keel.

Comedy

A dream in which the dreamer attends a comedy symbolizes the frivolous and superficial pleasures the dreamer will participate in. If he dreams about a comedy, it refers to enjoyable and pleasant tasks.

Comet

A dream about a comet implies that the dreamer will experience unexpected problems, but he will solve them

A B C D E F G H I J K L M N O P Q R S T U V W X Y Z

and become renowned. If comets appear in a young person's dream, they predict the death of a loved one and grief.

Comic songs

If a dreamer hears comic songs in a dream, it means that he will give up on an opportunity to advance his business in favor of the pursuit of pleasure. Dreaming about singing comic songs predicts a long period of fun and enjoyment followed by trouble.

Command

If a person is commanded in a dream, it means that he will be thoroughly reprimanded for behaving rudely toward his superiors. If he dreams of giving a command, he can expect to receive some kind of honor. However, if he gives the command in an overbearing way, he can expect to run into difficulties. Another meaning for receiving commands in a dream states that the dreamer will succumb to the negative influence of people who are stronger-willed than he is.

Commandment

If a person reads or hears the Ten Commandments in a dream, it means that the dreamer will make mistakes that even the cleverest advisors will not be able to rectify.

Commerce

If a person dreams about commercial dealings, it means that he makes the most of opportunities. If he dreams about negative aspects and consequences of commerce, it foretells serious problems and financial loss. If there is an improvement in commerce in the dream, it implies that the dreamer will solve his problems.

Committee

A dream about a committee indicates that the dreamer will be inveigled into performing an unpleasant task, or that other people will decide to give him a futile job to do.

Compact disk

A dream about a CD implies that the dreamer will soon become involved in a new romantic liaison that will go very well.

Companion

If a person dreams about his spouse, it means that he will have minor worries and possibly become ill. If he dreams about companions from his social circle, it means that he is being distracting from important issues by the pursuit of frivolous and superficial pastimes. If a person dreams about his spouse as loving, it is a sign of a warm, happy home with lovely children.

Compass

A person who dreams about a compass has reached a crossroads. Generally, before an important decision, various thoughts regarding the correct path to choose rise up from the subconscious. The dreamer may well be on the threshold of an important business or personal decision, and it briefly seems to him that the earth is giving way under his feet, just like a mountain climber who has lost his way. The dreamer must take a few days or weeks off in order to examine the moves he is about to make carefully and cautiously.

Competition

There are two interpretations of a competition in a dream: the first is the desire to overcome the fear of losing. The dreamer cannot bear losing, and every failure is hard for him to deal with and distorts his ability to see himself objectively. The source of his fear of failure and losing (in studies, games, or any other sphere) apparently lies in his childhood.

Whether he is aware of this or not, his desire to get rid of this obsessive need to prove to himself that he is capable of impressive achievements and the fear of not succeeding at the task at hand is great. This fierce desire is reflected in the dream, and it serves as the answer: if he wants to, he can overcome his fears of losing and failure, and this depends only on him.

The second common interpretation of a dream about a competition is also connected to the steadfastness of the dreamer's character. It hints that soon the dreamer will have to resist a temptation and not give in. He will have to muster his psychological forces in order to avoid being swept into an adventure or succumbing to powerful urges, and he will have to be strong enough to control them. If he does not do so, he is liable to face unnecessary damage that could have been prevented by his will power.

Completion

If a person dreams about completing a task, it means that he will soon be so proficient at his work that he will be able to decide how he wants to spend his time.

Complexion

If a person dreams about having a lovely complexion, it is a very good sign, since happy events are in the offing. If the dream features a bad, blotchy complexion, the dreamer must brace himself for disappointment and illness.

Computer

If a person dreams that he is working on a computer, it means that he will be given more responsibility at work. If the dreamer does not know how to operate a computer, he can soon expect to be given a task that will be overwhelming for him.

Concert

If a person dreams about a symphony concert, he can expect to enjoy really refined pleasures. If a businessman dreams about this kind of concert, he can look forward to financial profits. If young people have this dream, it is a sign that they will find perfect love.

If the dreamer attends a rock or pop concert, it means that he is hanging out with the wrong kind of people. He will also suffer losses in business.

A B **C** D E F G H I J K L M N O P Q R S T U V W X Y Z

Concubine

If a man dreams that he has a concubine, it means that he is trying to hide his true colors and conceal the real nature of his business from the public eye, and he runs the risk of disgrace. If a man dreams that his concubine is unfaithful, it means that he will have a run-in with his former enemies, and this will cause problems. If a woman dreams that she is a concubine, it means that her own promiscuous conduct will bring about her downfall.

Confectionery

If a dream features stale confectionery, it means that one of the dreamer's enemies is pretending to be his friend and will disclose the dreamer's secrets to his competitors.

Conference

If a person dreams about a business conference, it means that his financial situation will improve.

Confetti

If a dream features wedding festivities that are barely visible because of all the confetti in the air, it means that the dreamer wastes too much time on trivial things rather than focusing on important issues.

Conflagration

A dream about a conflagration appears in various forms, and can be interpreted in different ways. There is a 180-degree difference between a dream that features a conflagration and a dream in which the dreamer succeeds in extinguishing it.

If a person sees a house on fire in a dream, it is a sign that he is about to enjoy good luck. His financial situation will improve and he will enjoy health and a satisfying family life.

If a person sees fire breaking out or flames and a conflagration without a clear source in a dream, the dream indicates repressed anger that is erupting suddenly without any prior warning. The dream implies that because of the dreamer's nature, which keeps everything that bothers him inside, he can be expected to explode, quarrel, and find himself in an ongoing fight that he had no intention of starting.

If a person sees a conflagration in a multistory building, it implies that he will suffer from losses and worries. He may be deeply disturbed by financial and business matters, but the dream can also refer to matters of the heart and love.

If a person sees his friend's house going up in flames, it is a hint that he will succeed in overcoming an enemy or a rival of some kind, and this need not necessarily be the same person whose house went up in flames in the dream.

If a person sees a gigantic conflagration consuming a house, it predicts that the dreamer can expect to receive an inheritance, or that he has his eye on a large inheritance that is supposed to reach him in the near future.

A dream in which the dreamer himself is injured during a conflagration attests to the fact that he can expect to become embroiled in rows with relatives. The dispute is liable to erupt because of some trivial issue and turn into a massive row that will lead to ugly battles.

If a person sees trees being consumed in a conflagration

A B C D E F G H I J K L M N O P Q R S T U V W X Y Z

in a dream, it is a warning dream: the dreamer possesses some kind of secret information that would cause a great deal of embarrassment – not only to the people involved, but also to the dreamer himself – if he were to reveal and disseminate it.

If a person dreams about burning garbage, it is a prophetic dream, according to which a woman who is connected to his life is about to go through mental torment. If a woman has this dream, the interpretation refers either to her or to one of the women in her vicinity.

If, in contrast, a person succeeds in fighting the conflagration and extinguishing it, whether it was in the house or somewhere else, it is a good dream, since the dreamer is about to receive unexpected good news that will make him very happy. The element of surprise will be so great that the dreamer will have a hard time digesting the news.

Confusion

If a person dreams of chaos, a mess, untidiness, or, alternatively, feels that disorder or confusion reign in his life, or that a lack of clarity is dominating his thoughts, the dream is a kind of warning dream against unexpected hitches or mild accidents. The dreamer cannot avoid them, and he has to be a little more alert about the everyday actions he performs. The "accidents" or the "hitches" will occur at the most unexpected moment, so that other than preparing himself for them psychologically, he cannot do anything to avoid them. The dream "shakes" the dreamer out of his apathy in order to make him take control of his life.

A B **C** D E F G H I J K L M N O P Q R S T U V W X Y Z

Conjurer

A dream that features a conjurer implies that the dreamer will have to deal with problems along his path to happiness and prosperity.

Conscience

If the dreamer is bothered by his conscience in a dream, it means that he will be tempted to do wrong and must try to resist the temptation. If he has a clear conscience in a dream, it means that his reputation is good.

Conspiracy

If a person dreams that he is a victim of a conspiracy, it means that he is about to make a mistake in the running of his affairs.

Consumption (TB)

If a person dreams that he has consumption, it implies that the dreamer is jeopardizing himself somehow. He should stay with his friends.

Contempt

If a person dreams that he is in contempt of court, it means that he is guilty of committing a social or professional gaffe without any justification.

Contest – See Competition

Convent / Monastery

If a person dreams of entering a convent or monastery, it is a sign that he will no longer have enemies or worries. If the person meets a priest in his dream, however, it means that he will endlessly search for a cure for mundane problems and stress. If a young girl dreams about a convent, her moral conduct is questionable.

Conversation

If a person sees himself conversing with a woman about other people in a dream, it is a sign that idle gossip will lead to a loss or a lack. The gossip will circulate in the dreamer's house and cause irreversible damage.

If a person sees himself conversing with someone else in a dream, and the content of the conversation is not clear, the dream implies that the dreamer should pay attention to the content of his conversations and guard his tongue, since careless words are liable to cause him damage.

If a person dreams about two strangers conversing, it is a sign of confusion and of an inability to focus on the important things in life – a kind of temporary chaos that goes hand-in-hand with the routine of the dreamer's life. The dream does not augur well, and the dreamer must organize his days and his desires and define the goals he wants to achieve in life. If not, he will ultimately lose his way.

A dream like this also implies financial problems or problems in the dreamer's workplace. Perhaps someone in the dreamer's workplace is trying to trip him up, and this is why he has not been promoted. Moreover, the dreamer may soon expect other damage to occur in the economic realm, such as the possibility of falling victim to theft, extortion, vindictiveness, and so on.

Convict

If a person sees a convict in a dream predicts bad tidings and disaster. If he dreams that he himself is a convict, it means that he is worrying about something that will soon be clarified. If a woman dreams that her lover is dressed like a convict, it is a sign that she will begin having doubts about his love.

Cook – See Baker

Cookie / Biscuit

When cookies appear in a dream, it means finding a life partner and entering into a committed and legal relationship. The dreamer is about to meet the person who will be the perfect match for him. If he is already in a relationship, the dream implies that the relationship between him and his mate will keep on improving as time passes.

If a dreamer sees himself eating a cookie or a wafer in a dream, the dream indicates that the dreamer tends to blame other people for his situation or his suffering. When unpleasant things happen to him, he immediately seeks to place the blame on the people around him, never on himself. This tendency is way overdone. Not only do people tend to comment to him about it, but he himself is subconsciously aware of it; however, he refuses to admit to it wholeheartedly. The tendency to lay the blame for his

A B C D E F G H I J K L M N O P Q R S T U V W X Y Z

troubles, for mistakes he made and for his suffering on other people will cost him dearly in the end, since people will keep away from him and will sever their relations with him. He has begun to feel this happening, and therefore the dream is warning him and "suggesting" that he mend his ways.

Cooking

Cooking in a dream generally means health problems in the chest and in the digestive system. While the connection between cooking and smells and tastes is also linked to things that indicate the person's sexuality and to problems from which the dreamer suffers in the sexual realm, it generally indicates physical problems in the dreamer's body – mainly in the chest and the digestive system, as mentioned above

The dream serves as a kind of warning or signal regarding health problems, so it is a good idea for the dreamer to be more aware of himself and his body, and even undergo a general physical exam. The problem could eventually crop up in another part of his body rather than in his chest or digestive system, but it is important to discover it as early as possible.

As for the reference to sexual problems, it is possible that the dreamer is suffering from problems in sexual performance, but their source may be physiological, that is, connected to the sexual organs. It is a good idea for the dreamer to be examined by a gynecologist or a urologist in order to rule out possible problems.

Cooking stove

A dream about a cooking stove means that the dreamer will be able to avoid a lot of unpleasantness.

Copper

A dream in which the dreamer is in a copper mine or finds a pile of copper indicates an unsuccessful incident at work or in business. Instead of finding gold – the shiny and precious metal, the dreamer finds the relatively poor substitute of the metal he was really seeking.

He must be careful of taking the advice of true experts or of those who claim to be experts in their field. Deals in all areas pop up like mushrooms after the rain. There is no rush, and in this case, the saying that haste is from the devil should be the guiding light of the decision-makers.

The secret is to be patient. It will pay off.

Copperplate writing

A dream about this style of writing warns against expressing conflicting views at home, since these could lead to domestic strife and disharmony.

Coppersmith

A dream that features a coppersmith symbolizes a nice but poorly remunerated job.

Copying

A dream about copying indicates that the dreamer's plans will not work out.

Copying machine

A dream about a copying machine is a warning: the dreamer must be on the alert for people who want to steal property or ideas from him. He must be more cautious.

Coral

Coral that appears in a dream as it normally appears in natural surroundings – in the form of a reef – is a warning dream. In general, it warns of a disease that is liable to afflict the dreamer, or of a poor physical condition and physical or mental debility that is liable to cause his body's systems to collapse. When the body is weak, or when the dreamer is not in peak psychological condition, he is susceptible to diseases, and his immune system cannot carry the load.

The dream also warns of damage that is liable to be caused to the dreamer because of taking erroneous steps or opting for wrong moves that can lead to destruction or, heaven forbid, disaster. The dreamer must be very aware of his deeds and moves in life. He must be more alert than ever and aware of the possibility that a bad influence is being exerted over him, and it is guiding him along wrong paths or causing him to make incorrect decisions. The dream implies that the dreamer has to pay more attention than ever to the decisions, moves and ways he chooses to make in his life; moreover, he must be aware of everything that occurs in his immediate surroundings. The higher his level of awareness of himself and of external influences, the easier it will be for him to secure his path.

The source of the symbol of coral in a dream is the bitter fate of sailors whose ships foundered on coral reefs, causing them to drown in the depths of the sea. There is a hypothesis that states that people whose work or lives are connected to the sea are more inclined to dream about coral, but evidence that has been collected from different dreamers has indicated that it is a universal symbol that also appears in the dreams of people who have no direct connection with the sea, and even in the dreams of people who live far from the sea and who have never seen or been to the sea in their lives.

Cork

If a person dreams that he is pulling out corks at a banquet, it means that he will soon experience prosperity that will enable him to improve his standard of living and quality of life. If a young woman dreams about champagne corks, it means that she will have a handsome, lively lover who pampers her. This dream admonishes her to listen to her parents' advice.

Corkscrew

A dream about a corkscrew is a warning dream: it warns the dreamer to curb his urge to satisfy his desires, since they are leading him down a very perilous path.

Corn / Cornfields

If a dreamer sees a lush green cornfield, it means that the farmer will have a good harvest and prosperity, and the dreamer will enjoy harmony and happiness. If a person sees squashed ears of corn in a dream, he should brace himself for disappointment and bereavement. If he is busy husking corn in the dream, he can expect a successful and happy life. If he watches other people husking corn, it means that the dreamer will rejoice in their prosperity.

Dreams that feature young corn are positive, since they portend success, renown, riches and fulfilled desires. A dream about eating green corn is a sign of harmony.

Corner

If a person dreams that he is hiding in a corner because he is afraid, it is a bad dream. If he sees people gathered in a corner in his dream, he is warned that his enemies are plotting to bring him down. A person close to the dreamer may prove to be disloyal.

Cornmeal

A dream that features cornmeal indicates that the dreamer's most heartfelt wishes will come true. If a person dreams that he is eating a loaf baked from cornmeal, it means that he is unwittingly placing stumbling-blocks in his own path.

Corns

If a person dreams that he is suffering from painful corns, he should be warned that his enemies are plotting against him, and this is causing him mental agony. If he gets rid of the corns in his dream, he will receive a large inheritance. If a woman dreams that she has corns, it implies that her life will not be easy, especially as far as other women are concerned.

Coronation

A dream about a coronation indicates the dreamer's close ties with celebrities and VIPs.

Corpse

A dream about a corpse hints that the dreamer is preoccupied with the topic of death or with the disappearance of something dear to him that he is about to lose or that is already lost and gone. If a businessman dreams this dream, some people interpret it as a hint of the total loss of everything to do with business, money and funding. It is possible that the dream hints at the destruction of the dreamer's good name, and, consequently, at loss and at what that entails, namely – an occupation or an important source of income.

If a young person has this dream, it hints at the loss of love or the end of a relationship. It could be a disappointment in love, a separation from a beloved person, or even a divorce. A corpse that appears in a young person's dream also hints at powerful despair and at the loss of hope. The bad mental state in which the dreamer finds himself might be causing him to lose interest in life, and everything seems futile. He has no desire or will to invest in his life, in the people around him, or in anything that constitutes his world, and his mood causes those around him to sink into a black depression. If the dreamer has children, he must watch his behavior and try to snap out of his severe mental state at all costs in order not to hurt them.

A B C D E F G H I J K L M N O P Q R S T U V W X Y Z

Corpulence

If a person dreams that he is corpulent, it implies that he will be rich and live well.

Corridor

If a dream features an unfamiliar corridor, it means that the dreamer faces an important decision that does not depend on external factors.

Corset

A dream about a corset means that the dreamer does not know for sure why people are paying attention to him.

Cot

The sight of a cot in a dream predicts accidents, diseases and accidents. If a person sees a row of cots in a dream, it means that the dreamer will be in the same boat with lots of other people.

Cotton

A dream about cotton is a positive dream. If a person dreams about cotton growing or about cotton being ready for picking, it is an indication of wealth and prosperity, as well as of plentiful crops for farmers.

Cotton candy

A dream about cotton candy predicts a pleasant trip in the near future.

Couch

If a person sees himself sitting relaxed on a couch in a dream, it means that his hopes are unrealistic. If he does not pay careful attention to every single detail of his business, his hopes will not be realized.

Cough

If a person suffers from a nagging cough in a dream, it is an indication of a poor state of health that can improve if he is only given the right care. If a person sees someone else with a cough in a dream, it means that the dreamer will suddenly find himself in an unpleasant situation from which he will eventually extricate himself.

Counselor

A dream about a counselor means that the dreamer is quite talented at offering counsel. He prefers his own counsel to that of others. He should exercise caution when acting upon his instincts of "right" and "wrong."

Countenance

If a person sees a beautiful and innocent countenance in a dream, it means that he can look forward to a certain amount of pleasure in the future. If, however, he sees an ugly, scowling countenance in a dream, he can expect nothing but bad things to happen.

Counter

A dream about a counter means that the dreamer is

prevented from succumbing to injurious temptations by his diverse interests and activities. However, if a person sees an empty or dirty counter in a dream, it is a prediction of a negative meeting that will cause the dreamer to lose his peace of mind.

Counterfeit money

A dream about counterfeit money predicts that the dreamer will experience problems with some difficult and worthless person. This dream is always negative – it does not matter whether the dreamer is the person paying the counterfeit money or the recipient of it.

Counterpane

If a dream features a clean counterpane, it is a very good sign, since it indicates fulfilling professions for women. If the counterpane in the dream is dirty, there are worrying situations and illness in the offing.

Counting

If a person counts his sweet and joyful children in a dream, it implies that he will not have any grief from them and they will succeed in life. If he counts money in a dream, it is an indication that he will always be able to cover his debts. If he counts money for someone else, it means that he will have bad luck and suffer losses.

Country

If a person sees a fertile, lush, well-watered country in his dream, it means that things just don't get much better than this as far as he is concerned. He will become extremely rich and will be able to live wherever he wants. If he sees a dry, barren country in his dream, he should brace himself for hardships, hunger and illness.

Court

If a person dreams about a court or about giving evidence in court, it is a sign that he has made some kind of deal that is not above board, and that he will have to account for it in the future. His conscience is bothering him about the fact that the handsome profits he expects to receive as a result of this spurious deal will come to him in ways that are not pure and honest. Having said that, the temptation is enormous, since apparently the sums of money that the dreamer is about to receive because of that particular dishonest move are very large.

If the person who is giving evidence in court in the dream is the dreamer himself, and not someone else, the dreamer is liable to find himself at the center of attention – perhaps even in the headlines – but not in a positive way at all. The publicity concerning his actions will not be sympathetic.

If a person dreams that he wins in court, it means that he can expect only good things and great success at anything he undertakes, especially anything linked to success at work and financial matters. He may receive a reward or a promotion at his workplace in the near future.

Courtship

If a woman dreams about being courted, it is a very negative dream, since her romantic hopes will eventually be dashed after a brief and pleasurable fling. If a man dreams about courting, it means that he is not worthy of finding a partner.

Cousin

If a cousin appears in a dream, it is a prediction of sorrow, sadness and disappointment. If a dream features a cordial relationship between cousins, it signifies an unbridgeable rift in the family.

Cow

A dream about a cow is a good dream that refers to the dreamer's imminent success and happiness. Generally, it refers to the dreamer's sound economic situation thanks to a correct and successful financial investment. His economic ease goes hand in hand with peace of mind and inner calm, and these will bring on a chain of positive experiences for the dreamer.

Milking a cow in a dream is interpreted as good luck for the dreamer's household. The dream implies that the dreamer will be surrounded by good, loving and reliable friends who wish him well. These friends are not two-faced, but rather love the dreamer genuinely. He can trust them.

Cowslips

If a person dreams about gathering cowslips, it means that a close friendship will come to a wretched end. If he sees cowslips in full bloom in his dream, he is going through a devastating crisis in his life – it is so bad that it might even mean the breakup of a happy home.

Crab

If a dream features a crab that is not in its natural habitat – that is, not in the sea, but rather on land or on a plate, for instance – the dream does not have a positive meaning. It symbolizes sorrow, pain, trouble and grief. The forthcoming period might hold one or more of these things in store for the dreamer, and the dreamer is already beginning to pick up early signs of that. The dream is preparing him for a difficult period he has to go through, and implies that he will not have any joy from the forthcoming period.

In contrast, the meaning of the dream is the reverse if the dreamer sees the crab in its natural habitat, that is, in the ocean, when it is in the water or on wet sand. A dream like that hints at a great deal of satisfaction for the dreamer as a result of his efforts or hard work. While the achievement may not be big, it will give the dreamer a lot of joy and pleasure. In most cases, the achievement will be in the realm of love and matters of the heart: a not particularly large investment on the part of the dreamer will yield impressive results. He will succeed in attaining what he hoped for: the attention of another person, a person he loves and whose heart he has been hoping to win, and so on. Achievements like these will be his in the forthcoming period without any special effort, but they will cause him elation, great excitement, and a special inner feeling.

Conversely, if the dream features a crab withdrawing into a shell or into a hole in the sand and shutting itself off from the world, it is a sign that a treacherous person is threatening the dreamer's tranquillity. Even if the dreamer is not aware of it at this moment, he must be on his guard during the forthcoming period, since a certain person is plotting against him. The dreamer can draw his own conclusions as to whether this is a matter of work, family or the heart. His suspicion and alertness will quickly direct him to whom and what is involved.

Cradle / Crib

If a dream features a cradle with a lovely baby in it, it signifies that the dreamer will be prosperous and will enjoy the love of sweet children. If a dreamer sees an empty cradle, he is suffering from a lack of confidence or health problems. If he rocks a baby in a cradle, it is an indication of marital problems and illness in his family.

Crane (bird)

If a dream features cranes flying north, it is a very bad omen in the business realm, and it predicts disappointment for a woman. If a dream features cranes flying south, there will be a joyous reunion of friends. Furthermore, it indicates the ongoing faithful relationship of lovers. If a person sees a crane landing in a dream, it implies that strange incidents are about to occur.

Crane (mechanical)

Dreams about a crane can have a double meaning. On the one hand, the dreamer will go up the social ladder and associate with people in whose company he would never have even dreamed of being a short time previously. Connections like these can serve as a springboard on the social and financial ladders alike if the dreamer knows how to navigate his steps cautiously and out of a cold economic calculation.

On the other hand, a dream about a crane is also liable to serve as a warning sign for the dreamer. From a bird's-eye view, from a great height, things do not always seem as they really are. This is not the right time for a proposal of marriage or for a new financial deal. Things must be examined from all angles and over-enthusiasm must be avoided, since it is liable to lead to potentially disastrous consequences and financial and emotional losses.

Crawfish

When a dream features a crawfish, it means that the dreamer will have a lot of hassles in love.

Crawling

If a person dreams that he hurts his hand while crawling on the ground, it indicates that he will be given lowly and humiliating tasks to perform. If he crawls over rough ground in a dream, it means that he has not fully exploited the opportunities he was offered. If he crawls in the mud in a dream, it means that his credibility in business is under suspicion.

Cream

If a person sees cream in a dream, it is a good dream, predicting prosperity – unless he is a farmer. If he is a farmer, a dream about cream indicates a good harvest and a harmonious family life. If a person dreams about drinking cream, his good luck will begin at once.

Credit card

A dream that features a credit card indicates that there will be a significant improvement in the dreamer's finances. This may stem from an inheritance or from new ways of earning a living.

Creek

The appearance of a creek in a dream symbolizes brief journeys and new experiences. If a creek is seen to be overflowing in a dream, the dreamer will have temporary troubles that he can easily overcome. If a person sees a dry creek in a dream, it means that he will be disappointed because something he wanted has been given to someone else.

Cremation

If a person sees corpses being cremated in a dream, it means that the dreamer's influence in the world of business will be severely curtailed by his enemies. If the dreamer sees himself being cremated, it is a warning dream: he will be totally wiped out in business if he heeds anyone else's counsel but his own.

Crew

If a person sees the crew of a ship about to set sail in a dream, it means that he will unexpectedly cancel a trip, and this will be to his disadvantage. If he sees a crew battling to save a ship during a storm, it is a storm of impending catastrophe.

A B **C** D E F G H I J K L M N O P Q R S T U V W X Y Z

Cricket

If a cricket appears in a dream, it means that the dreamer belongs to a supportive society that imbues him with basic confidence. He derives his strength from it. The dreamer is very satisfied with his social situation, with his status, and with the way the people around him relate to him. He is happy with his lot and is generally pleased. He is thankful for what he has and makes the most of every possible situation.

Cries

If a person hears cries of distress in a dream, it means that he is about to encounter grave problems. However, he will manage to solve them and even profit from them because of his alertness. If he hears a cry of surprise in a dream, he can expect to receive assistance from an unexpected quarter. If he hears a cry for help in a dream, it is a warning sign that friends or relatives are ill or in distress. If a dream features the cries of wild animal, it means that there has been a serious accident.

Crime

A dream that features a meeting with a criminal is a warning dream: it warns the dreamer against people of dubious repute. If the dreamer sees himself as a criminal in his dream, the dream is telling him that he is blithely unaware of other people's hardships.

Criminal

If a person dreams that he associates with a criminal, it

A B **C** D E F G H I J K L M N O P Q R S T U V W X Y Z

means that he will be haunted by people with immoral and criminal designs who want to exploit him for their own benefit. If he sees a criminal fleeing in his dream, he runs the risk of becoming privy to other people's deep dark secrets. This is a dangerous situation, since he will be hunted down in order to prevent him from disclosing them.

Cripple – See Disabled Person

Crochet work

If a person dreams about crochet work, it is a warning against becoming involved in some ludicrous matter as a result of his curiosity concerning other people's business. The dream warns him not to be too forthcoming with his confidences.

Crockery

If a dream features an abundance of clean, tidily arranged crockery, it means that the dreamer is a good homemaker. If the dreamer is involved in business and finds himself in a crockery store in his dream, it means that he will make profits. If the store he enters is untidy, he will suffer financial losses.

Crocodile

A crocodile in a dream attests to the fact that even though the dreamer is unaware of it, one of his friends or acquaintances is plotting against him and planning his downfall in underhand ways. He is doing everything behind the dreamer's back, and is inciting the dreamer's closest friends against him. The dreamer does not imagine that someone close to him could do such a thing, because in general, he trusts the people around him implicitly. However, he should know that the person in question usually behaves in the diametrically opposite way – he is exceptionally nice, presents himself as someone who is really making a special effort on the dreamer's behalf, and appears to be seeking the dreamer's company and friendship.

The dream, therefore, warns the dreamer to wise up. He actually knows what's going on, but does not want to accept it; rather, he represses it. The "friend" wants to gain the dreamer's trust, but the latter knows that this behavior is not genuine. His unconscious is warning him not to succumb and fall into the trap set by the schemer.

If a person dreams that he kills a crocodile, it implies that he has managed to overcome some problems temporarily. Even if they recur, he will cope with them and overcome them again.

Cross

A cross in a dream means that there is trouble in store for the dreamer. It is a warning that he should take precautions. If a person sees someone carrying a cross in a dream, it means that he will be required to contribute to charity.

Crossbones

A dream about crossbones serves as a warning to the dreamer: other people are trying to cause him trouble and prevent him from enjoying prosperity.

Crossroads

A person dreams that he is at a crossroads, facing an important decision in life. This could be a personal or romantic decision and it could be one that concerns business and work.

Traveling straight ahead in the intended direction means that things will go well and success is assured. If a person dreams that he turns his car around and retraces his steps, it means that he is on a dangerous path and must return to the starting point.

Croup

If a person sees a child with croup in the dream, it may indicate a mild illness in the family, but it generally means good health and harmony.

Crow

A dream about a crow symbolizes grief and misfortune. If a person hears a crow cawing in a dream, it means that other people will influence him to give away his property for some completely illogical reason. If a young man dreams about a crow, it means that he will be seduced by women's wiles.

Crowd

A dream about a crowd is a good omen, in most cases – if most of the people are wearing brightly colored outfits. If a person sees a crowd of well-dressed people at some kind of festivity, it means that he will enjoy good friendships. However, if the atmosphere at the festivity is ruined in any way, it means that his friendships will be jeopardized, and instead of friendly and beneficial ties, he will suffer unhappiness and distress. If a person sees a crowd in a dream, it is a sign that there is dissent in the family and political discontent.

Crown

A dream about a crown symbolizes a change in the dreamer's lifestyle: it predicts lengthy travels and new relationships. However, it also foretells a serious illness. If the dreamer sees himself wearing a crown, he will lose personal possessions. If he places a crown on someone else's head, the dream indicates his excellent nature.

Crucifix

If a person dreams about a crucifix, it is a warning dream: there is impending trouble for both him and other people. If he kisses a crucifix in a dream, it signifies that he is resigned to his troubles. If a young woman dreams that she is carrying a crucifix, it means that she is renowned for her modesty and kindness. She wins the love of other people, and this contributes to her personal gain.

Crucifixion

A dream about a crucifixion means that the dreamer's hopes and expectations have been completely dashed; he has nothing but frustration left.

Cruelty

If a person dreams that someone is cruel to him, the

dream warns him that he will experience disappointment and problems in some area. If he dreams that the cruelty is directed at someone else, it means that he will have to perform an unpleasant task that will be very disadvantageous to him.

Crust

If a dream features a crust, it is a sign of incompetence. It also indicates that horrific consequences can be expected because someone has not acquitted his duties as he should have.

Crutches

If a person dreams that he walks with crutches, it signifies that he depends on other people for assistance and advancement. If he sees other people on crutches in a dream, it means that he will be very disappointed in the results of his hard work.

Crying

Crying in a dream means that the courage the dreamer demonstrates will enable him to overcome hitches and other unexpected and undesirable "surprises."

If a person sees his friend or someone else who is close to him crying, it could be a prophetic dream that signals a cry for help from that person. The dreamer "senses" that person's distress, as it is expressed in the dream, and he must try to extricate him from his situation. The friend is embroiled in a serious problem, and if a person close to him helps and lends him an ear, it can perform miracles for him.

Crystal

A dream that features crystal does not bode well: it foretells either a decline in business or a deterioration in personal relations. This dream frequently occurs prior to an electric storm.

Cubs – See Animal Young

Cuckoo

If a person sees a cuckoo in a dream, it means that a friend's sudden fall from grace will bring the dreamer's happiness to an abrupt end. If he hears a cuckoo in dream, it is a terrible omen, since it predicts the serious illness or death of a faraway friend, or a serious accident in the dreamer's family.

Cucumber

A dream about a cucumber predicts a serious disease from which the dreamer is about to suffer. The dream does not hint at the seriousness or nature of the disease (in other words, we do not know whether it refers to a serious disease such as cancer or a chronic illness that has no cure, or to a disease such as pneumonia that can be treated relatively easily). Since the dream only implies a difficult period from the health point of view, we cannot know how long the period of suffering will be, and what the implications will be for the dreamer – whether his recovery will be easy or whether he will have to cope with the disease for a long time. Having said that, the dream prepares the dreamer psychologically for the possibility that he will contract a serious disease that he will have to fight. Psychological preparedness in a case like this can be very helpful in coping with the disease.

Cunning

If a person dreams about cunning, it means that the dreamer will pretend to be cheerful in order to find favor with rich, happy people. If he dreams that his associates are cunning, it means that they are taking advantage of him for their own profit.

Cup

If a person dreams about a cup, it is a sign that the hard work he has invested will pay off for him, since he is about to win recognition. People will praise him and appreciate his efforts and his talents, and he will feel rewarded in return.

If a person dreams that he is holding a full cup in his hands, it is a sign of good fortune. Luck will shine on him and he will be very successful in whatever he does.

If the cup in the dream is empty, or almost empty, the dream implies a period of lack. The lack will be reflected mainly on the economic level and not on the emotional level, but it will only continue for a short time until the dreamer gets back on track. Then it will pass.

If the glass of the cup is dirty or dark, the dream implies that difficulties, problems and worries will accompany the dreamer in his work. He will have to muster mental strength and a great deal of patience in order to overcome the problems that stand in his way. If he does so, he will be able to extricate himself from them relatively easily.

If the glass of the cup in the dream is light and transparent, the future holds wonderful things for the dreamer. He will forget about the problems of earning a living, since he will enjoy an abundant income. He can delete these worries from his heart and rest assured that a successful future is awaiting him.

If the liquid in the cup is spilled in the dream, it implies problems and tension among the members of the dreamer's household. These family troubles will cause the dreamer to distance himself from the members of his family, and the differences of opinions will cause him not to want to be involved in what is going on.

Curb

If a person dreams about stepping on to a curb, it means that he will enjoy a meteoric rise in the business world and will be accorded high esteem. If a person sees himself falling or slipping off a curb in a dream, it is a warning that he will become embroiled in all kinds of trouble.

Currants

If a person sees red currants in a dream, it means that he is avoiding someone he cannot encounter face to face. If he picks currants in a dream, it shows that he has an optimistic personality – he is a person who always sees the half-full cup.

Currying a horse

If a person dreams about currying a horse, it is an indication that he will have to work very hard – physically and mentally – in order to fulfill his aspirations. If he dreams that he does a good job of currying the horse, he will achieve whatever he is seeking to achieve.

Curses

The meaning of hurling curses changes in accordance with the meaning of the dream, but it depends mainly on the person who is hurling the curses:

If the dreamer is the one who is cursed in the dream, and if there is no clear reason for this, the dream implies that the dreamer has certain enemies who seek to harm him, and he is completely unaware of them. It is possible that while the intentions of people who are close to the dreamer – such as members of his family or close friends – are not pure, the dreamer hasn't the faintest clue that this is the case. The dream is a kind of warning dream that hints that although everything seems fine, hidden intentions simmer beneath the surface, and they are motivated by dark forces.

If it is actually the dreamer who curses other people or comes to them with severe accusations that are accompanied by insulting words and unpleasant expressions, the dream hints that the dreamer is a vigorous and ambitious person, and that he will accomplish his goals at any cost. He is a person with "elbows," audacity and nerve, and will not let go of the goals he has set himself until he has achieved them.

Curtain

A dream about a curtain generally attests to the difficult and shrewish nature of the dreamer, which makes it hard for him to have good human relations with the people around him.

If a person dreams about drawing a curtain in a dream, it implies that bad days are in the offing, and that he is about to fall into a trap. It is possible that people whom the dreamer considers to be close to him and concerned about his welfare will actually turn out to be enemies who seek to harm him and are conspiring against him. In any case, the dream hints that a warning will come at the right time, before anything bad happens to the dreamer. The dreamer will find out in time that people are scheming against him and will make the appropriate preparations. The warning will arrive in time, before any irreversible or irreparable damage can be caused to the dreamer.

A dream that features a new curtain is a sign that an important guest will soon be arriving from far away. Even if the dreamer is not expecting him or prepared for him right now, the guest is on his way, and this will be a pleasant surprise for the dreamer. The guest will be the bearer of good news, and his visit will be enjoyable and useful. He could be a relative who lives abroad and has not seen the dreamer for a long time; however, this surprise visit could equally occur in the work setting, when a professional associate of the dreamer pays him a surprise visit in order to tell him some special news.

Dirty curtains in a dream are a sign of a friend who has tremendous debating and bargaining powers and wears the dreamer down by not giving him any peace. This person creates problems with which the dreamer finds it difficult to cope. The dream implies that the dreamer must ignore him and move forward.

A torn curtain in a dream serves as a warning: The dreamer must not take any action that he is not completely sure of, otherwise he will regret it later. The dream implies that the dreamer must be certain of any step he plans to take, and examine his moves carefully before carrying them out, otherwise it will be to late to change them. The way things develop is very sensitive, and the dreamer is standing at a crossroads. He must take care to choose the correct path and avoid unnecessary mistakes.

A colorful curtain in a dream is a sign that a vacation is in the offing and the dreamer is about to take time off from his affairs and "veg out." His preferred place is... at home! Yes, the dream implies that the dreamer prefers to take a few days of R&R at home rather than travel to a distant place or take a vacation that will use up his energies. Staying at home is recommended, and he should take advantage of the full potential of a few days at home in order to charge his batteries and really come back a new person.

If a person sees a net curtain in a dream, and it is clear to him that the main point of the dream is the fact that the curtain is made of net, it is a warning dream: The dreamer must be careful of mosquitoes that spread diseases. A dream like this mostly occurs between seasons, when the fear of disease-bearing mosquitoes is greatest (for example, the outbreak of Nile Fever), or during journeys to distant and exotic places such as the Far East, where it is still necessary to take precautions against malaria-bearing mosquitoes.

Cushions

If a person dreams that he is reclining on silk cushions, the dream indicates that he will enjoy a life of ease at other people's expense. If the dreamer sees cushions in his dream, both his love life and his business will thrive.

Custard

If a married woman dreams that she is making or eating custard, it signifies that she will have to be hospitable to an unexpected guest. If a dream features disgusting-tasting custard, the dreamer's hopes for happiness will be dashed, and he will only have grief.

Customs house

If a dream sees a customs house in a dream, it means that he is experiencing competition in his profession. If he dreams that he enters a customs house, he will have to compete for a position he has long yearned for – if it is offered to him. If he dreams that he is coming out of a customs house, the dream indicates that he will suffer a financial loss, a drop in status, or a failure.

Cut

A dream featuring a cut in its various forms and aspects mostly attests to the dreamer's fear of, lack of faith in and inability to trust those around him. He does not want to place his trust in someone close whom he does not trust for some reason, and even though he is under pressure, he wants to break off that relationship. He feels that he is being crushed under a steam-roller of pressure and wants to be free and independent.

If a person dreams that he cuts himself deliberately, the dream symbolizes family problems and the huge effort that the dreamer is investing in his work. The dreamer feels as if he has to break loose from all that, and does not feel tranquil.

A B C D E F G H I J K L M N O P Q R S T U V W X Y Z

A
B
C
D
E
F
G
H
I
J
K
L
M
N
O
P
Q
R
S
T
U
V
W
X
Y
Z

A dream in which the dreamer sees himself cutting himself deliberately, to the point of wanting to commit suicide, implies a feeling of relief and liberation from all the pressures and all the things that do not allow him to live his life as he wants. The dream expresses a feeling of a weight being lifted and the renewed ability to experience real life. The dream hints at the courage and confidence that the dreamer did not know he possessed; these qualities come to the fore suddenly and release him from his feeling of "prison."

Cyclamen

The appearance of a cyclamen in a dream generally implies goods things for the dreamer: good news from far away; promotion at work; a reconciliation with a person with whom the dreamer quarreled; an improvement in the dreamer's love life, and so on. Having said that, a dream like this could in fact indicate problems in the dreamer's sex life. In most cases, a dream that features a cyclamen indicates impotence in men, and even if it is not a matter of impotence, the dream hints at other physical problems that prevent the dreamer from enjoying a perfect sex life. The source of the physical problems may be psychological, and the dreamer must find out what is disrupting his daily life and ruining his nocturnal life.

When a woman dreams about a cyclamen, it refers to the problems she has with men, and usually indicates bad relations with a particular man or with the men in her life in general. She is not successful in building a healthy relationship with a man or in creating a good long-term relationship.

Generally, her relationships end in disappointment. The woman does not know how to set limits: she either gives too much of herself to her partner, to the point of total self-negation, or she does not give of herself at all, and does not invest in the relationship. Her extreme behavior prevents any relationship she enters into from developing, since ultimately one of the sides loses interest in it and it falls apart.

A dream that features a wilted and drooping cyclamen indicates that the dreamer is not quite clear about the limits of his ability. He assesses himself far beyond what he is actually capable of, and often experiences downfalls and disappointments, since his expectations exceed his true ability. He may have been brought up to think in this way, and he refuses to recognize the facts that keep hitting him in the face. Ultimately, he will have to acknowledge his true ability, because if he does not, he will not succeed at anything. Instead of fostering an image of a successful person, he will have to cope with an inferior self-image. If he recognizes his limitations and the extent of his abilities, he will be able to avoid unnecessary embarrassing disappointments, or alternatively, enjoy huge success – on condition that he lowers the level of the tasks he undertakes.

Cymbal

If a person hears the clash of cymbals in a dream, it means that someone he has known for a very long time is on the verge of death.

A
B
C
D
E
F
G
H
I
J
K
L
M
N
O
P
Q
R
S
T
U
V
W
X
Y
Z

D

Daffodil

A daffodil in a dream has several meanings:

In most cases, the daffodil symbolizes a problem with the dreamer's sexual identity. In his everyday life, the dreamer may not be aware of the inner conflict that is raging within him, or he may be repressing it. However, the dream raises the problems from his subconscious to his conscious and forces him to deal with them. Some people claim that a dream that features a daffodil not only attests to problems in the sexual realm, but to actual deviant tendencies. Even if these have never actually manifested themselves, they are hidden somewhere in the depth of the dreamer's mind, and the dream warns him not to give free rein to his urges in a deviant manner that is not considered acceptable in the "normal" society in which he lives.

If a dream features a daffodil in its natural outdoor habitat, near a source of water, the interpretation of the dream states that the dreamer will have a happy life, even if he is not rich. His home will be filled with light, and he will enjoy the fruits of his labor and will rejoice in his lot with his family and children.

If a dream features a daffodil that is not in its natural habitat – that is, in a vase, for instance – it implies that the dreamer is behaving arrogantly and haughtily, and this behavior will engender many difficulties and troubles for him. If he goes on like this, he will cause himself nothing but pain and sorrow.

Besides that, he can be sure that new enemies will emerge at every turn – and this in itself means new and complex problems.

A dream about picking daffodils is a sign that the dreamer can soon expect to go on an adventure-packed journey that involves backpacking, camping and sleeping outdoors.

Dagger

A dream about a dagger attests to the fact that the dreamer does not trust the people around him, even though they are supposed to be the people who are closest to him. His feeling of basic trust in them has been eroded as it has never been before. His suspicion of the people around him and his inability to trust them create a feeling of extreme loneliness in the dreamer. He must try to do whatever he can to revive his former feeling of trust in his associates.

Daisies

A dream about daises almost always predicts happiness, health and economic security for the dreamer.

If a person dreams about white daisies, the dream implies a period of goodness and purity that will be reflected in a new and true love. The dreamer can expect to enter a good period in which he will experience love at its most intense, as he has never experienced it before. In most cases, this kind of couple relationship will become official in the future.

If the daisies appeared on a black "heart" in the dream, it is a warning against jealousy. The dreamer may be jealous of someone else, but some other person may equally be jealous of him. Be that as it may, jealousy blinds people and evokes evil spirits. If the dreamer is suffering from jealousy, he must calm himself down and "kill" every emotion like that in himself. If the dreamer is suffering from someone else's jealousy, he should stay away from him as much as possible and try to avoid coming into contact with him.

Dahlia

If a dream features fresh, brightly colored dahlias, the dreamer can look forward to good fortune.

Damask rose

If a person sees a damask rose bush in full bloom, it means that someone in the dreamer's family is about to get married. The dreamer's hopes will materialize. If a woman dreams that she is given a bouquet of damask roses during the spring, it means that her lover will be faithful to her. However, this is not the case if she is given the roses during the winter.

Damson

If a person sees trees full of purple damson fruit, it augurs well: he will enjoy tremendous prosperity. If he eats the fruit in his dream, the dream predicts sorrow.

Dance master

If a person dreams about a dance master, it means that he does not concentrate on important things, but prefers to waste his time on frivolous and superficial matters.

Dancing

A dream about dancing always predicts good things: gifts, surprises, parties. A new romantic liaison is also within the realm of possibility. If a woman dreams that she is asked to dance by a handsome man, it implies a new romance on the horizon – and the same is true for a man. Circle or line dances imply that the dreamer will be involved in some kind of social activity that will give him a great deal of pleasure and success from an unexpected quarter.

Dandelion

If a dream features dandelions that are fresh and young, it implies that the dreamer will be happy in his love life and prosperous in financial affairs.

Danger

A dream in which danger threatens the dreamer actually attests to a new beginning and wonderful opportunities that are about to crop up in the dreamer's path. The greater the danger that threatens the dreamer, the greater his chances of success in the future. Having said that, if the dreamer sees himself saved from great danger at the last moment, it means that in spite of his very great chances for success, he has to be careful and not rely on others. He must exercise discretion and logic in every single issue.

A B C D E F G H I J K L M N O P Q R S T U V W X Y Z

Darkness

Darkness in a dream usually implies a feeling of a loss of direction. Nothing is going right for the dreamer, and he feels confusion, inner emotional turmoil, a lack of clarity of thought, of repose and of peace of mind. He is distracted by every little thing, finds it difficult to concentrate on important things, and feels that he has temporarily lost his grip on life.

When the person is wandering around in the dark in a dream and doesn't find his way hints that although the dreamer's path is not easy, eventually his inner instincts will guide him by serving as kind of warning signals. He will succeed in emerging from the dark into the light and surviving and succeeding.

Dark-skinned person

A dream about a dark-skinned person indicates that the dreamer lacks excitement and drama in his life. If he sees such a person in his dream, it might be an indication of sexual tension.

Dates

There are two radically different interpretations for a dream about dates. One attests to the fact that the dreamer's conscience is not clear: either he regrets something he did, or he is sorry that he acted in a certain way; his heart is tormenting him about it. He may have acted in haste or played a prank on someone for which it will be difficult for that person to forgive him. He must know that there is a way back, and if he knows how to ask forgiveness at the right opportunity, not only will he clear his conscience, but he will cheer up the person he wronged with his inappropriate behavior.

A dream that features dates can serve as a hint that soon one of the dreamer's friends or a member of his immediate family is going to get married. In any case, a happy occasion is on the way, and he can already go out and buy himself an outfit for the wedding.

Daughter – See Son / Daughter

Daughter-in-law

A dream about a daughter-in-law predicts that something out of the ordinary is about to happen. The nature of the event depends on the nature of the daughter-in-law: it will be a pleasant event if the daughter-in-law is pleasant, and the opposite if she is not.

Day

If a dream features a nice day, the dreamer can look forward to positive relationships and an upward trend in his life. If it features a dull, gloomy day, it is a sign of loss and failure.

Daybreak

If a person watches day breaking in a dream, it means that he will carry out various projects successfully. If, on the other hand, the scene of the daybreak is unclear or slightly out of kilter, it means that he will experience setbacks in business rather than success.

Dead

A dream about the dead is usually a warning dream. If a person dreams that he is talking to his dead father, he is about to clinch a bad deal, and must be cautious. If he sees his dead mother in a dream, it is a warning that he should show more love and compassion for other people. If a dream features his dead brother or a dead relative or friend, he will be asked for charity.

Deaf (person)

The image of a deaf person, as it appears in a dream, has one definitely symbolic meaning, and that is: "What you don't know won't hurt you." The dreamer prefers not to get involved and not to know, otherwise he will be compelled to express an opinion or take sides in a matter in which he prefers to be objective. He knows that the closer he gets to the heart of the matter, the more he will be expected to take a stand, and he shies away from that.

Death

If a dream features death, it does not refer to death in reality at all: on the contrary, it means that the dreamer can look forward to a good, long life. If a person dreams about the death of someone who really is ill, it means that the patient will recover in the near future.

Debt

If a person dreams about a debt, it is a prediction of hassles in both business and love. However, if he dreams that he can pay back his debts, his situation will improve.

December

If a dream features the month of December, it means that the dreamer will become wealthy, but will lose his friends. The friends will replace the dreamer with other people in their hearts.

Deck

If a person dreams that he is on the deck of a ship during a storm, it hints at impending disaster for the dreamer. However, if the sea is calm in his dream, he will be successful.

Decorate *(a room)*

If a person decorates a room with flowers in a dream, it implies that business will improve.

Decorate *(for action)*

If a person is decorating other people or sees others being decorated for heroic deeds, the dream signifies that he will be a person of distinction, even though he will not be famous.

Deed *(to property)*

If a person sees a deed in a dream, it is a symbol of a lawsuit. The dreamer should choose his lawyer with care if he is to have any chance of winning. If hc signs anything in his dream, it does not augur well.

Deer

The deer in a dream symbolizes an authoritative figure, generally a father figure, mainly because of its branched horns. The dreamer would like to resemble some authoritative person and follow in his footsteps. The dream implies that the dreamer admires a person of high standing who has special charisma and exerts an influence over him, whether consciously or unconsciously. The dream expresses the dreamer's desire to adopt properties similar to those of the admired person.

A dream about a deer, or about pursuing a deer, also implies that the dreamer is going to be seized by fear of something, but he will succeed in overcoming it.

A dream in which the dreamer sees himself killing a deer hints at the dreamer's prior knowledge that soon someone is going to take his life through no fault of his own. It is a warning dream.

If the person dreams that he receives a deer as a gift, the dream hints at good things: he can expect substantial advancement in the future, mainly in the economic realm. He will enjoy wellbeing, and will have the pleasure of seeing an investment that he made yield good profits. Good and positive things await the dreamer in the foreseeable future.

Defeat

If a person is defeated in a fight, it means that he will lose his rights to property. A dream about a defeat in battle mean that the dreamer's prospects will be ruined by the other people's bad transactions.

Delay

A dream that features a delay implies a deliberate conspiracy against the dreamer's advancement by his enemies.

Delight

A dream about feeling delight about any event is a positive sign in any circumstances. When a person sees an exquisite landscape in a dream and feels delight, he will be very successful both on the social and business levels.

Demand

The dreamer will be slightly perturbed by a demand for charity, but eventually his good reputation will be restored. If a dream features an unreasonable demand, it implies that the dreamer will become a leading member of his profession.

Demons

A dream about demons implies that the dreamer is in a state of anxiety and fear. This stems from personal reasons that vary from person to person. Even though the present time is difficult, there is hope and an excellent chance for improvement in the future. If these dreams occur over time, and make it difficult for the dreamer to function normally, he should seek support and help from someone who can be trusted in order to make a change.

A B C **D** E F G H I J K L M N O P Q R S T U V W X Y Z

Dentist

If a person dreams that a dentist is working on his teeth, it signifies that someone the dreamer is in contact with has caused him to doubt his sincerity and intentions.

Depression

A mental state of depression mainly appears in a dream when the person is thinking about such a state of mind or is about to succumb to a state of depression himself. A dream like this can actually serve as an excellent lever for extricating oneself from a bad state of mind. The dream implies that a golden opportunity will crop up for the dreamer and enable him to start over and initiate moves that will help him get out of a depression or some similar negative state of mind. If he exploits the opportunity that is about to come his way, he will be able to get out of the difficult state he is in and improve his situation. He must not hesitate to exploit this opportunity. Deep inside himself, he knows that he has the power to do so, and that he only has to grasp the stick that is being offered to him in order to get out of the whirlpool he is in. He must locate the proffered stick, grasp it, and pull himself out either by his own efforts or with outside help.

Derrick

A dream that features a derrick is an indication of obstacles and difficulties on the dreamer's path to success.

Desert

Dreams about desert treks have many meanings. A

person who dreams that he is walking in the desert, thirsty and suffering, expresses the whisperings of his heart. His life is not thriving; it is arid. The wild landscape is worth a visit or a few artistic photographs, perhaps, but it is not suitable for living in, at least not for Western man. The person who dreams about walking in the desert is going through a difficult period. He must try to work at extricating himself from the mess he is in.

Another kind of dream, in which the dreamer reaches a desert oasis, may serve as a hint that there will be a positive development in his life. Sometimes, after making a huge effort, one reaches the peak (or the water, in this case).

Desk

If a person sees himself sitting at a desk in a dream, it means that he will encounter unexpected bad luck. If he sees money on his desk in the dream, he will extricate himself from his difficulties.

Despair

If a person sees himself in a state of despair in his dream, it implies that he will have to endure numerous trials and tribulations in his profession. If he sees other people in despair, it is a sign that someone close to him is in distress.

Detective

If a person dreams that he is being tailed by a detective, and he is innocent, it means that fame and fortune are right around the corner. If he is not innocent, his reputation will be ruined and his friends will abandon him.

A
B
C
D
E
F
G
H
I
J
K
L
M
N
O
P
Q
R
S
T
U
V
W
X
Y
Z

Devil

A dream about the devil is sometimes a prediction of an easier and better future. In most cases, however, the devil is a symbol of temptation and seduction – so this dream generally has a negative connotation.

Devotion

A dream about a devout farmer means that he will raise plentiful crops and will live in peace with his neighbors. For people involved in business, this dream serves as a warning against deception.

Dew

If a person dreams that dew is falling on him, he can expect to succumb to fever and illness. If he sees the dew sparkling on the grass in his dream, he will be accorded respect and riches. There is every chance that he will soon marry very well.

Diadem

If a person dreams about a diadem, it means that he will soon be accorded some great honor.

Diamond

This predicts a serious incident or difficult phase, such as family quarrels or domestic disarray. A dream that features a diamond that gets lost reinforces the hint at negative events in the future. Sparkling diamonds in a bag or on a tray mean failures in personal matters, such as love.

A dream about fake diamonds attests to a negative event, such as a serious disease contracted by someone who wishes to cause the dreamer harm. A dream about a theft of diamonds attests to losses that can be expected, and if the dreamer buys diamonds, it means profits.

Diary

A person who dreams about a diary must be ready for an unpleasant incident. The jealousy and possessiveness that the dreamer feels toward someone close are liable to cause him emotional turmoil. These negative emotions create obstacles in his path to happiness and peace of mind. A dream about a diary can also indicate that someone close to the dreamer is excessively possessive of him. This causes him a feeling of suffocation and he is liable to explode at this person at any moment.

Dice

Dice quite naturally symbolize gambling. If the dreamer's financial situation in real life is good, it means that he will make a lot of money from gambling. If his financial situation in real life is bad, he will lose a lot of money from gambling.

Dictionary

If a person consults a dictionary in a dream, it implies that he is too dependent on other people's opinions and advice in the management of his own affairs; he is quite capable of running them perfectly competently himself.

A
B
C
D
E
F
G
H
I
J
K
L
M
N
O
P
Q
R
S
T
U
V
W
X
Y
Z

Difficulty

A dream about difficulties represents temporary embarrassment for anyone involved in business, but if he manages to get himself out of his difficulties, he can look forward to prosperity.

Digestion

In most cases, a dream that features problems in the digestive tract attests to some kind of health problems of which the dreamer is unaware in his everyday life. However, in the dream, they rise up from his subconscious. His body is well aware of the truth and cannot deny it.

Some people interpret digestive difficulties in a dream as a hint that the dreamer has come up against serious differences of opinion from the people around him, and he is breaking off relations with people who were considered to be very close to him. This tendency to break off relations and deny the people around him is a part of the dreamer's general process of wising up and internalizing the true reality that surrounds him.

Digestive system

Any dream about the functions and problems of the digestive system (including vomiting and diarrhea) is a sign of health or nutritional problems.

Digging

In a dream, digging is an indication of a battle for survival. If a person digs a hole and finds something shiny buried in it, the dream implies an improvement in his luck. If there is nothing but mist in the hole, it means that the dreamer will suffer from bad luck and misery throughout his life. If the dreamer sees the hole filling with water, it means that despite his efforts, nothing is going the way he wants it to.

Dinner

If a person dreams about eating dinner alone, it implies that he has reason to reflect on life's necessities. If he is a guest at a dinner-party, it means that he will soon be invited to enjoy the hospitality of people who can well afford to offer it.

Dirt

A dream that features dirt in various forms indicates that the dreamer's conscience is bothering him. Sometimes the dirt appears in the framework of an additional activity: the dreamer sees himself cleaning up dirt (he is trying to clear his conscience); the dreamer sees someone else cleaning up dirt (a hint that the dreamer should turn to a professional for help); the dreamer sees himself generating dirt (a warning sign against forbidden acts).

Dirt in the form of stains – see the entry for *Stains*.

Disabled person / Disability

A dream about a disability or a disabled person implies that the dreamer does not do enough for society. He must invest more in the community, volunteer, or get involved in activities for the good of other people. The very fact that he does not contribute anything of himself bothers him, weighs on his conscience and frustrates him. If he can find a suitable channel through which he will be able to contribute and mobilize his services or talents for the benefit of others who are less fortunate than he, he will finally feel that he has made the most of his life and that he is realizing lofty aspirations and goals.

If a healthy person sees himself as disabled in a dream, he is recuperating from a disease. Even if he was not physically ill, he is going through the stages of recovering from a mental breakdown.

If a person dreams that he is recovering from some kind of disability, the dream implies that the success he wants to achieve in a particular field will be delayed. The delay will not be long, but success will not come as soon as he had hoped.

If a person sees disabled children in a dream, it means that he still has to go through many more difficulties on the way to the success and achievements he is waiting for so eagerly.

If a person dreams about one of his relatives being disabled, it is a sign that he will get a good job or that he will receive good news in the near future.

A dream about a disabled enemy is a warning sign for the dreamer about a crash in business. He has to be on the alert so that he does not fail to notice some kind of business move that is liable to undermine his ventures. The trap is a certainty, and he should be on the lookout for it.

If the dreamer sees a friend who is disabled in his dream, it is a sign that certain complicated and uncertain matters are about to come right.

If a person dreams that he becomes permanently

disabled, it is a sign that he is about to receive compensation for something that happened to him.

If a disabled person dreams about a wedding, it is a sign that he will soon have a very good chance of leading an independent and good life. It is a positive dream that can certainly encourage the disabled person, since it predicts a happy, full and good life for him.

If a disabled person dreams about caregivers, it is a sign that he can expect unpleasant incidents with members of his family. Some bone of contention in the family will erupt and cause disappointment, complication and confusion.

If a disabled person dreams about his family members, it means that someone is embezzling his money. He must pay attention, check his expenditures carefully, and not accede to requests or entreaties for help. They are not always honest.

Other interpretations:

A dream about disabled people implies that resources, time and talents must be channeled in new directions, especially when it is a matter of assisting people who need help. If a person dreams that he himself becomes disabled, he is going through a difficult phase that is causing him fear and anxiety. Even before anything has happened to him, he is already feeling limited and dependent on others.

Be that as it may, the dreamer should examine the question of what is causing these feelings. On the other hand, he should channel his energy into contributing to the community and particularly to disabled people in order to come to terms with his dreams and fears.

Disaster

A dream about a general, undefined disaster attests to the fact that there are one or more elements in the dreamer's workplace that are undermining him. The person who is trying to engineer the dreamer's downfall is striving very energetically to do so under his very nose, and is making sure to wipe out the traces, so that the dreamer has absolutely no idea of what is happening around him.

A dream about a disaster where the dreamer was present is a sign that he will have the dubious fortune of making profits at the expense of other people. Whether this is conscious or unconscious, the dreamer is about to "earn" something at other people's expense. He will enjoy the fruits of someone else's labor.

If a person dreams that a disaster befalls other people, the dream is telling him that he should refrain from conflicts. He must aspire to achieve a situation as few disputes as possible with other people, even if it is sometimes very difficult for him to restrain himself.

A dream in which a person sees himself in a situation in which he is fleeing from a disaster hints that the dreamer will overcome difficulties that crop up in his path, thanks to his decency and integrity. He is a person who behaves according to the idiom, "Cast thy bread upon the waters, for thou shalt find it after many days" [Ecclesiastes 11:1] – and indeed this will be the case. His previous decent conduct toward other people will pay off in the future. Although he did not do anything in order to be awarded a prize, the reward will come in one way or another.

A dream in which the dreamer sees himself saving someone else from a disaster implies that soon he will find himself at a crossroads in his life. This will be significant for his future, since he will have to make fateful decisions that will determine his future path.

Discotheque

A dream about a discotheque is a sign that the dreamer will soon be confused, obsessed and distracted about a new relationship.

Disease

If a person is afflicted with a disease in a dream, it may indicate a mild and temporary illness. Alternatively, it may be a sign of a disagreement of some kind with a relative.

Disgrace

If a person dreams that he is worried about the conduct of his children or his relatives, it means that he will be dogged by anxiety. If he dreams that he himself is in disgrace, it means that he has lowered his moral standards and is about to lose his good reputation. Moreover, his enemies are on his trail.

Dishes

If a person handles dishes in a dream, it augurs well. However, if he breaks them, the dream has the opposite meaning. If a dream features shelves full of clean dishes, it is an indication of a successful marriage. On the other hand, a dream that features dirty dishes signals discontent and hopelessness.

A
B
C
D
E
F
G
H
I
J
K
L
M
N
O
P
Q
R
S
T
U
V
W
X
Y
Z

Dishwasher

A dream that features a dishwasher means that a conflict in the dreamer's personal life is about to be resolved.

Disinherited

If a person sees himself disinherited in a dream, it is a warning for him to scrutinize his conduct in his personal and business affairs. If a young man dreams that he is disinherited because of mutinous conduct, he can rectify the situation by marrying well. For a woman, this dream is a warning of misfortune that results from unbecoming behavior.

Dispute

If a dispute in a dream is about something trivial, the dream implies illness and unjust judgments. If the dreamer becomes involved in disputes with knowledgeable people, it means that he has great potential, but has not fully exploited it.

Distance

If a person's dream involves the concept of distance, it usually refers to long journeys and travel. If he dreams about being far from home, it means that he will soon depart on a journey in which strangers will ruin his life. If a person sees friends at a distance in a dream, it is a sign of disappointment.

Distress

If a person dreams that he is in distress, it is a good dream, since it is an indication that his financial situation will improve considerably.

Ditch

A dream about falling into a ditch signals personal loss and humiliation. On the other hand, if the dreamer jumps over the ditch in his dream, he will refute any allegations of guilt against him.

Ditch-digging machine

A dream that features a ditch-digging machine indicates that a deep dark secret is soon to be disclosed. The dreamer must prepare himself psychologically to deal with it.

Dividends

If a person dreams about dividends, the dream foretells increased profits or plentiful crops. If he fails to receive the desired dividends in his dream, it implies failure in love and mismanagement in business.

Diving

A dream about diving into clear water means that an embarrassing situation of some kind has terminated. If a person dreams about diving into muddy water, he will be plagued with worry about his affairs. If he sees other people diving, it implies congenial company.

A B C D E F G H I J K L M N O P Q R S T U V W X Y Z

Divining rod

A dream about a divining rod portends bad luck.

Divorce

A dream about divorce has a different meaning for a married person than it has for an unmarried person who has a partner. However, the two types of dreams have one thing in common: In both cases, the dream attests to the fact that the dreamer has problems with his partner in the sexual domain. This domain desperately requires reinforcement and attention. It could be that because of the length of the couple's relationship, there is less passion in the sexual domain. In any event, a dream like this serves as a reminder that the dreamer must invest in his relationship, especially in the sexual domain and the reinforcement of mutual sexual passion.

If the person is not married, the dream predicts only good things: The dreamer will have an enjoyable, full and happy married life. He can expect his spouse to be absolutely faithful to him. Even if there are crises in their married life, these will be resolved satisfactorily, since the couple will emerge from them strengthened, more loving and more faithful. The dream can remove any worries he may have about his married life. It will go well, and he can have full confidence in his partner.

In contrast, if the dreamer is single but has a partner (whom he may be about to marry), he must think very carefully before taking the crucial step he is about to take. For him, the dream serves as a kind of warning, since deep in his heart, he is not yet ready to make the relationship official. The dreamer may not be completely sure of his partner, and he may also not be sure of the strength of his love for his partner. He wonders about the degree of compatibility between them as well as the extent of true emotion he feels for his partner. In such a case, the dream serves as a warning sign, instructing the dreamer to slow down and reexamine his overall relationship before he takes the crucial and irrevocable step.

Docks

If the dreamer sees himself at the docks, it is an indication of an inauspicious journey that will be haunted by the menace of accidents. If he sees himself wandering around the docks in the dark, enemies will pose a threat to him. However, if he wanders around the docks in the sunlight in his dream, no harm will come to him.

Doctor

If a person dreams that he consults with a doctor in a clinic, it attests to the fact that he is in urgent need of help. If he runs into the doctor at a social gathering in a dream, it is a sign of good health and prosperity, since he will not have to pay the doctor.

Dog

A dog that appears in a dream symbolizes good fortune from the economic point of view. If a person dreams that he finds a dog in an unfamiliar place and brings him home, it attests to the fact that the person can expect good news. If a person dreams that a dog attacks him, it means that family quarrels are in the offing. A pack of barking dogs means that a matter of cardinal importance is about to arise and spark opposition among friends and associates. If a pack of dogs appears in a dream, chasing the dreamer, it means that he has leadership powers and gets other people to follow him. A puppy is a sign of something new that is about to happen or an unexpected guest who is about to visit.

If a person dreams about a sleeping dog, it is a sign that he has been feeling very comfortable and relaxed recently, especially among his immediate family. A dream about two dogs playing is a hint of harmony between the members of a couple. A fight between two dogs is a warning sign for the couple – disagreements and gossip are liable to cause a serious row. A dog that pounces on another dog or on a child and attacks him means that malicious gossip that someone is spreading about the dreamer is liable to harm him. There could also be legal complications.

A dream about a dog is interpreted both according to the situation in which the dog appears in the dream and according to its color, type, size, and behavior in the dream. In most cases, a dream about a dog is interpreted positively, as in "man's best friend," but a dream about a dog can also be a warning dream, a prophetic dream, or a dream that clarifies situations in the dreamer's life.

Hearing a dog bark is a sign that this is the right time to do business and to go ahead and make a deal the dreamer has only thought about in the past, but was afraid to actually put into practice. If the dog barks at strangers in the dream, it is a hint that disputes in the family are liable to hurt the dreamer, and for this reason it is advisable to act promptly to solve them.

A pack of dogs in a dream implies that joy and happiness will soon appear in the dreamer's life. Even if he is going through a difficult phase, the dream predicts that it is coming to an end, and will give way to happier and more felicitous days. If the dogs in the pack bark, the dream hints that something big is about to be realized. In other words, a plan that was hidden in the dreamer's drawer for a long time is about to be implemented.

If the dreamer stands in the middle of a pack of dogs, the dream implies that he is blessed with great powers of leadership, and is capable of leading many people with his words. His leadership is accepted by large groups, and he should use this power judiciously and not exploit it for negative purposes.

A poisoned dog in a dream: This is also how things look in the interpersonal relations of the dreamer's family, or between him and his partner. These relations are also poisoned and are about to reach the point of separation. If the poisoned dog is not the dreamer's dog but rather other people's dog, the dream warns the dreamer of unnecessary gossip and slander that rebound on him like a boomerang. He must refrain from spreading gossip and keep away from evil talk that shames others.

A seeing-eye dog in a dream (not a blind person's dream) implies that the dreamer's conscience is bothering him because of inappropriate behavior. The dream serves to imply that he should fast, give charity or a donation, pray and volunteer in order to atone for his actions. Only in this way will the dreamer's conscience be cleared. If not, it will keep on bothering him.

Dogs' colors are interpreted in the following ways:

A white dog indicates that the dreamer is likely to win a substantial sum of money in the near future. The win may come from gambling or from participating in a serious business deal.

A gray dog attests to the fact that the dreamer has one loyal friend on whom he can rely blindly, without the slightest doubt as to the purity of his intentions.

A black dog implies that the dreamer is surrounded by treacherous friends who are a danger to him and his well-being. It is difficult for the dreamer to know exactly who the friends in question are, but a simple little test would suffice to find out who the true friend is and who the treacherous one is.

A brown dog featuring in a dream implies that the dreamer feels that the people around him do not trust him completely. In spite of his efforts to portray himself as a trustworthy person, something in his behavior betrays a lack of credibility and integrity. He should scrutinize himself in order to put his finger on the thing that is preventing him from being able to depict himself as the person he wants his comrades to see.

A small or very small dog implies that the dreamer is in hostile surroundings, where there are people who want to harm him.

A big, fat dog implies a failing love life: the dreamer is about to lose his lover. His love life is collapsing in front of his eyes, and he can't blame anyone but himself.

A biting dog implies that the dreamer has been burned by someone close whom he trusted implicitly, and who betrayed his trust. The dreamer's faith in the people around him in general has been undermined, and he is no longer able to give of himself unstintingly to other people, for fear of being burned again.

A dream about puppies attests to a powerful sexual urge and the desire to satisfy it in every possible way indiscriminately: All welcome! The dreamer has a very powerful sexual urge, and he satisfies it with casual partners.

Various characteristics of canine behavior in dreams:

A drooling dog implies that the dreamer will lose some kind of lawsuit against him. Despite his efforts to be acquitted – including retaining the best lawyers – the dream hints that his fate has been sealed in advance, and he has no chance of proving his innocence.

A dog running after a bitch attests to the fact that the dreamer is hiding something from his lover (this is true for both sexes). Their relationship suffers from deceptions, denials and lies.

A dog baring his teeth in a dream is a kind of warning sign that the dreamer is liable to become infected with a serious disease that does not pass easily, and he will have a hard time recovering from it. He must take extra precautions in his contacts with people, especially regarding sex with casual partners.

A neglected dog that looks like a stray dog means that bad luck plagues the dreamer. Discouraging news will arrive soon, and the dreamer will be the recipient of bitter tidings. He must know that soon he will be forced to deal with serious and terrible things that will take him by surprise unless he takes the hint provided by the dream into account.

A
B
C
D
E
F
G
H
I
J
K
L
M
N
O
P
Q
R
S
T
U
V
W
X
Y
Z

Dolphin

The appearance of a dolphin in a dream is generally positive, and hints at advancement in life, whether at work – in rank and status – or in other areas of life. A dolphin in a dream is generally interpreted as a sign of luck, success and especially the great happiness the dreamer will enjoy.

Another meaning given to a dream featuring a (single) dolphin is the dreamer's yearning for the spiritual, not the material, which makes him seek the meaning of life in mysticism and magic. He has a tendency – albeit not conscious – to believe in things that are beyond comprehension and logic and to make them responsible for his situation. If something particularly good happens in his life, he attributes it to good luck. Similarly, he attributes unhappy events to an evil spirit, the evil eye, and so on. He tries to find the solutions to problems that crop up in his life in things that are connected to the esoteric. For instance, when he reaches a crossroads, he will opt to consult people who read cards, coffee grounds or the stars rather than seek the help of psychologists or other advisors. He is not an earthy person, but rather one of those who tend to be labeled as "floaters" who do not have their feet firmly planted in reality.

If a person sees a school of dolphins in a dream, it is a warning dream, warning the dreamer against approaching danger, or opening his eyes to an existing danger that he is aware of but has not paid attention to its extent and its size. The dreamer must be alert and make provision for every possibility of danger that is liable to arise at any moment. If he knows how to anticipate the danger and be prepared for it, he will be able to cope with things more easily, and will not be left with traumas or psychological scars.

Dome

If a person dreams about observing an unfamiliar panorama from a dome, it means that he is about to undergo a change for the better. He will be held in high regard by strangers. If a dreamer sees a dome from a distance, it implies that he will never fulfill his ambitions, and the person he loves will not reciprocate his feelings.

Domino

If a person dreams about winning or losing a game of dominoes, it attests to the extent of the dreamer's sensitivity toward his ego. If he dreams that he won a game of dominoes, he is a person who loves flattery. He loves receiving compliments from people about his success, and enjoys other people's positive attitude toward him or their admiration for him. This causes him so much happiness that his cool and logical judgment is liable to be undermined. Some people interpret winning a game of dominoes in a dream as the dreamer's ability to "walk between the drops." In other words, he can be in the eye of the storm without being harmed. He knows when to say the right sentence, when to remain silent and how to behave so as not to arouse the ire of the people around him. From this point of view, he is a master, and this ability often helps him emerge unscathed from crises and difficult periods.

If the dreamer loses a game of dominoes in his dream, the dream implies that although he thinks that his personal problems bother no one but him, this is not the case: The people around him are also disturbed and even affected by his problems. Sometimes these things have a bad effect on his surroundings, so it is no wonder that the people around

A B C D E F G H I J K L M N O P Q R S T U V W X Y Z

him occasionally get involved in his problems, since the latter have a direct bearing on the people's lives.

Donkey

There are several interpretations for the appearance of a donkey in a dream:

If a Jew dreams about a donkey, the dream might contain a hint that the donkey symbolizes redemption, and that the person sees an imminent solution to a problem that is bothering him: "The days of the Messiah have come." For a person who is in distress but is optimistic deep inside, the donkey in a dream expresses the hope and inner self-confidence that a solution to a problem he is wrestling with has appeared on the horizon.

If a child or youth dreams about a donkey, it attests to the fact that the dreamer feels alone or isolated in the society in which he lives. The dream implies the child's social distress and the sadness he feels because of it.

A dream in which the dreamer is riding on a donkey hints at progress in something that is bothering the dreamer, even if it is very slow. The goal the dreamer seeks to accomplish is within reach, but it will take time for him to accomplish it, and he has to be patient. In general, there is a hint that he is suffering from sexual problems of some kind and is repressing them. The dream encourages the dreamer not to hide the problems and not to sweep them under the carpet, but rather to deal with them and try to solve them. The dreamer must realize that there is a reason why he dreamed a dream like this at this particular time, and that something inside him may be signaling to him to begin to deal with the problems that are bothering him.

A dream that features a donkey braying implies that the dreamer is on a kind of "liberating" journey from hardships that are connected to some kind of family trauma. The dreamer may be experiencing a painful family relationship, an unpleasant separation or a really bitter acquaintance, and he is now going through a process of detaching himself from the enormous pain that has accompanied him over the recent period of time.

A dream in which a donkey is tied up attests to the dreamer's fierce will power and to his great mental powers and rare mental abilities. With his great mental power, he can "move mountains" if he wishes. He just has to mark his objective and go for it. The dream implies that he has to take advantage of his abilities, fulfill his desires, accomplish the goals he has set for himself, and make his fantasies about his advancement in life into a reality.

Doomsday

If the dreamer hopes to live until doomsday, it would be a very good idea for him to keep a close watch on all his possessions and affairs because cunning friends are all too ready to make off with them and leave him destitute. A young woman who dreams about doomsday should reject flashy but unsuitable men and marry the sincere, loving man near her.

Door

There are many interpretations for a door in a dream, in accordance with how the door appears: open, locked, closed, revolving, and so on.

If a person sees a closed door in a dream, it means that

he has to be careful of hasty and irresponsible decisions, especially in anything to do with money matters – gambles or a hasty investment are liable to lead to the loss and destruction of significant things that he has spent long years building. A locked door in a dream, too, behind which the dreamer hides things, is a warning sign against unnecessary expenses, extravagance and pointless spending.

Another meaning of a closed door in a dream states that people the dreamer knows may be trying to hide something from him. This is not always to his detriment. They may actually be doing so for his own good, so it is not advisable for him to dig too much, to ask and to investigate, since the secret is bound to be revealed sooner or later.

If a person sees an open door in a dream, it implies that this is the right time to make changes and initiate various actions that will lead to renewal.

Even if this does not look "sure" and the dreamer is deliberating whether this is really the time to make changes, the dream hints that he has no reason to deliberate, since every change will be for the best and will lead to success and prosperity in many spheres.

An open door in a dream also implies that something bad may come from an unexpected quarter. The dreamer must prepare himself for it, at least from the psychological point of view. It could involve the health of a family member, but it could also be bad news concerning money and property.

If a person sees a revolving door in a dream, it has a positive meaning. He is about to undergo positive experiences such as embarking on fascinating journeys to special places he never dreamed of visiting, or else he will receive good news he was not expecting. He may be about to undergo enjoyable experiences from other unexpected quarters. Without the dream, the news would surprise him totally.

A door can appear in a dream when it is in a large or small building, in a palace, in a hut, in a skyscraper, in a house and so on. Each of the interpretations will relate to the building in which the door appears, as it was seen in the dream. It must include most of the details together and take into account the "background" upon which the door in the dream was seen.

Doorbell

A dream about a doorbell heralds unexpected news or a summons to visit a sick relative.

Doorman *(in a hotel or luxury building)*

If a dream features a doorman, it implies the dreamer's intense yearning to go on trips to other countries. Another possible meaning of this dream is the dreamer's desire to make far-reaching changes in his life.

Dough

A dream that features dough implies that the dreamer is tortured by worries concerning his assets, money he has to receive or spend, or property that is worth a lot of money. Worry haunts him day and night, and this is expressed in the dream.

In most cases, it is the person who has many assets who is disturbed in this dream, and this bears out the saying, "The more you have, the more you worry." Nevertheless, a person of few means may have a dream about dough, and then the meaning of the dream, from his point of view, is fear of a shortage of money, inability to obtain the money that is vital for his existence or inability to fulfill financial obligations.

Dough may also appear in the dream of someone who has just won a large sum of money and does not know how to invest it so that it will maintain its value. It may also appear in the dream of a person who invested money in business, gambling and bets, and expects to lose it... or double or triple it.

Dove / Pigeon

Any aspect of a dove in a dream is interpreted in a positive way, whether it is a carrier pigeon, a flock of doves or a single dove.

When an ordinary white dove appears in a dream, it hints at the essence of all the good in the world: a calm and good life, harmony with the people around the dreamer, good fortune in whatever he does, a satisfying and happy family and social life, success at work and income, a great deal of love surrounding him wherever he goes, and a lot of satisfaction from life.

A carrier pigeon or a flock of doves in a dream is a hint that good news is on the way. Generally, this is news from far away. This could be a hint at an unexpected trip to an exotic destination or to a place the dreamer always dreamed of visiting.

If the dreamer sees a dove in a dream and hears it cooing loudly, the dream indicates that warm romantic ties will become a reality. It could be a hint at making a romantic relationship official, and at a potential wedding, or it could imply that a romantic relationship the dreamer is entering is about to become warmer, and his interpersonal relationship with his partner will be closer and better than ever.

Downpour / Pouring rain

A dream about a real downpour has two main meanings: the first states that the dreamer is in a state of fear and anxiety with regard to failure in the economic or commercial realm, a failure that can cause him total collapse. The case of a person who is actually in such a state and dreams about a downpour is also important – his dream indicates that the situation will actually occur and go on until the bitter end; in other words, it is a self-fulfilling prophecy.

However, another version of the interpretation of a downpour in a dream claims that it is a typical dream attesting to prolonged sexual frustration, and from that point of view, it is actually a "wet dream" that implies that soon the dreamer will soon experience sexual release.

Dragon

A dream that features a dragon implies that the dreamer must take himself in hand and not rely on others, on luck or on fate. He tends to seek redemption and help in elements over which he has no control, while in fact only if he takes his fate in his own hands will he be able to extricate himself from the bad situation he is in. Only if he first helps himself will luck then come to his aid.

A dragon breathing fire in a dream is a sign that the person must learn from his past mistakes and not repeat them. If he does not learn from his past mistakes or learn

A B C D E F G H I J K L M N O P Q R S T U V W X Y Z

the relevant lessons, a disaster is liable to befall him. If the fire-belching dragon dies, the dreamer can expect to receive bad news, and must prepare himself for it.

According to the Chinese tradition, seeing a dragon in a dream attests to the fact that the dreamer's partner is cheating on him. It is also possible that even if no real infidelity actually occurred, the partner did in fact contemplate it. One way or the other, the problem still exists and the dream hints at a difficult struggle awaiting the dreamer with his partner.

According to the Western tradition, a dream about a dragon generally attests to the fact that the dreamer is involved in a relationship with a commitment – or is on the way to it. In such a dream, there is a broad hint for the near future, and it is a sign that the dreamer is soon going to get married.

Drainpipe

A dream that features a drainpipe brings good news, and in most cases hints at the good life the dreamer can expect, as well as at health and wealth that are about to become his lot. Having said that, a drainpipe in a dream sometimes implies problems. This interpretation is particularly correct when the dreamer sees himself climbing a drainpipe in a dream. A dream of this kind means that the dreamer cannot cope with the problems facing him, and that he is trying to find an escape route for himself. Ignoring the problems will not help solve them, and ultimately the dreamer will have to deal with them one way or another, sooner or later.

A dream featuring a drainpipe with water flowing down it implies that the dreamer has a hidden enemy who is trying to hurt him. The dreamer is not yet aware of the danger he is in, but he should open his eyes, since complacency is liable to cause him damage. The person who is trying to hurt him has clear motives. He wants to take the dreamer's place – in the workplace or at home. The dreamer's standing is in jeopardy, and if he does not act immediately to find out who is plotting against him, he is liable to be stripped of his status without the possibility of restoring it to its former glory.

Drama

If a person watches a drama being acted out onstage in a dream, it refers to happy reunions with faraway friends. If the dreamer feels bored while watching a drama, it means that he will be landed with a tedious companion at some event. If he writes a drama, it attests to the fact that he will suddenly experience problems and debt, but most surprisingly will amazingly unscathed.

Drawers

If drawers appear in a dream, it indicates that there are irksome secrets in the dreamer's surroundings. These could be family disputes that are based on information that has been hidden for years. It could be some other problem, such as a person who suddenly discovers that he is adopted after finding a document in a hidden drawer. In general, the dream indicates a need to open up and air out old drawers and rooms in the house, literally and metaphorically.

Dream

A dream about a dream means distancing oneself from reality or wanting to distance oneself from reality. This kind of dream expresses the dreamer's desire to sink as deeply as he can into imaginings, fantasies and a world in which anything can happen. The difficulty of acknowledging reality causes him to want to get as far away as possible from it, and one of the ways to do so is by dreaming about dreaming. People who dream about a dream within a dream are usually in a state in which even when they are completely awake, they are generally daydreaming in order to avoid encountering reality. It is a dangerous situation, one which is liable to lead to various addictions as an additional flight from reality, such as an addiction to alcohol, drugs, food, strict diets and so on.

If a person dreams that he is telling someone else about a dream he dreamed the previous night, the dream reflects existing reality. The person is very aware of his situation and of the reality that surrounds him, and does not deny anything.

If a person dreams that he wakes up suddenly from a dream, there is no difference between dream and reality from his point of view. His dreams are actually an imitation of reality, and they are so real that there is hardly any difference between them and reality itself. Dreams of this type are dreamed by very realistic and down-to-earth people who are not blessed with a highly developed imagination. Their awareness of their surroundings is extremely high, and they are very self-critical in their way of thinking.

Dressing

If a person dreams that he experiences difficulty while dressing, it implies that he is being harassed by evil people. If he fails to dress in time to catch a train, it means that he will suffer the consequences of other people's incompetence. He should depend on no one but himself.

Dried fruit

If a dream features dried fruit, it means that the dreamer must guard himself against the results of a hasty decision. During times of distress or trouble, the dreamer will make a decision whose negative results will soon be evident. The dreamer must deal with the results of the hasty decision and not run away from them despite the inherent difficulties.

Drill

If a person dreams that he himself is operating a drill, the dream attests to the feeling of power and strength he will need in the forthcoming period of time. He can expect a struggle and perhaps even a crisis in business or at work. The dreamer will need all his talents and abilities to get through the rough period that is approaching, but he will come out on top. In contrast, if a dream features a drill that is pointed at the dreamer, it means that he feels threatened. It is important to try and remember who is holding the drill. Almost certainly that person poses a threat to the dreamer; even if this is not so in reality, in the dreamer's thoughts he is perceived as an enemy. It is advisable to check into this matter thoroughly and see whether the fears are justified and have some bearing on reality or whether they are

A B C **D** E F G H I J K L M N O P Q R S T U V W X Y Z

A B C D E F G H I J K L M N O P Q R S T U V W X Y Z

unfounded. All this should be done before the atmosphere becomes oppressive.

Drinking

There is a difference in the interpretation of the dream according to the type of beverage that appears in it:

If a person dreams that he drinks an alcoholic beverage such as wine, beer or some other intoxicating liquor, the dream implies that he can expect to suffer a financial loss as a result of a failed venture. A loss of money or property will lead to an increase in the desire to achieve, and this will lead to hard work.

Having said that, a dream about drinking alcohol attests to the dreamer's open nature – a nature that helps him make friends with other people, thereby winning their trust. In most cases, the person is easygoing and friendly, has a sense of humor, and enjoys being surrounded by friends. He likes expanding his circle of acquaintances and introducing new people into it in order to bring variety into his world.

A dream in which a person sees himself drinking himself into a blind stupor symbolizes obvious success in all areas, especially the social realm.

A dream about becoming drunk from drinking absinthe means that the dreamer is acting irresponsibly with innocent people, and he will squander his inheritance.

A dream about drinking water, in contrast, hints that in the near future, one of the dreamer's close friends or associates will suffer a disappointment. This will also affect the dreamer, who will be involved in it in some way.

Driving

A dream that features driving can have several interpretations. Driving round and round a traffic circle means that the dreamer is in some kind of psychological distress. He cannot find a way out of the vicious circle of problems he is in. An economic or emotional entanglement is making him feel as if he is in a whirlpool. A dream in which the person is driving along a narrow and dangerous road next to a deep chasm can also attest to a certain problem. While the dreamer displays courage and resourcefulness, he must be doubly cautious in order not to fall into the traps that lurk on all sides. He might be betrayed or let down by family members or business partners. When someone other than the dreamer is driving, it means that he is tired and feels the need to transfer the control of the situation to someone else.

Dromedary

A person who dreams about a dromedary camel is on the verge of coming into a generous amount of wealth and regard, which he will bear in a dignified manner. He will be magnanimous and charitable.

Drought

A dream about a drought is a very negative dream: it foretells internecine war and bloodshed, in addition to maritime calamities and land disasters. There will be vendettas between families, and diseases will rampage. On a personal level, the dreamer will have a very hard time keeping his business afloat.

Drowning

A dream about drowning in the sea or in a swimming pool or in any other pool of water serves as a warning dream. There could be losses in any area of life, material or others. The dreamer may lose property, but he may equally lose someone close or various abilities and talents.

A dream in which the dreamer sees himself about to drown implies that economic cooperation with someone close will yield handsome profits for both of them in the near future.

A dream about other people who are drowning or about to drown does not augur well. The health of the person who featured in the dream is in jeopardy, or there may be some other danger that will have repercussions throughout his life. Such a dream is also interpreted as a hint that the dreamer is protected against evil-doers who are plotting against him.

A dream about saving someone close from drowning is a sign that the dreamer will be very successful in anything concerning love and marriage.

A dream that features a sinking ship is a sign that soon the dreamer can expect to find himself in the middle of a scandal or get in trouble with the law and stand trial. People may tell lies about him, but in any case, he will feel embroiled and will plunge into a whirlpool of troubles and problems from which it will be difficult to extricate himself.

Drugstore

A dream that features nothing but a drugstore is a sign that the dreamer is about to enter a phase of temporary sadness and depression. The good news in the dream is that these feelings will pass.

However, the dream predicts a bad feeling that will afflict the dreamer and will be expressed in melancholy that will shroud the dreamer in gloom. It will be so difficult for him that he is liable to have suicidal thoughts. He must make every effort to force himself to detach himself from these negative thoughts. He must force himself to go out and see friends. He must try not to be alone, but to be surrounded with people who are close to him all the time, people in whose company he can be frank and to whom he can tell his troubles and unburden his heart. This process of psychological release may alleviate his mental pain until this period gradually passes.

If a person dreams that he enters a drugstore in order to buy medications, it is a sign that he will suffer from medical problems – in fact, he may already be incubating some kind of disease of whose existence he is still unaware. These health problems will not solve themselves. He will have to be examined by a physician in order to solve the problem, if there is one, as soon as possible.

Drum

If a person hears the dull beat of a drum in a drum, it is a sign that he is being summoned to the assistance of a faraway friend who is in trouble. If a person sees a drum in a dream, it attests to his congenial nature and his loathing of disagreements and quarrels. For tradesmen, farmers and sailors, dreaming about a drum is a good omen.

Drunkenness

A dream about drunkenness is basically a negative dream, since being drunk on alcohol is an indication of a dissipated character. The dreamer will be disgraced when he resorts to theft.

On the other hand, drunkenness as the result of an excessive intake of wine predicts luck in business and love, as well as ecstatic literary and esthetic experiences. If the dreamer sees other people drunk in a dream, it is a prediction of unhappiness.

Duck

In general, the appearance of a duck in a dream implies that positive things are about to happen to the dreamer, and that good news or changes that will cause joy, happiness and good luck are in the offing. The dreamer is facing a period filled with good and positive surprises that will bring him repose, peace of mind and financial success. If the dreamer has recently encountered problems he could not solve, or if he faced a serious dilemma or debate and could not decide which path to take, the appearance of a duck in a dream implies that the problem he was facing is about to be solved. The solution will be positive and will bring nothing but good consequences.

If a person dreams about a duck that is served up to him as a meal, or if he dreams that he himself is cooking a duck for a meal, it is a prophetic dream. It attests to the fact that the dreamer is about to face a new era in his life that will bring him great economic prosperity as well as a good and comfortable life. If the dreamer is already wealthy, the dream implies that he will soon become doubly so, and he can expect to become famous and well-known.

If a person dreams that he is being pursued by ducks, the dream is even more powerful, implying that success is pursuing him. Even if the dreamer sits with his arms folded and does nothing to further his success in life, this kind of dream assures him that success will shine upon him. He can rest assured that certain steps, certain behavior or a certain action on his part will lead to a great deal of success in the future, even if he neither intends nor expects it.

(Remember to differentiate between a duck and a goose – see entry. A goose is generally characterized by flying.)

Duet

A dream about a duet symbolizes peaceful, harmonious coexistence between lovers. Furthermore, is implies half-hearted rivalry between business people. However, musicians see this as blatant competition and a struggle to be top dog. A singing duet in a dream indicates that unpleasant news is in the offing, but it will soon be eclipsed by more pleasant things.

Dumb

A dream that features a person who is "dumb" warns the dreamer against revealing a secret. Deep down inside, the dreamer knows that he is keeping a secret that resembles a ticking time-bomb, and that if he reveals it, the world order is liable to change, and not for the better. The dream warns of being carried away by evil urges that tempt the dreamer to loosen the ties on his tongue. The damage that will be caused as a result of the revelation of the secret will be irreversible, and the dreamer must employ tremendous self-discipline in order not to reveal it.

A B C D E F G H I J K L M N O P Q R S T U V W X Y Z

Dun

If a person sees himself receiving a dun in a dream, it is a warning dream: it is imperative that he see to his affairs – both business and love – and make sure not to neglect them.

Dungeon

If a person sees a dungeon in a dream, it means that his wisdom will enable him to emerge triumphant from the trials of life. If a woman dreams about a dungeon, she herself will be the cause of her own ostracism because of her indiscreet conduct.

Dunghill

If a person dreams about a dunghill, it signals prosperity that will come from very unexpected quarters. If a farmer dreams about a dunghill, it is a sign of good luck, of a plentiful harvest and of numerous livestock. If a young woman has this dream, it implies that she will marry a rich man whom she has not yet met.

Dusk

A dream about dusk is a sad dream because it signals premature aging and unrealized hopes. Subsequent to this dream, business affairs seem to grind to a halt for a long time.

Dust

If a person dreams that he is covered with dust, it means that other people's lack of success will affect him as well.

If he uses his brains, he will overcome this setback and continue along his path to success.

Dwarf

A dwarf that appears in a dream in his classic form is interpreted according to ancient traditions mostly as a bearer of good luck. The dreamer is about to go through a good, positive phase during which he will recharge his batteries in a way that will make it easier for him to cope with life during subsequent phases that are not as good.

If an especially ugly dwarf appears in a dream, it predicts that a certain person or element that ostensibly looks small and insignificant is about to cause the dreamer harm and constitute a stumbling-block in his path to realizing his wishes and accomplishing his goals in life.

If a smiling, positive dwarf with a benevolent expression appears in a dream, it implies that should the dreamer land himself in a situation of distress, special and essential help will come from an unexpected quarter.

If a particularly malicious dwarf appears in a dream, inspiring a bad gut feeling, the dreamer can expect to go through a very difficult period that will be caused predominantly by his unrestrained utterances. The fact that he does not care who he is talking to and lashes out left and right will cost him dearly in the end. It will cause him damage that he did not imagine in his wildest dreams.

Sometimes, a dwarf appears in a dream as part of a circus performance. If such a dwarf does indeed appear in a dream, it is a sign that the dreamer will be the focal point of disputes that were sparked by malicious gossip that he helped proliferate.

Dye

If a dream features the dyeing of cloth, it is a sign of good or bad luck – depending on the color: blue, red and gold indicate prosperity, while white and black are signs of every kind of grief.

Dying

A dream about dying is usually linked to an obligation the dreamer has toward someone or something. Sometimes it attests to the fact that the dreamer did not honor agreements, did not do things he was required to do, or did not fulfill a request or a wish that he was asked to fulfill. Even if he was not obliged to do so, there is an uncomfortable feeling inside him, as if he did not meet expectations and did not do what he was instructed to do.

If a person sees himself dying in a dream, it means that severe guilt feelings about something he did are weighing heavily on his heart, and he regrets his action with all his being. He knows that even if he attempts to atone for it, nothing he does will diminish the terrible feeling in his heart in the least. The feeling of guilt is unbearable, and he is having a hard time finding a way out to mend his ways.

If a person sees another person who is close to him dying in a dream, it means that the dreamer wants to shake off the person who is the subject of the dream with all his heart. He does not want any contact with him, and longs for the moment when he no longer has an obligation to him. The person may have hurt the dreamer badly in the past. Alternatively, the dreamer's obligation to this person may be too burdensome for him, and he wants to free himself of any feeling of responsibility toward him. The dreamer's immediate desire is to detach himself emotionally from the person who is dying in the dream. It could be that feelings of dependence and an inability to be self-standing as a result of this bond are involved. The dreamer is trying with all his might to remove any obligation he has ever had toward the person he is dreaming about. He feels as if the bonds that bind him to the dying person are very difficult to remove – but nevertheless, he knows that it is possible if he makes a mental effort.

Dynamite

If a person sees dynamite in a dream, it is a sign that change is in the offing and that he is about to expand the scope of his affairs. If he is fearful in the dream, it means that a hidden enemy is undermining him, and if he is not cautious, that enemy will ambush him at a vulnerable moment.

Dynamo

If a dream features a dynamo, it means that the dreamer will succeed if he is meticulous in his business practices. If a broken-down dynamo appears in a dream, it indicates that the dreamer is coming close to enemies whose aim is to get him embroiled in trouble.

A B C D E F G H I J K L M N O P Q R S T U V W X Y Z

E

Eagle

An eagle in a dream attests to the person's character and abilities. The dreamer is blessed with a strong, uncompromising character, and he aspires to accomplish the goals he has set for himself, even if he has to push himself to the very limit. The dreamer is blessed with impressive abilities, and he possesses very incisive intuitive powers by means of which he can realize telepathic abilities. Some people think that he is gifted with a special "sixth sense" that affords him the possibility of observing things that are beyond human comprehension. The eagle indicates spiritual illumination and a very high mental capacity, and implies that the person will fulfill himself in the very best possible manner by making the most of all his abilities and extracting the maximum from his talents.

Earrings

If a person sees earrings in a dream, it means that he can expect to receive good news and get an interesting job. Broken earrings in a dream indicate vicious gossip about the dreamer.

Ears

A dream in which the dreamer sees ears means that an enemy is eavesdropping – possibly electronically – on his conversations.

Earth

Generally speaking, earth that appears in a dream is a good hint for the future. If the earth in the dream looks good and "healthy," it attests to material wealth, spiritual wealth, financial prosperity, abundance and a happy life for the dreamer.

If the dreamer sees himself (or someone else) digging in the earth, the dream implies that he is looking for treasure or something he perceives as treasure, and that he still has a long way to go. It may be a quest for true love, integrity, material wealth or anything else the dreamer considers a "treasure."

A dream in which the earth looks like ash or has a burned and smoky appearance is a sign of a bitter disappointment that is liable to be the dreamer's lot. A big investment may not yield profits, and may prove to be a bad investment. A feeling of a lack of fulfillment, a lack of success, failure, and helplessness will contribute to the mess.

If the earth in the dream is barren and arid, the dream indicates that the dreamer is not being honest and straight with himself. He is afraid of dealing with the truth or with reality, and close family members or other things may be in his way, causing him to ignore these things intentionally. Moreover, he is a person who does not listen to the opinions of those around him enough, and relates to them derisively and contemptuously. This behavior can backfire and hit him like a boomerang.

If the earth in the dream is fertile and rich, and its color attests to its qualities, the dream implies that excellent business opportunities are on the doorstep, and they will serve as the key to economic success and a springboard to other financial and economic successes in life.

Earthquake

A dream about an earthquake means that the dreamer is about to undergo a very significant revolution in his life – there will be far-reaching changes that will ultimately lead to an extremely positive development. It might be a change in social status such as marriage – or alternatively divorce from an unsatisfactory mate. There could also be a change in workplace. Overall, a dream like this augurs well.

Eating

Eating in a dream does not foretell anything good. It is a sign of consecutive disappointments, failure in things in which the dreamer expected success, and preoccupations about earning a living. Besides that, the dream also hints at the fact that the dreamer is not an energetic person – on the contrary, he is idle and lazy by nature, and so success is in no hurry to shine upon him. He lazes his life away and does nothing to extricate himself from trouble; this causes him to alienate the people around him.

If a person dreams that he is eating alone, the dream implies that the dreamer is in the process of losing his status and that a significant deterioration in his life has begun. He no longer has the esteem of the people around him as he did in the past, and his candle is burning down. Moreover, in the near future, the dreamer may lose a person close to him due to a separation. One of his associates who no longer wants to be in his proximity will break away.

In contrast, if a person sees himself eating with someone

else in a dream, the meaning of the dream changes: the dreamer will have the good fortune of being in the proximity of a person who will prove to be a sincere and genuine friend, and the dreamer will never be alone. There will always be someone who comes to his aid in times of need. Besides that, the dream attests to the dreamer's future economic stability and to his increasing self-confidence.

Eavesdropping

If other people are eavesdropping on the dreamer, it portends trouble. If the dreamer is eavesdropping on other people, he can look forward to happy surprises.

Ebony

Any dream concerning an object made of ebony foretells strife and dissent in the dreamer's house.

Echo

If a person hears an echo in his dream, it means that he is suffering from bad times. If he is ill, he may lose his job, and his friends will not be there for him.

Eclipse of the sun or moon

Generally, a dream about an eclipse of the sun or moon foretells an imminent disaster: the discovery of a partner's infidelity, problems at work, losing a job, or diseases. A loss of money can also be expected. However, after a difficult period, just as the sun and moon emerge from the darkness and illuminate the heavens once more, so the situation will improve.

A B C D **E** F G H I J K L M N O P Q R S T U V W X Y Z

Ecstasy

If a person dreams about ecstasy, it implies that he can look forward to a visit from a dear and distant friend.

Edifice

The interpretation of the dream lies in the height of the edifice. An edifice of average height indicates changes in the near future. A higher-than-average edifice predicts brilliant success in the near future.

Eel

If the dreamer manages to hold on to the eel, this is a good dream. If the eel wriggles out of the dreamer's grasp, his luck will not last. If a person sees a dead eel in a dream, it means that he will conquer his most dangerous enemy. For lovers, seeing an eel in a dream implies marriage.

Egg/s

The appearance of eggs in a dream is usually a good sign, hinting at good things that are about to happen to the dreamer. Eggs attest to the fact that luck will shine on him, and they are usually a sign that his economic situation is about to improve beyond recognition. If the eggs are in a basket, the dreamer is about to receive large sums of money as a result of hard work, an investment that yielded good results or a win at gambling (in a casino or in some type of lottery).

If the dreamer sees many eggs in his dream, it is a hint of an increase in his family. If he sees a pair of eggs in a nest, it symbolizes a loving and supportive family whom the dreamer can trust; he can be sure that he will have someone to rely on in time of trouble and that there will always be someone at his side.

Eggs as a warning: Eggs in a dream can also hint at less joyful things or give a warning.

A single egg in a nest is a sign that the person suffers from loneliness. This refers to an internal-psychological feeling of loneliness and not just a lack of friends in everyday reality. Even if the dreamer is surrounded by friends and enjoys an active social life, the dream brings out the dreamer's inner feeling, since he actually feels lonely and does not have anyone with whom he can share his inner experiences and feelings.

When the dreamer sees eggs breaking in his dream, it implies unresolved disputes that are bothering him, and conflicts and complications in which he is involved. These conflicts may be with other people in his immediate surroundings or with himself. His mind may not be at rest, and he may not be succeeding in resolving a crisis in which he is involved. It is also possible that he is disturbed by nagging guilt feelings, and until he does the right thing in order to get rid of them, they will not give him any peace. Breaking eggs in a dream can hint at a lack of luck in life and at the fact that nothing works out. Luck is "stuck" and does not shine upon the dreamer.

If the dreamer sees rotten eggs in his dream, the dream indicates that the dreamer feels that his nakedness has been revealed to everyone, and that everyone sees his shame. He is vainly trying to hide something he has done, of which he is very ashamed. The dreamer knows that he cannot hide his shame for very long, and is going through inner torture.

A dream that features brown eggs is a sign that news is

A B C D E F G H I J K L M N O P Q R S T U V W X Y Z

about to arrive from someone abroad. It is not clear whether it is good or bad news, but it will reach the dreamer in the form of a letter, a telegram or an e-mail.

If the dreamer sees eggs thrown at him in a dream, the dream attests to the fact that some kind of gossip is bothering him. In this case, it is malicious gossip that causes the dreamer public disgrace. He may have transmitted some item of gossip to other people, or he may be the subject of this gossip. One way or another, his inner feelings are intermingled with a feeling of profound shame.

Egg yolk

A dream that features an egg yolk implies that good times are in the offing. If a person who gambles dreams about an egg yolk, it means that he will have luck at gambling.

Elbow

A dream about an elbow says a lot about what the dreamer thinks of himself. He does not admit to this in reality, but deep inside himself he knows that he is the right person in the places that are most wrong for him. He is talented, but he does not work in a job in which he can make the most of his talent. He lives in a place that is completely unsuitable for his character and personality, and it is possible that even his partner is not suitable for him, and so on. He feels that he has to change his entire way of life, but is too lethargic to do it, besides being afraid of doing so. In fact, the dream emphasizes the fact that the dreamer has always allowed time and the forces at work around him to influence his future without taking hold of the helm of his life himself. He has not navigated his life himself, but rather has been influenced by the people around him, by his parents, by his superiors at work, and so on. Deep inside himself, he knows that he can no longer permit the future to solve his problems, and that he has to take himself in hand and assume responsibility for his life.

Elderberries

If a person dreams about leafy and fruit-laden elderberry bushes, it signifies a happy home in the country as well as enough money for enjoyable activities such as traveling.

Election

If a person dreams that he is at an election, it significes that he will get involved in some controversial matter that will do him no good financially or socially.

Electric blanket

A dream about an electric blanket predicts that the dreamer will soon be in need of support and comfort.

Electricity

If a person dreams about electricity, it is an indication of unexpected changes in the dreamer; these will not particularly be to his benefit. If the dreamer reacts badly to electricity, he is in grave danger. If he sees a live wire in his dream, it means that enemies will conspire to ruin his painstakingly developed plans.

A B C D **E** F G H I J K L M N O P Q R S T U V W X Y Z

Electric mixer

A dream about an electric mixer is an indication of an increased social life.

Elephant

A dream about an elephant is a positive dream that attests to the fact that the dreamer will enjoy a great deal of joy and satisfaction in his life, and success and fortune will shine on him in every area of life: family, love, work, friends, and so on.

If the dreamer sees himself riding an elephant, he will enjoy comfort and prosperity in his life.

If the dreamer sees other people riding an elephant, it is a sign that he will soon receive help from a close friend. A dream like this attests to a close and strong friendship the dreamer has with someone close to him, a friendship that will prove itself over and over again. This dream also implies that during the course of his life, the dreamer will meet many people who will become his close friends and will envelop him in warmth and love. The dreamer will never be alone, since there will always be someone who will come to his aid.

A dream that features a herd of elephants is a sign that the dreamer will enjoy a life of happiness and great wealth. Despite his prospective wealth, his friends will reveal themselves to be true friends.

If a person feeds an elephant in his dream, it is hint that the dreamer will become famous or will reach key positions and will hobnob with important, powerful people as a result of his occupation.

Elevator

A dream that features an elevator can have different meanings and interpretations according to the situation. If the dreamer gets into an elevator crammed with people, it attests to the fact that he is in competition with other people, probably in the work arena. He must behave with restraint and caution. A stuck elevator means that there is a dead-end situation that is causing the dreamer mental anguish. This can refer to both the personal and the business realms. An ascending elevator hints at success. A descending or falling elevator attests to a forthcoming disappointment. If the dreamer sees himself in an elevator with his family, it means that there is an urgent need for a talk with all the people who appear in the dream. He must find out whom among those present feels cheated or disillusioned. Communication can help him find a solution or at least ease the situation.

Elixir of life

A dream about the elixir of life is a positive dream that heralds new joys and new opportunities.

Elopement

If a person dreams that he elopes, he will be considered unworthy of his position by the married establishment and his reputation will be in jeopardy. If an unmarried person dreams about an elopement, it is an indication of disappointments in love and male infidelity.

A
B
C
D
E
F
G
H
I
J
K
L
M
N
O
P
Q
R
S
T
U
V
W
X
Y
Z

Eloquence

If the dreamer appears eloquent in a dream, he can expect to hear good news about somebody for whom he is working.

Embalming

If a person sees the process of embalming in a dream, it implies that he is going to experience a reversal of fortune. If he himself is being embalmed, it means that he will keep company with the wrong people.

Embankment

If a person dreams about driving along an embankment, it foretells problems and heartache for him. If he manages to continue driving without anything bad occurring, it means that he will be able to use the prediction for his own benefit.

Embracing

If a person dreams that he embraces his/her spouse indifferently, it is a sign of possible illness and domestic disputes and rows. If he embraces relatives, they will become ill and unhappy. For lovers, it is a sign of fights following infidelity. A dream about embracing a stranger foretells unwanted guests.

Embroidery

A dream that features embroidery is a good dream for a woman: it means that she is resourceful, thrifty and tactful.

If a married man dreams about embroidery, it signifies an addition to his household.

Emerald

If a person sees an emerald in a dream, it signifies a trouble-fraught inheritance for him. If a lover sees his beloved wearing an emerald in a dream, it is a sign that he is about to be dumped. A dream about purchasing an emerald is a warning that the dreamer is about to incur losses as a result of a bad deal.

Emperor

If a person dreams that he meets a foreign emperor during his travels, it means that he will be going on a long, futile and unenjoyable trip.

Employee

If a person sees one of his employees being belligerent or offensive in a dream, there will be trouble. If the employee is pleasant, everything will be fine.

Employer

A dream about an employer can contain various meanings. A conversation with an employer can hint at a promotion at work. On the other hand, it is liable to hint at a disappointment. It is possible that despite the dreamer's attempts to communicate and express his feelings and requests to the management in his workplace, he is not receiving a positive reply. Although the results are not clear-cut, the fact that the dreamer is keeping the channels

A B C D **E** F G H I J K L M N O P Q R S T U V W X Y Z

of communication open should be applauded. A clear and assertive conversation will achieve positive results, even if this takes time.

Employment

A dream about employment is an unlucky dream, because it indicates business failure, unemployment and illness. If the dreamer himself is unemployed at a given moment, he can rest assured that thanks to his industriousness, he will find a job. If the dreamer employs others, he will suffer losses.

Empress

Dreaming about an empress indicates that the dreamer will receive high honors, but will not be popular because of arrogance. A dream of an empress and an emperor has no particular significance.

Emptiness

A dream about an empty container or about a feeling of emptiness warns of a bitter disappointment that the dreamer will have to cope with and that will debilitate him severely, both physically and mentally.

Enchantment

A dream about being enchanted is a warning to the dreamer not to be seduced by evil in the guise of something pleasurable. If the dreamer resists enchantment in a dream, it means that people will seek his advice and enjoy his generosity. If he tries to enchant others, he will degrade into evil.

Encyclopedia

If a person sees or uses an encyclopedia in a dream, it means he will forgo life's comforts for literary acclaim.

Enemy

A dream that features the defeat of enemies implies overcoming business setbacks and enjoying prosperity. It is always a good dream for the dreamer. If the enemies in the dream overcome the dreamer, it means trouble. If enemies spread slander about the dreamer in a dream, it means that he will suffer setbacks and failure in his profession or business. If the dreamer kisses an enemy in his dream, it means that he is effecting a reconciliation with a friend with whom he quarreled.

Engagement

A dream about an engagement is usually a sign of bad tidings. Contrary to logic, a dream about an engagement, which in everyday life attests to a new and fresh beginning, symbolizes almost the exact opposite in a dream: failure and loss.

Generally, if a person dreams about an engagement between himself and his partner, they can expect rows, disputes and basic disagreements about their life together and their relationship.

A dream about an engagement between the dreamer and a partner from a high social class is a sign that they can expect scandal on the way to the altar. This scandal will not enhance the relaxed atmosphere in their married life, and there will always be hidden tension simmering beneath the surface.

If a person dreams of announcing his engagement to his partner, it is a sign that the partner is in no rush to make a commitment, and is not in favor of the engagement and the marriage at all. The partner's objection raises doubts about the quality of the relationship and the extent of the mutual trust between the two.

If a person dreams about breaking off an engagement, the dream implies that many disappointments are in the offing, and that the dreamer must not cherish many hopes, since they will burst like a balloon. He must be able to accept things as they are and not see what does not exist. Reality will give him a slap in the face, and he had better be prepared for it. In this way, the blow will be less painful.

If a person dreams about an engagement that both he and his partner want, their future life together will be good and rose-colored, and will flow smoothly.

Engine (of a car)

If a person dreams that he is stuck in a car whose engine has stopped running should take precautionary measures. These refer to the purchase of something big that entails a large outlay of money. Whether this is the purchase of a new apartment or some kind of appliance (including a car), the dreamer must consult with an expert before making the deal. The dream also implies a possibility of failure in anything to do with spurious money matters. This is not the right time to invest in shares or to gamble.

Engineer

If a person sees an engineer in a dream, it signifies happy reunions after exhausting journeys.

English

If a foreigner dreams that he meets English people, it means that he will fall victim to the egoistic intentions of others.

Entrails

A dream about human entrails symbolizes devastating, awful despair, with no glimmer of hope. If a dream features the entrails of a wild animal, it means that the dreamer will defeat an enemy. If a person tears out another person's entrails in a dream, it signifies that he is willing to stoop to sadistic behavior in order to further his own interests. A dream about the dreamer's own child's entrails portends the downfall of one of the two.

Envelope

A dream about an envelope is a hint of news that will arrive from an unexpected quarter. A white envelope means good news. A colored envelope means news in the romantic sphere. A black envelope hints at a sad event such as the illness of a distant relative or a friend. If the dreamer sees himself opening an envelope in a dream and finding money, he can expect a very big surprise in the financial realm. A win in a lottery or some similar framework will turn things upside down and change his life unrecognizably.

Envy / Jealousy

If a person dreams that he is envious of someone else, it portends possible disappointment. If another person is envious of the dreamer in a dream, it heralds success and good luck.

Epaulets

A soldier who dreams about epaulets will be in disfavor for a short time, but will soon receive a promotion. If a woman dreams about meeting a person with epaulets, it means that she is on the verge of involvement in a scandal.

Epidemic

A dream that features an epidemic is a sign of mental deterioration and anxiety caused by unpleasant tasks. People close to the dreamer will be exposed to illness.

Ermine

If a person dreams that he is wearing ermine, it is a sign of wealth and high status. The dreamer will be immune to poverty and misery. If he sees someone else clothed in ermine in a dream, it means that he will associate with rich and cultured people. A lover who sees his beloved in ermine in a dream can be assured of fidelity; however, if the ermine is moth-eaten or soiled, the opposite is true.

Errands

A dream about going on errands is implies amicable relationships at home and with friends. If a young woman dreams that she sends someone on an errand, she will lose the man she loves because of her indifferent behavior.

Escalator

A dream about riding the up escalator is a sign of professional progress. A dream about the down escalator is a sign of being stuck in a professional rut. If the escalator is out of order and the dreamer has to walk up it, he will not receive the promotion he expected.

Escape / Fleeing

A dream about fleeing generally hints at the ability to overcome hostile elements that are seeking to harm the dreamer.

If the dreamer sees a stranger fleeing in his dream, the dream implies that the person is not very close to the dreamer, but the dreamer knows him and tries to make contact with people who seek to harm him, and even try to conspire against him.

A dream in which the dreamer sees himself fleeing with his lover is a sign that the dreamer will suffer a bitter disappointment in love. Things will not go as he expected, and his lover will abandon him suddenly. It will take him time to get over it.

If a person sees someone close to him fleeing in a dream, the dream contains good news: that person is awaiting the birth of another child in the near future, thus increasing his family.

A dream in which the person sees himself fleeing from a loved one is a sign that a love affair is about to terminate. It is not worth digging in his heels and clinging to this relationship, since it is destined to fall apart. Even if the dreamer tries to revive it by force, he will not be able to do so, since it has been sentenced to die, so it is preferable for him to get out of it as quickly as possible and move forward.

A dream about fleeing from an enemy hints at the

A B C D **E** F G H I J K L M N O P Q R S T U V W X Y Z

unpleasant conclusion of a relationship in which the dreamer is involved. The dreamer's disillusionment will be huge, and he will have to brace himself for disappointment and for the difficult emotional period that will follow.

A dream in which a person sees himself fleeing from fire is a sign of victory, success and conquest. The dream mostly implies success in areas connected to law courts – an acquittal, the clearing of the dreamer's name, and so on.

A dream that features an escape from drowning attests to the fact that following a period of worry and anxiety, there will be calmness and tranquillity. The dreamer will be able to enjoy inner calm after a stormy period in which he was involved in a serious crisis.

A dream in which the dreamer feels that he is in a trap from which he cannot escape attests to the fact that the people around him will respect him because of an act of heroism he performed. Other people will think the world of him because of some exceptionally daring deed he performed or will perform.

If attempts to escape in a dream fail, it is a sign that the dreamer is imprisoned in a vicious circle of personal problems that have not yet been solved. He grapples and argues with them, and is caught in a kind of net that does not permit him to see things clearly so that they can be solved.

If a person dreams of escaping from difficulties, it is a sign that he will experience temporary success in everything to do with personal things such as career, family or money matters.

Estate

If a person dreams about inheriting an estate, it indicates that he will indeed receive a bequest one day, but it will not be what he is expecting. If a woman dreams about an estate, it is a sign that she will receive an extremely modest inheritance.

Eulogy

A dream about a eulogy implies that good news will arrive from a close acquaintance. In most cases, the news concerns a relationship. The acquaintance may be about to get married or make a long-standing relationship official.

If a person sees himself eulogizing someone in a dream, the dreamer can expect to be accorded a great deal of respect. A certain event will cause people around him to hold him in far greater esteem than they do now, and his glory will increase greatly among many of his acquaintances.

If the person sees other people eulogizing in a dream, it is a warning dream, hinting that the coming days hold risks. It is advisable for him to think about his moves and not act hastily. Moreover, this may be linked to national events, so it is a good idea for the dreamer to stay away from crowded places such as stormy, crowded demonstrations and so on for the moment.

Europe

If a person dreams about traveling in Europe, he will soon go on a trip during which he will become acquainted with foreign customs. He will profit both educationally and financially.

Eve and the apple

A dream about the story of Eve in the Garden of Eden usually symbolizes the dreamer's ability to resist temptation.

Evening

Twilight in a dream implies success and prosperity for the dreamer. He will enjoy the fruits of his labor, both from the material and the spiritual points of view.

The evening hour in a dream – especially if it is a pleasant evening with good weather – predicts that the dreamer will soon liberate himself from inhibitions that have accompanied him all his life. Throwing off the restraints will cause him to experience a new life. He will permit himself to do things that he never dreamed he could do and enjoy pleasures that he never thought he could enjoy. The everyday problems and troubles that usually preoccupy him will disappear without a trace.

Evergreen

A dream about evergreens is a wonderful dream for everyone: it predicts wealth, happiness and knowledge. If a person dreams about icicles on evergreens, the dream is an omen of a promising future being spoiled.

Exchange

A dream about an exchange implies clever business dealings. If a young woman dreams of exchanging boyfriends with her friend, she should follow this through if she wants to ensure her future happiness.

Execution

If a person sees an execution, it means that he will suffer because of other people's carelessness. If he dreams that he is about to be executed, but his execution is miraculously stayed, it means that he will vanquish his enemies and become rich.

Exile

If a woman dreams about being exiled, it is a sign that she will be compelled to travel and miss out on an event she was looking forward to.

Explosion

A dream about a bomb or an explosion implies a change in the fixed order of things that will soon take place in the dreamer's life. This could involve moving to a new home as a result of an unexpected sum of money or a work offer that will cause him to move house. The dream may also indicate some problem at home that will crop up and cause a temporary upheaval. Eventually, things will get back to normal.

Eyebrows

A dream about eyebrows is a sign of scary obstacles in the dreamer's path.

Eye doctor

A dream about an eye doctor warns the dreamer to keep his eyes open and be aware of his situation so that he does not miss any opportunities that may come his way.

Eyeglasses / Binoculars

A dream that features eyeglasses or binoculars attests to the dreamer's desire to see the things that are facing him in a clearer light. This desire will soon lead him to examine things in another light, and affairs that were not clear to him before will suddenly become clear. Confusion and chaos will give way to a feeling of control, order and logic. Things that he did not understand become clear and comprehensible. What was previously opaque and seemingly meaningless will now become something that is taken for granted. As a result of this new feeling, there will be a considerable improvement in the dreamer's life. Order will prevail once again and create a feeling in him of being able to take responsibility for his life and for everything that happens to him. He will stop feeling as if he is being dragged along by the current and will begin to feel that he is holding the reins of his own life.

Eyes

A dream that features eyes can imply that the dreamer is going through a phase during which he has to be on the alert and keep his eyes open, otherwise it will cost him dearly. The area the dream hints at depends on its content. It could be his family, his spouse, his workplace or his business. In any case, there is a high probability that someone is stalking the dreamer and seeking an opportunity to trip him up or make him fail. On the other hand, the dreamer can prevent the situation from deteriorating if he uncovers the plots against him in advance.

F

Fables

A dream that features reading or narrating fables indicates that the dreamer will pass the time pleasantly. He also has a literary inclination. If he dreams about religious fables, it means that he will become very pious.

Face

A dream about a face that is of no relevance to the dreamer is a sign of approaching trouble. The dreamer will suddenly become embroiled in troubles he had no wish for.

If a dream features the dreamer's face, it is a sign that he will soon become a party to secrets that will exert a huge influence on his life.

An angry face in a dream is a sign that extreme emotions of rage and pain will cause the dreamer to succumb to an illness and he will not be able to function properly.

A sad, pale face in a dream symbolizes worry that is liable to affect everyday life and cause additional complications.

A round, laughing, friendly and smiling face in a dream is a sign that the dreamer can expect great happiness. He will enjoy the best of all worlds: a lot of money, good health and wonderful friendships. His love life, too, will enjoy renewed impetus, and he will be happy and calm.

A dream in which the dreamer sees himself surrounded by faces of people he recognizes and knows is a sign that he can expect a trip to a faraway destination, or that he will soon be moving house.

If a dream features an especially pale face, it means that the dreamer is neglecting his health, and this can cause him to succumb to serious illnesses. He has to take swift preventative action in order to curb the deterioration of his health. If he does not watch out, he is liable to contract diseases that will be difficult to cure.

If the dreamer sees an exceptionally ugly face in his dream, it means that he is operating out of bitterness. The motivating factors in his life are frustration and irascibility, and he has to find out the source of the bitter feelings that are painting his life in such gloomy colors.

If a person sees a face that is full of sorrow in a dream, it is a warning dream according to which the dreamer must change his way of life and his habits. Even though it is difficult to change habits, it is not only possible but it is desirable.

Factory

A dream about a factory symbolizes the dreamer's past and the things he has done in his life. If other people appear in the dream, the dreamer sees himself as a partner in the creative process. An operational factory means that the dreamer has an active and fruitful professional and private life as well as family and social life. An abandoned or empty factory means that he can expect a drop in business or in his economic situation. This may also refer to his private life. The dreamer must scrutinize his life very carefully.

Failure

Contrary to what might be expected, if a lover dreams about failure, it is actually a prediction of success. However, if a businessman dreams of failure, it is a warning dream: he must prepare himself for losses and mismanagement. These will bring him down if he does not do anything to correct them.

Fainting

A dream about fainting predicts illness in the family and bad news about people who are far away.

Fair

The meaning of a dream about a fair is varied. The dreamer may find himself wandering around a fair and buying odd things. This means that the dreamer is bothered by things to do with spending money and is looking for a way to limit the extent of his expenditures. Another possibility is that the dreamer will find what he wants at the fair.

This means that the dreamer will succeed in a transaction. If a person dreams about an unpleasant incident at a fair – for instance, the theft of his money or involvement in a brawl or fistfight – he should beware of spending money, at least for a period of a few weeks. If he is hasty, he is liable to get in trouble. He may encounter swindlers or invest in a business that is on the verge of bankruptcy, and so on.

A
B
C
D
E
F
G
H
I
J
K
L
M
N
O
P
Q
R
S
T
U
V
W
X
Y
Z

Fairy

A dream that features a fairy bodes well for everybody, since it is the embodiment of beauty.

Faithless

Oddly enough, a dream about being faithless is a positive dream. A dream about faithless friends means that the dreamer's friends hold him in high regard. If a lover dreams that his beloved is faithless, it is a sign of a happy marriage.

Falcon

A dream that features a falcon means that people will envy the dreamer's wealth. Furthermore, it indicates vicious gossip.

Fall

If a person dreams that he falls and this frightens him, it means that he will be successful after a long, uphill battle. If he dreams that he is injured in the fall, he will lose his friends and run into trouble.

Fame

A dream in which the dreamer or someone close to him becomes famous is a good sign. Fame and glory will come as a result of some deed, invention or financial venture that will place the dreamer in the public eye. One thing will lead to another and the chances of massive economic success are higher than ever.

If a person dreams that other people achieve fame, the dream means that soon the dreamer will receive help from friends who will offer it unstintingly.

A dream in which the dreamer achieves fame implies that the dreamer has reached the summit of a particular field and enjoys the highest status possible in that field. He must be aware of the fact that after he has exhausted his abilities, the high position he is in can only decline. He should accept that fact with love and understanding, since it is impossible to be at the top for any length of time.

A dream about great fame and high status also implies that the dreamer must remember what modesty is and what things were like before he acquired his present status.

Family

If a person dreams about a happy family, it implies health and comfort. Having said that, a dream about illness or dissent in a family is a prediction of disappointment and unhappiness.

Family tree

A dream about a family tree symbolizes many worries in the realm of the family. It implies that the dreamer will seek his pleasures elsewhere.

Famine

If a person sees famine in a dream, it does not bode well: it predicts business failure and illness. If the dreamer's enemies die of famine in his dream, he will be successful.

A B C D E **F** G H I J K L M N O P Q R S T U V W X Y Z

Famish

If a person dreams that he is famished, it means that a project of whose success he was sure is on the way to failure. If he dreams about others being famished, it is a sign of bad luck both for the dreamer and for other people.

Fan

A dream about a fan indicates that the dreamer is involved in a romantic affair. This could well be with someone close, such as a distant relative or someone introduced by distant relatives. Waving a fan is a warning sign of a negative development for the precise reason that the affair is developing under the eyes of "acquaintances," and this fact attracts a great deal of criticism and comments that are often unwanted. If a dream features a situation in which a fan falls or gets lost, this is not a good sign, but it could be a matter of temporary difficulties that will pass with time. Ultimately, the development of the relationship and the question of whether it will last for a long time depend on many factors that are not connected to the person who is having the dream. The best solution to situations of this kind is to wait patiently for developments.

Fancy house

A fancy house in a dream need not be decorated or adorned or contain particularly luxurious accessories. It is enough that the dream features a very spacious, luxurious and impressive house, such as a villa. Dreaming about a fancy house can have contrasting meanings depending on whether the dreamer sees himself entering the house – or leaving it.

If he sees himself entering the house, it is a good sign, for he can look forward to a very good period during which he will receive good news. He will be blessed with a full and good life, and will be held in high esteem by the people around him. Success will shine upon him from every point of view – professionally, in his marriage and family, and socially. He does not ask for the world, and is generally easy to please. The dream hints to the dreamer that what he can expect in the near future is a "simple" and good life that will run smoothly, without upsets, unexpected problems, struggles or disappointments.

In contrast, if a dreamer sees himself leaving a big, fancy house, he can expect problems in the near future and he will have to deal with them. He will experience worries and severe tension that will accompany him for a long time, and there will be great confusion. The advice of a close friend, seeking to clarify things, can be of use to him. The feeling of the lack of clarity is liable to cause him a loss of self-confidence as well as feelings of impotence, depression and embarrassment.

Farewell

If a person dreams about bidding someone farewell, it means that he will receive bad news about friends who are far away. If a young woman bids her beloved farewell in a dream, it means that he no longer cares about her.

Farm / Ranch

A dream about farm work attests to a good and fulfilling family life. The dreamer is surrounded by the love of the members of his family, and this gives him a great deal of confidence and a feeling of tranquillity as a result of which nothing bad will happen to him. The dream also attests to the dreamer's life of wealth, since he succeeds at anything he does and enjoys the fruits of his labor.

A dream in which a person sees himself hiring strangers to work on his farm implies that the dreamer has to mend his ways because he is following spurious paths.

If a person sees himself working on a farm by himself, he can expect material success way beyond what he expected. The profits will be much higher than he expected, and economic ease will come in the near future. In addition, a dream like this implies that the dreamer will receive assistance; it is already on the way. Somebody who sensed the weight of the burden that the dreamer is carrying is coming to his aid and will soon be there to help him.

If a person dreams about a thriving farm, the dream implies imminent marriage or a romantic involvement for the dreamer in the near future.

If a person who is in love dreams about a visit to a farm, it is a sign of happiness with a partner, of a fruitful relationship and of success in family life.

The dream implies that the dreamer's married life will be good and that his partner is blessed with qualities of tolerance, integrity, reliability and an ability to express warmth and love to other people, and especially to the dreamer.

A dream that features a farm that is neglected, not properly cared for and looks abandoned is a warning dream. It serves to warn the dreamer about his laziness and about other properties such as conceit and deriding others: if he does not mend his ways, he is liable to find himself literally poor and destitute – both on the material level and

A B C D E **F** G H I J K L M N O P Q R S T U V W X Y Z

because of the fact that people will stay away from him, and he will not have friends who will stand by him.

If a person dreams that he takes over a farm and seizes ownership, it is a prophetic dream. The dreamer will soon receive an inheritance and will have a great deal of money. His luck is approaching a turning point and will change for the good. If the farm taken over by the dreamer is small, the dream attests to the fact that the dreamer has big aspirations that will lead him to great and respectable achievements.

Farmer

A dream about a farmer working the land, in which the dreamer sees himself talking to the farmer, hints at material and economic prosperity. The dreamer will soon get a promotion or see the fruits of some investment in the financial realm, so that his situation will improve. The dream links working the soil to "Mother Earth," who gives of the good of the earth. This abundance will also come the dreamer's way, and he will simultaneously enjoy both material wealth and happiness and satisfaction in the personal, social and family realms.

Fat

If a person dreams about becoming fat, it predicts a change for the good in his life. If he dreams about others being fat, it is a sign of prosperity.

Fates

A dream that features the Fates is a prediction of misery and quarrels.

A
B
C
D
E
F
G
H
I
J
K
L
M
N
O
P
Q
R
S
T
U
V
W
X
Y
Z

Father

It is important to differentiate between a dream in which the dreamer's father addresses him directly and a dream in which the father appears, but the dreamer does not engage in conversation with him, and there is no discourse between them.

If a conversation occurs between the dreamer and his father in the dream, the dream has a happy meaning (prior to clarifying the nature and content of the conversation, since these have their own meaning in the dream). Such a dream implies a joyful future that brings good, happy news. This is also true for dreamers whose fathers have died and they speak to them when in fact they are seeing an image that is no longer in this world. Every "encounter" with a father (alive or dead) in a dream, in which the father addresses his child and wants to have a conversation with him, is a sign of something good, of an event that will bring joy and elation.

If the dreamer sees his father in a dream, but the father does not address him and simply appears in the dream as a background image, the dream mainly contains a warning. The dreamer is not aware of problems or of a complicated situation in which he is embroiled. He is liable to uncover a situation concerning himself that is neither good nor particularly flattering, and the dream serves as a kind of signal from the subconscious to the conscious, with the aim of raising a problem that the dreamer is ignoring to the surface. It seems that there is a weak or vulnerable point in the dreamer's life, or that he trying to ignore various worries and problems. If he ignores them, the situation will worsen. If he heeds the signals the dream is sending him, he will know how to deal with these problems before it is too late.

Father-in-law

If a person dreams about his father-in-law, it is a sign of disputes with relatives or friends. If the father-in-law is healthy and happy in the dream, it is a sign of a harmonious domestic situation.

Fatigue

A dream about fatigue attests to the urgent need of a change in the dreamer's priorities. Overload is causing a feeling of fogginess, helplessness and an inability to enjoy life. The dreamer must take a vacation. During the days or weeks he is detached from the daily routine, he can make more fateful decisions about a suitable change.

Faucet

A dream about a faucet with water pouring out of it unceasingly is a sign that business will boom and the dreamer will see the fruits of his labor. He is about to clinch deals that will bring in a great deal of money.

If the faucet is dripping slowly in the dream, it is a sign that things in the dreamer's life will move very slowly, in slow motion. He will not see rapid results of his toil, and things he begins will be concluded only after a lengthy period of time, sometimes without positive results. Having said that, this does not mean that things will run unsatisfactorily. It mainly means that there will be delays.

A dream about a faucet, especially if the dreamer is

A B C D E F G H I J K L M N O P Q R S T U V W X Y Z

keeping a secret, hints that the secret will leak out and will eventually be revealed. The dreamer will not be able to avoid the exposure of the secret, even if he does his best to prevent it.

Favor

If a person dreams about asking favors of someone, it is a sign of a comfortable lifestyle, lacking for nothing. If the person dreams about granting favors, it means that he will suffer a loss.

Fawn (animal)

If a dream features a fawn, it is an indication of true, loyal friends and fidelity in love.

Fawn (behavior)

If a person dreams about someone fawning over him, it implies that enemies who are pretending to be his friends are in the vicinity.

Fax machine

If a person receives a fax in a dream, it attests to the fact that the dreamer is about to receive bad news regarding his profession or business. If he dreams about sending a fax, it means that he will suffer a severe disappointment at the hands of one of his business associates.

Fear

If a person feels fear in a dream, it implies that

enterprises he will embark on in the future will fail. If a woman feels fear in a dream, she is warned to brace herself for disappointment in love.

Feast

A dream in which the dreamer sees himself partaking of a big feast with numerous participants implies that a quarrel between him and his partner is in the offing. The quarrel may not be a lovers' spat, but rather a quarrel between friends. However, in any event, the dream implies a conflict that can be expected between the dreamer and the people close to him.

If an unmarried person dreams this dream, it is a prophetic dream that predicts a marriage that will not turn out well and will end in divorce.

If a widow has this dream, it is a sign that she will soon meet a person she likes. This person will break down her emotional barriers, and she will feel that she can marry him and start a new life.

Feather

Dreams about feathers can have various meanings. It is important to try to remember the color of the feather in the dream. A small white feather hints that the dreamer is going through a good phase that will last for several more years at least. A pink feather is also a good sign. A yellow feather (yellow symbolizes gold and jewelry) implies a sum of money that will come from an unexpected quarter. A gray or black feather serves as a warning sign: a disease or even the loss of someone close can be expected in the near future.

A B C D E **F** G H I J K L M N O P Q R S T U V W X Y Z

A dream in which the dreamer covers himself with an eiderdown attests to his feeling of satisfaction and happiness, comfort and warmth. On the other hand, a situation in which the eiderdown is taken away from him means that he is prone to feelings of anxiety and is afraid of his status being undermined.

February

If a person dreams about February, it is a sign of sickness and melancholy. If he dreams about a bright day in February, it means that some unexpectedly good thing will happen.

Feeble

A dream about being feeble means that the dreamer is not in a beneficial occupation, and is fraught with worries. It would be a good idea for him to effect a change in his lifestyle.

Feet

If the dreamer's own feet feature in a dream, it is a sign of despair and domination by others. If a person dreams about other people's feet, it signifies his assertiveness as regards his rights and status in life. If he dreams about washing his feet, it is a sign that he is being exploited. Sore feet in a dream are an indication of domestic strife. Red, swollen feet in a dream are a sign of a family crisis – separation, for instance – which will engender gossip.

Fence

A fence in a dream usually appears as a background to the "events" of the dream, and not as an independent factor. People frequently omit to report that they saw a fence in a dream, and only remember it in the second or third recounting of the dream.

In general, a dream about a fence attests to the fact that the dreamer is in a situation in which he has temporary problems, but he will soon overcome them, recover, and quickly resume his normal efficient functioning.

If the dreamer sees a hedge, it is a sign that he is looking for defenses against people who can invade his space and spoil things for him. For instance, if the dreamer is a scientist or is engaged in research or computer science, he may fear a situation in which a competitor arrives at the solution to a problem on which he is working before he does, or that someone else will beat him to the end of a large project on which he has spent a long time.

If a person dreams that he destroys part of a fence that surrounds him or his home, it is a good sign: The dreamer is about to solve a problem or find refuge from something that is bothering and haunting him.

A green and flowering hedge in a dream is a sign that the relationship in which the dreamer is involved is sincere and attests to true love. Having said that, there could be difficulties during the forthcoming period of time (but the dreamer must know that these difficulties are only temporary), and he must rely on the stable basis upon which his relationship with his partner is founded.

If a young woman dreams about a fence, it attests to her desire to settle down – that is, to get married or have children, and to live a full and orderly life. The fence symbolizes repressed emotions of motherhood and family that were hidden in her subconscious, and can now burst forth in full force.

Fern

A dream about ferns is usually a dream that reflects the dreamer's adventurous urge. The dreamer is a person who loves to hike, travel to distant and unfamiliar places and explore new treasures, different places and foreign cultures. Even if he could travel his whole life through, he would not quench his thirst and curiosity about the world. His passion is enormous, and if a large thicket of ferns, creepers and other jungle-like vegetation appears in the dream, it refers to exaggerated sexual lust – the kind that is insatiable. He is obsessive about sex and can engage in it from morning to night. If he did not have to take a break in order to sleep, he would be engaged in it 24 hours a day.

Ferry

A dream about a voyage in a ferry is generally a bad sign. Luck will abandon the dreamer. He should refrain from making any kind of financial deals or from opening a new business for at least six months. His patience will pay off. A voyage on a stormy river intensifies the hint given by the dream.

If the dreamer sees a voyage on a crowded ferry on calm waters, it refers to an unpleasant incident that will begin "smoothly" but will end badly. Other people will be involved. The dreamer must not take responsibility or blame himself for what happens. The only way to lessen the damage is not to sign papers, not to get further involved and not to initiate new investments, but to await developments patiently.

Festival

A dream about a festival indicates the shedding of conservative values in favor of new, superficial pleasures. Although the dreamer will never lack anything, he will not be self-supporting, either.

Fever (temperature)

A dream about a high fever warns the dreamer - a serious disease. The dream implies that the person is going through a sensitive period and must take care of himself because if he does not do so, he is liable to become ill.

A dream about a high fever also warns against taking the wrong steps for which the dreamer is liable to pay dearly. He is likely to get into embarrassing and unpleasant situations that will reflect on his future for a long time.

If a person sees a thermometer in his dream, it implies that a disease can be expected in the family. The disease will afflict one of the members of the household and will have long-term effects on the entire family.

Fiddle

A dream about a fiddle is a positive dream, since it predicts domestic harmony and joyous events.

Fiend

If a person encounters a fiend in a dream, it is an

A B C D E F G H I J K L M N O P Q R S T U V W X Y Z

indication of promiscuity, immorality and a bad reputation. If he dreams of a fiend, he is being warned against false friends. If he defeats a fiend, it means that he will thwart harmful schemes against him.

Fife

If a person hears a fife in a dream, it means that he will have to defend his honor or that of a close acquaintance. If he sees himself playing a fife in a dream, it means that his reputation is good.

Fig

A fig in a dream means unexpected surprises, generally pleasant ones. The dreamer can expect to receive good news or something that will make him happy, such as a large and meaningful gift or surprising and joyous occasions. A dream like this also hints that the dreamer can look forward to a life of ease, and he will not be troubled by any particular worries concerning his income.

The dream implies that the dreamer will have good fortune in life and will succeed in extricating himself from difficult and unpleasant situations without any particular difficulty. Good fortune will shine on him in his love life, too, as well as in everything to do with health and welfare.

Fighting

A person who dreams that he is involved in fighting is at the height of recuperating from a serious disease, or he is in the throes of external and internal struggles. It is a difficult period, which attests to the dreamer's desire to extricate himself from the situation he is in and with which he is not at all satisfied. It could be a time when he is reaching an emotional crossroads. If this is the case, the dreamer is exhausted from the struggles and battles he is experiencing in his emotional life and is ready for the necessary change. A victory in a dream indicates that the dreamer is optimistic and believes that what he is doing is correct. Failure means that the dreamer is very tired. One way or the other, he has to reach a decision as soon as possible regarding the issue at hand.

Figures

A dream about figures is a negative dream, since it implies mental anguish and misdeeds. The dreamer will suffer great losses if he is not careful of what he says and does.

Filbert

In a dream that features filberts, the dreamer can look forward to peace, domestic harmony and prosperity. If he dreams that he is eating filberts, it is a sign of good friendships for young people.

File

If a dream features a personal file that belongs only to the dreamer, it means that someone is very keen to find out about the dreamer, and wants to know private details about him. He is well advised to be on the lookout and find out who the person is and what he is up to.

If a person sees a work file in a dream, it implies that

because of a new idea the dreamer devised, he has made new enemies who are envious of him. Jealousy is at the root of their desire to take revenge, so the dreamer should watch out, pay attention to his moves and plan them meticulously.

Fillings (teeth)

A dream about fillings indicates that something of value that the dreamer has lost will be found after causing him a great deal of anguish.

Finger/s

A general dream about fingers has one meaning: the dreamer is about to be criminally charged. Even if it is traffic violation or a mild misdemeanor, he can expect to stand trial. However, if additional details of the dream are recalled, the meaning can change.

If the dreamer dreams about pains in his fingers, he can expect joy and celebration in the near future. This could be because of the birth of a child or a wedding, but it could also be because of a religious custom.

If one of the dreamer's fingers is wounded, cut and bleeding in the dream, it is a sign that the dreamer's image in anything to do with managing his assets has been tarnished. Actions he took recently engendered a downfall or a collapse, and this also damaged the dreamer's image from the professional point of view.

A dream about cutting fingers also implies a loss, quarrels, conflicts and malicious gossip that will be the dreamer's lot in the near future.

If a person dreams that he lost one of his fingers, it is a sign that he is in the process of abandonment or separation.

A beloved person is abandoning him and leaving him on his own. The dreamer's psychological state is bad, and requires that he muster great mental forces in order to keep going. If the abandonment process has not yet begun, the dream hints that it will do so very soon.

A dream in which the dreamer sees his finger broken is a sign that soon he will exchange vows at the altar. If he is married, he will soon be present at the wedding of someone close to him, and he will be there until the vows are exchanged.

A dream in which fewer than five fingers can be seen on the dreamer's hand is a sign of a good, rosy future.

If more than five fingers are seen in a dream, the dreamer will undergo a lofty spiritual experience in which he will receive messages pertaining to what happened to him in his previous incarnation. Even if the dreamer is totally skeptical and does not believe in reincarnation, the message he will receive will be completely clear.

Fingernails

A dream that features dirty fingernails implies that disgrace is imminent in the dreamer's family due to the bad behavior of the younger members. If a person sees well-groomed nails in a dream, it is an indication of cultural proclivities and achievements, as well as thrift.

Fire

A dream about fire is a warning dream: It warns the dreamer of problems and complications that are liable to arise in the near future. He will have to cope with worries that will prevent him from sleeping at night.

If an unusual kind of fire is seen burning in a dream (for instance, a pillar of fire in the sky), the opposite is true: the dreamer can expect great happiness, and a very joyful event is in the offing.

A dying fire in a dream is a sign of poverty and shortage that are about to be the dreamer's lot. It is a good idea to plan ahead for hard times and for a difficult period from the financial point of view. Things the dreamer wanted to do will have to be postponed for other, better times.

If the dreamer sees a member of his family going up in flames, the dream warns of a disease that he will contract, a disease like some kind of infection or inflammation that manifests itself in a high fever.

If the dream features an item of clothing burning and going up in flames, it implies that the dreamer will become the victim of a scandal. He will have to go through a difficult period of false accusations accompanied by shame and humiliation. The disgrace will be enormous, but eventually the dreamer will find a way out of the mess.

If a person sees a huge conflagration raging, it is a sign that he is debating about a personal problem that he cannot solve. His inability to extricate himself from the awkward situation he is in makes him feel restless and lack self-confidence and mental serenity.

If a person sees a house on fire in a dream, it is a sign that he is soon going to lose something meaningful and big in his life. The foundations of his family life may be undermined, but the dream could also refer to health problems that will interfere with his performance, or to an inability to function normally in certain areas.

If the fire in the dream is accompanied by black soot, smoke and ash, the dream is an indication of changes that are about to take place in the dreamer's life. These will happen suddenly and unexpectedly. There could be surprising changes in his place of residence, work or family. In most cases, the changes will be for the best, and will engender increased joy and happiness.

If a person sees himself going up in flames in a dream, it implies that he is bothered by something in his occupation, since he is involved in *luftgescheften* – airy matters – the kind that don't seem to him to be a proper profession, but rather depend on other people's favors.

A dream featuring glowing embers like the fire in a fireplace, for example, is a sign that the dreamer is a considered and rational person who fulfills his aspirations slowly but surely. He does not rush to accomplish his objective, often opting for indirect but sure ways that he knows will definitely lead him to his objective without "surprises" on the way.

Extinguishing a fire in a dream – especially using soil or sand – is a sign that soon the dreamer will be recompensed very substantially. This may take the form of sums of money or some other material thing. However, it may also take the form of a demonstration of love or admiration for the dreamer on the part of the people around him, or any other manifestation of affection and appreciation that is a recompense for his conduct or some other action.

Firebrand

A dream that features a firebrand is auspicious if the dreamer is neither burned nor frightened by it.

A B C D E F G H I J K L M N O P Q R S T U V W X Y Z

Fire drill

If a person dreams about a fire drill, it is a sign of strife concerning a financial matter.

Fire engine

If a person sees a fire engine in a dream, it means that certain worrying issues will be resolved satisfactorily. If he sees a fire engine breaking down in a dream, it is a sign of loss or mishap.

Fire fighter

If a person sees a fire fighter in a dream, it is a symbol of loyal friends.

Fireplace

A dream that features a fireplace symbolizes prosperity on the financial level. This is especially the case if a person sees himself sitting beside the fireplace on a winter's day, surrounded by his family, since it is a sign that he will be successful and that his financial status is about to improve significantly. Deals, investments, and hard, persistent work will bear fruit. Life will be easier in everything to do with the dreamer's financial status.

Firewood

If the dreamer's occupation concerns firewood, and he dreams about firewood, it means that he will be successful as a result of hard work.

Fireworks

If a person sees fireworks in a dream, it is a sign of good health and enjoyment.

Firing squad

The dreamer is going through a difficult time in which he has to make fateful decisions. He feels that his time is running out, exactly as if he is standing in front of a firing squad. If the dreamer is a soldier in the firing squad itself, he is well advised to try and recall the figure standing against the wall. If it is a familiar person, it is almost for sure that the dreamer feels that he is exerting unwarranted pressure on that person, whether it is in a personal or a work relationship.

Firmament

This is a bad dream. If a person sees a star-filled firmament in his dream, it means that he will have a very difficult time fulfilling his ambitions, and that his enemies will attempt to undermine him. If the dreamer sees people he knows in the firmament, it means that he will be involved in doing injurious things that will have an adverse effect on others.

Fish

There are many different interpretations for the appearance of a fish in a dream, and they depend on the way the fish appears:

Fish meant for eating – if a person sees fish that is to be eaten, such as herring or smoked salmon, in his dream, the

A B C D E F G H I J K L M N O P Q R S T U V W X Y Z

dream hints at good and pleasant things and implies that the dreamer can expect happiness as well as economic and social success in his life. His family may expand in the near future, or he may enjoy great and impressive success in business (if he is self-employed) or at work (if he is an employee). If fish dishes from his mother's or grandmother's house feature in a dream, it attests to the fact that the dreamer is very attached to his family and to things that symbolize domestic bliss in his eyes. A dream about frying fish implies that the first stirrings of an affair will become a full-blown, hot and stormy affair.

A lone fish in a dream means happiness and wealth in life. If a married person who has a son dreams this dream, it indicates that the son is very successful and is blessed with unique talents. The dream implies that the son is very clever – almost a genius. He is so brilliant that he may have the ability to invent things and be original in his field. These talents can enable him to reach serious and high positions in life, and will also bring him honor and money. The dream can also mean that the dreamer has a friend or someone particularly close to him who is operating on his behalf, even if the dreamer knows nothing about it. This mysterious "stranger" is operating for the benefit of the dreamer and is fighting his battle simply out of admiration and love for him. These actions do not depend on anything and are performed unconditionally with a full heart.

A school of fish in a dream has a similar meaning, except that several people rather than only one person are working behind the scenes for the dreamer's benefit and on his behalf. A group of people may also be operating on behalf of the dreamer in order to help him reach a certain position that he is striving to reach, such as winning an election campaign or competing for a more important position at work.

A dream about fishing in which the dreamer sees himself or his friend busy fishing is a sign that one of the people close to him is not being sincere and honest with him. Somebody is plotting against him and is weaving treachery and lies.

If a person dreams about fishing with a net, and his net is full, is a sign that he will make a great deal of money and enjoy an excellent financial situation. Investments he chooses to make will yield profits, and he will know nothing but ease and prosperity in everything to do with money matters.

In contrast, if a person dreams about a fishing rod that did not catch a single fish, or about a net that caught nothing, the opposite will happen: a financial loss and a shortage of money and the wherewithal to live. The dreamer will suffer from a poor financial situation, and he will have to be psychologically prepared for that.

Fish eggs

This dream predicts that soon the dreamer will feel that he has reached a state of rest and security! He can look forward to emotional serenity in every area of life. Evidently, the reason for this will be finding a partner or a new love that will generate greater self-confidence. The dreamer, who up till now has been going through an unpleasant phase in his life, is facing a serious change and a sharp turning point. Most of the things are about to change for the better, and, as mentioned above, the outstanding thing will be the dreamer's inner change and

A B C D E F G H I J K L M N O P Q R S T U V W X Y Z

emotional calm. Tension, anxieties and unconscious fears will all give way to a more orderly world, to more solid ground and to much greater faith in his own ability.

The appearance of fish eggs in the dream of a person who is suffering implies that soon his sufferings will cease and he can expect great relief. He will attain the emotional serenity that he has not had for some time. Tension and feelings of anger or nervousness are about to disappear. They will be replaced by feelings of calmness, consolation and compassion. This is the time for the dreamer to iron things out with people who were close to him but from whom he is now estranged, and reach compromises on topics that were matters of principle to the dreamer. (It seems that in the past he insisted on a certain path that ultimately led nowhere.)

If fish eggs appear in the dream of a person who is not suffering but rather is going through a relatively good phase in life, it means that in the forthcoming period, the dreamer will be able to change his ways of thinking without worrying whether this appears to be a loss of face. If the dreamer needs to effect changes in his life – changes that he was afraid that he would pay too dearly for –he can now do it without feeling that he has missed out on something.

Fishing / Angling

If a person dreams that he catches fish while fishing, it is a positive dream. If he does not catch any fish, it is a negative dream.

Fisherman

A dream about a fisherman signifies that the dreamer is about to enjoy a period of unprecedented prosperity.

Fishhooks

A dream about fishhooks implies that if the dreamer makes the most of the opportunities available to him, he can achieve wealth and fame.

Fish market

A dream about visiting a fish market is a happy dream. However, if the dreamer sees rotten fish in his dream, he will experience distress that will not be identifiable as such initially.

Fishnet

If a person sees a fishnet in good repair in his dream, he will have a lot of minor pleasures and profits. However, a torn fishnet in a dream means trouble and disappointment.

Fishpond

A dream about a muddy fishpond is an indication of illness. A dream about a clear fishpond teeming with fish implies prosperity and a pleasant life. If a young woman falls into a fishpond in her dream, she will be happy in love. An empty fishpond in a dream indicates that dangerous enemies of the dreamer are in the vicinity.

Fits

If a person dreams that he has fits, it means that he will fall ill and lose his job. If he sees other people having fits in a dream, it means that his social circle will be plunged into dissent.

Flag

The meaning of a dream about a flag changes according to the manner in which the flag appears in the dream, its size, color, shape, etc.

If a person dreams about a flag in the simple sense, but other than the fact that the flag was an important motif in his dream, he does not remember any particular color or the way the flag blew, it reflects his good and pleasant nature as well as his peace of mind and patience.

If a person dreams about waving a flag, the dream attests to an achievement-oriented nature, to competitiveness, and to a desire to be accorded respect by others and to be admired. The dream implies that the person must take "time out" from his occupations, work and so on, and relax. He can do this by taking a trip or a vacation, or by adopting a more laid-back lifestyle and engaging in relaxing activities such as meditation, swimming, sports, and so on.

If a flag that looks torn appears in a dream, it attests to a feeling of shame that is bothering the dreamer. He must look deep inside himself in order to find out what is causing this feeling, and do everything in his power to avoid feeling shame.

If the flag of a particular country appears in a dream, the dreamer must look for his personal link to that country and perhaps to the people who live there. It is possible that by means of the flag that appeared in the dream, they also figured in it somehow.

The colors of flags in a dream also constitute symbols, and they too have special importance:

A white flag implies that although the dreamer wanted to operate according to his emotions, logic ultimately overcame impulse, and he operated according to reason and not according to emotion.

A blue flag means that the dreamer will enjoy prosperity, wealth and financial success, even if these things come at the expense of other people or by exploiting other people.

A yellow flag implies that the dreamer is about to go through serious and far-reaching changes in his life. These will be very important for the distant future.

A green flag means prosperity and happiness in the dreamer's love life. He will succeed in attaining the thing to which he has been aspiring in everything concerning his love life, and can expect a period of success in the realm of the relationship and sex.

A red flag in a dream represents a warning against rows, disputes and plots, mainly in the field of work, and less in the social-family realm.

A black flag constitutes a broad hint at bad luck that is about to strike the dreamer. If he sees this flag in a dream, he should refrain from doing things that involve unnecessary risk. This is not the ideal time to go out on a survival hike or invest money in things that are not certain, or, in general, to get involved in unnecessary ventures. The dreamer must be cautious and responsible in the forthcoming period of time and take this warning dream suitably seriously.

Flame

Dreams about fire and flames generally symbolize something good. Rows, anger and problems at work will undergo an unexpected about-turn in a positive direction. Just as fire consumes and burns everything in its path and

A B C D E F G H I J K L M N O P Q R S T U V W X Y Z

then everything starts again, so the dreamer will find a way to grow in the scorched earth. On the other hand, a flame that causes a huge blaze and completely destroys a house or an entire city is not necessarily a good sign. This kind of dream may imply financial difficulties in the future, but not a terminal situation that cannot be resolved. Sometimes, a dream about a blaze, flames and fire indicates a desire to destroy what exists and rebuild. In such a case, the dreamer should find out what is bothering him and try to fix what can be changed.

Flash Flood

If a person sees a flash flood in a dream, it is an indication of danger on the horizon. If he overcomes a flash flood or a powerful current of water, it is an indication of overcoming obstacles and achieving success as a result of hard work.

Flax

A dream that features flax is a sign of prosperity.

Flax Spinning

A dream in which a person sees the spinning of flax is a symbol of industriousness and thrift.

Flea

A dream about one or more fleas means that danger is lurking on the threshold. It could mean that the dreamer will contract a serious disease. The source of evil might be different, however, and could come from an unexpected quarter such as an enemy or a hidden person who wants to hurt him.

This dream also attests to the fact that confusion reigns in the dreamer's life at the moment: he is not sure where he is going, what the general direction of his life is, and what the aims he should seek to accomplish are. The uncertainty in his life causes him to run into irksome everyday problems that require attention. This uses up a lot of his energy, and he is swept into a vicious circle without being able to stop and plan his steps wisely.

Fleeing / Flight

If a person dreams that he is fleeing, it implies that he is about to receive bad news about people who are far away. If anything flees from the dreamer, it means that he will be victorious in any disagreement.

Fleet

If the dreamer sees a rapidly sailing fleet in his dream, it means that there will be a positive turnabout in sluggish business.

Flies

If a person sees flies in a dream, the dream indicates daily concerns, illness, contagion and enemies.

Floating

A dream about floating in the air is very widespread. In most cases, it indicates that the dreamer should focus his efforts on one objective. If a person dreams about floating

A B C D E F G H I J K L M N O P Q R S T U V W X Y Z

in water, it implies that he will overcome apparently insurmountable obstacles. If the water in the dream is muddy, his success will not give him much joy.

Flood

A dream that features a flood, like a dream about an earthquake, attests to significant events that will lead to renewal and far-reaching changes. These will not be calamities, but rather changes that will be to the dreamer's advantage. In the forthcoming period of time, situations that could be interpreted as unpleasant may occur, but within a short time, there will be a turnabout that will lead to a drastic change.

A dream about a flood is interpreted according to its consequences: the flood is parallel to the word "danger." If a person dreams that he is swept away in a flood and cannot save himself, this is how his life looks. He is swept along in the current, has no control over it, and cannot get himself out of the situation. It is not a good idea to seek external help in order to extricate himself from this shameful situation.

In contrast, if a person dreams that he is not swept away by the flood, but rather has gotten the better of it and has pulled himself out of it safely, he can expect to encounter obstacles on his path to success. However, success will be his, and he will enjoy everything it implies. The dream also hints at a strong character: perseverance, sticking to the goal, hard work and industriousness. All these attributes will greatly advance the dreamer, and they attest to the fact that he will succeed in achieving what he wants. He will also know how to enjoy the fruits of his labor, and he will get the best and the most out of it.

Flour

If a person dreams about flour, it is a symbol of a simple but contented life. If he dreams about trading in flour, it is a sign of risky speculation.

Flower

A dream that features one or more flowers can have many meanings, and the interpretation changes according to the context of the flowers in the dream. In general, flowers in a dream symbolize security, calmness and tranquillity, which come to the fore mainly on the economic, emotional and health planes. Usually, the emphasis is on the emotional plane, and the appearance of flowers in a dream is almost always linked to warm and sincere emotions of love and affection in a couple.

If a person sees himself picking flowers in a dream, it is a hint that his friends are loyal and honest and wish him well; he can rely on them. These friends will accompany the dreamer along his path for a long way and will share enjoyable experiences as well as a common language with him. The meaning of a dream like this is eternal friendship that is worth more than its weight in gold.

Blooming flowers in a dream mean that the future holds a great deal of happiness for the dreamer – especially in anything to do with sex and marriage. The dreamer will meet a partner with whom his emotional and physical union will be unique. A union like this, which is like finding a soul mate, is not enjoyed by everyone, and the dreamer will have the privilege of tasting the sweetness of a unique experience that generates a great deal of joy.

If a young woman dreams about flowers, it is a sign that soon she will meet many men who will court her energetically, and her sexual feelings will grow. The blooming stage will end when she finds the one man who suits her from among all of her admirers.

If a person dreams about pruning flowers, he can expect large profits from a deal he made or from hard work in which he invested all of his efforts and energy. Having said that, it could also refer to financial profits from some kind of win or from a large and unexpected inheritance.

On the subject of inheritances – if the dreamer dreams about receiving flowers from overseas, it is a clear sign that he is about to inherit a large sum of money.

A dream in which flowers appear in their natural habitat – that is, not in a bouquet or in a vase, bur rather in a flower garden – it prophesies a future that is not particularly pleasant: powerful storms or other natural disasters such as an earthquake or a volcanic eruption are liable to cause the loss of a great deal of property. However, the loss will only be material, not loss of life.

If a dream features artificial flowers (made of plastic or silk, as well as dried flowers that are called "immortal" flowers), the dream attests to the fact that the forthcoming period of time will not be successful in business matters. This is not the right time to get involved in large-scale ventures, to sign contracts or to make other business commitments such as partnerships of various kinds. Such ventures will not succeed and are liable to lead to a significant monetary loss.

If a person dreams that he receives a flower from someone he loves, it means that luck is on his side and shines on him wherever he goes. Even if he did not plan his steps wisely, he will always be rescued from harmful situations in the end because of his luck.

Discarding a flower in a dream implies bad relations between the dreamer and someone close to him or the people around him in general, both in the family and at work. Anger, furious outbursts and frustration are liable to lead to rows and negative relations that will be difficult to repair.

If a dream features a single flower in a jar, it is a hint of the sexual passions that infuse the dreamer and of the stormy and surprising romantic experiences he can expect to have in the near future. The dreamer will be swept away in an unprecedented burst of emotions, and will particularly enjoy yielding to sexual temptations and physical experiences that are new to him, even though he thinks that he has already experienced everything in life.

A dream that features a flower among thorny bushes means that the dreamer will be successful in a romantic conquest despite the difficulties on the way. The opposition of some factor on his path to happiness will cause him a great deal of mental anguish, but this will give way to growing determination on the part of the dreamer to attain his wishes at almost any price. He will do anything in order to possess the person he wants, even if he has to break off relations with people who are dear to him but are a stumbling-block in his path to his big love.

If a dream features a dried flower, it is a sign that experiences and memories from the past will flood the dreamer during a certain period of time, and will not let him rest. That "going back in time" stems from nostalgia or from the desire to attain emotional status in the present like the status he enjoyed in the past. Having said that, this will be a brief and transient stage, and at a certain point the memories will stop bothering him and will disappear as suddenly as they appeared.

The colors of flowers in a dream also have special significance:

White flowers tell us that the dreamer is about to encounter minor difficulties in his everyday life. However, he will have no trouble overcoming them. The path to achieving his goal will not be easy. Some people interpret a dream with white flowers as indicating disappointment in love and romance. Great expectations in this area will lead to a bitter disappointment – to the point of a total loss of faith in love.

Yellow flowers mean that the dreamer is facing great difficulties and the path to achieving his goal will be filled with obstacles and problems.

Red flowers are a sign that one of the people close to the dreamer will die. A certain acquaintance will become ill or be involved in some kind of accident that will end very badly.

Pink flowers almost unequivocally attest to the fact that the dreamer is in love. Even if he denies his emotions and refuses to acknowledge them, the feeling that is growing inside him is that of love, and he cannot run away from it. Denial will not help in this case.

Light-colored flowers in a dream are a sign that a certain experience the dreamer is going to have will be accompanied by a feeling of sadness and melancholy. The feeling will be bad but not depressive, and he will get over it quite quickly.

Colored flowers in a dream indicate achievements in the

economic field and in anything to do with finance and money. The dreamer will enjoy the fruits of his investments or his hard work. He will achieve a high economic ranking and will have to watch out for other people's jealousy.

If a dream features flowers in a particularly splendid bouquet, it is a sign that the dreamer is a hedonistic type. He loves to lavish the best on himself, to buy himself the best-quality things and to go out to fancy places. The dreamer does not make do with anything mediocre, but always wants the best.

Flute

When the sound of a flute is heard in a dream, but the dreamer is not the one playing it, this attests to the fact that the dreamer can trust his friends. He is surrounded by people who love him and are very faithful to him, and will never betray him or wish him ill. He is well protected and in very supportive and loving surroundings. The dreamer himself, too, is a very responsible person, and his friends know that they can rely on him in time of need. They also know that they can lean on his strong, broad shoulders at any time.

If a person dreams that he himself plays the flute, the dream implies that he has great musical talent. If the dreamer knows this, and he really does play some kind of musical instrument or is involved in music, the dream serves to bolster his faith in himself.

However, if the dreamer is not involved in music, the dream serves as a hint that he has great musical talent that he should develop. He should become involved in some kind of music so that he does not miss out on the great pleasures in store for him as a result of developing his great hidden talent. He may be unaware of it, or he may be aware of it, but he is doing nothing to develop it.

Flux (diarrhea)

If a person dreams about having diarrhea or believing that he has it, it is a sign that either he or one of his family will be struck by a fatal illness. If other people have it, it means that the dreamer will fail at something because of the lack of cooperation of others.

Fly

A dream about a fly clearly refers to troubles that are bothering the dreamer in his everyday life. In most cases, when a person dreams about a fly, he manifests sharp eye movement that attest to the fact that he is "following" the flight of the pesky fly. People who have dreamed about flies generally report that in the dream, they heard the buzzing of the fly, and the fly seemed bigger than it usually was in reality. The dreamers were in the grips of "agitated" sleep rather than tranquil sleep. The dream implies that the dreamer is in a tense and possibly even an anxious situation, and that he cannot find a way out of it. The problems do not allow him any rest, and plague him throughout his waking hours and while he is asleep.

The never-ending thoughts that buzz through the dreamer's head day and night disrupt the normal course of his life. He becomes agitated during the day as well, and cannot concentrate on his routine. The people around him, who cannot help noticing it, also suffer from the dreamer's behavior. The incessant worries will only be forgotten if the dreamer decides to take the bull by the horns and tackle the problem that is haunting and bothering him. Only if he deals with it properly will he find a satisfactory solution and resume a calm, normal course of life.

A dream about a fly may also imply that the dreamer is wasting his energies on apparently stupid things that do not give him anything in return, and this is causing him a constant feeling of weakness. This mental weakness also causes him a feeling of tremendous physical weakness. The dreamer loses his characteristic vitality, and his general feeling is that of a balloon that has had the air let out of it – a feeling of being a "dishrag." A dream like this serves as a kind of "enlightening" dream and hints to the dreamer that he has to desist from the useless activity that is causing the feelings mentioned above.

Flying

If a person sees himself flying in the sky in a dream, it implies that he does not have both feet firmly planted on the ground. He is not aware of the gravity of his financial situation and is making no attempt to save money and reorganize his economic strategies. A dream about flying high indicates marital troubles. A dream about flying with black wings is a sign of keen disappointments. A dream about flying with white wings over green vegetation means success in business and love. If a woman dreams that she flies from one place to another, she will have to resist false declarations of love, and will face the danger of illness and the death of someone close to her. If a young woman dreams that she is shot at while flying, it means that her enemies are doing everything in their power to prevent her ascent up the ladder of advancement and promotion.

Flypaper

A dream about flypaper means illness and the dissolution of friendships.

Flytrap

A dream about a flytrap means that conspiracies are being schemed against the dreamer. A dream about a flytrap full of flies means that minor embarrassments will save the dreamer major ones.

Foal

If a dream features a foal, it indicates new enterprises in which the dreamer will be very successful.

Fog

If a dream features foggy conditions, it is a warning dream against being dazzled or taken in by a huge scam.

If a person dreams that he himself is standing in the fog, it is a sign that things he dreamed of achieving will actually come to pass, even though it may not be in the way he thought, but rather completely differently – in an unexpected way, full of surprises.

If a person sees fog in the distance only, the dream does not augur well. There are problems and troubles on the horizon. Problems and misunderstandings are creating a barrier between the dreamer and the people close to him – including his good friends – and they are liable to lead to a breakdown in communication and a serious short-circuit. The dreamer may find himself alone, no longer surrounded by lots of friends as he has been up till now. The price for standing up for his principles may sometimes be too high.

Some people interpret a dream that features fog as a dream that predicts failure in business, financial loss and a great deal of serious damage.

Folder / Binder

If a person dreams about a folder, it means that he needs to consult with friends or receive their help.

Following

A dream in which the dreamer is following someone means that the latter is considered "suspicious." The dreamer may not be sure of the loyalty of one of his family members or of someone with whom he is involved in business or money matters. He must examine the situation carefully in order not to hurt people who are guiltless. If there is "black and white" proof, the dreamer can stop worrying, since the moment is approaching when he will be able to turn to the person involved and present him with the incriminating evidence. If the dreamer sees himself being followed in a dream, it means that certain people around him, on whom he usually relies, are liable to betray him. This stems from a deep-seated feeling of a lack of trust, which requires that everyone involved act with extra caution.

Food

If a person sees himself eating and enjoying himself, it predicts good and happy times to come: his aspirations will be realized.

A B C D E **F** G H I J K L M N O P Q R S T U V W X Y Z

Foot

If a person sees a foot in his dream, he should interpret the dream according to the part of the foot that was most prominent in the dream:

The sole of the foot: This is a sign and a warning signal against serious medical problems. Get a medical checkup as soon as possible!

The heel: See the entry for *Heel* in this book.

The top of the foot: One of the people with whom the dreamer is on good, possibly even intimate terms is betraying him.

Only the toes, in addition to the meanings under the entry for *Toes*: The dreamer should prepare for a painful loss of money, even though it is not big.

The feeling of an irksome smell of a "smelly" foot in a dream: The dreamer suffers from sexual problems that he tries to repress.

Footprints

A footprint (whether of a bare foot or of a shoe) in a dream often implies an "Achilles heel" – the dreamer's most vulnerable point. The dreamer is suffering from someone's hostility and lust for revenge. For this reason, he must be careful of him and watch out for him.

If a dream features footprints that are incomplete because of a lot of walking, or because of pain while walking, it predicts that worries and problems are liable to be the dreamer's lot in the future. This dream does not augur well. The dreamer must brace himself for a difficult confrontation in the future.

The above interpretations are also correct for dreams in

which the footprints are heard rather than clearly seen. There may also be nothing more than an uncomfortable sensation of wearing shoes with high heels.

Forehead

If a dream features a smooth forehead, it means that the dreamer is held in high regard for his good judgment and equitable nature. If a person dreams about an ugly forehead, it means that he is discontent with himself. If the dreamer caresses the forehead of his child, it means that the latter will be praised because of his talent. If a young woman dreams about kissing her lover's forehead, it means that he will be upset at her behavior

Forest

A dream about a forest has many interpretations, and these change according to the appearance of the forest:

If a person sees himself entering a dense forest and not finding his way out, the dream implies that he can expect to encounter hardships that will be difficult for him to extricate himself from in everyday life as well.

If a dream features a forest in which the trees are taller than usual, it implies that the dreamer will get into financial difficulties and complications, such as debts and so on. The dream also hints that the dreamer is dabbling in several areas of business, and this is a sure formula for disaster, from the point of view of "not seeing the business failure for the business deals." The dreamer must concentrate on one area in which he can specialize, and in this way he will reduce his chances of failure.

If a person sees himself alone in a forest without a living

A B C D E F G H I J K L M N O P Q R S T U V W X Y Z

soul around him, the dream implies the opposite: the dreamer can anticipate extensive social activities, and he is soon likely to find himself at the center of social events – the very "life and soul of the party." He will be surrounded by friends and people who seek his company.

If the dreamer sees himself in a forest with other people, it is a warning dream that hints that he will be the victim of a scam and that he must take care and be on the lookout for people who want to harm him.

A forest in which the trees are very dense implies that the dreamer loves his friends and associates, and they care about him a lot. They will never abandon him, and will always inquire after his health and well-being. These are true friends who are near him in everyday life, and prove themselves in times of need.

If a person sees a forest catching on fire in a dream, and the fire spreads to all of the trees in the forest, it is actually a positive dream that announces the imminent arrival of good and positive news for the dreamer.

A dream in which the dreamer sees the members of his family walking through a forest and hiking in it hints that soon the dreamer's lover will leave him, or that he is about to leave his lover. Whatever the case may be, the relationship is about to end.

If a person sees a misty forest in a dream and only remembers a general view of a forest when he wakes up, he must interpret the view of the forest as an obstacle in his path to accomplishing some kind of goal.

Fork

A dream about a fork is a warning dream: the dreamer should be aware that his enemies are trying to undermine him.

A B C D E F G H I J K L M N O P Q R S T U V W X Y Z

Form

A dream about something that is ill-formed is an indication of disappointment. A beautiful form in a dream indicates good health and prosperous business.

Forsaking

If a young woman dreams about forsaking a friend or her home, it means that she will be badly let down by her lover, who will not live up to her expectations.

Fort

If a person dreams about defending a fort, it means that his honor and possessions will come under attack and this will cause him great worry. If a fort is attacked and captured in a dream, it means that the dreamer will defeat his biggest enemy and will be successful.

Fortress

If a person dreams that he is defending a fortress during some kind of battle, the dream means that that person has experienced some kind of crises that compelled him to defend his honor or status. Perhaps his wife cheated on him or the position he wanted was given to someone else. The person will dream about fortresses and castles that he defends fiercely and is even prepared to sacrifice his life for them. The results of the battle express the dreamer's determination and the extent of his belief in his powers.

Fortune

If a person squanders a fortune in a dream, it means that he will be hounded by domestic worries.

Fortune-telling

If a person dreams about having his fortune told, it means that he is bothered by some irksome matter and should be careful before agreeing to its solution.

Fountain

A fountain full of water that appears in a dream undoubtedly brings glad tidings of abundance, happiness and financial ease. A fountain into which the dreamer throws coins implies a possible win at gambling or in a lottery.

There is no doubt that this is the suitable time for the dreamer to try his luck. A person who dreams that he is jumping into a fountain can expect happiness and joy in the near future.

Fowl

A dream about fowls implies a passing concern or illness.

Fox

A fox in a dream means that the dreamer has been led astray by false and deceptive rumors that contain no element of truth. Because of these rumors, disputes and quarrels have erupted, and the dreamer has been overcome by jealousy. The dream should teach the dreamer to stick to the truth and not believe rumors that are spread by evildoers. If he feels any doubt about the rumors that have reached his ears, the dream affirms his inner feeling that they are simply empty, malicious rumors. He must stop believing them, otherwise the disputes and other upsets will continue.

If a person pursues a fox in a dream, it is a sign that the dreamer is not sufficiently focused on the reality around him and is detached and "floating." He must get back to reality, and then his ideas will have a chance of materializing. Daydreaming and living a life of detachment from reality will not help the dreamer progress.

Fraud

If a person dreams that he practices fraud, it means that he will cheat his boss, live an immoral life and lose his good reputation. If the dreamer is defrauded in the dream, it signifies that his enemies are trying in vain to destroy and discredit him. If he accuses someone of fraud in a dream, he will be offered a high position.

Freckles

If a woman dreams that she has freckles on her face, it means that her happiness will be diminished by numerous unpleasant incidents. If she sees the freckles in a mirror in a dream, it is a warning dream: she will lose her loved one to a rival.

A B C D E **F** G H I J K L M N O P Q R S T U V W X Y Z

Freezer

A dream about a freezer implies that a situation that has made the dreamer anxious is about to resolve itself.

Freight train

A dream about a freight train is a good dream, since it heralds advancement for the dreamer.

Friend

A dream in which the image of a close friend appears implies that this friend is in need of the dreamer's help and support. Evidently, this friend has gotten into trouble or has a problem from which he is finding it difficult to extricate himself. The dream hints that he needs the dreamer's help.

A dream in which the dreamer sees himself arriving for a visit at the home of a friend/s is a sign that his relations with the friend/s is about to improve and get onto the right path.

If a person sees his friend happy in a dream, it means that in the forthcoming period of time, he will feel a pleasant feeling of pride and great tranquillity.

A dream about a separation from a friend implies that painful experiences await the dreamer on the horizon. He must be prepared to suffer a blow from an unexpected quarter that will cause him sadness and depression.

A dream in which the dreamer sees himself arguing with a friend is a sign of waking up from a sweet illusion and the shattering of sweet dreams. The bitter truth will come knocking at the door and there will be no way to avoid it.

If a person sees a friend calling for help in a dream, it

means that unexpected tidings are in the offing. In contrast to what is expected, this is actually good news that will bring a breath of fresh air from distant places.

A dream in which the dreamer sees his friend embracing him actually attests to that very friend's treachery. This is a two-faced friend who speaks and behaves in a certain way and acts in another way completely. Under no circumstances must he be trusted.

If a young woman dreams that her boyfriend is making love to another woman, it means that in the near future he will make indecent proposals to engage in deviant behavior.

Meeting new friends in a dream is a sign of imminent mourning. It could be the death of a family member, but it could also be the death of a close acquaintance.

If a person dreams that his friend has betrayed him, it is a warning dream: the dreamer must protect himself from and be careful of temptations and the fraudulent conduct of a member of the opposite sex. He should be on the alert and not be ensnared by suggestions that can lead to heartbreak or a breach of trust in the other party.

Frightened

Being frightened in a dream is a symbol of transient anxieties.

Frog

A dream that features one or more frogs is always interpreted in a positive way. It is a dream that only heralds good things, and anyone who has a dream like this is really fortunate.

The dreamer will enjoy everything good in life: He will

A B C D E **F** G H I J K L M N O P Q R S T U V W X Y Z

be successful at work and at everything to do with earning money; his labors and efforts will produce nothing but good things; he will enjoy good health and a long and enjoyable life; good luck will shine on him in everything to do with his home and family; he will make a good choice of partner, and his relationship with his partner will be enjoyable and exciting throughout the years, even in old age. The emphasis of a dream that features a frog is in fact on the person's emotional life and everything to do with his spirit. Those aspects will be highly developed in his life, and will add an extra, deeper dimension to everything he does.

Frost

If a dream features frost on a dark morning, it means that the dreamer will be exiled to a faraway country, but will ultimately enjoy a peaceful life. If he sees frost sparkling in the sun, it is a sign of enjoyable things that he will abandon later in life.

Fruit

In order to interpret a dream that features a specific type fruit, the reader should consult the entry for that fruit. If a dream features many different types of fruit in a general way only, the dream has a positive meaning. In most cases, it indicates that good news and good times are in the offing. Even if the dreamer is going through a difficult and disappointing phase and cannot see the light at the end of the tunnel, the dream tells him that this phase is coming to an end and that better days are on the way.

A dream about fruit mainly predicts an era of plenty and comfort accompanied by economic ease and peace of mind in everything to do with money and finances. When the economic realm stabilizes, the dreamer will enjoy peace of mind in all the other areas of life as well.

If a person sees himself eating fruit in a dream, he can expect success in all areas of life. He will soon become aware of this, since the success will be reflected on different planes such as work, romance and health.

If a person sees other people picking fruit for him, it implies that soon he can expect to become involved in disputes and bitter conflicts with neighbors. As a result, there could be legal problems or rows that are so serious that the dreamer will consider moving out of his present home.

A dream in which the dreamer sees himself selling fruit is a warning dream reminding him that everything has a price. He will have to face the consequences of his actions and pay for pleasures and other things that gave him enjoyment, since sometimes these were at other people's expense.

Fruit seller

A dream about a fruit seller is a warning dream: the dreamer must be warned of financial loss and the inability to recoup his losses.

Fuel / Gasoline

This dream issues a warning: it indicates that the dreamer must distance himself from any situation that might lead to a confrontation with those close to him.

A B C D E F G H I J K L M N O P Q R S T U V W X Y Z

Funeral

A person who dreams that he is at a funeral need not necessarily think that some kind of death-related disaster will befall him. This kind of dreams hints at possibly spurious financial transactions. He must be more careful than usual not to be tempted by various deals that cannot be checked out thoroughly.

A dream about a funeral may also attest to the fact that the dreamer is very keen to "bury" his past, to forget everything that has happened to him in the past, especially bad things, and turn over a new leaf. A dream about a funeral serves as a hint of many new possibilities that are about to open up before the dreamer. Caution is highly recommended in such cases.

Fur

A dream about dry fur foretells wealth, good fortune and happiness. A dream about wet fur predicts success only after an about-face in the dreamer's life. If a person dreams about trading in fur, it is a sign of prosperity and a broad range of interests. If the dreamer sees himself dressed in fur, it means that he is far from being destitute or poor. If a person sees good fur in a dream, it symbolizes wealth and honor. If a woman wears expensive furs in a dream, she can look forward to marrying a clever man.

Furnace

A dream about a functioning furnace is a sign of good fortune. A malfunctioning furnace in a dream implies problems with children or employees. If a person dreams that he falls into a furnace, the dream foretells succumbing to an enemy in business.

Future

A dream about the future symbolizes thrift and eschewing extravagance.

G

Gaiety

If the dreamer sees himself at a party or in any other situation in which he is laughing and happy the whole time, it refers to an event in which he will participate in the near future, such as the wedding of a close family member, a big party at work or an unexpected invitation that will take the dreamer to a new place. At this event, the dreamer will meet someone who will open the door to huge success, probably in the financial realm.

Gaining weight

A dream about gaining weight foretells bad times for the dreamer in the near future.

Gaiters

If a dream features gaiters, it predicts amicable rivalries and fun.

Gale

If a person dreams that he is caught in a gale, it means business losses and problems for working people.

Galloping

In most cases, galloping in a dream attests to success or to a track that leads directly to success. Generally, the dreamer sees himself galloping on a horse, but not always. In any case, a dream like this predicts rapid success, without obstacles or delays. The dreamer will see the fruits of his success almost immediately and will be spared the worries that are usually the lot of anyone who wants to attain something and encounters difficulties on the path to success. The achievements will come immediately, almost on a silver platter.

Gallows

If a person sees a friend on the verge of being hanged on the gallows, it means that he must cope with terrible emergencies with a cool head, or catastrophe will follow. If the dreamer himself is on a gallows, he can rest assured that he has false friends. If a person dreams about rescuing someone else from the gallows, he will gain possessions. If the dreamer hangs his enemy in his dream, it means that he will be successful in everything.

Gambling

A general dream about gambling refers to an unfair situation the dreamer has experienced. The inappropriate or insincere behavior of friends caused the dreamer to feel shame, as if they derided him and betrayed his trust in them. This feeling is liable to engender a situation of loss, mainly in material matters. The dreamer may be about to lose money or other assets. In most cases, it is not a spiritual loss.

If a person dreams about gambling with dice, the dream implies that he will be lucky in business, in work and on the family and conjugal level. He can expect to go through a good phase, and he must be calm and rely on luck, not just on himself. He must let go of his habit of thinking a great deal about a step he is taking and let things flow and happen by themselves.

A dream about a gambling table, on the other hand, implies that every investment or gamble the dreamer is about to make is liable to end in disappointment, so he is well advised to examine his current financial situation minutely before rushing to get into a venture.

A dream in which the dreamer sees himself active in a lottery hints at a loss in business: a deal that was "cooked up" recently may not work out, but the reference is only to business- or commerce-related matters, and not to other areas of life.

Game

A dream about a game prophesies prosperity for the dreamer. He will abound with ideas that will lead to financial well-being for him and his entire family.

If a person dreams that he is participating in a competitive game, he can expect to receive good and happy news about one of the people close or particularly dear to him.

If the dreamer only watches a game passively and does not participate in it, it means that he is jealous of one of his friends, and he is ashamed of this and is trying to repress it. Jealousy can be dangerous. He should do everything in order to expunge this emotion. If not, things are liable to turn out badly.

If a person plays backgammon in a dream, he can expect victory in a certain field, possibly at work.

If a person dreams that he stands dominoes next to each other in such a way that the lightest touch can bring down the entire row, the dream implies that he should be cautious in a particular investment that is in the offing. It is liable to turn out to be a scam, or lead to a painful downfall.

A dream about games of chance attests to the fact that the dreamer is in the habit of taking risks. It also warns of fraud that is being perpetrated in a calculated and sophisticated manner against him. He must be doubly careful in whatever he does.

Game (hunting)

Any dream about hunting game means success, but as a result of selfishness. If the dreamer hunts and does not kill any game in his dream, it implies mismanagement and loss in business.

Gang

A person who dreams about belonging to a gang is actually expressing a deep need to belong. In many cases, dreams of this type occur after moving to a new area. The dream expresses the dreamer's worries about his social standing. If a violent brawl develops with members of a gang, the dreamer is already in the process of distancing himself socially. He is afraid of intimacy and of getting into relationships with commitment. Belonging to a gang gives him a kind of protection against one-on-one personal relations.

A B C D E F **G** H I J K L M N O P Q R S T U V W X Y Z

Gangrene

If the dreamer sees anyone with gangrene in a dream, it predicts the death of a parent or close relative.

Garbage

If a person sees heaps of garbage in a dream, it is a sign of bad business and social scandal.

Garbage can

A dream that features a garbage can does not augur well. It attests to the fact that the dreamer is surrounded by deceitful and fraudulent people who want to harm him and are plotting against him. They are devising tricks and trying to trip him up.

However, if the trick is not too sharp or clever, the dreamer will succeed in overcoming the enemies who want to hurt him and will find his way out of the mess. In spite of the obstacles they place in his path, he will be able to overcome everything and be calm, quiet, self-assured and intrepid.

Garden (small)

If a dream features a garden in front of the house, it means that the dreamer's marriage will be fruitful and successful, and the dreamer will be happy with his spouse.

If the garden in the dream is well cared for, the dream hints at a win of a sum of money that is not large, but is significant for the dreamer. It could be a win in a lottery or some kind of bet.

A garden that is neglected in the dream implies that the

dreamer must use his intellect in a cool and considered way in everything to do with money matters. He must neutralize his emotions and gut feelings and operate only according to existing data, calculations and plain logic. If the dreamer takes decisions in which emotions are involved, he will not succeed in the ventures he is facing.

Garden (large)

A large, flowering garden in a dream symbolizes peace of mind, tranquillity, calmness, prosperity and growth. The dreamer will enjoy all of these things if his life, and will appreciate his serene existence.

If a vegetable garden appears in a dream, there is cause for concern. The dreamer must be alert to any change that may endanger him or his family, or cause him to fail. He must take extreme precautions to avoid a bitter disappointment that he is liable to suffer in the future.

Gargoyle

If a person dreams about a gargoyle, it indicates that he will have a falling out with a close friend. If a gargoyle comes to life in a dream, it means that sadness and mishaps are in the offing.

Garlic

A dream that features garlic is interpreted according to the dreamer's taste: If he likes garlic, it is a positive dream predicting success. If he is revolted by garlic, it portends bad times.

A
B
C
D
E
F
G
H
I
J
K
L
M
N
O
P
Q
R
S
T
U
V
W
X
Y
Z

Garret

If a person dreams about climbing up to a garret, it means that he occupies himself with theories and leaves others to battle with the bitter realities of life. If a poor person dreams about a garret, it means that his situation will become easier.

Garter

If a lover dreams that he finds his sweetheart's garter, he will soon lose her to a rival. If a woman loses her garter in a dream, it means that her lover is jealous. If a married man dreams about a garter, it means that his secret affairs will soon be disclosed to his wife.

Gas

Dreaming about gas is a sign that the dreamer will misjudge others and will suffer pangs of conscience for it. Asphyxiation by gas means that the dreamer's extravagant behavior will lead to trouble. Extinguishing gas means destroying one's own happiness.

Gasoline

A dream about gasoline is a warning dream about getting embroiled with people who are dear to the dreamer. Generally, this means his family members. He is advised not to get into conflicts, disputes and crises with the people close to him. Futile clashes within the family will only lead to bad relations that are liable to leave their mark for many years. The dream implies that it is worthwhile refraining from futile arguments that do not serve anyone, as well as from anything that is liable to undermine relations with family members or with the people who are closest to the dreamer. The dreamer has to display forbearance, learn to curb his impulses and try to refrain from conflicts that he will later regret.

Gate

An open gate in a dream is a sign that there are new opportunities in the dreamer's path, and he should take advantage of them.

A closed gate in a dream is a sign of social problems that are the dreamer's lot, and these constitute an obstacle to his fitting into society. He does not feel that he is a part of a circle of friends; on the contrary – he always feels rejected and unpopular. The lack of acceptance of the dreamer on the part of the people around him is a result of his behavior, and he has the power to change things. A closed gate in a dream also refers to the dreamer's bad mental condition, which could be characterized by depression or emotional detachment. At the moment, there is no solution to this, but as time goes by, the gate will open.

If a person sees a specially designed gate or a particularly beautiful gate in a dream, it implies that he is in love, or that he is experiencing a powerful sexual attraction to a member of the opposite sex.

A broken gate in a dream attests to the obstacles in the dreamer's path toward advancement in the business realm. Delays and hitches are preventing the dreamer from advancing, and this is frustrating him. He is prevented from advancing to a higher station, but if he acts with determination and elbows his way, he will succeed in attaining what he wants.

A B C D E F G H I J K L M N O P Q R S T U V W X Y Z

If a person sees himself swinging on a gate in a dream, it is a sign that he loves to relax and do nothing. He is not a person who pursues achievements, and a career is of no interest to him. The more peace and quiet he gets in life, the more he enjoys it.

If a person sees himself walking through a gate, he can expect to be astonished by surprising news. He will receive news that will astound him and cause him to think again about his path in life. The surprising news may be for the best, and his life may be about to take a surprising positive turn.

If a person sees a gate closing in a dream, it means that he can expect to clinch a special deal at work with a handshake and with a feeling that success is on the doorstep.

A gate that is locked with a chain is a sign that the dreamer feels safe in his life. Nothing undermines the stability and the feeling of security that envelops him, even if it sometimes seems as if things are going out of control all around. He is always sure that he and his family are safe and nothing threatens them.

Gauze

A dream about gauze symbolizes uncertain luck. For a lover to see his sweetheart dressed in semitransparent gauze in a dream, it means that he can influence her positively.

Gavel

If a person dreams about a gavel, it means that he will have to do some futile but quite pleasant task. If a gavel is used in a dream, it means that the dreamer's friends will patronize him.

Gazelle

The appearance of a gazelle in a dream implies that the dreamer chooses to live his life alone rather than in a family setting. The gazelle symbolizes the person who lives alone, and hints at disputes and quarrels in the family, or at disagreements that are not easily settled.

If a person sees a gazelle being hunted in a dream, the dream does not augur well, and hints at the pain and sorrow that will be the dreamer's lot. These could stem from a bitter failure that the dreamer will bring on himself.

A dream that features a fleeing gazelle is a sign that the dreamer is popular and that he is about to acquire new friends on whom he can rely. The dreamer is a congenial person who likes the company of people and enjoys making new friends. He is an open and easy-going person who does not engage in malicious gossip and is always willing to come to his friends and offer to help them. This is also the reason why the people around him really and truly love him.

If a person dreams about killing a gazelle (not necessarily while hunting), it is a warning dream that implies that a serious disaster is about to take place. It prepares the dreamer psychologically for the unexpected event that will bring disorder and chaos in its wake.

Gemstones

In general, a dream about gemstones attests to the fact that the dreamer is about to receive good tidings. This dream portends happiness alongside financial prosperity.

A B C D E F **G** H I J K L M N O P Q R S T U V W X Y Z

If the gemstones in the dream are cracked, broken or distorted, it is a warning dream. A complex relationship is about to end – whether it is a relationship between lovers, between spouses or between close friends. The circumstances may change, the wheel may switch direction several times, and the winds may blow in different directions, but one thing is for sure: the end. Fate has decided that this relationship is over, and you can stand on your head, try to kiss and make up, and so on, but it won't help; it's finished. Period.

A dream about gemstones that were brought in for repair is a sign that there is a chance of reconciliation between lovers, married couples, friends or acquaintances who quarreled.

A dream about a gemstone set in a brooch that adorns an item of clothing implies that the dreamer is going through a period of sadness and depression that dominate his life. He is dissatisfied with his situation, and no matter how much he scrutinizes it and examines himself, things always seem futile to him. The lack of hope and anticipation in the dreamer's life causes him severe distress, and he is sometimes even liable to suffer from cardiac pains or other dangerous physical conditions.

If a person dreams that he has lost precious stones that were in his possession, the dream implies a feeling of a lack of luck. The dreamer feels as if he is liable to lose what he has as well, and he cannot get rid of this feeling.

A dream about gemstones set in expensive jewelry is a good sign for the future. The future will be rosy, and the dreamer can expect pleasant surprises, happy occasions and exciting events.

A dream in which the dreamer sees himself purchasing

precious stones is a sign that he can expect good deals and handsome profits as a result of astute business moves. From the economic point of view, prosperity and wealth are foretold, and the profits will be far greater than he ever dreamed of.

Genitals

If a person dreams about malformed or diseased genitals (male or female), it means that he will be tempted into an illicit and scandalous liaison, which will be destructive. If he dreams that he exposes his genitals, it means that he is about to lose his good reputation.

Geography

A dream about geography means that the dreamer will travel far and wide.

Germ

In a dream like this, thoughts of germs occur, or there is talk about them. Generally, it is a matter of a health problem that the dreamer is ignoring even though he knows it exists, and it will end up by erupting one of these days. The subconscious raises the problem to the surface in order to warn the dreamer that he must relate to his condition and not neglect the disease or the health problem that is simmering inside him.

A dream featuring germs also attests to the dreamer's character: this could also be a manifestation of hypochondria that the dreamer is not always prepared to acknowledge. His fear of diseases and their cures is so great that it does not leave the dreamer alone.

A B C D E F **G** H I J K L M N O P Q R S T U V W X Y Z

Getting lost

A dream in which the dreamer sees himself getting lost (in the forest, in the streets of the city or in a labyrinth) attests to the feelings of frustration and insecurity the dreamer suffers from.

A dream in which the dreamer sees someone he knows getting lost implies that the relationship between the dreamer and this person conceals a big secret.

A dream in which the dreamer sees someone he does not know getting lost implies that the dreamer needs professional help in order to deal with his lack of self-confidence.

A dream in which the dreamer sees himself rescuing someone who has gotten lost hints that soon the dreamer will find a partner who will help him solve his self-confidence problem.

Ghost

If a dream features the appearance of a ghost and a conversation with it, it indicates that the dreamer has difficulty in coping with someone's death. A dream like this is also indicative of the desire to make contact with the world beyond.

Giant

If a person dreams that he is being pursued by a giant, the dream attests to the fact that he is in some kind of danger. People might be getting fired at work. It is necessary for him to cut down on expenses and brace himself for a period of belt-tightening.

On the other hand, if a person dreams that he himself is a giant, it means that he is going through a phase in which he feels power and control over what is happening to him in life. Even so, he must display sensitivity and refrain from stepping on other people, literally, on his way to the top.

Gift

The meaning of a dream about a gift varies according to the content of the dream.

If a person receives a gift from a person he loves in a dream, he can expect success and good luck in everything he does.

If the dreamer receives a gift from a person he knows, not necessarily someone he loves, it is a sign that he is not advised to rely on the giver of the gift and trust in him. If he relies on him, he is liable to fall into a trap. Even if the person offers the dreamer advice, he should ignore it. It should be assumed that this person is a swindler, and it is advisable to avoid getting into any kind of conflict with him. He may be plotting against the dreamer and may intend to deceive him, so the dreamer should stay away from him.

If a person dreams that he receives several gifts, he should relate to the giver with healthy suspicion. He should not place his trust in him until he is absolutely sure of his intentions.

A dream about giving a gift is a sign of bad luck.

Giving gifts to people who are close and familiar to the dreamer is a sign of hope. Even if the present time is uncertain, and things are vague and even depressing, the future holds good things. Things will work out well, and the dreamer will have a rosy future and a lot more than he does now.

If the dreamer receives a gift from an important person in a dream, the dream implies that the people around the dreamer accord him a great deal of respect, appreciate his work and, in a certain way, admire him and his personality and talents.

If the dreamer gets a gift from his son, it is a sign that the dreamer can expect a whole heap of trouble, and will have to deal with difficult things that he did not expect and never dreamed he would have to face.

If the dreamer gets a gift from his daughter, it is a sign of objections. The dreamer is about to encounter a wall of resistance. No matter what he says or wants to achieve, he will encounter objections around him. The lack of cooperation will ultimately cause him to pay dearly.

If a man dreams that he receives a gift from a woman, it is a sign that soon a true, warm and sincere relationship with a woman will begin, and will become a great friendship. It may not necessarily be a romantic or erotic relationship. The dream hints at a particularly fruitful friendship, with the emphasis on fidelity and great personal integrity.

If a woman dreams that she receives a gift from a man, she can soon expect a drastic change in her life. This change will be expressed on several levels, and is actually liable to cause her to change her way of life. This cannot be changed, since it is something dictated by fate, predestined, so that any attempt to divert things to another track is doomed to failure in advance.

Many dreams feature rings as presents. In most cases, a dream like this attests to a meeting with a rich person, whether it is with the dreamer's future partner who is rich or a very rich person, and this meeting will exert an influence on the dreamer's life.

Gig

If a person dreams about traveling in a gig, it means that he will have to forgo a nice trip because of an unwelcome guest. Illness is also predicted.

Giraffe

A giraffe in a dream is a warning sign for the dreamer: life and death are in the power of the tongue. The dreamer must be very cautious in whatever steps he takes and calculate them carefully and wisely. He must take care not to inadvertently blurt out something that is quite inappropriate.

A giraffe also warns of the dreamer's unrestrained urge to spread gossip or slander about other people. He should think twice before he speaks about his associates, and should be particularly careful of revealing secrets that were confided to him by other people who trusted him blindly.

If a man dreams about a giraffe, the dream has an additional meaning: He may be suffering from impotence or from other problems linked to his sexual performance. If a married man has this dream, his defective performance is affecting his relations with his wife, and the dream raises the problem and asks for a solution. If a married man sees a giraffe in a dream and does not believe that there his sexual performance is deficient in any way – even though it is quite clear and obvious to him that his relations with his wife are flawed – the dream opens his eyes and indicates that the source of the flaws in their relationship is indeed sexual, even if he refuses to notice or acknowledge it. The moment he sifts through his actions and his sexual conduct, he will discover that there is a problem. A simple conversation with his wife will explain how he has to improve his performance or his general attitude toward sex.

Girdle

If a person sees a tight girdle in a dream, it means that people with hidden agendas will influence him. If he sees a velvet or jewel-studded girdle, it means that wealth is more important to him than honor. If a woman dreams about a girdle, it is a sign of respect.

Girl

A dream about a bright, healthy girl is a sign of good luck and domestic happiness. A dream about a thin, pale girl, on the other hand, implies that there is a sick person in the family, as well as unpleasantness.

Giving birth (animal)

A dream about an animal giving birth to its young attests to the power of the dreamer in his struggle against his opponents. Even if he has enemies, even if there are people who are conspiring against him or sabotaging him, he will succeed in overcoming these obstacles and will emerge victorious from the battle. The dreamer's strengths and powers will be revealed in all their glory in the near future, and will teach the dreamer about his powers, since he himself is not aware of their existence. Those "forces of darkness" that are operating against him are doing so in secret, and even if their activities are not visible at the moment and the dreamer has no idea that he has any enemies, he will eventually become aware of it. He must not be surprised, because, as mentioned above, he will find great coping powers within himself, and these will enable him to succeed and accomplish his goals despite the obstacles that will be placed in his path in the future.

Glass

If a person sees himself peering through glass in a dream, the dream implies that he can expect problems, since he does not know how to plan his actions or see several steps ahcad. His inability to anticipate what is going to happen in the future leaves him confused and troubled by problems that could be solved if he were to direct his attention toward what is about to happen.

A dream about breaking glass attests to the dreamer's frustrations, usually because of a lack of luck. Even though he knows how to channel his actions after devoting thought to them and planning every step, success evades him. This is because of bad luck and not because of the things he did.

A dream in which the dreamer sees a window being broken implies trouble in the offing. The dream warns of extreme complications, since the troubles are inevitable. However, by preparing himself psychologically for them, the dreamer can effect changes, and the unavoidable bad luck will affect him in a far more moderate way.

If a person dreams about cleaning a window, the happiness and tranquillity he normally enjoys are in jeopardy.

A B C D E F **G** H I J K L M N O P Q R S T U V W X Y Z

A B C D E F **G** H I J K L M N O P Q R S T U V W X Y Z

Glass (for drinking)

If a person dreams about drinking from a glass in an unfamiliar place, he is liable to find himself in an unpleasant and even dangerous situation. Raising a glass of wine at home predicts a happy event. A dirty glass means success in business. A broken glass means danger.

A person who dreams that he has been injured by a broken glass must take precautionary measures. Sometimes a dream like this can indicate the break-up of a business partnership. A new examination will help prevent disappointments in the future.

Glass blower

A dream that features a drinking glass means that the dreamer will effect a cosmetic change in his business that will not be of any help to him.

Glass house

A dream about a glass house symbolizes the devastating consequences of flattery. If a young woman dreams about living in a glass house, it is a warning dream: she is warned of trouble and losing her good reputation.

Gleaning

If a person sees gleaners busy in a dream, it is a sign of prosperity for him and of abundant crops for the farmer. If the dreamer is involved in gleaning, he will come into possession of an estate that he will have to fight for.

Gloom

A dream about gloom is a warning of imminent loss and bad luck.

Glory

If a dream features glory, it is a sign that the dreamer has reached the summit of his achievements and from here on, it is only downhill.

Gloves

If a person loses a pair of gloves in a dream, it is a sign that he is about to suffer a loss in a bad financial deal. He must weigh up his business moves with extreme caution, especially if a large financial transaction is involved. A person who dreams about finding gloves can expect to have a row with a close friend and possibly even a total break-up. Losing one glove, especially if this occurs in a woman's dream, implies the possibility of a wedding.

Glue

A dream about glue symbolizes pampering, high financial standing, great personal security and senior status in anything to do with business. In most cases, the dream encourages what the person knows in reality or experiences in his everyday life. If the dreamer does not feel like this in reality, the dream refers to his sub-conscious. Despite the various feelings the dreamer experiences in his everyday life, deep down inside he is a person with strong self-confidence who knows how to value himself and is well aware of the superior abilities with which he is blessed. The dream serves to fortify him against reality as well and remind him that he can actually rely on himself. In short, he recognizes his self-worth.

If a person dreams that he uses glue in order to mend something, it is a warning dream. The dream serves to warn the dreamer of complications in the financial realm. Although he may have thought about his steps carefully, does not rush into ventures or gambles and is responsible, not always does everything go the way we plan, and now he has to prepare himself for a difficult situation in which he will have to cope with additional difficulties.

Goat

A goat in a dream heralds prosperity in the financial realm. In general, it implies that the dreamer will soon come into a large sum of money that will be paid to him as remuneration for a deed or work he did. The payment will be much bigger than the dreamer expected, and this will be a nice surprise. It is also possible that the dreamer will be given some kind of grant – not necessarily for things he did, but as a gesture or token of appreciation for his conduct.

The appearance of a goat in a dream also symbolizes virility, and therefore if the goat appears in a woman's dream, its appearance should be linked to a lover or to a man she desires. If the goat appears in a man's dream, it attests to the amount of importance he ascribes to his virility – according to the context of the general topic of the dream – and it should be interpreted in that way.

Goblet

If a person dreams about drinking from a silver goblet, it

predicts bad business results. If he dreams about ornate goblets, it implies that he will receive favors and good things from strangers.

God

In a dream, the concept of God can appear not only in the form of a defined figure, but also as a feeling (a feeling of "knowing" or communication regarding anything linked to divinity, a feeling of touching divinity, and so on), where the figure of God is not actually "seen."

In general, people who dream about God are people who believe in God – but this is not always the case. Sworn atheists and total non-believers also dream about God.

A dream in which the dreamer sends a prayer of supplication to God implies that the dreamer will soon see the fruits of his toil – happiness and prosperity, mainly in the economic sphere.

If a person dreams that he is involved in divine labor as a form of ritual worship – offering sacrifices, special prayers, pilgrimages, and so on – the dream implies that a disease is in the offing, and it warns against the collapse of the body's immune system. The dreamer is about to suffer from physical debility, and he will be overcome by great fatigue. Those are the symptoms of a disease that is connected with the collapse of the immune system, and, besides the need to treat the disease itself, the body is warning of its inability to cope with everyday tasks. In most cases, total rest is expected to help overcome the disease. As soon as the first symptoms appear, it is advisable for the dreamer to relate to his state of health with due seriousness and not go on with his regular activities. He should take time off to rest.

A B C D E F **G** H I J K L M N O P Q R S T U V W X Y Z

If a person dreams that he hears God speaking to him, it means that he is about to undergo a unique experience that will bring sublime happiness and tremendous pleasure. It will be physical and mental pleasure at the same time, a kind of joining of body and soul and a feeling of elation at the highest level. This physical-spiritual experience will be very significant in the dreamer's life, and will change his life and his world-view for the next three years.

A dream in which the dreamer feels as if God has wrapped His arms around him or as if he is enveloped in something godly means that a prayer offered by the dreamer will not be answered. Despite his supplications and repeated requests, and although he feels that he has done everything to ensure the achievement of the goal he is praying for, his wish will not come true, and his prayer will not be answered.

If a person sees God face to face in his dream, the dream foretells happiness and wealth. His home will be filled with joy, and even if he does not become a tycoon or a property owner, this will not stop him from being rich in his own eyes. He will always be happy and content, and radiate light onto the people around him. People will want to be in his company and will enjoy his incorrigible optimism.

If the dreamer feels that God is giving him what he desired in the dream, it is a prophetic dream. Accordingly, the person will have the good fortune to realize his aspirations and his goals in life. The dreamer is an ambitious person, and even if the path toward the accomplishment of the goals he set himself is not easy, he will ultimately see himself accomplishing everything he set his heart on.

Goggles

A dream that features goggles is a warning dream: the dreamer must not be conned into lending money to companions of dubious repute.

Gold

The interpretation of a dream about gold changes in accordance with the circumstances in which it appears in a dream. In most cases, gold in a dream symbolizes wealth and success – wealth from both the material and spiritual points of view.

If a person finds gold in his dream, it is a sign that he can soon expect to come into an inheritance from a source that is not yet entirely clear to him. This may result from the death of someone close to him; however, the inheritance may come from an unexpected source, such as a solitary neighbor or distant acquaintance who dies and leaves a great deal of property, some of which will be bequeathed to the dreamer. Finding gold in a dream also implies that the dreamer is a very ambitious and achievement-oriented person who generally accomplishes his goals. The dream is a sign that he will go far and will be accorded respect and esteem, wealth and fame. The dreamer will be held in high esteem because of his achievements and he may even become famous in his field of occupation since he persists and sticks to his goal and is very thorough in everything he does.

In contrast, if a person dreams of losing gold, the dream implies a loss of money and the onset of a difficult financial era. He is about to experience a serious financial situation, but the dream indicates a loss of money and not of other assets, such as real estate or the like. A dream like this also attests to the dreamer's conceited nature, and hints that he neglects important issues that could change his fate and affect his life. Eventually, he is liable to regret this bitterly.

If a person dreams about working with gold (making jewelry, gold-mining, and so on), his luck is about to change for the worse. Nothing will succeed; everything will look hopeless and terrible. Even if he tries to improve his situation, it will not help, since this has been dictated from above. He must bend with the storm and let it pass over him. He should not try to change his luck, since there is no chance that he will succeed in doing so.

A dream that features fake gold, and the dreamer knows that the gold he sees is fake and not real, is a dream that attests to the fact that the dreamer can expect imaginary wealth. On the surface, it may seem as if he is as rich as a king, but everything is imaginary and fake. He himself knows the truth, but enjoys using his fake wealth to wield his power. When the bubble bursts, he will find himself in a truly ridiculous situation. He should pay attention to the hints contained in the dream.

If a person dreams about involvement with gold in a business context, it is a sign that he is high-spirited and full of vitality and loves to create things, initiate moves and always be in action. His brain does not rest for a moment, and he always strives to perfect his work methods. Just as his brain is never inactive, nor is his body. He is constantly racing around and loves being in perpetual motion. He does not let up for a moment, and for this reason he can expect a brilliant future in anything he does.

A dream that features the color gold rather than the actual metal is a warning dream. The dreamer must refrain from doing business in the street, on dark corners, and in spurious places. Anything that smacks of criminal activities will be disastrous for the dreamer. He must follow legal and official paths and eschew shortcuts, otherwise the results will be catastrophic.

If a person dreams that an item of jewelry or some other object he owns is gold-plated, he can expect to be promoted in his workplace or to be given praise, honor or appreciation by his superiors.

A dream that features throwing gold away is a dream that foretells days of profound sorrow and pain.

A dream in which a person sees himself simply touching gold hints at a possibility of finding a new hobby or another field of occupation that the dreamer has never tried before. The dream is about to reveal a whole world that is completely new and marvelous to the dreamer, and he will be swept into it and totally caught up in it.

Goldfish

If a person dreams about a goldfish, it predicts that he will embark on exciting adventures and enjoy a good marriage. If however, he sees dead goldfish in his dream, it is a sign of bitter disappointments and of heavy burdens.

Gold leaf

If a dream features gold leaf, it is an omen of a successful future.

Golf

If a person dreams about golf, it indicates pleasant

A B C D E F **G** H I J K L M N O P Q R S T U V W X Y Z

daydreaming and wishing. If anything bad happens in golf in a dream, the dreamer can expect to be humiliated by the thoughtlessness of another.

Gong

If a dream features a gong, it is a false alarm of illness or a sign of an extremely annoying loss.

Goose

A dream about a goose implies that the dreamer can expect trouble from enemies of some kind of whom he is as yet unaware. The dream is a warning about them as well as about some kind of serious failure or disappointment that is in the offing. The dreamer may be expecting to hear news concerning something on which he has pinned his hopes. He must brace himself for the possibility that the things he prayed for and anticipated probably won't materialize. The dream is a kind of sign for him, warning him of the possibility.

On the other hand, a dream about a goose can also be positive, implying the dreamer's success in everything connected with intelligence and wisdom. Success may be awaiting him in the workplace, on a certain exam, or in anything else in which he is required to prove his intelligence. The next year also contains success in the material realm. The dreamer will become rich or find the right path from the economic point of view. Joy and happiness in the personal realm will follow hard on the heels of wealth and material ease.

If a person sees several geese in a dream, he will be successful in the social sphere. He will soon be popular with those around him, and people will seek him out. If he was not too popular up till now, the situation is about to change, and soon he will be invited to social events, where he will be the life and soul of the party.

(See the entry for *Duck* and the comment at the end of the definition.)

Gooseberries

A dream about picking gooseberries is a sign of improvement after domestic or business-related problems. The dreamer is warned not to eat green gooseberries which will cause bad things to happen. Seeing gooseberries in a dream means that the dreamer will get away with not doing some repulsive task.

Gossip

If a person dreams that he participates in low gossip, he will suffer the embarrassing consequences of having gone overboard in his confidences to the wrong person. If he dreams about being the object of gossip, however, it is a sign of unexpected good things in the offing.

Gout

A dream of suffering from gout means that the dreamer will be driven to distraction by the stupidity of some relative, and will also lose money because of the same person.

Grain

A dream about grain is an excellent dream, since it predicts wealth and happiness.

Grandparents

If a person dreams about a conversation with his own grandparents, it is indicative of almost insurmountable difficulties, but the dreamer will ultimately overcome them by taking good advice.

Grapefruit

A dream about a grapefruit is linked to the dreamer's state of health. A grapefruit in a dream may be perceived as a symbol of health because of the age-old "propaganda" that convinces people that "grapefruit = health."

A grapefruit on a tree in a dream symbolizes health and longevity for the dreamer.

If a person eats a grapefruit in a dream, it attests to the fact that he does not feel well, and that he is worried about health problems. Something connected to his health is bothering him, and he is not calm.

If a person sees himself squeezing a grapefruit in a dream, it is a sign that various people around him are not healthy. Their condition may also affect the dreamer somehow, and if he suspects that something is not right with someone around him, he must say something about it to that person. He may be adversely affected by their condition, since there could be situations in which, for some reason that is linked to poor health, they are liable to behave in a way that will cause the dreamer harm. However, they may also be coming down with a disease, and the dreamer is liable to catch it from them and become ill.

If a person sees other people squeezing grapefruit in a dream, it is a dream that augurs ill: the funeral of one of his friends is in the offing.

A dream featuring a rotten grapefruit is a sign that someone close to the dreamer is betraying his trust. The dreamer has placed his trust in unreliable people who say terrible things about him.

If a dream features several grapefruit that are unblemished and are particularly beautiful, it predicts that a new love is on the threshold. It will be a sweeping and serious love that may even lead to marriage.

A segment of grapefruit in a dream implies that the dreamer or someone close to him is suffering from a feeling of jealousy. This terrible feeling is liable to lead to potent rivalry that will culminate in the breakup of a long-term friendship.

If a person dreams about a grapefruit as a dessert after a meal, the dream predicts bad things regarding family matters, and particularly attests to the fact that rows and quarrels can be expected among the members of the family. Tension will run high in the home, and rows will become everyday occurrences.

Grapes

A dream that features grapes implies that the dreamer pursues material things and ascribes great importance to anything that represents money. This is especially true of big grapes in a dream. The bigger the grapes, the more it is a sign that the dreamer tends to pursue mammon and luxuries.

White grapes in a dream mean are a sign that the dreamer is in a better position than his enemies or those who wish him ill; he has the upper hand. It will not be easy to subdue him and cause him to fall.

A B C D E F **G** H I J K L M N O P Q R S T U V W X Y Z

Dark grapes in a dream are a sign that the dreamer is plagued by problems concerning his income. He may be in difficulties in the business he runs or at work, if he is an employee. Some kind of threat in the workplace constitutes a danger to his continued career there, and these fears are expressed in the dream.

If a dream features grapes in the form of bunches on the grapevine, it means that the dreamer can expect a long and full life. He will manage to have many experiences during his life and to "taste" much of what life has to offer. He is a person with a lust for life who does not let an adventure or any kind of experience pass him by.

If a person sees grapes being eaten by someone or by children, the dream serves as a sign that he will suffer from many worries and will be bothered by many things that will give him no peace. However, having said that, the dreamer will be in such a position that he will be able to influence his surroundings and be the one who makes the decisions and calls the tune. He is the one whose opinion will be the decisive one – he will have the last word.

If the dreamer sees himself feeding grapes to his partner in a dream, it predicts that he will soon be involved in a romantic liaison. If the dreamer is already involved in such a liaison, the dream predicts that the relationship will be successful, honest, warm and filled with mutual love.

Purchasing grapes in a dream is a warning that the dreamer is liable to fall victim to a scam, particularly in the realm of business, and this is liable to land him in serious financial problems.

The sale of grapes in a dream is a sign that the dreamer will not know a lack of anything, and will enjoy economic and material abundance. The dream attests to the fact that the dreamer is a cool-headed person who generally knows how to plan his steps wisely, so that his investments yield dividends and he can enjoy the fruits of his labor.

Gathering grapes in a dream is parallel to collecting a large amount of money in life. The dream predicts that the dreamer will enjoy great abundance. Practicing a lucrative profession, or alternatively, getting into a promising venture that will prove itself by delivering high returns will ensure the dreamer's financial future.

Grapevine

The meaning of a grapevine in a dream changes in accordance with how it appears in the dream:

A dream that features a grapevine full of grapes is a sign that the dreamer's family will increase in the near future. Another meaning is that success is on the threshold, and the dreamer will see the fruits of his labor, but only after hard work and great exertion. He will have to prove himself properly before he gets to see the fruit of his labor.

If the grapevine is in full bloom in the dream, there is a hint of an imminent marriage that will take place after only a brief period of acquaintance. The relationship with the future partner will be fast and short, but intense and sweeping.

A "wrecked" vine in a dream is a sign that the dreamer gets embroiled in things easily and afterwards it is very difficult for him to extricate himself.

He must know how to identify such "traps" so that he can avoid them in time.

A B C D E F **G** H I J K L M N O P Q R S T U V W X Y Z

Grass

In general, when a dream features grass that looks like a lawn, it indicates that the dreamer will soon achieve spiritual serenity and will be liberated from prolonged suffering – particularly spiritual or psychological suffering. The dream is also a sign that the dreamer is entering a good phase during which he will enjoy good health. If he does not feel well, or is suffering from some physical ill, from now on his general physical state will improve and his health will be excellent. A dream in which the grass appears green and particularly "healthy" is a sign that the dreamer can expect a happy life. He will derive great satisfaction on all levels – financial, health, and love and marriage.

Withered grass in a dream implies that if the dreamer neglects his health, he is liable to reach the point of no return and will not be able to go back and function normally. His condition is liable to deteriorate so much that the dreamer may even bring disaster on himself. The dream serves as a kind of warning that he must listen to his body and his physical condition, since if he does not identify the illness at an early stage, it is liable to be too late.

Frozen or dry grass in a dream is a sign of the loneliness the dreamer is suffering. The loneliness in question is on the spiritual and emotional level, since the dreamer can be surrounded by people who love him and care about him, and, in spite of that, he can feel great loneliness.

A dream that features grass can also imply that the dreamer will achieve illumination or reach high degrees of concentration during meditation – the kind he has never experienced before – that will cause him to change his attitudes to the point of changing his approach to life in general.

Grasshopper

This dream indicates that a threat is hanging over the dreamer's head.

Grave

If a person dreams about a grave, the dream symbolizes everything the dreamer is lacking: health for a sick person, money for someone of limited means, marriage for single people, etc.

A dream about walking on a grave is an indication of a bad marriage or early death. A dream about an empty grave means disillusionment and losing friends. A dream about being buried alive means that the dreamer is about to make a terrible mistake that will be exploited by his enemies. If he is rescued in the dream, the mistake will ultimately be rectified.

Gravel

If a person dreams about gravel, it implies futile business ventures. A dream about gravel mixed with sand indicates loss of property as a result of bad speculation.

Gravy

If a person eats gravy in a dream, it means ill health and unprofitable business.

Grease

If a person dreams that he is covered in grease, it predicts that he will be with well-groomed but unpleasant strangers.

Greek

A dream about reading Greek means that the dreamer's ideas will finally be heeded and adopted. A dream about failure to read Greek means that the dreamer has technical problems.

Green

The color green has the following symbolic interpretations in dreams: green clothing: prosperity and joy; green fields: prosperity and abundance for all.; green fruit: futile efforts, hasty actions; green grass with dry patches: illness or business-related problems; freshly cut down green trees: pleasure clouded by unhappiness.

Greyhound

A dream about a greyhound is a good dream. If the dog is following a young girl in the dream, the dreamer will receive an unexpected bequest. If the dreamer owns a greyhound, he will find friends where he expected to find enemies.

Grindstone

A dream that features turning a grindstone indicates an energetic life that leads to prosperity. If a person dreams that he is sharpening tools on a grindstone, he will marry well. If he dreams that he is dealing in grindstones, it means that he will have a small but honest income.

Groans

If a person hears groans in a dream, he is warned that he has to act smartly if he wants to prevent his enemies from hurting him. If he is groaning with fear in a dream, he will be thrilled with the upward swing of his business and with nice encounters with friends.

Groceries

A dream about fresh, hygienic groceries signifies a pleasant life without hardship.

Grotto

A dream about a grotto is a sign of unsatisfactory friendships. The dreamer's quality of life will decline from relative comfort to insufferable poverty.

Grove

A dream about a grove is interpreted in several ways. If a person sees a particularly dense grove in his dream, the dream implies that "he can't see the forest for the trees." The dreamer lost the direct path to his objective a long time ago, and he has gotten lost in his desire to follow a whole lot of paths. He must stick to one path and follow it. In everyday reality, this means that he should stick to a routine. The more he persists in following the difficult path, and does thorough work, the more success is guaranteed and his dreams and objectives that he set himself in life will be realized.

If the grove is especially green in the dream, it is a hint of a positive turning point that can be expected to occur in the dreamer's life. Soon something will happen that will cause a sharp and even dramatic change – for the better – in his life. He must take this opportunity with both hands and not let it slip away.

If the grove in the dream is particularly dense, and resembles a small, tangled forest, it is a sign that soon a certain person will appear. This person will look after the dreamer and will travel a considerable distance just to see that he is well and in good health and that everything is fine with him.

If a person sees himself alone in a grove, it is a sign that he is about to be involved in happy events.

A dream in which a fire suddenly breaks out in a grove and destroys it is a warning dream that implies that the dreamer must make preparations for his old age. Possibly worries about a pension are disturbing his well-being, and this is the time to see about it in order to be comfortable in the future. Some people interpret a dream about a fire in a grove as a good prophecy, or as a dream that hints that good news is in the offing.

A dream in which a person sees himself strolling leisurely through a grove hints at a large inheritance on the horizon. Even if this is not realistic at the moment, the inheritance will come from an unexpected source and will cause the dreamer to improve his standard of living.

If a person sees his family members in a grove, it is a sign that soon someone he loves will betray him. This does not necessarily refer to a romantic betrayal. The betrayal could come from a child, from a work-mate or from some other person he holds dear. This person could do something that the dreamer deems a betrayal.

Guardian

If a person dreams about a guardian, it means that the dreamer will be treated considerately by his friends.

Guidance

Whether the dreamer sees himself guiding other people in a dream, or whether he sees himself being guided, both possibilities imply that he will soon meet a person who will exert an enormous influence on his life – perhaps even a crucial influence. The dreamer may even have encountered this particular personality already, and he is still unaware of the power and the influence he has over him, but there is no doubt that he has the ability to remodel the dreamer's life and cause him to change his opinions or way of life. This person will not exert a negative influence – on the contrary, his influence will bring about positive changes in the dreamer's life and is essentially positive. His good effects on the dreamer will radiate outward to the people around him and cause better and more positive energies to radiate from him.

If a person dreams that he is looking through guidebooks or books that help a person improve his life by giving various pieces of advice, it is also a dream with a positive meaning. It hints at new beginnings and at the fact that he is on the threshold of a new era and of new possibilities and opportunities in life. This is the time for him to make changes, study and open himself up to things to which he was previously closed or oblivious. The dreamer's new ability to "open his eyes" to things that he did not notice before can enable him to get more out of life and feel that he is experiencing the power of life in full.

A
B
C
D
E
F
G
H
I
J
K
L
M
N
O
P
Q
R
S
T
U
V
W
X
Y
Z

Guitar

If a person dreams that he has a guitar, it is a sign of merrymaking and being deeply in love. A dream about playing a guitar symbolizes domestic harmony.

Gulls

A dream about gulls prophesies dealing amicably with stingy people. A dream about dead gulls means estrangement from friends.

Gun / Pistol

A dream in which the dreamer sees himself firing a gun implies that a substantial investment he made will not yield significant results. The mediocre results will not reflect the dreamer's investment and hard work. This is especially true for a person who works in the financial realm and is not in the least suited to it. The dream hints that it would be better for him to quit this field in favor of other areas that are more compatible with his character and talents.

If a person dreams about holding a gun, without making use of it, the dream means that he is not someone who is well liked. Other people do not display any affection or love for him. In most cases, this is a result of his attitude toward them.

If a person dreams that his enemy is holding a gun, the dream hints that the dreamer has totally lost his grip. He suffers from worry and anxiety that are so extreme that he finds himself in a state of a basic lack of control as regards anything that happens to him. He is confused, cannot control himself, and is prone to unrestrained attacks of hysteria.

Gutter (of a roof)

The gutter in all its forms in a dream means that the dreamer can expect a long and anxiety-free life. If a person dreams about climbing up a gutter, it indicates that he wants to run away from solving his problems.

Gutter (of a street)

If a person sees a gutter in a dream, it is a sign of dissipation. He will cause others misfortune. If he finds something valuable in a gutter in a dream, his right to a particular piece of property will be queried.

Gymnast

A dream about a gymnast means bad luck in business ventures.

Gypsy

If a person dreams about a gypsy, he is warned to watch out for a swindler who will make him suffer in the future. If the dreamer himself appears as a gypsy in a dream, it is a sign that in the future he will move to another country in search of happiness.

If a person dreams about visiting a gypsy camp, it means that he will receive an important proposition. If a woman dreams that she has her fortune told by gypsies, she will make a rushed and bad marriage. If she is married, a dream about gypsies means that she will be unjustifiably jealous of her husband. If a man talks to a gypsy in a dream, it is a warning to him about losing of valuable assets. Trading with a gypsy in a dream predicts a loss of money as a result of speculation.

H

Haggard

If a person sees a haggard face in a dream, it is a sign of bad luck in love. If the dreamer's own face appears haggard and unhappy, it means that women are rendering him incapable of dealing with his business affairs properly.

Hail

If a person dreams about being caught in a hailstorm, it is a warning dream: he can anticipate failure in any enterprise. If he sees hail falling while the sun is shining, he will be bothered by small worries that will soon disappear. If he hears the pounding of hail in a dream, it is a bad omen.

Hair

The meaning of a dream that features hair changes in accordance with the manner in which the hair appears – its color, its vitality, and so on.

If a dream features healthy hair, full and shiny, it is a sign of sure success. Even if the dreamer is hesitant about a certain action he has to perform, and fears that he will not be able to do it, he can rest assured that he will do it well and his success will exceed all expectations.

If a person dreams about body hair, it is a sign that he is plotting and his thoughts are not pure.

If a woman dreams of not having hair – either on her hair or in other places on her body – it is a sign that she is a haughty and conceited person, and for that reason, she is also isolated. People tend to avoid her company, and she knows this, but finds it difficult to change her nature. For this reason, she lives in constant frustration and in a kind of vicious circle she finds it difficult to get out of.

If a person sees lovely hair that he particularly likes in a dream, it is a sign that he can expect good luck in his life. Even if plans he has dreamed up and devised are not easily implemented, suddenly, without prior warning, things will work out better than he could have expected.

A dream that features hair of a peculiar shade or an unconventional color (blue or green, for instance), it is a sign that the dreamer, for some reason known only to him, feels frustrated. He is filled with worry, suffering, fears, and agitation.

If the hair in the dream appears tied back, it is a sign that the dreamer has lost love because of stupidity. Moves that were not very smart caused him to lose something dear to him, and it is doubtful that he can ever get it back. This stupid step haunts him and gives him no rest.

Dyed hair in a dream attests to a fake image. The dreamer does not show his true self outwardly. He puts on an act for the people around him as if he were someone else. This may stem from fears and anxiety that he will not be popular, but this lie is with him constantly and poses a serious threat. His desire to get rid of the fake image he presents to others emerges in the dream and does not let up.

If a person sees graying hair in a dream, it is a sign that things he heard in the past are beginning to come true. Rumors, stories or gossip of some kind that were baseless

A B C D E F G H I J K L M N O P Q R S T U V W X Y Z

and that the dreamer believed not to be true are now taking shape and becoming something real and threatening.

If a person sees his hair in a dream and is dissatisfied with it, it is a sign that he must make a greater effort and work extremely energetically in order to accomplish the goals he set for himself in life and overcome the obstacles in his path.

If a person sees hair being torn out in a dream, it attests to the sadness or deep sorrow that will be his lot. This may be linked to a loss of some kind, so the dream may imply imminent mourning.

If a person dreams that his hair is curly, even though in reality his hair is straight, the dream serves as a hint that people are gossiping about him, and that he has to be aware of and alert to changes in the way the people around him relate to him.

Hairbrush

If a person sees a hairbrush in a dream, it is a sign that the dreamer's affairs have been mismanaged. If the dream features an old hairbrush, it portends illness.

Hairdresser

If a person dreams about a hairdresser, the dream is a mirror of the dreamer's dejection and melancholy. It is also a warning of a possible scandal, both for men and for women.

Hairstylist

A woman who dreams about her hairstylist is developing

feelings for this person that go beyond the service she receives from him. The dreamer may be lacking attention from her partner or from her family, and she sees in her hairstylist the figure of a friend and a potential admirer. The dreamer is in a state of mental depression, at least to a certain extent, and tends to develop additional relationships outside of the existing ones in order to feel feminine, admired and desirable. She must be careful of being swept into an affair that could cause heartbreak.

Hairy hands

If a person dreams about hairy hands, it signifies that he is plotting against innocent people; it also signifies that he has enemies who aim to stop him. Hands covered with hair in a dream also imply that the dreamer will never be prominent among his associates.

Halter

If a person dreams that he is placing a halter on a young horse, the dream predicts success in business and love. If he leads a donkey by the halter in a dream, it means that he will have a great deal of clout with both sexes.

Ham

A dream about ham is a warning against treachery. If a person sees thick slices of ham in his dream, it means that he will overcome all competition. If he dreams about eating ham, he will lose something of value. A dream about dealing in ham portends health and prosperity.

A
B
C
D
E
F
G
H
I
J
K
L
M
N
O
P
Q
R
S
T
U
V
W
X
Y
Z

Hammer

A hammer in a dream can be interpreted in two ways:

If a hammer appears in a general way in a dream, it implies that the dreamer can expect to be given a substantial promotion at work. Having said that, a dream like this also warns against economic instability in the form of taking unnecessary risks or getting involved in spurious deals that are ultimately liable to cause the dreamer big losses. He must be more aware of his expenses and be cautious in anything to do with financial matters.

A hammer that resembles the one that is used to call gatherings such as auctions and meetings to attention attests to the fact that the dreamer enjoys a significant social position. The dreamer is right in the middle of things, and everyone looks up to him. He is one of the social leaders, and in this capacity determines the general feeling, the preferences of the people around him, and the opinions that other people will adopt. His influence on his surroundings is enormous, and this fact is evident in his actions.

Hand

A person who dreams about a tight-fisted hand should beware of legal embroilments. If the dreamer is facing a lawsuit, he should make sure that he is working with suitably professional people. Perhaps it's a good idea to change strategies and choose another possible direction. If dirty or stained hands appear in a dream, they are a warning against friends who gossip. There could also be an unpleasant incident. Bound hands in a dream hints at some kind of diametric change. Failure and sadness will soon be replaced by happiness. The information relates to both personal and professional life.

If a person dreams about his own hands, it is a positive sign of success in the family and work realms.

A strange hand stretched out toward the dreamer means help from an unexpected quarter.

Hands holding a file or an envelope imply creative ideas that are taking shape and are about to bear fruit.

The right hand is generally linked to a message about close family members.

The left hand relates to children in the home.

A hand that is involved in an accident means that it's time to pay back an old debt.

A hand that is involved in a fire means losing a job.

Handbills

If a person dreams that he is distributing handbills, the dream predicts that he will be involved in lawsuits and disputes. If he sees himself printing handbills, it is a sign of bad news.

Handcuffs

A dream about handcuffs generally attests to temporary success, mainly in the realm of business and finance. The dreamer does not relinquish the reins and carefully oversees the path along which he is traveling so that he veers neither to the left nor to the right. In this way, he succeeds in business and in financial investments.

If the dreamer sees himself wearing handcuffs in his dream, it implies that he is involved in a harmful relationship (one that is virtually impossible for him). He

A B C D E F G **H** I J K L M N O P Q R S T U V W X Y Z

A B C D E F G **H** I J K L M N O P Q R S T U V W X Y Z

wants to get out of it, but he is "tied up" in it for reasons that do not permit him the liberty he yearns for.

If the dreamer tries to take the handcuffs off and liberate himself in the dream, it is a sign that he wants to break out of a framework. He is a non-conformist who finds it difficult to accept the burden of the laws of society and toe the line. He wants to map out his own special path, but feels bound by the fetters of the laws around him that do not permit him to give free rein to his abilities. When he tries to do so anyway, he is considered a freak.

If the dream features broken handcuffs, it is a sign that the dreamer wants to flee from every ill and evil, even if this entails great sacrifice or hurts other people.

Handicap

If a person dreams that he is handicapped, he can look forward to an improvement in his status and in other areas of life. If he dreams about overcoming a handicap, it means that he will overcome obstacles along his path. However, if he dreams that he is unable to overcome a handicap, the obstacles in his path will remain.

Handkerchief

A dream about a handkerchief indicates a surprising change that will take place in the dreamers' life or in the life of someone close to him. Almost certainly, it refers to an event in the romantic realm. A new acquaintance will lead to unexpected developments. An engagement or a wedding can be taken into account. If the dreamer is married or involved in a committed relationship, he is well advised to look into what's going on with his partner.

Handshake

A dream in which two parties shake hands attests to a fierce desire for reconciliation. There may well be a positive change at work or in other areas of life. This kind of dream generally hints that a positive era is in the offing for the dreamer. It is highly likely that there will be an improvement in the overall family dynamics. Moreover, the dreamer will live with himself more easily and will learn to accept his shortcomings.

Handsome

If a person sees himself as handsome in a dream, it means that he is excellent at doling out flattery. If other people are handsome in his dream, it means that he will spend his time in the company of people who do not enjoy the best reputation.

Handwriting

If a person dreams that he identifies his own handwriting, it means that enemies will exploit his opinions in order to thwart his aspirations for a particular position.

Hanging

A dream in which the dreamer sees himself or one of the people close to him hanged actually predicts good things.

If the dreamer sees himself hanged, he can expect to have a brilliant career in whatever field he chooses. He will make the most of his talent and will derive satisfaction from his work and his actions. Moreover, he will be proud of his occupation and his achievements. His satisfaction will be

A B C D E F G **H** I J K L M N O P Q R S T U V W X Y Z

great – among the members of his household as well, since he will become more easygoing, pleasant and pleased with himself.

If a dream features another person hanged, it is a sign for the dreamer that one of the people near to him is about to enjoy fame and glory. Word of his actions will travel far and wide, and he will be accorded a great deal of prestige and honor. People will be impressed by his talents and abilities, and their recognition of him will increase.

Happiness

Even though it would seem that a dream about happiness is a positive dream, the contrary is actually the case: a dream about happiness portends times of hardship and danger, particularly in the workplace.

Harbor – See Port

Hare / Rabbit

A dream about a hare generally attests to the dreamer's problems with anything to do with sex. The hare symbolizes inhibitions and the inability to achieve sexual fulfillment, and indicates that the dreamer is subject to severe pressures in everything concerning the sexual area of his life. Having said that, if the hare is in flight or in a race, the dream implies that changes are about to happen to the dreamer. He will change his surroundings – his residence or his workplace – and his status will also change. This change will be reflected mainly in his financial situation – for instance, an improvement in his income, prosperity in business, a promotion at work, and so on.

If the dreamer sees a rabbit "participating" in a magician show (coming out of a hat or appearing in the show in some other way), the dream implies that a deal he made recently will fall through, and his expectations will prove to be unfounded. He can expect disappointment in anything to do with investments he made, and it is even possible that he bought a pig in a poke.

If the hare is "personified" in a dream and speaks in a human language, there is a hint that the dreamer is drawn to mystical and magical activities, to mystery and to everything to do with cosmic and unknown things.

If a person dreams that he is eating a rabbit, or that he is hunting one, it attests to the fact that he is an envious person who cannot participate in other people's happiness. He is a belligerent and quarrelsome person who does not know how to compromise and be flexible, and he tends to get into futile arguments with those around him. He revels in other people's downfall and does not know how to give praise. As far as he is concerned, nothing touches rejoicing at someone else's calamity.

Harem

If a person dreams that he keeps a harem, it means that he is wasting himself on base pleasures. If a woman dreams about belonging to a harem, it means that she generally pursues married men.

Harlequin

If a person dreams about a harlequin, it is a warning

dream. He can expect trouble. If he dreams that is dressed as a harlequin, he will make serious mistakes that will cost him dearly, both in money and in moral conscience.

Harlot

If a person dreams about being with a harlot, it means trouble both financially and socially. If he dreams about marrying a harlot, he will be placing his life in jeopardy at the hands of an enemy.

Harness

A dream about a shiny new harness is an indication of a nice trip.

Harp

A dream in which the dreamer sees himself at a party or concert where a harp is being played means that disappointment is in the offing for him. If the dreamer himself is playing the harp, it is a hint that he wants to be in a situation in which he has greater control over things. At the moment, it seems to him that other people are telling him what to do. He feels that he has no effect on what is happening around him, and this intensifies his inner feeling of frustration.

Harvest

A dream about a harvest is an excellent dream that symbolizes an abundance of wealth and success in all areas of life. A person who dreams that he is harvesting a field of crops of any type can invest a little bit of money in various financial deals. An investment on the stock exchange is a wise step, and tremendous success is assured. Good luck is shining on him, and this is the time to act, big time.

Hash

If a person dreams about eating hash, it is a sign of trouble and unhappiness that will undermine the dreamer's health. If he dreams about cooking hash, it indicates that a woman will be jealous of her husband.

Hassock

A dream involving a hassock indicates that the dreamer will hand over his power and possessions to someone else.

Hat

The meaning of a dream that features a hat changes in accordance with the circumstances. If the dreamer sees himself purchasing a hat and putting it on, it means that disappointment awaits him. If the dreamer loses his hat, he will soon have a pleasant surprise. He may receive a gift or some kind of package in the mail from an unexpected quarter. If a person dreams that he finds a hat in the street, for instance, he must be careful in public places. He is liable to lose his wallet or fall victim to pickpockets. If a person dreams that he cannot take his hat off, it means that pains are starting, warning him about a possible illness.

Hatchet

A dream about a hatchet is a warning dream: as a result of profligacy, the dreamer will fall victim to the plots of people who are jealous of him.

Hate

If a person dreams about hating someone, it is a warning dream: it warns the dreamer that he is liable to cause that person an injury, and that he will suffer financial losses and worries. If a person dreams that he is hated unjustifiably, it means that his friends and associates are positive and faithful. Usually, however, a dream about hate is a bad dream.

Hawk

If a person sees a hawk in a dream, it means that he will be cheated. If he dreams about shooting a hawk, it means that he will finally overcome stubborn obstacles. It also means that he will probably triumph in a competition with his enemies. A dream about a dead hawk signifies defeating enemies.

Hay

A dream about mowing hay is a good sign – it signifies a plentiful harvest for farmers. A dream about newly cut hay indicates prosperity. If a person dreams about carrying, storing and loading hay, he can look forward to good luck. If he sees himself feeding cattle with hay in a dream, it means that he will help someone who will reciprocate by promoting the dreamer to a higher position.

Head

If a person sees a well-shaped head in a dream, it means that he will meet powerful people who will be of assistance to him in important undertakings. If he dreams about his own head, it is a warning of trouble in that part of the body. The sight of a bloody severed head in a dream is a sign of bitter disappointments and dashed hopes. If a person dreams about having an aching head, it is a sign of worry.

A dream about a swollen head means that the dreamer's life will basically be positive. A dream about a child's head is a sign of enjoyment and prosperity. If a person sees an animal's head in a dream, it is a sign of base desires and material pleasures. If the dreamer washes his head in a dream, he can expect important people to seek his advice and judgment.

If the dreamer sees himself wounded in the head, it is a sign that he has hidden enemies. A dream about having two or more heads indicates a meteoric rise in life, but one that will not last long.

Headache

A dream about a headache indicates that one of the dreamer's friends is in need of his help.

Headgear

A dream about lavish headgear is a sign of success and fame. A dream about old, worn headgear means that the dreamer will have to forfeit his possessions to someone else.

Headlights

If the dreamer is dazzled by the headlights of a car in a dream, it means that he should take steps quickly in order to prevent possible complications.

A B C D E F G **H** I J K L M N O P Q R S T U V W X Y Z

Hearing aid

If a person dreams about using a hearing aid, it means that he did not pay enough attention to something of great significance to him.

Hearing voices

If a person hears pleasant voices in a dream, it signifies a reconciliation. If the voices in the dream are strident, he can expect trouble and disappointment to follow.

Hearse

If a person sees a hearse in a dream, it is a sign of domestic strife and trouble in business. It also signifies the illness or death of someone close to the dreamer. If a person dreams that a hearse crosses his path, he will have to tackle a sworn enemy.

Heart

A dream about a heart – that is, a heart shape and not a real flesh-and-blood heart – is always interpreted as the dreamer's desire to find the great, true love of his life. Even if the dreamer is in a good relationship, a dream about a heart still implies his aspiration to find the "big" love that comes once in a lifetime.

A dream about a flesh-and-blood heart is a warning sign about health problems. Go to the doctor!

Heartache

If a young woman dreams that she has a heartache, it

means that she will suffer from the poor treatment she receives at the hands of her lover.

Heaven

If a person dreams about going up to heaven, it means that he will not be accorded esteem, and his joy will turn to sadness. If he dreams about being in heaven and meeting Christ, it means that he will suffer many losses. A dream about climbing up to heaven on a ladder means an unprecedented rise in status without much joy.

Heaviness

A feeling of heaviness in a dream indicates that the dreamer is going through a difficult phase. He is vacillating about matters of crucial importance, and the decision is difficult for him. It is advisable for him to decide in advance on a certain period of time for weighing up the problematic topic and set an exact date when the decision must be reached. The doubts and waiting will not help. Heaviness in the legs characterizes a dreamer who feels that he is in a rut. Perhaps quicksand appeared in the dream, with his feet sinking into it, and this is causing a "genuine" feeling of heaviness. In such a case, the dreamer must hurry to get out of the emotional mire. The longer he waits, the more he'll lose his powers and then he'll have difficulty coping with the consequences.

Heavy rain – See Flood

Hedges

Evergreen hedges portend prosperity and happiness. Bare hedges portend unhappiness and mistakes in business. Being caught in a thorny hedge means that the dreamer will be held back in his work by partners or subordinates.

Heel

A dream about a broken heel means that the dreamer will have to confront problems and hardship in the near future.

Heir

If a person dreams about being an heir to property, it means that he risks losing what he has. Sometimes good things come as a result of this dream.

Helicopter

If a person sees a helicopter hovering over him, it is a sign that a guest is about to arrive. If the helicopter seems menacing, the visitor will be dangerous. Hearing the noise of a helicopter in a dream indicates an imminent journey.

Hell

A dream about hell is interpreted in different ways according to whether the dreamer is religious or secular, Christian or a Jewish, and so on. The prevalent interpretation for a secular person who dreams about hell is that he is perceived by society as a money-chaser who will do anything for mammon. The people around him perceive him as super-materialistic, as someone who is interested in nothing but money, and as someone whose existence and deeds are motivated by money alone. People are generally repelled by those types, and so the dream constitutes a kind of warning for the dreamer, telling him that he has to change his behavior patterns so that he can become more likeable and acceptable to other people.

Since money is at the top of the dreamer's list of priorities, he often gets into a state of mental and physical suffering, which is reflected in physical pains and severe mental pressures. He is inclined to burst out at the people around him and be patently insufferable – both to his family and to the people who work with him. It is no wonder, therefore, that a situation like this is conducive to making numerous enemies and causing people to wish for the dreamer's downfall. They would rejoice if he were to lose his money and assets. In such a case, not only will he find himself without means, but he would have no friends at his side in his darkest hour.

Another interpretation of a dream about hell involves the guilt feelings that gnaw at the dreamer and are expressed as a "punishment" in the dream. The dreamer clearly knows that he did something forbidden and unworthy that hurt someone else, so his conscience is working overtime. He knows that he must atone for his deeds and grapple with reality, however painful and bitter it may be, if he really wants to "purify" himself and turn over a new leaf.

Helmet

A dream about a helmet implies that sadness and loss can be prevented if the dreamer acts wisely.

Hemp

A dream about hemp is an indication of success in all undertakings.

Hemp seed

A dream about hemp seed is an indication of deep, enduring friendship, as well as the opportunity to make money.

Hen / Rooster

A dream about a hen with chicks indicates the need to plan ahead meticulously before acting. If a person hears a rooster in a dream, it is a sign of exaggerated self-confidence.

Hen's nest

A dream about a hen's nest symbolizes domestic harmony and delightful children.

Herbs

Following a dream about herbs, the dreamer will experience some hassles, but these will be replaced by fun. A dream about poisonous herbs indicates enemies. On the other hand, dreaming about beneficial herbs mean good business and friendships.

Hermit

If a person dreams about a hermit, it signifies distress and solitude due to disloyal friends. If the dreamer dreams that he is a hermit, he will take great interest in current affairs. If he dreams that he finds himself in a hermit's hut, it is a sign of great altruism and magnanimity toward both friends and enemies.

Heron

A dream about any kind of bird is generally a good dream that predicts positive things. The appearance of a heron in a dream is interpreted like a dream about a stork – positive changes can be anticipated in the life of the dreamer. If the person is involved in a conflict or if there has been a misunderstanding between him and a person close to him, the dream predicts that there will be peace and reconciliation once more. The dream also implies the inner tranquillity that the dreamer will enjoy. If he is at odds with himself or does not find repose for his soul, he will feel as if it is easier for him (with himself) in the forthcoming period of time. He will be less severe with himself and will tend to accept himself as he is, overcoming inhibitions and the desire to change according to the dictates of society or fashion.

On the other hand, some people interpret a dream about a heron in almost precisely the opposite way: the dreamer's desire to keep the things that had been part of his life, bowing to conservatism and a desire for a lifestyle that preserves the tradition that makes him special. In a dream like this, his tendency toward intellectual or emotional stagnation comes to the fore, as does his inability to become more flexible and adapt to his surroundings, to his times, or to changing situations vis-à-vis his own situation.

A B C D E F G **H** I J K L M N O P Q R S T U V W X Y Z

Herring

A dream about a herring indicates an uncomfortably tight financial situation from which the dreamer will finally extricate himself.

Hide (*of an animal*)

If a person sees an animal hide in a dream, it is a sign of a secure job and prosperity

Hiding-place

If a person hides in a hiding-place in a dream, it is a sign that he will soon receive bad news.

Hieroglyphs

A dream in which a person sees hieroglyphics foretells that the dreamer's hesitation in an important matter will cause him trouble and financial losses. If the dreamer is able to decipher hieroglyphics in his dream, it means that he will overcome bad things.

High school

A dream about a high school means progress in love as well as in social and professional affairs.

High tide

If a person dreams about high tide, it is a sign of progress in his ventures.

Hills

A dream about reaching the top of hills is good. However, if the dreamer does not get to the top, he will have to grapple with envy and setbacks. A bald hill in a dream is a sign of famine and suffering.

Hippopotamus

A dream about a hippopotamus implies a revelation of the subconscious according to which the dreamer is suffering from feelings of inferiority. He is not satisfied with himself in any possible way – physically or mentally. The dreamer feels as if he is not succeeding in fulfilling the expectations of his surroundings, and that he is rejected or not accepted. These feelings do not always have a basis in reality, and it is very possible that this is just the dreamer's inner feeling of which he is aware in some way. Having said that, the dreamer may be suffering from a problem of obesity that causes his low self-image. It is also possible that the dreamer looks excellent by any standards, but feels clumsy, fat or heavy, even though he is none of these things in reality. The constant negative inner feeling of being a "loser" prevents him from succeeding and advancing in life. He is incapable of daring to try new things, and his eroded self-confidence creates a stumbling-block in his path. The dream implies that this image is a figment of the dreamer's imagination. If he could only shake himself free of it and see himself in a less critical and more objective light, he would succeed in achieving the objectives to which he aspires and accomplish at least some of the goals he has set himself in life.

A dream about a hippopotamus also implies that the

A B C D E F G H I J K L M N O P Q R S T U V W X Y Z

person has a hidden enemy who clings to him like a shadow and obscures his actions. The dreamer is the victim of endless plots by that person, who seeks to harm him. This enemy is stronger than he is, and his attempts to evade him or overcome him are fruitless.

Hips

If a person admires curvy hips in a dream, it means that his wife will yell at him. If a woman admires her own hips in a dream, she will be disappointed in love. If she dreams that her hips are narrow, it predicts that she will suffer from illness and disappointment.

Hissing

If a person dreams about hissing, it signifies that he will be outraged by the cavalier treatment meted out to him by new acquaintances. If they actually hiss at him in the dream, it means that he runs the risk of losing a friend.

History

If a person dreams about reading history, it means that he will have a very nice time.

Hives *(on body)*

If a person sees hives on his child in a dream, it means that the child will be obedient and healthy. If he dreams about strange children with hives, he will be worried about his own children.

Hoe

If a person sees a hoe in a dream, it means that he will have to work hard to support others. A dream about using a hoe means that the dreamer will avoid poverty by working hard. If a woman dreams about hoeing, she will be self-sufficient.

Hogs

A dream about fat, healthy hogs mean positive changes in business. A dream about lean hogs mean hassles with children and employees. If a person hears hogs squeal in a dream, it is a sign that he will receive bad news from faraway friends; it can also imply death or losses in business. A dream about feeding hogs signifies an increase in the dreamer's assets. If a person dreams about hogs eating fruit in an orchard, he will lose property while trying to take something that does not belong to him. A dream about dealing in hogs means that the dreamer will make a lot of money, but he will have to work very hard for it.

Hole

A dream about a hole implies a family problem that the dreamer is grappling with. The problem causes him a great deal of emotional suffering and even depression. His depressed state of mind engenders a state of fear of failure and undermines his basic confidence.

If the hole in the dream is particularly large, the dream symbolizes the profound disgrace that will be the dreamer's lot because of society's behavior toward him. Because of a particular certain move, action or choice he makes, he is

A B C D E F G **H** I J K L M N O P Q R S T U V W X Y Z

liable to get into a situation in which the esteem in which he is held by the people around him will dwindle, and in its place will come scorn, mockery and contempt.

Holiday

A dream about a holiday is a sign that interesting strangers will enjoy the dreamer's hospitality.

Holy Communion

A dream about taking communion is a warning dream: the dreamer will give up his opinions in order to pursue some superficial pleasure. If a person dreams that he feels worthy of taking communion, but is denied it, it means that he will receive a position that he never dreamed possible. If he feels unworthy in his dream, he will have trouble.

Home

A dream about visiting one's old home presages good news. If the old home is dilapidated in the dream, it warns of the death or illness of a relative. If a person returns to a bright and pleasant home in a dream, it imlies domestic harmony and prosperity in business.

Homesick

If a person dreams about being homesick, it means that he will miss out on the chance to go on enjoyable trips.

Homicide

A dream about homicide predicts that the dreamer will

suffer great humiliation at the hands of others, and his despair will distress others.

Hominy

A dream about hominy implies love that is a great diversion from study and business preoccupations.

Honey

A dream about honey is generally a very positive dream. It symbolizes success, the fruits of a good investment, and enjoyment of life.

Honey in a dream symbolizes mainly business/economic success as well as joy and happiness.

If a person sees himself eating honey in a dream, success will shine upon him in the realm of romance. In anything to do with matters of sex, compatibility and success in choosing a mate, he can expect great success, far beyond the norm.

If the dreamer sees himself receiving honey, great social achievements are in store for him. He will be loved by the people around him and popular with other people, and will feel that he is at the center of things. Even if he does not feel that way right now, things are about to change for the best, and the dreamer will feel wanted and sought after by other people.

If a person sees himself licking honey in a dream, it is an erotic hint. The dream implies the fulfillment of hopes for anyone who is in love or is in the process of establishing a relationship. The part played by sex in the type of relationship that is being built is big and significant. The dreamer may not be in a relationship, and may not be building such a relationship, but the dream attests unequivocally to the fact that he is in the grips of fierce passion and the desire to release it. He is in a sensory whirlpool that is making his head spin. He must try to control himself so that he does not make mistakes.

Honeysuckle

A dream about honeysuckle is an indication of prosperity and domestic bliss.

Honor

A dream about honor signifies that the dreamer must take precautions in money matters and lead a more economical lifestyle.

Hood

If a young woman dreams that she wears a hood in a dream, it means that she will soon try to seduce a decent man.

Hook

If a person sees a hook in a dream, it is a sign of heavy, unpleasant burdens in store for the dreamer.

Hoop

If a person dreams about a hoop, it is an indication that he will make friends with important people. People will come to him for advice. If a person dreams about seeing anyone jumping through hoops, it indicates problems that will ultimately be solved.

Hops

A dream about hops implies energy, thrift and the ability to exploit any business venture to the hilt.

Horn (animal)

The appearance of an animal's horn in a dream, such as a deer's horn, an elk's horn, a rhino's horn, or even an elephant's tusk are all interpreted as symptoms of the dreamer's sex-related problems. The dreamer may be experiencing difficulties in sexual performance because he is suffering from a physical problem in his genitals, but the problem may have psychological roots.

A sexual problem is not necessarily linked to the dreamer's sexual exploits. It is not impossible that the dreamer is facing a difficult dilemma connected with the sexual realm and does not know what to decide or how to act. Perhaps the dream attests to the dreamer's sexual infidelity, which is troubling him greatly. If he cheats on his partner solely in order to satisfy his sexual lust, and he suffers from heavy guilt feelings, the dream is the "sign" that will bring him back to the straight and narrow path, since it expresses the voice of the dreamer's conscience. With a strong will and some effort, the dreamer can kick the cheating habit and return to a happy and sexually fulfilling relationship.

Horn (brass)

If a person hears a horn playing in a dream, it predicts excellent news. If a dream features a broken horn, it is a sign of death or mishap. If a person sees children playing horns, it signifies domestic harmony. If a woman dreams about blowing a horn, it means that she wants marriage more than her lover does.

Hornet

If a person sees a hornet in a dream, it attests to broken friendships and financial loss. If a woman is stung by a hornet in a dream, it means that her rivals want to ridicule her in front of her admirers.

Horoscope

If a person dreams about having his horoscope drawn up, it predicts a long journey and changes in business matters. If a dream features the stars being pointed out to the dreamer while being read, he can expect disappointment instead of luck.

Horse

A horse in a dream attests to positive things that are about to occur in the dreamer's life.

Having said that, when the horse appears in contexts that are not good in the dream – for instance, if the horse has run away, or the dreamer falls off the horse while riding it and so on – the interpretation is reversed and implies negative things.

A dream that features a horse that is not in any specific context indicates that the dreamer is about to experience a positive event that will be accompanied by great profit (usually financial). It attests to huge success, both in social and family life and in business, and indicates that the dreamer is blessed with a powerful sexual drive that is a general expression of his lust for life and of every manifestation of vitality.

The colors of horses in a dream:

A white horse attests to the fact that the dreamer can expect to derive great satisfaction from actions he has performed recently, especially in the business realm.

A black horse attests to the fact that the dreamer has several so-called friends who are not true friends, even though their behavior would indicate that they are. The dreamer can imagine which friends are in question here, and he should take care and exercise caution with them.

A red horse attests to the fact that the dreamer will soon find a new love in his life. If he is already involved in a relationship or is married, the dream implies that the relationship will thrive and the interpersonal relations between the couple will become stronger and closer. The dreamer has someone to rely on and lean on in times of trouble.

A brown horse implies that the dreamer is characterized by high spirits. He loves to help people, he has endless *joie de vivre*, people love to be in his company, and he radiates congeniality and happiness. His happy nature also brings him financial stability and equilibrium in the material realm, and this nurtures his ability to be cheerful and happy.

A yellow horse implies that the dreamer is determined to implement his plans, and he can do this even when something stands in his way. He will overcome all obstacles on his path to achieving his goal, and will be successful.

A gray horse is an indication of a prophetic dream that

A B C D E F G **H** I J K L M N O P Q R S T U V W X Y Z

indicates that if the dreamer has lost something, whether it is a material thing such as money, a valuable object, or something like that, or something of great sentimental value, he will soon find it. It may be returned to him by someone who finds it by chance, but it may equally be returned to him by the person who stole it, changes his mind, and gives it back to him somehow.

A piebald horse indicates that the dreamer loves to involve himself in spurious ventures that yield minor profits. His desire for an "easy buck" is innate, and he cannot kick this bad habit.

If the dreamer is riding a black horse in his dream, the dream acquires a negative meaning and implies that the dreamer can expect failure. As mentioned above, the failure will be in the economic realm – a drop in business, a bad investment, and so on.

Riding a horse in a dream implies economic prosperity, profits as a result of a good and successful deal, and good, loyal friends. Some people interpret riding a horse as becoming wealthy – not as a result of hard, back-breaking work, but rather as a result of a meeting with a rich lover.

Falling off a horse in a dream is a hint that there will also be a drop in the value of the shares owned by the dreamer. If the dreamer does not own shares, the meaning of the dream is a financial downfall – but one that is not too serious. The dreamer will soon recover.

A fleeing horse implies a financial loss and a loss of property. Having said that, a dream like this also attests to a great disappointment. Generally, the disappointment in question is the result of the hopes the dreamer pinned on an important deal that did not materialize.

A dream about a racehorse attests to the fact that the dreamer is involved in a dispute with his friends, and this is bothering him. If the dreamer is not involved in a dispute with his friends, the dream hints that he soon will be.

Losing a horse in a dream implies the loss of friends in reality. The dreamer feels that he is about to lose one of his good friends, and the anxiety he feels about losing that friend rises to the surface in his dream. It is never too late to turn the clock back.

A horse that obeys the dreamer – If a person dreams that while he is riding a horse, he commands the horse to do as he says, and the horse reacts with unconditional obedience, the dream implies that the dreamer will soon be accorded honor and respect. He may find himself in a situation that will make him very famous, and many of his acquaintances as well as people who do not know him personally will relate to him with great respect.

A wild horse that cannot be controlled and that roams around freely and gallops to its heart's content through the countryside attests to the fact that the dreamer will soon clinch successful real estate deals. If the dreamer is a merchant or a businessman, it will be a deal that will yield excellent results. If the dreamer is not involved in business, he may find himself purchasing a new apartment in the near future, and this may be a very successful deal for him.

A horse in water – If a person sees a horse wallowing in the mud or swimming in water in his dream, the dream indicates the dreamer's feeling of wretchedness, of powerlessness, and of his inability to contend with things and stand up for himself. The dreamer feels as if he is gradually sinking into a cloud of sadness and does not see the way out of the situation in which he has become embroiled.

A limping horse – If a dream features a limping horse, it implies that the dreamer is not managing to fulfill his desires because of some kind of unexpected opposition that is undermining his ability to get what he wants. This opposition can come from several quarters: someone from his family who is putting a spanner in the works and seeks to harm him, or someone the dreamer knows at work, feels that the dreamer is a threat to him of some kind, and for this reason is placing obstacles in his path.

A dream about riding a horse wildly attests to wild and unfettered sexuality. The dreamer gives free rein to his desires, is used to living according to the patterns of life he has adopted, and is considered to be an aberration in the conservative society around him.

If a man dreams about riding a horse wildly, the dream implies an unconscious fear of impotence. Even if the man feels that he is in his prime, fears of whose existence he is completely unaware rise up from his subconscious.

If a woman has this dream, it is a sign that she is expressing her hidden fear of a failed marriage: the fear of long-term commitment to something for which she is not yet psychologically prepared is being aroused. She is afraid that she is taking an unwise step by moving toward marriage, and the consequences strike terror in her heart.

Horse race

If a woman dreams about a horse race, it implies she will soon have marital problems. If a man dreams about a horse race, it is a warning dream: he must be on the alert for danger from an unexpected quarter. He must take care and be cautious.

Horseradish

If a person dreams about horseradish, it predicts congenial friendships with amicable and smart people. It is also a sign of prosperity. A dream about eating horseradish means that other people will take the mickey out of the dreamer in a nice way.

Horseshoe

If a person dreams about a horseshoe, it means that he will embark on a sea voyage in the near future.

Horse trader

If a person dreams about a horse trader, it means that risky ventures will be extremcly profitable. If a person dreams that he is cheated by a horse trader, it signifies that he will have bad luck in love or business. If the horse the dreamer receives in the trade is better than his previous one, it means that his capital will increase.

Hospital

A dream about a hospital attests to a fear of illness and death. (This does not apply to people who work in a hospital and are used to spending many hours there every day.)

A dream like this, in which the dreamer sees himself lying in a hospital bed, surrounded and treated by a team of nurses and doctors dressed in white, attcsts mainly to the fears and anxieties that beset the dreamer. The fear is of the future, of the future in general and of what it holds. The dreamer's ignorance and uncertainty about everything concerning his future evoke great fear and terror in him. He cannot cope with the unknown, and he feels impotent when he has no ability or tools to deal with the situation. If he had organized his life in a tidier and more conscious way regarding his possibilities in the future, the majority of his fears and worries would disappear. The unknown and the fear of "what tomorrow will bring" are the reasons for his feeling of destruction and helplessness.

If a person dreams of being in a psychiatric hospital, it is a sign that soon there will be a drastic change in his social status. It could take the form of a significant promotion at work or of an extreme move, such as from one country to another. The change will be sharp and extreme, and will be reflected in the essentially different manner in which the people around him relate to him. The dreamer will be held in higher esteem, and the people around him will deem it important to hear what he has to say. Moreover, they will seek his counsel and his recommendations.

Hotel

If a dream features a hotel in which the dreamer is staying, it attests to the fact that the dreamer is tired of his life of routine and is seeking excitement, change, adventure and new and exciting experiences.

There may also be a hint that the dreamer is about to embark on a long journey or trip in which he will get to see new landscapes, cultures or people, and these will light up his life and make him look at life from a different perspective.

If the "stay" in the hotel was accompanied by an

unpleasant feeling of being uncomfortable or unwilling to be there for some reason or other, the dream constitutes some kind of warning dream against hasty decisions or irresponsible actions. The dreamer does not weigh his actions wisely. He must be more considered in his moves and think well – from every possible angle – about the consequences of his actions. He must not be hasty, and he must be considered and rational.

Hot pepper

A dream about a hot pepper expresses feelings of pride resulting from the success of someone close to the dreamer.

Hounds

If a person dreams about hunting hounds, it is a prediction of positive changes and pleasures. If a woman dreams of hounds, she will love a man of a lower social class. If she is being pursued by hounds in a dream, she will have many admirers who do not care much about her.

House

In general, a dream about a house actually implies a desire for liberation and freedom as opposed to the fixed state symbolized by a house. The dream hints at the unconventional adventures, experiences and undertakings that can be expected.

If a person sees a tall house in his dream, it means that he is about to get a promotion at work, or go up in rank from the point of view of his talents in other areas.

If a person sees a low house in his dream, it is a sign that his work relations in his workplace are about to break down. The poor relations will engender a difficult and depressing atmosphere in which work disputes will break out every now and then. A difficult phase lies ahead, and it will only pass after changes are effected in the higher echelons at the workplace.

If a lone house standing in a deserted place appears in a dream, it is a sign of a drastic change for the good in the dreamer's situation. A highly irksome problem he encountered recently will be solved. In general, it is an economic problem, but it could also be a mental problem or troublesome thoughts that do not allow the dreamer to rest. The problem will soon disappear.

If a dream features a house that looks destroyed, it predicts anguish, depression and a series of difficult experiences that are about to afflict the dreamer: financial losses, health problems, some kind of loss, and so on.

If a new house is seen in a dream, it is a sign that the dreamer and his partner will enjoy a relationship of love and trust. Their relationship will bloom, and they will be happy in each other's company for a long time.

Housekeeper

If a person dreams about being a housekeeper, it means that he is happy with his tasks and occupations. If he dreams about employing a housekeeper, it means that he dreamer will be comfortably off.

Hug

A hug in a dream generally means that the dreamer wants to hold out his hand to someone in his family or his circle who needs help. He is prepared to be of assistance to him without asking for or expecting anything in return.

If the intention of the hug in the dream is to display affection only, the dream implies that the dreamer likes respect and obedience.

If the hug is given with unconcealed joy, the dream hints that soon the dreamer can expect to get married or meet someone new who will be very important in his life.

A dream in which a hug is given sorrowfully with the intention of consoling predicts quarrels and misunderstandings that the dreamer will unwittingly encounter with the people around him or with someone else who is close to him.

If a person dreams about a romantic or an erotic hug, the dream predicts that in the near future, the dreamer will come into an inheritance. In most cases, this will be money, but the inheritance could also be valuable objects that will come into his possession.

Humidity

A dream about humidity implies a fierce struggle against enemies. It warns that the dreamer will be completely defeated. It also indicates that he will be cursed and will not be able to view the future with any optimism.

Hunchback

A dream about a hunchback heralds good news if it is dreamed by a person who suffers from a hunchback or some other kind of back deformity: it implies that thc dreamer will enjoy success and good fortunc in the near future. He will succeed in money matters as well as in

A B C D E F G H I J K L M N O P Q R S T U V W X Y Z

matters of the heart. If the dreamer is not married, a dream about a hunchback attests to the fact that he can expect a pleasant surprise in his love life, too. If the dreamer is married, this dream implies that his marriage will thrive and will soon be rejuvenated.

If, however, a hunchback appears in the dream of a person who does not suffer from health problems concerning his back, the dream does not augur well. This is especially true when a person sees himself touching someone else's hunchback in a dream. He is about to lose money and suffer from everything that is linked to the psychological realm as well. Moreover, he may develop sensitivity in the abdominal region, which may cause a stomach upset or another problem, leading to debility from the health point of view.

Hunger

If a person dreams about hunger, it is a bad sign, because it is indicative of a lack of domestic harmony. For lovers, a dream about hunger predicts a bad marriage.

Hunting

A dream about hunting wild animals implies that the dreamer will be involved in an event in which highly respected people will participate. Having said that, influential people who can endanger the dreamer's status or lay a trap for him are expected to attend this event.

He must take every possible precautionary measure, but at the same time act tactfully and diplomatically, without appearing to be suspicious.

Hurricane

If a person sees a hurricane rampaging in a dream, it means that he will suffer from extreme tension in his attempt to save his business from disaster. If he is trying to rescue someone from the ruins of a house, it means that he will move to a new home and make changes, but will not achieve happiness. If he sees the casualties of a hurricane, it means that he will be sad about other people's troubles.

Hurt

If a person dreams that he hurts someone in a dream, it means that he will hurt other people cruelly. If he himself is hurt, his enemies will overcome him.

Husband

If a woman dreams that her husband is leaving her for no reason, it means that a very bad period she is going through will be followed by reconciliation. If she dreams about her husband's death, grief and disillusionment are in the offing for her.

Hut

If a person dreams about sleeping in a hut, the dream predicts illness and dissatisfaction. If a dream features a hut in a green pasture, it means prosperity, but not constant happiness.

Hyacinth

A dream about a hyacinth predicts a heart-rending

separation from a friend, which, however, will ultimately turn out for the better.

Hydrophobia (rabies)

If a person dreams that he has hydrophobia, it indicates that he has enemies. It also means that there will be changes in his business. If he sees other people suffering from hydrophobia, it means that his work will be interrupted by death. If he dreams that he is bitten by a rabid animal, it means that he will be betrayed by his closest friend in the middle of a storm of scandal.

Hyena

A dream about a hyena is a sign of misfortune and trouble, as well as of unpleasant encounters with acquaintances. A dream about an attack by a hyena foretells an attempt that will be made to ruin the dreamer's reputation.

Hymns

A dream about hymns is a sign of domestic happiness and reasonable prosperity.

Hypnotist

If a person dreams that he is in a hypnotic state, it means that his enemies have him in their thrall. If he is the one who has others in his thrall, it means that he will dominate his surroundings.

Hypocrite

If anyone acts hypocritically toward the dreamer in a dream, it means that disloyal friends have betrayed him to his enemies. If he himself is a hypocrite, he will act falsely with his friends.

I

Ice

If a person sees ice in a dream, it is a sign of trouble and a warning: evil people will try to sabotage the dreamer's work. If he sees ice floating in a clear stream, it means that his contentment will be disrupted by the malevolence of jealous friends. If he dreams that he is walking on ice, it means that he will risk solid benefits for fleeting pleasures. Eating ice in a dream is a sign of illness, as is drinking ice water.

Ice-skating

A dream about ice-skating is a warning dream: it warns of flattery, or of a shaky relationship with the person whom the dreamer loves the most. If the dreamer sees himself ice-skating, it warns him that he may lose his job.

Ice-cream

A dream that features ice-cream indicates that the dreamer will be successful in ventures he undertakes. If a person dreams that children eat ice-cream, it implies joy and prosperity. If a dream features ice-cream that has gone sour, it means that the dreamer's joy will be marred. Melted ice-cream in a dream means that he will not consummate his pleasures.

Icicles

If a person sees icicles falling off trees in a dream, it means that his worries will evaporate. If the icicles are on the eaves of houses in a dream, it signals poverty, lack, and illness. If the icicles are seen on the fence, on trees or on evergreens, it is a prediction of bad things and an unhappy future.

Ideal

If a woman dreams about the ideal man, it means that she will have uninterrupted enjoyment and happiness. If a bachelor dreams about the ideal woman, it means that he will soon experience a change for the better in his affairs.

Idiot

If a person sees an idiot in a dream, it predicts losses and disputes. If the dreamer himself is the idiot, he will suffer humiliation and sadness on account of plans that did not succeed. If a person dreams about children being idiots, the future holds nothing good for him.

Idle

A dream about being idle means a failure to attain one's objectives. If a dream features idle friends, it means that they will encounter a problem.

Idols

If a person dreams about worshipping idols, it means that he will not advance on account of the fact that he

A B C D E F G H I J K L M N O P Q R S T U V W X Y Z

allows little things to get to him. A dream about iconoclasm means that the dreamer will succeed in spite of the obstacles. If a person sees other people worshipping idols, it means that he will quarrel with his friends.

Illness

A dream that features an illness attests to the fact that the dreamer is afraid that somebody in his family – or he himself – will become ill. These fears may be based on actual facts or may serve as a mirror to the fears and anxieties in the dreamer's heart with no particular justification. In principle, dreams about illnesses serve as a sign of positive events in the future.

Illumination

A dream that features strange illuminations implies failure on every count. If a person sees illuminated heavens with distorted heavenly bodies in a dream, it means grief and sorrow in the extreme. If the dreamer sees illuminated snakes or other crawling creatures, it means that his enemies will go to any length to crush him.

Images

If a person sees images in a dream, it is a sign of failure in love and business. Ugly images in a dream refer to domestic strife.

Imitation

A dream that features some kind of imitation means that the dreamer will be deceived.

Immortality

If a person discusses the immortality of the soul in a dream, it means that he is on the way to higher knowledge and the opportunity to discuss things with cultured people.

Implements

If a person dreams about implements, it means that he cannot put his plans into practice. A dream that features broken implements means illness, death, or business failure.

Imps

A dream about imps is a forecast of trouble as a result of some casual fun. If the dreamer himself is an imp in the dream, his own stupidity will lead to poverty.

Inauguration

If a person dreams about an inauguration, it intimates that the dreamer will reach the highest position he has ever had.

Incantation

The use of incantations in a dream indicates conflicts between spouses or lovers. If other people repeat the incantation in the dream, it signifies that the dreamer's friends are not being genuine in their behavior.

Incarceration

A person who dreams that he is being incarcerated feels

as if he has failed in his missions and is in a whirlpool from which there is no way out. He should check out the reason for his distress and take appropriate action. If a person dreams that a member of his family or an acquaintance is incarcerated, it means that he is worried about what will happen to them. He sees that they are about to get in trouble more clearly than they do. Dreams of this kind are liable to occur before a wedding or similar events, when the dreamer has no faith in the success of the marriage. His fears of what the future holds are expressed in the dream, and although they do not necessarily constitute a self-fulfilling prophecy, they certainly hint at future difficulties.

Incense

If a person dreams that he burns or smells incense, is refers to dear friends and a promising future.

Incest

A dream about incestuous actions means that the dreamer will fall into disgrace from a high position. In addition, he will suffer financial losses.

Incoherence

A dream about incoherence is usually a manifestation of a state of great agitation and nerves as a consequence of rapid events.

Income

If a person dreams about receiving his income, it means that he might defraud someone or cause his family anguish.

If someone in his family receives an income in a dream, it means that he will be successful. If his income is not enough, it means that trouble is in store for people close to him.

Increase

A dream about an increase in the dreamer's family means that he may face failure in some plans and success in others.

Independence

If a person dreams about being very independent, it is a warning dream: it warns him of a rival who wants to hurt him. If a person dreams of becoming independently wealthy, it means that his future looks rosy.

Indifference

A dream about indifference implies brief, amiable friendships.

Indigestion

A dream about indigestion is an indication of an unhealthy, depressing environment.

Indigo

If a person sees indigo in a dream, it means that he will swindle friendly and innocent people out of their possessions. A dream about indigo water is an indication of a sordid love affair.

Indistinctness

If a person sees things indistinctly in a dream, it is a sign of disloyalty in friendships and unsuccessful business ventures.

Indulgence

If a woman dreams about indulgence, it means that she will be harshly criticized for her conduct.

Industry

If a person dreams about being industrious, it means that he will spend a lot of time and effort devising plans and ideas for advancement, and these will pay off.

Infant

Almost every dream that features an infant is a positive dream. An infant symbolizes health, happiness, joy and tranquillity. In most cases, a dream that features an infant attests to the dreamer's hidden talents that have not been developed and expressed. The dreamer feels frustrated about this, and his frustration comes to the fore in his dream.

If a woman dreams about an infant, it means that she will soon be holding her own infant in her arms. Many women who are pregnant as well as women who are undergoing fertility treatment dream about an infant.

If a particularly beautiful infant appears in a dream, it indicates the happiness that the members of the dreamer's household will enjoy, as well as the true friendship the dreamer shares with one of his friends.

A happy infant in a dream predicts that joy and happiness will be the dreamer's lot. It is a dream that augurs well and attests to the fact that the dreamer will enjoy good and happy days.

If a widow dreams that she is pregnant, it is a sign that she will enjoy tranquillity and serenity all her life.

A diapered infant in a dream is a sign of a promising love life.

A dream in which the dreamer is holding an infant very close to his chest is a dream that is characteristic of a person who already has an infant at home. In such a case, it is a sign that there is another infant on the way. If the person does not have an infant at home, it is a hint that there soon will be.

If the appearance of an infant in a dream is negative, the meaning of the dream is not positive either:

An ugly infant in a dream is a hint that the dreamer can expect to suffer a large financial loss.

A sick infant in a dream is a warning about treacherous friends or about a disease that has not yet been discovered in one of the members of the dreamer's family.

An infant crying in a dream implies that the dreamer can expect rows to break out in his family. The dream serves to warn him about such rows, which can be avoided if people are willing to compromise.

An infant that appears helpless in a dream is a sign of a disappointment in love. The dreamer has pinned too many hopes on a relationship that has no future. He should detach himself emotionally from his partner as soon as possible in order to minimize the pain.

If the dreamer sees an infant taking its first steps in a dream, the dream implies difficulties in business. These

A B C D E F G H I J K L M N O P Q R S T U V W X Y Z

will be serious difficulties that will have repercussions on his financial future.

An infant in a stroller means that the dreamer can expect pleasant surprises. He may receive good and surprising news from far away.

An infant who is making noise in a dream for no reason and is causing everyone discomfort is a sign that soon the dreamer can expect to go through a tough and stressful period. It will not be easy in the least, but it will end quickly. He is advised to muster his strength in order to cope with the forthcoming phase in the best possible way.

If a dream features an infant that smells good and clean, it is a sign that one of the dreamer's friends is a loyal person who can be relied upon completely. He will always come to the dreamer's assistance because he loves the dreamer truly.

Infidelity

A dream about the infidelity of the partner's mate (having sex with someone else) indicates the opposite of what is true in reality: It is a sign that the partner's mate is faithful to him in reality, and can be relied on completely in every area.

If a person dreams that he is being unfaithful to his mate, the dream indicates that someone is exploiting him or extorting him. He is being subjected to a campaign of intimidation and threats by someone and is suffering from fear and anxiety.

If a woman sees herself cheating on her husband in a dream, it implies an unexpected pregnancy or uncertainty regarding the state of pregnancy.

If the dream about infidelity involves partners who are

not yet married, the dream predicts a breakup: each of them will soon find another partner.

Infirmary

If a person dreams about leaving an infirmary, the dream symbolizes escaping from enemies who cause the dreamer a lot of concern.

Infirmity

A dream about an infirmity is a negative sign, referring to bad luck in business, health and love. The dreamer should not underestimate his enemies. If he dreams that other people have infirmities, it means that he will be unsuccessful and disappointed in business.

Influence

If the dreamer hopes to advance by means of the influence and intervention of people in high places, he will be disappointed. If, however, he dreams that he is influential, his prospects are excellent. If he sees influential friends in a dream, he will be free of anxiety.

Inheritance

If a person dreams about receiving an inheritance, it means that he will realize all his wishes and objectives. If he dreams about inheriting jewelry, it signifies unexpected, but not altogether positive, prosperity.

Injury

If someone does the dreamer an injury in a dream, it means that he will soon be very irritated by some mishap.

Ink

If a person dreams that ink is spilt on his clothing, he will be the butt of many little nasty digs. If he dreams that he has ink on his fingers, it means that his jealousy will lead him to hurt someone else, unless he controls himself. A dream that features red ink is a sign of serious trouble. A dream about making ink is indicative of a lowly occupation, and a dream about bottles of ink implies enemies and failure in business.

Inkstand

A dream about full inkstands is a sign of malicious slander disseminated by enemies. If the inkstands in the dream are empty, it means that the dreamer will have a narrow escape from public censure for some alleged injustice.

Inn

A dream about a well-appointed, comfortable inn indicates prosperity and an enjoyable life. A dream about a wretched, miserable inn is a sign of failure, undesirable jobs and unwanted journeys.

Inquest

A dream about an inquest indicates bad luck in friendships.

Inquisition

A dream about the inquisition means nothing but trouble and distress. If a person is brought before an inquisition in a dream, he will be powerless in the face of vicious slander.

Insanity

If a person dreams about being insane, it is a terrible forecast if it occurs at the beginning of a project. It could involve the dreamer's ill health. If other people are insane in the dream, it means that the dreamer will have unpleasant contact with poor, distressed people. He should be extremely careful after this dream.

Inscription

If a person sees an inscription, it indicates that bad news is in the offing. If he is reading inscriptions on tombs in the dream, he will become seriously ill. If he writes an inscription in a dream, he will lose a dear friend.

Insect

A dream that features an insect or insects attests to the fact that the dreamer can expect a difficult period accompanied by anger, temper tantrums, quarrels and hardships that he will have to vent and give free rein to. However, the dream hints that the dreamer's outbursts will not cause any damage. He must be prepared for the fact that he will be beset by disappointments and that there will be difficulties in various areas of his life that will dampen his *joie de vivre* during the forthcoming period of time.

The problems that will preoccupy him will mainly result

from unsuccessful business dealings, failed deals or a lack of profits, but they will be minor and not really significant. The dreamer will be able to overcome them relatively easily.

Another interpretation of a dream about insects, especially if they appear in the dream crawling on the dreamer's body or clothes, is that it serves as an expression of the dreamer's feeling of revulsion regarding something that he has come across in his everyday life.

Insult

A dream that features an insult indicates that the dreamer can expect to go through a difficult stage that is full of changes. Although it is not in the least certain that the events will be terribly serious, he will feel insulted and hurt. There could be drastic changes, such as a change of jobs or of place of residence.

Intemperance

If a person dreams about being intemperate in love or other emotions, it is a prediction of illness, financial loss or a drop in esteem.

Intercede

If a person dreams that he intercedes in behalf of someone else, it means that he will be offered assistance in time of need.

Interpreter

If a person dreams about an interpreter, it means that he will become involved in unprofitable matters.

Intersection

A dream about an intersection signifies exactly that: The dreamer has come to a crossroads in his life and must make decisions that will affect his destiny.

Interview

A dream about an interview hints that there will be a promotion in the near future and good news from a close acquaintance.

Intestines

The appearance of intestines in a dream is extremely negative. It foretells a catastrophe that will cause the death of the dreamer's friend. If he sees his own intestines in a dream, it means that he will contract a disease that will cut him off from his surroundings.

Intoxication

A dream about intoxication is an indication that the dreamer is harboring secret immoral desires.

Inundation

If a dreamer sees cities or countries under water, it is a prediction of catastrophes and enormous loss of life. If he dreams that people are swept away in an inundation, it is a sign of death and despair. If he sees an extensive area under clear water, it signifies prosperity after what seemed a hopeless battle.

A B C D E F G H I J K L M N O P Q R S T U V W X Y Z

Invalid

A dream about invalids means that the dreamer is in the company of disagreeable people who want to jeopardize his interests. If he is an invalid in a dream, it warns of negative conditions.

Invective

If a person dreams about invective, it is a warning against outbursts of anger against close friends. If other people spew invective in a dream, it means that the dreamer's enemies are entrapping him.

Inventor

If a person dreams about an inventor, it implies that he will soon be well known for some special project. If he dreams that he is inventing something, he will be successful in his plans and in financial matters.

Inviting

If a person dreams about inviting people to his home, it means that some disturbing event is in the offing. If he receives an invitation in a dream, it means that he will hear bad news.

Iron (metal)

A dream about iron is a very bad sign. A dream that features an iron weight implies worries and financial loss. A dream about old rusty iron symbolizes poverty and disillusionment. A dream about a red-hot iron means lack of success due to misguided enthusiasm.

Iron

A dream about an iron can mean that the dreamer is going through a comfortable phase in his life. Particularly for a woman, the action of ironing constitutes a symbol of a serene life that is expressed, among other things, in her concerns for the needs of her family.

On the other hand, the dreamer may well be attempting to smooth out creases in the clothes, just as he is trying to straighten out the problems in his life. Feelings of frustration and dissatisfaction have been accompanying him for a long time, and now is the time to open up his heart and talk about them with the people concerned. If a person dreams about an iron scorching an article of clothing, the dream implies a serious crisis in the relationship, with very little chance of making amends.

Ironing

A dream about ironing is interpreted in different ways according to the situation in which the dreamer sees himself ironing. In general, it is a positive dream that attests to the onset of a good and harmonious era with the people around him, and hints that he can get whatever he wants by being charming.

If a person dreams about ironing with a lukewarm iron and not with a very hot iron, as is usually the case, the dream hints at the male-female realm: the relationship with his partner is not "flowing" as it should, but the lovers may eventually become accustomed to each other's quirks and get the most out of the relationship. The dreamer and his partner are still finding it difficult to function together as a team, and they have to learn to know each other well until their relationship begins to fit the definition of optimal relations between the members of a couple.

If a person dreams about ironing with an especially hot iron, the dream implies that he acts according to his impulses rather than his common sense. Instead of listening to his conscience and inner logic, behaving according to moral dictates and opting for the path of decency, he operates according to his instincts and allows his impulses to dictate the path he takes. The dream is a warning dream, admonishing the dreamer to "take himself in hand" before it's too late, pull himself together and begin acting according to reason and not just according to emotion and impulse. It is a dream that is characteristic mainly of men who cheat on their wives or of women who cheat on their husbands.

If the dreamer sees himself ironing happily, joyfully and cheerfully (especially if he is normally a person who loathes ironing in reality), it is a dream that attests to the fact that the dreamer is a peace-loving person. The people around him enjoy being in his company and seek him our. The dreamer will have a good and peaceful life, since he brings *joie de vivre* wherever he goes.

A dream in which pressure is exerted on the dreamer to force him to do the ironing – whether pressure is exerted on him to do something he does not want to do or whether it is pressure of time – the dream implies that the dreamer must refrain from unnecessary conflicts. He is a person who tends to get into unnecessary arguments and taunt anyone who irritates him; he is not in the habit of letting anyone get the better of him. If he knows that being with a certain person will lead to a conflict with him, he is advised to refrain from being in the same place with that person, and so on. The more he extricates himself from problematic situations that lead to conflicts, the more pleasant and smooth-flowing his life will be.

Island

If a person dreams about being on an island in a clear-water stream, it is an indication of good journeys and good fortune in business. If a woman dreams about an island, it also means a happy marriage. A dream that features a barren island means exactly the opposite, due to the dreamer's outrageous behavior. Seeing an island in a dream is a positive sign for the dreamer's future after many struggles.

Itch

A dream in which a person scratches himself or rubs his body attests to the fact that in his everyday life he is bothered by unnecessary things that should under no circumstances take up his time, thoughts or energy. The dreamer has certain emotional problems that he intensifies for no real reason. Sometimes it seems as if he enjoys the self-torture and agony that preoccupy him so much. In order to regain his peace of mind, he must calm down and occupy himself with things that will restore tranquillity and repose to his soul. He should meditate or do other calming things, such as a massage that will relax his body. Perhaps he should get away from everything by going on vacation.

A dream about an annoying itch or rash on the body frequently occurs in people who are about to get married, and they are anxious about it. Emotional problems in lovers sometimes cause this dream. In such a case, the dreamer should examine the nature of his relationship with his potential spouse very carefully, before he makes a mistake and it is too late.

Ivory

A dream that features ivory is a lucky dream. If a person sees large pieces of ivory in a dream, it implies unadulterated enjoyment and financial gain.

Ivy

Among the numerous plants that appear in dreams, ivy holds an honorable position, perhaps because it is common in many gardens and is grown as a decorative plant in many places.

Ivy symbolizes a fierce emotional attachment to something or someone in a dream, a tie that affects the dreamer and his actions. In most cases, it means that the dreamer is connected to the traditions of his parental home and to the way of life according to which he was raised. It is very difficult for him to go against it, and he shies away from breaking the rules and acting in a way that is incompatible with the way he was raised and educated. This inner conflict causes him to wrestle with several of the truths according to which he was raised, and to reexamine them in the mirror of reality and according to the beliefs and world-views he has developed for himself as an adult.

There could also be an attachment to a certain person who has a great influence on the dreamer's path and is a dominant personality in his life. He manifests almost blind admiration for a figure such as a father, mother, uncle, friend or teacher, who sketched out his path and greatly influenced the dreamer's world-view. Deep inside himself, the dreamer reexamines what that path is and whether he is still keen on following and adopting it.

A B C D E F G H I J K L M N O P Q R S T U V W X Y Z

J

Jackdaw

A dream about a jackdaw is a bad sign because it foretells illness and disputes. If the dreamer catches a jackdaw in a dream, he will defeat his enemies. If a person kills a jackdaw in a dream, it means that he will receive disputed property.

Jade

A dream about jade indicates that the dreamer has luck in life as well as someone looking after him from above and protecting him from harm. An expensive jewel given to the dreamer attests to the possibility of winning a large amount of money or coming into an inheritance.

If a person dreams about a journey during which he reaches a foreign place in which there are great quantities of jade stones, he can expect to receive exciting news from an unexpected quarter. The news will surprise the entire family and is liable to causes disputes. In any case, the dreamer is likely to receive a large sum of money.

Jail

Dreams that feature a jail have many possible interpretations. First and foremost, the dreamer may fear that he is liable to find himself in jail because of an illegal transaction or some kind of financial embroilment. It is also possible that the dreamer, who has been in trouble for a long time, subconsciously wants to go to jail, since it constitutes a secure place for someone who has already despaired of all the other possibilities. A jail in a dream also expresses a fear of assuming responsibility. Dreams about a jail can also hint at the possibility of some kind of commitment.

If the dream is relatively pleasant, it means that a wedding, the purchase of a home or any other kind of deal that involves commitment is in the offing. If the dream is bad, the dreamer is suffering a great deal and believes that he has no luck in life. The walls are closing on him from all sides and he has no plan for improving his situation.

Jailer

If a person sees a jailer in a dream, it means that his interests will be jeopardized by treachery. The dreamer will fall under the spell of bad women. If he sees a jail being overrun by a rowdy mob, he will be in extreme danger of having money extorted from him.

Jam

If a person dreams about eating jam, it is a sign of nice surprises and trips. If he sees himself making jam in a dream, it is an indication of a happy home and good friends.

Janitor

A dream about a janitor signifies mismanagement, undisciplined children, and uncooperative employees.

A
B
C
D
E
F
G
H
I
J
K
L
M
N
O
P
Q
R
S
T
U
V
W
X
Y
Z

January

A dream about the month of January implies that the dreamer will be landed with unwanted companions or children.

Jar

A dream that features a jar is a sign of good fortune. If the dreamer carries a jar (full or empty) on his back, it means that very soon he will reach a turning point in his life and can expect a pleasant surprise. Not only will he enjoy material success, but there will also be other family developments. The fuller the jar, the greater the surprise awaiting him.

Jasmine

A dream about jasmine serves to open the dreamer's eyes and tell him that he has hardly exploited the talents and abilities he is blessed with. In fact, the dream is "shouting" that the dreamer is wasting his life, and that with a little effort he could achieve much more than what he has achieved until now.

Another interpretation of a dream about jasmine implies that the dreamer has never been fortunate enough to experience complete enjoyment in his life, and there is always something that curtails the happiness in his heart and does not let him be happy for any length of time. It could be a trauma that accompanies him and does not let him rejoice wholeheartedly. Moreover, it could be linked to his nature, which simply does not let him express joy fully because he is incapable of "letting his hair down" and always maintains a high level of self-control. The dream serves to hint that full and complete happiness could be his if he could only allow himself to shake off the mental bonds that prevent him from doing so.

Jasper

A dream about jasper is a good sign, since it refers to love and success.

Jaundice

If a person dreams about jaundice, it is a sign of prosperity after a setback. If the dreamer sees others with jaundice in a dream, he will be hounded by business worries and disagreeable companions.

Javelin

If a person dreams that he has to defend himself with a javelin, it means that his most private affairs have become public knowledge in order to prove him guilty of perjury; only after a lot of litigation will he establish his innocence.

If a person dreams that a javelin wounds him, his enemies will defeat him. If he sees others carrying javelins, it is a threat to his interests.

Jaws

A dream about ugly, distorted jaws symbolizes disputes and bad feelings between friends. If a person dreams about being in the jaws of a wild animal, it means that his business and domestic harmony are being jeopardized by enemies.

Jaybird

A dream about a jaybird is predicts congenial visits with friends and pleasant conversation. A dream about a dead jaybird implies domestic conflicts and trouble.

Jealousy

If a person dreams that other people are jealous of him, it means that he is soon going to succeed and the people around him will be jealous of him.

If a person dreams that he himself is jealous of someone else, he should examine himself and his actions during the forthcoming period of time. There is every chance of a real disappointment in the romantic realm, and before rushing off to buy a diamond ring, book the church and buy bridal clothes, he should go into the matter carefully and weigh up the situation once more.

Jelly

If a person dreams about eating jelly, it refers to many agreeable interruptions. If a woman makes jelly in a dream, she will have happy reunions with friends.

Jester

A dream about a jester implies that the dreamer neglects important things in favor of the pursuit of trivial things.

Jewel

The meaning of the appearance of a jewel in a dream – no matter what kind – is that the dreamer is fortunate.

In most cases, a dream about a jewel predicts that the dreamer will find new paths and discover new horizons in the near future, and will enjoy whatever these offer.

Receiving a jewel as a gift in a dream is a sign of great happiness in the person's love life and marriage. The dreamer's life with his partner will be fulfilling, enjoyable and full.

Having said that, dreams that feature jewels in bad circumstances have less auspicious interpretations:

Losing a jewel in a dream is a warning against getting involved in gambling or in an unsuccessful venture, or signing a risky contract.

If a dream features a broken jewel, the dreamer can expect to suffer a bitter disappointment in his life.

If a dream features an emerald set in an item of jewelry, it warns of a deterioration in the state of health of one of the dreamer's close family members. He should be on the alert, since the disease may be in its initial stages and has not yet manifested itself externally.

If a person dreams about agate, it means that some kind of business dealings are in the offing.

Jewelry

If a person dreams about jewelry, it is a sign that that he is lucky. A dream that features broken jewelry presages disappointment. If a person dreams about receiving jewelry as a gift, it signifies a happy marriage. If a person dreams about losing jewelry, it implies gambling-linked troubles.

Jew's harp

A dream about a jew's harp indicates a slight

improvement in the dreamer's affairs. If he plays a jew's harp in a dream, he will fall in love with a stranger.

Jig

A dream about dancing a jig is a sign of happy, lighthearted and joyful pastimes. If the dreamer's sweetheart dances, it implies a cheerful disposition.

Jockey

A dream about a jockey means that the dreamer will be pleased to receive a gift from an unexpected quarter. If a jockey is thrown from his horse in a dream, the dreamer will be asked to offer strangers assistance.

Jolly

A dream about being jolly in company means that the dreamer will be blessed with well-behaved children and success in business. If the jollity is marred at all, he will have worries.

Journey

A dream about setting out on a journey can hint at several possible directions: money worries, losses, a desire to escape from a given situation, and so on. A dream of this type indicates that the dreamer is in a particular kind of distress or at least in an uncomfortable situation. Perhaps he feels a desire to take a vacation as a result of cumulative fatigue over a long time. A journey that breaks down in the middle implies a failure that can be expected in business. The situation must be examined carefully. It is advisable to refrain from making important decisions, at least in the coming month.

Journeyman

A dream about a journeyman indicates that the dreamer wastes money on futile trips. If a woman dreams about a journeyman, it means that the trips are unexpected but nice.

Joy

A dream about joy that is not genuine, such as joy at someone else's downfall, is a hint that the dreamer can expect mentally exhausting rows that will bring out the evil in him. Moreover, the rows will cause him to feel prematurely old.

A dream about genuine joy is not necessarily positive, either. On the contrary, in most cases, a dream like this does not augur well – rather, it serves as a warning to the dreamer that soon he will have to be cautious and suspicious and not act hastily. He must plan his moves wisely and not rush to fulfill every whim that comes into his head.

The dreamer is liable to be bombarded with difficulties, so he should prepare himself. If a person who is close to the dreamer appears in the dream, and he is happy and rejoicing, these things are true for him too: he is liable to encounter difficulties and problems both at work and in the family, and he should be warned about it as soon as possible.

A
B
C
D
E
F
G
H
I
J
K
L
M
N
O
P
Q
R
S
T
U
V
W
X
Y
Z

Jubilee

A dream about a jubilee means that the dreamer will be involved in many happy events.

Judge

If a person dreams about a judge, it is a clear indication that he must not be quick to judge other people or determine their guilt or innocence. If he dreams about appearing before a judge, it means that he will be involved in a dispute that can only be settled in court.

Judgment Day

If the dreamer is optimistic about escaping punishment on Judgment Day, he will accomplish some complicated work. If he is not optimistic, he will fail.

Jug

A dream about a jug is a symbol of good luck. If the jug is full, it is a sign of extremely good luck, as well as of true friends who are rooting for the dreamer's welfare. A dream about a broken jug indicates illness and employment setbacks. A dream in which a person drinks wine from a jug signifies excellent health, optimism and *joie de vivre*. If the dreamer drinks an unpleasant-tasting drink from a jug, it means that the anticipation of happy events will turn into disillusionment and disgust.

Juggler

A dream about a juggler in a circus or in some kind of

show attests to the fact that there is someone in the dreamer's surroundings who wants to cause him to fail, plots against him and makes every possible effort to accomplish this objective. If the juggler falls during the dream, the dreamer has been "saved." If the dreamer himself is the juggler, it attests to the fact that he is going through a difficult phase in which he has to make maximal efforts in order to succeed in his various roles. The dreamer may well feel as if he is the juggler who is doing what other people consider to be impossible.

Another meaning of a dream of this type is that the dreamer is a person who needs a lot of attention in general, and during this time in particular. For this reason, he is liable to be pushed into high-risk situations, get caught up in adventures, and get involved in dangerous and daring feats without any justification and, as a result, attract a lot of attention from his family and friends. The dreamer may also feel that he is needlessly endangering himself and is beginning to fear the risks he is taking upon himself.

July

A dream about the month of July is a dreary dream, but a sudden change will occur and the dreamer will enjoy unprecedented happiness.

Jumping

A dream about jumping is not a good omen: it means the dreamer can expect hardships, disappointment or frustration. A dream about jumping rope is a sign that the dreamer's associates will be dazzled by a daredevil display. If he dreams that he jumps rope with children, it means that

A B C D E F G H I J K L M N O P Q R S T U V W X Y Z

he is overbearing and bossy, and his children will not accord him any respect. If he dreams that cattle jump over a fence into his property, he will receive unforeseen help. If they jump out of his property in his dream, he can expect to suffer losses.

June

A dream about the month of June predicts great success. If a woman dreams that the country is drought-stricken, it implies that she will experience grief and bereavement.

Juniper trees

If a person dreams about juniper trees, it is a symbol of happiness and wealth emerging from misery and poverty. This dream bodes well for a person recovering from an illness. However, eating or picking juniper berries predicts problems and disease.

Jury

A dream about a jury is indicative of the dreamer's dissatisfaction with his job, and he will look for a new one. If the dreamer is acquitted by the jury, his business will be successful. If he is convicted, he will be mercilessly crushed by his enemies.

Justice

If a person dreams that he demands justice from somebody, it means that he has been falsely accused by people who are out to destroy him. If someone demands justice of him in a dream, it means that his good reputation and conduct are in question, and it is almost certain that he will not be able to defend them adequately.

A
B
C
D
E
F
G
H
I
J
K
L
M
N
O
P
Q
R
S
T
U
V
W
X
Y
Z

K

Kaleidoscope

A kaleidoscope in a dream is a symbol of rapid changes that will not be of great value.

Kangaroo

A dream about a kangaroo, especially if the creature appears in its natural habitat, hopping around in its characteristic manner and disappearing into the sunset, means a problematic relationship. The dreamer is enjoying the best of both worlds and is unable to focus on the relationship he is in. His volatility causes his partner to feel that s/he is not at the top of the dreamer's list of priorities. The dream may be implying that the dreamer has a *penchant* for someone else or that he is cheating on his partner. One way or the other, if the dreamer wants to preserve his relationship, he must show his desire to invest in it and not engage too much in other occupations. Moreover, he must refrain from spending too much time with other people, since this hints at a lack of satisfaction with his relationship.

Katydids

A dream about these large green grasshopper-like

insects does not bode well: they are a sign of bad luck and of the fact that the dreamer is dependent on others.

Keg

A dream about a keg symbolizes the dreamer's struggle to free himself from a situation of tyranny. If the keg is broken in the dream, it implies that the dreamer will be separated from people he loves.

Kennel / Doghouse

A dream about an empty kennel is a sign of something serious that is about to happen. This could well refer to a financial downfall, embroilment in business, and a substantial drop in assets. The person who dreams about an empty kennel must be very careful not to take any step that entails any kind of monetary outlay. If a person dreams about a kennel with a dog in it, he must also be careful. If the dog is large and threatening, bares its teeth and barks, it is a hint of legal complications, gossip and suspicions in which the dreamer is going to become embroiled. He must plan for the future by consulting with an experienced lawyer and ensuring that the paperwork is in order. A small and aggressive dog is a sign that despite the complications, the dreamer will succeed in defeating the people who are plotting his downfall.

Kettle

If a person sees a kettle in a dream, it means that there is a lot of work ahead of him. If the kettle has not boiled in the dream, it warns of a loss of assets. If the water in the kettle has boiled, it predicts changes, success and good luck.

Key

This hints at new directions. It is almost certain that this is the right time to open a new business or make a romantic relationship official. The purchase of property or an investment is also recommended and will be a huge success. If the dreamer gives a bunch of keys to someone, it hints that he trusts that person implicitly. A bunch of keys that gets lost means that the dreamer is locked inside himself and cannot make the most of the opportunities that come his way. He is advised to wait for new developments.

Keyhole

If a person spies on others through a keyhole in a dream, it means that he will make mischief by disclosing someone else's secrets. If he sees other people spying on him through a keyhole in a dream, it means that other people are prying into his affairs for their own benefit. If a person is unable to find a keyhole in a dream, it means that he will unwittingly hurt a friend.

Kidney

If a person dreamsg about kidneys, it is a warning dream, warning him of a serious illness or marital problems. A dream about overactive kidneys indicates that the dreamer will be involved in a juicy affair. A dream that features underactive kidneys means that a scandal will erupt, and it will not be advantageous to the dreamer.

Kid

A dream about a kid indicates that the dreamer lacks scruples when it comes to pleasure-seeking. He will break other people's hearts.

Killing

If a person kills an unarmed man in a dream, it presages trouble and sorrow. If the killing occurs in self-defense, it means victory and advancement.

King / Queen

The person who dreams of being a king or queen has aspirations of controlling the people around him/her. This unrealistic desire is liable to get him into undesirable situations such as rows and arguments for which he will pay dearly. He can expect to become involved in serious disputes unless he gets a hold of himself as soon as possible and changes his conduct. The dream can also imply unexpected success in business, but the dreamer must be doubly so as to avoid disappointments.

Dreams about royalty are always a good sign. If the dreamer sees himself reaching the royal palace and being received graciously, he will soon be accorded great honor and will reach a turning point in life. He may be about to meet influential people who can help him in many ways, for instance with his social and financial standing.

If the dreamer himself has royal status, it is an especially good sign. The dreamer will win a large sum of money or receive a particularly good job offer.

Another meaning of a dream about royalty is that the dreamer is not held in sufficient regard and deserves better.

A
B
C
D
E
F
G
H
I
J
K
L
M
N
O
P
Q
R
S
T
U
V
W
X
Y
Z

Kiss

A kiss in a dream has many different interpretations, according to the way in which it appears:

If a person dreams that he kisses someone in his family, it is a sign that he can expect a great deal of happiness in life on all levels. He will be satisfied with everything he has and know how to enjoy life.

A dream in which the dreamer kisses his partner is a sign that his lover is beginning to be indifferent toward him.

If a person dreams that he kisses a stranger, it is a warning dream. It warns of events occurring around the dreamer that are liable to harm him, but he is not in the least aware of them. Generally, these are events that are liable to place the dreamer right in the spotlight of a scandal, causing him shame and humiliation.

If a person dreams about a polite kiss that he gives a stranger, he is about to receive some kind of prize. The prize could be given to him at his workplace, but it could also be a prize in some kind of gambling activity, such as a lottery or a casino.

A dream about giving one's mother a kiss is a sign that success is on its way.

A dream about giving one's father a kiss means that the dreamer and his household are soon going to have joyful experiences.

If the dreamer kisses someone on the face, he can expect success in the near future, and this will be accompanied by great honor. People will greatly admire his actions and talents, and he will be welcomed in circles that were previously closed to him.

A kiss on the hand in a dream is a sign of good luck for the dreamer.

If a man dreams that he gives a married woman a kiss, he will not be happy. Even if he has everything he desires, he will always be lacking the one thing that will make him truly happy. He will always have the feeling that he has missed out on something.

If a man dreams that he kisses a single woman, it is a sign that he is liable to become embroiled in a scam from which he will emerge the loser.

A dream in which the dreamer sees himself kissing a dead person is a sign that he can expect to live a long life. He will have a long life on this earth and will enjoy good health. He will feel like a young person when he is old, since he will have a lot of energy.

If a woman sees herself kissing a male friend in a dream, it is a sign that she does not value herself sufficiently. She feels that she is a failure, that she is not successful, and this takes its toll in all areas of her life and inhibits her advancement.

A dream in which the dreamer sees himself kissing the ground of a foreign country is a sign of humiliation. He feels humiliated and despised for something that happened in reality and he is not aware of it.

A dream about kissing the ground in the Holy Land is a sign that kings are about to honor the dreamer. He will be elevated above the common people and will earn the admiration and love of many people because of his forthcoming renown.

If a man dreams that he kisses a woman's back, he is liable to be the victim of a woman's deceit. She will operate various manipulations on him, he will succumb, and that is how he will fall into her net and believe her lies.

A B C D E F G H I J **K** L M N O P Q R S T U V W X Y Z

Kitchen

If a person dreams about a kitchen, it means that he will have to cope with an unexpected and depressing emergency. If a woman dreams about a kitchen, it attests to satisfaction with family life and loyal friends.

Kite

A dream in which the dreamer sees himself flying a kite implies a loss of pride and a fall from the social point of view. The dreamer is smarting from the inner failure and he feels bad.

Having said that, things can change through hard work that requires a great deal of effort on the dreamer's part, but will eventually pay off.

Making a kite in a dream is a warning dream against deceptive visions and worthless imaginings.

If the kite the dreamer is flying reaches especially enormous heights, it means that the dreamer's aspirations will be realized. Moreover, a dream of this kind attests to the dreamer's character. He is not afraid of expressing his opinion out loud, even if it is not popular. The dreamer often feels that he must externalize his emotions and that he has to express the whisperings of his heart in whatever way possible.

If a person dreams that the kite he is flying tumbles to the ground, it is a prophetic dream. The dreamer can expect to receive an unpleasant message or announcement in the near future.

Kittens

A dream about kittens symbolizes endless problems and hassles, and the only way to end them is to kill the kittens. A dream about a plump white kitten means that a woman will be in danger of being deceived, but her common sense will avert it.

Knapsack

If a person dreams about a knapsack, it indicates happiness not in the company of friends.

Knee/s

A dream about hurt, bleeding, wounded or bruised knees hints at general problems the dreamer will encounter in the near future. Having said that, he will have to display patience and forbearance, since time will elapse before he succeeds in extricating himself from them. He will have to cope with the problems, no matter how difficult they are, and muster a great deal of psychological strength, mainly because of the fact that the problems will continue for a long time.

If the injury to the knees made them look broken in the dream, losses in the dreamer's love life can be expected. The crisis will be serious and even inevitable.

If the knees are at their best in the dream, that is, smooth and lovely and unblemished, the dream hints at abundance, success and good fortune in all areas. Joy and happiness will be the dreamer's lot, and this will radiate out into his surroundings. People will seek his company and compliment him on his achievements and on his appearance.

A B C D E F G H I J **K** L M N O P Q R S T U V W X Y Z

Knife

In most cases, a knife in a dream does not augur well. Generally, it refers to family quarrels, disputes and problems. However, if the knife is seen slicing bread, for instance, the dream indicates that the dreamer can be assured of repletion. "Repletion" means that he will never have problems of income.

As mentioned above, a dream about a knife usually attests to disputes, to quarrels and to misunderstandings with other people. This is even truer if the dream features a rusty knife. Since the disputes can reach the point of violent and extreme behavior, the dream hints that this extreme behavior must be toned down, and it is necessary for the dreamer to try to calm down and be patient and tolerant. If necessary, he should consult with a professional person.

If a dream features the dreamer's partner threatening him with a knife, the dream implies that the assailant is in danger of impotence and the loss of his sexual prowess. This reality may be disrupting the relationship between the couple to such an extent that it is expressed in a dream in the form of a threat with a knife.

If the knife in the dream has a handle that looks like a cross, it means that the danger of attack from some quarter is stalking the dreamer. The attack could come in the form of an outburst of rage from a close associate, but it may also be expressed in some way at work. He should brace himself psychologically for an unpleasant incident of this kind that can make his life difficult for some time.

If the dreamer receives a knife as a gift in a dream, it hints that the end of the friendship between the dreamer and the giver of the gift is on the horizon.

Knife grinder

A dream about a knife grinder warns the dreamer that people will treat his possessions with a complete lack of respect.

Knight

A dream about a knight has many meanings, which change according to the "picture" of the knight in the dream and according to the circumstances in which he appears. The myth that it is mainly women who dream about knights (on white horses) is incorrect. Men also dream about knights, generally in matters of dominance/subservience, or as a reaction to a state of dispute or war.

If the knight appears in his "classic" form (wearing armor and bearing a sword) in the dream, it implies that a person with whom the dreamer is not on good terms – and to whom he does not relate as a friend – will change his attitude, and their relationship will improve. They may not become bosom pals, but the situation in which they virtually turn their backs on each other will definitely change for the better, and they will no longer bear a grudge against each other.

If the dreamer himself is the knight, it means that the dream heralds good news, mainly of joy and happiness for the dreamer. This could be a family event such as a wedding or the birth of a child in the offing.

If a person dreams that someone close to him is a knight, the dream implies that if there are people who wish the dreamer ill, he will succeed in defeating them. No one can harm him, and he will deflect evil designs with ease.

If a young girl or a woman dreams about a knight, the

dream prophesies that the dreamer is about to be part of a special adventure, or that she is about to make an unexpected move that will bring new opportunities into her life. The dreamer is about to be swept away to make a change in her life in a direction she had not thought of previously, whether in her profession, in her studies, or some kind of trip.

A dream in which the knight attacks the dreamer or assumes a belligerent stance toward him is a sign that the dreamer will fall victim to a scam or a con job. Somebody will try to cheat him – possibly successfully – if the dreamer does not wise up and keep his eyes open.

A dream in which the knight is riding on a white horse implies that the solution to any problem that is bothering the dreamer is on the horizon: he will find the right path and follow it until he reaches the successful conclusion of some affair that is disturbing him. He must be open-minded so that he can look around and find the right path to follow.

If the most important feature of the dream is the armor worn by the knight, the dream symbolizes protection. The dreamer is protected mainly by his friends, who afford him basic security in everything he does in life.

Knitting

A dream about knitting attests to the dreamer's yearning for a state of repose and serenity that will affect his life and channel it toward a different lifestyle than the one he is leading at present. The dreamer leads a particularly busy life and he wants a change. Overall, a dream about knitting is an indication of good news and a rosy future. If the knitting needles fall down in a dream, it is a warning sign.

The dreamer must be particularly alert to a person close to him who is jealous of him and is liable to do anything to hurt him.

Knocker

A dream about a knocker means that the dreamer will be compelled to seek other people's advice and succor.

Knocking

If a person hears knocking in a dream, it is a sign that serious news is in the offing. If he dreams that he is woken up by knocking, the news will be extremely serious.

Knot

A dream that features a knot implies financial problems and money losses. A dream about tying a knot is a sign of independence and assertiveness.

L

Label

If a dream features a label or sticker indicating a name or an item, it foretells a future full of surprises.

Labor

If a person sees animals laboring under heavy loads in a dream, it means that he will enjoy prosperity, but he will mistreat his subordinates. If a person sees people laboring, it means that he will enjoy profits and health. If he himself labors in a dream, it is an indication of success in any future undertaking.

Laboratory

A dream about a laboratory implies time wasted on useless things when it could be put to better use.

Labyrinth

A dream about a labyrinth is a sign of business troubles as well as domestic conflict and lovers' quarrels. A dream about a dark labyrinth symbolizes transient but serious trouble and illness. A dream that features a labyrinth of green vines means success after certain failure. A dream about a labyrinth of railroads predicts long, boring and futile trips.

Lace

If a person sees lace in a dream, it is a sign of fidelity in love and a rise in status. If a woman dreams about lace, she will realize all her ambitions and desires. A dream about purchasing lace symbolizes wealth. If a person dreams about selling lace, it means that he is living beyond his means. A dream in which the dreamer is making lace is a sign of finding a wealthy, good-looking husband. If a person dreams about decorating wedding clothes with lace, it means that a woman will have many admirers, but she will not be getting married for a very long time.

Ladder

A dream in which the dreamer sees himself climbing up a ladder safely is a sign that he is about to be promoted at his workplace as a result of his industriousness, his persistence, his perseverance and his ability to stick to the goal. The dream augurs well for the dreamer in everything he turns his hand to. His wishes will be fulfilled, too. He will experience extraordinary prosperity and happiness.

If a person sees himself climbing up a particularly tall ladder in a dream, it is a sign that he will soon reject his lover, whether this is because of the fact that their love is over, or for other reasons, such as various types of utilitarian considerations.

If a person sees himself going down a crooked ladder, it is a sign that he will succeed in accomplishing his objective, even if the path leading to it is winding and difficult.

If a person sees himself going down a regular ladder, it is a sign that his plans will fail dismally.

If a person dreams that he feels dizzy while climbing up a ladder, it is a sign that a big event is about to occur in his life – an event that will be accompanied by huge profits. This event could occur at the dreamer's workplace, but it could also be a private event such as a celebration, party or wedding.

Climbing a rope ladder in a dream is a sign that the dreamer is about to earn a sum of money.

If a person sees himself carrying only a ladder in a dream, it is a sign that he is about to save someone. Even if he does so completely unwittingly, a certain action he performs will save a person who is associate with him.

If the dreamer sees other people climbing up a ladder in a dream, it is a sign that he has loyal friends and that he can rely on them completely. They will help him in times of distress and trouble.

A dream in which a person sees himself jumping from a ladder implies that soon there will be a "jump" in his social status.

His situation will improve from every point of view, since this jump will also bring him larger profits in business or a higher salary in his workplace.

If a dream features a falling ladder, or if the dreamer's efforts to climb up the ladder fail, the future does not augur well. He should be careful of things to come.

If a dream features a ladder leaning against a wall of the dreamer's home, someone in the dreamer's family is being disloyal to him. This person is showing signs of treachery, and is liable to reveal and spread deep secrets.

Ladle

If a person sees a ladle in a dream, it means that he will be lucky with a companion and with children. A dream that features a dirty or broken ladle predicts a terrible loss.

Ladybug

If a dream features this red insect with the black spots, it is a sign that the dreamer will soon come across a golden opportunity that will allow him to realize his greatest dreams.

Lagoon

A dream about a lagoon indicates that misuse of the dreamer's intellectual resources will drag him into confusion and uncertainty.

Lake

A dream that features a lake is a promising dream: all of the dreamer's investments will succeed, big time! He will enjoy the fruits of his labor, and the patience and forbearance he displayed in the past will bear fruit and certainly pay off. If in the past he thought that his investments were going down the drain, now it will be clear to him that it was worthwhile casting his bread upon the waters, even indirectly.

If the dreamer sees that the water in the lake is especially clear, it implies that his life has reached a positive turning point. He can now implement long-awaited plans easily; he is about to be liberated from worries or from something that was bothering him, which was his lot up till now. He will be overcome by a feeling of relief and fullness, and will feel that he is making the most of his life. The feeling of "missing out" on something because he did not experience it completely or did not fulfill his potential will dissipate. In parallel, his self-confidence will increase, and he will experience a feeling of better control over his life and over his ability to realize his talents.

Lamb

If a person sees frisky lambs in a dream, it is a sign of friendship and happiness. For the farmer, it heralds prosperity. If a dream features a dead lamb, it is a symbol of sorrow and death. The bleating of lambs in a dream will inspire the dreamer's generosity. A dream about slaughtering lambs means wealth at the expense of peace of mind. A dream about eating lamb chops means that the dreamer will worry about his children. If a dream features wolves or dogs tearing lambs apart, it means that innocent people are suffering at the hands of unscrupulous swindlers. If a person dreams about owning lambs, it is a sign of prosperity and comfort. A dream about shearing lambs is a sign of a cool, money-loving nature. A dream about carrying lambs means that the dreamer will bear the burdens of the people he loves happily. If he sees lambskins in a dream, it means that other people have been deprived of their joy and comfort.

Lame

If a woman dreams about someone lame, it predicts disappointment and bitterness in her life.

Lament

A dream about lamenting the loss of possessions or friends implies that joy and prosperity are in the offing. If a person laments the loss of relatives, it means that an illness will come along and seal friendships.

Lamp / Flashlight

A dream about a broken lamp implies that the dreamer is liable to find himself in a period of darkness in his life. He will be beset by disasters and hitches, mainly on the domestic level. He must be careful of fires or floods. A dream about a flickering light hints at the dreamer's unclear situation. This refers mainly to men-women relationships. He must take care not to make hasty and unfounded decisions, because he is liable to find himself deceived and disappointed.

Lamppost

If a person sees a lamppost in a dream, it means that he will be helped by a stranger in time of need. If he bumps into a lamppost in a dream, he is in danger of being swindled by enemies. If he sees a lamppost in his path, it means that he will have many problems in his life.

Lance

If a person dreams about a lance, it is a sign that he has powerful enemies. If the dreamer is injured by a lance in a dream, it means that he will be angered by an error of judgment. If he breaks a lance in a dream, he will succeed in overcoming obstacles that were insurmountable until now and achieve success.

A B C D E F G H I J K L M N O P Q R S T U V W X Y Z

Land

A dream that features fertile land is a good sign. However, barren land in a dream is a sign of failure and despair. If a person sees land while he is sailing on the ocean, he can anticipate great wealth and joy.

Landing (of an airplane)

A dream about a landing prophesies imminent difficulties, and these are expected to dampen the dreamer's mood, make him depressed and cause him to lose his optimism. Having said that, the difficult period will pass, since the dreamer will know how to deal with it and get back into a positive routine. The dreamer will eventually achieve a feeling of "purification." He will feel that he has learned a lesson from the difficult period he went through, and is now able to rebuild himself.

Lantern

If a person sees a lantern glowing in the dark, it means that he will come into sudden wealth. If the lantern suddenly disappears in the dream, financial affairs will go bad. If he dreams about carrying a shining lantern, it is a sign of altruism. If he dreams about breaking it, it means that the dreamer will injure himself while helping others. A dream about losing a lantern means business losses.

Lap

A dream about sitting on someone's lap implies being protected from problems. If a woman dreams that someone is sitting on her lap, she can expect to be criticized. If she holds a cat on her lap in a dream, she is in jeopardy of being seduced by a treacherous enemy.

Lapdog

If a person dreams about a lapdog, it indicates that friends will help the dreamer out of a predicament. If the dog in the dream is bony and sickly, the dreamer will suffer a setback in business.

Lard

A dream that features lard indicates an increase in prosperity. A dream about lard-covcred hand means disappointment.

Lark

A dream about a lark prophesies joy and happiness. It relates mainly to the dreamer's married life, and predicts a good life together, full of excitement, power, gaiety and joy. The dreamer will find a partner who will complement him in every way, a kind of "kindred spirit" with whom he will feel as comfortable as it is possible to be. A dream about a lark implies that the dreamer was really "born" to married life. He is the type of person who succeeds in extracting the full potential from marriage and from a life with a partner who completes him. His married life will be stable and healthy, the kind of relationship that can serve as a paradigm for marriage.

A B C D E F G H I J K L M N O P Q R S T U V W X Y Z

Laser

If a person dreams about a laser, he is warned not to waste his time and thoughts on trivialities when he should concentrate on important matters.

Latch

If a person dreams about a latch, it means that he will turn a deaf ear to an appeal for assistance. A dream about a broken latch implies that the dreamer will quarrel with his friends. He will also become ill.

Lateness

If a person dreams that he is late even though he tried to arrive on time, it attests to the fact that people value his opinion and are keen to hear what he has to say.

Latin

If a person dreams that he is studying Latin, it is a sign that his opinion about important matters of state has prevailed.

Laudanum

If a person takes laudanum in a dream, it attests to his weak character and his liability to be influenced by others. If he dreams that he prevents others from taking laudanum, it means that he will be the bearer of excellent news. If he dreams that he is administering laudanum, the dream implies that a member of his household will become mildly ill.

Laughter

Laughter in a dream, whether it is the dreamer or other people laughing, refers to a joyful event that will occur soon. There are very good chances of an interesting and unexpected development that will cause the dreamer and the members of his family joy and possibly even financial profit.

Laundromat

If a person dreams about doing his laundry in a laundromat, it signifies the end of an unsuccessful relationship, and a good new one in its place.

Laundry

In general, the meaning of this dream is instability. Just as laundry flaps in the breeze, so there will be uncontrollable changes in the dreamer's life, causing undesirable consequences. If a person dreams about clean laundry that reaches the threshold of the home, it hints at an urgent need for change and for setting several areas of life in order.

It is possible that the time has come to tidy or paint the house. It is reasonable to assume that there are several areas or rooms that have been neglected. They should be cleaned and aired as quickly as possible in order to achieve a situation of progress and flow.

Laurels

A dream that features laurels is a rare dream: it symbolizes honor, glory, fame, love and wealth that will

A B C D E F G H I J K **L** M N O P Q R S T U V W X Y Z

soon enter the dreamer's life. If a young woman dreams that she is placing a laurel wreath on her lover's head, she can rest assured that she will find a faithful, famous man.

Law

A dream about legal matters, judges, lawyers, lawsuits, pleading in court and so on serves as a warning dream and does not augur well. The meaning of such a dream is that the dreamer is liable to take a dive in a major deal, signing a contract, or any other matter linked to money. The dream implies that deals or financial decisions the dreamer is about to make in the near future are liable to be fateful and determine his financial future for a long time to come. Fate is not favorably inclined toward him, so he has to take extra precautions in everything to do with finances, investments, and long-term commitments or decisions in this realm.

Lawn

A dream in which a lawn or grass appears is mostly a sign of the dreamer's full, tranquil, quiet and fulfilling life. Another meaning of such a dream is a signal to the dreamer that his place of residence has a good influence on him. The dream may occur during a period when the dreamer is thinking of making changes in his life and moving house or moving to a different area. The dream implies that everything the dreamer needs is within reach, and that he must not move out of the area where he lives, since the great success that is still awaiting him in life will come precisely because of that area. This is not the time to move out and to wander off to other realms.

If a person dreams that he is mowing the lawn, it is a

prophetic dream that implies that a particular wish or ambition of his is about to be realized or will be completely fulfilled.

If the person who dreams of a lawn is in love, the dream informs him that he will soon be united with the object of his love – that is, a wedding or a marriage contract is in the offing. Even if the dreamer does not wish to get involved in a commitment at the moment, he will soon change his mind and eventually find himself in a process leading to marriage.

If a person dreams that the lawn in his garden is green, the dream attests to the fact that everything will be excellent in the future. However, if the grass is greener on the other side, the dream implies that the dreamer will be gnawed by tremendous jealousy for someone or something (he knows exactly what). The feeling of jealousy that is germinating inside him will give him no rest, and if he does not combat it and learn to overcome it, he will suffer from it and will not be able to live a full and tranquil life.

Lawnmower

A dream about a lawnmower symbolizes a tedious social duty the dreamer will have to perform.

Lawsuit

A dream about a lawsuit attests to the fact that the dreamer is embroiled in a complicated relationship. The source of the problems in this relationship is a simple misunderstanding. The dream indicates that the misunderstanding is on the verge of being clarified, and the relationship will be normal and enjoyable once more.

In most cases, a dream like this refers to a simple and comfortable life, free of worries and pressures. The dreamer does not normally break the routine, and he does so only infrequently. Having said that, a tiring life of routine like that is liable to be devoid of excitement and adventure.

If a person dreams about a lawsuit and is actually involved in one, the dream has no meaning. It is only meaningful when the background to the dream is a life of routine.

Lawyer

A dream about a lawyer indicates that the dreamer is going through a phase of uncertainty regarding an issue of some kind and is looking for a qualified person who will give him professional advice. His problem might involve property, but it might equally be concerned with something to do with his private life. In either case, the dream attests to a feeling of distress that will disappear if the dreamer does indeed seek professional assistance.

Lazy

If a person acts or feels lazy in a dream, it means that he will make a mistake in a business venture and this will culminate in disappointment. If a woman dreams that her lover is lazy, she will not have any luck in finding the right man.

Lead

A dream about lead does not augur well: lead is a sign

of failure. A dream about lead ore foretells accidents and business failure. A dream about smelting lead means that the dreamer will engender failure because of his impatience. A dream about a lead mine means that the dreamer's friends will regard his income with suspicion. A dream that features white lead means that the dreamer is endangering his children by his carelessness.

Leak

A dream that features a leak in the plumbing of a house or even in one of the faucets attests to a situation of stagnation in a particular area of life. If it is not resolved, it is liable to cause serious damage. It is reasonable to assume that it concerns the romantic or emotional realm. There could be a problem between one of the parents and the children, especially with the rebellious one among them. The infidelity of a partner is also a possibility. Now is the time to take some time off and look into things at home, before matters get completely out of hand.

Leaping

If a young woman dreams about leaping over an obstacle, it means that her wishes will come true after a lot of vicissitudes.

Learning

If a person dreams about learning, it means that he will enjoy acquiring knowledge. If he dreams about going into places of learning, he will enjoy fame and fortune. If a person dreams about learned people, it is a sign that his friends will be well-known and interesting. If a woman dreams of rubbing shoulders with learned people, she will fulfill her ambitions of status and fame.

Leather

Leather is a sign of business success and success with women. If the dreamer is dressed in leather, he will have luck in a particular venture. Leather ornaments denote fidelity. Heaps of leather are a sign of wealth and joy. Dreaming of being a leather merchant means that changes in one's business dealings must be made if the dreamer is to be successful.

Leaves

If a dream features green, fresh leaves on a tree, it prophesies success in the emotional realm, successful love affairs, a great love that will sweep the dreamer off his feet, and special experiences that he will enjoy with his partner.

If a dream features autumn leaves, or yellow, withered and dry leaves, the dreamer is also suffering from autumn in his heart. His heart is empty and sad, and he is inundated with great sorrow. In general, mental sorrow and pain come from disappointed love, but they might also stem from a mistake the dreamer made and is sorry about. The dreamer may have made a mistake for which he is going to have to pay for a long time, and he cannot atone for his deeds in any way. Remorse is torturing him and is not letting him rest.

If a person dreams about walking on leaves, the dream implies that he is occupying himself with useless things rather than with important ones, and he is wasting his time. He must concentrate on the crux of the matter and on the true meaning of things, and stop thinking about the marginal stuff that is preoccupying him unjustifiably.

Lecture

If the dreamer sees himself lecturing in front of an audience, it is a sign that his career is taking off. In the future, the dreamer will gain satisfaction from his profession. He will derive a great deal of interest and enjoyment from what he does, and will enjoy a lot of professional satisfaction. Success will shine upon him, and he will feel appreciated. The honor that he will be accorded by people who belong to the professional community around him will provide him with a great deal of pleasure and happiness, and he will feel that he is fulfilling his potential and making the most of his abilities.

Ledger

If a person keeps a ledger in a dream, it implies difficulties and disappointments. If he makes mistakes in a ledger in a dream, it is a prediction of quarrels and minor losses. If he loses a ledger, it implies losses as a result of carelessness. If a ledger is destroyed by fire in a dream, it means that the dreamer's friends will be responsible for his misfortune. If a person dreams that a woman is keeping his ledger, he will sustain financial losses because of mixing business and pleasure.

Leeches

If a person dreams about leeches, he is going to be attacked by his enemies. If leeches bite the dreamer in a dream, it is a warning of danger from a surprising quarter.

A
B
C
D
E
F
G
H
I
J
K
L
M
N
O
P
Q
R
S
T
U
V
W
X
Y
Z

Leeward

If a sailor dreams about sailing leeward, it is a sign of a happy voyage. For other people, this dream implies a pleasant trip.

Leg

If a person's legs are conspicuous in a dream, it means that he is logical, self-aware and self-confident and has many good friends. If a person dreams about admiring lovely female legs, it means that he will make an idiot of himself over a woman.

A dream about misshapen legs indicates that the dreamer keeps bad company and makes stupid deals. A dream that features a wounded leg implies losses and disease. A dream about a wooden leg means insincere conduct toward friends. A dream about the inability to use one's legs is a sign of poverty. If a person dreams about having three or more legs, it refers to the fact that many of his most cherished business ventures will never come off.

If a woman dreams about admiring her own legs, she is conceited, and finds her lover disgusting. If she dreams that her legs are hairy, she will be a domineering wife.

Legerdemain

If a person dreams that he practices legerdemain or sees other people doing so, he will become embroiled in a difficult situation from which he will have a hard time extricating himself.

Legislature

If a person dreams about belonging to the legislature, it means that he will brag about his wealth and will mistreat his family. He will not be given a promotion.

Legume

A dream about a legume implies financial success and prosperity in business.

Lemon

A dream about a lemon in any of its forms (eating a lemon, squeezing a lemon, growing a lemon, making lemonade and so on) is a "sour" dream – it does not augur well:

If a person dreams that he himself or someone else is eating a lemon, he can expect a great disappointment in life, accompanied by humiliation and a feeling of destruction and bitterness. The dreamer may have a particular goal in his sights that he is dying to accomplish, but he has to be prepared for the fact that it is highly likely that he will not be able to attain his goal for some reason. This goal could be winning the heart of a person the dreamer loves, studies he wants to pursue, a profession he intends to acquire, or a certain status he yearns to reach – he will have to resign himself to the fact that he will not be able to fulfill his heart's desire and will be disappointed. Moreover, the dreamer may feel humiliated because of some move he made or a move that other people made that affected him. The feeling of rejection and inner repression will be terrible, but if he maintains his strength of mind, he will be able to overcome the crisis and move forward.

In most cases, a dream about a lemon indicates that a powerful feeling of jealousy will cause unexpected problems. Jealousy of someone else may even erupt in the dream itself and will cause many problems in his life. However, the dreamer himself may be the object of other people's jealousy, and even if this is the case, he will go through a difficult phase that will disrupt his life.

A dream in which the dreamer sees himself picking lemons in an orchard attests to the fact that there are people who are stealing from him, but he is completely unaware of this. If he shakes himself and looks around, he will see that this is the state of things, and he should wake up and take care of it before it's too late.

If a person dreams that he is growing lemon trees in his yard or garden, the dream implies that there is a certain family member who is doing the dreamer an injustice. The dreamer may be aware of it and is not reacting because he wants to maintain peace and unity in the family, but he must be aware of the fact that this injustice causes cumulative damage, and he is well advised to arrest it and get rid of it.

There is one case in which a dream about a lemon has a positive meaning: If a person dreams about lemon juice, that is, about a squeezed lemon or lemonade, the dream implies that if there are people close to the dreamer, such as his family or good friends, who are suffering from a disease, they will recover and feel fine.

In contrast, if the dreamer's enemies are ill, the dream hints that they will not be fortunate enough to recover from the disease.

Lemonade

If a person sees himself drinking lemonade in dream, it means that he is allowing others to take advantage of him so that they can finance some fun activity they want to engage in.

Lending

A dream about lending money indicates the dreamer's inability to pay debts. If he dreams about lending other things, the dream implies that his exaggerated largesse will lead to poverty. If the dreamer refuses to lend things, it is a sign of his assertiveness. If others offer to lend the dreamer objects or money in a dream, it implies good friendship and wealth.

Lentils

If a person dreams about lentils, it is a sign of conflicts and a negative environment. If a young woman has this dream, her parents will force her to opt for a man she does not love.

Leopard

A dream about a caged leopard is a warning dream: it warns of an enemy who is attempting to hurt the dreamer. However, he will not succeed. A dream about killing a leopard means success. If a person sees a leopard attacking him, it implies that he will encounter difficulties along his path to success. A dream about leopards in the wild escaping from the dreamer implies problems in business and love, but they will be overcome. A dream about

A B C D E F G H I J K **L** M N O P Q R S T U V W X Y Z

leopard skin means that the dreamer will suffer at the hands of a false friend.

Leprosy

If a person dreams that he has leprosy, the dream predicts sickness, monetary loss and ostracizing by other people. If he sees other people with leprosy in a dream, it means disappointment in love and business.

Letter

A dreamer who receives a letter in his dream can expect exciting news in the near future. It may well be news of progress in business, but there is also a possibility that someone from the past will establish ties that will become especially significant – possibly even romantic. If the dreamer sends a letter to someone else in a dream, he is going through a difficult phase and has been waiting for new developments for a long time. There could be a trip abroad following a tempting work offer. The matter must be weighed up carefully. Not every offer that comes along constitutes a suitable solution, despite the problems that exist in reality.

Lettuce

Lettuce in a dream attests to the fact that the dreamer is a healthy person and enjoys every aspect of life except one – the realm of love, marriage, sex and family life, even though he is generally proud of his children and derives a great deal of satisfaction from them.

In general, the dreamer is satisfied with what he has

achieved in his life, and he even defines himself as "happy." He does not suffer from any particular problems and his life flows smoothly. However, his sex life and everything to do with his marriage is on the rocks. He cannot shake off the tensions inherent in the topic, nor can he achieve what he wants to achieve regarding this topic, despite many attempts on his part. The dream hints that everything is actually fine in his life, and that he must let things take their course. Eventually, they will also work themselves out. The perpetual tension in which he lives in the attempt to save his marriage simply interferes with the normal course of his life. He must go with the flow, and everything will come right.

Liar

If a person dreams that other people are liars, it implies that he will no longer back a plan that he himself proposed. If a person is accused of being a liar in a dream, it means that he will be worried because of dishonest people. If a woman dreams that her lover is a liar, she will lose a good friend.

Library

If a person dreams about being in a library, it implies that he will become bored with his occupation and will seek knowledge. If he is in a library but not because he is seeking knowledge, it means that he wants to deceive his friends.

A B C D E F G H I J K L M N O P Q R S T U V W X Y Z

Lice

A dream about lice implies that the dreamer is hounded by feelings of social alienation or inferiority as well as by worries of ill health. A dream that features lice on cattle is an indication of famine and ruin. A dream about body lice denotes that the dreamer's conduct toward the people around him will be bad. If a person dreams about becoming infected with lice, it is a prediction of disease and an indication of a fear of death.

License

A dream about a license indicates disputes and losses. If a woman dreams about a marriage license, she will soon become involved in a bad relationship.

Lie

A dream in which the dreamer sees himself lying is a sign that he is aware of the fact that his behavior is not appropriate, does not reflect well on him, and makes him an object of contempt. This feeling is unbearable, and he feels tremendous regret and remorse for what he has done.

If a person dreams that another person lies to him or tries to cheat him, it means that someone close to him wants to hurt him and defraud him somehow. The dreamer must be on guard so as not to fall victim to the scam. Similarly, someone might be trying to defraud the dreamer in the business context, and he must be extremely alert at work in order to preempt trouble.

A dream about a lie in general indicates that the dreamer is aware of the fact that lies have short wings, and in the end the truth will come out. If a person dreams that he has been cheated, it is possible that he was involved in some illegal affair or spurious venture. The dream warns against getting involved in such ventures in the future as well as against the other party involved in the venture.

Lie detector

If a person dreams that he has to take a lie detector test, it means that he will soon be the focus of some scandal.

Life insurance salesman

If a person sees a life insurance salesman in a dream, it implies that he will soon meet someone who will be beneficial to his business. If the salesman is distorted in any way in the dream, it does not augur well.

Lifeboat

If a person dreams about being on a lifeboat, he can expect to escape from something bad. A dream that features a sinking lifeboat means that the dreamer's friends will be partially responsible for his predicament. If a person dreams that he is lost in a lifeboat, it means that he will be overwhelmed with hardships. If he dreams that he is saved, he will be spared disaster.

Light

Light in a dream generally implies temporary success at everything the dreamer does. Even if the more distant future holds the dreamer's "downfall," the dream indicates that the temporary success can be so great that he can "save up" for a rainy day.

The intensity of the light in the dream alters its meaning:

Dim light symbolizes a depressed mood, depression, the blues, and a feeling of profound distress. This kind of dream can often hint at the onset of a disease in the dreamer. Sometimes he does not yet know about the disease, so he should go and get a checkup as soon as possible.

Bright light indicates the opposite: the dreamer's health is good, he enjoys a good, full and rich life, and the wellbeing he radiates to those around him causes them to like him and revel in his presence.

Light that emanates from a source such as an illuminated light-bulb is a sign that the dreamer can expect to inherit in the near future. The inheritance will make him wealthy, and his standard of living will rise dramatically.

If a person sees a light that has been extinguished in a dream, it hints that danger lurks for him in matters of love. The dreamer is liable to lose something valuable as a result of a bad relationship, and therefore he must be strong enough to break off such a flawed relationship as quickly as possible.

If a very distant light features in a dream, it is a prophecy of a safe return from a long journey (not necessarily the dreamer's journey). It could be the safe return of a person close to the dreamer – such as a partner, parent or child – who traveled to a distant country and is about to return safe and sound.

The light of a candle or candelabra hints that the dreamer is interested in things that are linked to spirituality or mysticism. These topics attract the dreamer, and for him, the world of mystery constitutes an enchanted world that draws him with invisible ropes, sometimes against his will.

Lighthouse

If a person dreams about a lighthouse in a storm, he is going to have trouble and sadness that will then be replaced by happiness and prosperity. If he sees the lighthouse from a calm sea in a dream, his life will be pleasant and tranquil.

Lightning

Seeing lightning in a dream predicts that the dreamer can expect changes for the good in most areas of his life: He is about to switch jobs and move house and enjoy far better conditions than he had previously. The dreamer will also be highly successful in business or in various financial investments. This is especially true for people involved in agriculture: they can expect good and abundant crops (this is linked to their talents and abilities as well as to environmental conditions – a rainy year, and so on).

If a person dreams that he is struck by lightning, it is a warning dream, warning him of an accident or some other injury that is liable to disrupt his life all of a sudden. Having said that, some people interpret a dream like this as a prophecy of a rapid recovery from a disease to which the dreamer will soon succumb.

If lightning is accompanied by thunder in a dream, it implies a golden opportunity to get rich and make fast and easy profits. Moreover, there is a hint of a good love life and a successful relationship.

Lightning rod

If a person sees a lightning rod in a dream, it predicts that the dreamer's favorite project is in danger of collapse.

If he sees lightning strike a lightning rod in a dream, it is a prediction of an accident or bad tidings. If he dreams that he is having a lightning rod installed, it means that he should be instructed as to how to initiate a new venture so that it will not end in disappointment. If a person dismantles a lightning rod in a dream, it implies a positive change in plans. If a dream features many lightning rods, all kinds of trouble can be expected.

Lily

If a person dreams about a lily that blooms out of season, the dream hints at a disappointment awaiting him. If he holds great hopes about something, he must lower his expectations because the disillusionment that will result from a big disappointment is liable to be severe.

A lily that appears dry and wilted in a dream is a sign that the dreamer does not trust his friends and that he does not have faith in them.

The people who call themselves "friends" are nothing other than people who wish him harm. The dream stresses what the dreamer is in the habit of internalizing and ignoring – his dissatisfaction with his friends and his basic inability to believe in them.

Another interpretation of a dream about lilies mainly refers to Christians: they tend to link the symbol of the lily to sanctity, such as a holy person, a sacred ritual and so on. The lily is also linked to symbolism and symbols and to rituals in general, and not just to the ones linked with religion.

Lime (fruit)

If a person dreams about eating limes, it signifies bad luck and illness.

Lime (mineral)

A dream about the mineral lime predicts a passing disaster followed by unprecedented good fortune.

Limekiln

A dream that features a limekiln informs the dreamer that there is nothing in the immediate future – either in business or in love.

Limousine

A dream about a limousine predicts sudden and unexpected good luck.

Limping

A dream about a friend, an acquaintance or even a stranger who limps indicates failure and disappointment in the economic or emotional realm. What seems to be a certainty will not stand the test of reality. In contrast, if a person dreams that he himself limps, it means that he is going through a difficult phase. He feels that he is not in control of the situation, and as a result, he must postpone taking important decisions, especially the kind that concern a large financial outlay and signing contracts. His consolation lies in the fact that the situation is going to change in the near future.

Line

If a person sees himself standing on line in a dream, it attests to the fact that a relationship with an old friend, severed as a result of a quarrel, will be soon be patched up.

Linen

If a person dreams about linen, it is a sign of happiness and prosperity. If he sees someone dressed in linen clothes in his dream, it means that he is about to receive good news about an inheritance. If a person dreams that he is wearing good, clean linen, he will have a wonderful life. If the linen in the dream is dirty, there will be the occasional period of grief and bad luck.

Lion

If a lion appears in a dream, but not in any particular context, it implies that one of these days, the dreamer will receive help from a friend. At the precise moment when he is in trouble, help or redemption will come from one of his close friends. In addition, it is a positive sign that attests to success in all fields. The dreamer has nothing to hesitate about concerning his future path, since the dream promises him numerous significant achievements in every area of life.

If a person sees the lion's den in his dream, it is a sign that the immediate future will bring good news and that the coming year will be a successful one for the dreamer, both materially and spiritually.

If the lion is in a cage in the dream, it means that even if the dreamer has enemies, or if there are people who are out to get him, he will ultimately get the better of them and overcome them, and will succeed in attaining what he wants. His enemies' plans to harm him will be foiled.

Fighting a lion in a dream indicates the dreamer's superiority in anything to do with his powers of persuasion. Armed with nothing but the power of his words, he can convince people who oppose him and his opinions to change their minds and stand by him. In this way, he can also defeat his enemies and overpower them.

If the dreamer wrestles with a lion and beats him, the dream hints that the dreamer should compromise on his points of view and not stand up for them at any price. Flexibility of ideas and thoughts and the ability to display pragmatism may help him later on. He must try to avoid conflicts at all costs.

Lioness

Dreams about lionesses or lions attest to good fortune and blessings that will soon be the dreamer's lot. Dreams that feature a lioness with cubs undoubtedly indicate a person who protects his family jealously, especially during hard times. An improvement in the situation can be expected in the near future, thanks to the dreamer's courage. Dreams about a small lioness roaming around the area of the house predict a proposal of marriage or a similar romantic proposition. A lioness or a lion in a circus act may imply that the dreamer feels that he is in a dangerous place in which there is far more than what meets the eye. There could be tension in the workplace and the dreamer does not have a great deal of faith in the person who works with him or in his superiors. In the future, the dreamer will display strength and daring that will help him cope with the situation and advance in the directions he wants.

Lips

If a person sees full, fleshy and healthy lips in a dream, and they are bright red, it is a sign that he can look forward to joy and happiness in the future, and that he will find himself at the center of attention. The dreamer loves attention and knows how to get it. Being in the spotlight is a basic need for him, like an actor's desire to occupy center stage. From his point of view, when he accomplishes his goal of being at the center of attention of the people around him, he will have achieved everything in life and will be happy with his lot.

If a person sees pale, thin, colorless lips in his dream, it is a sign that pain and sorrow will be his lot, mainly as a result of his shattered self-respect. The dreamer may be suffering from some kind of abuse that is causing him to lose his self-respect and feel wounded. This makes him feel sorrow and despair and places him in a situation from which it is extremely difficult for him to extricate himself. He needs a great deal of reinforcement from his surroundings in order to continue functioning and feel joy and happiness once more.

Liquor

If a person dreams about buying liquor, it implies that he wants property that does not belong to him. If a person sells liquor in a dream, it is a sign of imminent criticism. A dream about drinking liquor means that the dreamer will obtain money in a slightly shady way; his companions will try to get him to spend it on them, as will women. A dream about liquor in bottles implies very good luck. If a woman is drinking liquor in a dream, it means that she has an easy-going, superficial character and lifestyle, and does not harbor any jealousy or hard feelings.

Listening / Eavesdropping

Listening in a dream generally appears in the form of the dreamer seeing himself eavesdropping on someone else, or as the victim of someone else's eavesdropping. Listening is not done overtly, and it contains an element of concealment, secrecy and attempting to plot against someone else.

If a person actually sees himself eavesdropping on someone else (in order to reveal that person's secret to a third party, or in order to "shadow" him), the dream implies that the dreamer can anticipate pleasant surprises. He may receive good news from far away or find himself at the center of a happy event.

If a person dreams that someone eavesdropped on him, the dream serves as a warning against getting embroiled in serious situations. The dreamer is not aware of certain processes that are occurring in his life and are liable to get him embroiled in troubles. Whether he ignores occurrences of which he is aware or whether things are done without his knowledge, he has a great chance of getting into difficult situations from which it will be hard for him to extricate himself. If he has not been aware of his situation up till now, the dream must ignite a red light in his mind, and he must change his ways and act before it is too late.

Liver

If a person dreams about any liver disorders, it indicates that his partner will be cantankerous, and strife will reign in his home. If he dreams about eating liver, it means that his beloved has been seduced by someone else.

Lizard

A dream in which a lizard appears in a house is interpreted positively: a small treasure will be revealed to the dreamer.

This "treasure" need not appear in the usual sense of "treasure" that we're used to from fairy tales – money and other material things – but it could reach the dreamer in the form of something he is longing for and is likely to make use of in the future. This could be passing an important exam, winning something that is very meaningful to him, receiving something he has not been able to lay hands on, and so on.

A lizard that is seen in some other context in a dream implies that a secret belonging to the dreamer is liable to be revealed by some completely unexpected element. The revelation may be linked to a letter that was meant for the dreamer but was opened by the wrong person or by people seeking to harm the dreamer. A lizard may also indicate that the source of the evil will come from an evil person, a swindler, a cheat, who is in the dreamer's immediate surroundings and of whose existence the dreamer is blithely unaware.

Loaf

A person who dreams about a loaf of bread is worried about the bad financial situation he is in at the moment. The dreamer is very worried and does not know what he has to do in order to solve the problem.

Loan

A dream about a loan can have several meanings. If a person dreams that he loaned money to other people, it means that the dreamer's friends are about to change their minds about something very central to his life. He must be prepared for the fact that people are liable to "switch sides" and present him with opinions that are different than and opposite to his own about a particular matter of principle.

A dream in which someone asks the dreamer for a loan hints at financial losses that are liable to occur in the near future and undermine the dreamer's financial situation. He must be aware of this and act accordingly in order to prepare himself for this situation.

If a person dreams that he is unable to return money that he has borrowed, the dream actually implies the opposite: soon the dreamer's financial situation will improve, and he will accomplish the tasks he set himself and will be able to return sums of money he borrowed, even if the sums are large and significant.

Lobster

If a person sees lobsters in a dream, it is a sign of great prosperity. If he eats them in the dream, it means that he will get into superficial company. A dream that features

A B C D E F G H I J K **L** M N O P Q R S T U V W X Y Z

lobsters in a salad indicates that the dreamer will make the most of pleasurable things. If he dreams that he orders a lobster, it means that he will occupy a high post, with many people subordinate to him.

Lock

A dream about locks of any kind implies a difficulty. The difficulty, which has not yet come to the fore, may occur in the field of work or family. The dreamer is liable to find himself in a place he did not expect to be in, facing difficulties and problems. A dream in which the dreamer comes to a room with a closed door hints at difficulties at work. A locked box attests in most cases to personal problems, probably with the dreamer's partner.

A lock that opens easily indicates that a certain problem will be solved.

A dream in which there is a battle and a struggle to open the lock hints that even if certain problems are solved, this will not be to the dreamer's satisfaction.

In order to ease the situation, it is necessary to initiate a talk between the parties involved in the problem that has arisen. Communication, even if it does not lead to agreement, at least clarifies the situation.

Locket

If a young woman dreams that her lover places a locket around her neck, it means that she will soon be married and have lovely children. If she loses the locket in the dream, it portends that her life will be destroyed as a result of bereavement. If a lover dreams that his sweetheart returns his locket to him, he must brace himself for disappointment. The woman of his dreams will not relate to him in the manner he likes. If a person dreams about breaking a locket, it means that a woman will have an erratic husband who is completely inconsistent in business and in his relationship with her.

Lockjaw

If a person dreams about having lockjaw, it means that he can expect trouble as the result of someone else's treachery. If a woman sees somebody else with lockjaw in a dream, her happiness will decrease as a result of friends giving her unpleasant things to do. If cattle get lockjaw in a dream, it means that the dreamer will lose a friend.

Locomotive

A dream about a speeding locomotive is a sign of a vast increase in fortune and journeys to faraway places. A dream that features a stationary locomotive implies trouble and stagnation in business. Moreover, trips will be canceled.

A dream about a locomotive collision denotes anguish and financial loss. If a person hears a locomotive in a dream, it means that he can expect to receive news from far away. He will also effect beneficial changes in business strategies. If a person hears the whistle of a locomotive, it predicts the arrival of a long-lost friend, or the offer of a good job.

A B C D E F G H I J K L M N O P Q R S T U V W X Y Z

Locust

A dream about a locust has a special meaning, especially if it appears in the form of a swarm of locusts. The dreamer is disturbed by some kind of threat hanging over him. He may be going through a stressful period during which he has to make fateful decisions – the kind that will determine his future. The threat hanging over him does not emanate from something external, but rather stems from the dreamer's everyday life. In other words, the dream does not refer to a threat that comes from another person, but rather to certain things that constitute a threat for him. If the locusts appear in the form of a large swarm that covers the sky, the dream implies that the dreamer is in some kind of suffocating situation: the sky has darkened, and not because of clouds or natural elements, but because of the onset of something else that is unexpected and threatening. The sensation of a lack of air, space and freedom hints to the dreamer that he is operating incorrectly, and that he has to change his ways, his customs and his habits. One of those factors is bothering him, and this comes out in the dream since he refrains from tackling it in his daily life.

Lodger

If a woman dreams of having lodgers, it means that she will be unwillingly privy to bad secrets. A lodger who leaves without paying means that she can expect trouble with men. If the lodger pays, it is a good sign, meaning financial gain.

Looking glass

If a woman dreams about a looking glass, it means that he will soon encounter shocking treachery that can lead to wful quarrels or breakups.

Loom

If a person sees a loom operated by a stranger, it is an ndication of trouble. However, there is also a measure of iappy anticipation. If a person dreams that a good-looking voman is operating the loom, it is a good omen for lovers: t implies compatibility and many interests in common. If he dream shows a woman weaving at an old-fashioned loom, it means that she has a good husband and beautiful children. If the loom is idle in the dream, the dreamer will have to deal with a petulant, time-consuming person.

Lord's Prayer

If a person dreams that he recites the Lord's Prayer, it means that hidden enemies are placing him in jeopardy, and he will need all the help he can get from his friends. If he dreams that someone else says the prayer, it means that his friend is in danger.

Loss

A dream about a loss does not bear glad tidings; rather, it serves as a kind of warning dream about the future. This is true not only regarding a loss, but also if the dreamer sees himself being injured in some way or suffering some kind of blow in a dream. In such a case, the dreamer must be alert to what is going on in his life. He must be sensitive to the people around him, since someone is trying to set a trap for him. He must pay attention to the changes that are occurring around him and to every hint that can indicate approaching danger. These are difficult days for the dreamer, and if he takes one injudicious step, does not pay attention to small details or behaves incorrectly, he can place himself at risk and unwittingly spark changes that are liable to be disastrous for him. The dream warns against complacency, and it is advisable to relate to its messages.

Lottery

If the dreamer is involved in the draw, it means that he is wasting his time, and will have to go on a futile journey. If his number comes up, his winning will cause him anxiety. If others win in a lottery, it means lots of fun, laughter and socializing. Any kind of lottery in a young woman's dream means that she is not entirely responsible, and will marry someone on whom she cannot rely. Dreaming of a lottery indicates bad business connections and temporary love relationships.

Louse

A dream about a louse or lice generally occurs along with an irksome feeling of itching. A person who dreams about lice generally scratches his forehead during the dream.

A dream about lice that has no immediate connection to lice (that is, it does not occur after lice have actually been found in the dreamer's head, or after he has undergone treatment for getting rid of them) attests to the dreamer's mental inhibitions. In most cases, he is a person who suffers

A B C D E F G H I J K L M N O P Q R S T U V W X Y Z

from feelings of inferiority; he feels that he is not good enough for anything because he is not qualified to perform simple tasks. He does not feel that he is an integral part of the society in which he lives. Rather, he feels rejected, unwanted and useless in every way. The dream serves as a mirror for his emotions and inner feeling of being despised and worthless.

Love

It is impossible to relate to a dream about love exclusively, since we are talking about an emotion. (In a dream, only an emotion that is manifested in a scene or in an action is discussed.) Therefore, we can relate to love in a dream in accordance with how it is manifested in the dream.

If the dreamer is having an affair with a member of the opposite sex in the dream, the dream presages success and happiness in his love life. The dreamer's relationship with his mate will prove itself, and he will enjoy a good, happy and sizzling love life.

If lovers have a row in a dream, it is a sign that the couple are about to enter into a whirlpool of conflicts and disagreements, mainly about family matters. Problems in family life and misunderstandings with close or distant family members will cause arguments and a bad atmosphere between them.

If the person dreams that he is in love with two people at the same time, the dream implies that he is betraying the trust of someone close to him. Acts of deception or denial directed at a close person are liable to lead to a serious rift that will have an unhappy ending. The dreamer tries to conceal the truth, thereby toying not only with the other person's trust, but also with his emotions.

If a woman dreams that she loves her husband, it is a sign that disputes and rows with neighbors are in the offing. Unresolved problems with people nearby will crop up and come to the surface.

If a person dreams that he loves his wife, the dream means that he can expect an exciting surprise soon. It is almost certain that he is about to win a money prize of some kind, or undergo a change in status at work or in his place of residence – something that will be the equivalent of winning the lottery.

If a woman dreams that other people love her husband, it attests to the fact that she has been cheated on. The dream signals her that she must scrutinize her married life. Even if everything seems to be great on the surface, things of a completely different kind are going on beneath the surface. The dreamer must be alert, pay attention to what is going on around her, and be heedful of her surroundings. If not, she is liable to discover that she is a cuckold. Needless to say, everyone knows that her husband is cheating on her – except her.

If a man dreams a similar dream, that is, that other people love his wife – the dream implies that he must be careful of friends that pretend to be soul mates but in fact seek to harm him, and will take the first opportunity to stab him in the back. The dreamer must be alert and try to identify the fake smile that may one day constitute a serious stumbling-block in his path to success.

If a person dreams about writing love letters, it means that people are gossiping about him behind his back. He must be aware of this, since even if the gossip is not particularly malicious, it can still hurt him. The reason for the gossip may lie in the dreamer's inappropriate deeds, and he must examine himself carefully in order to see that he has not erred in his conduct.

If a person dreams of reading love letters, he will soon receive good news. Life will smile on him, and if he is feeling depressed, he will soon go from "darkness to light" and his personal feeling will improve beyond recognition, thanks to the imminent good news. This news will change the entire picture, and will have a long-term positive effect.

If a person dreams about someone he loves dearly, in a special way, and for whom he feels emotions that he has never felt for anyone else, the dream has two main meanings: (1) He will attain a great deal of happiness in his love life, even if this does not necessarily happen with the object of his love, but rather with someone else. (2) He can expect problems on the interpersonal level with people who are close to him – friends and acquaintances. Disputes about various topics (mainly differences in world-views, political views, etc.) will cause people who he considers to be closest to him to keep their distance and display a lack of interest in him.

If a man or a woman dreams about a lover, the dream prophesies marital problems. The problems are not a "death knell," and they can be resolved if the parties are willing and determined to do so. Having said that, if the two sides are not serious about overcoming their marital problems, their marriage is liable to go downhill until it ends in divorce. From this point of view, the dream constitutes a warning about jeopardizing married life. If the marriage and the state of being married are important to the dreamer, he/she should relate to this dream very seriously.

A B C D E F G H I J K **L** M N O P Q R S T U V W X Y Z

A dream about unwanted love attests to the fact that the dreamer may have heart problems, i.e., physiological problems in the heart. For this reason, he should undergo medical tests. However, it is also possible that the dreamer has serious mental problems; in this case, he should seek psychological treatment. The problem may be temporary or of short duration only, but it plays a significant role in the dreamer's ability to lead a healthy life.

If a person dreams that he is in love with himself – even if in reality he does not think this is the case in the least – the dream serves as a sign that he should be modest and not flaunt his abilities and achievements. Exaggerated conceit is liable to embroil the dreamer in such complications that he will find it difficult to extricate himself from them.

If a person dreams that he is not successful in love, it implies that not only will he be successful in this realm, but his success will be enormous, and his marriage will be successful and happy. He will live a full and interesting life, without a moment of boredom, with a beloved person from whom he will learn a great deal and who will also be able to return his love.

A dream about the love of work attests to the fact that the dreamer does not detest any job, and generally does his work well. The dreamer is one of those industrious people who do their work faithfully. In addition to being totally dependable, they work quickly and accomplish the tasks they are given competently. For this reason, they enjoy promotions, earn good salaries, and generally love their work. The dreamer belongs to the category of people who, even if their lives are not perfect in other aspects, are very successful at their jobs and in their careers, and this compensates for the other areas that are less brilliant.

If a person dreams that he loves his children, it is a sign that he will enjoy great happiness in his life, overshadowing the difficult things. Even if he does not have an easy life, and has to work hard to earn a living and make ends meet, he will be a "rich" man from the point of view of his family life. His children and grandchildren will love him, take care of him, respect him, cherish him and appreciate him until the day he dies.

Lover

When people dream about a lover, they have to examine what's going on in their emotional realm. The dreamer may be suffering from sexual or emotional deprivation. Even if he/she is in a relationship, it can be assumed that the excitement and novelty have dissipated. The dream implies that something must be done about this in order to keep the "third rib" a fantasy that will not be realized.

Loveliness

If a person dreams about lovely things, it means that all the people close to the dreamer will benefit. If a lover dreams about his sweetheart's loveliness, he will soon marry and be very happy. If a woman sees her own loveliness in a dream, she will have a lot of happiness in life.

Lozenges

Lozenges in a dream are an indication of minor successes. If a woman eats them or throws them away, her joy in life will be jeopardized by the digs of jealous people.

A
B
C
D
E
F
G
H
I
J
K
L
M
N
O
P
Q
R
S
T
U
V
W
X
Y
Z

Lucky

A dream about being lucky is in fact a lucky dream. The dreamer's wishes will come true, and he will enjoy the things he has to do. If he is in despair in real life, this dream affords hope for new joy and prosperity.

Luggage

A dream about luggage denotes unwanted troubles. The dreamer will have people he really can't stand hanging around his neck like albatrosses. If he dreams that he carries his own luggage, he will be so involved in his own misery that he will be unaware of other people's unhappiness. A dream about losing luggage is indicative of domestic strife. If a single person dreams about losing luggage, it means that he is about to go through broken romances or engagements.

Lumber

A dream about lumber indicates numerous difficult, distasteful and poorly paid tasks. If a person sees piles of burning lumber in a dream, it predicts an unexpected windfall. A dream about sawing lumber means bad business deals and general bad luck.

Lute

If a person plays the lute in a dream, it is a sign of good news from faraway friends. If he hears lute music, it predicts nice things.

Luxury

If a person dreams about wallowing in luxury, it is a warning that his capital is diminishing rapidly due to his corrupt and hedonistic lifestyle. If a poor woman dreams of luxury, it means that her circumstances are going to change.

Lying

If a person lies in a dream in order to escape penalty, it means that he will behave in a contemptible manner toward an undeserving person. If the dreamer lies in order to cover for a friend, it means that unjustified criticism will be leveled at him, but he will get past it and become well known. If he hears other people lying in a dream, it means that they are trying to cause his downfall.

Lynx

If a person sees a lynx in a dream, it is a reference to enemies who are trying to ruin the dreamer's business and jeopardize his domestic life. If a woman dreams about a lynx, it means that another woman is after her lover. If she kills the lynx in her dream, it means that she will beat her rival.

Lyre

If a person listens to lyre music, it is an indication of innocent pleasures, congenial company and smooth-running business dealings. If a young woman dreams that she is playing a lyre, she will receive all the love of an excellent guy.

A
B
C
D
E
F
G
H
I
J
K
L
M
N
O
P
Q
R
S
T
U
V
W
X
Y
Z

M

Macaroni

If a person dreams that he is eating macaroni, it is a sign of small losses. If he sees large amounts of macaroni in a dream, it means that he will save money by being very thrifty. If a young woman sees macaroni in a dream, it means that a stranger will enter her life.

Mace (tear gas)

If a person dreams that he uses mace to defend himself against assailants, it is a warning dream: he is being warned about a danger that he can avoid if he is on the lookout for it.

Machinery

A dream that features machinery implies that a difficult project will finally succeed. If a person sees old machinery in a dream, it means that enemies are conspiring against him. If he gets caught in machinery, he will suffer financial losses and trouble.

Machines

A dream in which the dreamer appears in a large machine room attests to dreams of greatness and soaring ambitions. The dreamer wants to get out of the place he's in and spread his wings in other directions. At the moment, reality is shutting him in and limiting him, but the dreamer is a person of vision, imagination and courage, and is about to realize his dreams and embark on a successful and highly lucrative project. If the dreamer reaches a place where there are many large machines that are not operating, it means that he must be careful not to be drawn into a financial venture that will soon be proposed, despite the fact that "on the surface" it looks completely safe to him. An experience of this kind is liable to become complicated and end up in failure.

Mad dog

If a person dreams about a mad dog, it means that in spite of his efforts, he will fail in his endeavors and may become very ill. If the mad dog bites him in the dream, it implies imminent insanity or disaster for him or someone close to him. If he sees a mad dog in a dream, it is an indication of hostile attacks on the dreamer and his friends. If he manages to kill the dog, he will lead a successful life.

Madness

A dream about madness does not attest to problems in the dreamer's life, but rather the opposite – the dreamer will solve problems that have been plaguing him for many years and that have disturbed him greatly. He will succeed in attaining tranquillity and preserving his sanity and a secure and peaceful life.

A dream about madness also implies great economic success. If the person is about to make a big purchase, clinch an important deal, or make a special investment, and he has this dream, he can rest assured that the deal or investment will succeed and yield good dividends for a long time.

If a person dreams that he himself is a patient in a mental hospital, it is a warning sign. His tense mental condition may not hospitalize him, but will doubtlessly take a high psychological toll. This is the time to do some soul-searching, to make a change in his priorities in life, and to devote more time to repose and family. If a person dreams that he meets one of his acquaintances or family members in a hospital, it is a hint that that person is suffering from a physical or mental disease. This is the time to have some tests done.

Magic

If a person dreams that he performs magic, it foretells positive changes in his life, particularly in the areas of finance and health. If others perform magic in his dream, the dreamer will benefit from it. If a person sees a magician, it is an indication of interesting journeys for academics.

Magistrate

A dream that features a magistrate is a warning dream: it warns of impending lawsuits and financial losses.

Magnet

If a person dreams about a magnet, it means that he will fall under the influence of deleterious forces; he may be seduced by a woman. If the dreamer is a woman, it means that she will gain wealth and patronage.

Magnifying glass

If a person sees himself looking through a magnifying glass in a dream, it that he is failing to complete projects successfully. If a woman dreams that she has a magnifying glass, it means that she is looking for relationships with people who will leave her.

Magpie

A dream that features a magpie is a warning dream: it warns the dreamer of disputes and unhappiness.

Mail

There are several interpretations of this topic as it appears in a dream. Of course, it depends on the way it appears. If a person sees a post office in his dream, without any distinguishing features, it attests to the fact that the dreamer did not keep a promise he made or did not pay a debt he owed. Apparently, the dreamer neglected a commitment he promised to fulfill and now his conscience is bothering him about it. He should find out where the problem lies and solve it soon in order to alleviate his mental distress.

A dream about mail also implies that the dreamer was badly insulted by someone and is unable to get over it.

If a person sees himself entering a post office in a dream, there will soon be extreme changes in his life. He must be psychologically prepared for them, since they will occur very suddenly.

If a person sees himself purchasing stamps in a dream, he can expect unpleasant things for which he should prepare himself, too. These could occur in his workplace, but it is also possible that one of the members of his family will give him an unpleasant surprise.

If the dreamer sees himself coming to the post office in order to pick up a letter, he must be ready for changes in his place of residence. While he may not be expecting any change in his place of residence, there is going to be such a turnabout in his life that he will be forced to change it.

Mailman

If a person dreams that he is a mailman, the dream implies that he is liable to lose property – probably an apartment or a house – or some kind of real estate.

This kind of dream also attests to the fact that the dreamer is inundated by worries that stem from fears of complications on the professional/business level, but the complications he fears may also stem from the social domain. The worries, fears and anxieties will not pass until the dreamer examines their character, nature and true source. The dreamer is preoccupied with worries that are unfounded and do not have any serious reason. He is so wrapped up in his worries and in his relentless feeling of anxiety that it will only embroil him later on in anything to do with his occupation or profession. He will also have a hard time maintaining normal relations with the people around him and is liable to get himself into conflicts with others. It will not be surprising, therefore, if a dream about himself as a mailman will keep on recurring until the problems mentioned above have been solved.

Some people interpret a dream about a mailman as a dream that hints at letters or news on the way to the dreamer.

Making up

A dream in which a person sees himself making up with someone with whom he had a quarrel or row is interpreted literally – it is a positive dream.

If a person dreams of seeing a person or several people that he cannot view in a positive light (in reality) because of recent problems or disputes with them, and he makes up with them in the dream, it is a hint that his conscience is telling him to make up and achieve a reconciliation. Even if he has to give in, "bend," or not necessarily appear to be the victor, it is important for the dreamer to take a step toward mending the breach. If he does not, his conscience will continue to bother him about it in subsequent dreams.

Malice

If a person dreams that he feels malice toward someone, it means that his friends will dislike him for his bad nature. If others act maliciously toward the dreamer in a dream, it means that he is being undermined by an enemy in the guise of a friend.

Mallet

A dream that features a mallet means that the dreamer will suffer mistreatment at the hands of friends because he is ill. Strife will reign in his home.

Malt

If a person dreams about malt, it is an indication of a good, wealthy life. A dream about drinking malted beverages is a sign of risky undertakings that will work out very profitably.

Man

If a woman dreams about a man – especially if he is a complete stranger to her – the dream contains glad tidings: she will soon receive good news, or something in her life will work out, even if she does not make any special effort. If the man in the dream was particularly handsome, it is a sign of difficulties and serious quarrels for the dreamer, especially with her mate.

A tall man in a dream is a sign of good fortune. The dreamer will have wealth and happiness in most areas of his life. He will not have to face any particular obstacles, and he will live a bourgeois life without hair-raising adventures, but never in poverty or in need.

A fat man in a dream is a sign that the dreamer is liable to lay himself open to unsuccessful ventures. These may be expressed in some form of gambling or incautious behavior that is a sign of irresponsibility. However, it is possible that even if the dreamer takes all the necessary precautions, he will still suffer the consequences of an unsuccessful venture that he will be dragged into even if he does not want it.

A man who is scolding in a dream is a sign of shame or a feeling of disgrace that clings to the dreamer as a result of perverted gossip. The dreamer knows that something is working against him and that people are talking behind his back, and even if this is nothing but unfounded malicious gossip, he will have a hard time shaking it off and proving that he is innocent.

If a bearded man appears in a dream, it is a hint that the dreamer will lose control. He may get into a difficult situation that he cannot resolve, and he is therefore in a state of anxiety to the point that he cannot function normally and think rationally.

A bald man in a dream is a sign that abundance, health and wealth will accompany the dreamer along his path. He will lack for nothing, at least not for any material things. The economic stability and the attendant peace of mind will grant the dreamer mental strength and the ability to cope with difficult situations and withstand mental crises.

A dream about an arrogant man or the type who cannot conceal his supcriority is a sign that there is someone who is secretly in love with the dreamer and is doing everything to ensure that the dreamer does not find out. It could be someone who is married, and this would account for his desire to hide his infatuation. In spite of this, the dreamer has a good idea as to the identity of the person who wants to conceal his affection.

A good-looking and impressive man in a dream is a sign of the dreamer's self-satisfaction. The dreamer is pleased with himself, with his achievements in life, and with his abilities and talents. All these will enable him to accomplish goals and be able to realize things that generally remain unfulfilled dreams for other people.

If a man dreams about a man whom is a stranger to him, it is a sign that the dreamer can expect untold wealth. He will be as rich as a king, and there will be no bounds to his financial capabilities. Having said that, precisely because of his enormous wealth, he can expect obstacles in the

A B C D E F G H I J K L **M** N O P Q R S T U V W X Y Z

romantic realm. He will always suspect that his partner does not love him for himself, but rather for his money. He is one of those people whose happiness can never be complete because of the tiny element of doubt that always threatens to turn into a gigantic issue that will lead to a total lack of belief in the partner's sincerity.

A man dressed in white in a dream is a sign of good fortune in most areas of life, and of the fulfillment of the wishes and goals the dreamer set himself.

A man dressed in black in a dream is a sign of a lack of luck in life, mainly in anything to do with the desire to achieve. He always "almost" succeeds in accomplishing the goal he set himself, but something always happens to prevent him from enjoying the fruits of his labor, and disappointment almost always awaits him in life.

Manager / Manageress

This dream augurs well. Almost certainly the dreamer will soon receive a promotion, recognition and financial recompense at work. If the dreamer sees himself at work during an argument with his superiors, this means that he does not rely on them. Despite his undermined faith, there will be an improvement in his situation. If the dreamer sees himself in the position of manager, it means that the good news is really in the offing. The dream must teach the dreamer that he has to rely more on himself and that his abilities are valued by his superiors, even if ostensibly there are professional disputes and conflicts that he misinterprets as personal ones.

Manicure

A dream that features a visit to a manicurist serves as a hint of a romantic development. The dreamer wants to improve his external appearance, so he goes to do something that symbolizes grooming and taking care of himself. There is no doubt that a person who maintains a pleasant external appearance and also has a suitable inner feeling, is looking for some kind of romantic relationship, which will appear soon.

Man-of-war

A dream about this type of ship implies long journeys and separations. It also refers to a danger of political unrest. If the ship is sailing on rough seas in the dream, disputes with other powers may affect the dreamer's personal business.

Manners

If a person sees ill-mannered people in dreams, it implies failure in projects due to the nastiness of one of the associates. A dream that features well-mannered people indicates changes for the better.

Mansion

If a person sees himself going into a mansion in a dream, he can look forward to good news and wealth. If he dreams about leaving a mansion in a hurry, or of a haunted room in a mansion, it portends difficult problems that he will have to solve. If he sees a mansion from a distance in a dream, it means promotion.

A
B
C
D
E
F
G
H
I
J
K
L
M
N
O
P
Q
R
S
T
U
V
W
X
Y
Z

Manslaughter

If a woman dreams of being linked to manslaughter in any way, it means that she is afraid of being named in some scandal.

Mantilla

The appearance of a mantilla in a dream indicates an unsuccessful undertaking that will hurt the dreamer.

Manure

A dream that features manure is a very good sign, since it predicts good things – especially for farmers.

Manuscript

A dream about an unfinished or mislaid manuscript implies disappointment. A dream about a completed manuscript means that the dreamer's expectations will be fulfilled. If a person dreams that he is working on a manuscript, it means that he is anxious about something; if he keeps on working with determination, he will be successful. If a person dreams that a manuscript is rejected, he will be very upset, but his dreams will eventually come true. A dream that features a burning manuscript is a sign of success and profit.

Map

If a person dreams about a map, it is a sign that he can expect some kind of change in his life to occur. This change may be good or disappointing. If the dreamer sees himself looking for a map, it means that he will change direction in life because of a sudden insight that shows that he is not too thrilled with his present condition.

Marble

If a person dreams about a marble quarry, it implies financial success but social failure. A dream about polishing marble refers to an inheritance. If marble breaks in a dream, the dreamer will incur the disapproval of his colleagues because of immoral conduct.

March

A dream about the month of March is an indication of setbacks in business.

March (music)

A dream about marching to music implies that the dreamer wants to enter the military or public life. It warns him to take all the aspects of the professions into account. If a woman dreams about men marching, it means that she has set her sights on an important man.

Marching

Marching along a bad road attests to the fact that the dreamer is going through a tough period and does not enjoy good communication with the people around him. A nocturnal march along a dark road or in a spooky place like a cemetery indicates the unpleasant feelings of helplessness and anxiety that are weighing on the dreamer.

A
B
C
D
E
F
G
H
I
J
K
L
M
N
O
P
Q
R
S
T
U
V
W
X
Y
Z

Mare

A dream about a mare grazing in a field implies prosperity in business and congenial company. A dry field is an indication of good friends but poverty. If a young woman dreams about a mare, it means that she will have a good marriage and lovely children.

Marigold

A dream about a marigold admonishes the dreamer to make do with a simple life.

Marijuana

A dream about the marijuana plant, without any particular connection to its narcotic properties, hints at a disease that is incubating in the dreamer or at a very bleak mood, bordering on depression, from which he is suffering. The dream serves as a kind of confirmation of the fact that the dreamer is suffering from a bad psychological feeling, and that he needs help to get him out of this state.

A dream in which the dreamer sees himself smoking marijuana as a narcotic is a dream about things that are unattainable from the dreamer's point of view. The dream symbolizes a practical inability to accomplish the goals the dreamer has set himself and that he wants to achieve.

If a person dreams about smoking marijuana with a member of the opposite sex, the dream attests to the fact that he is experiencing a full and complete love, and even more – he feels that anything concerning his love life is solid. In contrast, he is suffering from a lack of confidence in everything to do with the difficulties of life and the everyday problems that life presents.

Mariner

If a person dreams about being a mariner, it implies that he will embark on a long, agreeable journey to faraway places. If he sees his ship sailing off without him, he can expect trouble from adversaries.

Market

If a person dreams about being in a market, it is an indication that he is thrifty and industrious. If he sees an empty market, is a sign of depression and sadness. If a woman sees a market, it attests to good changes.

Marmalade

If a person dreams about eating marmalade, it is a prediction of illness and unhappiness.

Marmot

If a person sees a marmot in a dream, it is a warning dream: it warns of enemies in the guise of pretty women. If a woman has this dream, it means that temptation will cross her path.

Marriage / Nuptials

If a woman dreams that she is marrying an old and ugly man, it portends great trouble and illness for her. If a person sees a marriage with brightly dressed guests in a dream, it means joy. Somber dress at a marriage in a dream means bereavement and sorrow. If a person dreams about anything bad connected to marriage, it is a prediction of

A B C D E F G H I J K L **M** N O P Q R S T U V W X Y Z

catastrophe in the dreamer's family. If the dreamer is present at a marriage, he will have joy and prosperity.

Mars

A dream about Mars is a bad sign: friends will treat the dreamer cruelly, enemies will try to bring him down. If a person dreams that he is rising up toward Mars, he will be blessed with an acute sense of judgment that will place him far ahead of his friends.

Marsh

A dream about walking through a marsh implies ill health as a result of overwork. The dreamer will bear the brunt of a relative's bad behavior.

Martyr

If a person dreams about martyrs, it warns of hypocritical friends, domestic strife and business losses. If the person himself is a martyr in a dream, he will lose his friends and be vilified by enemies.

Mask

If a person dreams about a mask, he must take into account that he can expect a disappointment. It could well be that a person the dreamer relied on has betrayed him behind his back. It could also be a professional dispute and not necessarily something that happens on the social level.

In any case, the dreamer must be cautious and examine the events carefully. There is also a possibility that the dreamer himself played a part in front of another person or

A B C D E F G H I J K L **M** N O P Q R S T U V W X Y Z

other people, and he is liable to be exposed. Anyway, honesty and sincerity are to be recommended.

Mason (trade)

A dream about a mason is auspicious for the dreamer – both financially and socially.

Mason (secret order)

If a person sees members of the Masonic Order in full costume in a dream, it means that the dreamer will have others to worry about and provide for besides himself.

Masquerade

If a person dreams that he is participating in a masquerade, it means that he is wasting time on trivial things and neglecting important matters. If a woman dreams about a masquerade, it means that she will be deceived.

Mast

If a person sees a ship's masts in a dream, it refers to a long, pleasant voyage, new friends and assets. If he sees the masts of wrecked ships in a dream, it means changes for the worse and sacrifices in the dreamer's life. If a sailor dreams about a mast, he will soon embark on an eventful voyage.

Master

If a person dreams about having a master, it implies that

A B C D E F G H I J K L **M** N O P Q R S T U V W X Y Z

he is not competent enough to be a leader; he requires the direction of a stronger person. If he dreams that he is the master of many underlings, it attests to the dreamer's acute judgment, high status and massive wealth.

Mastiff

If a person feels frightened of a big mastiff in a dream, it implies that he finds it difficult to rise above mediocrity. If a woman dreams about a mastiff, she will marry a kind, clever man.

Mat

A dream about a mat is a sign of grief and worry.

Match

If a person dreams about matches, the dream predicts change and wealth. A dream about striking a match in the dark predicts sudden news and change in fortune.

Matting

A dream about matting is a sign of good prospects and news from distant loved ones. If a dream features old or torn matting, worries are in the offing for the dreamer.

Mattress

If a person dreams about a mattress, it is a sign of new obligations in the near future. A dream about sleeping on a new mattress means contentment with one's life. If a person dreams about a mattress factory, the dream refers to shrewd business partners and wealth.

Mausoleum

A dream about a mausoleum means the illness, demise or misfortune of a renowned friend of the dreamer. If the dreamer is in a mausoleum, it means that he is ill.

May

A dream about the month of May is a sign of enjoyment and prosperity. If there are extreme vacillations in the weather in the dream, the good times will be marred by sorrow and cares.

May bugs

The appearance of May bugs in a dream indicates that the drcamer will have a sour partner instead of a sweet-tempered one.

Meadow

A dream that features a meadow is a prediction of joyful reunions and the anticipation of prosperity.

Meal

An unsatisfying "main" meal in a dream is a sign that the dreamer is facing hard times, especially times of shortage. He is about to lose some of his assets and will have to minimize his expenses. If he does not budget carefully, he is even liable to go hungry. In any case, he will fccl the shortage, and he will have to toil hard in order to return to the standard of living to which hc is accustomed.

If a dreamer sees himself eating breakfast alone in a

dream, he is facing a difficult test in his life, one in which he will have to prove himself. He is not sure whether he can do that, despite the fact that it is be a crucial factor in his life, so he is petrified of failure.

Lunch in a dream implies that the dreamer is about to go on a pleasant trip or a relaxing vacation. This is not planned and will happen unexpectedly.

If the lunch in the dream is a business lunch or an official meal, it hints at a promotion at work or a move up the social ladder. In both cases, the move up will be accompanied by much praise and many compliments for the dreamer, and it will be very significant for him.

A family dinner in a dream is a sign that soon there will be a happy event in the family – the birth of a child, a wedding, and so on.

Measles

If a person dreams about having measles, it is an indication that he will be plagued by worries and anxieties concerning his business. If other people have measles in the dream, the dreamer will be anxious about their state of health.

Meat

The meaning of meat in a dream varies according to the type of meat, the nature of its preparation, and the way it looks in the dream:

If the dream features beef, and the person who dreamed it succumbed to the temptation of following devious paths or doing things he regretted, it hints at "repentance," that is, a return to the correct path and to what is right for and worthy of him.

A dream about pig meat (this interpretation is appropriate for a Jew or a Moslem) is a sign that the dreamer will overcome unwanted emotions. He may be having difficulty getting rid of a certain trauma, such as the inability to overcome the emotions he feels for someone whom he loved and who terminated a relationship with him, and so on.

If mutton features in a dream, it is a sign that the dreamer will have a happy life. He will not know lack, and will live in the "fleshpots."

If a person dreams about chicken or turkey meat, it is a sign that he will be granted spiritual inspiration or religious visions. He will develop his spiritual talents extensively, since he is gifted with them in any case, and will reach a higher spiritual plane than the one he is on at the moment.

If a person dreams about cooked meat, especially if he himself cooked it, and sees himself eating it, the dream hints at a mixture of good and bad: on the one hand, it implies positive things that await the dreamer and considerable advancement in most areas of life, but on the other, it indicates that not everything in his life will flow smoothly. The dreamer will indeed succeed in realizing most of his aspirations and goals in life, but not always will the path to their realization be easy, and he may encounter disruptions and hitches here and there.

If a person sees (or tastes) raw meat in his dream, that is, meat that is not sufficiently cooked, the dream hints at a chance of the dreamer being exposed to physical humiliation. There could be a hint of some kind of physical abuse, but it could also be mental abuse and a heavy feeling of shame that weighs on the dreamer.

If a person dreams about eating well-cooked beef, he can

A B C D E F G H I J K L **M** N O P Q R S T U V W X Y Z

expect serenity and tranquillity in life, particularly in anything to do with the spiritual and mental aspects of his life. In other words, even if he runs into serious material problems and unpleasant hardships, he will always know how to overcome them spiritually, since he the extent of his tranquillity and peace of mind is such that they will help him solve the problems he is facing.

Mechanic

A dream about a mechanic means that the dreamer will move house and enjoy an improvement in his business and an increase in his income.

Medal

If a person dreams about medals, it is an indication of rewards as a result of hard work. If he dreams about losing medals, it is a sign of bad luck brought about by other people's treachery.

Medication / Medicine

If a dream features medicine, it is interpreted according to the way in which it appears:

If a person dreams about medicine inside a medicine chest, the dream implies that he can expect great but insignificant joy.

If a person sees himself taking medication in a dream, it is a sign that he is facing a difficult period of struggles on various levels: economic, social and personal. The crises will be resolved, but he will have to muster strength and a great deal of patience until the storm blows over.

If a person takes medication and he is hospitalized in an institution, the dream implies that the dreamer is right. He is facing some kind of battle in which he has to justify his deeds. He is completely at one with himself and has to prove that he is right. The dream encourages him and reinforces his claim that he is right.

If a person dreams that he takes particularly bitter medicine, which leaves a very bitter taste in his mouth, it is a sign that an unknown person is trying to conspire against someone who trusts the dreamer. Someone is trying to hurt that person, and it is advisable to warn him before it is too late.

If a person dreams that he gives his friend medicine, it is a sign that they will smooth things out between them and will resolve their differences. The agreement is mutual, and they can once again trust each other and rely on each other.

A dream in which the dreamer gives a child medicine hints that the dreamer can expect to have to work hard, but not necessarily with children. He is facing a difficult and backbreaking period during which he will have to toil hard in order to achieve something he is longing for.

Medicinal herb

When a person dreams about a medicinal herb, it means that he is grappling with big challenges in his life. If he has not succeeded in persisting in the battle with these challenges up till now, he is now facing a breakthrough. The ability to accomplish objectives that were out of the dreamer's reach until now hints at a step up in his life. The proof itself that he is capable of accomplishing goals that seemed unattainable to him up till now reinforces his recognition of his abilities, and now he can strive for additional objectives that previously appeared unattainable to him. His self-confidence is also increasing, and his self-esteem is greatly improving as compared to the past.

Medium

If a person dreams about a medium, a witch or a female enchantress can expect to go through a difficult phase. The medium generally appears in a dream as a figure that links the world of the living and the world of the dead. The dream implies that the dreamer or someone close to him can expect a crisis. It could be an accident, an illness, or any other serious event.

Melancholy

If a person feels melancholy in his dream, he will be disappointed by something he thought would be successful. If other people are melancholy in the dream, the dreamer's business will be badly disrupted. For lovers, it is warns of a breakup.

Melon

If a person sees melons growing in a dream, it means that he can expect changes for the better in his life, which is full of worries at the moment. A dream about melons indicates illness and business failures. A dream about eating melons implies that the dreamer will be anxious as a result of hasty actions.

Memorial

If a person dreams about a memorial, it means that he will have to exercise kindness and forbearance with sick and unfortunate relatives.

Menagerie

A dream about a menagerie signals a whole range of problems.

Mendicant

If a woman dreams about a mendicant, her ambitions will be interrupted by negative things.

Mending

If a person sees himself mending dirty clothes in a dream, he will choose the wrong time to rectify an injustice. If he is mending clean clothes in the dream, he will be prosperous. If a young woman dreams about mending, she will be of valuable assistance to her husband.

Mercury

If a person dreams about mercury, it means that due to the intervention of enemies, inauspicious changes will take place in the dreamer's life. If a woman dreams that she is suffering from mercury poisoning, it is an indication that her family will abandon her.

Mermaid

A dream about a legendary figure such as a mermaid

A B C D E F G H I J K L **M** N O P Q R S T U V W X Y Z

attests to the dreamer's romantic soul, and hints at special experiences of a romantic nature he is about to share with his partner. Some people interpret a dream that features a being that does not really exist as the dreamer's fierce desire for a love he knows is unattainable. He is searching for an impossible love that cannot exist in reality.

A person like this, who clings to wishes that cannot come true, is not sufficiently down to earth, and he must shake off the wishes of the dream and acknowledge the reality in which he lives. The dream hints that he is chasing the unattainable, and that the love he wants for himself is impossible and can never exist in reality.

He should discard the illusion as quickly as possible, because if he doesn't, he is liable to find himself in a situation in which real life passes him by. The sooner he comes to grips with reality and recognizes it, the sooner he can enjoy what there is and succeed in accomplishing his goals in life.

Merry

If a person dreams about being merry or about being with merry people, it means that he will enjoy life for a while and his business will thrive.

Meshes

A dream about being enmeshed means that the dreamer will be set upon by enemies. If a young woman dreams about being enmeshed, she will stray off the straight and narrow path and eventually be abandoned. If she succeeds in extricating herself from the meshes in the dream, she will avoid being the object of vicious gossip.

Message

If a person receives a message in a dream, it indicates change. If he sends a message in a dream, it predicts awkward predicaments for him.

Metamorphosis

A dream about a metamorphosis indicates changes in life, which can be good or bad.

Mice

If a person dreams about mice, the dream predicts domestic conflicts, professional problems and two-faced friends. A dream about killing mice is a symbol of defeating enemies. If a young woman dreams about mice, it is a sign that she has hidden enemies and is being deceived. If she dreams about a mouse in her clothes, it predicts that she will be involved in a scandal.

Microscope

A dream about a microscope indicates failure in projects or business ventures.

Microwave oven

If a person uses a microwave oven to prepare a meal in a dream, it implies that the dreamer can expect a visit from unwelcome guests.

Midwife

If a person sees a midwife in a dream, it is a sign of

illness and near death. It is a bad omen of slander and distress for a young woman.

Milestone

If a person sees or passes a milestone in a dream, he will experience fears and doubts about love or business. If he sees a fallen milestone, it means that his affairs will be undermined by mishaps.

Milk / Milkman

Milk in a dream has various interpretations according to the context in which it appears:

A dream in which milk or a milkman appears is a good dream in most cases, prophesying a good life, prosperity, wealth and happiness, the fulfillment of wishes and desires, and so on. The greater the quantity of milk in the dream, the more numerous the good things that will happen in the wake of the dream and what it represents.

Having said that, when milk appears in the following contexts, there may be a reversal of fortune:

Spilled milk in a dream predicts misery, a period of depression and sadness that will take over the dreamer's life. If, in contrast, the dreamer himself spills the milk, there will be another reversal of fortune, and the dream will portend prosperity and growth in his life.

A dream in which the dreamer drinks sour milk is a sign of family problems based on a sex-related problem. Women will suffer from a gynecological problem and men will suffer from fertility problems.

A dream in which the dreamer sees himself purchasing milk augurs well. He will receive predominantly good news from afar, and it will affect his life.

A dream in which the dreamer sells milk hints at the disappointment, tension and worry that will be the dreamer's lot.

A dream that features nothing but milk that is boiling over is a sign that the dreamer has great ambitions to invest in a plan that is supposed to bring him economic abundance. He has not yet achieved results, but he certainly invests a great deal in order to accomplish his coveted goal.

A dream in which the dreamer sees himself drinking boiling milk and getting scalded implies that the personal problems that are plaguing him will be solved, but it will be a slow and nerve-racking process. The dreamer must be infinitely patient, but it will ultimately pay off.

A dream about a bath of milk hints at the dreamer's character: He is a hedonistic person who loves the pleasures of life. He will do anything for an hour of the pampering and personal pleasures that always head his list of priorities. He is a person who does not save money when he has it, even if there certainly are things he can do with it, but rather rushes off to spend it on pleasures and pampering – mainly physical ones (massages, a good meal, and so on).

Milking

If a person dreams that he is milking a cow with abundant milk, it means that he will achieve success after a great deal of trouble.

Mill

If a person sees a mill in a dream, it is a sign of good luck and prosperity. A dream that features a dilapidated mill signifies disease and bad luck.

Miller

A dream that features a miller implies an improvement in the dreamer's surroundings. If a woman dreams about an unsuccessful miller, she will be disappointed by her lover's financial situation.

Millionaire

A person who dreams that he is a millionaire is expressing his desire to get rich quickly. The dream does not augur well, especially in the near future. The dreamer must be cautious in every deal and check it out carefully from every possible angle. He must particularly avoid gambles. However, in the more distant future, the dreamer will have an unexpected adventure following which an interesting and profitable opportunity will fall into his hands. This almost certainly refers to a chance meeting as a result of which the dreamer will become acquainted with an influential person who can introduce him into a circle of business people and financiers who will open up a world of new opportunities to him.

Millstone

If the dreamer sees a millstone in his dream, or dreams that he is carrying a millstone, the dream attests to the fact that the dreamer is investing a great deal in his work or in his interpersonal relations, but is not being properly rewarded. He always feels as if he is "investing and sinking." He does his best, expends energy and resources in order to accomplish his goal, but instead of being granted what he deserves in return, he is usually disappointed. He is constantly frustrated by the fact that the reward is never in proportion to the investment.

Mine

If a person dreams that he is in a mine, the dream indicates business failure. If he dreams that he owns a mine, it implies wealth. If he works in a gold mine in a dream, it means that he will try to deprive other people of their rights. He should avoid scandals at home.

Mineral

If a person dreams about minerals, it implies that his life will improve.

Mineral water

If a person drinks mineral water in a dream, it means that he will succeed in his endeavors and will be able to satisfy his cravings.

Minister

If a person sees a minister in a dream, it is an indication of changes for the worse and undesirable journeys. If he hears a minister preach in a dream, it means that he will be persuaded to do wrong. If he dreams about being a minister, the dream indicates that he will try to deprive others of their rights.

Mink

A dream about a mink attests to the fact that the dreamer

will have to defeat cunning enemies. If he kills minks in his dream, he will be victorious. If a woman dreams about loving mink furs, she will fall in love with an insanely jealous man.

Mint

There are several interpretations for a dream that features mint. One states that the appearance of mint in a dream is a sign that the dreamer will soon come into a large inheritance, even if he had no idea of where such an inheritance would come from while he was dreaming. This inheritance will change his life and steer it along a different path than the one with which he has been familiar up till now.

Another interpretation of mint in a dream states that the dreamer can expect to have an unusual adventure, and even if he is not an adventurous person and is not crazy about surprises and unplanned and unexpected things, he will find himself in the middle of an adventure that he never imagined he would get into.

A further interpretation states that mint implies problems of adaptation that the dreamer will encounter. This could refer to a move to a new home or to a new neighborhood. It could refer to a new job to which he will have to become accustomed, and so on. It could also refer to much smaller and more banal things that can nevertheless be a nuisance, such as getting used to a new daily routine, a new boss at work, to new eyeglasses, and so on.

Minuet

If a person sees the minuet being danced, it is a sign of

a pleasant life with good friends. If the dreamer himself dances a minuet in a dream, he will be successful in business and happy at home.

Mire

If a person dreams about going through the mire, it means that his cherished plans will have to be delayed due to changes occurring around him.

Mirror

If a person dreams about looking at himself in a mirror, it refers to self-awareness and self-understanding. After a long period of deliberation and inner confusion, the dreamer understands a problem that he has not been able to solve. He finds himself and knows where he has to go from now on. If a person dreams that he is looking in a mirror but does not see his reflection because the mirror is transparent, it implies an imminent illness. He should go to the doctor and undergo general tests.

A broken mirror implies a possible disaster, so the dreamer is advised to drive carefully.

The appearance of a strange face in a mirror means that the dreamer is not pleased with himself and the way he has been acting recently. He is disappointed with himself and suspects that he has betrayed his own principles to the point that he does not recognize himself in the mirror. This is the right time for a vacation and some soul-searching.

Miser

A dream about a miser is a warning dream: it warns the

A B C D E F G H I J K L **M** N O P Q R S T U V W X Y Z

dreamer that because of his egoism, he will not find true love and happiness. If a woman dreams about being befriended by a miser, she will be accorded love and wealth because of her cleverness and tact. If a person dreams about acting in a miserly way, it means that he will behave disgustingly toward other people. If he dreams that his friends are misers, he will be affected by other people's troubles.

Mist

If a person is shrouded in mist in a dream, it implies that his luck is not solid. If the mist in his dream clears, his troubles will pass. If he sees other people in a mist in his dream, he will profit from their troubles.

Mistletoe

A dream about mistletoe is a very happy, festive dream, since it promises good times. If bad omens appear alongside the mistletoe in the dream, however, the good times will be replaced by disappointment.

Mixer

If a person dreams about an electric mixer, it means that he is about to enjoy a more active social life.

Mockingbird

If a person sees or hears a mockingbird, it means that he will be invited to friends for a nice visit. Furthermore, business matters will run smoothly. If a woman sees a dead or wounded mockingbird in a dream, she can expect to quarrel with her partner in the near future.

A B C D E F G H I J K L **M** N O P Q R S T U V W X Y Z

Models

A dream that features a model means that the dreamer will waste his money on his social life, and this will lead to quarrels and recriminations. If a young woman dreams about being a model, it predicts a complicated love affair that will cause her anguish due to an selfish friend.

Molasses

A dream about molasses attests to the fact that the dreamer will receive an invitation that will lead to pleasant surprises. If he eats molasses in the dream, it means that he will be disappointed in love. If the molasses is smeared on his clothing, he may suffer business losses and receive unwanted marriage proposals.

Mole (animal)

Some kind of danger is hovering over the dreamer. Some people interpret a dream about a mole or ferret, which dig up mounds of earth, as a warning dream against one person or a group of people who are conspiring against the dreamer and threatening the integrity of his family or the stability of his ties in the workplace. The same elements who are undermining him by secretly "digging" things up against him and who seek to harm him will only be successful in their mission if the dreamer ignores their presence and does not pay attention to what is going on bchind his back. Thc sooncr hc rctaliatcs against the people who are undermining him, the sooner he will succeed in overcoming their evil intentions.

Mole (on the skin)

A mole on the skin indicates conflicts and illness.

Molting (birds)

A dream about birds molting indicates inhuman and immoral treatment of the unfortunate and downtrodden by the wealthy.

Monastery

A person who dreams about a monastery is someone who is undergoing a spiritual process and urgently needs to distance himself somewhat from his regular surroundings because of difficult events that he has gone through recently. There could be a trip to a distant and isolated place in which the dreamer can collect his thoughts and make important decisions that will affect the course of his life in the future. A dilapidated monastery means that the dreamer, who needs a break, cannot allow himself this time because of certain considerations that seem very important to him at this stage. Postponing his deep personal need is liable to cause him to slip back even further. He should not put off for tomorrow what he can do today.

Money

Dealing with money in a dream is liable to be interpreted as a warning and also as a good sign for the future. If the dreamer receives money in his dream, he can expect an income, but he has to plan his steps carefully. If he loses a large sum of money, he can expect difficulties and arguments regarding money. If a person dreams that he goes to a money-changer, he can expect a problem. If the dreamer finds a pile of money in an unexpected place, the dream implies a big surprise. This could be a big money win or it could be the danger inherent in a certain deal that is not as sound as it first seemed. The dreamer is liable to lose his money just as quickly as he found it. If the dreamer discovers that someone close to him has found a sum of money in a hidden place, it is a sign that someone close is trying to deceive the dreamer and exploit him. Over-cautiousness that will be interpreted as excessive suspiciousness will turn out to be the correct move later on.

Monk / Priest

If a person dreams about a monk or a monastery, he can expect a surprise in the near future. It seems that the dreamer is moving toward a new beginning, apparently in the spiritual realm. If the dreamer sees himself as a monk (or if a female dreamer sees herself as a nun), this attests to the psychological need to break away from the tumult of life. The dreamer's previous pace of life no longer suits him. He needs a change, and quickly. The change will in fact occur because of a certain event that will surprise the dreamer and cause him to deviate from his routine and state of stagnation and actually do something. There could well be a trip abroad.

Another version: A dream about a monk augurs well. An unexpected development will lead the dreamer in a new direction. He will change his way of life and will achieve a state of calm and peace following the many difficulties and problems that plagued him in the past. It is highly possible that the dreamer will move to a new place – somewhere quieter and more rustic. He can also expect a change in workplace or in occupation that will offer "calmer" directions. A change in his emotional life is in the offing, too, as is a new romantic development.

Monkey

There are several interpretations of the appearance of a monkey in a dream, and they change in accordance with the dreamer or the situation in which the monkey appears:

A monkey in a cage is a sign that the dreamer is not satisfied with his relationship with one of the people close to him, and he feels embarrassed and ill at ease with him. Even though there may be close ties between the dreamer and that person, in his heart, the dreamer feels that his relations with that person are not whole-hearted. If he plucks up his courage and opens up to the person, the situation may change for the better.

A monkey in the jungle is a sign that the dreamer can expect to win something during a happy event. This dream has different meanings: The dreamer may be about to meet the love of his life at a party to which he will be invited, but it is also possible that the dreamer will be invited to a particular function where he will win a big prize in a lottery. The possibilities are numerous, and the dreamer can expect good things.

If a poor person dreams about a monkey, especially if the dream features a small monkey, it is a sign that the dreamer can soon expect to make a profit of some kind. He can expect to win something or receive a sum of money from an unexpected quarter, but having said that, the profits will not be big.

If a rich person dreams about a monkey, it is a sign that his business is facing a danger that stems mainly from burglars or from someone who is liable to rob the business. The business may also be facing bankruptcy, but this is a rare possibility. Another possibility is that the dreamer is cheating on his taxes. This fraud is liable to be discovered, and the dreamer can expect to pay heavy fines that will undermine his business standing.

If a person dreams about little monkeys (especially if they are in a cage), it is a sign of falling in love. The dreamer may already be well aware of whom the object of his affections is, and his feelings of love that rise up and overflow are expressed in this dream. It is also possible that even if the dreamer is not yet falling in love, the dream implies that in the near future he will find himself involved in such a process, and this will have a great effect on him in the near future.

A dream about a baby monkey nursing from his mother's teats expresses the dreamer's great hopes regarding love. Deep in his heart, the dreamer wants to make his relationship with his partner official. If the dreamer is in the process of falling in love, he is expressing his hidden wishes for the continuation of the relationship by means of this dream, as well as his desire to establish a very serious relationship with the person he loves.

Monster

Dreams that feature a monster attest to extreme anxiety, unfocused fear and escape from reality. An extremely tough phase is causing the dreamer to see the black side of everything. If he does not take time off to muster his

A B C D E F G H I J K L **M** N O P Q R S T U V W X Y Z

strength, he can expect a deterioration in his physical and mental state, even to the point of hospitalization. Confusion, uncertainty and mental chaos are in the offing. This is a warning sign that the situation must be dealt with immediately.

Moon

Dreams about the moon have many meanings, especially emotional ones. It is a good idea to examine the dreamer's personal contexts regarding the concept of the moon. A bright moon sailing across the heavens can attest to the love and fidelity that are given and received by the dreamer. A dream about a cloud-covered moon generally attests to the season of solitude that is not suitable for renewing or initiating romantic ties. A dream about a moonless night indicates feelings of envy and suspicion despite an existing love relationship. In contrast, a full moon attests to a good general situation and to the satisfaction of everyone concerned. A moon that illuminates the heaven with powerful light implies a feeling of happiness in a romantic relationship, even though the economic situation is bad. A dream about a red moon indicates forthcoming wars.

Morgue

If a person dreams about visiting a morgue, it implies that he will receive terrible news about the death of someone close. If he sees many corpses in the morgue in his dream, he will be informed about a great deal of grief and trouble.

Morning

If a person sees morning break, it is a sign of good luck and pleasure. If the morning in the dream is cloudy, it means that the dreamer will have to deal with weighty issues.

Morocco

A dream about Morocco predicts that the dreamer will receive a lot of assistance from an unexpected quarter. His love will be reciprocated with fidelity.

Morose

If the dreamer appears morose in his dream, everything will go wrong for him when he wakes up. If other people are morose in the dream, he will be condemned to disagreeable tasks and associates.

Mortgage

If a person dreams that he takes a mortgage, it means that he is in financial trouble that will cause him embarrassment. If he dreams about granting other people a mortgage, it means that he does not have enough money to pay his debts.

Mortification

A dream about feeling mortified about one's conduct means that the dreamer will suffer humiliation in front of those he wished to impress. He will experience financial loss.

A B C D E F G H I J K L **M** N O P Q R S T U V W X Y Z

Moses

If a person dreams about Moses, it predicts a happy marriage and prosperity.

Mosquito

A dream about a mosquito implies quarrelsome and belligerent people who are plotting to harm the dreamer. He must be careful of them – their bite is liable to be destructive. These enemies are seeking an opportunity for revenge and threaten to cloud his happiness and his *joie de vivre*. The dream serves to give him an hour's prior warning so that he can prepare for battle.

Moss

If a person dreams about moss, it means that he will work as an employee. If, however, the moss grows in fertile soil in the dream, he will gain recognition.

Moth

If a dream features a moth among the clothing in a house, the dream implies that the dreamer has established business ties with a friend, and he must cut these ties immediately. These ties could be employing a friend at work or making a deal with a friend (such as purchasing something from him). Every kind of tie that mixes friendly relations with business relations must be terminated immediately. Any other dimension that is added to the pure relations with a friend is liable to cause a breakup of the relations, and the sinister relations will overpower the true friendship between them.

A moth that appears outside of the house in a dream implies that the dreamer is engaged in a flirtation with someone who is unsuitable for him. This perverted attempt to initiate a relationship in such a simplistic and superficial way is liable to bring a whole slew of negative gossip down on the dreamer's head and cause him to lose his good reputation. Misleading gossip and rumors are liable to ruin the good reputation he has nurtured for years.

Mother

A dream in which the dreamer's mother appears is linked to the nature of the dreamer's relationship with his mother, and reveals things about it.

The appearance of the mother in a dream generally means good luck and happiness. Because of the tendency to consider the mother figure as the most important factor for basic security – she is the one that can contain everything – and for the primeval nature of man, it is customary to interpret such a dream as an indication of a pregnancy or of an imminent birth in the family.

If the mother in the dream looks as if she is in danger, the dreamer can expect to be accorded great honor in life. He will be very popular, and people will ask his advice and respect everything he says.

A dream in which the mother is seen bringing something to the dreamer or throwing something at him is a sign that the dreamer is about to change his lifestyle. This new lifestyle and the new codes according to which he will behave may lead to a considerable improvement in his economic status and will be effective in everything to do with financial matters.

If a person dreams that he lives with his mother, it means that he is seeking a feeling of security. The dreamer seems to be going through a period haunted by fears and anxieties, and he feels the need for a shield.

A dream in which a conversation takes place between the dreamer and his mother – even if the dreamer does not remember what the conversation was about – predicts that good tidings and happy news will reach the dreamer.

If a person dreams about his mother's death, the dream attests to the fact that the dreamer is in immediate danger, and that he has to be aware of every step he takes in order not to cause a disaster to befall him.

A dream in which a mother embraces her son (the dreamer) is a sign that fate holds good things in store for the dreamer. Even if the situation seems difficult to him, and things are bad, and even if his economic and social standing are at a low, this is a temporary state of affairs, since fate has decreed that his life will be good, full and happy. Everything is a matter of time, and he must cheer up since these things will soon happen.

If a person dreams about striking his mother, it is a warning dream that indicates a disaster that is about to befall the dreamer and his family. The disaster is liable to strike the family without warning, and will be expressed in loss of life or property.

If a person dreams about killing his mother, the dream indicates that death in the family is inevitable. The death will be the result of an accident – a traffic accident, an accidental poisoning, and so on.

Mother-in-law

A dream about a mother-in-law implies a lack of peace of mind when it comes to domestic happiness. It is possible that the dreamer has not found a good way to terminate some kind of dispute, and he is very disturbed by this. If there really are disputes with a mother-in-law, the dreamer is bringing things to the conscious surface in order to set them straight. He cannot continue living a normal life without bringing the dispute to an end, and this is haunting him in his dreams as well. The dream may also imply that the dreamer must conclude unresolved matters or disputes concerning family members in general – not necessarily the mother-in-law herself. As long as the dreamer does not resolve the matter, he will be at odds not only with the people around him, but also with himself. He should take a break and get to the bottom of it, find out what is needed to clarify the matter and terminate conflicts and disputes as fast as possible.

Motor

A dream about a motor symbolizes the desire to be a leader and to be at the hub of things.

Motorcycle

If a person dreams about riding a motorcycle, it means that he will be in control of his relationships. If a person watches other people ride motorcycles in a dream, it means that he is in a rut while others are advancing in their personal and professional lives.

Mountain

In general, a dream about a mountain reflects the extent of the dreamer's desire to reach the top, achieve success and realize his aspirations and goals in life. In most cases, a dream about a mountain implies that the dreamer will in fact accomplish his goals and realize his wishes.

If a person dreams about climbing a mountain without any hitches, and the climb is easy, fast and successful, the person can expect life to be like this, too – he will have no trouble overcoming obstacles in life and bypassing stumbling-blocks, and luck will shine upon him.

If, however, a person dreams that the ascent up the mountain was difficult and tortuous, full of pitfalls and problems that he encountered on the way, he will not succeed in overcoming the obstacles that await him in life, and even if he tries over and over again, the bitter truth will slap him in the face.

If the dreamer sees himself running into people along his path during the course of the dream, it is a sign that even though his path to success is full of difficulties, he will come across people who will help him reach his goal, and he will avail himself of their assistance.

If a person sees a snow-covered mountain in a dream, it prophesies that the dreamer is about to receive a favor from a person who is almost a complete stranger to him.

A dream in which the mountain is especially high and is reminiscent of the Alps or the Himalayas attests to the fact that the dreamer does not give up or throw in the towel on the way to his goal. He is single-minded in his struggle to accomplish the objectives he has set himself, and engages in a crucial and uncompromising struggle for survival. In the end, of course, he will achieve his goal, since he will not give up until he has fulfilled all of his desires.

A low mountain in a dream hints that the dreamer is about to take a vacation and get away to a place where he can relax after the mental pressures and enormous fatigue that are the results of the struggles he has had to endure recently.

The weather during the climb up the mountain is important as far as the dreamer's path to success is concerned. If the weather is fine and clear, his success will come rapidly, without any particular problems or obstacles on the way. If the weather is dark and gloomy, the melancholy atmosphere will also prevail along his path to accomplishment in life. The dreamer will experience difficulties, disappointments and frustrations, but will ultimately achieve repose and security.

Mourning

A dream about mourning or a funeral symbolizes the dreamer's deep pain or sorrow. It sometimes implies an emotional or material embroilment on the part of the dreamer. He feels as if he is stuck in some kind of deep, suffocating quicksand from which he cannot escape.

If a person dreams that he is mourning his parents, the dream implies that he is embroiled in a legal matter or that he is in a dispute with a partner, a neighbor, or some other person who is "close." His embroilment is not simple and really weighs on his heart.

If a person dreams that he is paying a sympathy visit, the dream is a warning sign: the dreamer must avoid getting involved in some kind of accident. This not only applies to

A B C D E F G H I J K L **M** N O P Q R S T U V W X Y Z

traffic accidents, but to accidents in general. It could be a domestic accident or a work accident, but it could also be an "emotional accident."

If a person dreams that he is mourning his partner/spouse, the dream attests to the fact that there are disputes within the family or severe complications that must be resolved amicably. Anger, annoyance, insults or other residues are liable to leave the family split and not supportive, as it should be.

A dream in which the dreamer sees himself as one of the mourners in a house of mourning implies a drastic change in habits or conduct. The person is about to make a 180-degree change in his life. This may possibly stem from a courageous decision to change something that he has wanted to change for a long time, and can only do so now. Alternatively, it may stem from a lack of choice. It is possible that the change will mainly be emotional, but any change the dreamer decides to effect in his life will be for the best.

If the dreamer sees many people mourning in one place (not necessarily in a house of mourning or at a funeral), and the general feeling and atmosphere in the dream is gloomy, the dream prophesies a long journey to a distant place with people who are not particularly amiable, and with whom the dreamer will not feel comfortable.

Mouse

A dream that features a mouse is interpreted according to the context in which the mouse appears in the dream.

A mouse that appears by chance, without being connected to anything in particular, is interpreted as delegating authority to someone who is not to be relied on: the dreamer is inclined to trust somebody who does not deserve his trust. Even though the dreamer delegates responsibility to the person whom he believes to be reliable, that person is liable to reveal himself to be completely untrustworthy and incapable of accomplishing tasks, no matter how simple they may be. The dreamer's expectations of him go way beyond the person's abilities. The disappointment he causes the dreamer is liable to be severe, and the dreamer's wising up to the impossibility of this relationship is inevitable.

If a dream features a mouse that is caught in a trap, it implies that despite the dreamer's attempts to carve out a respectable name for himself, he will not succeed in doing so. He will be widely slandered, and this will happen because of some stupid thing he did. Taking a stand that was inappropriate or focusing on the minor details will get the dreamer into unpleasant situations in which people will not hold him in high enough regard. Instead of carving out a respectable and worthy name for himself, he will cause exactly the opposite to happen. A dream like this is also liable to indicate failure in business, such as a deal that is not clinched or an investment that does not yield dividends.

A dream that features a cat catching a mouse is a sign that the dreamer will earn fame that will demonstrate his talents in front of others, and he will succeed in overcoming his enemies or his rivals. Generally speaking, this relates to some area of work, but the victory may be attained in other areas as well.

A dream that features a dog catching a mouse is a dream that predicts good things: all of the dreamer's troubles will come to an end. Everything that is bothering him, every stumbling-block in his path, every obstacle will go away. The dreamer can look forward to good days, and the future looks rosy.

If mice play in a dream, it is a sign that the dreamer can expect to go through a difficult phase, during which he will have to deal with malicious gossip. He will find himself the victim of a malicious verbal attack that will cause him great shame, even though he is completely blameless.

Mousetrap

If a person sees a mousetrap in a dream, it means that he has to be careful of people who want to take advantage of him. If there are mice in the trap in a dream, the dreamer will probably fall into the hands of his enemies. However, if he sets a trap of his own, he will defeat his rivals.

Mouth

A dream that features a big mouth means great future wealth for the dreamer. A dream that features a small mouth means financial problems for him.

Mud

Dreams about mud are a sign that the dreamer is going through a period of uncertainty regarding his situation. He is evidently going through a transition period between jobs or homes. In any event, things are not sufficiently clear to him, and his plans have not yet been finalized. The dreamer is in an interim state that bothers him and makes him tense and restless.

If a muddy road or an especially impassable muddy path

A B C D E F G H I J K L **M** N O P Q R S T U V W X Y Z

appears in a dream, it indicates that the dreamer is gradually losing his self-confidence. He is going through a bad phase, during which things are happening to him and undermining his confidence and his belief in his abilities and powers.

If particularly filthy mud appears in a dream, it is a sign that the aches and pains suffered by the dreamer will stop abruptly. A disease or some other physiological factor that causes pain or suffering will cease. Physical pains are about to end.

Muff

If a person dreams about wearing a muff, it implies that he is protected against life's vicissitudes. If a lover dreams about his sweetheart wearing a muff, someone else will take her away from him.

Mulberries

If a dream features mulberries, the dreamer will be unable to realize his desires because of illness, and he will have to alleviate the suffering of other people. A dream about eating mulberries is a sign of bitter disappointment.

Mule

A dream about riding on a mule means that the things in which the dreamer is involved are causing him tremendous worry. If the ride in the dream is uneventful, he will be successful. If he dreams about being kicked by a mule, it is a sign that he will be disappointed in love and marriage. A dream about a dead mule symbolizes breakups and social

A B C D E F G H I J K L **M** N O P Q R S T U V W X Y Z

ostracism. If a woman dreams about a white mule, she will marry a wealthy foreigner or some other rich but incompatible man.

Murder

A dream about murder can have many interpretations, depending on the circumstances. A dream in which the dreamer murders someone generally predicts a bitter dispute with serious consequences. If the dreamer sees himself murdered, it is a sign that he is in danger and is plagued by fears and anxiety. He is not in a good situation, but a little resourcefulness and original thinking can prevent a further deterioration of the situation.

Muscles

If a person dreams that his muscles are developed, he will face enemies, but will defeat them. A dream about undeveloped muscles is a sign of the dreamer's inability to succeed in business. If a woman dreams about muscles, it predicts that she will have a life of hard work and difficulties.

Museum

A dream that features a museum means that the dreamer will experience a variety of things while seeking his perfect niche. These things will enrich him more than formal learning. If he dislikes the museum in the dream, it is a sign of irksome worries.

Mushrooms

The appearance of mushrooms of any kind in a dream indicates that the dreamer will expand his circle of friends and will make new friends. Even if he does not attribute particular importance to this right now, the expansion of his social circle will play a significant role in his life in the future.

If a person sees himself picking mushrooms in a dream, it predicts great economic success for him in everything to do with business and financial investments. The financial security he will have will enable him to engage in the areas that interest him and to develop unique and unusual hobbies.

If a person sees himself eating mushrooms in a dream, it attests to some kind of health problem to which he should pay attention, even though it is not a question of a serious disease, but rather something mild and transient.

If a person sees poison mushrooms in a dream, the dream warns the dreamer against negative experiences he will undergo in the near future. He must be aware of the fact that the forthcoming period of time will not be easy for him, and he is liable to get into unpleasant, embarrassing and difficult situations with which he will have to cope.

Music

If a person hears harmonious and pleasant music in a dream, it symbolizes success and a good life. If, on the other hand, he hears discordant and cacophonic sounds, the dream attests to domestic conflicts, unruly children and disruptions during a journey or long trip.

A
B
C
D
E
F
G
H
I
J
K
L
M
N
O
P
Q
R
S
T
U
V
W
X
Y
Z

Musk

A dream about musk is a sign of unforeseen happy events, as well as harmony and fidelity between partners.

Mussels

A dream about mussels is a sign of unexceptional prosperity, but a happy and contented domestic life.

Mustache

If a person dreams that he has a mustache, it is a sign of impertinence and selfishness, which will cost him an inheritance. Moreover, it implies that he will treat women very badly. If a man dreams about shaving off his mustache, it indicates that he is trying to reform himself and return to the straight and narrow path. If a woman dreams about admiring a mustache, her moral standing is in jeopardy.

Mustard

If a person sees mustard growing in a dream, it is a sign of prosperity for the farmer and wealth for sea travelers. If he dreams about eating mustard, it is a warning dream: it warns against accepting bad advice and of taking some unconsidered action that will cause him trouble.

Mute

A dream about a mute person indicates that the dreamer is unable to convince others to think like he does. He tries to take advantage of them using smooth talk.

Myrrh

A dream about myrrh is a sign of satisfactory returns on investments. If a young woman dreams about myrrh, she will meet a wealthy person.

Myrtle

If a person dreams about blooming, green myrtle, it signifies pleasures and fulfilled desires. If a young woman dreams about wearing myrtle, she will make a good marriage at a young age. However, if the myrtle is dry, she will miss out because of her own conduct.

Mystery

If a person is puzzled by mysterious events in a dream, it means that he will be bothered by strangers' problems and demands for assistance. It is a reminder of unpleasant duties, and foretells business setbacks. If the dreamer contemplates the mysteries of creation in a dream, it is a sign that his life is about to change and rise to a higher plane, promising him joy and prosperity.

A B C D E F G H I J K L **M** N O P Q R S T U V W X Y Z

N

Nails (on fingers and toes)

If a person dreams that he has long nails, it means that he will receive a large sum of money in the near future. Apparently, the long nails will serve not only to improve his appearance, but also in the battle for the money, since many people will try to jump on the bandwagon and grab a share of the loot.

Broken and neglected nails can indicate that the dreamer is going through a very difficult phase and that the effort he is investing in his work has turned into a burden. Taking a vacation is the most recommended plan of action.

Nails (metal)

A dream about nails implies hard work and small earnings. If a person deals in nails, it means that he will have a respectable job, even if it is not a high-status position. A dream about rusty or broken nails portends illness and failure in business.

Naked

If a person dreams about being naked, the dream predicts scandal. If he sees others naked in a dream, it means that he will be unable to resist negative temptations.

If he discovers that he is naked and tries to cover up, it means that he wants to forgo all his dubious pleasures and get back on the right path. If a person sees himself walking or swimming naked and alone in a dream, it means that his spouse is very loyal. If he dreams about walking naked among clothed people, this dream also presages a period of scandal.

Name

If a person hears someone calling his name in a dream, it could mean that one of his acquaintances needs him or requires his assistance. Even if this is not immediate, it is a sign that soon someone will need the dreamer's help or services. He can be useful not only from the technical point of view, but also from the psychological point of view – in giving advice, in listening to difficulties and in sharing his thoughts about how to solve them. The person is considered to be a good listener, and often finds himself in the role of the "psychologist on duty" among his friends and acquaintances.

If the name of a person who is known to the dreamer through someone else is mentioned in a dream, the dream refers to a severe emotional disappointment that the dreamer will suffer. He must prepare himself for a situation in which people will betray him, turn their backs on him, and profoundly undermine his faith.

Napkin

If a person dreams about a napkin, the dream foretells happy events in which the dreamer will take part. If a woman dreams about dirty napkins, it means that she will be caught in an embarrassing situation.

A B C D E F G H I J K L M **N** O P Q R S T U V W X Y Z

Narrow passage

If a person suffers from a feeling of suffocation and a lack of air while dreaming about being in a narrow passage, it is a reference to his very powerful sexual drive or feelings of pressure and anxiety.

Navy

If a person dreams about the navy, it means that he will have to tackle weird and serious obstacles. Ultimately, however, he will overcome them and become prosperous. He can look forward to fun trips. If the navy is in chaos, the dreamer will have bad luck in love and business.

Nazi

Dreams that feature Holocaust elements such as Nazi soldiers imply that the dreamer is in a state of depression, mainly because of events in the distant past. The dreamer feels threatened and is worried about his fate. A dream in which a concentration camp appears also attests to the fact that the dreamer feels isolated in the extreme and sees himself as being in a dangerous situation to the point that his physical existence is in jeopardy. He is advised to take a break and try to overcome the bad feeling that is liable to have an adverse effect on his everyday functioning.

Nearsighted

If a person dreams about being nearsighted, it implies that he will suffer humiliating failure and can expect unwelcome visitors. If a young woman dreams about being nearsighted, it means that she will run up against unforeseen competition. If the dreamer's sweetheart is nearsighted in a dream, he will be disappointed in her.

Neck

If a person dreams that he receives a compliment about his neck, it means that he has a full love life. If he admires someone else's neck in a dream, it is a prediction of the breakup of a relationship. If he sees his own neck in a dream, his life will be disrupted by domestic strife. If a woman dreams that her neck is thick, it warns her that she will become really bitchy if she does not take care.

Necklace

A broken necklace, bits of which are strewn over the road or on the floor, attests to a process of dismantling, disappointment and frustration. This type of dream can symbolize both health problems and family problems. It is advisable to undergo medical tests or to pay closer attention to the family. In contrast, a beautiful (and whole) necklace around the neck indicates that the dreamer is going through a good phase in life. The adornment serves as an expression of its owner's esthetic sense as well as his financial possibilities.

Necromancer

If a person dreams about a necromancer and his practices, it means that he is in danger of falling under the influence of malevolent strangers.

Need

A dream about being in need implies unsuccessful business ventures and bad news about friends. If a person sees other people in need in his dream, both he and other people will suffer from hard times.

Needle

Dreams that feature a needle have many meanings in accordance with the situation and events in the dream. If the dreamer finds a needle, it means that new friends are about enter the dreamer's life, even though perhaps the dreamer does not believe that things will happen in this way. This is because he has moved to a new home or a new workplace. In any event, a significant improvement can be expected in the social realm. A dream about a broken needle attests to the opposite. A serious argument is liable to lead to isolation. A dream that features a tray of needles or a pincushion containing needles generally serves as a warning about a difficult and depressing situation, when, instead of abundance and plenty, everything is prickly and harmful.

Needlefish

If a person dreams about needlefish, it portends unpleasantness with friends for reasons unknown to the dreamer. If he catches a needlefish in a dream, it signifies that he will overcome an obstacle in his path. If he eats a needlefish in a dream, it means that the obstacle has been overcome.

Needlepoint

If a person dreams that he is doing needlepoint, it implies that he is curious about what the future holds for him. He will receive answers to many questions; his rivals will no longer bother him, and his family will love having him around. If a person practices multicolored needlepoint in a dream, it is an indication of a lively social life. If he sees a monochrome needlepoint design in a dream, it is a warning not to let fear of the unknown prevent him from realizing his aspirations. If he finds a cushion worked in needlepoint in a dream, new opportunities are predicted. If a woman dreams of holding a needlepoint purse, she can look forward to romance and excitement .

Needlewoman

A dream that features a needlewoman is a sign of an external change that will bring about a change in the dreamer's life; it also foretells harmony at home. If a person sees a needlewoman at work in a dream, the dream augurs well. If she is asking for work, the dreamer should actively make a change before it simply happens to him. If the needlewoman has come to demand payment for services rendered, the dreamer should be careful when he gets up.

Negligee

If a person dreams about a negligee, it is a prediction of an innovative love life with a partner with similar tastes. If he sees a negligee in a box in his dream, it means that long-existing relationships are still satisfying. A dream about a woman wearing a negligee predicts a love affair that will turn the dreamer's life upside-down.

A B C D E F G H I J K L M N O P Q R S T U V W X Y Z

Neighbor

If a person sees his neighbors in a dream, it means that a great deal of time will be wasted on quarrels and gossip. If the neighbors are angry or upset in the dream, it is a prediction of disputes.

Nephew

If a person dreams about a handsome nephew, he can expect to receive a windfall. If the nephew in the dream is not handsome, the dreamer can expect nothing but unpleasantness and disappointment.

Nervousness

A dream in which the dreamer sees himself overcome with feelings of nervousness attests to the fact that he can expect good news very soon. Waiting for it is no doubt nerve-racking, but the dreamer can console himself with the fact that success is assured. If the dreamer sees other people who are nervous in his dream, this attests to a serious incident that is liable to cause unpleasantness. There is a high probability of a family row. There is a possibility of problems at work and even dismissals. In any case, there is no need to worry. Everything will turn out well.

Nest

If a person sees birds' nests in a dream, it means that there is a possibility of a lucrative business proposition. If a young woman dreams about birds' nests, she will move house. A dream about an empty nest implies sadness because a friend has left. A dream that features a nest with bad or broken eggs is a sign of failure and disillusionment. If a person sees doves building nests in a dream, it is a sign of domestic harmony and world peace.

Nets

If a person dreams that he catches something in a net, it means that he is unscrupulous in his dealings with others. If he dreams about an old, torn net, it means that his property is mortgaged or otherwise entailed – and this is a sign of trouble.

Nettles

If a person dreams about nettles, he can expect to be treated with impertinence by employees or children. If he sees himself walking through nettles without being stung in a dream, it is a sign of prosperity. If he is stung in a dream, it is sign of self-loathing and making others unhappy. If a woman dreams that she is walking through nettles, it means that she will find it difficult to decide which proposal of marriage to accept.

News

A dream about news is interpreted exactly opposite to its contents:

If a person dreams about receiving good and happy news, he can expect the opposite in his life – he will have to cope with a difficult period, full of problems and crises. Bad things will happen to him, making him worried and troubled.

If the news in the dream is bad and threatening, worrying and serious, the opposite will be true in the dreamer's life: a good phase is in the offing, and gladdening and heartwarming news will reach him in the near future. In addition, he can expect success in the field of work, and he will earn a higher salary. Besides solving the economic difficulty, there will be a good phase in the life of his family, and the dreamer will feel as if he can achieve much more in his life than he expected.

Newspaper

The interpretation of a dream that features a newspaper varies according to the manner in which it appeared:

In general, a newspaper implies that the dreamer's good name and the good reputation he has carved out for himself are in jeopardy. He is about to lose the esteem of the people around him because of stupid and thoughtless behavior that may destroy what has taken him years to build up. Even people who have trusted him for years are liable to turn their backs on him.

If a person dreams about working for a newspaper or of being involved in the process of printing a newspaper, it implies that the dreamer is not satisfied with his work or with the friends around him, and he wants to make a radical change in his life. He is seeking new thrills and interesting experiences, and he wants to meet new people and change his social life.

A hopeless attempt to read a newspaper in a dream, when the letters become jumbled or skip around, attests to failure in life, to an inability to cope with economic problems and to a fear of business and of a lack of success at work in general. This is liable to render the dreamer totally powerlessness. He must therefore be aware that it is possible to rehabilitate himself from the worst thing that can happen to him from the material point of view.

He must try to see the half-full glass.

Newspaper reporter

If a person dreams that he is not pleased to see reporters in his dream, he will be plagued with idiotic quarrels and small talk. If he himself dreams that he is a newspaper reporter, he will undergo a variety of adventures and trips, not all of them positive. All in all, however, he will earn respect and profit.

New Year

A dream about the New Year symbolizes prosperity and joy in love. If the dreamer considers the New Year a real nuisance, the ventures he undertakes will be successful.

Niece

If a woman dreams about her niece, it is a prediction of unforeseen problems and futile anxiety.

Night

A dream about night, or a dream in which there is a feeling of night, can be interpreted in three different ways. These are determined according to additional elements in the scene of the dream.

A dream about night attests to the dreamer's problems and frustrations in the sexual realm if there is a "sexual" atmosphere in the dream.

A dream about night attests to the economic problems of a person close to the dreamer if the dream contains elements that indicate the economic realm. Sometimes the dreamer will see the image of the person concerned in the dream. A dream about night attests to the dreamer's lack of self-confidence if the interpretation negates the previous possibility.

Nightgown

If a person dreams about wearing a nightgown, it implies a mild illness. If he sees other people wearing nightgowns in a dream, it signifies bad news and business problems. If a lover sees his sweetheart dressed in a nightgown in a dream, it means that he will be given his walking papers.

Nightingale

The appearance of a nightingale in a dream attests to the fact that the dreamer is a romantic person with a sensitive and occasionally vulnerable soul. The dream implies that the dreamer will soon find himself in situations he loves being in: romance will dominate his life in the forthcoming period of time, but only for a short time. Consequently, he should refrain from becoming too emotionally involved with his temporary partner. The dreamer is a vulnerable person, and in order to avoid serious disappointments, he is well advised to relate to every romantic affair as something transient and temporary. If he cherishes false hopes, it will be ten times more difficult for him to cope with the consequences of the loss of the relationship later on.

Because of the nightingale's clear song, a dream about it also attests to a pleasant and clear period of time in the offing for the dreamer. It contains no question marks, and flows smoothly.

Nightmare

If a person dreams about having a nightmare, he can expect conflicts and failure in business. If a young woman has this dream, it predicts disappointments and unmerited insults. This dream serves as a warning about her health.

Ninepins

There is nothing good about a dream that features ninepins. A dream of this kind warns the dreamer that he is wasting his time and energy. He should exercise greater judgment when choosing his friends.

Nobility

If a person dreams that he rubs shoulders with the nobility, it means that his aspirations are misdirected: he seeks frivolous pleasures instead of higher spiritual goals. If a young woman dreams of the nobility, it means that she will choose a man on the basis of his looks rather than his inner qualities.

Noise

If someone dreams that he is in a noisy room, he can expect to get to a place in which he will have to impose order. Evidently, this is the workplace. He can expect a professional promotion and a salary raise.

Nomad

If a person dreams that he or someone else is a nomad or a wanderer, he has an urgent desire to effect a change in his life.

Noodles

A dream that features noodles is not a good dream: it is a sign of abnormal urges and appetites.

Nose

In general, if a person dreams about a nose, he tends to increase the size of his nose in the dream or vice versa – to reduce it to miniscule dimensions. The interpretation of the dream changes accordingly. If a person sees himself with an exaggeratedly larger nose than the one he is blessed with, the dream implies that he will enjoy economic abundance and prosperity in everything regarding the realm of money and material things.

If a person dreams that his nose is significantly smaller than his nose in reality, it is a sign that the dreamer will suffer from great shame that will be caused by a member of his family. An action, utterance, standpoint or opinion of someone in his family will shame the entire family, and, consequently, the dreamer. This matter will be so embarrassing and humiliating that it will endanger the dreamer's social status.

A dream featuring another person with an exceptionally large nose hints that soon the dreamer will be granted abundance and good things by an especially rich person. The latter, who comes from an unexpected place, will lavish good things on the dreamer, and will in fact be the solution to all of his economic and financial worries.

Nosebleed

If a person sees himself in a dream with blood pouring out of his nose, the dream warns that the dreamer must be careful of someone who is taking out his wrath, anger and fury on him, or is liable to do so.

This dream also serves as a warning against health problems that the dreamer is liable to encounter in the near future, mainly because his lifestyle is not healthy. He must adopt new life habits, avoid smoking, rest more and not work too hard, engage in sports and refrain from making too great an effort or from situations that cause him unnecessary tension and mental pressures. This dream constitutes a kind of warning sign. It is advisable to take it seriously and not dismiss it and carry on as usual.

Notary

If a person dreams about a notary, it means that he has unfulfilled desires, and will probably become embroiled in lawsuits. If a woman dreams that she has dealings with a notary, it means that she tends to risk her reputation for the sake of momentary pleasures.

Note

If a person dreams that he receives a note, it means that even though he will require the help of his friends, they will refuse to offer it.

Notebook

If a person dreams about a notebook, it indicates that he has problems when it comes to breaking away from his past.

November

A dream about the month of November is an indication of very ordinary success in all areas.

Nudity

If a person dreams that he is wandering around nude among people, he suspects that someone is trying to expose him and his secret in public or to frame him with something with which he actually has no direct connection. The dreamer can relax, since he has nothing to hide. Except for the embarrassment he may be caused, he will emerge morally and financially strengthened and enriched from any scandal and gossip that will spring up around him. Another meaning of a dream of this kind could be that the dreamer feels that he is being blamed for something and is actually trying to shake off the suspicions and accusations. He has nothing to worry about, in any case; everything will come right in the future.

Numbers

A dream in which the dreamer counts numbers or people attests to increased activity in the near future, which may involve successful economic deals or counting money that will come from an unexpected quarter. A specific number in a dream can be a hint of a forthcoming win in the lottery. If the dreamer dreams about numbers a lot, he is advised to keep paper and pencil next to his bed and write down what appeared in his dream. Even if it doesn't help, it certainly won't hurt. If the dream is about counting money without a clear end result, there is a hint of possible problems in business. The dreamer must not sign a new contract or close a deal without an especially thorough check. He should consult with a professional in order to get a second opinion that is objective and can save him from a fall.

The meanings of the numbers in a dream are as follows:

Number 1

A dream about the number 1 implies the dreamer's desires and wishes. The dreamer is a person with a powerful libido – his sex drive works overtime. His urges are enormous – both the sexual urge and his other energies. He is a very vital person who needs a lot of action in order to provide an outlet for his abundant forces and energy. He operates in "turbo" mode, and many people find it difficult to be with him for any length of time because they find it exhausting. The number 1 in a dream implies that the dreamer has to take his abilities and channel them into positive things and build himself up.

Number 2

A dream about the number 2 implies that the dreamer is in a relationship that is about to end, but he continues to cling to it and refuses to let go. He is not doing the right thing. The dream hints that the affair is on the decline and nothing can revive it. The dreamer has to let go and get on with his life.

Number 3

In most cases, a dream about the number 3 implies that the dreamer will achieve spiritual illumination. He is close to himself, he has the ability to neutralize the conscious and penetrate his subconscious. He is gifted with a very great spiritual capability and he must channel his path in such a way that he attains the illumination he expects. Some people interpret a dream about the number 3 as implying that help will arrive from an unexpected quarter.

Number 4

The number 4 in a dream indicates that the dreamer has great inspirational powers and exerts tremendous influence over the people around him. The dream implies that this power will increase. However, it can also work against him, so he has to channel it into positive things. People tend to follow his advice and are very influenced by his opinions and views. The dream implies that since his abilities will increase, the dreamer must take this into account and be modest and considerate.

Number 5

The number 5 in a dream does not relate to the dreamer himself, but rather to one of the members of his family. He will have a powerful and good romantic liaison after a lengthy series of failures. The number 5 is the lucky number of the person hinted at in the dream.

Number 6

A dream about the number 6 implies expected

advancement at work. The dreamer will seek… and find. The huge efforts he made in the past will bear fruit, and he will soon get a promotion or a substantial salary raise in his workplace. The promotion will contribute both to the bolstering of his status in the workplace and to much greater financial stability.

Number 7

A dream about the number 7 implies that although the dreamer did something that seemed exaggerated to him, and he thought he was a "sucker," in the end it will pay off, and he is about to receive a small bonus or special prize for his efforts. He must learn from this, as in "Cast thy bread upon the waters: for thou shalt find it after many days." In spite of the feeling that he did far more than what was required, in the end it will turn out that his efforts were not in vain.

Number 8

The number 8 in a dream serves as a warning. It warns the dreamer of losing what he has, and admonishes him to protect it and not to do anything hasty that will cause him to lose it.

Number 9

A dream that features the number 9 attests to the fact that the dreamer's conscience is bothering him because of something he did. He cannot come to grips with what he has done, and knows that there is no atonement for it. The dreamer must try to ask forgiveness in every possible way in order to clear his conscience. If he does not, he will continue to agonize and will never be able to calm down.

Number 10

The number 10 in a dream implies that the dreamer can expect to go through a good phase that will bring him a lot of happiness. The dreamer will have an enriching and joyous experience followed by a happy time in his life. The great joy will stem from both spiritual and material factors – mainly from making the most of his "self" and from the ability to reach his inner truth and bring it out.

Number 11

A person who dreams about the number 11 will stand trial twice in the near future. The cause of these lawsuits is an ongoing dispute. It could be a dispute between neighbors or within the family, but it could also be caused by business matters. The forthcoming period of time will be filled with tension, and it will not be easy to get through it. The dreamer must muster a lot of patience in order to get through it unscathed. When it ends, he will attain rest and security.

Number 12

The dreamer wants to have everything – and quickly. He does not have the patience to work hard and he does not feel like building his life layer by layer, reaching his goals in this way. Haste is the work of the devil, and the dream warns him precisely of this. The desire to get everything quickly is liable to bring him to the edge of the abyss, and he could ultimately lose the little he has. He must calm down, plan his steps slowly and carefully, and make do with what he has.

Number 13

The number 13 in a dream implies that the dreamer is in a relationship against his will. He feels a tremendous obligation toward the relationship and his partner, and although he already despises it and wants out, he is unable to do it. But he cannot keep behaving in this way. The bubble inside him has to burst eventually. He should free himself from the relationship he does not want to be in, even if the price can sometimes be heavy.

Number 14

A dream that features the number 14 implies losses. In most cases, the losses are financial, but not always. There could also be spiritual losses. A dream of this type is a warning dream against the loss of everything the dreamer possesses. He must protect everything he has fiercely, because the loss is inevitable. The more he protects it, the less he will lose.

Number 15

The number 15 in a dream attests to the fact that the dreamer wants to help others. He has a great capacity for giving, and he wants to give of himself to the community and society. Even if things have not been put into practice up till now, it's never too late, and he can start at any time. He will derive great satisfaction from it, and society will benefit from it, too.

A B C D E F G H I J K L M **N** O P Q R S T U V W X Y Z

Number 16

A person who dreams about the number 16 can expect ease and love. The dream predicts that during the forthcoming period of time, the dreamer will attain these things, which eluded him until now, despite many efforts and serious attempts. Now the things will flow and reach him effortlessly – as if fixed from above. Love will come by itself, as will the life of ease that he has to do nothing to achieve.

Number 17

A person who sees the number 17 in a dream will soon enjoy only good things, both materially and spiritually. The state of his bank account will be excellent, and so will things on the social, romantic, family and work levels. He can expect peace and quiet.

Number 18

A dream about the number 18 indicates a sparkling person who loves to live life to the full, and for this reason is extraordinarily active. Having said that, he undertakes tasks that are too much for him. He is liable to collapse one day without knowing exactly why. The reason is that he is overloaded. The dreamer does not feel that he is doing more than he is capable of because he is used to this pace. He must slow down and take a breather occasionally so that he does not find himself exhausted.

Number 19

A dream that features the number 19 symbolizes the fact

that the dreamer is collapsing under the burden. He is suffering from an overload in his everyday life, and only he can change the situation. It is in his hands. If he slows the pace down, he will also enjoy other things in life, such as family life, engineering quality time for hobbies, and so on. His life can change radically. This would also be important for his health, since if he continues the pace of life to which he is accustomed, he is liable to contract some kind of heart disease or other ailment that will be the direct result of his incorrect lifestyle. Correct nutrition, watching his health, physical exercise – all these can help him change the course of his life and set him on another, better, path.

Number 20

A dream about the number 20 implies that the dreamer is confused and he does not know how to organize his day, and for this reason tends to miss out on many things in his life. He is the ultimate latecomer, and he already has a terrible reputation for being someone who cannot be relied on in anything to do with punctuality. He must be more punctual and learn to organize his day in a more correct manner. He won't be the only one to benefit: everyone around him will benefit, too.

Number 21

A dream that features the number 21 implies that a move planned by the dreamer will succeed beyond his wildest expectations. The dreamer toiled long and hard on a certain project whose stages he had to plan meticulously. It will succeed, and the dreamer will see the fruits of his labor.

Number 22

A dream about the number 22 contains a spiritual and symbolic significance. The dreamer is engaged in the world of the spirit and succeeds in experiencing things that ordinary mortals, who do not dabble in the spiritual world, will never reach. His inner world is rich and overflowing, and he does not need friends or people around him in order to be happy. The spiritual level he has reached is very high, and he dabbles in the occult. He can expect many more discoveries in this field, and will rise to higher spiritual levels.

Number 23

A dream about the number 23 is a warning dream, warning the dreamer against the envy and jealousy of the people around him who cannot resign themselves to the fact that he is more successful than they are, or that he possesses more than they do. The dreamer must be careful of their jealousy, which can be expressed in terrible deeds. He must behave modestly and not flaunt his achievements publicly so as not to inflame the jealousy that is burning in any case.

Number 24

A dream that features the number 24 implies that the dreamer will be at the center of an affair in which something that he opposes will be imposed on him, but he will not be able to do anything about it. He can expect a tough battle, and despite his vigorous resistance, he will not be able to withstand the well-oiled machine that is exerting pressure on him. In spite of this, he has to try to be loyal to his inner truth at any cost.

Number 25

A dream about the number 25 symbolizes very weighty matters. The dreamer is a man of the book, who likes to get to the bottom of complex issues and grapple with very important things.

This often deters people who do not understand what he is saying and do not always comprehend the meaning of the issues he raises. If he wants to make friends, he has to learn to be more down-to-earth and willing to invest in other things.

Number 26

A dream about the number 26 prophesies that something profitable is in the offing. The dreamer will find himself in the midst of a deal that he did not plan in advance, and that will yield large profits. This will change his way of life radically, so he has to be careful and plan his moves judiciously in anything to do with ventures of any kind.

Number 27

A dream about the number 27 implies that the dreamer is a person who is easily swayed by others, adopts a large variety of opinions, and does not have an opinion of his own that he can stand up for and that forms the mainstay of his personality.

The dreamer is responsible for the people around him not according him his due respect. They scoff at him and do not ascribe any importance to his opinion, which changes from day to day. He must listen to his inner self, adopt opinions that reflect his world-view, and stick to them.

Number 28

A dream that features the number 28 symbolizes love affairs. The dreamer is about to get involved in a love affair that will sweep him along like a twig in a raging torrent. He will be so enamoured that he is liable to lose his individuality in the waves of adoration he feels for his partner. He must try and curb himself, for if he does not, he will find himself on the fast track to losing the object of his love.

Number 29

A dream about the number 29 indicates that the dreamer can soon expect to receive an invitation to a party. The dreamer, who is not accustomed to socializing, is likely to find himself in the role of the heart and soul of this party and surprised at his ability to charm other people. Although deep inside himself, he is familiar with his hidden abilities, he is still surprised by them, and this is a good and pleasant surprise.

Number 30

This dream predicts that the dreamer is about to hear a piece of gossip that, to his great astonishment, can extricate him from a shameful situation he has gotten himself into. Juicy information that is going to reach his ears soon in the form of gossip will help him get out of the crisis he has been in for a long time. He has to exploit this information for his benefit in spite of the fact that he does not feel comfortable doing so.

Number 31

The number 31 in a dream implies that, thanks to the stubbornness he displayed, the dreamer is about to succeed in accomplishing a goal he set himself. His ability not to let go of things even when it is difficult but to keep on grasping them relentlessly, can be chalked up to his credit. He owes his success to his stubbornness, to his ability to stick to his goal, and to his character that does not let him rest until he sees things working out well from his point of view.

Number 32

A dream about the number 32 implies that the dreamer has suffered a fall, out of which, by virtue of his astonishing abilities alone, he has managed to extricate himself and start over with renewed strength and extraordinary energy. Although the dreamer has endured a very rough period, during which he experienced a bitter failure, he can now expect success as a result of his abilities and because of his great personal charm.

Number 33

A dream that features the number 33 hints that a disease is in the offing. Some kind of disease is incubating in the dreamer, but he is not yet aware of it. This could be a minor problem whose roots are already planted in his body, such as a back problem that is about to manifest itself as a more significant disease, but it could also be something much more serious. For this reason, the dreamer is well advised to have a general and comprehensive physical exam in order to form an advance prognosis and treat the incipient problem while it is still in its infancy.

Number 34

The meaning of the number 34 in a dream is essentially similar to that of the number 28. The love the dreamer is about to experience is addictive. He is liable to find himself negating his own personality in the face of his partner, who is going to sweep him away in a wave of great love. He must learn to maintain the stability of his self in this sweeping relationship.

Number 35

A dream that features the number 35 is a warning dream about family disputes. The dreamer must work toward peace in the home and do everything to prevent the dispute. It is in his hands, and he really can bring peace to the home. The dream implies that the dreamer is blessed with a special talent to influence the people around him. He is very charismatic, and one word from him is important and crucial to the family. He must take advantage of his character in order to restore calm to the home.

Number 36

A dream about the number 36 is a special dream, since it predicts that the dreamer can expect to be endowed with great spiritual illumination. The dreamer engages in spirituality, and for a long time has yearned to achieve the illumination, the lofty and the perfect that only a few people on earth achieve. The dream prophesies that the dreamer will actually experience the illumination he has anticipated so eagerly, and reach the highest level of spirituality that exists.

Number 37

The number 37 indicates that the dreamer is in a tricky situation – on the one hand he wants love, and on the other, he despises commitment. The dream implies that he can indulge in non-committal love flirtations without any pangs of conscience. He has time until he has to commit to a long-term relationship, and he can certainly enjoy an uncommitted relationship. The dream "authorizes" him to do so.

Number 38

A dream about the number 38 affords the dreamer the possibility of recognizing his achievements. The dreamer tends to diminish his self-worth and depict himself to others as a mediocre person, while the opposite is true – he is creative, talented and successful, and he must learn not to be ashamed to say this aloud and observe the extent of the esteem he deserves from the society he lives in. Sometimes one does not have to be so modest; it is a good idea to know how to stress achievements and abilities as well.

Number 39

The person who dreams about the number 39 must be careful of the emotion of jealousy that is bubbling inside him. He is liable to drown in this terrible emotion, which can destroy him. Jealousy is liable to lead to hatred, and hatred is liable to lead to terrible deeds. The dreamer must try with all his strength to avoid the destructive emotion of jealousy and slough it off it in favor of more gentle emotions. If he is unable to do this by himself, he should seek counseling and not hesitate to take all the necessary steps required to quash these evil emotions.

Number 40

A dream about the number 40 is a simple dream, which implies that soon the dreamer will go to some kind of performance that he will enjoy. He may have missed a performance that he considered important, and this prophetic dream hints that soon he will be able to enjoy it and that his wish will come true.

Number 41

A dream that features the number 41 symbolizes the total disgrace that will be the dreamer's lot. The dreamer may have done something that he is very ashamed of and is trying to conceal, and now it is too late, since his action is already public knowledge. There is nothing he can do but ask forgiveness if he did something bad to somebody that is causing him to feel such shame, or he must take another step to erase the disgrace, the sooner the better.

Number 42

If a dream features the number 42, it is a warning dream that predicts an accident. The dreamer is liable to find himself involved in some kind of accident, and the dream serves to warn him of it. It could be an accident involving

A B C D E F G H I J K L M **N** O P Q R S T U V W X Y Z

vehicles, but for that matter it could also be a work accident or some other kind of accident. The dreamer must be very careful with what he does, act moderately and think well before taking any step.

Number 43

A dream about the number 43 implies that the dreamer relishes shifting the blame to other people's doorsteps. Ultimately, this is liable to cost him dearly. People do not like to carry other people's guilt. He must learn to take responsibility for his actions and confess to his errors or misdeeds. He must not continue placing the blame on others, particularly if he is the guilty party and not they. He will soon find himself ostracized and in a difficult and uncomfortable position.

Number 44

A dream that features the number 44 attests to the fact that soon the dreamer will move to new surroundings and he will have to adapt to life in the new place. He has to take into account that a change of place leads to a change of luck – for good and for bad. If the move entails a change of residence for his children, he should involve himself in the move in order to make it easier for them in every way.

Number 45

The number 45 in a dream foretells that something valuable is about to get lost. It will not help the dreamer to prepare himself for this event in advance, or even to put all his valuables in a safe. Something dear to him is about to disappear, and he cannot prevent it. There are things that are dictated from above, like fate, and this is one of them. For this reason, he should not make an effort to hide and conceal his things, but rather learn to accept the loss of the valuable object with equanimity, since nothing can change the bitter dictate.

Number 46

A dream that features the number 46 implies that the dreamer is a creative person. He is very talented, and this will be very beneficial to him in his life – from finding a congenial place of work to finding an interesting partner with whom to establish a family. His talent and the creativity are hereditary, so he will also enjoy the fruits of his children's creations.

Number 47

A dream about the number 47 indicates that even if the dreamer falls ill in the near future, he can expect a speedy recovery. Even if the diagnosis of the disease seems pessimistic and indicates something serious, the dream predicts a relatively speedy and easy recovery. For this reason, the dreamer can discard any worries. Everything will be all right in the end, and will get back to normal.

Number 48

A dream in which the number 48 appears implies that the dreamer can expect to find himself in the midst of disputes that do not really concern him. He will get involved in them by accident, completely by mistake, but will find it difficult to extricate himself. He has to brace himself for such an event, which will not make his life easier. Having said that, the moment he frees himself from the situation and the disputes are resolved, he will learn a lesson for life, and will never again find himself in the midst of scandals.

Number 49

A dream about the number 49 symbolizes hedonism. The dreamer loves to enjoy life and what it offers him, particularly everything the realm of sex and its pleasures can give him. The dream implies that soon the dreamer will "star" in a stormy love affair that will be reflected in sexual pleasures provided by his bed partner. These physical pleasures interest and fascinate him, and he is never satiated, even after a long time.

Number 50

The number 50 implies that a matter of principle to which the dreamer adheres is causing a dispute with his neighbors. The dispute is liable to get worse if the sides do not reach a compromise, but the dream takes the side of the dreamer and his standpoint, and vindicates him. He must stick to his belief and fight for what he considers right, since this will ultimately emerge.

Number 60

A dream that features the number 60 does not augur well. It is a dream that predicts the death of someone close to the dreamer, causing grief and longing. This cannot be changed because it has been dictated "from above." The dreamer can do nothing more than get through this difficult period and let himself mourn, express his grief and move on, because life goes on, and it is stronger than anything else.

Number 70

A dream about the number 70 predicts that the dreamer will rise in rank. This may be reflected in a promotion at work, bringing with it prestige and a salary raise, but it could also be a rise up the hierarchical ladder of one of the security institutions, such as the military, law enforcement agencies, and so on, if the dreamer serves there. A rise in rank can also be reflected in the spiritual realm – the dreamer rises in spiritual rank, reaching new and marvelous places.

Number 80

A dream about the number 80 refers to the dreamer's concern about adulthood, old age and death. This is very natural, and generally this dream is dreamed by elderly people for whom age really does pose a threat. However, coping with the ravages of adulthood and aging can help with the fear of old age: physical exercise, using the mind and mental activity, socializing with people – all these can blot out the fear and erase it.

Number 90

A dream that features the number 90 is similar in meaning to a dream about the number 80, with one difference: it also warns against visiting an old people's home. It is not advisable to pay such a visit, unless it has special importance. A visit like this is liable to cause the dreamer a bad feeling about his advancing age, and this can easily be avoided.

Number 100

A dream about the number 100 implies that the dreamer can expect to reach great illumination. He has achieved high ranks of spirituality, he is close to himself, he is familiar with the lofty and the occult, and now he can expect *the* major experience of any spiritual person – illumination. When he is an illuminated person, his entire life will look different, and he will be able to guide generations of acolytes, who are also seeking the light, in his way.

Number 200

A dream about the number 200 hints at the existence of reincarnation. Even if the dreamer does not believe in reincarnation, the dream implies that such a thing really does exist, and that there is tremendous significance to the secret of life.

Number 365

A dream about the number 365, which indicates the number of days in a year, is a sign that the dreamer can expect a sweet and successful year. During this year, he will experience nothing but good things, and will see the fruits of his labor. He will enjoy wealth and happiness, and will derive great satisfaction from his family, from his job and from his social and romantic life.

Number 500

Like 200, the number 500 also implies the existence of reincarnation, except that here there is a hint from a previous incarnation for the dreamer. If the dreamer adds the content of his dream to the number he dreamed about, he will be able to receive a hint about his previous incarnations, since his distance past has returned to him in this incarnation.

Number 666

The appearance of the number 666 in a dream symbolizes evil. The dreamer must be careful because the devil is after him. He must safeguard himself, be very cautious in everything he does in his everyday life, since the devil is looking for an opportunity to attack him.

Number 1000

A dream about the number 1000 hints that the dreamer will drown in heavy debts in the future. He is therefore advised to be cautious and level-headed from now on, since the debts are inevitable, but he can minimize the damage by keeping his finger on the pulse and being thrifty rather than extravagant. In this way, he will succeed in preventing a further deterioration in the situation that is awaiting him in the future.

Numbness

If a person feels numb in his dream, it is a forecast of illness and anxieties.

Nun

If a religious person dreams about nuns, it indicates that he is in the throes of a conflict between material pleasures and matters of the spirit. If a woman dreams about nuns, it predicts widowhood or a breakup with her partner.

If a woman dreams that she is a nun, it reflects her feeling of discontent with her life. A dream that features a dead nun is an expression of the dreamer's despair about his partner's infidelity and his financial losses. If a nun dreams about discarding her habit, it means that she is unsuitable for her calling.

Nuptials

If a woman dreams about her nuptials, it is a forecast of lovely events that will bring her joy and respect.

Nurse (male or female)

The appearance of a nurse in a dream means that the dreamer is experiencing or is about to experience a tragic event such as an accident or a loss of some kind that will change his life. In many cases, the dream attests to the dreamer's bad feelings toward one of his parents, who, he feels, does not believe in him or trust him. In such a case, the feeling of loss that the dreamer is experiencing is on the psychological level. This disturbs him so much that he is unable to shake off the distressing feeling even in the dream.

If the dreamer sees a nurse in his dream, but she is not wearing a white uniform, he can expect an era of health and happiness. He will feel well, and will be free from physiological and mental diseases and problems. His good physical feeling will affect all the other areas of his life on different levels, and he will feel mental health and vigor.

A nurse wearing a white uniform in a dream refers to the dreamer's neglect of everything concerning health. This may refer to bad eating habits, a lack of exercise, a tendency to smoke or indulge some other habit that is bad for his health. This is a sign that the dreamer should go and have a general checkup and begin to adopt a healthier lifestyle. The everyday subconscious and conscious fears of disaster-filled consequences as a result of not paying attention to the right lifestyle are expressed in the fact that they come to the surface in a dream.

Nursing (infants)

If a woman dreams about nursing her infant, it means that she will enjoy what she does. If a young woman has this dream, she can expect to hold responsible, respectable jobs. If a man dreams that his wife is nursing their infant, everything he does will go smoothly.

Nut

A dream that features nuts heralds good and happy things, especially the advent of a new love into the dreamer's life. Not only is the dreamer's future happiness great and accompanied by a lot of satisfaction, but his future partner will be very rich and will provide the dreamer with economic security. The dreamer's social status is also about to change for the better as a result of his new relationship, and the people around him will accord him great respect.

Eating nuts in a dream hints at the dreamer's extravagance. He acts irresponsibly regarding his day-to-day expenditures and must be more cautious. If not, he is liable to become embroiled in a series of serious financial complications and problems from which it will be difficult to extricate himself. If he manifcsts greater self-discipline, and acts in a more organized and calculating way, he can evade all the ills that are threatening to bring him down if he continues with his wayward lifestyle.

Nutmeg

A dream about nutmeg is a sign of financial prosperity and successful journeys.

Nymph

If a person dreams about nymphs frolicking in clear water, it means that intimate desires will be realized in an explosion of pleasure and ecstasy. If he dreams that the nymphs are not in water, it is a sign of disillusionment. If a young woman sees nymphs bathing in a dream, she will have pleasure and joy, but they will not be innocent; she will use her charms to corrupt men.

O

Oak tree

A dream about an oak tree is a sign that the dreamer can expect a long life, a life of ease in which he will enjoy wealth and happiness. This dream augurs nothing but good for the dreamer, and its tidings are positive. The dreamer can know that even in moments of crisis, anxiety or fear, he must be absolutely certain that fate holds tremendous success in store for him. None of the crises will cause him real problems in life, and he will always manage to overcome them easily and emerge strengthened from them, with renewed faith in himself and in his abilities.

Another interpretation of a dream about an oak tree is that it is a sign of the dreamer's good health. Even if the dreamer is not feeling well at the moment, or is worried about health problems, the dream implies that soon his state of health will improve, and he can expect to enjoy a good and healthy quality of life. The symbol of the oak tree as a source of good health originates in the ancient belief according to which healers would refer to oak trees, which were thought to be sacred, when healing patients.

Oar

A dream in which a person sees himself handling oars is a sign of disappointment for him, because he will have to make many sacrifices for the well-being of other people. If a person dreams about losing an oar, it implies that he will not be able to realize his ambitions.

A dream that features a broken oar signifies that some event the dreamer was looking forward to will be postponed.

Oasis

The dreamer can expect to go through a tough stage, at the end of which he will reach safe ground. During the forthcoming period of time, the dreamer will find himself in startling and complicated situations. He will feel lonely and short of money, to the point that he might leave his home and go out to seek a living from other sources that are located further away geographically.

He may well get into situations that will require him to make a far greater effort than he is accustomed to making. He need not worry. The final result will be positive.

Oath

If a person dreams about taking an oath, it is a prediction of conflicts and arguments in real life.

Oatmeal

If a person eats oatmeal in a dream, it means that he deserves to enjoy the wealth he has worked so hard for. If a young woman dreams about preparing oatmeal, she will soon be responsible for other people's fate.

Oats

If a person sees oats in a dream, it is a good sign, particularly for farmers. A dream that features rotten oats is a sign of sorrow that will replace joy. A dream about a horse eating oats implies that the dreamer has unfinished tasks at hand.

Obedience

If a person dreams that he is obedient to someone else, he can expect a normal, pleasant period in life. If he dreams that other people are obedient to him, it is a sign that he will have wealth and power.

Obelisk

If a person sees an obelisk in a dream, it means that sad news is in the offing. If he dreams that lovers are standing beside an obelisk, it is a sign that they will break up.

Obituary

If a person dreams about writing an obituary, it means that he will soon have to do things that are distasteful to him. If he reads an obituary in a dream, it means that disconcerting news will arrive soon.

Obligation

If a person dreams that he obligates himself in any situation, he will be upset by other people's complaints. If other people obligate themselves to him in his dream, he will be accorded the esteem of his friends and family.

Observatory

A dream about an observatory hints at the dreamer's desire to realize a dream that looks too distant and difficult to realize. The dreamer is an ambitious person whose goals are clear to him, but they are way above average. The dreamer may be aspiring to achieve fame and glory on a national or international level in a particular professional field. To this end, he must work hard and be patient. Rome was not built in a day, either. His patience will pay off and he will realize most of his aspirations if he plans his moves wisely.

Occultist

If a person dreams about listening to the teachings of an occultist, it means that he will try to lead other people to higher planes of tolerance and justice.

Ocean

In a dream, the ocean is perceived as an endless sea – a sea that extends from horizon to horizon.

If the dream features a stormy ocean, it means that the dreamer is using the dream to express his fears about an imminent danger that will apparently emanate from an enemy of some kind or from someone else who wants to harm the dreamer.

If the dream features a calm ocean with "smooth" waters, the dreamer can expect a good, rosy future – a future without dangers, filled with interesting adventures and journeys to unusual places. The dreamer is neither a particularly curious nor a particularly spontaneous person, but life holds surprises in store for him, and he will find himself reaching distant shores that he never dreamed he would visit.

If the dreamer does not remember the horizon, but only the ocean around him, the dream indicates his urgent psychological need to escape the bonds of the world and go someplace else. He wants to detach and distance himself from everything around him in order to calm down and live a serene and peaceful life for a certain length of time. His objective is to renew his energies so that he can ultimately resume the rat race.

October

A dream about the month of October is a sign of success in all undertakings. In addition, new friendships will be formed.

Oculist

If a person dreams about consulting an oculist, it means that he is not satisfied with his progress in life, and will employ other means in order to advance.

Odor

If a person smells sweet odors in a dream, it means that he is being taken care of by a beautiful woman and is thriving. If he smells disgusting odors, he should brace himself for bitter quarrels and irresponsible employees.

Offense

If a person is offended in a dream, he will be furious at

having to justify himself for minor misdemeanors. If he gives offense in a dream, his path to success will be fraught with obstacles. If a young woman dreams that she is offended or that she offends, she will regret having disobeyed her parents or jumped to hasty conclusions.

Offerings

If a person dreams about making an offering, it means that he will be servile and obsequious until his level of responsibility is raised.

Office (public)

If a person dreams that he holds office, he will be successful, even though his ambitions prompt him to take risks occasionally.

If he dreams about failing to be appointed to a certain post, it indicates that he will suffer serious disappointments in his business. If he dreams that he is dismissed from office, the dream implies that he will lose valuable possessions.

Office (workplace)

In most cases, dreams about an office are dreams in which the dreamer has a job – whether it is as an office worker or an office manager who is responsible for what goes on in the office and for the people who are subordinate to him.

If a person sees himself working in an office in a dream, the dream implies that money matters are bothering him and undermining his peace of mind. He is so preoccupied with these financial matters that he is neglecting other important things that are going on around him. The dream serves to draw the dreamer's attention to this, and to cause him to be more heedful of his immediate surroundings. He may be neglecting his children and other family members, and this is liable to have negative repercussions later on.

If a person dreams that he is managing an office by himself, the dream serves to confirm that he is an ambitious person, just as he views himself. When he sets himself a goal, he aspires to accomplish it at almost any price, and will do whatever he can to succeed in doing so. He is a champion at improvisations, and knows how to extricate himself from tricky situations. With this knowledge as well as his ability to adapt to different situations, he can go very far indeed.

Officer

A dream about an officer indicates that the dreamer is in need of an authoritative figure in his life to map out a path for him.

Offspring

If a person sees his own offspring in a dream, it is a sign of joy and cheerfulness. If he sees the offspring of domestic animals, it means an upswing in prosperity.

Ogre / Giant

A dream about an ogre or a giant implies that the dreamer is facing a gigantic task and requires great courage to tackle it. He must try to muster this courage in order to accomplish the task he is facing. It will be worth his while.

A dream about an ogre refers to big problems in the dreamer's path, which are causing him to become "stuck." He feels that he is unable to advance in any direction, but the dream augurs well. Ultimately, he will be able to overcome the difficulties and emerge triumphant.

If a person dreams that he himself is an ogre, the dream implies that he tends to overestimate himself, to boast and to patronize other people, and he must curb these urges, since they do nothing but alienate the people he loves.

If a person dreams about meeting an ogre, he is assured of success in every aspect of life, especially money.

A dream in which the dreamer sees himself killing an ogre is a sign that he has abundant means of accomplishing his objectives at his disposal. There are no stumbling-blocks along his path, and he must make the most of this.

If a dream features a particularly monstrous ogre, the dreamer can expect success in all areas. He can forget about his fears, since regardless of what he does and which path he chooses, everything in his life will turn out extremely well.

If a person dreams about an ogre that appears in someone else's life, it is a sign that he will be successful in his love life. He will succeed in winning the person he wants, even if he has to fight and get rid of other lovers.

Oil

A dream about oil warns against being tempted into believing the words of a close friend who does not always say what he is actually thinking.

The interpretations of dreams about oil differ between

men and women. If a man dreams about oil, the dream serves as a warning against disappointments and failures that are liable to lead to a period that is full of frustration and rage. The dream predicts that in the immediate future, the dreamer is liable to run into difficulties that will undermine his peace of mind. Moreover, there could be delays in important moves in his life, which could be critical for his future. The dreamer is liable to fail, and he must take this into account.

In contrast, the meaning of the dream is radically different if a woman dreams it. When a woman dreams about oil, it is a sign of the respect that she will be accorded and of a happy marriage. She will be fortunate to have a husband who appreciates and respects her very much, and maybe admires her so much that she will be pampered all her life. Her husband will express his love and respect for her in various ways such as helping her in the house, raising the children and taking an interest in her everyday experiences. In other words, he will participate in her life as a full-fledged partner.

Oilcloth

If a person dreams about oilcloth, it means that the dreamer is about to be treated with aloofness and betrayed. If he deals in oilcloth in his dream, it refers to underhand business practices.

Ointment

A dream that features ointment signifies that the dreamer will establish warm and profitable friendships.

Old person

A dream that features a very old person speaking to the dreamer hints that the latter is well advised to take the useful advice of a person on whom he relies and whom he knows to be a person he can trust. His openness to listen to a person with experience in life can only help him and will have a positive influence on his future path.

A dream about an old person can also be interpreted as a prophetic dream, according to which the dreamer can expect to get rich easily. This may come from gambling or from a successful business venture that will enable him to get rich quickly.

It is a good idea to keep the money that will flow in for harder times and not to squander it.

A dream that features an old, wrinkled woman hints at a lack of happiness in the offing. Even though the present state of things gives no indication of this, the dreamer must prepare himself for gray and dismal days of sadness and depression.

If a person dreams that he does business with an old person, the dream implies that he has to act modestly and be more refined in his dealings. He must learn not to act in an extreme manner but rather to be a little more sensitive toward other people and behave cautiously rather than act hastily.

A dream in which the dreamer sees himself dressed as an old person is a sign that in the future, he will enjoy a great deal of fame and honor.

If a person dreams that he acts in an "old" way and feels very old in a dream, he can expect to quarrel with a young girl.

Olive

The following interpretations of a dream about olives or olive trees are mainly true for people who grew up in the Mediterranean region. This is because the associations and attitudes of people who did not grow up in a landscape of which olive trees are an inherent part are different, as is the interpretation of the dream.

A dream about olive trees symbolizes the calm, relaxed and happy family life the dreamer can expect to lead.

If a person dreams about olives – not necessarily growing on trees – he can expect wealth and happiness. The greater the number of olives in the dream, the greater the chances of the dream coming true.

If a person sees black olives on the tree, it is a sign that there will soon be a birth in his family.

Omelet

If a person sees an omelet served in a dream, it is a warning dream: it warns him of false flattery and deceit at his expense. If he dreams that he eats an omelet, someone he thought he trusted will make demands of him.

One-eyed person

A dream about a one-eyed person is a dire warning of plots and intrigues against the dreamer's happiness and good fortune in life.

Onion

If a person dreams about a scallion (a green onion), the dream predicts a state of sadness and sorrow that is about to

A B C D E F G H I J K L M N **O** P Q R S T U V W X Y Z

befall the dreamer and his family. The painful event will be accompanied by tears and weeping. It is possible that the death of someone in the family is to be expected soon.

An onion in a dream also augurs ill. It attests to the fact that the dreamer is going through a very difficult phase, mainly because of the revelation of a certain truth that tortures the dreamer's soul. It also hints that the dreamer can expect to suffer financial losses that will bring economic worries in their wake.

Another serious problem that crops up in addition to the rest is that the dreamer's associates do not stand by him and do not give him their full backup – precisely during the difficult period he has to go through. Therefore the dreamer is compelled to cope with the new financial difficulties that are facing him by himself while those around him object to his decisions and plans, but do not offer any alternatives.

A dream in which the dreamer sees himself peeling an onion implies a situation in which the dreamer feels as if he is "Don Quixote" fighting windmills. He is fighting to achieve a certain objective that he has set himself, but it makes no difference which method he chooses for accomplishing it – he does not succeed in doing so.

The path of Sisyphean hardship he is following debilitates him and plunges him into despair. However, in order to succeed and overcome the difficult period, he has to try again and again, and not throw in the towel.

Opera

A dream that features an opera house, or a dreamer who sees himself watching an opera, attests to the fact that the dreamer has influential friends who make sure to pamper

A B C D E F G H I J K L M N O P Q R S T U V W X Y Z

him and to share their wealth with him. They are in the habit of entertaining him at their expense, of taking him on journeys or luxury trips, and so on.

If the dreamer sees himself participating in the opera as one of the members of the troupe that is putting on the performance, the dream indicates that he is giving free rein to his desires and artistic talents. The dreamer is gifted with unique artistic abilities, and they are seeking an outlet. The dream is a sign for the dreamer to begin to work toward a certain goal and express his hidden talent. If he does not do this, he will suffer from constant frustration for the rest of his life.

If the dream features opera music that is unpleasant to the dreamer's ear – to the point that he actually suffers because of it – it means that the dreamer can expect to go through a period of crisis. During this time, he will have to cope with difficult inner struggles, with a troubled soul, and with a lack of mental tranquillity in order to get on with the rest of his life.

Opium

A dream that features opium implies that strangers will employ subtle means in order to sabotage the dreamer's chances of success.

Opponent / Rival

If someone dreams about an opponent, it means that he can expect good news. This generally refers to the workplace or to a "battle" for social status. It could also refer to political advancement. If the dreamer is involved in an argument with his opponent and beats him, it is a sign of a possible "explosion" – a verbal or other kind of argument in which the dreamer will ultimately have the upper hand. If the dreamer encounters his opponent in an arbitrary place, such as an entertainment venue or a shopping mall, it means that the opponent has no intention of using too much force, and the dreamer's anticipated advancement is in the pipeline.

Opulence

If a young woman dreams of unbelievable, exquisite opulence, it is a warning: she must take care not to be taken in and find herself in a humiliating and awful situation.

Orange

The appearance of an orange in a dream hints at good health and at the fact that the dreamer is about to have good luck. This is particularly true if the orange in the dream is ripe and sweet. The "healthier" the orange looks, the more it symbolizes health and good luck. The dreamer will be fortunate and will enjoy growth in life from all points of view, but the most significant of all will be his economic growth. The dreamer's financial status will improve beyond recognition, he will begin to enjoy the good life, he will be able to permit himself pleasures that he previously considered to be luxuries, and he will live an easier and more comfortable life, without the daily hassles that preoccupy him today.

A rotten orange in a dream symbolizes a lack of happiness and love: the infidelity of the dreamer's partner, the inability to trust the partner, or a lack of mutual cheer. This situation will make the dreamer bitter and frustrated, and he should wake up and take care of it. If he does not, he is liable to find himself in a situation in which it will already be too late, and there will be nothing to fix.

If a dream features several oranges in a basket, it implies that the dreamer is facing a temporary separation from a person he loves. However, the dreamer will return to that loved person later on, and the ties between them will be closer and better. Even if the separation causes a great deal of sadness, the dreamer should know that the situation is only temporary, and he should be happy about the fact that the reunion will improve their relations.

If the orange in the dream was unripe or bitter, it means that the dreamer does not speak clearly to the people around him. It seems that the people surrounding the dreamer do not always understand him, and this sparks friction, disputes and misunderstandings. The confusion and lack of clarity that are causing the misunderstandings are ultimately liable to be harmful to the dreamer, and he will find himself helpless in the face of situations that he never had any intention of getting into.

Orang-utan

If a person dreams about an orang-utan, it means that he is being used to promote someone else's selfish schemes. A dream about an orang-utan is a sign of an unfaithful lover for a young woman.

Orator

If a person dreams that he is influenced by the words of an orator, it means that his head will be turned by flattery, and he will help undeserving people.

Orchard

An orchard symbolizes a good life, and hints at the dreamer's yearning for the lost paradise. The dreamer yearns for an idyllic world and a perfect life, which he cannot ever attain, of course. It is difficult for him to cope with everyday hardships, and he frequently finds himself escaping to other worlds, to the realms of the imagination.

A dream about the lost paradise can also be interpreted as something specific that the dreamer longs for without ever being able to attain it. The knowledge that his quest is futile in advance frustrates the dreamer and causes him to seek refuge in dreams and imaginings.

Orchestra

A dream about an orchestra has different meanings:

If a person hears an orchestra playing harmonious sounds in a dream, and the melody is pleasant to his ears, the dream attests to the fact that he can expect to receive material and spiritual help from his friends in a harmonious way, like the sounds of the orchestra in the dream. The help will be offered happily, without hesitation, and out of a sincere desire to extricate him from the situation in which he has landed himself.

Another interpretation of an orchestra playing states that the dreamer is about to become very famous because of his deeds. His name will be known far and wide, and he will enjoy fame and honor.

If a person sees himself playing and being active in an orchestra in a dream (it makes no difference what instrument he is playing, what kind of orchestra he is playing in, or what type of music is being played), the dream implies that in the near future he will receive a promotion at work. The people around him, especially his superiors at work, are about to recognize the dreamer's talents, and he will be promoted, along with improved working conditions and a higher salary. Playing in an orchestra in a dream and cooperating with other people symbolize his ability to work in a team harmoniously and gaining the recognition and admiration of the team.

Orchid

An orchid in a dream signifies the stormy sexual desires that are hidden in the dreamer's soul and are seeking a way out. The dreamer does not give free rein to his desires. He is too busy with mental self-flagellation in everything concerning matters of sex, and does not permit himself release. He is a person who is very preoccupied with his explosive sexuality for the very reason that he does not give it free rein. The orchid is linked to fierce sexual passions, crazy love and sweeping emotions that are not expressed fully in the way the dreamer would like to experience them in real life. The orchid symbolizes repressed emotions, repressed desires and burning passions that have no outlet in reality. It is a dream that serves as an opportunity for the dreamer to take an objective look at the way he chooses to live his love life, and urges him to be more liberated and free in his sex life and in his relationships in general.

Organ

If a person hears powerful organ music, it indicates solid wealth and good friends. If he sees an organ in a church, it is a sign of despair due to death or separation in the family.

If he plays the organ competently, he will enjoy renown and good fortune. If he hears lugubrious singing accompanied by an organ, it means that distasteful tasks are in the offing for him. He can also expect to lose friends or his job.

Organist

If a person sees an organist in a dream, it indicates that he will have problems because of a friend's careless behavior. If a young woman dreams about being an organist, it is a warning dream: she should refrain from being so demanding in love, otherwise she runs the risk of her lover leaving her.

Orgy

In general, a dream about an orgy in which people are having sex, but the dreamer is not directly connected to what he is seeing, means that friends of the dreamer are facing a trial in which they are about to lose their shirts. The dream indicates losses and downfalls or crashes, mainly of people around the dreamer and not of the dreamer himself.

If the dreamer sees himself taking part in an orgy, it is a sign that he is the object of malicious gossip. This gossip is liable to embroil him in complications, and it will not be easy for him to extricate himself from the new situation in which he is inadvertently about to land. If he tends to conceal things and live under a shroud of secrecy, he should discard anything that could be a reason or pretext for mystery so that the evil tongues do not target him.

If the dreamer sees himself and his partner taking part in an orgy, the dream is a warning: It foretells that such serious disputes and rows will flare up between them that reconciliation will be impossible. Separation will be almost inevitable. Conflicts like that will become par for the course for the couple, and they will just become worse. The dream constitutes a kind of requiem for the dreamer's relationship, and if he still wants to salvage it, he must rally quickly and try to save it in any way possible.

If the dreamer sees a movie about an orgy in a dream, it implies that he is about to drop all the bonds of hypocrisy and modesty that characterized him up till now in favor of more liberated and even wild behavior. The dreamer is about to give free rein to his urges, which he has not dared to indulge for a very long time. He is about to participate in a sensual adventure that will sweep him away to places he has never been before, and this new openness will cause him to look at life differently than in the past.

Ornament

If a person wears an ornament in a dream, it means that he will be awarded a marvelous honor. If he dreams that he receives ornaments, it is a sign of luck. If he gives them away in his dream, it is a sign of carelessness and wastefulness. If he loses ornaments, he can expect to lose his job or partner.

Orphan

If a person dreams about comforting orphans, it will cause him to forgo his own pleasures in order to help them. If the orphans in the dream are the dreamer's relatives, he will have new obligations that will cause him to lose friends.

Orphanhood

In contrast to the feelings of sadness evoked by the dream, it implies a positive development. If a person who dreams that he himself is orphaned or that someone he knows loses his parents, it actually predicts the appearance of a new and unknown figure on the horizon. This person serves as a dominant and powerful figure and will influence the dreamer's life for a long time. This person may previously have lived abroad or in a distant town, and the dreamer's ties with him are very tenuous. Now there will be a physical and emotional *rapprochement*, perhaps because of moving house or frequent trips that will bring the dreamer into contact with this figure who will bring only good things into his life. New opportunities will open up before the dreamer. He may change jobs, move house or make a change in the status of a romantic relationship.

Ostrich

An ostrich in a dream can attest to two things that are happening to the dreamer: one on the physical plan and the other on the mental plane.

On the physical plane, a dream about an ostrich indicates that the dreamer or one of his associates (generally, a member of his family) is not in the best health. Even if he has not noticed it yet, the disease exists, and he should go for a checkup and pay attention to the health problem. (Even if he is aware of it and it doesn't really bother him, it is still advisable to have it seen to – the sooner the better.) The same goes for his relative. If the dreamer knows of someone in his family who is suffering from a health problem, the dream should encourage him to convince the person to go for a checkup and to receive treatment for the problem from which he is suffering.

As we said above, a dream about an ostrich also indicates the mental plane. Such a dream hints that the person feels as if his head is in the clouds and he is all-powerful. He permits himself far more than he is capable of. Arrogance and conceit will get him nowhere. On the contrary, the dream hints that his lack of humility can engender bad experiences and cause him to enter a difficult phase. The dreamer's inappropriate behavior may make the people around him jealous of him to the point that they curse him with the "evil eye." He must resist the temptation to show off things he is proud of, especially things concerning money and finances, so that they do not destroy him.

Otter

If a person dreams about otters frolicking in clear springs, it is a sign of happiness and good fortune. If a single person has this dream, he may marry soon afterwards. Furthermore, spouses may be particularly affectionate.

Ottoman

If a person dreams that he and his sweetheart are relaxing on an ottoman and talking about love, his rivals will cause trouble in order to demean him in the eyes of his lover, and he will have to marry her quickly.

Ouija

If a person dreams about working on an ouija board, the dream portends failed plans and partnerships. If he dreams that he does not work on the ouija board, it is a warning dream: he is neglecting business for pleasure. If the board writes fluently in the dream, there will be good results.

Oven

If a person dreams about an oven in which tasty food is cooking, the dream implies that he can look forward to a period of prosperity and growth. Everything he does will turn out well and produce excellent results.

An oven in a dream is also an indication of the dreamer's nature. He is a person who needs attention, loves being at the hub of things, and needs people to lavish love and warmth on him. These things are more important to him than anything else. His fierce desire for recognition and social status take precedence over all his other aspirations, and they are the ones that afford him confidence and daring. A dream like this implies that the dreamer feels threatened and is afraid to lose the social status that he worked so hard to earn.

Overalls

If a woman dreams about a man wearing overalls, she will be deceived as to the true nature of her lover. If she is married and has this dream, she will be taken in by her husband's frequent absences: far from being work-related, they stem from infidelity.

Overcoat

If a person dreams about an overcoat, it means that other people will cross the dreamer. If he dreams that he borrows an overcoat, he will be penalized for other people's mistakes. If he sees or wears a new overcoat in a dream, his wishes will come true.

Owl

A dream about an owl generally serves as a warning dream. It mostly warns against two main things:

The people around the dreamer do not wish him well, and he must take care and keep his eyes and ears open, since they are up to something that is liable to harm him. The hostility could come from his domestic, business or social surroundings. He is well aware of where the evil is liable to emanate from.

The dream warns against the dreamer's intuition, which is betraying him at the moment, and therefore he should listen to the voice of reason and follow the rational side of it. Emotion is swaying him and is liable to cause him great disappointment. This is the time to operate in a thought-out and systematic manner – according to reason and not according to the dictates of his heart. If he does so, he will not be disappointed.

Some people do not necessarily interpret a dream about an owl as a warning dream, but rather as the forerunner of the sad and melancholy mood into which the dreamer has sunk. An emotional collapse, pain or disappointment are causing him to go through a difficult phase mentally, but he is strong enough not to sink into depression, and this phase will soon pass.

Ox / Bull

A dream about an ox generally indicates good things, since the ox is the symbol of decency, integrity, seriousness, determination and good and correct deeds. An ox in a dream attests to the fact that the dreamer is blessed with these wonderful qualities, which will lead him to success – both social and financial. People will hold him in very high regard because of his special nature, and will seek his company. In addition, they will accord him respect in view of the fact that he is considered by the people around him to be a courageous and fearless person who knows how to make the right decision at the right time.

An ox or bull in a dream also implies that the dreamer has made a good and correct investment that will yield excellent profits and make the dreamer very happy. The investment could be a financial one or an investment in the workplace, but the choice of a life partner can also be considered "a good investment" as a result of which the longed-for happiness will be achieved.

If a person sees an angry or bellicose bull in a dream, it predicts that the dreamer can soon expect to enter into a successful relationship with a member of the opposite sex, and establish a long romance that will make him happy. If a single person has this dream, he may soon meet his intended partner and the couple will make a life together.

An ox plowing in a dream means that inquiries are being made about the dreamer behind his back. Someone is investigating him and wants to know as many details about him as possible. These could be people who want him to join their ranks in some kind of private company or society, and that is why they are making inquiries. However, it is also possible that someone wants to establish a relationship with the dreamer and is making inquiries in order to know as much about him as possible before approaching him.

If several oxen appear in a dream, it implies that it is time to take risks. The dream encourages adventure, gambling and unusual things to which the dreamer is not accustomed and generally eschews. This time, he must dive in at the deep end since this is the time to do things he has never dared to do.

A white ox or bull in a dream attests to the fact that the dreamer can expect great wealth accompanied by a position of power and honor.

Oysters

If a person dreams about eating oysters, it means that he will cast off his sense of decency and morality in order to pursue base pleasures. He will also pursue financial gain shamelessly. If he dreams that he deals in oysters, he will stop at nothing to win a woman or gain wealth. If a person sees oysters in a dream, it is a prediction of wealth and children.

If a dream features oyster soup made of fresh milk, it indicates conflicts and some trouble, but there will be a reconciliation. A dream that features oyster soup made of buttermilk means that the dreamer will have to do some distasteful things. The dream hints at quarrels, bad luck and the breakup of friendships.

Only if the person dreams that he wakes up while eating the soup can this be prevented.

Oyster shells

If a person sees oyster shells in a dream, it attests to the fact that the dreamer will not be able to lay his hands on someone else's assets.

A B C D E F G H I J K L M N **O** P Q R S T U V W X Y Z

P

Pacify

If a person dreams that he is trying to pacify people in pain, it attests to his good nature. If a young woman has this dream, it means that she will have a good husband or friends. If a person dreams that he is pacifying other people's anger, it means that he will further other people's progress. If a lover is pacifying the jealousy of his sweetheart in a dream, it is a sign that he loves the wrong person.

Package

Receiving a package in a dream is a sign that the dreamer and his household are about to experience changes. In most cases, this refers to moving to a new home or renovating the present family residence. However, a dream like this sometimes implies an addition to the family in the shape of a new baby. In any case, these changes will be for the good and will bring greater joy and happiness into the dreamer's life and into the life of his family, as well as an improvement in their standard of living and quality of life.

In most cases, opening a package in a dream or carrying a package implies the dreamer's problems with his children or his concerns about their health and welfare.

A dream in which the dreamer sees himself carrying a particularly large and heavy package implies endless problems – a real plague of problems from which there does not seem to be any way out. Having said that, dealing with the problems slowly and steadily, and attempting to solve them one by one, will yield satisfactory results. The main thing is not to run away from them, but to deal with them.

If a person dreams about preparing a package, it is a sign that he is about to go off on a short and enjoyable trip or vacation that will recharge his energy, and he'll come back as good as new.

If the dreamer carries a package in a dream, he is suffering from health problems that are preoccupying him and keeping him awake at night. It is also possible that the dreamer is disturbed by the inappropriate behavior of his or other children, causing him suffering or sorrow.

Receiving a package in a dream is a sign that the dreamer has admirers clustering around him and is the recipient of enormous outpourings of love and warmth. The dream aims to bring him down to earth and reality and remind him that he is just a human being.

Packet (cargo ship)

If a person sees a packet docking, is a sign that there is a treat in store for him. If he sees the packet depart, he will suffer minor losses and disappointments.

Packing

A very common dream is one in which the dreamer sees himself packing objects, but does not complete the task. In such a case, the dream implies the dreamer's general feeling of frustration and bitterness. He feels that he is not fulfilling his potential and realizing his abilities and talents.

If the dreamer manages to complete the task of packing, it is a sign that he feels the need to effect a change in his life. The routine is killing him and he wants to change his surroundings and the atmosphere. He may be in need of a more profound change, such as job retraining, a change in his life habits, and so on.

If a person sees himself packing for a long journey in a dream, it is a sign that worries concerning business matters will keep him locked up at home, and he will be stuck in his place without being able to set himself free.

If a person sees family members or other people who are close to him packing suitcases, it is a sign that soon the dreamer will be blessed with happiness and tranquillity at home.

If the dreamer sees something being packed for a delivery, he is betraying someone's trust, and this is bothering him and weighing on his conscience.

Page (person)

If a dream features a page, it means that the dreamer will rush into a marriage with an unsuitable person. If a young woman dreams about being a page, she is going to make a fool of herself in some prank.

Pages

If a person sees blank pages in a dream, he can expect to make valuable and pleasant acquaintances that can propose interesting and varied initiatives and will enrich the dreamer's world.

In contrast, if the pages in the dream look too bright and clean, the dreamer can expect to go through a difficult phase that will be characterized by a lack of repose and a lack of caution. Having said that, he can get out of it quickly if he makes sure not to sink into it but to cling to his inner faith in his talents and abilities.

If, however, the pages are dirty and torn, it means that the dreamer's chances during this time are not good, and he will find it difficult to get out of it, free himself of it and start over. In order for him to be able to muster the strength to extricate himself from the situation in which he finds himself, he will have to slow down, not take chances and not gamble about things that are not certain – in short, keep a low profile.

Pagoda

If a person sees a pagoda in a dream, it means that he will go on a long-awaited trip. If a young woman sees herself in a pagoda with her lover in a dream, she will come up against many obstacles on the way to marriage. A dream about an empty pagoda warns of a breakup.

Pail

A dream that features full pails of milk is a sign of happiness and prosperity. A dream about an empty pail signifies hunger and crop failure. If a young woman dreams about carrying a pail, she will be employed as domestic help.

Pain

A dream about pain implies positive developments in the future: good health, financial profits and prosperity. A dream about a headache indicates that the dreamer is disturbed by business matters. Pains in the region of the heart mean that he is involved in emotional issues. Perhaps this is the time to make an important decision such as breaking off a relationship or making it official. In any event, the decision will yield good results. Pains in the legs and arms attest to excessive effort on the part of the dreamer. He may be trying too hard to advance at work. Actually, the obstacles are not as big as they seem to him. He can continue making an effort, but he should reduce the pace. A positive outcome is guaranteed.

Painting

A dream about painting the walls of a house or painting a picture predicts positive events and innovations in the dreamer's life.

Just as the spring is the symbol of nature's renewal, so painting and paint are the obvious signs of the desire to change and renew things. This does not simply refer to the physical plane, but also to the emotional plane. It is a sign to do a thorough spring-cleaning and throw out old objects, air out the house and renovate. Success can be expected in the near future.

If a person sees something freshly painted, it indicates that something he has long been wishing for will come true. A dream that features paint stains on clothes mean that other people's criticism will hurt the dreamer. If the dreamer himself holds the paintbrush and paints in his dream, it means that he is pleased with his job.

Paintings

If a person dreams about seeing beautiful paintings, it indicates that her friends are two-faced. If a young woman dreams about painting a picture, her lover will be unfaithful to her and leave her for another woman.

Palace

If a person finds himself in a palace or great hall in a dream, it is a warning that he will encounter unforeseen problems. If he did not see the entrance to this palace in his dream, it means that he can expect good news regarding romance. If he sees himself wandering through a palace and admiring it in his dream, it is a sign that he is advancing.

Palisade

If a person sees palisades in a dream, it means that he will alter carefully devised plans in order to please strangers, but this will be disadvantageous to him.

Pall

If a person sees a pall in a dream, it is a sign of sorrow and bad luck. If the person dreams that he raises the pall from a corpse, the dream predicts the death of a loved one.

Pallbearer

If a person dreams about a pallbearer, it means that one of his enemies is trying to provoke him by casting doubt on his honesty. If he sees a pallbearer in a dream, it means that he will become a nuisance to his friends and to institutions.

A B C D E F G H I J K L M N O **P** Q R S T U V W X Y Z

Pallet

A dream about a pallet implies that the dreamer will be preoccupied about his love affairs. If a young woman dreams about a pallet, it is a symbol of a rival.

Palmistry

If a young woman dreams about palmistry, she will be held in suspicion. If she dreams that she has her palms read, she can expect to be popular with men, but criticized by women. If she dreams that she herself reads palms, it is a sign of her intelligence.

Palms (of the hands)

If a person sees hands that are far from the body in a dream, it shows that the dreamer and those around him do not understand each other. A dream about hairy palms indicates that the dreamer has a wild imagination. A dream that features dirty palms indicates jealousy. A dream about folded hands is indicative of emotional stress. A dream about bound hands demonstrates that the dreamer is very restrained.

Palm tree

A dream about palm trees is a very optimistic dream. If a young woman dreams that she walks down a palm-lined avenue, it means that she will have a happy home and a good husband. If the palm trees in the dream are dry, her joy will be clouded by a sad event.

Palsy

If a person dreams that he has palsy, it is a sign that he is involved in spurious deals. If he dreams that his friend has palsy, the latter's fidelity is questionable, and the dreamer's life might be affected by an illness.

Pancake

A dream about eating pancakes is an excellent dream, since it refers to success in all endeavors. A dream about making pancakes indicates a well-run, economical household.

Pane of glass

If a person dreams about handling a pane of glass, it signifies that his affairs are uncertain. If he dreams that he breaks the pane of glass, it signals failure. If he sees himself talking to someone through a pane of glass in a dream, it means that there are problematic obstacles in his path.

Panorama

A dream about a panorama implies a change of job or address.

Panther

If a person sees a panther in a dream and is frightened, he can expect business and personal contracts to fall through unexpectedly due to the interference of people who seek his downfall. If he dreams about killing the panther, he can look forward to success. If he is threatened by a panther

A B C D E F G H I J K L M N O **P** Q R S T U V W X Y Z

in a dream, it means business disappointments and broken promises. If he hears the frightening roar of a panther in a dream, it means that bad news is on the horizon.

Pantomime

If a person sees a pantomime in a dream, it means that he will be betrayed by friends. If he dreams that he is participating in a pantomime, it means that he will be offended and unsuccessful.

Pants

If a person sees pants in a dream, it means that he will tempted to do improper things. If he dreams about putting pants on inside out, it means that he will be totally mesmerized by something.

Paper

Dreams about paper can have many meanings. A person who dreams that he is in a paper factory with gigantic rolls of paper around him on all sides feels threatened. If he is a well-known public figure, it is possible that an article about him is about to be published in the newspaper. It will cause him damage and expose details about his life that he has no wish to reveal. Small pieces of paper that are rolling around the house, on the floor or on the carpet, serve as a reminder that the dreamer has to put his life in order from every possible point of view. The dreamer feels that he has no control over his life. Piles of papers in all the corners of the house or papers flying around the rooms attest to inner and outer disorder alike.

Parables

If a person dreams about parables, it means that he is incapable of making a decision regarding a business dilemma. Parables are also a symbol of infidelity and misunderstandings.

Parachute

This dream expresses the dreamer's desire to be as free as a bird. The dreamer feels trapped by either financial or personal obligations. He wants to escape from reality. The dream may also hint at a drop in assets. The dreamer must take precautions. The parachute also reflects the dreamer's ability to take risks. He has courage and a highly developed sense of adventure. If a parachute does not open in a dream, it means that the dreamer is suffering from fears in certain areas of his life. The future seems vague and bleak and he feels alone in the fray. In contrast, if the parachute opens at the last moment and he lands safely, it means that he has strong powers of survival and endurance that help him overcome every obstacle.

Parachuting

A dream about parachuting means that the dreamer is in need of a special vacation that will come to pass in the very near future. The dreamer yearns to liberate himself from the bonds he has been feeling lately and be free and happy.

A dream that features sky-diving indicates that the dreamer is a courageous person who is prepared to take far-reaching measures in order to succeed. Moreover, he can expect an interesting development in the business realm and economic success in the forthcoming stretch of time. A parachute dive that ends in crash on the ground means that precautionary measures must be taken in order to avoid failure.

Parade

This dream indicates the dreamer's desire to put down roots in his surroundings. It also indicates an escape from loneliness and a desire to find a new circle. It refers to a person who seeks a framework after a long period of disorder. A dream about a parade can reflect the person's desire to remain mobile while fitting into a group.

The dreamer may have been living alone for some time and this is the time to come back and blend into life in society once more.

Paradise

A dream that features paradise attests to the dreamer's future happiness in all domains, to great personal fulfillment and to the love that will prevail in his home.

If a person dreams that he himself is living in paradise, the dream is telling him that he must forgive someone against whom he bears a grudge. Even if there are people who hurt the dreamer, only forgiveness will enable him to live in peace with himself. He is not a quarrelsome and angry person, and only if he appeases his soul will he succeed in living in peace with himself and his surroundings.

If a person dreams that he is not wanted in paradise, he must view the dream as a warning: It is warning the dreamer of an imminent accident that he may be able to avoid if he is sufficiently alert and quick-thinking. The danger is approaching, and he must do everything to avoid it.

If a person dreams that he is in paradise with his beloved (this goes for a female dreamer, too), and they are making love, the dream prophesies tremendous financial success. The dreamer and his family will enjoy a life of comfort and wealth and will never want for anything.

According to another version: Paradise in a dream can appear in different contexts. If a person dreams that he himself is in paradise, the dream hints at his ability to fulfill his potential and make the most of his abilities. The dream also implies that the dreamer will have a life of great happiness in every sphere. If a person sees himself in a dream in paradise, it is a sign that his way of thinking is in the process of moving in a more spiritual direction. If he has been occupied with the material world up till now, his point of view is changing and moving toward the mind and the spirit. Spiritual development interests him far more and takes him to realms of infinite happiness.

If a person dreams that he is on the road to paradise, that is, he is walking toward paradise, but still has not gotten there, the dream presages a happy marriage for him.

A dream in which a person dreams about an entire life being lived inside paradise implies that the dreamer must forgive people against whom he bears a grudge, even if they hurt him deeply in the past. Things will come right very easily if he does so.

If a farmer dreams about paradise, he can expect a large crop and an abundant harvest from his fields and plantations.

If a person dreams that he is in paradise, but senses that

he is not wanted there, the dream hints that an accident will occur in the near future. The dreamer must take great care and be psychologically prepared for the traumatic event that is about to befall him.

If a person dreams about being in paradise with his partner, the dream implies that he will have a life of financial abundance and will not have any material problems. However, the dream does not promise happiness – only wealth.

Paralysis

If a person dreams about paralysis, it predicts disappointments in business and in literary pursuits. For lovers, a dream about paralysis portends a breakup.

Parasol

If a married person sees a parasol in a dream, it is a sign of illicit pleasures. If a young woman dreams about a parasol, she will have many affairs on the side, and will revel in concealing them from her lover.

Parcel

A dream about the delivery of a parcel means that someone dear to the dreamer will return unexpectedly. If a person is carrying a parcel in a dream, it attests to an unpleasant chore that has to be done. If he drops a parcel on the way to delivering it, it means that the dreamer has neglected something important.

Pardon

If a person dreams that he seeks a pardon for a crime he never committed, it means that he is worried about business, but it will work out. If he is guilty, he will have hassles. If he dreams that he receives a pardon, things will work out after a lot of trouble.

Parents

A dream about parents is difficult to interpret because it cannot be interpreted literally according to the relations between the dreamer and his parents. This is because if the parents appear in the dream, it has bearings on the dreamer's relations with other family members who do not appear in the dream.

In most cases, this kind of dream teaches about difficulties in the family (not necessarily with the parents).

A dream that features the dreamer's parents without any additional meaning may be a hint that the dreamer is soon going to find himself at the center of a trial, and this is troubling him. Not for nothing do parents appear in the dreams of people who are facing trial, since they feel subconsciously that they are being tried twice – both by the judge in the trial and by their parents, who judge their every deed from the day they are born.

A dream about a visit to the parents' home (even if the parents do not actually appear in the dream) hints at unpleasant news the dreamer is about to receive. He must prepare himself psychologically so as not to be surprised.

If a person whose parents are dead dreams about parents, the dream implies longevity, prosperity and good health.

If a person sees one of his parents standing naked in a

A B C D E F G H I J K L M N O P Q R S T U V W X Y Z

dream, it hints at difficulties in the family, at disputes and at extreme differences of opinion.

A dream in which the dreamer sees himself hugging his parents implies an imminent betrayal. This applies to any kind of betrayal and not necessarily a betrayal between the dreamer and his parents. The betrayal can also occur between him and his mate, between him and a colleague at work, between him and a business partner and so on.

Park

If a person dreams about walking through a well-kept park, it signifies that he will enjoy his leisure. If he dreams that he is with his lover in the park, it predicts a happy marriage. A dream that features a neglected park is a sign of serious setbacks.

Parrot

If a dream features a parrot, it means gossip and scandal. The dreamer is the victim of a vicious rumor mill. Possibly his behavior is provocative and causes scandals. Having said that, the opposite may also be true: the dreamer is the one who cannot stop himself from gossiping about others, since he is a gossip by nature. A dream like this may also hint at what gossip is liable to do, and the dreamer expresses his fear of malicious rumors or vicious gossip by dreaming about a parrot.

If a person sees a parrot talking to him fluently in a dream, it is a prophetic dream. If he remembers the parrot's words, he should know that they will come true in reality.

Parsley

If a dream features parsley, it is a sign of triumph after a struggle. A dream about eating parsley signifies good health along with responsibility for a large family.

Parsnips

A dream about parsnips indicates success in business but trouble in love.

Parting

A dream about parting from loved ones predicts minor hassles. On the other hand, a dream about parting from enemies is a sign of good luck in love and business.

Partner

If a person dreams that his partner breaks merchandise, it means that he is going to cause damage to the business. If the dreamer scolds his partner for the breakage in the dream, the loss will be recouped to some extent.

Partnership

If a person dreams about forming a partnership with a man, it portends unstable money matters. On the other hand, if he dreams about forming a partnership with a woman, it means that he will want to conceal some enterprise from his friends. A dream about dissolving an unpleasant partnership predicts happiness. However, if it was a good partnership, dissolving it will lead to bad luck.

Partridge

If a person sees partridges in a dream, it is a sign that he will enjoy good luck in the near future. If he dreams about killing them, it means that he will amass wealth and distribute it to other people. If he dreams about eating partridges, the dream indicates that he is enjoying the perks of a high position. If he sees flying partridges in a dream, he can look forward to a good future. A dream about trapping partridges means that the dreamer's hopes will be realized.

Party (group)

If a person dreams that a party of strangers mugs him, it means that his enemies are joining forces against him. If he comes out unscathed in the dream, it means that he will overcome any obstacles in business or love.

Party – See Celebration

Passenger

If a person sees incoming passengers in a dream, it is a prediction of positive things for him. However, if he sees outgoing passengers in a dream, it is a sign of a missed business opportunity. If the dreamer is one of the departing passengers, he is dissatisfied with what he does and will try to make a change.

Password

A dream about a password means that the dreamer will be given assistance during some imminent trouble.

Pastry

If a person dreams about pastry, it means that he will be taken in by a swindler. If he dreams about eating pastry, he will have true friendships. If a young woman dreams that she prepares pastry, her intentions will be clear to other people.

Pasture

A dream about a pasture is a wonderful dream that symbolizes abundance, tranquillity, peace and health. The dreamer is on the threshold of a new era that has everything: changes in the personal realm, the possibility of moving to a new home, and financial success.

Patch

If a person dreams that he has patches on his clothing, it means that he will do his duties humbly. If he sees other people with patches in a dream, it is a sign that poverty and wretchedness are in the offing. If a woman dreams that she patches her family's clothing, it signifies a great deal of love but a lack of money. If a young woman dreams that she tries to hide her patches, it means that she will attempt to conceal flaws in her character from her lover.

Patent

If a person dreams about securing a patent, it means that he takes a lot of trouble with everything he does. If he does not secure a patent in his dream, he will fail in undertakings that are beyond his capabilities. If he dreams of buying a patent, it is a sign that he will have to go on a futile journey.

Patent medicine

If a person dreams about taking patent medicine in order to cure himself, it is a sign of his determination to succeed. And he will, much to the chagrin of his rivals. If a person sees or produces patent medicines in his dream, he will enjoy a meteoric rise to prominence.

Path

A dream that features a path indicates that the dreamer is at a crossroads and has to make some brave decisions.

A gravel path means that the path to success is still long and that there are many difficulties to be overcome before the dreamer achieves his goal. A winding path through a field of flowers paints a pastoral picture of the dreamer's life. The path itself, rather than the goal, is important. Life is going to the dreamer's satisfaction, so it can be defined as good.

A path paved with stones or marble predicts a meteoric rise up the social ladder, leading the dreamer to huge financial success.

Paunch

A dream about a large paunch is a sign of great wealth alongside a complete lack of finesse. A dream about a shrunken paunch means hardship and disease.

Pauper

A dream about being a pauper does not augur well for the dreamer. If he sees paupers in a dream, it means that he will have to be generous.

Pea

A dream about a pea is a sign of glad tidings: the dreamer can expect a wonderful era of prosperity, economic and social blooming, success in everything regarding financial matters, and numerous achievements. Even if the dreamer is going through a difficult phase at the moment, and does not have a feeling of satisfaction or of fulfilling his potential, he must be patient. The good times are on the threshold, and they will change his world.

If a person dreams about a sweet pea, it means that together with the era of prosperity in the various areas, he will find a new love that will be accompanied mainly by pampering feelings of softness, gentleness and sensitivity. In the wake of love, there will also be *joie de vivre* and everything it can do for the dreamer. The pea also symbolizes perfection in conjugal and family life. The dreamer will be offered great understanding by the members of his family, as well as total support for anything he chooses to do, because they rely on him and on the steps he decides to take.

Peach

A dream that features a peach attests to the dreamer's powerful sexual urges. He has to satisfy them very frequently since he is a sensual person who loves the pleasures of the body. The meaning of a peach in a dream is also expressed in the fact that it hints at the dreamer's need for caresses, love, warmth and embracing his partner. His desire for contact is enormous, and sometimes, in order to appease his simmering urges, he should calm down with the help of a good body massage or soak in a tub or hot-tub, as well as other kinds of physical pleasures.

Another meaning of the appearance of a peach (or peaches) in a dream is the happiness and tranquillity engendered by the dreamer's partner, who gives him a lot of love. The love that envelops the dreamer will nourish him and generate a great deal of self-confidence in him. This will come to the fore in other areas of his life as well, and will cause him to make the most of his abilities in almost any field he chooses.

Peacock

A dream about a peacock serves to warn the dreamer about excessive pride and inappropriate conceit that are liable to bring disaster on him. A little modesty and humility won't hurt, sooner rather than later. The dreamer's bragging is liable to hurt him in the most painful place, so he must relate to this dream as a warning dream at the last minute and set things straight before something happens and the clock cannot be turned back. The dream may not only serve as a warning against the dreamer's perverted and irresponsible behavior, but also against the behavior that characterizes the dreamer's entire surroundings – his friends, acquaintances and relatives, who behave in this way and have a bad influence on the dreamer.

If a peacock appears in a woman's dream, it is also interpreted as a warning dream, except that it has a specific meaning: It warns against a man who is coming into her life – a lover or a life partner – with whom she has to be very careful in her dealings. He is the kind of person who she should "test" in order for her to trust him completely and be one hundred percent certain that he is Mr. Right. Only in this way will she be able to ascertain his reliability and the seriousness of his intentions.

Peanuts

A dream about peanuts implies that the dreamer is a very sociable person who makes friends easily. He is popular, and the people around him enjoy being in his company. His opinions are also widely accepted, and the people close to him tend to consult with him from time to time. His circle of friends is wide, and, as the years go by, keeps on expanding. The dreamer is accustomed to being at the center of things in everything to do with social matters, and enjoys this status. He frequently becomes the life and soul of the party.

Pear

If the dreamer sees a pear in his dream, but does not see himself eating it, the dream is a warning of juicy and predominantly malicious gossip that is taking place behind his back. The dreamer may inadvertently be drawing "fire" to himself as a result of a certain type of behavior, but it is also possible that other things are causing this gossip – things that have nothing to do with the dreamer, but rather stem from jealousy. This type of gossip is liable to spawn unfounded stories about the dreamer. For this reason, he should not be surprised if one day he hears that completely fictitious things are being said about him. If he continues acting in an ordinary and natural way and does not get upset about the gossip, it will gradually die down.

If the dreamer sees himself eating a pear in a dream, he must relate to the dream as a warning dream that is telling him that there is something wrong with his health. He must pay attention to this warning and have himself checked over, even if he does not feel anything out of the ordinary

A B C D E F G H I J K L M N O **P** Q R S T U V W X Y Z

and feels well. It seems that something is "cooking" in his body, and the dream is giving him a sign.

Pearls

If a person dreams about pearls, he can be assured of a successful business and a good social life. If a young woman dreams that her lover sends her pearls, they will have a wonderful, harmonious relationship.

Pebbles

If a young woman dreams about pebbles, the dream signals that she is egoistic and implacable. If she sees a path strewn with pebbles in her dream, it means that she can expect to have lots of worthy rivals.

Pecans

If a person sees himself eating pecans in a dream, it implies that he will implement a plan with total success. If he sees them growing on a tree, it means that he will have a long, happy life. If the pecans are rotten in the dream, he can expect failure in business and love. If he dreams that he has difficulty cracking them and then finds small nuts, it means that he will be successful, but in a minor way.

Peddler

A dream about a peddler is a sign of financial success occurring in an unusual way.

Pelican

If a person has a dream about pelicans, it symbolizes a mixture of success and failure. Failure can be overcome if he catches a pelican in his dream. If he dreams about killing a pelican, it means that he ignores other people's rights.

Pen

The meaning of a pen in a dream is renewed contact with a close friend from whom nothing has been heard for a long time. The dreamer is about to renew old ties with a person who was once very close to him, and of whom he lost track.

A dream in which the dreamer sees himself holding a pen and writing with it attests to the fact that strange events are about to happen to him. It is advisable for the dreamer to be prepared for unexpected surprises that will not always be congenial. Advance psychological preparation will prevent panic and a loss of control when the unexplained things become a reality.

If a person sees someone else holding a pen and writing with it in a dream, he must be careful of an alien element that is hostile to him and is plotting his downfall. He must keep his eyes open and be prepared for any trouble that may come his way.

Penalties

If a person dreams that penalties are imposed on him, it means that he is rebelling against duties he has to perform. If he dreams about paying a penalty, it is a sign of disease and financial loss. If he dreams that he wriggles out of a penalty, it is a sign of his triumph.

Pencil

If a person sees a pencil, it means that he can look forward to holding good jobs. If a young woman dreams that she writes with a pencil, it means that she will marry well. If she erases what she has written in the dream, her lover will let her down.

Penguin

A dream about a penguin is generally not a common dream. Having said that, when a person reports seeing a penguin in a dream, it is a sign that his soul is in need of freedom and liberty, and that he is unable to be locked into a framework. The dream attests to the fact that the person loves adventure and enjoys discovering new places and exploring things he does not know. The dreamer is exceptionally curious and is not afraid of anything. His determination, courage and resourcefulness in stressful situations are admirable. He is a person who does not shy away from new experiences and seeks excitement. What other people consider crazy, he considers completely normal. The dream attests to a longing for seeking out the unusual, the new and the exciting. It seems as if the dreamer is insatiable and always aspires to learn more and achieve the impossible. His fields of interest are numerous and broad, and he does not rest on his laurels – he wants to learn more, to go on exploring the world.

Penis / Vagina

A dream about a penis or vagina is given a sexual interpretation that depends on the dreamer's character.

Penitentiary

If a person dreams about a penitentiary, it signals that he will become involved in ventures that will not be to his advantage. If he dreams that he is an inmate of a penitentiary, it means that he has an unhappy home and is failing in business. If he escapes from the penitentiary in his dream, he will overcome problems.

Penny

If a person dreams about pennies, it means that he is wasting his time and jeopardizing both his business and his relationships. If he dreams about losing pennies, it means failure. If he finds them in his dream, it is a sign that he has good prospects of advancement. If he sees himself counting pennies, the dream indicates that he is thrifty.

Pension

If a person dreams that he draws a pension, it means that his friends will come to his assistance. If he does not receive a pension, the dream indicates that his enterprises will fail and he will lose friends.

Pepper

If a person dreams that his tongue is burnt by pepper, it means that his love of gossip will get him into trouble. If he sees red pepper growing in a dream, it means that he will marry a thrifty and independent woman. If he sees pods of red pepper in a dream, it means that he will jealously defend his rights. A dream about grinding black pepper means that he will be deceived by unsavory people. If he

A B C D E F G H I J K L M N O P Q R S T U V W X Y Z

sees himself sprinkling pepper on food in a dream, it is a sign that he has treacherous friends.

Peppermint

If a person dreams about peppermint, the dream predicts interesting business developments and agreeable ways of spending his leisure time. If he sees peppermint growing in a dream, it indicates an amusing activity with an element of romance in it. If a person sees peppermint in a beverage, he will make the acquaintance of an interesting and attractive person.

Perfume

A dream about perfume always has a positive meaning and hints at good things that will happen to the dreamer.

If a small bottle of perfume appears in a dream, or the dreamer "sniffs" it in his dream, it is a sign of a great love that will emerge in his life. A special romantic relationship is about to develop, bringing great happiness with it. This relationship will be successful and will improve with age like good wine.

If the scent of the perfume is powerful and intoxicating in the dream, the dream symbolizes great happiness or a unique experience, the memories of which will fade quickly. This need not necessarily have a negative connotation. If, for instance, the dreamer goes through a breakup and a separation from someone he loved, the cherished memories will soon give way to new experiences that will help the dreamer move forward and meet new partners.

Perspiration

If a person dreams that he is perspiring, it means he will get through some scandal completely unscathed.

Pest

If a person dreams that he is anxious about some kind of pest, it means that he will have worries. If other people are bothered by pests, the dreamer will be upset by negative developments.

Pestering / Harassment

A dream about any kind of pestering or harassment means that gossip, idle chatter and small talk are liable to cause harm.

Petticoat

If a person sees new petticoats in a dream, it means that people will scoff at him for taking pride in his possessions. A dream that features dirty or torn petticoats is a warning dream: it warns of a threat to the dreamer's good reputation. If a woman dreams that she has clean silk petticoats, it means that she has a good, attentive husband. If she dreams that she forgets to wear a petticoat, it is a sign of bad luck. If she dreams that her petticoat slips down in public, it means that she will lose her lover.

Pewter

A dream that features pewter is a sign of financial difficulties.

A
B
C
D
E
F
G
H
I
J
K
L
M
N
O
P
Q
R
S
T
U
V
W
X
Y
Z

Phantom

A dream about being pursued by a phantom is a prediction of strange and disturbing experiences. If a person dreams that a phantom flees from him, it means that his troubles will decrease.

Pheasant

A dream about a pheasant indicates that the dreamer loves amusing himself with his masculinity, showing off his abilities and boasting about his exploits. If a woman has this dream, it means that she tends to look for masculine characteristics in her man. She prefers a man with prominent physical properties to a man whose strong point is his intellect.

A dream about a pheasant tells the dreamer that his economic situation will improve and that he can expect to become wealthy. He will not encounter material problems, and from this point of view will live an untroubled life characterized by ease and prosperity.

In certain cases, a dream like this can also indicate a change in workplace. The change will mainly be in content and will not involve any drastic improvement in salary. In other words, this is not a matter of a promotion, but of a shift from one area of interest to another, a change of workplace or moving to another field within the present workplace.

Phosphorus

A dream about phosphorus symbolizes fleeting happiness. If a woman dreams about phosphorus, it is a symbol of great but temporary success with admirers.

Photograph

A person who dreams about a camera or about photos and pictures is likely to find himself packing his suitcases in the near future. There is a high probability of a business trip to a distant destination, and the dreamer must take precautions and safeguard personal and business secrets, even during chance encounters. The world is small, and a situation could arise in which important information falls into the wrong hands.

Photography

A dream that features anything to do with photography foretells a long journey. If a woman dreams about a camera, it means that she will soon have a heartwarming meeting with a man.

Physician

If a young woman dreams about a physician, it means that she is ruining her good looks on superficial pleasures. If she is ill and dreams about a physician, she will soon be well. If he appears anxious, her troubles will increase.

Piano

If a dream features a piano, it predicts a happy event. If a person hears beautiful piano music in a dream, it is a sign of success and health. If he hears discordant noises from the piano, he is going to suffer various annoyances. If he hears sad music, it is an indication of bad news. A dream that features a broken-down piano that is out of tune implies that the dreamer is generally dissatisfied with his own achievements as well as those of his children and friends.

Pickax

If a person dreams about a pickax, it is a warning that an enemy is seeking his social downfall. A dream that features a broken pickax is a sign of very bad luck.

Pickles

If a person sees pickles in a dream, he will waste his time on worthless things if he does not use his discretion. If a young woman dreams that she eats pickles in a dream, she will have a very ordinary job as well as rivals who will bring her down unless she uses her judgment.

Pickpocket

If a person dreams about a pickpocket, it means that an enemy will hurt him. If a young woman dreams that her pockets are picked, it means that she will be the object of someone's envy and malice. If she dreams that she herself picks someone's pockets, she will be ostracized for her crude behavior.

Picnic

If a person attends a picnic in a dream, he can look forward to success and enjoyment. If the picnic is spoilt by a storm or some other interruption in the dream, he will suffer temporary setbacks in business and love.

Picture

If a person dreams that he takes a picture off the wall, it is a sign that his present stage in life is about to end, and a new, more promising one is about to begin. He can start to summarize the phase he has just gone through and learn lessons and draw conclusions in order to apply them in the coming phase.

A dream in which the dreamer is looking at a picture or photograph, such as at an exhibition, attests to the dreamer's reflections on his unfulfilled talents.

If the dreamer sees himself in a picture or photograph, the dream implies that he is struggling with many difficulties. He will overcome them thanks to the encouragement and backing of his family and friends. He must know that he is not alone in the struggle.

If a person sees a framed picture on the wall in a dream, he must struggle with a big challenge facing him and do anything to succeed. He knows that he has the ability to do this, and there is no reason for him to fail. His fierce desire to be at the top and to achieve the best sometimes works against him because it is not always possible.

Pier

If a person dreams about standing on a pier, it signifies that he will overcome obstacles and earn the highest honors and prosperity. If he sees himself trying to walk on a pier in his dream, but fails to do so, it is a sign that he will lose the honor he values so much.

Pies

If a person dreams about eating pies, it is a warning dream: it warns the dreamer to watch out for his enemies, who want to harm him. If a young woman dreams about making pies, she will be an inveterate flirt.

Pig

Among the peoples of the East, especially in China, a dream about a pig is interpreted as a good dream that attests to prosperity, wealth and handsome profits for the dreamer. He will be blessed with great financial success and abundance, and this will not only be enough to set up the members of his family for life, but also future generations.

In contrast, according to Western culture, a dream featuring a pig or a wild boar is not seen as something positive. It attests to evil and repulsive impulses that accompany the dreamer – these may be his impulses, which prevent him from succeeding and serve as a stumbling-block along his path to the goals he has set himself, or other people's impulses. The dream may imply that the dreamer is surrounded by envious people and even by people who hate him, and he has to be careful of them, since they are liable to harm him – directly or indirectly.

If a dreamer sees a small pink piglet in a dream, the dream hints that the dreamer is fighting a tough rival for a beloved woman's heart. The rival is also threatening to capture her heart. This rivalry causes the dreamer great distress, but also reawakens his dormant energies.

If a dreamer sees more than one pig in his dream, and the pigs are in a filthy sty, the dream attests to the fact that the dreamer is agonizing about something he did or about his inappropriate behavior. This is causing him a great deal of anguish as well as sadness and shame. He feels self-reproachful that he did not fix things when they could still be fixed, and he feels as if he's missed the opportunity.

If a person dreams about one or more pigs grunting and making loud porcine noises, the dream hints that unpleasant news is in the offing. This news will come from the dreamer's workplace or it may be connected with his career in a general way. The news is not too bad, but there is no doubt that it is the kind of news that will make him think twice about his professional future.

Pigeon

If a person sees and hears pigeons in a dream, it is a sign of domestic harmony and good children. For a young woman, this dream means a happy marriage at a young age. If a person dreams that he shoots pigeons for sport, the dream reveals a cruel streak in his nature. It warns him against seeking immoral pleasures. If a person sees flying pigeons in a dream, it predicts harmony and news from faraway acquaintances.

Pilgrim

If a person dreams about pilgrims, it means that he will depart on a long journey, leaving his dear ones behind, in the mistaken belief that it is in everyone's best interests. If he dreams that he is a pilgrim, it implies poverty and uncaring friends. If a young woman dreams that she is approached by a pilgrim, it is a warning that she will be swindled. If the pilgrim goes away, she will become aware of her weakness of character and will try to correct it.

Pillow

Generally, dreams about pillows serve as a warning sign. The dreamer does not feel comfortable and his sleep at night is disturbed by a pillow – a near and familiar object that actually turns out not to be so near and familiar. A pillow with feathers flying around in it hints at a possibility of the break-up of a financial partnership, and possible worries and confusion with friends or business partners. It is advisable to devote some thought to factors that are bothering the dreamer.

Pills

Pills in a dream are interpreted in different ways. In most cases, pills are not interpreted as something to do with diseases and cures. In general, a dream in which pills appear (and it doesn't matter how they are packaged – it could be in a regular package or in a little bottle) hints that the dreamer can expect to go on a journey, a long trip or a voyage. In any case, he will go far away physically from his home and his acquaintances for an extended period of time.

One interpretation of pills in a dream is less pleasant: Some people interpret this dream as bearing bad tidings. The dreamer's luck is deteriorating, and this can have very unpleasant repercussions in all areas of his life. While there is nothing he can do to prevent this, it would not hurt to keep his eyes open and prepare himself for things to come in order to diminish the vicissitudes that are about to befall him.

Pimple

In a dream, pimply flesh is a symbol of nagging worries. If a person sees other people with pimples in a dream, it means that he will be burdened with other people's hassles. If a woman dreams that her beauty is spoilt by pimples, her conduct will be censured by her friends.

Pincers

A dream about pincers is a bad sign. If a person dreams that he is pinched by pincers, it signifies that he will have to deal with infuriating worries.

Pineapple

A pineapple in a dream implies success in various areas of life, particularly in anything to do with work, studies or business. The dreamer will find himself riding the wave of success mainly because he is that special type of person who knows how to take life as it comes. The appearance of a pineapple in a dream does not merely hint at the regular type of happiness that will accompany the dreamer throughout his life, but also at a feeling of genuine gaiety and cheerfulness that characterize him. He has no need to pour out the bitterness of his heart to friends or a psychologist. He is one of those types who are soothed by music. He can break out in a wild dance and derive emotional tranquillity from a "self-treatment" like that. The friends who are close to him also have tremendous *joie de vivre*, and the supportive surroundings in which the dreamer lives enable him to live his life in joy and happiness.

If a person sees himself eating a pineapple in a dream, it means that luck is at his side in every sphere, and even if he is besieged by dread, fear and anxiety at different stages of his life, he must know that luck is with him. He will always get out of the unpleasant situations he got himself

into with the upper hand, and will be stronger than he was prior to the crisis. All in all, he will not have many difficult moments in his life.

A
B
C
D
E
F
G
H
I
J
K
L
M
N
O
P
Q
R
S
T
U
V
W
X
Y
Z

Pinecone

A pinecone in a dream has various interpretations, depending on how it appears in the dream.

A dream in which the pinecone is closed attests to the fact that the dreamer's family is tight-knit, supportive and loving. For the dreamer, his family is the basis, the nucleus of everything in his life. He draws his strength from his family, he relies on his family in times of crisis, and it is his family that endows him with the basic confidence to dare to embark on adventurous experiences occasionally.

In contrast, if the pinecone in the dream is open, the contrary is true. This attests to the fact that the dreamer's family is not tight-knit and is in the throes of coming apart. The lack of support and the fact that the dreamer does not have powerful backing behind him causes him an anguished lack of self-confidence. Even if it sometimes looks as if his self-confidence is way up in the sky, it is just an act concealing a beaten and fearful soul.

If the pinecone is lying on the ground in the dream (with other pinecones scattered beside it), this symbolizes serious insults hurled at the dreamer, and from which he finds it difficult to recover. The dreamer took the things that were thrown at him to heart and he cannot get over them. The pinecone hints at a wounded and tortured soul in need of help.

If the dreamer sees a pinecone that is not in any particular context in the dream, he can expect a substantial gambling win in the near future. He can also expect to meet an interesting figure who will become close to him – to the point of being a good friend who will be significant in the dreamer's life.

If the dreamer sees himself collecting pinecones in the forest, the dream implies that in the near future, the dreamer can expect to come into a large inheritance.

Pine tree

A dream about a pine tree implies that the dreamer will eventually enjoy success, but he will have to toil hard and go through hell to attain it. He needs pertinacity and prodigious will power to accomplish the objectives he has set himself. Even though the path will be strewn with thorns and obstacles, he will undoubtedly succeed if he persists and sticks to his goal.

Another interpretation of a dream about a pine tree, connected to the European traditions, links the pine tree to holy places and wizards and magi. This interpretation views the pine tree as a symbol of mystical powers or of black magic that accompany the dreamer. The dreamer himself may be gifted with mystical powers, or possibly someone close to him, a family member for instance, is the one who has the gift and uses it to influence the dreamer. The dreamer himself may be gifted with special powers of which he is unaware; he must develop his talents and bring them to the fore.

Pins

If a person dreams about pins, it is a sign of domestic conflict and lovers' quarrels. If he dreams about swallowing a pin, it is a warning dream: it warns of accidents and dangers. If a person dreams about losing a pin, it refers to minor losses and arguments. If he sees a bent or rusty pin in his dream, it means a loss of other people's respect as a result of his sloppy habits. If he dreams that he is pricked by a pin, it signifies that someone is bothering him.

Pipe (plumbing)

If a person sees various utility pipes in a dream, they are an indication of a caring and prosperous community. If the pipes are old and broken, the dream is a sign of illness and stagnation in business.

Pipe (smoking)

Smoking a pipe in a group means that the dreamer is at the height of a dispute that will be resolved peacefully.

On the other hand, a dream that features an extinguished pipe can attest to an ambivalent situation. The dreamer is advised to be careful of people who look like friends or well-wishers, but they may well have hidden agendas that are different from what they propose.

Caution will pay off, especially if there is an important deal in the offing. There could well be a happy family event such as a wedding or an engagement. In such a case, the dreamer must be careful of financial commitments. He must get every agreement in writing.

Pistol

If a person dreams that he owns a pistol, the dream indicates his base nature. If he hears one go off in a dream, one of his enterprises will fail. If he dreams about shooting a pistol, it means that he will be irrationally jealous of someone and will persecute them.

Pit

If a person dreams about looking into a deep pit, it indicates that he will take absurd business risks. If he sees himself falling into a pit in a dream, it is a sign of sorrow and disaster – unless he wakes up as he falls. If he dreams that he goes down into a pit, he knowingly risks health and property for greater gains.

Pitcher

If a person dreams about a pitcher, it is an indication of his pleasant and generous nature. He will be successful. A dream about a broken pitcher signifies losing friends.

Pitchfork

A dream that features a pitchfork symbolizes the dreamer's struggle for self-improvement and prosperity. If he dreams that he is attacked by a person brandishing a pitchfork, it means that he has enemies who want to harm him.

Place

A dream in which the dreamer sees himself visiting a different, alien place can serve as a hint of an approaching trip. Apparently, it is a business or work trip that will culminate in success. There is every chance of a romantic adventure as well. It is advisable to remain alert and cautious and to refrain from signing any type of documents or making verbal promises that do not have any clear and tangible backing.

Plague

If a person dreams about a plague epidemic, it implies that he will suffer extreme failures in business and domestic misery. If the dreamer dreams that he is sick with the plague, it means that he will have to make enormous efforts to keep his business afloat. If he dreams about attempting to flee the plague, it means that a serious problem is hounding him.

Plain

If a young woman crosses a green, fertile plain in a dream, she will have a good life. If the plain is arid and barren, her life will be lonely and unpleasant.

Planet

If a person dreams about visiting other planets, he will soon experience new and fascinating things.

Plank

If a young woman dreams that she is crossing murky water on a rotten plank, she will suffer from an indifferent lover, have problems and risk her good reputation.

Plant / Vegetation

Green and healthy vegetation in a dream means that the dreamer can expect good things such as exciting surprises or positive news that will affect his future. The greener and fresher the plant in the dream is, the more positive and joyful the news on its way to the dreamer is. The emphasis is on the great significance of the news that is on the way. The news is not something the dreamer is expecting, and it will surprise him without him suspecting that the change is about to happen.

Plantation / Orchard

A person who dreams about hiking or working in an orchard is going through a happy phase in his life. The link to nature, whether the hike is for enjoyment or work, expresses the dreamer's inner feeling – repose and tranquillity. If the dreamer finds a dangerous person or animal in the plantation, it is an expression of his feelings of worry toward his "perfect" world at this stage.

Plaster

If a dream features undecorated, plastered walls, it means a very delicate success. If a person dreams that pieces of plaster fall on him, it is a sign of total catastrophe. If he sees plasterers working in a dream, it means that he will have enough money to live fairly comfortably.

Plates

If a woman dreams about plates, she is thrifty and will marry a good man. If she is married, she will keep her husband happy by managing the house well.

Play (theater)

If a young woman sees a play in a dream, it means that she will marry for money and the pursuit of pleasure. If she dreams that she has trouble getting to or from the play, or if

A B C D E F G H I J K L M N O P Q R S T U V W X Y Z

there are ugly scenes, she will have an unexpectedly rough time ahead of her.

Playing (music)

Generally, a dream that features an element of an orchestra or a group of players is an indication of good news or some kind of happy event, such as a romantic attachment, a family event or an improvement in the dreamer's financial situation. Playing in an orchestra means a process of cooperation among the members of a family or at work, in the political party or some other social group to which the dreamer belongs.

Pleasure boat

A dream about a pleasure boat expresses the dreamer's need to get out into the open, to go on a fancy vacation, and to feel as if he is making the most of life and is living it to the full. The longing for a vacation, freedom and fulfillment of his wishes is what is causing the dream.

The dreamer is going through a difficult phase in his life. He feels that he is working too hard, is not resting enough, and is frustrated by the situation he finds himself in. He feels like that not only at work, but also at home, where life is not a bed of roses. The desire to take a vacation serves as a kind of desire to flee from the reality in which he is living and into a fantasy world.

Plow

If a person dreams about a plow, it is a sign of unprecedented success. If he himself plows in a dream, it signals joy and prosperity. If he watches people plow in a dream, it means increased knowledge and property. If a young woman watches her lover plow in a dream, she will have a good, wealthy husband and a happy life.

Plum

A dream about a plum is a good dream that predicts that the dreamer will have a life full of happiness, laughter, and *joie de vivre*. The dreamer, who is blessed with a highly developed sense of humor and an easygoing and peaceful nature, will make the most of these qualities. Even in difficult or painful situations, he will be able to mobilize his optimistic nature in order to see the "half-full glass."

The people around him will enjoy being in his company, since an easygoing nature like his creates a pleasant atmosphere, and spending time with him is soothing. He is easygoing with both friends and family. He is a successful family man who devotes time and attention to his spouse and children. The members of his family are exceptionally open, and his children see him not only as a parent, but also as a guide and a good friend.

In the Eastern Europe countries, a dream like this is mainly thought to be a warning dream: in most cases, it is interpreted as a hint that the dreamer has a friend or acquaintance who is plotting against him. Someone close to the dreamer wants to hurt him, not necessarily physically, but in other ways (for instance, causing him to lose his job or his business, getting him involved in a family dispute, and so on). If he tries very hard, the dreamer can work out who this person is and act quickly to foil the plot.

Pocket

When a dream features a pocket, it generally represents a womb. The dreamer's state of mind at the time of the dream should be taken into account. The dreamer may well be going through a particularly difficult time, and the fact that he dreams about a womb indicates his desire to go back and find shelter in the safest place in the world – the place where he was before his birth, the place in which he had everything he needed, and all he had to do was breathe. The dreamer, who is in a difficult situation, wants and needs to take some time out for withdrawing into himself, for thinking and for making new decisions. After his soul-searching, he will be able to set out along a new and more successful track.

Pocketbook

If a person finds a pocketbook full of money in a dream, it indicates good luck. If the pocketbook is empty, the dreamer will suffer a grave disappointment. If a person dreams about losing a pocketbook, it indicates that he will quarrel with a good friend, much to his detriment.

Poison

If a person dreams that he is preparing poison for someone else, it means that he bears a very big grudge that is liable to develop in a negative direction. He should find out who is causing his frustration and get away from him as quickly as possible. Life is too short to waste, and the future indicates positive developments. In contrast, if the dreamer sees himself poisoned in his dream, it means that there is someone who is conspiring against him. Malicious gossip and libel may land him in court, where he will have to prove his innocence. He must exercise great caution, both at work and in his private life.

Poker (cards)

A dream about playing poker is a warning dream: if a person dreams about playing poker, it warns him against falling into bad company. If young women dream about playing poker will compromise their moral reputation.

Poker (for the fire)

A dream that features a red-hot poker or fighting with one means that the dreamer will tackle his problems courageously.

Polar Bear

If a person dreams about polar bears, it means that he will be taken in by things that look positive – including enemies in the guise of friends. A dream about a polar-bear skin means that the dreamer will overcome all resistance.

Polecat

A dream about a polecat is a warning dream: a person close to the dreamer is scheming against him and wants to harm him. He is employing crooked means of deception, misleading him intentionally, and so on. He is operating secretly so that it does not occur to the dreamer that this is what he is doing. His conduct is false, and it is difficult for the dreamer to recognize this since the person in question is extremely sly.

A B C D E F G H I J K L M N O **P** Q R S T U V W X Y Z

In contrast, the picture is quite the opposite if the dreamer sees one or more people in his dream defending him against the polecat. If such a person appears in the dream, the dreamer can place his trust in him because the dream implies that the person is rooting for him and will stand by him in times of crisis. The dreamer can trust him implicitly, because he is a true friend who does what he can for the dreamer with all his heart.

If the person sees more than one polecat in a dream, that is, a pack of polecats, he must hurry to have a medical check-up because the dream implies that he is suffering from some kind of health problem that has not yet shown any signs or manifested itself fully. The sooner the dreamer checks what this means and discovers the problem when it is still in its beginning stages, the less he will suffer from it. If the person goes to the doctor and the exam reveals nothing, the dream must be interpreted as predicting some other bad thing for which it is worthwhile preparing himself – at least psychologically. This will come in the form of bad news from far away or some kind of problem that is liable to crop up in the workplace. If the dreamer is an employee, the problem will concern his job in the workplace; if he is self-employed, he will have a problem finding clients.

Police

If a person dreams that a police officer attacks him, he can expect a lawsuit in the near future, and it is not at all certain that he will win it and come out on top.

A dream about a police precinct or about anything else that is connected to the police means that the dreamer will soon get out of a crisis he is in. He will receive help with a problem that has been bothering him lately and giving him sleepless nights. Thanks to that same help, he will succeed in extricating himself from the crisis, begin to live a new and full life, and regain his peace of mind.

If a person dreams that he is a police inspector, he has a tendency toward self-castigation. He tends to blame himself not only for all the things that happen to him, but also for the things that happen to others – even though objectively he did not cause them and had no connection with them whatsoever. This self-castigation undermines his repose and his stability, and he must have it treated without delay.

A dream that features a police officer dragging the dreamer is a sign that the dreamer can expect to be arrested soon. Even if he has never been detained and has committed no offence, he may suddenly be involved in an incident that will result in him being arrested.

If a person dreams that a police officer comes to his aid, he must be careful of becoming involved in a robbery.

A dream in which a complaint is made against the dreamer attests to the fact that he must pay more attention to his appearance. He must make sure that is better dressed and turned out. He neglects his appearance, and this affects the manner in which people relate to him.

If a married person dreams that he calls the police, it is a sign that his partner is liable to cheat on him. The reason for the infidelity is his lack of attention to his partner. The partner feels that he/she is being neglected, and for this reason is looking elsewhere and seeking attention from another quarter. This dream should be perceived as a warning sign.

If a person dreams about a job he has been given in the

A B C D E F G H I J K L M N O **P** Q R S T U V W X Y Z

police force, it is a sign that he has an enemy who is undermining him and seeking to do him harm. He must keep his eyes open.

A dream about a conflict with a police officer is a sign that the guilt feelings the dreamer is suffering from allow him no rest. He is well aware of what is causing them, and he is so embroiled in them emotionally that they do not let him sleep at night and bother him throughout the dream. In order to get rid of these tiresome guilt feelings, the dreamer has to find out the extent of his guilt and pay the price he has to pay in order to get rid of this feeling.

Polishing

If a person dreams about polishing something, his achievements will lead him to high positions.

Politician

If a person dreams about a politician, it signifies bad friends and events that waste both time and money. If he dabbles in politics in his dream, his friends will behave angrily and disagreeably toward him. If a young woman dreams about being interested in politics, it is a warning dream: she must guard herself against being swindled.

Polka

A dream about dancing the polka signifies agreeable pastimes.

Pomegranate

A dream about a pomegranate is a joyful dream: the

dreamer will enjoy a great deal of happiness, will be held in high regard by the people around him, and will be accorded great respect by the people who come into contact with him. This will contribute to a greater feeling of self-confidence and self-esteem.

If a dream features a pomegranate tree with very red fruit, the dream has a sexual meaning: the dreamer is afraid of cheating on his partner or of his partner cheating on him. He is in a relationship that is not completely genuine; honesty is not one of its strong points. The little lies, improprieties and dishonesty between the dreamer and his partner are liable to cost them dearly. The sooner the dreamer discovers the true face of things and grapples with them, the more he will help both sides, especially himself, because his conscience will stop tormenting him.

Pond

If a person sees a pond in a dream, it signifies a calm, smooth life. A dream that features muddy pond is a sign of domestic conflict.

Pony

A dream about a pony is a sign of success in business ventures.

Poor

If a person dreams that he or his friends are poor, it signifies trouble and loss.

A B C D E F G H I J K L M N O **P** Q R S T U V W X Y Z

Poorhouse

A dream about a poorhouse is a sign of disloyal friends who associate with the dreamer only so that they can get their hands on his money and possessions.

Pope

If a person sees a pope in a dream but does not speak to him, it means that he will be subservient to a master. If he speaks to the pope in his dream, he can expect to be accorded great honors. If the pope appears sad or upset in the dream, it is a warning dream: it warns the dreamer against sorrow and immorality.

Poplars

A dream that features blooming or leafy poplars is a good omen. If a young woman dreams that she stands under such a tree with her lover, all of her wildest dreams will come true. If the trees are bare and dry in her dream, she will suffer disappointment.

Poppies

If a person dreams about poppies, it is a sign of transient, superficial pleasures and business successes. If the dreamer inhales the scent of a poppy, it means that he will fall victim to impudent flattery.

Porcelain

A dream that features porcelain implies favorable business conditions. If the porcelain is broken or dirty, it is a sign of mistakes that will have serious consequences.

Porch

If a person dreams about a porch, it means that he will embark on new adventures that will make him feel very unsure. If he dreams that he is standing on a porch, it means that banal worries are bothering him. If he sees himself building a porch in a dream, it is a sign that he will be assuming new obligations. If a young woman dreams that she is on a porch with her lover, it means that she suspects the purity of someone's intentions.

Porcupine

If a person sees a porcupine, it indicates his reluctance to undertake any new enterprises or make new friends. If a young woman dreams about a porcupine, she will be afraid of her lover. A dream that features a dead porcupine means that the dreamer sloughs off anger and gives up his possessions.

Pork

A dream about eating pork is a sign of terrible trouble, but seeing it predicts triumph for the dreamer.

Porpoise

If a person sees a porpoise in a dream, it means that he is incapable of maintaining other people's interest, so his enemies are pushing him to one side.

Porridge

A dream about porridge is a warning dream: it implies

that people around the dreamer are liable to conspire and plot against him, and want to harm him. For that reason, he is well advised to keep away from the people closest to him and be suspicious of everyone until he can discover the source of the evil. Friends on whom the dreamer relies are liable to turn out to be dangerous, and he must stay away from them as best he can.

Port

If a person dreams about ships anchored in a port, it is a sign that he will soon put new and original enterprises of his own devising into practice. A plan that he has been devising for a long time is about to be implemented.

A dream about difficulty in climbing on board ship is a sign that any plan the dreamer is trying to implement at the moment is doomed to failure. He is advised to wait.

A dream about a port also implies that the dreamer is going through a period of worries and hassles that are preoccupying him and giving him no rest.

If a person dreams about ships entering the port, it is a sign that even if the relations with the people around him are bad, things will be resolved in the very best way. Giving in or compromising on the part of one of the sides will eventually lead to clearing the atmosphere and getting things back to normal.

Not only that, but the bad relations will give way to warm and pleasant ties of friendship.

Porter

If a person sees a porter in a dream, it is a sign of bad luck and tumultuous events. If he sees himself as a porter in a dream, it is a sign of a decrease in his status. If he dreams about hiring a porter, it implies success and its attendant joys. If he sends a porter away in a dream, charges will be pressed against him.

Portfolio

A dream about a portfolio indicates the dreamer's displeasure with his job and his desire to make a change.

Portrait

If a person dreams about looking at a portrait of a handsome person, it is a warning dream: it warns the dreamer that certain pleasures have a treacherous side to them. This dream brings bad luck.

Postman / Mailman

If a dream features a postman, it is a sign that the dreamer is worried about financial, business-related, or social difficulties.

Post office

A dream that features a post office indicates that the dreamer has a guilty conscience concerning an outstanding debt or commitment. It is a sign of bad news and bad luck.

Postage

If a person dreams about postage stamps, it means lucrative and organized business affairs. If he attempts to use canceled stamps, it means that his reputation is in jeopardy. Torn stamps in a dream are a sign of obstacles in the dreamer's path to success.

Postcard

If a person dreams about receiving a postcard, it means that he will receive sudden tidings – and these will generally be bad.

Pot

If a person dreams about a pot, it means that he will be bothered by minor hassles. If a woman's dream features a boiling pot, it is a sign of happy duties. A dream about a broken or rusty pot signifies disappointment.

Potato

A dream about a potato implies two main things, and partially serves as a warning dream: It warns the dreamer against giving vague advice to friends; he is liable to get himself in trouble. The dreamer can also become embroiled in a situation in which he gives someone else advice and changes things for that person in an unfavorable way. By doing this, he will not only place the person who asked for advice in jeopardy, but he will also jeopardize their friendship. Things may never be the same as they were before.

A dream like this, as mentioned above, is also a hint of other things that relate to the dreamer's life: He can expect a life of ease and wellbeing, particularly in the emotional realm. While he will also enjoy financial ease, a dream like this stresses the fact that the dreamer will enjoy peace of mind, repose, stability and tremendous satisfaction from his social life and his love life (this also refers to his future marriage). The dream symbolizes progress in life and the accomplishment of the important goals the dreamer wants to achieve.

Potsherds

A dream about potsherds predicts a period of happiness and joy, as well as of economic prosperity.

Potter

If a person dreams about a potter, it is a sign of satisfaction with work. If a young woman sees a potter in a dream, she will have a good social life.

Poultry

If a person dreams about poultry, it is a warning dream: it warns the dreamer against a profligate lifestyle. If a young woman dreams that she chases poultry, it means that she will pursue superficial pleasures.

Powder

A dream about powder is a sign of unscrupulous people who are in contact with the dreamer. He can beat them at their own game if he is on the ball.

Prairie

If a person dreams about a prairie, it indicates a comfortable, affluent lifestyle and steady advancement. If he dreams about a grassy, flower-filled, gently hilly prairie, it is a sign of happy events. A dream about an arid prairie means that the absence of friends will cause the dreamer to feel lost and unhappy. If he is lost on a prairie in a dream, it is a sign of sadness and bad luck.

Prayer

In general, a prayer in a dream symbolizes respect, tranquillity and happiness for the dreamer.

If a person dreams that he himself is taking part in prayer, he can soon expect to go through a good, enjoyable and happy phase.

If a person sees a group of people praying in a dream while he stands to one side and does not participate in the prayers, it is a warning dream: consciously or not, the dreamer's actions are causing sorrow and pain to the people around him.

If a person prays for the health and safety of someone else in a dream, he will earn greatness, and the people around him will admire him greatly and will appreciate him and his acts. His reputation will precede him, and he will be accorded respect and admiration.

If a person dreams that he is saying a silent prayer, the dream attests to the fact that a deal he has made will be canceled. Having said that, it is all for the best, since from the outset the deal was not sound and was shrouded in fraudulence. Its cancellation can be viewed as a blessing.

If a person dreams that while he is praying, he asks someone else to pray instead of him, it is a bad sign that predicts negative events in the dreamer's life.

If a woman dreams that she is praying and lighting candles, her home will be filled with peace and happiness.

If a person dreams that he is praying alone without anyone else present during his prayers, it is a hint that he is very popular with his friends and colleagues, and that he loves to spend time with them. He knows how to be a good friend, to give his friends the credit they deserve, and to offer assistance in times of need.

A dream in which the dreamer sees himself coerced into praying against his will, it is a sign that in reality he is helpless, and his powerlessness is causing him to request help and be in need of other people's assistance.

Preacher

If a person dreams about a preacher, it means that he is not perfect, and he will have problems. If he dreams about being a preacher, it predicts losses in business. If a person hears a preacher in a dream, it is an omen of bad luck. If he becomes involved in a dispute with a preacher in a dream, it means that he will lose a contest. If a preacher leaves the dreamer, business will pick up. If the preacher looks sad in a dream, the dreamer will suffer recriminations.

Precipice

If a person dreams about standing over a gaping precipice, it is a sign of imminent catastrophe. A dream about falling over a precipice means disaster for the dreamer.

Pregnancy

A dream about pregnancy mainly symbolizes a new beginning or the desire to turn over a new leaf or start a new chapter in life. In general, this fierce desire stems from a feeling of dissatisfaction with everyday life, from failure in certain fields, and from a feeling of not having fulfilled one's potential.

If a woman dreams of being pregnant, the dream implies good health as well as the fact that while various temptations may crop up along the way, the dreamer succeeds in overcoming them and persisting in the right way of life. The direct result of that is normal and good health.

In contrast, if a married woman dreams of pregnancy, she must check to see that everything is normal in her relationship with her husband. In general, this dream hints at problems that constitute an obstacle that must be overcome in order to move ahead.

If a man dreams that his wife is pregnant, it implies that whether his wife is actually pregnant or will soon become pregnant, the newborn will be a son.

If a widow dreams about pregnancy, it means that a wedding is in the offing. She is about to meet a man who will be the person with whom she can start a new relationship. After a long period of being unable to trust men and shying away from new and commitment-filled relationships, the time for change is about to come. The dreamer is about to find herself in the middle of an affair that will shake up her life, make the adrenaline flow, and cause her a great deal of joy and happiness.

If a widower dreams about a pregnant woman, it is a sign that he is surrounded by good people who are dear to him, want things to be good for him and want to help him. He can rely on them in times of need or trouble.

If a young girl dreams about pregnancy, the dream

implies that the pregnancy is still far away and that she will marry late.

If a young man dreams that his girlfriend is pregnant, it is a sign that he is suffering from pangs of conscience. Feelings of remorse about something bad that he did are torturing him. He tries to overcome them, but until he smoothes things over, his chances of being able to extricate himself from his difficult situation are poor.

Presents

If a person dreams about receiving presents it indicates that he will be extremely lucky.

President of the United States

If a person dreams about speaking to the President of the United States, it means that he has political leanings and ambitions.

Priest

A dream about a priest is a sign of bad luck. It is a negative dream. If a woman dreams that she is in love with a priest, it means that her lover has no conscience and no morals. If a person dreams about confessing to a priest, the dream predicts grief and humiliation. Any dream about a priest means that the dreamer will be the cause of unpleasantness to the people close to him.

Primrose

A dream about a primrose predicts happiness, comfort and tranquillity.

Printer

If a dream features a printer, it means that the dreamer will suffer from economic difficulties if he is not careful. If a woman dreams about some kind of relationship with a printer, it means that her parents will not approve of her choice of friends.

Printing press

If a person dreams that he is at a printing press, it implies gossip and slander. If he dreams that he is running a printing press, the dream predicts bad luck. If a woman's lover is associated with a printing press in her dream, it means he has neither time nor money for her.

Princes, princesses and royalty

Dreams about princes and royalty imply that the dreamer aspires to improve his social status. It is possible that he will soon get into the company of upper-class people who will lead him in new and unexpected directions. His chances of rising in social and economic status are excellent.

Prison

If a person sees himself locked up in prison, as if in a cage without a way out, the dream implies health problems. The dreamer's physical state is not good, and he is not in the best of health. This feeling has been incubating inside him for a long time, but apparently he has not noticed it. He has ignored his condition and kept on going, hoping that the feeling will eventually disappear. The dreamer has to be more alert to his condition, pay heed to his body and not neglect his state of health.

If a person dreams about an unsuccessful attempt to escape from prison, the dream implies a fierce desire to release the restraining bonds, to achieve freedom and to find one's own way without the dictates of the surroundings and society. The person feels as if the laws of society are holding him back, and that his mind – which is original and special in its way – is being forcibly "incarcerated." He cannot give free rein to his impulses, his abilities and his talents, because if he does, society will not look kindly on it. He is afraid of non-conformity, and the inner struggle that is raging inside him between the desire to break through the limits and the desire to be accepted in society is causing him unbearable emotional turmoil.

If, in contrast, a person sees himself making a successful escape from prison, he will accomplish the goals he set himself, he will have the chance to realize his wildest fantasies, his hopes will be fulfilled and his numerous plans will bear fruit.

Prisoner

A dream about a prisoner in general, not in a specific context, predicts a long life for the dreamer.

If a person sees himself as a prisoner in a dream, he is about to be found guilty in a fraud trial. If he sees someone else in a prisoner's uniform and in chains in prison, the dream implies that the dreamer is involved in criminal activities. Even if he is not aware of the gravity of his deeds, he is not exempt from the severe punishment that awaits him.

A dream in which prisoners are seen escaping from prison is a sign that malicious gossip will cause the dreamer's his entire world to collapse. Evil rumors will cause the people around the dreamer to view him in a negative way, even if he did not commit any sin or crime. This curse will plague him for a long time, and he will not be able to get rid of the stigma attached to his name.

Privacy

that his privacy is infringed, he will be disturbed by inconsiderate people. A woman who has this dream should mind her private affairs and not interfere with those of her partner.

Prize

If a person dreams about winning a prize, the dream actually means the opposite: He can expect massive financial losses.

Prize fight

If a person dreams sees a prize fight in a dream, it implies that he has difficulty controlling his affairs.

Prize fighter

If a woman dreams about a prize fighter, it means that she will lead a wild life.

Procession / Festive parade

A procession or a festive parade in a dream attests to the

A B C D E F G H I J K L M N O P Q R S T U V W X Y Z

fact that the dreamer is anticipating exciting events. His expectations engender a great deal of excitement in him, and this is expressed in the dream. He should lower his expectations in order not to be disappointed.

If a person dreams that he participates in a procession or a parade, the dream predicts the advent of a period full of changes and surprises. In most cases, the changes will be for the better and will benefit him, but things will not always be positive. There could also be less pleasant surprises. The changes will mainly take place in the dreamer's career and family life, but there could also be a significant change in his love life. The dreamer must take everything in proportion and prepare himself emotionally for the changes that are about to occur.

Profanity

A dream that features profanity symbolizes the dreamer's coarse, tactless behavior. If he dreams about others using profanities, he will soon be offended.

Profit

If a person dreams about profits, it is a sign of imminent success. If he receives a large sum of money, it is a warning of deception, denial and being led astray by one of his close friends.

Promenade

If a person dreams about promenading, the dream predicts agreeable, lucrative pastimes. If he dreams about other people promenading, it is a sign of rivalry.

Property

If a person dreams about owning a lot of property, it is a sign of financial and social success.

Prophet

This is a hint of a special experience or spiritual illumination. Alternatively, there could be a fateful turnabout in the near future, which will cause a significant change in the dreamer's life. A trip to a distant place or a surprising job offer will get the dreamer into a situation in which others will come to him in order to hear what he has to say and to consult him. This new state of affairs will lead to an improvement in his social status. He can also expect substantial financial remuneration for his work.

Prostitute

If a person dreams about being with a prostitute, it means that his friends will be justifiably angry at him. If a married woman dreams about a prostitute, she will become suspicious of her husband and quarrel with him. If a young woman has this dream, it means that she will not be honest with her lover.

Psychiatrist

If a person dreams about a psychiatrist, it means that he will soon receive advice and counseling. If he dreams that he is a psychiatrist's patient, it predicts emotional turmoil.

Publisher

If a person sees a publisher in a dream, it means he has literary aspirations. If a woman dreams that her husband is a publisher, she will be jealous of his female acquaintances. If a publisher rejects the dreamer's manuscript in a dream, he must brace himself for imminent disappointment. If the publisher accepts the manuscript in the dream, the dreamer's hopes will be realized. If the publisher loses the manuscript in the dream, the dreamer will be hurt by unknown parties.

Puddings

If a person dreams about puddings, it symbolizes disappointingly small profits. If he sees himself eating pudding, it denotes disappointments. If he makes a pudding in a dream, he will have bad luck in love.

Puddle

If a person dreams that he steps into a puddle of clear water, he will endure some minor hassle that will soon disappear. If the puddle in the dream is muddy, the hassle will not disappear so soon. If his feet get wet because of stepping into a puddle, it means that good luck will turn sour.

Pulpit

A dream about a pulpit is a sign of trouble and sadness. If a person dreams that he is in a pulpit, he is warned of illness and bad luck in business.

A B C D E F G H I J K L M N O **P** Q R S T U V W X Y Z

Pulse

If a person dreams about his pulse, it is a warning dream: it warns the dreamer to watch out for his health and business, both of which are in jeopardy. If he dreams about feeling someone else's pulse, it is a sign of lasciviousness.

Pulses (legumes)

Pulses in a dream mean economic prosperity. Even if the economic situation is difficult and there is no relief in the offing, things will soon change for the better. If the dreamer runs an independent business, he can expect it to prosper and provide him with large and respectable revenues. The dreamer can put his worries concerning his business aside and calm down: his business will grow and flourish and his economic situation will improve beyond recognition.

If a person who is an employee has this dream, the appearance of pulses in the dream indicate that problems he has at work, as well as the tensions or pressures, will all disappear, and he will be given a serious promotion along with a good salary.

His new post will calm him down regarding his economic situation, which will also change. Everyday life will be easier for him, and the new status he will be given in the form of tenure or other conditions that will provide him with economic security, will make life easier – both on the material and psychological levels.

Pump

If a dream features a pump, it is a sign that prosperity will come in the wake of hard work. It is also a sign of health. A dream that features a broken pump means that the dreamer has no chance of prospering because of family worries. If he sees himself working a pump, it means that he will have a good life.

Punch (beverage)

If a person dreams about drinking punch, the dream indicates his preference for a selfish, immoral life rather than a respectable one.

Punch, box, fist

If the dreamer sees a fist giving a punch in a dream, it symbolizes getting out of difficulties, and an attempt to get out of an embroilment in which the dreamer finds himself. Apparently, the dreamer is in some kind of difficulty from which he is trying to extricate himself, and this is manifested in a dream of this kind.

A fist in a dream, without any special context, is a sign of a quarrel. Generally, the background is penny-pinching, bone-picking about minor and insignificant matters, pettiness and childishness.

If the dreamer sees himself punching another person, it implies that he will lose an impending court-case. If he is the one who was punched, he will win the case in which he is involved.

If the dreamer catches a punch from somebody in his dream and is injured as a result, the dream foretells a prize. The dreamer will be given some kind of award, even though he did not make a special effort to attain or win it.

If the dreamer punched somebody else and injured him in his dream, it signifies the loss of a person close to him, such as a friend, and this will be very significant for the continuation of the dreamer's life. The loss is inevitable, and even if the dreamer is on the alert for such an event, he will fail to prevent it. It is the hand of fate, and the dream hints at the foreseeable future, which the dreamer is unable to change.

If the dreamer sees a boxing ring in which several boxers are fighting, it is a sign that he is about to get a promotion, either at work or in his military service. The promotion will be reflected both in a higher salary and in higher social standing. The people in the dreamer's everyday surroundings will appreciate him more, and he will be accorded greater esteem by his superiors and his subordinates alike. This is his opportunity to establish his new status and to win a permanent place for himself among the ranks of superiors, order-givers and decision-makers.

Pups

If a person dreams about pups and their innocence, it signifies a good, pleasant life. If the pups in the dream are strong and healthy, the dreamer will enjoy prosperity close friendships. The opposite is true if they are weak and sickly.

Purchases

If a dream features purchases of any kind, it is a sign of prosperity and career success.

Purse

If a person dreams about a purse that is stuffed with money bills and diamonds, he will enjoy harmony and love in life.

Pursuit

A person who dreams that people are pursuing him is going through a difficult phase and feels as if he is in a trap. He is plagued by fatigue and a lack of enthusiasm, as well as by a feeling of helplessness that bursts into the dream and persecutes him. He must examine the true causes of his feeling of failure and act accordingly.

Putting on weight

A dream about putting on weight augurs ill. Nothing will go right in the near future. Everything will go wrong. It is a temporary/transient bad patch, and it will pass, so it is important to relate to things in the correct proportion. Since the dreamer is in for a stormy period, full of unpleasant surprises, it would be better for him to keep a low profile, not to be conspicuous anywhere, not to begin grandiose projects and not to come out with pompous declarations. This is the time to bow his head until the wave washes over him. Maintaining industrial peace is the order of the day.

Putty

A dream about putty is a warning dream: it warns against risking one's fortune.

Pyramid

A pyramid is a symbol of change. If a person dreams about climbing thc pyramids, it signitics that hc will have to wait a long time before realizing his hopes and desires. If he dreams about studying the mysteries of the pyramids, it means that he will enjoy the mysteries of nature and will become well informed.

Q

A
B
C
D
E
F
G
H
I
J
K
L
M
N
O
P
Q
R
S
T
U
V
W
X
Y
Z

Quack (bogus doctor)

A dream that features a quack predicts that a disease will be treated incorrectly.

Quack medicine

If a person dreams about quack medicine, it means that he is collapsing under the burden of some kind of problem. However, by working hard, he can extricate himself from it. If he sees an advertisement for this type of medicine, ill-intentioned associates will cause him harm.

Quadrille

If a person sees people dancing a quadrille in a dream, he can look forward to leading a good social life.

Quagmire

If a person dreams that he is in a quagmire, it is a sign that he is completely unable to carry out his obligations. If he sees other people in a quagmire in a dream, it means that he will suffer the consequences of their failures.

Quail

If a person dreams about live quails, the dream augurs very well. If he sees dead ones in a dream, however, the forecast is bad luck. If he dreams about shooting quail, it means that his friends will be mad at him. If he sees himself eating quail in a dream, it implies that he leads a wasteful lifestyle.

Quaker

If a person dreams about Quakers, he can rest assured that he has true friends and carries out honest business dealings. If he dreams that he himself is a Quaker, it means that he will treat his enemies fairly. If a young woman dreams that she attends a Quaker meeting, it implies that she will have a good and faithful husband.

Quarantine

If a person dreams about being in quarantine, it means that his enemies will put him in an impossible position as a result of their scheming.

Quarrel

A dream about a quarrel is a sign of unhappiness. If a person dreams about being involved in a quarrel, it means that someone is insanely jealous of him. For a woman, a dream like this can mean conflict and scparation.

Quarry

This type of dream is characteristic of a person who has worked very hard for a long period of time. Only after a very long time does he finally see the fruits of his labor. In his dream, he may see that he finds some kind of treasure in the quarry. This is an encouraging sign, implying that the goal he set himself is nearer than ever.

Quartet

A dream about being a member of a quartet attests to happy times, prosperity and good friends. If a person hears a quartet in a dream, it means that he will foster lofty new aspirations.

Quay

If a person dreams about a quay, the dream foretells a long journey. If he sees ships while he is standing on a quay, the dream signals that things will work out for him.

Queen

If a person dreams about a queen, it indicates that he will soon be given help or assistance by the people nearest to him. If the dream features a queen who is old or tired, it means that the dreamer will not enjoy his leisure activities.

Question

If a person questions the worth of something, it means that he suspects his partner of cheating on him. If he asks a question in a dream, it means that he is embarking on a serious quest for the truth, as well as success. If he himself is questioned, he will not be treated fairly.

Quicksand

If a person dreams about being trapped in quicksand, it implies that his economic and social status will collapse. If he sees another person trapped in quicksand in a dream, it is a sign that other people will do anything in their power to prevent him from accomplishing his objectives. If he dreams that he cannot extricate himself from the quicksand, he will be completely crushed by bad luck.

Quills

A dream about quills is a positive dream. If the dreamer is a writer, a dream about quills implies success. If the quills in the dream are for decoration, business will boom.

Quilts

If a person dreams about quilts, it is a sign of good luck. If a young woman has this dream, it means that her smart, practical nature will appeal to a man, who will want to marry her. If she dreams that the quilt is clean but has holes in it, she will have a husband who cherishes her; however, she will not be attracted to him. If she dreams that the quilt is dirty, it is a reflection on her own conduct, and she will not marry a good man.

Quinine

If a person dreams about quinine, it is a sign of great happiness, but not of wealth. If he dreams that he takes quinine, not only will his health improve, but he will feel an upswing in his social and business life as well.

Quitting (a job) / Resignation

If a person dreams about quitting a job, especially if he has a senior position, the dream implies that his plans will be put into practice in the near future.

Quiz

If a person dreams about taking a quiz or exam, he can expect to be offered an important business opportunity very soon. If he dreams about failing a quiz, he must brace himself for losses in business. If he gets a good score on a quiz in a dream, it is a sign of good luck and a tranquil life. If he dreams that his mind goes blank during a quiz, it means that he cannot advance, nor can he overcome the obstacles in his path.

Quoits

A dream about quoits does not augur well. If a person dreams about playing quoits, it means that he will be fired from a good job. If he loses a game of quoits, it is a sign of bad luck.

R

Rabbi — See Religious functionary

Rabbit

The appearance of any kind of rabbit in a dream is a sign that the dreamer is a person who resists temptation and does not succumb to it easily. He is a person with a strong character who can say "no" when other people cannot. The people around him greatly admire the dreamer for this trait, and he often uses it for his own benefit.

The appearance of a white rabbit in a dream implies that the dreamer must remain good friends with one of his friends or acquaintances and straighten things out with him.

If a dream features a black rabbit, it attests to the fact that the dreamer is fickle in his opinions. He can hold one opinion, be convinced easily, and then change it. He is the type of person who is "dragged along," so he must be aware of himself and try to be more consistent in his opinions. In this way, he will also be held in higher regard by the people around him, since right now he is sometimes the object of mockery and scorn.

If a person sees a rabbit in flight, he can expect disappointment in many areas. His expectations should not be too great in case he is let down and the disappointment is too much to bear.

The appearance of a rabbit locked in a cage in a dream is a sign that the dreamer does not give his mind enough freedom. He feels that he has to "toe the line" in order not to hurt other people, but if he is unable to release the tensions that accumulate inside him, they will eventually erupt in violent ways or unexpected outbursts that will frighten the people around him or the members of his family. He must learn to liberate himself, and there are many ways to do that – either by meditation or some other mind/body relaxation, or by going away for weekends. The main thing is for him to know how to relax and allow himself to rest both physically and mentally.

Rabies – See Hydrophobia

Raccoon

If a person dreams about a raccoon, it means that his enemies are deceiving him by pretending to be his friends.

Race

A dream about a motor race or a running race is generally a positive dream. This is the time for action, opening new businesses and taking steps to improve one's social status. The dream hints that the dreamer is going though an important and crucial phase in his life. He is trying to accomplish certain goals that other people are also aspiring to reach. In order to succeed, he must make an effort and come up with creative means. Because of the pressure that work colleagues and family members are exerting on him, he feels alone in the struggle, without enough support. It is difficult to know how the race will end. The matter depends on the dreamer's staying power and determination. These capacities may come into play during the "trial period." He who hangs in there for the longest time will ultimately achieve the coveted goal.

Rack (torture)

If a person dreams about a rack, it implies that he is uncertain of the outcome of something that is causing him a great deal of worry.

Racket

If a dream features a racket, it predicts disappointment in something the dreamer was looking forward to.

Radio

If a person dreams about listening to a radio, it means that he will make friends with a congenial person with whom he can have fun. If he hears a radio in a dream, it is a sign of good luck.

Radish

If a person dreams about a bed of radishes, it is a sign of good luck from the point of view of friends and business. If he sees himself eating radishes in a dream, it means that someone close to him will cause him offense. A dream about sccing or planting radishcs is a positivc drcam, sincc it indicatcs that wishcs will comc truc.

Raffle

A dream about a raffle is usually a sign of disappointment. If the dreamer participates in a church raffle, he will be disappointed. If a young woman dreams about participating in a raffle, her hopes will never be realized.

Raft

A dream about a raft is an excellent dream that attests to the fact that the dreamer can expect to go through a good phase. A raft symbolizes going on a fascinating journey over the waves, which are a symbol of life itself. The dreamer will be successful as a result of his courage, uniqueness and originality. If the raft sinks, the dreamer must exercise great caution. There will be obstacles, but ultimately, success is assured.

Rage

A dream about being in a violent rage is an indication of conflict and violence among friends. If a person sees other people in a rage, he will suffer a spell of bad luck in his business affairs and social life. If a young woman dreams that her lover is in a rage, there relationship will be marred by misunderstandings and quarrels.

Raging – See Wildness

Railing

If a person dreams about a railing, it symbolizes barriers

in his path. If he is holding on to a railing in his dream, it means that he will take a gigantic risk in order to achieve what he wants – either in love or in business.

Railroad

If a person dreams about a railroad, it is a warning dream: he is warned to safeguard his affairs from his enemies. If the railroad in his dream is blocked, it is a sign of underhand business practices. If a young woman dreams about a railroad, she will go on a trip that will be very successful.

Rain

In general, rain in a dream is not a good sign. In most cases, it attests to embroilments, anger, disasters and various problems.

If the rain looks like it is falling in fine drops, the dreamer will have to cope with frustrating problems, with disappointments and with changing situations that he will have to know how to get out of. He can expect a difficult period of excitement alongside difficulties and stagnation, disappointments alongside glimmers of hope.

If heavy rain is pouring down, the dream hints that the dreamer can expect to go through a period full of tensions, worries and anxieties. This is liable to make him depressed or plunge him into bad moods, depression and nervousness. The tendency to get angry and have outbursts will accompany him for some time, until things calm down.

If a person dreams that he gets wet in the rain, he can expect complications in all aspects of his love life. If he is clever enough to heed the dream, he may prevent

A B C D E F G H I J K L M N O P Q **R** S T U V W X Y Z

unpleasant situations by telling the truth. If he is honest with himself and with the people around him, he will not find himself squirming to prove his innocence or to show that he is untainted by any sin.

Rainbow

A rainbow in a dream is always a good omen: It predicts joy, happiness, serenity and pleasure for the dreamer. It is a marvelous sign for lovers. If the rainbow appears low over green trees in a dream, the dreamer will be successful in anything he undertakes.

Raisins

If a person dreams about raisins, the dream symbolizes wastefulness and extravagance that must be curbed. If a person dreams about eating raisins, it means that his hopes will be disappointed.

Rake

If a person dreams about a rake, he should keep his eyes open – when he wakes up from the dream and comes back to reality – and examine the people close to him extremely carefully. Somebody is laying a trap for him, and if he is not careful, he will fall right into it and pay a heavy price for keeping his eyes closed as he has done up till now.

Ram

A dream that features a ram is a negative dream that foretells very difficult times in the near future. The dreamer should know that this prophetic dream is preparing him psychologically for the difficult struggle that is in store for him, and that he has to muster great emotional forces in order to get through this difficult period psychologically unscathed. He will go through a serious crisis, but will emerge from it strengthened. He will learn many lessons from it.

If a white ram appears in a dream, it is a hint that the dreamer must "go for gold" since he has nothing to lose.

If a person sees a black ram in a dream, it indicates that luck is not on his side and that he must try to get through the crisis ahead.

Another meaning of a ram in a dream states that the dreamer has rivals who are scheming against him and trying to sabotage him in any possible manner.

Ramble

If a person dreams that he is on a country ramble, it means that he will have a comfortable life, but will suffer because of the separation from people he loves. If a young woman's dream features a ramble in the country, it means that her home will be agreeable, but she will lose someone she loves at a young age.

Ramrod

A dream about a ramrod is an omen of negative events. If a young woman sees a bent ramrod in a dream, she will be badly let down by a friend or lover.

Ranch – See Farm

A
B
C
D
E
F
G
H
I
J
K
L
M
N
O
P
Q
R
S
T
U
V
W
X
Y
Z

Ransom

If a person dreams that a ransom is paid for him, it is a warning dream: someone will try and deceive him. If a woman dreams about a ransom, it is a sign of evil. This can be neutralized if the ransom in the dream is paid.

Rape

Dreams of rape certainly occur more frequently among women than among men, and generally portend a tragedy that is about to befall the dreamer. The dream does not signify an actual act of rape, but rather serves as a kind of warning of a catastrophic event that is in the offing and that will inflict great sorrow and deep pain. While it does not seem possible to avert the disaster, one can prepare oneself psychologically for such a traumatic event in order to soften the blow.

Sometimes, if the dreamer is a woman, such a dream may attest to abnormal relations between a woman and her husband or the partner with whom she lives. The dreamer must examine her relations with her partner closely, since the dream is a warning sign that something in those relations is not as it should be.

[A dream about rape has a different meaning when it occurs as a result of the dreamer's hearing, seeing or reading a news report about an actual rape, or if there is a fear of a rapist who is known to be roaming around the neighborhood and has not yet been apprehended. Then the dream must be interpreted literally as the fear that stems from an encounter with the rapist. The nature of fears and anxieties is to emerge in dreams, and such dreams must be related to in this way.].

Rapids

If a person dreams about being swept along by rapids, it means that he is neglecting his affairs for the sake of superficial pleasures and will pay dearly for this in huge financial losses.

Raspberry

A dream about a raspberry can be interpreted in three ways:

In most cases, the presence of a raspberry attests to the fact that the dreamer is in the company of people who like him and want the best for him – so he thinks – but in fact the opposite is true: his friends are treacherous people who are waiting for his downfall; the moment he needs them, they will turn their backs on him. He must be more alert to the people around him and scrutinize the relationship he is developing with them.

A completely different interpretation indicates a stormy love life. Accordingly, the dream implies the amount of free rein the dreamer gives his desires. The dreamer is a passionate person who enjoys making wild love and delights in the pleasures of the flesh. He is not turned off by any of the possible ways of satisfying his desires, even those that may be considered to be deviant or unconventional pleasures. Because of his almost uncontrollable attraction to physical pleasures, the dreamer is not in the habit of staying with any one partner for any length of time, but rather switches partners frequently. He loves to experience as much as possible, to notch up more and more conquests, and to prove his masculinity to himself (or, in the case of a woman, her femininity).

A B C D E F G H I J K L M N O P Q **R** S T U V W X Y Z

If a dream features a raspberry, it also means that because of the dreamer's conduct and the way he lives, an entire "industry" of gossip has sprung up around him. This is partially due to the fact that the dreamer leads a "different" kind of life, has the audacity to express himself, and flouts the opinion of society. This conduct generally sparks malicious gossip, even though many of those who talk behind the dreamer's back admire his daring conduct since he embodies all the things they dreamed of doing but did not dare to do.

Rat

A rat in a dream is a sign of a hidden enemy who is threatening to cause the dreamer harm. In general, a dream like this focuses on the dreamer's own problems with his surroundings. As mentioned above, a specific person is plotting to harm him. However, if the rat in the dream is seen to be running, the dream implies that the expected threat is not necessarily directed at the dreamer, but at someone close to him, or at one of his loved ones. A serious attack is expected to be perpetrated on a person who is close to the dreamer, and the dream serves as a kind of warning to the dreamer to safeguard himself from enemies, and particularly to look after his loved ones and the people who are close to him.

Rattle

If a person sees an infant playing with a rattle in a dream, it is a sign of a happy, thriving household. If a young woman dreams about a rattle, she will marry young. If a person dreams about giving a baby a rattle, it implies that he will be involved in unsuccessful deals.

A B C D E F G H I J K L M N O P Q **R** S T U V W X Y Z

Rat trap

If a person dreams that he gets caught in a rat trap, it is a warning dream: he will be attacked and robbed. A dream that features a broken rat trap signifies the end of an inauspicious relationship. If an empty rat trap appears in a dream, it means that the dreamer will not have to contend with rivalry and gossip. If the dreamer sets a rat trap, it means that he is aware of his enemies' evil intentions and can thwart them.

Raven

In our subconscious, a raven is linked to negative things, and it even has many ties to the world of black magic. In the stories and fables we were accustomed to hearing in our childhood, the raven always played a negative, evil and scary role. It is also well known that ravens are in the habit of attacking human beings and can constitute a serious nuisance – and even a peril. All of this causes the raven to be perceived by the vast majority of dreamers in a negative way. A dream about a raven is generally linked to sorrow, disappointment, trouble, disease, pain, panic, hardship, and so on. The general feeling that arises in most cases in a dream that features a raven is not positive – it is bad, irksome and sometimes even frightening. The atmosphere in the dream is not pleasant, and many dreamers who wake up from a dream that features a raven report bad feelings that are connected to vague fears, panic and restlessness.

A raven that is flying in a dream implies that the dreamer is going through a difficult phase and is experiencing deep psychological pain or feelings of great sorrow that he finds very difficult to overcome. If the dreamer does not feel like this, then another interpretation given to a raven flying in a dream involves heavy losses that the dreamer can expect in the near future, especially in the financial realm. However, it is certainly possible that the loss will also occur in other areas – in other words, the loss of a loved one, the loss of a good job opportunity, missing out on some chance to make a financial investment, and so on.

If a dream features a flock of ravens, it is a sign that a natural disaster is on the way and is going to strike in the near future. In both North and South America, a dream like this hints at powerful storms and winds such as hurricanes, tornadoes, volcanic eruptions, and so on. In other regions, a dream like this can indicate earthquakes, the collapse of buildings for some other reason, the advent of a harsh winter that can lead to floods that will cause disasters, and so on.

If a raven attacks the dreamer in a dream, it is a sign that the dreamer will succeed in overcoming all the obstacles in his path, especially the ones placed by his enemies, the people who hate him, or the people who are competing with him for similar posts.

Some dreams feature a raven that swoops down on the dreamer in a dream or "adopts" the dreamer and does not leave him alone. This is a sign that the dreamer is in a situation from which he finds it difficult to extricate himself or that he is at the height of involvement in an affair that is hard for him to get out of. Although he is sick and tired of the situation and can no longer bear the situation he is in, he cannot find a way out.

A particularly large raven in a dream attests to the fact that the dreamer must not rely on his friends. He is well advised to be suspicious of anyone around him, since even the ones who seem to wish him well are ultimately liable to turn out to be his worst enemies.

Razor

If a person dreams about a razor, it is a sign of bad luck and vicissitudes. If he dreams that he cuts himself with a razor, he will make a bad deal. A dream that features a broken or rusty razor implies great unhappiness. If a person fights with a razor, it means that he will have to deal with an extremely irritating person.

Reading

If a person reads in a dream, it means that he will do very well at a task that appears difficult. If he sees other people reading in a dream, it is a sign that he has very good friends. If he discusses reading in the dream, it implies that he will become more informed. If the reading is incomprehensible or inaudible, it is a sign of worries and disillusionment.

Reapers

If a person dreams about reapers working, it signals happiness and prosperity. If the field is dry and full of crop stubble, it is a warning dream: business will be bad. If the reapers are not working in the dream, there will be a setback in business. If a reaping machine has broken down in a dream, people will lose their jobs.

Reception

If a person dreams about being at a reception, it is a sign of forthcoming enjoyable social events. If he dreams that

A B C D E F G H I J K L M N O P Q **R** S T U V W X Y Z

there is an unpleasant incident at a reception, he will have anxieties.

Recipe

A dream that features a recipe book attests to the dreamer's good health. He is a person who knows how to look after himself and lead a healthy lifestyle from the point of view of both nutrition and physical fitness. Even if he goes through phases when he neglects these things, he never lets things get out of control, and immediately pulls himself up short in order to get back into shape and eat correctly again.

The dream also attests to the dreamer's sound mental health, as the saying goes: "A healthy mind in a healthy body." He knows how to safeguard his mental health and not get caught up in unnecessary tension or extreme psychological situations. He knows how to take a break even when he is going through periods of pressure. He also knows how to enjoy the moment, go on vacation every now and then in order to refuel body and soul, and all in all live a good and healthy life in every way.

Recitation

Any type of text that a person dreams of reciting – whether it is a poem, a recitation, a speech or a part in a play or show – attests to the dreamer's attempt to cope with difficulties and the ability to overcome them.

The difficulties can be expressed in the family setting, at work or in his social life, but there is no doubt that the dreamer is going through a phase of coping and grappling with problems and difficulties. The battle is not simple, and he is making an effort to deal with it and confront the problem. The desire and determination to overcome the difficulties and get through the difficult phase will pay off. The dream implies that the dreamer, in his uncompromising battle, will indeed succeed in accomplishing the mission he set himself, in overcoming the obstacles and the difficulties and in reaching his goal. Ultimately, it will be easier for him to deal with this confusion, and he will become stronger and will value himself more. His confidence in himself will increase, and in the future he will be able to cope more easily with similar obstacles and problems that crop up in his life.

Reconciliation

If a person dreams that he effects a reconciliation with someone with whom he has quarreled and broken off relations, it means that good news is in the offing.

Record player

A dream that features a record player signifies happiness and prosperity as well as a calm domestic life.

Red currants

A dream that features red currants or other berries attests to the dreamer's inability to cope with a problem and to his desire to ignore it and the reality of the situation he is in. Evading the problem by ignoring it or something similar will not solve it, but will just delay coping with it for another time that is liable to turn out to be more complicated. The dream implies that the dreamer must

A B C D E F G H I J K L M N O P Q **R** S T U V W X Y Z

come to grips with the subject, deal with it and try to solve the things while they are still "on a back burner," since otherwise it could be too late.

A dream in which the dreamer gathers red currants or berries among the trees implies the dreamer's healthy attitude toward the conflicts and problems he runs into in life: He always sees the half-full glass and manages to avoid plunging into melancholy, even if things are far from brilliant. He tends to see the positive side of everything, and by nature he is an optimistic person who always hopes for the best and is sure that things will eventually turn out well. Other people dub him an "incorrigible optimist." This quality always works in his favor and is never a stumbling-block for him. It gives him something else that is important – many friends who love to be near him, because he is always charming and does not get into depressed and difficult moods. He is well loved, and people seek his company.

Red pepper

If a person dreams about a red pepper growing, it is a symbol of an independent and thrifty spouse.

Refrigerator

If a person dreams that he puts ice into the refrigerator, he will quarrel with people. If he dreams about a refrigerator, it means that he will behave selfishly and rudely with someone who does not merit such treatment.

Reindeer

If a person dreams about a reindeer, it implies that he carries out his obligations well and is a loyal, steadfast friend. If he is driving a team of reindeer in a dream, he will have a lot of problems, but his friends will help him through.

Religion

A dream that features religious symbols must be interpreted according to the religion and culture of the dreamer, since things vary from religion to religion. Sometimes a symbol that symbolizes a certain thing in one religion can be interpreted to mean something else in another religion. In most cases, dreams about religion, religious symbols, religious leaders or a religious event in which the dreamer participated in his dream predict good, comfortable and pleasant times that will be meaningful for the dreamer. In general, dreams about religion are dreams with spiritual enlightenment.

A dream in which a person sees himself meeting with a religious functionary constitutes a type of spiritual enlightenment. In most cases, people wake up from such a dream feeling as if they have undergone a special spiritual and religious experience. Sometimes they have powerful experiences, the kind that can change their way of life or the way they perceive life. Such a dream can have great significance for the dreamer and a very powerful effect on him. Many people have dreams like this after the death of a person who was close to them or after going through some kind of trauma.

If the religious symbols appeared in a dream where the

atmosphere is tense and the dreamer feels worried or anxious, the dream implies that the dreamer can expect to go through a difficult period of worry and anxiety. The attempt to deal with the worries on the everyday level also appears in the dream and does not let up.

Religious functionary

The religious functionary that appears in a dream may be a rabbi, a priest or any other person whom the dreamer perceives as a religious functionary – be he Jewish, Christian, Buddhist, Moslem, etc. In such a case, the dream implies that the dreamer is about to go through a difficult and frustrating period with many question marks. He will have a hard time choosing the path that is right for him, and will be confused. Every step he takes will seem wrong to him, and he will be fraught with unexplained fears and anxieties. The problems that he will be obliged to face will not be simple, and disappointment will strike time and time again. He has to muster all his emotional strength in preparation for the difficult time ahead, but eventually, after he overcomes those obstacles, he will emerge fortified and with greater self-confidence.

Religious revival

If a person dreams about being present at a religious revival, it is a warning dream: he will have bad luck in business and domestic affairs. If he takes part in a religious revival, he will anger his friends as a result of his wayward behavior.

Remote control

If a person dreams about using a remote control, it implies that the dreamer will become involved in a manipulative relationship.

Rent

A dream that features renting a house foretells lucrative deals. If the dreamer does not succeed in renting out property, he will go through a period of stagnation in business. If he dreams that he pays rent, his financial affairs will be very satisfactory. If he dreams that he is unable to pay the rent, it is a sign of financial failure.

Reprieve

If a person dreams that he is reprieved, he will overcome an obstacle that has been bothering him. If a young woman dreams that her lover is reprieved, it is a sign of good luck for him, and this is significant for her.

Reptiles

A dream about reptiles of any kind is a warning dream. It hints at a lack of luck, and generally does not augur well. The dreamer has opponents or enemies who are plotting against him. Usually, these are friends who "switched sides," so it is difficult for the dreamer to believe that they would conspire against him so ruthlessly. These are treacherous friends who are jealous of him or of his status.

The dream also hints that in the forthcoming stretch of time, the dreamer will find himself deeply embroiled in merciless and bitter disputes that will not end well, and in

A B C D E F G H I J K L M N O P Q R S T U V W X Y Z

serious conflicts to which he is not accustomed. These could be problems that crop up at work, where he will have to stand up for his opinions and principles against people who would rejoice in his downfall. However, they could also be problems at home with his children, his spouse or his parents, and the dreamer will have to deal with them. The serious differences of opinion that will erupt between the members of his household are liable to make his life a living hell. The obstacles will come from an unexpected quarter, and he will not be able to identify them in advance.

The appearance of a snake in a dream is interpreted in the same way as Eve's temptation by a serpent in the Garden of Eden: nothing good can come out of what is being offered. The dream implies that even the most enchanting and tempting offers are liable to contain hidden dangers or a reward that will prove to be blatantly worthless. The dreamer must display a certain amount of suspicion when considering any tempting offer he happens upon, so that the ground under his feet does not suddenly cave in.

Rescue

A dream about rescue implies that the person can get out of difficult situations of grief and sorrow and move forward. The dream expresses the dreamer's ability to get on with life even after suffering severe traumas or painful blows. His innate strengths are numerous and powerful, and he knows how to use them correctly and avail himself of them to get on with his life.

If a person sees himself rescued from danger by fleeing, the dream implies that someone is misleading him, and he must keep his eyes wide open in order not to be led astray by false promises.

If a person dreams of saving a life, it is a sign that in the future, he will be rewarded for the good things and deeds he did.

A dream in which the dreamer sees himself rescued from drowning hints at danger that is lying in wait for the dreamer as he approaches deep water. In the forthcoming stretch of time, it would be advisable for him to refrain from swimming in a pool, in the sea or in any other place where there is a danger of drowning, such as in rivers, streams or lakes.

If the dreamer sees himself rescuing other people, it is a sign that his actions will be recognized, and he will be accorded honor and great esteem. If a person dreams that he rescued someone from drowning, the dream implies that he can expect to notch up significant financial achievements, and that his financial situation is seriously improving.

A dream about rescuing a person who is attempting to commit suicide implies that the dreamer is in the company of people who put on an act. These are not people who can be trusted and relied upon, but the opposite. The dreamer is in the company of impostors and charlatans who will do anything to get what they want out of him. He must be careful of them.

If a person dreams that he rescued children, it is a prophetic dream according to which the dreamer is about to receive an inheritance from someone he does not know. It could be a distant relative with whom he has not had regular contact, but the inheritance may equally come from a stranger whom the dreamer does not yet know.

Resignation

A dream about resignation is mainly a positive dream that augurs well. If a person dreams that he resigns from his job voluntarily, destiny holds success and prosperity in whatever he does in store for him, especially in the field of work. If the person is particularly ambitious and dreams that he resigned from his job, the dream heralds new and broad horizons that are about to open up before him. In most cases, a dream like this implies a change in career direction and the choice of a different field or occupation in which the dreamer will enjoy success.

If the person who has this dream holds a high position in his workplace, or if he is self-employed, commands businesses on a grand scale and employs many workers, the dream implies great prosperity in the workplace. The dreamer will be accorded a great deal of esteem by the people who work with him. There will also be even greater financial success later on.

If a person dreams about being fired from his job against his will, the dream attests to a drastic change in his fate. If the dreamer is poor and humble, the dream predicts that his fate is about to change and he will earn a lot of money or win a large sum of money that will bring him comfort and prosperity. If the person is very wealthy, fate may hold other days in store for him, a drop in his assets and a decrease in his property. This kind of person is advised to plan his actions wisely and save up for a rainy day.

Restaurant

A dream about a meal in a restaurant generally implies positive developments. A meal *en famille* and with friends attests to a good situation (economic, social and general). A romantic meal with a partner indicates a longing to spend more time together, but gives more than a hint that the situation is excellent. A meal with the extended family is a sign of a happy occasion in the family. It could be a wedding, an engagement, or just a birthday. This encounter will give the family members a feeling the likes of which they have not had for a long time – a mutual recognition of the important of the event and great excitement.

Resurrection

If a person dreams about being resurrected from the dead, it implies that he will overcome tremendous worries. If he dreams that other people are resurrected, it means that his friends will help him overcome his worries.

Resuscitation

If a person dreams about being resuscitated, he will suffer heavy losses, but he will get over them and achieve prosperity and happiness. If he dreams that he resuscitates someone else, he will establish new and satisfying friendships.

Revelation

A dream about a positive revelation is a prediction of good things in business and love. A dream about a negative revelation, however, warns of worries and bad luck.

Revenge

A dream about revenge implies a serious quarrel or

dispute that will erupt in the dreamer's immediate surroundings. It will almost certainly start with an exchange of words and will quickly become violent. The dreamer is the one who must take responsibility, display restraint and prevent the situation from deteriorating further.

Revolver

If a young woman dreams about her lover holding a revolver, she will have a terrible row with a friend and may well break up with her lover.

Rheumatism

If a person dreams about falling ill with rheumatism, it means that his plans will be subjected to an unforeseen delay. If he dreams that other people suffer from rheumatism, he will endure disappointments.

Rhinestones

If a person dreams about rhinestones, it is an indication of short-lived pleasures. If he dreams that a rhinestone actually turns out to be a diamond, it means that an apparently insignificant action will engender good luck.

Rhinoceros

A dream about a rhinoceros is usually a sign that the dreamer is an authoritative person who likes to impose his authority on others. Having said that, he sometimes behaves in a forceful and aggressive way that is unpleasant for the people around him. The dreamer is aware of his character, and things he tries to repress in his everyday life come back and rise up to the conscious level via his dreams. The situation must be resolved or at least dealt with, and it bothers the dreamer constantly. However difficult it may be, he must deal with his outbursts of forcefulness, especially if he wants to keep his friends. The dreamer's fear of the consequences of his behavior does not permit him any rest. He is very anxious, and he should see that the aim of the dream is to "shake him up" and make him change his ways.

If the person sees a rhino charging in a dream, it is reasonable to assume that the dreamer has encountered people around him who have decided to oppose him and not give in to him or accept his opinions in a particular matter. This disturbs and bothers him, but the dream serves to hint to the dreamer that he has to forgo his desire to change the opinion of the other side, since the battle has already been lost. This will save him unnecessary disappointment and frustration.

Some people interpret a dream in which the rhino's horn is very prominent as referring to problems in the sexual context, whether the dreamer is a man or a woman. The problems that preoccupy the dreamer could be about his/her sexual potency and prowess. These fears are apparently not groundless, and if they bother the dreamer, he should seek counseling or try to deal with the situation in some other effective manner. He must not ignore the problem, since it will not go away by itself – it will only get worse.

Rhubarb

If a person dreams about rhubarb growing, he can look

A B C D E F G H I J K L M N O P Q R S T U V W X Y Z

forward to enjoyable events. If he dreams that he cooks it, he will quarrel with a friend. If he dreams about eating it, he will feel dissatisfied with his present job.

Rib

A dream that features a rib is a sign of poverty and unhappiness.

Ribbon

If a person dreams that he is wearing a lot of ribbons, he knows that he is acting frivolously and that his conduct is liable to harm many of the people around him – among them the ones that are closest to him. The sorrow that he is liable to cause the ones he loves is great. He must try not to act frivolously, but rather be more responsible for his actions, think well before taking any step that can affect his life and the lives of the people around him, and plan his steps carefully.

A dream that features a ribbon that does not necessarily adorn the dreamer is a warning sign against extravagance. On the other hand, the dream indicates that the dreamer can expect joy and happiness, the wonderful times that he has been waiting for so long.

If the dreamer sees ribbons discarded in the trash, the dream warns of an impending disaster. He should avoid taking unnecessary risks and from undertaking projects he is not sure about.

A dream about ribbons floating on the water is a sign that the dreamer can expect calmness, repose, peace and quiet. Possibly a difficult phase he has been going through is about to come to an end. Alternatively, he may be facing a trip that will bring calmness or result in a drastic change in his life – truly revolutionary – that will engender changes in his habits and in his everyday life in the direction of repose, serenity and a healthier lifestyle.

A dream in which a bride wears ribbons is a warning dream that warns against the groom's intentions. His intentions toward her may not be pure. It is a good idea to display a certain measure of suspicion toward him, and examine and scrutinize his intentions and actions.

Some people also interpret the appearance of ribbons in a dream as a hint that a competition between lovers is liable to lead to a tragedy. If the dreamer is involved in such a competition, he would do well to hold himself back and not get in too deep, for fear that things will unexpectedly end up very badly, in the worst possible way.

Rice

A dream about rice has a positive meaning, and can be interpreted in several ways:

Some interpretations consider a dream about rice to be a prophetic dream that foretells finding an ideal life partner who is compatible with the dreamer in every way. This is how the dreamer's sex life will look as well, according to this interpretation – fulfilling and good. If the dreamer is not happy with his love life at present, the dream foretells that he is facing a drastic change in his situation, and that changes for the better are expected in the realm of relationships and sex.

There is another version according to which a dream about rice implies that the dreamer will get help from an unexpected source; alternatively, a new friendship will

A B C D E F G H I J K L M N O P Q R S T U V W X Y Z

A B C D E F G H I J K L M N O P Q R S T U V W X Y Z

emerge, and it will be there for him in time of need. One way or another, it is an optimistic dream that hints to the dreamer that he is not alone; there will always be help and succor nearby, even if the exact source is unknown to him at the moment.

If a person dreams that rice is thrown over him, the dream hints that he can expect triumphs and success in various areas of his life; luck is pursuing him.

If a dream features a bowl of rice, it implies a change for the better in everything regarding money matters: the dreamer can expect a large win or a large inheritance from a source from which he expected nothing. Moreover, he may come into that sum of money thanks to a good investment or participation in some kind of lottery. A win in a casino can have the same results. Whatever it may be, the dreamer can expect a large additional income and a significant change in his economic status.

If the dreamer sees himself eating rice, the dream implies that the dreamer is facing unnecessary expenses. Before purchasing items, he must think carefully whether he really needs them, and not just spend money on superfluous items. In addition, he must be aware of the fact that if he does not check what he is spending the money on, he may be throwing it down the drain, in which case he will have no one to blame but himself.

Cooking rice in a dream is a hint that the dreamer is about to make a good and profitable deal that will lead to good revenues as well as respect and success on other levels.

In the Italian tradition, a dream about rice is interpreted, for some reason, as a dream that augurs badly, and even foretells death in the family. The origin of this interpretation is unknown, and it is considered to be no more than a popular interpretation.

Riches

If a person dreams about possessing riches, it means that he will go far thanks to his industriousness and hard work.

Riddles

Riddles are a symbol of confusion and discontent. If a person is attempting to solve riddles in a dream, it means that he will undertake a project that will tax his patience and waste his moncy.

Ride

A dream about riding does not augur well: it often predicts illness. If a person dreams about riding slowly, it means that he can expect disappointing outcomes from business dealings. If he dreams about riding fast, it implies prosperity at the risk of danger.

Riding school

A dream that features a riding school warns of a friend's treacherous behavior. The dreamer will manage to neutralize the bad effects, however.

Ring

Wearing a ring is a sign of success in new endeavors. If a person dreams about seeing others with rings, his dream symbolizes increasing wealth and many new friends. If he dreams about a broken ring, it is a sign of conflict, unhappiness in marriage, and breakups. If a young woman dreams about receiving a ring, she need no longer worry about her lover: from now on, she is the only one for him.

Ringing of a clock

The ringing of a clock in a dream hints at positive events. Just as the ringing of a clock wakes us up every morning in order to start the day, so a dream about the ringing of a clock offers a hint of a new beginning. This could well be linked to business matters: more and more opportunities and developments will arise in the dreamer's path, and if he is clever and courageous enough to take matters in hand, his chances of success are very great.

Ringworms

If a person dreams about seeing ringworms on his body, it means that he will soon come down with a mild illness and suffer from aggravating worries. If he sees ringworms on other people in a dream, he will be plagued by demands for charity.

Riot / Tumult

If a person dreams about displays of violence, rage or wild behavior, it means that his conscience is not clear; it would be a good idea to reevaluate his actions carefully. If a person sees riots in a dream, it is a sign of disappointments in business. If he sees a friend killed in a riot, it portends bad luck, illness or death.

Rising

If a person dreams about rising to a high position of some kind, it means that he will become rich thanks to learning and promotion. If he rises into the air, he will enjoy himself tremendously and receive a large windfall. However, he should beware of unwelcome publicity.

Rival

If a person dreams about a rival, it means that he will not be assertive enough and will be overlooked by important people. If a young woman dreams about a rival, it is a warning dream: she must stick with her present lover and not risk making erroneous choices.

If the dreamer is taken in by a rival, it means that he is not paying enough attention to his business. If the dreamer himself is the successful rival, he will have luck in his career and his love life.

River

A dream about a river refers to changes that can be expected in the dreamer's life. If the water is turbulent and dark, there will be difficulties. Sailing on a river means that there is a chance of loss and problems. This could refer to someone close contracting a disease or a deterioration in the situation at work. A dream about a river in which the dreamer is sailing along completely at ease and fishing means that he is yearning for a simpler lifestyle. An overload of the emotional and psychological system is liable to lead to a general breakdown. This is the time to take a vacation and do some soul-searching.

Road

If a person dreams about a dirt road or a bad road, he is liable to find himself in the streets. In other words, the dream refers to a change that sometimes entails a crisis. He may be fired. A dream about a road with a field or flowers blooming on each side of it implies that success in some kind of financial deal can be expected. If a person dreams about traveling along the road in a car with friends, he can expect to move to a new place. A drive along a winding road attests to difficulties in a particular process. The dreamer aspires to a certain goal and although he encounters difficulties, he can expect to be successful.

Roadblock

A dream that features a roadblock foretells a good period in life. The dreamer can expect to be promoted at work and will succeed in accomplishing his objectives.

Roast

If a person eats or sees roast meat in a dream, it signifies unhappiness and infidelity at home.

Robbery / Theft

If a person dreams that he himself is involved in a robbery, it means that he can expect success in the business arena. The change will occur suddenly, and the dreamer will have to take courageous action and know how to pay the price. It is highly probable that the change will occur in the workplace as a result of someone in a high position quitting suddenly. There is also a chance of a change in the dreamer's place of residence. If someone dreams that he himself is the victim of a robbery, he can expect some kind of disappointment.

Robin

This bird, which is common in Western countries, symbolizes the color red in dreams, and implies everything that the color red symbolizes – in the context of a bird. The general meaning of red is love, sex and continuity, and the context of the bird – which symbolizes goodness, peace and brotherhood in the dream – implies that the dreamer's financial situation is about to improve.

The combination of the color red that appears and the context of a bird implies success on the interpersonal level, in the romantic realm and in love. Soon there will be changes in the dreamer's love life. He will soon find a partner and attain the tranquillity he yearns for. In addition, the dream predicts a good and sound financial future that will accompany him along his path, in parallel to positive developments in love.

If a virgin dreams about this kind of red, her dream implies that soon she will lose her virginity, even if she does not have any kind of relationship with a partner at the moment.

If the dreamer is in a steady relationship with a partner, but is not married, the dream implies that their relationship will soon be legalized, and this will bring him happiness as well as wealth later on.

If the dreamer is married, the dream implies fertility and a successful sex life. The physical relations between the dreamer and his partner are good, and they complement each other in a way that makes them comfortable and fertile. It is possible that in the near future, a first or additional child can be expected.

The appearance of a robin in a dream can also hint at an expected reconciliation in the near future between the dreamer and a person who is close to him or particularly loved by him, with whom he quarreled. The dream implies healing the rift and resuming a normal and loving relationship.

Rock

A rock in a dream symbolizes a difficulty or danger. The larger the rock, the greater the difficulty or danger the dreamer will experience. A rock implies the difficulties the dreamer will encounter, and in most cases, these refer to one person who will constitute the major part of the difficulty or danger. The dreamer will have to deal with that person. In order to succeed in this mission, the dreamer must pay attention to the steps he takes along his path, and exercise great caution. If he is sufficiently alert to what is going on around him, he will be able to preempt the evil and succeed in coping with the difficulties presented by the person in question.

Rocket

If a person dreams about a rocket, it is a sign of dissatisfaction with his partner. It also indicates his desire for change or movement in the relationship. If he sees a rocket launch in a dream, it means that the problems will be solved. If he watches a rocket ascending in a dream, it means that he will be promoted, win the person he loves, and enjoy a strong marriage. If a person sees a rocket plummeting to the earth, it predicts a bad marriage. If he dreams that he is flying a rocket, he can surmount his problems.

Rocking-chair

If a person dreams about someone sitting in a rocking-chair – particularly a wife, mother or partner – it is a sign of material and economic stability, as well as personal happiness. A dream that features an empty rocking-chair is a sign that sadness and pain are going to be the dreamer's lot as a result of a separation from a person he loves – possibly by death.

Rogue

If a person dreams that he himself is a rogue, he may become ill, or he may act in a way that causes his friends embarrassment and unhappiness. If a woman dreams that her husband or lover is a rogue, it is a sign that a close friend will hurt her badly.

Rogue's gallery

If a person dreams about being in a rogue's gallery, it means that he will not be held in high regard by his associates. If he sees his own picture in a rogue's gallery in a dream, it means that he will suffer at the hands of an adversary.

Roller-skates

A dream about roller-skates is a warning dream. If the

dreamer sees himself roller-skating in his dream, he must be on the alert and guard himself from a possible accident. The dream does not warn only of an accident that may happen on the physical level – such as a traffic or domestic accident – but also of wrong choices, which constitute the "accidents" of life. The dreamer must be tuned into and alert to his surroundings and to himself, and map out his actions wisely, because any "accident" like that can disrupt the course of his life and have an (adverse) effect on his life path for many years.

Another interpretation of a dream about roller-skates regards the dreamer's status: The dream hints that malicious gossip that is being whispered behind the dreamer's back is liable to cause him to lose his property and his social status. He must be aware of this and do anything he can to get the people around him to turn a deaf ear to the slanderers. Maintaining his good reputation must be his guiding light in whatever he does.

Roman candles

If a person dreams about a Roman candle, it means that he will enjoy a meteoric rise to the pinnacle of success and pleasure. If he discovers that the Roman candle is empty in a dream, it means that he will be disappointed in something he has wanted for a long time.

Roof

A dream about a roof generally means advancement, especially if the dreamer sees himself climbing on a roof.

If the dreamer ascends and climbs onto a roof in his dream, it attests to the fact that he is on the right path and that he is advancing in the desired direction: in the future, he will see his aspirations being fulfilled.

If a person sees himself building a roof in a dream, it means that although he will have to expend a great deal of effort, toil and sweat in order to reach his goal, he will succeed in advancing nicely in life and going far.

Another meaning of building a roof in a dream states that the dreamer associates with undesirable friends, and there is a clear hint here that he must shake them off.

If a person dreams about mending a roof, the dream warns against stinginess and selfishness that will eventually cost the dreamer dearly. He must be generous and not tight-fisted –that is the only way he will succeed. If he behaves differently, there will be obstacles in his path and he will not manage to survive and achieve a state of repose and security.

If a person dreams about falling off a roof, the dream warns of bankruptcy, a decrease in assets, and an embroilment in a mass of lawsuits – an embroilment that will be endless.

Rooks

A dream about rooks means that even though the dreamer has true friends, their aspirations are far more modest than his. As a result, they will never be able to provide him with the level of pleasure and happiness he craves.

Room

A room in a dream always appears in a particular context, and the interpretation depends on how the room looks in the dream:

A dream featuring a room full of people, especially if the people that the dreamer identifies are very close to him, is a sign that the dreamer is about to get into trouble with people who are close to him – tangle or argue with them to the point of losing his basic trust in them.

A room in a dream that looks resplendent, beautiful and especially well furnished is a sign that the dreamer can rely on his friends and relatives to come to his aid in time of need and offer him help. He can depend on them blindly since they will never let him down.

A bathroom in a dream is a sign that the dreamer will enjoy impressive advancement in the field he has chosen, even if others doubted him initially, and even if he himself is not yet at one with what he has done.

A bedroom in a dream:

If a single person has this dream, the dream implies that he will get married sooner than expected. Even if a wedding is not yet in the offing (and even if there is no partner in evidence), the dream implies that he will get married much more quickly than he thought.

If a married person has this dream, the bedroom has mostly sexual connotations and hints at an unsatisfying sex life, at problems concerning sex or at indecent thoughts.

When the dreamer sees himself outside of a closed room in a dream, it implies an inexplicable fear that grips the dreamer without rhyme or reason – at least nothing that is known or clear to the dreamer. The fears can be of different types – claustrophobia, a fear of flying and so on.

Some people interpret a dream like this as a dream that

indicates that the dreamer's partner is not suitable for him or is unwanted. There may be a certain feeling of rejection toward the partner, and the dreamer represses it or is not conscious of it in reality.

If a hotel room appears in a dream, it hints at imminent romantic experiences for the dreamer that are about to be realized.

A dream that features a dining-room indicates that a window of opportunity in the financial realm has opened up to the dreamer. He may now have opportunities to make money from a deal that is at hand. He should make the most of it.

A clean and neat room in a dream is a sign of good luck in the dreamer's life.

A dream that features a dirty, untidy and chaotic room hints at problems awaiting the dreamer, stemming from the laziness or selfishness he displays. If he begins to initiate things, to share with others and to behave generously and politely toward the people around him, things will work out peaceably.

If a person sees an empty room in his dream – only four walls with no furniture, drapes or carpets – the dream implies that the dreamer will lack certain things in his life. This refers to material and physical things, not to spiritual things. From the material point of view, he will not attain what he wants, but this will not prevent him from being happy and joyful with his lot.

If an indigent person dreams about an empty room, the dream indicates that there will not be any change in the his status, at least not in the near future.

A B C D E F G H I J K L M N O P Q **R** S T U V W X Y Z

Rooster / Hen

If a rooster appears in a dream, it predicts that the dreamer can look forward to great wealth and an abundance of good things that will be accompanied by joy and happiness. Having said that, if a rooster or hen appears in a dream along with its chicks, the dreamer is disturbed by some kind of problem and feels anxiety that ruins his mood and makes him feel tense.

The crowing of a rooster in a dream is a sign of the dreamer's inflated self-importance. The dreamer has very high self-esteem, and even though this usually works in his favor, he must take care not to overdo it, since ultimately he is liable to lose the people close to him as a result of inappropriate haughtiness. A certain degree of modesty and humility can be of great help.

Roots

If a person dreams about the roots of trees or plants, it is a sign of bad luck in health and business. If he dreams that he takes roots in the form of a medication, it is a warning of imminent grief and illness.

Rope

A dream about climbing a rope implies slow but steady progress in the business realm. The path to success may be paved with obstacles and problems, but the direction the dreamer has chosen is correct. He must advance along it, planning his steps very cautiously.

If a person sees himself in a dream with a rope wound around him, the dream attests to the fact that the dreamer is embroiled in love matters and takes risks because of love. The dreamer may also be liable to break a promise to a friend.

A dream in which the dreamer sees his hands and feet bound implies that certain people want to embroil him in an unreliable contract that will ultimately cause him complications in his life and will bring down a whole lot of trouble on his head.

If the dreamer sees other people tied up with rope, the dream implies that someone else will break a promise to him.

A dream in which the dreamer sees a hanging noose warns of a criminal lapse and of falling foul of the law. The dreamer must be loyal to himself and not be tempted by casual, one-time thrills that are liable to get him into bad trouble for years to come.

A dream about a rope that is very difficult to unravel attests to numerous problems awaiting the dreamer as well as to hard times from the point of view of both business and work and of his interpersonal relations with the people around him.

If a person sees a torn rope in a dream, he has reached the end of a romantic affair. His relations with his partner are about to end. Having said that, it's not a "fateful" thing: if the relationship is important to him, and he works at it, he may be able to reverse the evil decree and breathe new life into the dying relationship.

Tying up a package in a dream is a hint that the dreamer is a domineering person who loves people to obey him and submit to his authority. His nature is sometimes a stumbling-block to him, and if he tries to change his ways, he will "win" friends. People who shy away from him today will seek him out in the future.

A B C D E F G H I J K L M N O P Q **R** S T U V W X Y Z

A dream in which a person sees himself jumping rope, like children do, means that the dreamer is looking for ways to escape from the routine. His dull everyday life is getting to him, and he feels that he needs to make some urgent changes and take an unusual step that will dispel the boredom and engender enthusiasm and a new blaze of *joie de vivre.*

Rosebush

A dream about a leafy rosebush without buds is a sign of approaching prosperity. A dream about adead rosebush is a bad sign, since it foretells bad luck and illness.

Roses

In most cases, a dream about roses is linked to romantic events in which the dreamer was involved, and which come to the surface in the dream. A dream about roses implies that the dreamer will have nothing but good things in his life, but even more so, it implies that his love life is thriving and satisfying, and his sex life is good and enjoyable. The dream attests to the fact that the dreamer will enjoy a great deal of inner happiness, and will be able to lavish love on his surroundings – especially on his partner.

If a person dreams that he is smelling roses in a dream, it attests to his naivety and to the fact that he is being exploited by others.

If a person sees a sick person smelling roses or holding roses in his hand in a dream, it implies that the (sick) person is in mortal danger.

A dream in which the dreamer sees himself gathering roses indicates that in the near future, the dreamer will receive a proposal of marriage. If the dreamer is not single, the dream hints that he will receive a good offer of some kind regarding work. He may be offered a promotion or another job that will be very attractive to him.

If a person dreams about gathering rosebuds, the dream foretells an increase in the family. This could be his immediate family, but it could also refer to an increase in his extended family as a result of the marriage of one of the family members or the birth of a new baby. Rosebuds on their own in a dream imply that great wealth is in the offing for the dreamer.

A dream about fading or wilting and falling roses is a sign that the dreamer will have to toil very hard in order to achieve the results he yearns to achieve. However, sometimes the dream also indicates that a plot to deceive the dreamer and mislead him is being hatched behind his back.

If a person dreams of given roses to someone (male or female), the dream attests to the fact that he is in modest surroundings that lavish good things and happiness on him.

Rosette

If the dreamer or someone else wears a rosette, it is an indication of superficiality. It may provide initial pleasure, but it will soon be a disappointment.

Rouge

If a person dreams about using rouge, it means that he will cheat someone in order to get something. If he sees other people with rouge on their faces in a dream, it means that he will be the victim of a scam. If he dreams that there

A B C D E F G H I J K L M N O P Q R S T U V W X Y Z

is rouge on his hands or clothes, he will be caught "red-handed" doing something unsavory. If he dreams that the rouge comes off his face, he will be humiliated in front of a rival and will lose his lover.

Rowboat

If a person dreams that he is in a rowboat with other people, he will have a merry and lively social life. If he dreams that the boat overturns, he will experience financial setbacks. If he dreams that he wins a rowing race, he will have luck in love and in business. If he loses the race, however, his rival will win the person he loves.

Rubber

If a person dreams about wearing rubber clothes, it means that he will be honored because of his moral character. If the clothes in the dream are torn or shabby, he should take care, because his reputation is in jeopardy. If he dreams that his limbs are as flexible as rubber, he runs the risk of becoming ill. There is also an implication of dishonesty in his business practices.

Rubbish

If a person dreams about rubbish, it implies that he is mismanaging his business.

Ruby

If a person dreams about a ruby, it is a sign of good luck in love and money. If a woman dreams that she loses a ruby, she should be warned that her lover no longer loves her.

Rudder

If a dream features a rudder, it implies an enjoyable trip abroad and new friends. A dream about a broken rudder is a sign of illness and disillusionment.

Rudeness

If a person dreams that he is rude to someone, the dream concerns his relationship with his partner.

Ruins

If a person dreams about ruins, it is a bad sign: ruined crops, bad health, failed relationships, failure in business. If he dreams about ancient ruins, it hints at a lot of travel. This will be very exciting, but the excitement will be tempered by sadness because of the absence of someone close.

Ruler

A ruler that appears in a dream implies that the dreamer is worried and feels very tense in his everyday life, even though there are no grounds for this in reality. He must stop worrying so much, since it is inhibiting his actions and his ability to advance toward his goals in life.

Another interpretation for the appearance of a ruler in a dream is the dreamer's fierce desire to be objective and unbiased. However, the appearance of the ruler in the dream implies that this is impossible, and not everything can be measured with a ruler, especially not family or professional values. Despite the desire to be rational and unbiased, the issues with which the dreamer deals in life are not the kind that can be "measured," nor are they the kind toward which he can remain impartial. Intervention here is essential.

Rum

A dream about drinking rum is a sign of *nouveau riche*. It also indicates moral coarseness.

Running

If a person dreams about running, it means that he is competing with someone in his vicinity. The dream does not attest to distress or any urgent problem, but the dreamer must carefully check out and identify his friends and his enemies. Only then will he be able to act wisely and take the correct course of action. In any event, he can expect to succeed.

Running away / Fleeing

If a person dreams that he is running away from something, it means that a close friend is plotting against him and joining forces with his enemies. If he sees someone close to him running away in a dream, it means that his family will soon expand.

A dream about an unsuccessful attempt to run away indicates that certain problems have not been solved. If a person dreams that he is running away from danger, it is a warning dream: it warns of inevitable losses. If he dreams that other people are running away from danger, he will be extremely distressed by his friends' troubles. If he sees cattle running in a dream, he is warned to be cautious when making deals or initiating new endeavors.

Rupture

If a person dreams about suffering from physical ruptures, it means that he will become ill or get involved in conflicts. If he dreams that other people are suffering from physical ruptures, he runs the risk of getting involved in a bitter fight.

Rust

If rust appears in a dream about tools or anything else made of metal, it is a sign that the dreamer can expect a disappointment in love. He may be pinning hopes that are too high on a love affair that will not yield positive results. The dream implies that the dreamer should not fall into the trap of empty illusions, and he should be prepared for the pain when the existing or emerging relationship terminates.

In most cases, a dream about rust attests to a lack of purpose in life, to a thin period in which the dreamer is not sufficiently satisfied with what he is doing. He is not at one with himself and does not like what he does for a living. The general atmosphere that prevails in his life is one of missing out big-time. For this reason, the dreamer should view a dream like this as a kind of hint that he should wake up and take steps to change the situation he is in. He must shake himself and try to change the situation so that his life will be fuller and more satisfying.

People who are unemployed and cannot find a job often dream about rust. They feel like idlers who don't deserve anything, and their self-confidence is at a very low ebb. The person who dreams this kind of dream and feels worthless must respond to the job offers he receives, even if he works in these jobs for a short time. The main thing is to get out of the rotten situation he has gotten into. Any kind of work he does for the sake of an income will lift his spirits and restore his self-confidence in his abilities. This will enable him to keep going and continue his search for better jobs.

Rye

If a person dreams about rye, it is a sign of prosperity and a rosy future. If he dreams that cattle go into a field of rye, it is also a sign of wealth.

Rye bread

If a person dreams about seeing or eating rye bread in a dream, it is the symbol of a happy and attractive home.

S

Saddle

The meaning of a saddle in a dream is adventure. The dreamer can expect to set out on an unexpected journey, hike or trip in the near future, during the course of which he will have weird and wonderful adventures that are totally unfamiliar to him. These new experiences will accompany him throughout his life, and will constitute some of his most important and meaningful memories. He can expect to reach distant places that he did not imagine visiting in his wildest dreams, and the events that he experiences on the way will be special and meaningful for the future. He may come across things that will change not only his view of the world, but also his hitherto iron-clad opinions about certain topics. The many changes that are about to occur will cause him to be a far more open and broad-minded person than he is today.

Sadness

If a person dreams that he is in a state of sadness, it attests to the recognition and internalization of a loss. The dreamer may have lost a close family member or some of his property. During the period he or she had to get through, there was not a whole lot of time for self-pity, depression or sadness. In contrast, now, when things are beginning to fall

A B C D E F G H I J K L M N O P Q R **S** T U V W X Y Z

into place, the person is allowing himself to express – even if it is only in dreams – his feelings of loss. The dreamer can expect renewed success if he perseveres with his practical actions toward his personal advancement.

Safe

If the dreamer sees an empty safe or a safe that has been broken into in his dream, it implies the bringing forward of a wedding. A full safe means the postponement of a wedding. If the dreamer himself breaks into a safe, it almost certainly means that a serious relationship that was supposed to be moving in the direction of the altar is liable to land up on the rocks.

Saffron

If a person sees saffron in a dream, it means that his hopes will be completely dashed because bitter enemies are plotting against him. They will sabotage his plans. If a person dreams about eating or drinking saffron-flavored food, it is a sign of family dissent.

Sage

A dream that features the sage plant is usually a prophetic dream that attests to the fact that the dreamer will soon notch up impressive achievements in his workplace. As a result, he will also be held in higher regard, and will advance both in status and in salary.

A dream about sage symbolizes rehabilitation and recovery because of the plant's medicinal qualities, so it is customary to attribute prophecies of a recovery from a serious illness that the dreamer or someone in his family is liable to suffer from to such a dream.

Sail

A sail expresses optimism, especially if it is white: wind, flowing and advancing toward new goals. A sail on a ship or a boat also attests to the dreamer's desire to return to past era, an era in which innocence and romance dominated his life. The dreamer feels that the pace of life is too fast for his liking, and so he is seeking an escape route. All in all, it is an optimistic and positive dream that predicts positive developments.

Sailing

A dream about sailing generally refers to a smooth flow of life, to prosperity and to happiness. The dream also hints that the horizon is wide open to the dreamer, so that he can do whatever he wants with his life. His life is one big party, everything is open in front of him, and he simply has to choose the path he wants to follow. He is not dragging any hassles along with him from the past. He is not a person who suffers from complexes or frustration, so he has every possibility of fulfilling his desires. The dreamer should be daring enough to take risks, since the chance of failure is very low.

Sailor

If a person dreams that he is a sailor boarding a ship that is sailing across the ocean, he can expect many adventures in the near future. Whether he travels to a faraway place or not, he can expect many essential changes in his life. A person like this may be informed by his wife that she wants to leave him. One of the children may decide to leave home earlier than expected. A person who dreams about a line of sailors disembarking from a ship will soon receive a big surprise from abroad. This could take the form of an important guest who will bring gifts or money.

Saint

A dream about a saint is a sign that the dreamer relies on a higher power for aid.

Salad

If a person dreams about eating salad, it is a sign that he will succeed in life. The dreamer is blessed with many talents, he has many abilities, and he succeeds in expressing them in various ways. He is popular with the people around him, and they recognize his talents and show him respect.

If a person dreams about eating a vegetable salad, it is a sign that he is liable to encounter health problems because he does not get enough rest. The pursuit of a career is squeezing the last drop of energy out of him, and he is not taking a break in order to charge his batteries. This will be to his detriment. If he expects glory to follow the recognition of his abilities and talents, he must know how to take a rest every now and again in order to renew his strength.

In contrast, a dream that features a fruit salad attests to the fact that the dreamer can expect the forthcoming period of time to be a good one from the romantic point of view. There is no commitment, but there is flirting, mischief and exciting fun and games. He should watch out for traps in his path, and he should bypass them without falling into them.

Salary

A dream about receiving a salary for a job refers to the dreamer's desire to see the fruits of his labor. He feels that success is dragging its feet, and he is impatient and wants speedy results.

A dream about a delay in the payment of a salary refers to the dreamer's ongoing frustration with everything to do with success in the financial realm. It is possible that even though he is doing his best, he is not successful in achieving a goal he set himself. Moreover, he is dependent on an external element for his success, and this intensifies his frustration and causes him a great deal of tension.

A dream in which the dreamer receives a raise in salary hints that he must be attentive and alert to what is going on around him. He is not aware of the processes that are taking place in his surroundings, and the dream serves as a kind of warning, signaling him that he is well advised to keep his eyes open, since he is missing opportunities and is behaving like an ostrich.

Sales

A person who dreams that he is selling his home or his personal belongings is in some kind of distress. He may want to sell his home because of financial difficulties or because he wants to purchase another, better one. One way or the other, the dream implies that haste is the work of the devil. The dreamer must not rush to make the deal. He must check the contract and the documents concerning the sale

A B C D E F G H I J K L M N O P Q R S T U V W X Y Z

or purchase over and over again. A person who dreams that he participates in a sale, such as an auction, is a person with a high level of self-confidence. The dream hints at successful deals in the near future, accompanied by financial profit.

Salmon

A dream featuring a salmon implies that the dreamer is going through a crisis of struggles. He must overcome obstacles in the near future and muster all of his forces in order to keep going. The salmon symbolizes success in the struggles and the ability to surmount the difficulties and triumph in contests. This is contingent on the dreamer's mobilizing all of his mental and physical strength and capabilities, and displaying the determination and courage to do anything in order to succeed and accomplish his goals. If he displays fierce will power and galvanizes all his wishes in order to achieve the goals he set himself, nothing will stand in his way and he will be able to do anything. If the salmon in the dream is especially large, it is a clear hint that the dreamer will soon enjoy a life of ease and a good time. He can expect material abundance that will also bring mental tranquillity and spiritual repose in its wake.

Salt

This is a positive dream that indicates that the dreamer is about to advance from the social point of view. If someone dreams that other people bring him sacks of salt, he is going to become rich from an especially surprising and successful venture.

The same goes for a person who sells salt, except that the

financial success will entail a great deal of effort on the part of the dreamer.

If a person dreams that he oversalts his food, it indicates that he feels that a lot of money is being wasted needlessly. He may well find that somebody in the workplace is embezzling funds and wasting the company's money. In the domestic realm, a temporary regimen of belt-tightening is in order.

Saltpeter

A dream about saltpeter is a very bad omen, since it portends grief and bereavement.

Salve

A dream about salve indicates that despite adverse conditions, the dreamer will thrive, and his enemies will become his friends.

Samples

If a person dreams about receiving samples of goods, it is a sign that his business in on the upswing. If he dreams that a salesman mislays his samples, it implies that he will have problems in business and love. If a woman dreams that she looks at samples she has received, a range of options will be open to her.

Sand

The main meaning ascribed to sand in a dream is wising up to illusions, but the interpretation differs according to the context in which the sand appears.

A B C D E F G H I J K L M N O P Q R **S** T U V W X Y Z

Sand that appears randomly in a dream indicates that the dreamer is about to come down to earth with a bump after a rude awakening from illusions or from a dream he had cherished for a long time. The shattering of his illusions will be painful and embarrassing, and he will feel very confused. He is going to find himself in a situation in which the earth is about to cave in under him, and he will have to adapt to a reality that will seem bitter and difficult to him. Even though his struggle will not be easy, and he will have to go through a long period of adaptation, he will emerge from it strengthened and smarter, and it will help him cope with changing and unexpected situations in the future.

Sand also implies that the dreamer can expect rows with his family as well as financial losses, embarrassment, and a lack of confidence as a result of insults.

If a dreamer sees sand dunes like the ones in a desert in his dream, he lacks confidence and does not rely on his talents or abilities. He doubts his strength to cope with changing situations and projects this outwardly.

If a person sees himself in quicksand in a dream, it is generally interpreted as something positive that presages good fortune for the dreamer. His status is rising, he will be accorded great respect from the people around him, since they hold his work and his achievements in high regard. If a single person has this dream, it is a prophetic dream that implies that his future marriage partner is very rich – in his own right and because of his rich family.

In contrast, if the dreamer sees someone else trapped in quicksand, the dream does not augur well: it implies that there are people who are waiting for his downfall and serve as a stumbling-block in his path to success. They will do anything to bring him down and make him lose all the glory and honor he has acquired through hard work. Moreover, the dream serves as a kind of warning dream that states that there could be problems in the business/financial realm in the future.

If a person dreams about burning hot sand, the dream implies that he should be proud of his abilities and bolster his self-confidence. The more he believes in himself, the more the people around him will appreciate him.

Sapphire

A dream about a sapphire is a sign of good luck in business and in choosing a partner.

Sardines

If a person dreams about eating sardines, it is a reference to bad things that will happen completely out of the blue. If a young woman dreams that she puts sardines on the table, she will be harassed by somebody's unwelcome attentions.

Sardonyx

If a person dreams about sardonyx, it means that he will improve his miserable surroundings by improving his financial situation. If a woman dreams of sardonyx, she will enjoy increased wealth. If she throws sardonyx away or loses it, it means that she will ignore the chance to improve her lot.

Sash

If a person dreams about wearing a sash, it means that he is trying to get a fickle person to fall in love with him. If a young woman dreams that she purchases a sash, it is a sign of her fidelity and the respect she will earn in the future.

Satan

A dream about Satan heralds better and lovelier days. Contrary to what may be expected, a dream like this augurs well and hints at a period of prosperity and ease for the dreamer. Even if he has to overcome difficult obstacles along his path to success, he will do so, and will eventually reach his objectives.

A dream about Satan is sometimes also interpreted as the dreamer's over-ambitiousness, which is liable to lead him to the edge of the abyss. He is liable to fall victim to a bribe or to other temptations and cause himself serious damage. He must be strong enough to resist the dark urges that threaten to suffocate him and cause his downfall.

Sausage

If a person dreams about making sausage, it is an indication of success in most of his endeavors. If he sees himself eating a sausage in a dream, it is a sign of a modest but attractive home.

Saw

In most cases, a saw appears in men's dreams, and a dream of this kind means something different for a man than it does for a woman.

A man whose dream features a saw is a man with all the characteristic properties of a macho – he likes to use his strong and well-built body to impress, he likes to do "masculine" jobs, and he can usually be depended on blindly, since his word is "a man's word." By nature he is thorough, likes to do things as well as he can and does not make do with the minimum. He behaves in this way with his female partners, too, and when he marries he is faithful, gives a lot of himself, invests in the relationship and loves to have his feelings reciprocated. The dream implies that he can expect a good and pleasant life. He will find the woman who is ideal for him, and if he is already married, the dream predicts a good future, a pleasant and fulfilling life, full of meaning and satisfaction.

If a woman dreams about a saw, the dream indicates that she will soon receive good advice from a friend. She should follow it it, since it will be helpful to her in life. The person who advises her is a good friend who wants things to be good for her and wants her to advance in life.

If a person dreams about a saw that he does not see, but rather only hears the sawing sound in the background, the dream is not positive, and it implies that he will be afflicted by weakness and debility in the near future. These symptoms are liable to cause a deterioration in his state of health as well as a disease that the dreamer will have difficulty shaking off. He must safeguard his mental strength and not let depression or mental pressure control him.

Sawdust

A dream about sawdust is an indication of serious mistakes that will lead to domestic strife and misery.

Scabbard

If a person dreams about a scabbard, it means that he will succeed in resolving a conflict amicably. If he dreams about losing a scabbard, it is a sign of overwhelming problems.

Scaffold

If a person dreams about a scaffold, it means that he will fail to win the heart of the person he loves. If he dreams that he goes up to the scaffold, it means that he has been judged unjustly by his friends for a misdemeanor he never committed. If he dreams that he comes down from the scaffold, it is an indication of his guilt, and he will be duly punished. If he dreams that he falls from the scaffold, he will be caught red-handed while scheming against other people.

Scaffolding

A dream that features scaffolding is a sign that one wrong step taken by the dreamer may cause a lover's quarrel and even lead to a breakup.

Scalding

If a person dreams about being scalded, it means that something he was looking forward to with great anticipation will be marred by a negative event.

Scales

A dream in which the dreamer appears as a person who

is working the scales means that he is an influential person with a highly developed sense of justice and good judgment. He knows how to analyze situations correctly, and, accordingly, it can be assumed that he is successful in life. He may well serve as an adviser for people who come to him to receive his support, encouragement and direction as a result of his public position or because of his personal charisma. Scales symbolize both courts of law and anticipated disputes. It is impossible to know the outcome of a legal process if things reach the point of an actual lawsuit.

Scandal

If a person dreams about being the subject of scandal, it means that he prefers the company of frivolous, immoral people to that of more solid companions. Following this dream, business will stagnate. If a young woman dreams that she discusses a scandal, a man who is not worthy of her will take advantage of her innocence.

Scar

A dream about a scar indicates the dreamer's inability to break away from his past.

Scarcity

A dream about scarcity is a bad sign, since it foretells sadness at home and poor business.

Scarf

If a person dreams about a scarf, it is not a good omen.

If he sees himself wrapped in a scarf, it means that he has a tendency toward depression. If a woman dreams about a scarf that bothers her when she wears it, it means that an intimate secret about her life will soon be disclosed.

Scarlet fever

If a person dreams about scarlet fever, the dream warns of illness or enemies. If he dreams that one of his relatives dies of scarlet fever, he will be brought down by treacherous behavior.

Scepter

If a person dreams about holding a scepter, it means that he will be elected to a weighty, responsible post thanks to his abilities, and he will not let anyone down. If he sees other people holding a scepter, it means that he will always be an employee, rather than self-employed or a boss.

School

In most cases, a dream that features a school that does not have any special significance attests to the dreamer's fear of facing some kind of test. The dream symbolizes the tension and anxiety engendered by his fear of failing, of not succeeding in his chosen path, and of "blowing it."

A dream about a school at almost any age is not good news. However, the meaning of the dream changes according to whether the dreamer is an adult or a youngster.

If a young person – of school age or recently graduated – dreams about school, the dream attests to the fact that the person hates taking responsibility and does not like to

assume any kind of burden. He prefers to do anything else – anything rather than being the one who decides things, takes a stand, supervises to check that things are running as they should and getting done. This does not mean that the dreamer is incapable of carrying out tasks or accomplishing missions. He can be a veritable workhorse and do things extremely well – he just doesn't want to be directly in charge of the tasks he is carrying out.

If the person who dreams about school is an adult whose school years are long behind him, it implies that he is uncomfortable about anything linked to his ability to realize his aspirations. It also hints at confusion and embarrassment when he tries to balance his aspirations against his ability to realize them. He finds himself depressed, frustrated and disappointed. Above all, he experiences a feeling of having missed out big-time. If only he could turn the clock back, he would do things completely differently. But since life does not let us go back and start over, he has to look into himself and find out if the goals he is setting himself are really beyond his capabilities. Perhaps less grandiose aspirations will succeed in restoring his self-confidence, since then he can realize at least some of those goals.

If a dream features a school with a more specific meaning, the dreamer must relate to the dream according to the definition, for instance:

A dancing school means that the dreamer is a person with a lot of *joie de vivre*, which will help him advance in life. His high morale and his ability to imbue any place with a feeling of vitality, joy and merriment and enthuse the people around him, win him many merit points. These will enable him to go far and to conquer several peaks in his life.

If a person dreams about a swimming school, it has one meaning: Be careful of burglars or robbers who are liable to break into your house, invade your privacy and undermine your peace of mind.

If a person dreams about a driving school, it means that he has to be careful of a defective vehicle! This does not necessarily mean that the vehicle belongs to the dreamer. It could be another vehicle that is liable to constitute a danger for him. One way or another, it is a warning dream against possible danger on the roads, and it is advisable to be doubly careful regarding anything that involves driving.

Scissors

If a person dreams about scissors, it is a bad sign: it presages conflicts between husbands and wives and between lovers. Business will not thrive. If a person dreams about having scissors sharpened, the dream refers to work the dreamer despises doing. A dream about broken scissors is a sign of breakups and strife. A dream that features lost scissors implies that the dreamer is trying to wriggle out of doing something he is reluctant to do.

Scorpion

If a dream features a scorpion, it is a warning dream: it warns the dreamer of enemies who want to hurt him. If he does not destroy the scorpion, he will be harmed by the enemies' attack.

Scrapbook

A dream about a scrapbook is a sign that the dreamer will soon meet disagreeable people.

Scratch

If a person dreams about giving another person a scratch, it implies that he has an irascible and critical nature. If he receives a scratch, he can expect to be hurt by the actions of a two-faced, conniving person. If he gets a scratch from a cat, it means that an enemy will steal a good deal to which he has devoted a lot of time.

Scratching

If a person dreams that he is scratched, it implies that there is someone who is seeking to harm him and slander him.

If a person dreams that he scratches someone else, his dream warns him against his critical nature. The dreamer has the ability to put other people on the spot for errors and point out their defects. He must do this delicately rather than bluntly, since people are liable to be badly offended by his conduct. He must tone down his criticism, otherwise he will make enemies needlessly.

If a person dreams that he scratches himself, his dream is prophetic, implying that the dreamer can expect to win in a lottery. This involves a substantial sum of money that will reach him without any effort on his part. The dreamer must plan his moves wisely when it comes to investing the money he has won, because, as the well known saying goes, "easy come, easy go."

Scratching one's head

If a person dreams that he is scratching his head, it means that strangers will flatter him, much to his

annoyance, since he knows they are trying to get something out of him.

Screech owl

If a person dreams about hearing the cries of a screech owl, it is a warning dream: he must brace himself to hear terrible news about the terminal illness or death of a close friend.

Screen

A dream about a screen is a sign that the dreamer suffers from emotional problems.

Screw

If a person dreams about seeing screws, it implies boring tasks and tetchy associates. A dream about screws also warns the dreamer to be thrifty and to pay attention to detail.

Sculptor

If a person dreams about a sculptor, it means that he will get a job that pays less but is of higher status. If a woman dreams that her lover or husband is a sculptor, it means that she will have clout with people in high places.

Scum

A dream about scum indicates that the dreamer will be bitterly disappointed by failures in his social life.

Scythe

If a person dreams about a scythe, it means that he will be unable to concentrate on his business or travel plans because of illness or mishaps. If he sees an old or damaged scythe in his dream, it means that he must prepare himself for business losses or separations from old friends.

Sea

If a person dreams about the sea, it indicates unrealized hopes, mainly in the spiritual realm. If a young woman dreams about skimming over the sea with her lover, she will soon experience conjugal bliss. If the dreamer hears the dull roar of the sea in his dream, it means that it is his lot in life to lead a lonely, loveless life.

Sea foam

If a woman dreams about sea foam, it is a sign of promiscuous behavior. If she dreams about decorating herself with sea foam, it symbolizes her quest for material things rather than spiritual, self-improving ones.

Seagull

In most cases, a seagull in a dream symbolizes the arrival of bad news from far away. The dreamer will soon have to prepare himself to receive news that will sadden him and cause him pain.

If the seagull appears in a dream without a context of water, the news will not necessarily be bad or serious, but will, in any event, come from far away.

A B C D E F G H I J K L M N O P Q R **S** T U V W X Y Z

Seal / Sea lion

If a person dreams about seals, it means that he is an over-achiever, usually unhappy with his present situation, who aspires to bigger and better things.

Seaman

A person who dreams about the sea and sees himself in the role of a seaman is expressing the desire to escape from a situation of restlessness and dissatisfaction. A dream about a gang of seamen expresses a feeling of wretchedness and homesickness. The group of men on a ship way out in the middle of the ocean takes the place of a real family far away somewhere.

If a person dreams about a seaman who arrives from overseas to visit him, he can expect a surprise in the form of a childhood friend who will come and visit him from far away.

A dream about a seaman can indicate the dreamer's suspicions regarding the fidelity of his partner (but this requires more in-depth investigation and the deciphering of other elements of the dream).

Seamstress

If a person sees a seamstress in a dream, it means that he will be prevented from doing something he wants to do because of unexpected events.

Seaport

If a person dreams about going to a seaport, it means that he will have the opportunity to travel and study, but someone will try to prevent him from doing so.

Search

A dream in which the dreamer sees himself searching for an object is a warning dream. It warns of taking hasty, impulsive actions that are liable to bring disaster down on him. He must plan his actions wisely, think twice before making decisions and carrying out tasks, and be alert to anything that could hint that something has gone wrong. The dream warns of haste, which comes from the devil, and hints to the dreamer that he is operating too fast – to the point of not paying attention to important details – and he is liable to pay dearly for this later on. The dreamer must learn to slow his pace down in order to prevent a problem or failure in the future.

If a person dreams that he is searching for a certain person and not for an object, the dream indicates that the dreamer has suffered a personal loss, sometimes an emotional loss, which is very difficult to bring back, and in most cases is not possible at all.

The dream may also indicate fear of losing something in the future. In most cases, people who dream a dream like this are possessive, and their fear of losing something that they own is so great that it bothers them morning and night. A dream about searching for a person reflects this.

Seat

If a person dreams that his seat is taken, it means that he will have no peace from people soliciting his help. If he gives up his seat for a woman, it means that someone is taking advantage of him.

A B C D E F G H I J K L M N O P Q R **S** T U V W X Y Z

Secret order

If a person dreams about any secret order, it is a warning against being selfish and scheming. If he dreams that the leader of the order dies, huge difficulties will eventually be resolved.

Seducer

If a man dreams about seducing a woman, it is a warning dream: it warns him to be on the lookout for people who are dying to frame him. If he dreams about trying to seduce the woman he loves, and she protests angrily, it means that she is pure and blameless. If she consents, it means that he is being exploited for his money. A young woman who dreams about being seduced can easily fall under the influence of unsavory characters.

Seeds

The appearance of seeds in a dream means that a large portion of the dreamer's big (sometimes even grandiose) plans for the future will actually begin to take shape soon and will be completed. Even if these involve wishes that seem exaggerated to the dreamer, an opportunity to make them come true will present itself. (For instance, a person who dreams that he will have his own yacht – a wish that is very unlikely to come true – is about to get his wish because of a friend who offers him a partnership, or because of winning an unexpected sum of money, and so on).

There are other interpretations for the appearance of seeds in a dream. One of them states: "You shall reap what you sow," that is, what you reap will be exactly in proportion to the effort you make. If you toiled and labored, you will reap good fruits, and if you did not bother to make an effort, that's how your "harvest" will look.

Another interpretation of seeds in a dream, especially if they do not appear in any specific context, states that seeds imply an imminent danger that is lying in wait for the dreamer, and he must protect himself from it. He must think carefully about the source of the danger, and prepare himself accordingly.

Seeds (grains)

When a dream features plentiful seeds crowded into a piece of fruit or a vegetable – and this could include kernels of corn on the cob, grains of wheat in the sheaf, sunflower seeds in the flower, and so on – the dream attests to prosperity, blooming, abundance and success in all areas including spiritual abundance, fulfillment and the expression of the dreamer's creativity.

In contrast, if the seeds in the dream are sparse and meager, the meaning is the opposite. The dreamer can expect to go through a phase of great financial difficulties and even poverty. He tends to be extravagant and spend money he does not have. He gets himself into a whirlpool of money loans and debts from which he does not know how to extricate himself. He uses up all of his savings and acts as if there is no tomorrow.

(Many) seeds in a dream on a backdrop of expansive wheat fields attest to a tremendous social and financial achievement on the part of the dreamer, and to the peace of mind and high-level spirituality that accompany him.

A B C D E F G H I J K L M N O P Q R **S** T U V W X Y Z

Selling

If a person dreams about selling his private property, it is a sign that he can expect financial difficulties in the near future. If he dreams about selling butter or fruit, it implies that he will not make very much profit. If he dreams about selling iron, he can rest assured that he will have very little success and unworthy friends.

Sentry

If a person dreams about a sentry, it is a sign of benevolent protectors and a tranquil life.

Separation

If a person dreams about a separation from a person who is very close to him, it means that he will have to adapt to a situation of submission or loss. This does not necessarily refer to a loss of life, but rather to a loss of something that was dear to the dreamer's heart, such as a friendship that ended or dismissal from his workplace. In any case, there is no need to worry, since the dreamer will get back on his feet and will quickly move on.

September

A dream about the month of September predicts good fortune.

Serenade

If a person hears a serenade in a dream, it means that he

will receive good news from faraway friends, and his hopes will be realized. If he is doing the serenading in the dream, he can look forward to wonderful things in life.

Serpents

If a person dreams about serpents, it is an indication of gloomy and depressed feelings and surroundings, and usually precedes disillusionment. If he hears Eve conversing with the serpent in the dream, it means that women will cause him to lose his money and reputation.

If a person dreams about bronze serpents, it predicts destruction and jealousy. If he sees serpents crawling in the grass in his dream, it means that he will be destroyed by treachery and slander. If a young woman sees a serpent in her lap, she risks being humiliated by dangerous rivals.

Servant

If a person dreams that he is surrounded by servants taking care of his every need, he can expect a rosy future. Good news in the financial real is in the offing, as is a successful deal or an unexpected inheritance that will bring him financial ease that he never thought he would attain. This is the time to start remembering all the aspirations that he shelved in the distant past.

If a person dreams that he himself is a servant, it means that he is subject to pressure at home or at work. The dreamer may feel exploited, like a person who listens to and meets the needs of other people but does not get enough in return. The dreamer must examine the situation vis-à-vis those people and express his feelings. A feeling of satisfaction and happiness will only come after he receives

– at least, according to the way he perceives it – the attention he deserves.

Sewage

A dream that features sewage is a warning dream. In most cases, it warns of things that are linked to the mind or to the dreamer's love life and marriage, but not only to those things.

The dream implies a flawed and unhealthy romantic liaison that is liable to embroil the dreamer in a complex relationship. This may end in an unsuccessful marriage. If the dreamer is already in a relationship with a partner but is not yet married, he should examine the nature of the relationship very carefully in order not to make the mistake of which the dream is warning him.

If the dreamer sees objects that have been thrown into the sewage, the dream hints that the problems or troubles that previously plagued him will gradually work out and disappear. Things that bothered the dreamer and gave him no rest are working out as well as can be.

A dream that features sewage also attests to the fact that the dreamer has hidden enemies, and that there are people who want to harm him and make him fail. The more alert he is to these intentions, the better he can avoid a conflict and the possibility of stumbling and falling. If the dreamer owns a private business, he should implement safety measures, since the people who are plotting against him are liable to trip him up in business and cause him a severe economic downfall.

Sex

Sexual and erotic dreams do not necessarily indicate a sexual urge and a desire for intercourse. A man who dreams about sex with another man is caught up in a bad feeling of a loss of faith in his own sex, almost certainly in the workplace. A woman who dreams about sex with another woman is yearning for warmth and closeness that she may not be getting from her present (male) partner. Dreams about sex with unknown partners indicate that the dreamer is tired of his routine and feels that he wants to have other experiences. This could well be a trip abroad. Dreams about masturbation express a feeling of loneliness and an unsatisfied sexual need.

Shadows

If a person dreams about shadows, it indicates that there will be a great improvement in his economic status as well as significant monetary profits.

Shakespeare

If a person dreams about Shakespeare, it means that important events will be clouded by gloom and sadness, and the passion will disappear from love. If he dreams about reading the works of Shakespeare, it is a sign that he will be involved in literary pursuits.

Shaking hands

If a person dreams about shaking hands with people of a lower station in life, it means that he will be accorded love and respect for his benevolent conduct. If, however, he thinks that the hand of one of the other people is dirty, he will discover that friends are in fact enemies. If he dreams about shaking hands with someone who has wronged him, he will quarrel with a close friend.

If a young woman shakes hands with an important leader in a dream, she will win respect and wealth. If she has to stretch upward to shake the leader's hand, she should brace herself for competition and obstacles. However, if she is wearing gloves, she will bypass them.

Shampooing one's hair

Shampooing one's hair in a dream implies that other people are envious of the dreamer and slander him. A dream like this also indicates that secrets will be revealed. The dreamer may have been a party to the exposure of certain secrets, but it is also possible that a secret concerning the dreamer has been revealed publicly, and for this reason he is hounded by gossip. A dream like this hints at a new era in which the dreamer will be less protected and will be subjected to the criticism of the people around him. It will not be easy for him, since he is about to be attacked coldly and aggressively by those around him, and sometimes even by people who are especially close to him.

Shanty

If a person dreams about a shanty, it means that he will leave home in order to improve his state of health. If he sees a shanty in a dream, it is a warning of financial loss.

Shark

A shark appears in a dream as the representative of various subconscious fears. A shark attests to fears, especially of things concerning source of income and investments. The dreamer is afraid that an investment he made will not turn out well. The fear may also stem from the fact that the dreamer does not have the financial resources to return a loan he took, and his fears do not allow him any rest. The shark represents the fear of a feeling of "no way out," since the loss of the investment or the inability to repay the loan will place the dreamer in a desperate situation. The dream characterizes very responsible people who sometimes face a situation in which they have are not in control of everything, as they normally are, and this is the source of their undefined fears.

Shave

If a person dreams that he considers getting a shave, it means that he will have grandiose plans for developing his business, but will be unable to muster the motivation to put them into practice.

Shaving

If a man dreams about being shaved, it means that swindlers will rip him off. If he shaves himself, it implies that he is in charge of his business and household, even though he has a bossy wife. If his face is smooth, he will lead a serene life. If it is rough and craggy, domestic strife is in the offing.

If a person dreams about a blunt razor, it means that he

will give his friends cause to criticize his personal life. If he dreams that his beard is gray, he will not display fairness. If a woman dreams about men shaving, she will pursue crude pleasures. If she dreams about being shaved, it means that she will be so masculine that she will repel men.

Shawl

If a person dreams about a shawl, it means that he is flattered and admired. If he dreams about losing a shawl, the dream predicts sadness and unpleasantness. If a young woman dreams about losing a shawl, she may be abandoned by a handsome man.

Shearing

If a person dreams about shearing lambs, it means that he lacks any kind of human feeling, and deals honestly, but coldly and calculatedly, with others. A dream about shearing sheep portends massive financial gains.

Shears

If a person dreams about shears, it means that he will become irascible and stingy with money. If he sees damaged shears in a dream, it is a warning that the dreamer's peculiar conduct will cause him to lose his friends.

Sheaves

If a person dreams about sheaves, it is a prediction of happy events and prosperity.

Sheep

A sheep in a dream means success despite difficulties. Even if the dreamer has been working hard to accomplish his goal, and even if he has been striving for a long time to attain his heart's desire and still does not see the light at the end of the tunnel, the dream hints that in another step or two... he will accomplish his objective. He must stick to his goal and not give up and quit the long path he has already been following for such a long time, since stubbornness pays off, and he will eventually enjoy the longed-for fruits. In the end, he will not only get these "fruits," but also a great deal of esteem from those around him and from anyone else who witnessed the long path he traveled and his ability to overcome all the obstacles in it.

Sheet Iron

If a person dreams about sheet iron, it means that he is relating seriously to other people's criticism – to his detriment. If he sees himself walking on sheet iron in a dream, it is a sign of disagreeable encounters.

Sheets – See Bed-linen

Shells

If a person dreams about shells, it means that good and positive things are in the offing: happiness, joy and financial and business success. If he sees himself walking among shells and collecting them in his dream, it is an indication of wastefulness. Moreover, the consequences of pleasure will be frustrating memories.

A B C D E F G H I J K L M N O P Q R S T U V W X Y Z

Shelter

If a person dreams about looking for shelter, it means that he is terrified of enemies. If he builds a shelter in a dream, it refers to his desire to escape from them. If he dreams about seeking shelter, it means that he will be caught cheating and will attempt to explain himself.

Shelves

Shelves actually have two meanings, according to the state in which they appear in the dream:

Empty or broken shelves, full of dust or dirt, attest to the fact that the dreamer is about to make a fundamental change in his life – a change in his profession, a separation from his partner, and so on. Chances are that this change will improve his situation.

Shelves that are loaded with goods (of all kinds) in a dream imply that the dreamer is a rigid person who shies away from any adventure and is afraid of any kind of change. It is advisable for the dreamer to become accustomed to the thought that change is an integral part of a normal way of life.

A dream that features shelves full of books, such as in a library, means that the dreamer is about to suffer from a medical problem that will limit his intellectual ability. He should go for a medical checkup.

Shepherd

If a person dreams about a shepherd, it attests to his hidden need to be involved in spiritual matters. If he watches shepherds tending their sheep in a dream, it is a prediction of a good harvest, as well as of happiness and prosperity. A dream about idle shepherds signifies death and illness.

Sheriff

If a person dreams about a sheriff, it implies fear of change. If he is elected sheriff, it means that he will take part in something that will result in neither respect nor gain.

Ship

A dream that features a ship predicts that good news is in the offing. The dreamer is about to receive news from afar that will be like music to his ears. Moreover, the dream attests to the fact that if the dreamer alters his conduct and adopts different, more relaxed and tranquil patterns of behavior, he will find himself on the right path. Obstacles that seemed to be standing in his path will disappear as if they had never existed.

Conversely, if the dreamer sees a shipwreck, it means that bad news is on the way. He must brace himself psychologically for hearing bad tidings, which may even be disastrous for him.

A sailing ship in a dream is a hint that now is the right time to invest in enterprises and take risks in anything to do with financial matters. This venture will prove itself to be correct in the future.

If a person sees a sinking ship in a dream, it means that the dream prophesies a terrible disaster and tragedy. This may be directly linked to the dreamer, but it is also possible that the disaster will strike one of his associates.

If a person sees himself sailing in a ship on calm waters,

and he feels secure in it, the dream implies that he can expect nothing but wealth and happiness. He will have a great deal of joy in his life, in his marriage and in his domestic life.

If a person sees himself sailing on a ship in the middle of the ocean without any dry land on the horizon, the dream predicts that he will never lack any material thing. He will be very successful from the economic point of view, and will be a wealthy man who does not know the meaning of poverty or lack.

A ship that is seen rocking on a stormy sea in a dream is a sign of a loss of money or property. Even if the dreamer does not have many assets, he must be prepared for the fact that he is about to lose the little he has. Having said that, it is only a material loss, and the dreamer can eventually make it up. It is not a loss of another kind. On the contrary – all the other planes of his life will remain stable, except for the brief stretch of time during which his self-confidence will be eroded because of the expected material loss. A vigorous psychological struggle with such a loss will quickly bring the dreamer back to normal and restore his basic feeling of confidence.

If a person sees himself on board ship with children and family members that are not his own, the dream predicts that he will have a happy home and will not lack for anything material.

If a person sees a small sailing ship in a dream, it indicates the existence of some kind of health problem. It is possible that a disease is incubating in the dreamer's body, and it would therefore be a good idea for him to go have a check-up as soon as possible. When that same ship appears with its sails down in a dream, it means that the dreamer can expect good news from an unknown source. His mood is about to change in the wake of the good tidings that are in the offing.

Shirt

If a person dreams about putting on his shirt, he will lose his partner because of his infidelity. If a dream features a torn shirt, it implies bad luck and miserable conditions. A dirty shirt in a dream is a warning of contagious diseases. If a person dreams about losing his shirt, it warns him of humiliation in love or business.

Shirtwaist

If a young woman dreams about a shirtwaist, it means that her lovely behavior will win her esteem. If she dreams that her shirtwaist is torn, she will get into trouble for immoral behavior. If she dreams that she tries on a shirtwaist, she will have a rival for the man she loves. If she gets the shirtwaist to fit her properly in her dream, she will win the man she loves.

Shoemaker

If a person dreams about a shoemaker, it means that he will not be given a promotion. If a woman dreams that her husband or lover is a shoemaker, she will get whatever she wants.

Shoes

If a person dreams that his shoes are dirty and scuffed, it is a sign that he will make enemies because of his critical nature. If he dreams that he has his shoes shined, business will pick up. A dream that features new shoes indicates a change for the better. If shoes pinch in a dream, the dreamer will be the butt of his friends' practical jokes. If a dream features shoes with laces untied, it warns of conflicts, illness and losses. A dream about losing shoes means abandonment and divorce. If a young woman dreams that her shoes are admired while she is wearing them, she should be wary of people she meets, particularly men.

Shooting

A dream about shooting attests to an abnormal situation in a personal relationship. It could stem from a couple's lack of compatibility: if one of them is an egoistic, miserly type, or the economic situation is bad, it is an indication of real hardship that is liable to lead, at least symbolically, to a gunfight.

A dream in which the dreamer is injured by shooting attests to a serious emotional wound. A dream in which other people are involved in a shooting incident attests to a possible betrayal on the part of people whom the dreamer considers to be his close associates. Perhaps it's time to check who his true friends are. If a person dreams that he has gotten stuck somewhere and is suddenly the target of a volley of shots, someone may be spreading malicious rumors about him. He must prepare himself for such a possibility, and it is advisable to listen well and check which of the dreamer's close friends is acting differently than usual.

Shop

A dream about a shop means that the dreamer will be thwarted at every turn by friends who are jealous of his advancement.

Shore – See Beach

Short

If a person dreams that he or one of his friends is short – shorter than in reality – it is a dream that augurs well: The dreamer will make significant and satisfactory progress in all areas of his life, and he will enjoy success.

Shortage / Hunger

Contrary to what one might think, a dream about a shortage predicts particularly good things and indicates a positive about-turn in the dreamer's life.

Shot

If a person dreams that he is dying as a result of being shot, it means that his friends will display unprecedented and sudden animosity toward him. If he dreams that he outwits death and wakes up, he will effect a reconciliation with his friends.

Shotgun

If a person dreams about a shotgun, it portends domestic problems and anxiety caused by employees and children. If he dreams about shooting with both barrels of a double-barreled shotgun, it means that he will have been aggravated to such an extent by the attitude of people in his professional life that he will drop all courtesy and etiquette and vent his anger.

Shoulder

If a person dreams about bare shoulders, it is a sign of positive changes and a new outlook on life. If he sees his own shoulders in a dream, and they look scrawny, he will need other people to amuse and entertain him.

Shovel

If a person dreams about a shovel, it refers to hard but not unpleasant work. A dream that features a damaged or old shovel means that his hopes will not be realized. If he sees himself stoking a fire with a shovel in a dream, it indicates that he can expect good times.

Shower (bathing)

If a person dreams about a shower, it symbolizes the desire for sexuality and love. If he dreams about taking a shower with a partner, it is an indication of a good sex life.

Shower (rain)

If a person dreams about standing in a shower of rain, it means that he will greatly enjoy devising and indulging in hedonistic pleasures.

Shrew (animal)

If a person dreams about a shrew, it means that he will have to attempt to cheer a friend up. The dreamer will no longer be able to cope with daily life.

Shroud

If a dream features shrouds, it portends illness and worry, as well as the malicious scheming of two-faced friends and a decline in business. If a person dreams about seeing shrouded corpses, it is a sign of tremendously bad luck. If the shroud is removed from a corpse in a dream, the dreamer will experience irreconcilable rifts with people close to him.

Sickness

This dream usually foretells sickness. If a person dreams about sickness, it is truly a sign of distress and illness in the family. Strife will also play a part. If he himself is sick, he is warned to take care of himself. If he sees any member of his family looking ill and wan in his dream, it means that a sudden and negative event will occur.

Side

If a person sees only the side of something in a dream, it means that an honest suggestion by the dreamer will be rejected. If his side hurts him in his dream, it means that his patience will be taxed by hassles and anxieties. If he dreams that his side is healthy and strong, he will be lucky in love and business.

A B C D E F G H I J K L M N O P Q R **S** T U V W X Y Z

Siege

If a young woman dreams about being in a siege, she will have to overcome all kinds of obstacles on her way to pleasure, but when she does, it will be worth it.

Sieve

If a person dreams about a sieve, it means that he is about to make a deal that will be to his detriment. If the sieve in the dream is very fine, the dreamer may be able to prevent something that is bad for him from happening. If the sieve in the dream is very coarse, the dreamer will lose assets that he has just acquired.

Sigh

If a person dreams that he sighs because of something bad or troubling, it indicates sudden sadness that will be assuaged by something good. The dream means that the dreamer does not owe other people anything. If he hears other people sigh, he will be upset by the poor conduct of close friends.

Silk

A dream about silk is interpreted differently for men and for women.

When a woman dreams about silk, or about spinning silk, she can expect a happy and fulfilling life. She will be blessed with love and happiness in her marriage. However, even though her life will be serene, there is a fly in the ointment: There are people around her she will have to confront, since they are not trustworthy and are liable to mislead her. They do not always have bad intentions, but the outcome is the same.

In contrast, if a man dreams about silk fabric, he will enjoy tremendous economic success. His business will thrive, and he will see the fruits of his labor. The great effort he expends on business affairs will yield dividends, and from this point of view, he will have a lot of satisfaction. Having said that, his love life does not look particularly promising. Even though chances are that he will find a mate, have children and raise a family, he will always have a feeling of having missed out on something. It is possible that his great investment in work and his pursuit of mammon do not leave him time for other things that are no less important. He will sense his loss over the years.

Silkworm

If a person dreams about a silkworm, it is an indication of an excellent, lucrative, prestigious job. A dream that features dead silkworms or cut cocoons is an indication of bad luck and difficulties.

Silver

A dream about silver is a warning dream: it warns against depending on money to bring happiness. If a person finds silver money in a dream, it implies that he is too critical and hasty in his judgment of others.

Silverware

Silverware indicates great happiness, whether this takes the form of a wedding or some other joyous occasion or the form of an unexpected financial triumph. Silverware on a festive table symbolizes the sense of security the dreamer feels with regard to his family and his social standing. In contrast, silverware that falls off the table hints at the dreamer's profound fears. There may be problems in the workplace. Perhaps his business has run into difficulties and he himself is attempting to solve the problems without sharing the worry and deliberations with anyone else.

Singing

If a person dreams about singing in happy surroundings, he can expect jealousy to mar his joy. If the song in the dream is sad, it means that there will be obstacles and problems in business. If he hears singing, it is a sign of exuberance and merry friends, and also indicates news from friends far away. If the dream features bawdy songs, it implies wastefulness.

Single

If a married person dreams of being single, it is a sign that his marriage will not be happy.

Sister – See Brother

Skating

Skating in a dream has two principal meanings, but additional meanings are attributed to special forms of skating such as ice-skating or roller-skating.

One way in which a dream about skating can be interpreted is as a warning dream! The dream warns that displays of flattery, obsequiousness or ingratiation are liable to be interpreted incorrectly, and nothing good will come of them.

Another way in which a dream about skating can be interpreted as a warning dream states that there is a chance that the dreamer's relations with the person closest to him, whom he loves dearly, may deteriorate. That person may interpret the fact that the dreamer does not pay attention to a particular thing as almost a betrayal. The dreamer must be very aware of the ways in which he expresses himself in order to avoid regrettable misunderstandings.

Roller-skating in a dream constitutes a warning against hasty and irresponsible decisions concerning significant issues.

Skating on snow or on ice implies that the dreamer can expect happy days. He is entering a good phase during which he will meet and enjoy the company of good people who give him the credit he deserves.

Skeleton

A skeleton in a dream implies that the dreamer can overcome the problems in his path and will soon succeed in solving them very effectively. He will be less stressed out and more serene and calm. His forbearance will be restored and he will be the patient person he was before.

If a person sees himself chased by a skeleton in a dream, he must relate to the dream as a warning: it implies that he is wallowing in complacency and is not sufficiently alert to what's going on around him. He is therefore liable to miss opportunities and not to notice important events occurring around him or people close to him who need his attention.

A situation lie this is liable to cause complications and problems, so it encourages the dreamer to pull himself together and start behaving differently. This situation is bad both for him and for the people around him.

If a person dreams about a skeleton he recognizes, it is something of a hint that a trauma that causes severe psychological damage is liable to be the dreamer's lot. He must be aware of this and prepare himself for it psychologically.

If a dream features a rival's skeleton, it is invoking the dreamer's guilt feelings regarding a regrettable accident in which he was involved. Even if in fact nobody blames him for causing it, deep down he feels guilty and knows that he had the power to prevent it, but did not do so. Frustration is haunting him and gives him no rest. Psychological treatment can be helpful in such a situation.

Skin

In most cases, a dream about skins implies that the dreamer's prestige, satisfaction and influence are in jeopardy.

If a person dreams about his own skin, the dream implies that he is a physical and material person and that those are the things that predominate in his life. He is not interested in spiritual things. He is a very earthy person who measures his and other people's achievements according to their material value.

If the dream features skin that is full of freckles, it prophesies that the anger that is simmering inside the dreamer is liable to cause serious problems within the family. He must tone down his anger and wrath in order to avoid causing problems that will have a major effect on the people around him.

If a person dreams about particularly smooth facial skin, he can expect to go through a period of time that is filled with pampering and pleasures. Since he is a full-blooded hedonist, the dreamer ensures that he is taken care of. He is about to enter a phase that is full of satisfaction, during which he will derive pleasure from the simple things in life such as good food, repose, the pleasures of the flesh and so on.

A dream that features a pock-marked skin implies that the dreamer is supposed to receive a large amount of cash from a spurious deal. The dreamer is not completely at one with the sum of money that has come into his possession because he knows where it comes from, and he is afraid to keep it for fear that his disgrace will become public knowledge.

Skull

A dream about a skull is a warning dream. It hints that the dreamer must examine his actions very well before taking any step, since he is liable to fall into a trap. Moreover, a dream like this attests to problems in every aspect of family matters; the dreamer tends to get involved in family intrigues and disputes from which he does not know how to extricate himself. He must refrain from getting involved in unnecessary family arguments or conflicts as much as possible, since the end is liable to be bad, unpleasant and difficult to resolve.

If the skull in the dream is lying in a field, the dreamer can expect disputes with the people around him about almost anything he can think of. He must show restraint and not get himself into situations from which he will have a hard time extricating himself later on. He must make a special effort to hold his tongue so that he does not say things he will regret and will not be able to take back.

If a person sees his own skull in a dream, it is a sign that he is a slave to his passions. He is so enslaved to his lusts that he often fails to control them and finds himself in truly embarrassing situations. He often suffers from remorse and contrition for things he did or for "conquests" that did not end particularly well.

Sky

A dream about the sky is always a welcome dream: it attests to the fact that the dreamer can look forward to good times. Even if the situation around him is difficult, it will be easy for the dreamer personally, and he will succeed in accomplishing his aims relatively easily.

If the sky in the dream looks blue, the dreamer can expect to enjoy especially good luck, and will soon experience spiritual elation and inner illumination, an experience that only a chosen few are privileged to undergo.

A dream about a clear sky predicts a romantic liaison that will begin in the near future. If the dreamer is married, it is a warning dream: ties with a person of the opposite sex who is not his partner could take a romantic turn and he is liable to find himself swept away in a sensual whirlpool that will lead him to a painful betrayal of his partner.

A cloudy sky in a dream is a sign of a lack of luck.

A red sky in a dream is a sign of receiving a great deal

of property – possibly by means of an inheritance. There could also be a big win in a game of chance. The dreamer is likely to become wealthy overnight.

A golden sunset sky appears in a dream when the dreamer feels threatened. The feeling is extremely powerful and the dreamer knows deep down inside who is causing this fear.

A dream about rising to the sky – It sometimes happens that the dreamer sees himself rising up to the sky or leaving his physical body and rising up to the sky. This dream attests to the fact that the dreamer will earn great honor and will enjoy prosperity and growth in the economic, physical and spiritual realms.

A dream in which the dreamer sees the color of the sky as flaming red is a sign that he can expect to live in great loneliness. Whether by choice or as a result of constraints, he will find himself living in solitude that will sometimes be a mercy for him, but at other times will weigh on him and cause him a feeling of desperation.

If a person sees stars falling from the sky in a dream, it implies that he will have difficulty bringing children into the world. The dream does not predict that the person will be childless, heaven forbid, but warns of the difficulties he will encounter.

If the sky looks dark in a dream, it predicts that the dreamer will find a sum of money by chance. He will come across a sum of money, and even if he wants to return it to its rightful owner, he will not succeed in doing so, and he will ultimately get to keep it.

A sky that lacks the light of the sun in a dream, that is, it is dark and shadowy, implies that the dreamer is liable to contract some kind of disease and that he must look after himself and take care. If he looks after himself properly, he will be able to avoid the disease.

If a person sees himself in the sky in a dream, it predicts immediate marriage, or tying a tight romantic knot for the long term. Even if the dreamer is not yet in a serious relationship, the dream predicts that soon he will find himself in such a relationship. The chances of the relationship leading to marriage are great.

Slander

If a person dreams that he is the victim of slander, it means that he is exploiting people's ignorance in order to pull the wool over their eyes. If he himself slanders someone in his dream, his egoism will cause him to lose friends.

Slaughterhouse

A dream about a slaughterhouse indicates that the dreamer will be accused of embezzlement. Moreover, his wife or lover will fear rather than love him.

Sleep

A dream about sleep is interpreted in different ways, according to the context:

A dream in which the dreamer sees himself sleeping attests to troubles and problems. It is a warning dream that serves to warn the dreamer and hint that he must pay careful attention to the steps he takes and not do anything hasty, otherwise things will end badly.

Some people interpret a dream about sleeping as a

warning against a sense of false security, a pretence that everything is successful and wonderful when in fact it's nothing of the kind. Such a pretence is liable to cost the dreamer dearly.

If a person sees himself getting ready to sleep, he can expect to receive unexpected good news from somewhere.

If a person sees himself sleeping beside a little child in a dream, it is a sign that he is yearning for an old love that may come back unexpectedly when he least expects it.

If a person sees himself sleeping with someone of the same sex, his dream implies that he is liable to get into embarrassing situations that will be difficult for him to get out of. Explanations will not help, and he is liable to suffer from a stigma that will remain all his life.

If a person dreams that he is sleeping with his mother, the dream indicates a powerful longing to adopt a baby. The maternal or paternal desire of the dreamer comes to the fore fiercely in a dream like this.

If a man dreams about sleeping naked, he can expect great happiness.

If a woman dreams about sleeping naked, it is a sign that she is having thoughts of sexual infidelity. She is not faithful to her husband or partner, and so she is not faithful to herself.

Sleigh

If a person dreams about a sleigh, it is indicative of failure in love and a quarrel with a friend. If he sees himself riding in a sleigh in a dream, it is a sign of injudicious meetings. If a young woman dreams that she is in a sleigh, it means that she will meet with disapproval regarding her choice of a partner.

A B C D E F G H I J K L M N O P Q R **S** T U V W X Y Z

Sliding

A dream about sliding, it is a warning dream: it warns the dreamer of a decline in business and infidelity in love. If he sees himself sliding down a grassy slope in a dream, it means that he will be ruined as a result of flattery and false promises.

Slighting

If a person dreams that he slights someone, he will not find repose, and his nature will become cantankerous and obnoxious. If he dreamer is slighted, his complaints will be justified.

Slippers

If a person dreams about slippers, it means that he is about to become embroiled in some plot or negative association – possibly with a married person. This will probably lead to problems and scandal. If he dreams that people admire his slippers, he will become involved in a love affair that will bring him nothing but humiliation.

Slot machine

If a person dreams about a slot machine, it is a prediction of good luck and wealth. If he plays a slot machine, he will soon have financial problems that he will not be able to settle.

Smallpox

If a person dreams about seeing people with smallpox, it

warns him that he is liable to contract a sudden, terrible and possibly contagious illness. In addition, his aspirations will not come to anything.

Smoke

Smoke in a dream is usually interpreted as the dreamer's feelings of regret. Deep down, the dreamer regrets something and is not at one with the path he has chosen. The dream is an indication of his deep regret about the way he opted to do things.

A dream about black smoke also attests to family problems that are liable to crop up. The relations between the members of the immediate and extended family are liable to be destroyed.

A dream about smoke can predict disputes and differences of opinion between the dreamer and the people around him – either in the workplace or among friends.

If a dream features smoke rising from a chimney, it is a sign that the veracity of news that has reached the dreamer has not been checked out. Before he believes every rumor that he hears, he should check it out carefully. It would not be surprising if it is a lot of nonsense.

Conversely, if a person dreams about white smoke drifting out of a cigarette, he can expect to go through a romance-filled period and everything it involves – moonlight serenades, strolls along the beach at sunset, and all the other clichés – but it will bring him a great deal of joy and happiness.

Smoking

Smoking in a dream indicates several things. First of all,

the dreamer is in an unclear situation, just like smoke obscures the eyes of people who are in a closed room. He does not see things in a clear light. He should not make decisions when he is in a state like this, because they would be doomed to failure. Group smoking also attests to the dreamer's desire to belong. However, here too the price he pays is heavy, and he should weigh up whether the whole business is worthwhile or whether he will come out the loser.

Snail

A dream that features a snail implies that in the near future, the dreamer will receive good news that will bring about a significant change in his life. The change will essentially be positive in everything to do with family matters. The dream may hint that the dreamer can expect a significantly higher standard of living in the future. While the good news might concern a promotion at work that would allow the dreamer to achieve a new status and earn a more substantial salary, it could also be connected to an addition to the family, to the success of one of the family members in a particular field (success in one of the children's exams, for instance), or the achievement of some other goal that was important to one of the members of the household and that has a direct effect on all of the family members.

The news will not be any old everyday good news that the dreamer is accustomed to receiving every now and then, but rather special and unusual news that makes him extraordinarily happy, and causes him great excitement to the point of tears of joy. A great torrent of happiness will flood the dreamer, and he will feel that he cannot contain all of the joy that has "landed" on him.

Snake

The appearance of a snake in a dream is usually not a positive sign for the dreamer. The snake implies that people in the dreamer's vicinity are conspiring against him. It indicates that the dreamer succumbs to urges and temptations that are liable to bring him to the verge of destruction. It implies that the devil is on the dreamer's doorstep and is threatening to burst in.

A snakebite in a dream is a sign that the dreamer is surrounded by denial and acts of fraud by one of the people close to him, in particular one of his acquaintances or close friends. This person is pretending to be one of the dreamer's good friends, but his friendship is false, and he is not a person whom the dreamer can trust.

If the dreamer succeeds in killing or stamping on a snake in his dream, the dream implies that the dreamer considers any way that will accomplish the goal facing him as legitimate, even if he has to trample on other people or use his elbows in the most brutal manner possible. On the way, the dreamer is liable to lose some of his good friends, but it seems that in this case, the end justifies the means.

Seeing more than one snake in a dream – several at one time – means that the dreamer needs (or thinks that he needs) mental therapy in the form of sessions with a psychologist or a psychiatrist. The dreamer feels that he is mental unbalanced and unstable, so the dream serves as a hint that his mind is calling for help.

A dream that features a snake in one of the rooms of the

dreamer's home or in the home of someone close to him is a prophetic dream that indicates that something bad is about to happen in that home.

If a snake is standing on its tail in a dream or is twisting upward in the manner of the snakes that dance to the sound of a flute, it is a sign that the dreamer will get into a situation in which he will have to stand trial. People's hatred and jealousy will accompany him during the difficult time ahead of him.

A dream in which the dreamer sees a snake suffocating him and winding itself around him attests to the dreamer's negative thoughts and to the planning of illicit acts in order to obtain something, usually money. The dreamer insists on planning moves that constitute some kind of infringement of the law, and his money will reach him in illegitimate ways.

Another version: A viper in a dream is the intensification of all the evil the snake represents.

In general, a dream about a snake is not a particularly good dream. There could be some kind of link to the personal realm, especially if there is some kind of sexual temptation. For instance, a man who dreams about his secretary turning into a snake can express his dissatisfaction with her and his suspicion of her in this way, whether he is sexually attracted to her or not. Generally, dreams that feature snakes do not indicate heightened sexual desires, but rather events that occur under the dreamer's nose and are usually not to his advantage. He is well advised to take care during the forthcoming period of time – even with someone he considers close.

Sneeze

If a person dreams that he sneezes, it means that unexpected news will cause him to change his plans. If other people sneeze in his dream, it is a prediction of tedious social engagements.

Snout

A dream about a snout signals dangerous times for the dreamer. He is plagued by vicissitudes and hounded by enemies.

Snow

In most cases, a dream about snow indicates the dreamer's personal feeling.

If a dream features dirty snow rather than the pristine white snow we might expect, it implies that the dreamer is about to be humiliated in a certain situation and lose his self-respect.

If a dream features melting snow, it is a sign of bad luck for the dreamer. He must wait for the storm to pass, since he is unable to alter this bad luck.

If a dream features white snow, it attests to the prosperity and happiness that are in store for the dreamer. He will succeed in attaining his wishes very easily and in accomplishing his goals without any difficulty, until he reaches a state of rest and security and can enjoy life.

A dream about cleaning up snow from the entrance to the house is a sign of the dreamer's fatigue – both physical and mental. This is a warning dream that serves to rouse the dreamer to action and hint to him that if he persists in his

A B C D E F G H I J K L M N O P Q R **S** T U V W X Y Z

way of life, he is liable to become completely debilitated and take to his bed. He must slow down, rest, go on vacation or take time off in order to recharge his batteries and overcome the crisis he is going through. If the snow is cleaned up easily and quickly, the dreamer will soon overcome the difficulties and obstacles in his path.

If snow falls heavily during a storm in a dream, it implies that the dreamer can expect a tremendous disappointment from something in his life. While he may be disappointed by the failure of a certain project, it could be a more bitter disappointment at the hands of a person close to him. The dreamer should prepare himself psychologically so that he is not taken by surprise.

If a person dreams that he slips on a snowy surface, it is a sign that something the dreamer wants to achieve is slipping away from him, and he is missing opportunities. For a moment it seems to him that he will succeed in attaining what he wants, and a moment later he realizes, to his great disappointment, that it has slipped away from him without his noticing. This pattern repeats itself, and for that reason it is advisable for the dreamer to try and find out where he went wrong and what he is not doing properly, so that he can mend his ways and prevent the phenomenon from repeating itself.

A dream in which the dreamer sees himself skiing on the snow is a sign that the dreamer is successful in overcoming all the obstacles in his path. He has the ability to overcome difficulties and problems, and sometimes he himself is surprised at his ability to do so. He is a strong person who does not give in or give up, and that is why he succeeds in getting what he wants and overcoming anything in his path.

Snuff

If a person dreams about snuff, it means that his enemies are turning his friends against him. If a woman dreams that she uses snuff, it refers to a situation that will lead to her quarreling with a good friend.

Soap

If a person dreams about soap, it means that he will have fun doing unusual things with his friends. If a woman dreams about making soap, she will have a comfortable life.

Socialist

If a person dreams about a socialist, his friends will no longer like him. He will channel his energy into imaginary tasks rather than into the business at hand.

Soda fountain

If a person dreams about being at a soda fountain, it means that he will finally obtain good things after countless frustrations. If he dreams that he treats others to sodas, it means that he will ultimately be successful in his endeavors, however unlikely that may seem at the moment.

Sold

If a person dreams that he has sold something, he can expect trouble as a result of unsuccessful deals.

A B C D E F G H I J K L M N O P Q R **S** T U V W X Y Z

Soldier

There are different interpretations for a dream that features a soldier or several soldiers. If the soldier is not a relative or an important figure in the dreamer's life, but rather an arbitrary figure, it is a sign that the dreamer is soon liable to find himself at the center of a battleground or at the heart of a dispute or row. Even if he did not intend it, he is liable to get embroiled in it against his will.

A dream about a soldier or soldiers also hints that soon there will be a rise in rank. This could be an improvement in the dreamer's status in the workplace, but it could also be reflected in a rise in other areas of life, such as an improvement in the dreamer's residence, in his living conditions, and so on.

If a wounded soldier is seen in a dream, the dream implies that the dreamer can expect monetary losses. In most cases, the losses will come from investments in shares or stocks.

A dream in which a soldier is fighting is a hint of missing one's family or a family member who is out of sight but not out of mind.

If a woman dreams about a soldier, it is a sign that she must avoid taking unnecessary risks. The dreamer has an inclination for adventurous behavior that is liable to end badly. She must think well before each important step she plans to take.

Somnambulist

A dream that features a somnambulist means that the dreamer may agree to a plan in all innocence, which is later liable to cause him worry and bad luck.

Son / Daughter

A dream about a son or a daughter hints at the nature of the dreamer's relationship with the son or daughter that appears in the dream.

If the feeling in the dream is of loyalty, that is, the son or the daughter of the dreamer is faithful to him and his way, respects him and makes him proud, the dream indicates that the dreamer considers the way in which he is perceived by others to be very important. It is very important for him to be accepted and for him and his actions be held in high esteem. His expectations of being granted his due respect are high. He cannot resign himself to an attitude of contempt, to his instructions being disobeyed, or to cases in which he is silenced.

If the son or daughter appears lost or ill in a dream, it is a sign that the dreamer indeed is afraid of a certain anticipated loss. The dream constitutes a kind of warning against a state of a lack of control or embarrassment that will result from the undermining of his self-confidence. The dreamer feels as if the strong foundations on which he has constructed his life are gradually crumbling. The dream warns of an inability to organize and stabilize things in their place once more.

Song / Singing

A dream in which the dream hears another person singing loudly and clearly attests to the fact that the dreamer can expect to go through a difficult phase from the point of view of accomplishing the goals he set for himself. He is liable to encounter obstacles and problems that will make things difficult for him. In spite of that, if he sticks to his goal and is patient and forbearing, he will overcome all the obstacles and attain tranquillity.

If a person dreams about hearing a song at a performance of a singer, it is a hint that some kind of health problem is liable to crop up in his family. In all likelihood, someone will become ill, but the disease will be curable. Having said that, the dreamer must preserve his strength for taking care of the sick family member, since this task will deplete him of both his physical and mental strength.

If a person dreams that he hears a song sung by a particularly bad singer, and the song grates on his ears, he can expect to suffer disappointments in life and may get into conflicts with people around him unintentionally. Such mistakes are liable to get him into serious difficulties regarding interpersonal relations with the people close to him, and he must take care to avoid them.

If a person hears birds singing in a dream, it implies that the dreamer can expect to enjoy happiness, joy, love and an easy life.

A dream that features particularly sweet and beautiful singing, which is pleasant to the dreamer's ears, is a sign that good news is in the offing. This is a prophetic dream according to which bad things that befell the dreamer will change for the better. A new and lovely phase is on the threshold.

If a person dreams about a representative song (such as an anthem, a football song or a school or work song), it is a sign that the dreamer's love life will be successful. Everything will go smoothly, without glitches or problems.

If a person dreams about a song that is considered a hit and is played frequently over the airwaves, it is a sign that he will be accorded a respectful welcome at every function.

People will hold him in high esteem because of his actions and his personality, and he will be shown a great deal of affection.

Soot

If a person sees soot in a dream, it is a sign of bad luck in business and predicts quarrels between lovers.

Soothsayer

A person who dreams that he is going to a soothsayer is undoubtedly in some kind of distress. He may be worrying needlessly about the fate of one of the members of his family or about a relationship at home or at work. If a person dreams that he is going to a soothsayer and hears good news, it means that his situation is relatively "good." A person who dreams that he receives "bad news" during the course of such an encounter must refrain from consulting mystics who are involved in predicting the future. The dream serves as a real warning about this. A visit of this kind will engender confusion and deep emotional depression. It would be preferable for him to wait patiently for developments.

Sorcerer

A dream about a sorcerer implies that the dreamer's aspirations will not be realized, and will undergo a transformation.

Sores

If a person dreams about seeing sores, he will suffer

A B C D E F G H I J K L M N O P Q R S T U V W X Y Z

mental anguish and a feeling of loss because of a disease. If he dreams about putting a dressing on a sore, it means that he will forgo his own pleasure for the good of others.

Soul

If a person sees his soul leaving his body in a dream, it means that he is about to indulge in futile, time-wasting pursuits that will erode his moral fiber and make him materialistic and miserly. If he sees another person's soul inside him, it means that an individual who is as yet unknown to him will come into his life and help him. If a person dreams about discussing the immortality of the soul, it means that he will have the opportunity to expand his knowledge and enjoy erudite conversations with intelligent people.

Soup

If a person dreams about soup, it predicts good news and nice things. If he sees other people eating soup, there is every chance that he will get married. If a young woman dreams about making soup, she will marry a rich man and will not have to deal with the humdrum details of housekeeping.

Sovereign

A dream about a sovereign portends an improvement in the dreamer's financial situation as well as in his social life.

Sowing

If a farmer dreams that he sows seed in freshly plowed

earth, he can expect a good harvest. If a person dreams about sowing lettuce, it means that he will be responsible for his own illness or death at a young age.

Space

If a person dreams about traveling through outer space, he will soon be liberated from a suffocating situation and will revel in the exhilaration of self-sufficiency and freedom.

Spade

If a person dreams about a spade, it implies the nuisance jobs and annoying tasks that the dreamer has to perform.

Sparrow

If a person dreams about sparrows, it means that he is enveloped in love and happiness. This means that he will have the forbearance and sympathy to deal with other people's misfortunes. If the sparrows in the dream are injured or dead, unhappiness or grief might ensue.

Specters – See Spirits

Speech

A dream about a speech hints at good news that will reach the dreamer in the near future. If the dreamer himself is giving a speech in a place where there are many people listening to him, he can expect recognition of his status. It may well concern recognition at work or socially. If the dreamer finds himself in a situation in which he is listening to someone else's speech, it implies that he will embark on studies or some kind of course. The studies and the encounter with new people will open up important and successful opportunities and events, probably in the business field.

Spell

Someone of the opposite sex to the dreamer is liable to cause embarrassment. The dreamer may also be afraid that the personal relationship he is in at the moment lacks sincerity. His partner is liable to take manipulative actions in order to get what he wants. The dreamer is not completely sure of the other party's credibility. He must check whether these feelings are based on facts or if they are the result of vicious gossip.

Spice

If a person dreams about spice, it means that he is liable to destroy his reputation as a result of his hedonistic habits. If a young woman dreams that she smells or eats spice, she will be taken in by a swindler.

Spider

Several meanings are ascribed to a spider in a dream. In most cases, the spider symbolizes the woman in the European culture, perhaps because the webs it spins are interpreted as traps from which there is no way out. This parallels the cunning of the woman's brain; she is clever enough to catch her man like a spider catches its prey. Thus, in most cases, the appearance of a spider in a dream is linked to a woman's domination over the dreamer's life – whether the dreamer is a man or a woman. The dreamer is controlled by the dominant female figure in his life. This could be the mother figure, the wife figure, the boss figure at work, the sister figure, and so on.

If the spider itself does not feature in the dream, but rather only its web, the dream implies that the dreamer's thoughts are occupied by marginal things, and that he must concentrate on useful things that will shift his thoughts from the chaff to the wheat. It would be a good idea for him to focus his full attention on his work and concentrate on it. In this way, he will prevent himself from being preoccupied with idle thoughts, and he will also derive much more benefit from his work. Busying himself with work will make him forget things that should not be preoccupying him, and in this way, some of his problems will be solved.

If a spider is seen hanging from its web or from something else in a dream, the dream refers to the fact that someone is stalking the dreamer and waiting for his downfall. In a moment of weakness, when the dreamer stumbles or displays signs of uncertainty, that enemy will find the way to attack him.

If the dreamer sees himself killing a spider in a dream, the dream implies that his problems have only begun, and that the problems he has been experiencing will become much worse. He must find a way to extricate himself from the situation into which he has gotten himself, otherwise it will be too late.

Spiderwebs

In most cases, spiderwebs in a dream attest to the dreamer's embroilment in a romantic affair. The dreamer has gotten into a problematic relationship from which it will be very difficult for him to extricate himself when he wants to do so. The dreamer is a sensitive person, so he tends to get involved in problematic relationships from which it is very difficult to get out.

If a person dreams about being surrounded by spiderwebs, as if he were flying in the air and was trapped in them, the dream implies that the dreamer is very daring, and by means of his inner strengths will be able to overcome any obstacle in his path and extricate himself from any difficulty or problem.

If a person dreams about spiderwebs in a dark place, so that the spiderwebs are not seen clearly in the dream, the dream predicts a good era that will bring joy and happiness. The dreamer will see himself as a fortunate person who has everything good going for him. Even if outwardly it does not look as if there has been any change in the dreamer's life, his inner feeling will be one of wholeness and tranquillity because he has attained everything he wanted in life. He will feel extraordinarily content, and will ultimately view himself as a happy person who has reached a state of rest and security.

Spinning

If a person dreams about spinning, he will undertake a project to which he is perfectly suited in every way.

Spinning top

A dream about a spinning top means that the dreamer will be bothered by minor hassles.

Spirits

If a person dreams about seeing spirits or hearing them knock at the door, it is a warning dream: it warns him of sudden troubles. If the spirits in the dream are wearing white, it means that the health of one of the dreamer's good friends is in jeopardy. If they are wearing black in the dream, deceit and infidelity will be the dreamer's lot.

If a person hears a spirit speak in a dream, it is a warning to listen to advice in order to prevent negative things from happening. If he dreams that the spirits hide behind the curtains, he is warned not to vent his emotions in order to avoid behaving foolishly. If he sees his friend's spirit gliding in the house in a dream, it means that he will suffer from disillusionment and a lack of confidence.

Spitting

If a person dreams about spitting, it means that enterprises that initially looked pretty good will end very badly. If he dreams that someone spits on him, quarrels and breakups are in the offing.

Spleen

If a person dreams about a spleen, it portends an argument with someone who will cause the dreamer damage.

A
B
C
D
E
F
G
H
I
J
K
L
M
N
O
P
Q
R
S
T
U
V
W
X
Y
Z

Splendor

If a person dreams about living in splendor, it means that he will rise to a much higher status in life. If he dreams that other people live in splendor, he will be pleased to know that his friends are very concerned with how he feels.

Splinter

If a person dreams that he is suffering from the discomfort of splinters, it means that his family or competitors will cause him a lot of trouble. If he gets a splinter in his foot while paying a visit, it portends an especially awful visit as well as losses in business because of inattention.

Sponge

If a person dreams about a sponge, he can be sure that he is being swindled. If he uses a sponge to clean a blackboard in a dream, someone else's stupidity will make him suffer.

Spools of thread

If a person dreams about spools of thread, it is an indication of unhappy feelings due to his inability to cope with the tedious tasks at hand. A dream that features empty spools symbolizes disillusionment.

Spoon / Teaspoon

Spoons and teaspoons in a dream mean that the dreamer enjoys a good financial situation and family harmony, and his life is filled with satisfaction and happiness. In contrast, if the dreamer sees them getting lost, it means that he is about to have an unpleasant experience as a result of the malicious gossip that someone is spreading about him. If a person dreams that he is stealing teaspoons, he is preoccupied by the bad economic situation. He is seeking easy solutions in the form of stealing small items that will put money in his pocket as quickly as possible.

Spring (season)

If a person dreams about the approach of the spring, it is a sign of good fortune and a happy social life. If the spring appears at the wrong time of year, it foretells of trouble and loss.

Spur

If a person dreams about wearing spurs, it is an indication of involvement in a highly controversial issue. If he dreams about other people wearing spurs, it means that enemies are conspiring against the dreamer.

Spy

A person who dreams that he is a spy and is taking part in a dangerous mission must be careful of risky propositions that will be offered him in the near future. Despite the tremendous temptation, he must not expect any success from the proposed projects. Another possible meaning is that the dreamer is not satisfied with his present lifestyle and yearns for a change – professional or personal. If there is some basis to this in reality, the dreamer is advised to find out why he is not satisfied with his life and act accordingly in order to effect a positive future change that is considered and controlled.

Spyglass

If a person dreams that he is peering through a spyglass, it means that there will be changes in his lifestyle that will be detrimental to him. If the dream features a broken or non-functional spyglass, it is a sign of disputes and conflicts with friends.

Squall

A dream about a squall predicts gloom and bad business.

Squinting

If a person dreams about a person who squints, he will be annoyed by unpleasant individuals. If he dreams about his lover or a beautiful woman squinting at him, he will be hounded by problems if he pursues women. If a young woman has this dream, her good name may be in jeopardy.

Squirrel

A squirrel in a dream implies that the dreamer will soon be given some kind of promotion. In most cases, this refers to a promotion at work, but the dream implies success in general. The dreamer will notch up a series of achievements in the near future, and these will improve his status – his financial status, his social status and his family status.

Even if success shines on him in only one area at first, this will "radiate" outward to all the other areas of life, and he can expect a significant improvement at all levels. The dream also hints that deep down, the dreamer is an achievement-oriented person for whom it is important to get far and be held in high regard. Even if he is not in the habit of manifesting this in his everyday life, in a hidden and personal way he has an ambitious personality, and always looks ahead toward accomplishing new objectives. He does not rest on his laurels. The forthcoming period of time will enable him to bring some of his hitherto hidden talents to the fore, and the people around him will acknowledge them.

A dream that features a squirrel in flight, as if he is fleeing from some other animal, implies that the dreamer has not behaved decently toward the people around him. The dream serves as a kind of warning sign for the future, since instead of waiting for revenge or a sharp reaction, the dreamer should smooth things over as soon as possible. If not, it is liable to come back at him like a boomerang and ultimately hurt him.

Stable

If a person dreams about a stable, it is a sign of good luck and profitable business. A dream that features a blazing stable may predict the actual event, or it could imply changes that will be to the dreamer's benefit.

Stag

If a person dreams about stags, it means that his friends are loyal and hones, and he will have good times with them.

A B C D E F G H I J K L M N O P Q R **S** T U V W X Y Z

A B C D E F G H I J K L M N O P Q R S T U V W X Y Z

Stage driver

A dream that features a stage driver is a sign of a weird journey the dreamer will undertake, in search of wealth and happiness.

Stains

Stains that appear on various things – clothing, tablecloths, leather and so on – are not interpreted literally, but rather in the context of the item on which they appear. The rule is that stains diminish the validity of the interpretation of the item on which they appear. If the interpretation is positive, the stain makes it "less" positive. If the interpretation is negative, the stain makes it "less" negative (but does not make it positive). Similarly, the number and size of the stains reinforces or diminishes their effect on the interpretation.

Stairs

A dream about going up stairs is a sign of excellent luck. A dream about going down stairs is a sign of bad luck in business and love. A dream about falling down stairs means that the dreamer will be despised and envied. If a person dreams about sitting on the stairs, it implies a general improvement in his life. If his dream features a broad, elegant staircase, it foretells wealth and a higher status. If he sees other people going down the stairs in the dream, joy will soon give way to unhappiness.

Stalagmite

Colored stalagmites in a cave or icicles in a dream are a

sign that something wonderful is about to happen in the dreamer's life. These marvelous natural creations – stalagmites – attest to the wonderful power and magic of nature. The dream implies that the dreamer does not have to make any particular effort. Good things will come to him, somehow, just like the stalagmites that are created below the earth. He will be very happy, will live in a beautiful and elegant place, and will forget all about what happened to him in the past.

Stall

If a person dreams about a stall, it is an indication of his unrealistic expectations of a particular situation.

Stallion

If a person dreams about a stallion, it is a sign that he can look forward to prosperity and status. If he rides a handsome stallion, he will enjoy a meteoric rise to fame and fortune, but his new status will corrupt him. If the stallion in the dream is rabid, the dreamer's wealth will cause him to become arrogant, and this will alienate his friends.

Stammer

If a person dreams that he stammers, it means that his joy in life will by marred by problems and ill-health. If he hears other people stammer in a dream, it means that he will be bothered and aggravated by nasty people.

Standard bearer

If a person dreams about being a standard bearer, he can look forward to having an enjoyable and varied occupation. If he sees other people who are standard bearers in a dream, it means that he will envy a friend.

Star

Stars in a dream are generally a sign of fecundity, happiness and financial success. A falling star means that something the dreamer has been aspiring to for a long time will soon be realized. Stars attest to the fact that the dreamer feels secure with his status and his personal situation in life and has luck and success in all areas of life. The dreamer's courage will raise him up to a place where he wants to be. If the dreamer sees a cloudy sky and it is difficult for him to see the stars, it means that disappointment or even a serious incident will occur, involving him or one of his friends.

If the dreamer sees himself reaching another planet and talking to its inhabitants or getting a visit from a person who claims to have reached another place in the universe, it means that he is undergoing a process of spiritual development and an expansion of his consciousness. He is opening himself up to thoughts and ideas that previously seemed fundamentally contrived to him.

Star of David

Dreams in which symbols of this kind appear doubtlessly serve as a sign that the dreamer is going through a spiritual-emotional process. He may well have undergone a powerful experience that left its mark on him. A large Star of David in a dream implies that help will come from a source that is linked to religion. It could be voluntary or some other organization that helps the dreamer with a problem he is struggling with.

Starving

If a person dreams that he is starving, he will have neither a job nor friends. If he dreams that others are starving, his present job and friends will cause him nothing but unhappiness.

Statue

If a person dreams that he is looking at a statue, it is a sign of a self-imposed change in his life. If he sees a statue in a dream, it implies that he will break up with his partner.

Staves / Sticks

A violent row with staves means that the dreamer is at the height of some kind of legal battle that will ultimately turn out very well for him. He need not worry too much, because despite the many difficulties along the way, the end will be good. Almost certainly, the dreamer will also be awarded an impressive financial settlement. If the dreamer sees himself stumbling and falling over a stick that is lying on the ground, it is a warning. We often fail to notice things that are right under our nose. He must be careful of traps that might unwittingly be set by associates or family members. Even if their intentions are good, they are liable to get the dreamer in trouble.

A B C D E F G H I J K L M N O P Q R S T U V W X Y Z

Stealing

If a person dreams that he or someone else steals, it is a sign of bad luck and a ruined reputation. If he is accused of stealing in a dream, it means that his actions will be misinterpreted, but the situation will become advantageous to him later. If he accuses someone else of stealing in a dream, it means that he will be totally inconsiderate to somebody.

Steam bath

If a person dreams about taking a steam bath, it means that his friends will be complainers. If he dreams about getting out of a steam bath, it means that his worries will pass.

Steeple

If a person dreams about seeing a steeple of a church, the dream signals ill-health and misfortune. If a dream features a broken-down steeple, it is a sign of a death among the dreamer's circle of friends. If he dreams that he climbs up a steeple, it is a sign of difficulties that he will overcome. If he falls off a steeple in a dream, he is liable to suffer from illness and business losses.

Steer (animal)

If a person dreams about a steer, it is indicative of his honesty and fairness, which are his most prominent character traits. If a dream features more than one steer, it means that now is the right time to take risks. (A steer, as opposed to a bull or cow, is characterized by his horns; see Bull.)

Steps

If a person dreams about going up steps, it refers to an improvement in the dreamer's circumstances. If he dreams about going down steps, it means the opposite. If he falls down steps in his dream, he will suffer sudden setbacks in business.

Stepsister

If a person dreams about having a stepsister, it is a sign of unavoidable worry and responsibility.

Stethoscope

A dream about a stethoscope is a very negative dream – nothing good comes of it, only bad luck, dashed hopes and trouble in love.

Sticks

A dream that features sticks signifies bad luck.

Stillborn

If a person dreams about a stillborn baby, it means that he will soon hear about a sad event.

Stilts

If a person dreams about walking on stilts, it means that his financial situation is shaky. If he dreams that he falls, or that they break, he will have serious trouble as a result of entrusting his business to other people.

A B C D E F G H I J K L M N O P Q R **S** T U V W X Y Z

Sting

If a person dreams that he is stung by an insect, he should brace himself for troubles and bad things. If a young woman dreams that she is stung, it portends sadness and guilt as a result of a relationship with a man.

Stockings

If a person dreams about stockings, it is a sign that he will get into bad company. If a young woman dreams that her stockings are worn or full of runs, her conduct will not be considered in the least; in fact, it is even liable to be immoral. If she dreams that she is wearing fancy stockings, she should be careful of how she conducts herself in the company of men. If she dreams that she is wearing white stockings, she is in for bad luck.

Stone mason

If a person dreams about watching stone masons at work, it is a sign of disappointment. If he dreams that he himself is a stone mason, it means that his job is unrewarding and his associates uninspiring.

Stone

A dream about a stone generally symbolizes a lack of love: the dreamer has not been given the attention he deserves in his life, and he feels other people's lack of affection and love. As a result, he constantly experiences a feeling of a lack of basic fulfillment and of ongoing frustration. He always feels that he has not been given the warmth and love he deserves.

A dream in which the person is walking on stones attests to the fact that the dreamer has experienced unnecessary suffering in his life, which he knows he could have avoided easily. This causes him to feel that he has missed out, that he could have achieved far more in his life, but was prevented from doing so.

Store / Shop

A dream about a store is interpreted according to the type of store that appears in it. If the dreamer sees a huge department store, the dream attests to the fact that the dreamer is about to experience a great burst forward, and from now on he can expect a new era in his life in which he will succeed in achieving what he wants and accomplishing his goals. If a meat store appears in the dream, it means that the dreamer is suffering from emotional anguish and that he is plagued by many problems that give him no rest. In this case, the dream indicates mental problems, and in most cases, they stem from pangs of conscience and a lack of honesty and integrity.

If a person dreams about an empty store, the dream implies that a whole lot of trouble is on the way. In other words, all of the dreamer's plans are about to go wrong at the same time, and he can expect a series of unpleasant incidents to occur. However, it will be a temporary setback and will soon pass.

A dream that features a full store implies that the dreamer can expect to be successful in something in which he has invested a great deal lately, and from which he anticipates receiving significant dividends. This will actually happen, and the achievements will exceed his expectations many times over.

If the dreamer owns the store he dreamed about, or works in it, the dream hints that difficult times from the financial point of view are in the offing. Certain difficulties will crop up in the business, and the dreamer has to brace himself in order to overcome the forthcoming difficult period and carry on.

If the dreamer sees himself working very hard in his store, it is a sign that he will succeed in overcoming the difficulties and obstacles that are awaiting him, and will succeed in business.

If a person dreams about himself wandering around a store among the shelves and the products, the dream implies that in the near future the dreamer can expect to enjoy small but meaningful pleasures from which he will draw the strength to continue working hard. There may be a fascinating journey in the offing for him, or a happy family event (the birth of a baby, a wedding, and so on), or he may attain something he has wanted for a long time.

Storeroom

A dream that features a tidy storeroom is a sign of economic prosperity, pleasure and abundance. A dream that features an empty storeroom is a warning against wrong decisions, especially in anything to do with money.

Stork

A dream about a stork is a positive dream that attests to the arrival of good news or to something new in the dreamer's life. If a person dreams about a single stork sitting in a nest, it implies that the dreamer can expect changes for the good in his life, and attests to an upward movement as well as the realization of the dreamer's other abilities that have not yet come to the fore.

The person looks toward the future and is finally able to break away from the bonds and difficulties of the past that have hounded him and from which he has been unable to break away until now. Now he can raise his eyes to the goal he is striving to accomplish and cast off past hardships or pain.

If a person dreams of two storks, the dream is prophetic and implies that in the near future, he will receive a proposal of marriage or find a true relationship – the kind he has long been yearning for.

A common interpretation of a dream about a stork is the one that implies an imminent birth in the family or something to do with a baby – only with a positive meaning, of course.

Storms

If a person dreams that he sees and hears a storm approaching, he will have bad luck in everything: business, health, friendship. If he dreams that the storm passes, things will improve somewhat.

Stranger

If a person dreams about an encounter he had with a stranger, the dream is a warning dream that illuminates a red light, advising the dreamer that there is a trap that he can expect to fall into soon. If he pays attention to this advance warning, it can be very helpful in preventing unpleasantness later on.

Another version: A dream in which a person dreams that he is a stranger arriving in a new place attests to the fact that he can expect good luck in any new place he is about to go to. Whether he is about to move house to a new area or about to begin working in a new workplace, luck will shine upon him, and he will have only good things in the new place.

Strangled

If a person dreams about being strangled, it predicts that he will be caught up in a confining and draining relationship. If he dreams that he is strangled by an unseen strangler, it means that he will be hurt by someone near to him.

Straw

A dream that features straw (usually in bundles in a field) means the end of a chapter in life. The dreamer senses that he has reached the end of one era and is facing the beginning of a new one, and is terrified of it. The unknown is the most frightening thing, and the dreamer wants to prepare himself for it psychologically. A dream of this type contains a kind of "lament" or feeling of mourning for the era that has ended and will never come back. The dreamer feels profound sadness or grief for the fact that those days will never return, and even if he could go back to them, nothing would be the same as it was before.

Many of the people who dream about straw are people who have reached the end of long relationships and have still not gotten over the crisis that resulted from their breakup with their partners. The dreamer is still in a state of crisis, which serves to help him sum up the outgoing era while resigning himself to the fact that it is over. He has to prepare himself for a "new tomorrow."

Strawberries

If a person dreams about strawberries, it is a good sign: promotion, enjoyment and wishes coming true. A dream about eating strawberries means happy love and a dream about buying and selling strawberries means that there will be good crops and joy.

Stream

A dream that features a stream augurs well. Water, currents and fish are all symbols of abundance, health and renewal. The dreamer is going through a process that leads him toward success in all areas of life, whether on the personal level or on the business level. Having said that, in spite of the signs of approaching success, anyone in the world of business must not forget to take the necessary precautionary measures.

Street

A dream about a street does not augur well. If a person dreams about walking down a brightly lit street, he will experience an unsatisfactory and fleeting sense of enjoyment. If he dreams that he is in a familiar street in a faraway town, it means that he will soon take a trip that will not be as enjoyable or worthwhile as he was led to believe. If he dreams about walking in a street, he is liable to have cares and bad luck, and will fail to realize his ambitions. If he dreams that he is in a street and is afraid of being mugged, it means that he is taking dangerous risks in his business or social life. If he sees a crowd in a street in a dream, it is a sign of excellent business and sales.

Streetcars

If a person dreams about streetcars, it means that people are plotting against him and sabotaging him. If he dreams about riding a streetcar, it means that his peace of mind will be clouded by jealousy and envy. If he dreams that he is riding on the platform, it means that he will take a huge risk in some matter. If he rides without mishap in his dream, he will succeed. A dream that features a streetcar with a high platform implies more serious danger; however, a low platform means a very low degree of success.

Stretcher

If a dream features a stretcher, it portends bad news. If the dreamer is using a stretcher, it means that he will have to do disagreeable work.

Structure

Every dream about a structure – a house, a warehouse, and so on – is interpreted first and foremost according to the identity of the structure. If we can define the structure by name (university, hotel, fortress, and so on), we will examine the meaning of the dream according to the entry that appears in this dictionary.

If the structure that appears in the dream is one that we are unable to define or identify, the dream teaches us that the dreamer must invest a great deal of thought and effort in ensuring his economic future. He is not doing enough in this area, and he would be well advised to mobilize his energies and talents to deal with the situation.

Struggle

If a person dreams that he is involved in a struggle, the dream attests to success that will come after a great deal of effort has been invested in accomplishing some kind of objective, whether it is in his personal life or at work. A dream about interfering in a violent struggle between strangers or acquaintances means that the dreamer has a highly developed sense of justice. What goes on in his world is important to him and he tends to defend the weak. However, the dream offers a word of caution and advises the dreamer not to interfere in every problematic situation he comes across.

Strychnine

If a person dreams about consuming strychnine under a physician's orders, it meas that he is taking huge risks.

Stumbling

If a person dreams about stumbling while running or walking, it implies that people will disapprove of him. Moreover, he will encounter obstacles in his path and will suffer damage to assets and the loss of his good reputation. If he manages to avoid stumbling in his dream, he will overcome the obstacles.

A
B
C
D
E
F
G
H
I
J
K
L
M
N
O
P
Q
R
S
T
U
V
W
X
Y
Z

Stumps

If a person dreams about a stump, it denotes troubles and a change in lifestyle. If a dream features fields of stumps, it attest to the dreamer's impotence in the face of attack. If a person dreams about uprooting stumps, it demonstrates his practical determination to cast off poverty, defeat rivals and get on in life.

Submarine

If a person dreams about a submarine, it is a symbol of an unsavory secret that will be disclosed unexpectedly and cause him a great deal of damage. If he dreams that he is on a submarine, he will unwittingly reveal bad news, causing chaos.

Subway

If a person dreams about riding in a subway, it is a sign of imminent troubles, mostly of a psychological and emotional nature. If he dreams about being stuck in the subway, his dream symbolizes a struggle with a moral issue that will require consideration and time.

Suckle

A dream that features a mother suckling an infant implies that the dreamer will enjoy success and happiness.

Suffering

A dream about suffering or pain prophesies that soon the dreamer will receive unexpected help from an unknown quarter. People who know of the distress he is in will find a way to help him without his discovering who is behind the initiative.

A dream about suffering or pain predicts that the dreamer can expect a happy phase in his life, one that will bring a lot of smiles and laughter.

Suffocation / Choking

A dream about suffocation expresses aggressiveness and force as well as the attempt to use them for accomplishing goals.

Suffocation or choking in a dream means trouble! If a person dreams that somebody else is choking him, it is a sign that a close friend is ratting on him. He must not rely on the person who is closest to him, but should be suspicious, since someone is denouncing him, placing the blame on him, and trying to frame him!

A dream in which the dreamer sees himself being suffocated attests to his enormous fear of the person who is suffocating him in the dream. Even if in reality the dreamer does not feel particularly afraid of the person who is suffocating him in the dream, he fears him without really being aware of it. That particular person might pose a threat to the dreamer for various reasons, and this is reflected in the dream.

A dream in which the dreamer suffocates someone else is a sign that he has especially strong negative feelings toward that person. The dreamer's wishes will indeed come true, but only by taking violent steps. Things will not be set straight by a good word or persuasion, but only by force. Only in this way will thc drcamcr succccd in achieving his coveted goal.

A B C D E F G H I J K L M N O P Q R **S** T U V W X Y Z

A B C D E F G H I J K L M N O P Q R **S** T U V W X Y Z

If the dreamer sees other people suffocating in a dream, it is a sign that he will only be successful at the expense of a friend. Only if he uses his elbows and tramples people underfoot will he get what he wants.

A dream about suffocation is often causes the dreamer to wake up suddenly in a panic when he experiences the feelings of real suffocation or of terror and nightmare that characterize such a dream.

Sugar

The appearance of sugar in a dream implies that the dreamer can expect a harmonious period of wonderful relations with his partner and his family, as well as huge success in his workplace.

A dream about sugar can have a few other interpretations. It can also imply the forbidden pleasures the dreamer will experience. If the dreamer is married, it is a sign that soon he will find a lover, or that he will experiment with different aspects of things that are forbidden by law. He will cross the barricades and partake of forbidden fruits.

If the person dreams about sugar that appears in the context of baking or cooking in the dream, it is a sign that he is surrounded by friends in whom he should not place his trust. They are not true friends and will not be of help to him when he needs them.

A candy in a dream is a hint that a love affair is on the horizon.

Sugar tongs

A dream about sugar tongs predicts that the dreamer will get to hear of bad deeds committed by others.

Suicide

A dream about suicide hints to the dreamer that he has to muster courage and stop pitying himself. Only if he finds his innate inner strengths and gets out of the struggle for survival will he succeed in extricating himself from the difficult situation in which he is embroiled. A dream about suicide expresses the need to find one's way out of the dead end when it finally seems as if all other possibilities are exhausted, and there is no other way out of the mess the dreamer has gotten himself into. The dream expresses the dreamer's desire to get out of the dead end he is in, and his innate ability to do so, even though he is not always aware of its existence.

Suitcase

If a person dreams that a suitcase belongs to him, it implies that he will soon have to tackle problems. If he dreams that the suitcase belongs to someone else, it means that he will go on a trip in the near future.

Sums (addition)

If a dream features an incorrect sum, it warns against unsuccessful commercial negotiations.

Sulfur

If a person dreams about sulfur, it is a warning dream: he must guard himself against the malicious plots hatched by other people. A dream about burning sulfur means that the dreamer should safeguard his wealth. If he sees himself eating sulfur, it is a sign of health and enjoyment.

A
B
C
D
E
F
G
H
I
J
K
L
M
N
O
P
Q
R
S
T
U
V
W
X
Y
Z

Sun

If a person dreams about a bright, vivid sunrise, it is a sign of happiness and wealth. A dream that features the midday sun symbolizes ambitions that are satisfactorily realized. A dream about sunset is a symbol of being past one's prime, with the attendant health worries. If the sun shines through clouds in a dream, the dreamer's troubles will soon disappear, to be replaced by good luck. If a dream features a peculiar-looking sun, or an eclipse, dangerous things lie ahead, but they are temporary.

Sunflower

A dream about a sunflower signifies sunshine, light and warmth.

Sunshade

If a person dreams about young women carrying sunshades, it is a sign of good fortune and happiness. A dream that features a broken sunshade is a sign of bad luck and untimely death.

Surgeon

If a person dreams about a surgeon, he must be on the lookout for dangerous business adversaries. If a young woman dreams about a surgeon, she will come down with a serious illness.

Surgical instruments

If a dream features surgical instruments, it means that

the dreamer will feel annoyed and offended that a friend is holding back on something.

Swallow (bird)

If a person dreams about a swallow, it implies a happy and serene home. A dream about a dead or injured swallow is a sign of deep sorrow.

Swamp

If a person dreams about walking through swamps, it symbolizes bad luck in money matters – especially bequests – and in love. If the swamp has green vegetation and limpid water in the dream, the dreamer will enjoy money and good times, but with a lot of risk.

Swan

A dream about a swan implies good things, especially a good relationship with one's partner and a happy family life. In general, it is a positive dream. A great deal of importance is attributed to the color of the swan that appears in the dream, so upon waking up, it is important to remember the swan's color. There is a difference in meaning between the appearance of a black swan in a dream and that of a white swan.

The appearance of a black swan in a dream attests to the fact that the dreamer's son or daughter is a good person with a pleasant temperament. He/She knows how to give of him/herself and is sincere and honest. He/She is not tight-fisted, and knows how to behave very generously with those around him/her.

A dream about a white swan is a prophetic dream. If the person who dreamed it is single, the dream predicts that he will find a suitable partner who will bring him pride and joy. The dreamer's relationship will be happy and good, and his married life will be successful and happy. His family life will also be good and fulfilling, and he will derive a great deal of joy from his future offspring, since they will be successful, and will accomplish the goals they set for themselves and notch up impressive achievements.

If a married person has this dream, the dream predicts that even if his married life is not going too well at the moment, his marriage and family life will soon improve and get onto an even keel. The future holds success on the personal level for him in everything to do with his relationship. Problems that occur in the present are just temporary, and together with his partner, he can achieve wholeness and satisfaction in his family and married life.

There is only one case in which a dream about a swan may be interpreted negatively, and that is when there are more than one swan in a dream, and they are black. In such a case, it is a warning dream, implying that the dreamer must be careful and wary of something that is threatening the tranquillity of his life. It can be something connected to work, such as a partner, or an unsuccessful deal, or something connected to his health. The dreamer must pay attention to the murmurings of his surroundings as well as to his health and the physical state of his body in order to preempt bad things and be ready for them.

Swearing (oaths)

If a lover dreams about swearing, it means that he will

no longer have faith in his sweetheart. If he dreams about swearing, it means that he will suffer a setback in business. If he swears in the presence of his family in a dream, there will soon be a quarrel because of his poor conduct.

Sweating

If a person sees sweat pouring from his forehead in a dream, it means that he is making a great effort to achieve the success he yearns for. He is trying to do everything in his power to realize his desires. His efforts will pay off, especially in anything to do with finances. If the dreamer is a person whose goal is to make money, his efforts, which are reflected in his hard work, will bear fruit, and he will achieve what he wants and become wealthy. Even if his goal is not financial but rather spiritual or social, success will shine upon him – perhaps not to the extent that it will shine upon a dreamer whose goal is to amass wealth.

Sweeping

If a woman dreams that she is sweeping, it means that she will be appreciated by her family. If the floors need sweeping in a dream, but they are not swept, there will be problems and bitter disappointment. If employees dream about sweeping, it gives them grounds to doubt the sincerity of other people's intentions.

Sweetheart

If a person dreams that he sees his sweetheart as pleasant and good-looking, he will find a lovely and well-established woman. If his sweetheart does not look so good in his dream, he will have serious doubts about his future with her. If he dreams that his sweetheart is ill, it means that both happiness and sadness are in store for him. If he dreams that his sweetheart is dead, it predicts a lot of bad luck.

Sweetness

A dream about eating something sweet refers to the dreamer's ability to resist temptation. He has a strong character, and is blessed with a special ability to stand up for himself, which sometimes borders on unnecessary stubbornness, but sometimes also pays off. If he decides to do something in his life, he does not give in to whims, and succeeds in accomplishing his objective. For instance, if he decides to go on a diet in order to reach a certain weight, he will not succumb to the temptation of eating calorie-rich dishes, and will obtain quickly good results, to his complete satisfaction.

Sweets / Candy

A dream about a pile of sweets on a table that is meant for the dreamer attests to his feeling of happiness. Abundance, health and a good income are the dreamer's lot, and he just has to be careful that his heart doesn't cause him to take a step that will cause him to lose what he has obtained through so much toil. A plate or basket of sweets that is taken from the dreamer is a hint at the possibility of loss. This refers to his personal life or workplace. It is very possible that because of cutbacks, he will lose his job or take a drop in rank. Frequently, a dream of this type also hints at the possibility of the termination of an existing

A B C D E F G H I J K L M N O P Q R **S** T U V W X Y Z

relationship because of a misunderstanding and a lack of communication. It is advisable to clarify things before it is too late. A person who dreams that he is distributing sweets is a generous person who does not hesitate to share the abundance he enjoys with other people. He must check to see whether the distribution of resources is a considered action and not an act of extravagance that is liable to cause the dreamer to get into financial trouble.

Sweet taste

If a person dreams that he has a sweet taste in his mouth, he will behave with self-control and magnanimity during a period of turmoil, and people will appreciate this. If he tries to dispel a sweet taste in his dream, it means that he will act contemptuously and tyrannically toward his friends.

Swelling

If a person dreams that his body looks swollen, it means that he will be prosperous, but his egoism will be a stumbling-block. If he sees other people swollen in a dream, his rise in life will be perceived with envy.

Swimming

In principle, a dream about swimming attests to an imminent change, and success will come from an unexpected quarter. If the dreamer sees himself swimming in stormy waters, he can expect to encounter difficulties. A dream about drowning hints at a possible failure at a task.

Swiss cheese

If a person dreams about Swiss cheese, it is a sign of great wealth about to be acquired by the dreamer, as well as healthy pleasures.

Switch

If a person dreams about a switch, it is a symbol of reverses of fortune and discouragement. A dream that features a broken switch is an indication of humiliation and troubles. A dream about a railroad switch is an indicating of losses resulting from journeys.

Sword

If a person dreams about wearing a sword, it means that he will hold a position of great dignity and respect. If he dreams that his sword is confiscated, he will be outwitted by rivals. If he sees other people carrying swords in a dream, it is a warning that serious disputes are about to erupt. A dream that features a broken sword is a sign of desperation.

Symphony

A dream about a symphony is an excellent dream, since it implies pleasurable entertainment.

Synagogue

If a person dreams about a synagogue, it is an indication of powerful enemies who are blocking his advancement. If he dreams that he climbs to the top of a synagogue from the exterior, he will defeat his enemies and be successful. If he dreams about reading the Hebrew words inscribed on a synagogue, it is a warning of financial catastrophe that he will eventually overcome.

Syringe

If a person dreams about a syringe, it means that he will be unjustifiably appalled at bad news concerning a relative's health. A dream that features a broken syringe signifies minor health setbacks and business worries.

A B C D E F G H I J K L M N O P Q R S T U V W X Y Z

T

Table

A dream that features a table can have numerous meanings: A conference table implies legal proceedings in which the dreamer will be involved. An operating table implies a medical problem – this is the time to have an annual checkup. A worktable or desk means success in a financial deal, and sitting around a table eating a meal with the family predicts that the dreamer can look forward to a period of financial abundance and happiness in the bosom of his family. An empty table with the dreamer sitting alone next to it means that he needs time for thinking and for some soul-searching. The dreamer feels that loneliness and massive responsibility are weighing on his shoulders, and this is the time for reorganizing his life and renewing his strength.

Tablecloth

A dream about a set table with a fancy tablecloth contains a hint for the future: financial ease will prevail in the dreamer's home even though things do not reflect anything like this at the moment. It is a dream that contains more than a hint of a possible development in the near future. A dream about a torn tablecloth attests to the fact that the dreamer's economic situation could deteriorate.

This may not be as bad as the dreamer fears, but without a doubt there will be a substantial drop. The dreamer must take advantage of the time that remains and put money aside for a rainy day.

Tacks

If a person dreams about tacks, it is a sign of conflicts and problems. If a woman dreams that she is hammering in a tack, she will defeat rivals. If she dreams that she hits her finger while doing so, she will be annoyed about unpleasant things she has to do.

Tadpole

If a person dreams about tadpoles, it means that he has gotten involved in ventures that are causing him anxiety. If a young woman dreams that she sees tadpoles swimming, she will get into a relationship with a rich but unscrupulous man.

Tail

If a person dreams that he has an animal's tail, he will suffer from peculiar incidents and trouble as a result of his own maleficence. If he sees himself cutting off an animal's tail in a dream, it means that his own carelessness will engender losses for him. If a person dreams about seeing only an animal's tail, it signals that he will have nothing but aggravation when he expected happiness. If he dreams about trimming a horse's tail, it implies success in business or agriculture.

A B C D E F G H I J K L M N O P Q R S **T** U V W X Y Z

Tailor

If a person dreams about a tailor, it is a sign that he is indecisive and easily swayed by other people. A dream about a tailor is indicative of anxiety about a trip. If a person dreams about arguing with a tailor, it predicts that he is going to be disappointed in the results of one of his ventures.

Tailoring

A dream about a tailor or about the profession itself means exchanging one thing for another. This could be reflected in changing one's mind, or an apartment, or a job, or a girl/boyfriend, and so on. In most cases, such a dream implies that the dreamer is not a decisive person. He is easily swayed and tends to accept every piece of advice he is offered, without being able to judge for himself. He is the type of person that is "dragged along." Every time someone expresses a solid and confident opinion, the dreamer follows it and adopts it immediately. The dream warns against this behavior. It calls on the dreamer's inner voice not to get caught up in beliefs that are not his, and to learn to stand up for himself and pay attention to his desires and to the things that characterize him. The dreamer must learn to do only things he feels at one with, and to be faithful to his path and beliefs.

Talisman

If a person dreams about wearing a talisman, it is indicative of good friends and the patronage of wealthy people. If a young woman dreams that her lover gives her a talisman, it is a sign that she will marry the man she wants.

Talking

If a person dreams about talking, it is a prediction of ill health in his family as well as business worries. If he dreams that other people talk loudly, it means that he will be accused of interfering. If he thinks people are talking about him, the dream warns of illness and unhappiness.

Tambourine

A dream about a tambourine predicts an extraordinary event that the dreamer will enjoy.

Tank (water)

If a person dreams about a water tank, it predicts unprecedented contentment and prosperity for the dreamer. A dream about a leaking tank implies business losses.

Tannery

If a person dreams about a tannery, it is a warning dream: it warns of contagious diseases and financial losses. If he dreams that he is a tanner, he will have to do disagreeable work because of his dependants. If he buys leather from a tanner, his financial status will be good, but his social life will not.

Tape

If a person dreams about tape, it means that he is employed in a job that is no more than badly paid drudgery. If a woman dreams that she purchases tape, she will be the victim of bad luck.

Tape recorder

If a person dreams about a recording made on a tape recorder, it means that things he said will come back to torment and incriminate him, particularly if the wrong people get to hear them.

Tapestry

If a person dreams about an ornate tapestry, it means that he will enjoy a life of wealth and ease. If the tapestries in the dream are in good condition, his wishes will come true. If a young woman dreams about tapestries adorning her room, she will marry a rich man who enjoys a high social status.

Tapeworms

If a person dreams about seeing or being affected with a tapeworm, it is a sign of imminent ill health and fun that has gone sour.

Tar

A dream about tar attests to the fact that thanks to the dreamer's good health, he will overcome obstacles and succeed in life. His strength and vigor will not let him down in difficult times, and will help him extricate himself from difficult and problematic situations. It is not easy to "break" him because of his great strength and because of the fact that he does not crumble psychologically, either.

If a person sees black tar lying on the road in a dream, or smells tar, it means that the good health he is blessed with will not fail him over the years and will safeguard him from all ills.

Tar on the soles of the dreamer's shoes or on his clothes is a sign of a journey or some other kind of adventure trip the dreamer will soon be taking. Even if the dreamer is accustomed to pleasure trips that do not involve treks or fascinating discoveries, he will soon find himself in the swing of such an experience, despite the fact that he did not plan it beforehand.

If a person sees a lump of tar floating on the water, he can expect to go on a particularly long journey. It could be a trip that is work- or study-related, but it could simply be a trip that takes longer than expected. Even if the original plan was for a short trip only, something will go wrong or crop up, causing the dreamer to postpone his return. This should be taken into account during his next trip, and it would be a good idea for him to take a few extra pairs of socks and underwear – just in case.

Boiling tar in a dream is a sign of interpersonal problems. The dreamer's rebellious nature or excessive stubbornness may be what gets him into problematic situations with the people around him. The dream implies that if he goes on like this, he is liable to find himself isolated and very frustrated with the situation. He should begin to be more flexible and submissive, if only to preserve his good relations with the people around him or with his neighbors, and to maintain a pleasant atmosphere.

Tarantula

If a person dreams about killing a tarantula, it implies that he will be successful after failing hopelessly. If he sees a tarantula in a dream, it means that he will be totally defeated by his enemies.

A
B
C
D
E
F
G
H
I
J
K
L
M
N
O
P
Q
R
S
T
U
V
W
X
Y
Z

Tardiness

Many people dream that they were supposed to get to a certain place at a certain time but did not get there on time, despite the enormous efforts they made to do so. Sometimes they even awaken from such a dream in a panic and in a cold sweat. A person who has a dream like this is very responsible and sensitive, and tends to be a perfectionist. This specific dream implies that the dreamer is well aware of the fact that the people around him hold him in high esteem and value his opinion in everything, and that he has sweeping natural charisma. That is why people tend to cluster in his shadow and eagerly await his pearls of wisdom. The things he has to say are highly esteemed by other people, and his ideas and advice are always received gladly and taken very seriously. The power he has vis-à-vis those around him and his ability to influence are so great that they are also liable to become an obstacle for him, and he must be very careful of this. One word that is out of place or that exerts an undesirable influence is enough for avalanches of fire and brimstone to be directed at him.

Target

If a person dreams about a target, it means that he will have to deal with an unpleasant matter instead of having a good time. If a young woman dreams that she considers herself a target, it is a warning that she may be badmouthed by acquaintances.

Tassels

If a person dreams about tassels, it means that his loftiest aspirations are about to be realized. A dream about losing tassels warns of an impending catastrophe.

Tattoo

If a person dreams that he has a tattoo, it will be necessary for him to go on a long and unpleasant journey. If he sees tattoos on other people in a dream, people will envy him because of love. If he dreams that he is a tattoo artist, his friends will reject him because of his *penchant* for weird experiences.

Taxes

If a person dreams about paying taxes, he will conquer the forces of evil in his vicinity. If he dreams that he cannot pay taxes, his endeavors will not succeed. If he dreams that other people pay taxes, he will have to ask friends for assistance.

Taxi / Cab

If a person dreams that he is running after a taxi and does not catch it, the dream indicates a feeling of missing out on an event that happened in the past or is about to happen. It could be a crisis in a relationship or in financial plans. If a person who dreams that he is riding in a taxi with a specific person, the dream hints at a possibility of an interesting encounter that could affect the dreamer's life in an extremely significant way. If, during a taxi-ride with another person, the conversation develops into an argument, it is an explicit warning to the dreamer not to get involved in the conflicts of work colleagues or strangers that come his way. This kind of argument is liable to deteriorate into real violence and lead to disaster.

Tea

A dream in which a person sees himself making tea implies that he is about to get embroiled in troubles from which it will be difficult for him to extricate himself.

A dream about tea in general attests to the fact that the dreamer must bolster his self-confidence. Only if he adheres to the path he has mapped for himself and is faithful to himself and his principles will he be happy and content with his lot. In this way, he will be able to realize his aspirations and attain satisfaction. He must be more resolute in the path he chooses in order to attain his desires, and then he will reap the real fruits of success.

If a person sees himself drinking tea outside of his house, the dream predicts a move to a new home. Even if the dreamer does not have any plans to move to a new house or apartment, something will soon happen that will cause him to do so.

Some people interpret a dream about tea as referring to negative gossip about the dreamer, which will cause him sorrow and torment.

Teacher

If a person dreams that he is a pupil facing a teacher in a classroom or a group, it means that he can expect financial problems. He is going through a phase of "going astray," so it would be a good idea for him to avail himself of a professional or someone close who can advise him in this field. The dreamer may well be going through a period of confusion. He may be at a crossroads from the social and personal points of view. Perhaps he has to make a decision concerning a new choice of profession or concerning a course of study. In any event, the dreamer seems to be requesting guidance from a figure of authority who will help him make certain decisions.

If the dreamer is a teacher in the dream, it means that he feels that he has a message to pass on to other people and has not yet found the requisite framework for doing so. He may also feel that people do not listen to him enough at home or at work, so he finds encouragement and release for his frustrations in a dream.

Teacups

If a person dreams about teacups, it is a prediction of enjoyable events. If he dreams about breaking teacups or seeing broken teacups, it means that good luck and happiness will be interrupted by some problem. If a person dreams about drinking wine from a teacup, it means that he will soon enjoy both wealth and pleasure.

Teapot

If a person dreams about seeing a teapot, is warns of bad news. If he dreams about pouring fresh, cold water from a teapot, it is a sign of sudden good fortune.

Tear

A dream that features a tear is an indication of extreme mood swings.

Tears

Tears in a dream generally attest to a wave of happiness, good things and joy that the dreamer is about to experience. Sometimes tears in a dream imply a transition from one extreme situation to its opposite – from joy to sadness or vice versa.

Tears also imply that the dreamer is about to receive a gift or something that he wanted for a long time. This will come as a surprise.

If a person sees his lover shedding a tear in a dream, the dream attests to the fact that soon he will be consoled when he gets into a crisis or a difficult state of mind. He will not have to go through the crisis alone because he has someone to lean on, depend on, and pour out his troubles to.

If a woman sees her husband shedding tears in a dream, this actually means that they can expect a good and happy marriage in which there will be understanding between them, and they will serve as helpmeets to each other.

Teasing

If a person dreams about teasing someone, it means that he will be popular because of his outgoing nature and sense of humor. Success in business will also follow. If he is teased in a dream, he will be liked by cheerful, wealthy people. If a young woman dreams that she is teased, she will fall in love quickly without getting married.

Teaspoon – See Spoon

Teeth

Teeth in a dream usually imply that the dreamer can expect health problems, or that his body is very sensitive, and so he has to take care and avoid situations in which he is liable to put his health at risk.

Having said that, the manner in which the teeth appear in a dream can be interpreted in different ways:

If the dream features lovely white teeth, it implies that the dreamer can expect prosperity, success and a good life.

A dream in which the teeth are not healthy-looking – that is, they are broken, crooked or missing – is a sign that the dreamer is liable to suffer from troubles, diseases and problems that he will have a hard time solving.

If a person dreams that he is having teeth extracted (a common dream), it is a sign that the people close to him are up to no good. They do not want the best for him, and he has to be careful of them. Their intentions are not good and pure, and they are liable to harm the dreamer.

If a person dreams that he hits another person in the teeth, it is a sign that he will soon be able to overcome difficulties and succeed in fields in which he feared failure.

If a person dreams that he undergoes dental treatment, it implies that he finds it difficult to express himself from the emotional point of view. There is an inner struggle between his desire to be liberated mentally and physically and his inability to express this in reality. This conflict frustrates the dreamer and is expressed in the dream.

Telegram

A dream that features a telegram attests to the need to hurry. The dreamer may need to make an important business decision or give an answer to his partner. The dream indicates the urgent need to make a decision and act upon it. However, the dreamer must be careful of erroneous information that is liable to lead him in the wrong direction.

Telephone

A person who dreams about a telephone is likely to get an important phone-call shortly after the dream. This could be an unexpected call from someone from whom the dreamer has not heard in a long time. It is also possible that a package or letter will arrive by mail. Dreams about a telephone may also serve as a warning sign that it is not advisable to listen to the gossip that is being spread by people the dreamer knows. Sometimes a telephone in a dream is linked to receiving a message from someone far away or deceased. In the case of a dream about a telephone conversation that is not clear, it is almost certain that the person at the other end of the line is not telling the truth and is trying to conceal his true feelings. A dream about a telephone conversation from a closed telephone booth indicates that the dreamer can expect a pleasant surprise – not from his family but from a stranger. An event like this can occur during a trip to a new or to a familiar place, during which there could be an interesting meeting with an unknown person.

Telescope

A dream about a telescope implies the possibility of changes in life, particularly in the professional realm. A small telescope means that several ideas the dreamer is turning over in his mind might merge and form a single comprehensive idea or perception that may lead the dreamer to new pastures. A dream about a broken telescope is liable to indicate that the occurrence of an important event may cause the dreamer some confusion. Since the event is unexpected, it may turn the tables on him. A new situation will require the dreamer to be prepared and plan carefully for the future. A large telescope pointing at the sky predicts that positive events are in the offing for the dreamer.

Television

If a person dreams that he watches television and is not very happy with what he is seeing, it means that other people can influence him too easily. If he dreams about being on television, it means that he is overly intrigued with his looks, and will be hurt as a result of this superficiality.

Tempest

A dream about a tempest portends catastrophic events and uncaring friends for the dreamer.

Temple

A dream about a temple can have many meanings. If the dream occurs after a visit to a place that resembles a temple or is an actual temple, it proves that the dreamer underwent a profound experience there. The place may have sparked emotions that were hidden deep in his heart: a strong desire for peace and quiet, a desire to escape reality, or a sense of wonder about beauty and harmony. He must spend time thinking about why these feelings arose in his heart exactly

A B C D E F G H I J K L M N O P Q R S **T** U V W X Y Z

at this time, and he should flow with the inner voices as much as possible.

If the dream occurs without any connection to an event that occurred in reality, it means that the dreamer is undergoing a spiritual process and is expressing his desire to reach deeper levels than that of his everyday, material life in his dream. The dreamer must find out whether there is something bothering him and whether there are things that he would like to change. If he decides to change professions or move house, this step will have positive consequences.

Temptation

A dream about temptation can have several meanings. If the dreamer sees himself tempted to stray from his usual straight and narrow path, he will not be tempted to do anything he would not normally do, despite his vacillations. This could refer to cheating on his partner or betrayal in some work-related issue.

In contrast, if the dreamer sees himself being betrayed, it means that there is someone who is trying to trip him up, but he will have the upper hand.

Tenant

If a landlord dreams about his tenant, he will have problems. If the dreamer is a tenant, he will suffer losses in business as a result of trying out ideas. If a person dreams that a tenant pays him, it is a sign of success.

Tennis

This is an aristocratic game that is considered to be popular among the middle and upper classes. Accordingly, the person who dreams that he is playing tennis is a person for whom social recognition and status are very important. He is prepared to invest a great deal of time and effort to be considered "acceptable. This may well be his normal character, but it is could also be a temporary phenomenon that is causing the dreamer to seek attention and to fight to accomplish the goal. His aspirations are mainly in the social realm and may emerge without prior warning – at work as well. The explosion of energy imbues him with power and influence. This is the time to ask the boss for a raise in rank and salary.

Tent

A dream about a tent is generally a prophetic dream that aims to instill a feeling of security in the dreamer. If the tent stands firmly on the ground and is held up by poles and taut ropes, it signifies stability, security and protection. The dreamer will be exempt from bad feelings such as sorrow, pain and anxiety.

In contrast, if the tent in the dream looks as if it is collapsing, leaning to one side, and unsteady in the wind, the dream warns of financial complications and monetary and property losses. The dreamer must be very aware of his economic moves and plan his path of action carefully so that he does not make mistakes that will cause him substantial monetary losses.

If the tent in the dream is particularly wide, the dream implies that the dreamer's situation is highly conducive to business and economic success. Every deal or financial venture he undertakes will culminate in success.

If the dream features a tent that is riddled with holes, it hints at a difficult financial period. The dreamer might become unemployed and have a hard time finding a new job. This is the reason for the stressful period from the financial point of view.

A dream that features a patrol tent attests to the fact that the dreamer's current job is temporary and that he will soon have to find another. There are several possible reasons for this: The job may not suit the dreamer's qualifications, so he himself will reach the conclusion that it does not suit him. It is also possible that the dreamer is not satisfied with his present salary. Changes may occur in his place of residence or in his personal status, preventing him from continuing to work in his present workplace.

Terror

If a person dreams about experiencing terror in a dream, it is a warning of setbacks and disappointment. If he dreams that other people are terrified, he will be adversely affected by his friends' troubles.

Text

If a person dreams about hearing a clergyman reading a text, it predicts a dispute and a breakup with a friend. If he dreams that he is arguing about a text, it is a sign of bad luck. If he dreams about attempting to remember a text, it signifies unforeseen problems. A dream about studying, rereading and thinking about a text implies overcoming many pitfalls on the way to realizing one's wishes.

Thatch

If a person dreams about a straw-thatched roof that leaks, it means that there is a possibility of danger, but if the dreamer is quick-witted enough, he can avoid it. If the roof in the dream is thatched with low-quality materials, the dreamer will experience unhappiness.

Thaw

If a person dreams about seeing the ground thaw after being frozen for a long time, it predicts prosperity. If he sees ice thawing, a problem that bothered him greatly will be solved satisfactorily and to his financial advantage.

Theater

A dream about a theater attests to the dreamer's fierce desire to get out of the dull routine and stand in the spotlight. Having already tasted success, he lives a monotonous and boring life and works at a difficult job that does not enable him to express himself properly. Metaphorically speaking, he feels a need to stand in the center of the stage – in other words, to be at the hub of things, express himself and his talents, earn the affection and love from the people around him, and become an admired and famous figure.

The dream encourages the dreamer to try his luck once more, and if he knows how to play his cards right, he may enjoy success again, as he did once before.

A dream about a theater also predicts that an admirer may pleasantly surprise the dreamer. The surprise may be linked to a declaration concerning the formalization of the relationship.

If the dreamer sees a comedy at the theater in his dream, he feels that the people around him are trying to bring a smile to his face. Their efforts stem from love and caring, and he should try and cooperate.

In contrast, a dream in which the dreamer sees a tragedy at the theater attests to the fact that there is someone who is trying to tug at his heartstrings and make him feel guilty about something he knows he has nothing to do with. The dreamer must be resolute and stand up for himself. If he is sure that he is right, the truth will ultimately emerge.

Theft – See Robbery

Thermometer

If a person dreams about looking at a thermometer, it is a sign of poor business and domestic strife. If he sees the mercury falling, the dream implies that business will deteriorate. If he sees the mercury rising, he will overcome difficulties. If the thermometer in the dream is broken, illness is in the offing.

Thermos flask

A dream that features a thermos flask is a sign of an imminent disaster.

Thief

If a person dreams about being a thief who is pursued by the police, it is an indication of problems in his business and social life. If he dreams that he catches a thief, it means that he will defeat his enemies.

A B C D E F G H I J K L M N O P Q R S T U V W X Y Z

Thigh

A person who dreams about powerful thighs will travel extensively during the stretch of time immediately following the dream. It could be a matter of business or personal trips – often unexpected ones. A dream that features a wounded thigh indicates a danger of being injured during a trip or some kind of struggle that requires great effort. It could be something linked to the workplace or a change that is expected in the dreamer's personal life, such as moving house or even a divorce. A right thigh generally indicates the approaching need to deal with personal and emotional problems. In contrast, a dream that features a left thigh attests to hidden and overt struggles in the workplace or with neighbors.

Thimble

If a person dreams about a thimble, it symbolizes unrealistic ambitions that cannot be fulfilled. A dream about using a thimble implies that he is accountable to many other people. If a woman dreams about using a thimble, it means that she will have to support herself. A dream about purchasing or receiving a new thimble signifies pleasurable new relationships. A dream about losing a thimble predicts distress and poverty. If a person dreams about seeing an old, battered thimble, the dream warns of an unwise decision regarding an important matter.

Thirst

If a person dreams about being thirsty, it means that his aspirations are too high. If he dreams that he quenches his thirst, he will realize them. If he dreams that other people are thirsty and slake their thirst, he will benefit from the patronage of rich people.

Thorn

A dream that features a thorn (of any kind) hints at the betrayal of a close friend. The dreamer may trust a person that he considers a close friend, but in fact that same "friend" is plotting against him behind his back. It is also possible that the betrayal is coming from the direction of the dreamer's partner, who is cheating on him with someone else without the dreamer's knowledge. A betrayal for romantic reasons is very painful from the emotional point of view, but a betrayal of the first kind can have very unpleasant side effects such as a loss of money or income. In any event, the dreamer must hone his senses and be a little more suspicious of the people around him. It turns out that things are more complicated than they appear on the surface.

Thread

A dream about thread is a sign that the dreamer can soon expect to go on short journeys to distant and exotic places where he will have magical and fascinating adventures.

A dream about a silken thread is a sign that the dreamer's life will comprise a good and happy routine. Occasionally there will be ups and downs, but generally the dreamer's life will flow smoothly, and he and his family will be surrounded by security and a feeling of tranquillity.

A torn or invisible thread in a dream is a sign that the dreamer is about to lose something important or experience a severe disappointment that will have repercussions in his life in the future. The picture looks especially gloomy because this will be a result of the dreamer's magnanimity. He feels exploited and badly hurt and will sink into a bad and depressed mood in the near future, until he gets over the expected loss.

If a tangled, knotted thread appears in a dream, it is a prophetic dream. It implies that the dreamer is about to be cheated and deceived. The dream serves to warn the dreamer about people who are plotting and scheming against him and the evil that will come from them. He must be alert to what is going on around him, otherwise bad things will happen to him, and he will fall into the plotters' net.

Sometimes, a dream features a thread of a particular color. The color is significant in the interpretation of the dream, and the dream must be interpreted according to the shape and color of the thread in the dream.

Threshing

If a person dreams about threshing grain or wheat, it is a sign of a thriving business and domestic bliss. If he dreams that there is much more straw than grain, he can expect business failures. If the dream features an accident or breakdown during threshing, the dreamer will suffer a tragedy.

Throat

A dream about a throat mostly occurs in the context of diseases.

However, if the dream features a feeling of burning, pain

A B C D E F G H I J K L M N O P Q R S T U V W X Y Z

or some kind of irritation in the region of the throat, it attests to the fact that good things will happen to the dreamer. The things that were confused in his life may begin to sort themselves out in the near future. Everything will return to its place and the dreamer will feel that he has achieved a measure of personal maturity and the ability to control his life. The worries, tensions and anxieties will gradually leave him, and in their place there will be a feeling of fullness, control, satisfaction and creativity. As soon as these feelings predominate in his life, the good energies will return to operate in his life, bringing him happiness and wealth, prosperity and success in everything to which he turns his hand. He must learn to detach himself from the things that lead him to a narrow way of thinking, to open his head and his heart, and to leave room for the good things that will come and take control of his life.

Throne

If a person dreams about sitting on a throne, he will enjoy increased wealth and status. If he dreams about getting off a throne, it is a sign of disillusionment. If he sees others on a throne in a dream, it means that he will prosper as a result of the intervention of other people.

Thumb

If a person dreams about seeing a thumb, it means that he will be popular with unsavory people. If a dream features a sore thumb, it is a sign of business losses and disagreeable associates. If a person dreams about not having thumbs, it is an indication of solitude and poverty. An extremely small thumb in a dream means temporary enjoyment. An extremely large thumb in a dream means meteoric success. A dirty thumb in a dream symbolizes the gratification of base urges. A long thumbnail in a dream warns of getting into evil habits as a result of the quest for unnatural pleasures.

Thunder

If a person dreams about hearing thunder, it is a warning of setbacks in business. If he dreams about being out in a thunderstorm, it predicts distress and grief. If he dreams about hearing deafening thunderclaps, it is a sign of disillusionment and loss.

Ticket

A dream that features a ticket implies the possibility of a trip in the near future. The dreamer may receive a notice in the mail containing a solution or an offer that will extricate him from an undesirable situation he has been in recently. It could be a job offer in a place that is far from his home or abroad. In principle, a ticket in a dream is a good sign, whether the dreamer receives the ticket or gives it to someone else.

Tickle

If a person dreams about being tickled, it signifies anxieties and disease. If the dreamer tickles other people, he will sacrifice happiness and joy because of his own stupidity and weakness.

Ticks

If a person dreams about seeing ticks crawling on his body, it signifies poverty and disease. If he squashes a tick on his body, it means that dangerous enemies are hounding him. If he sees huge ticks on his livestock in a dream, it means that enemies are trying to rob him of his possessions.

Tiger

The appearance of a tiger in a dream serves as a hint that things planned by the dreamer will not turn out the way he expected them to. The dreamer may have built up false hopes and plans that will ultimately not be fulfilled, and his disappointment will be as great as his expectations. For this reason, the dreamer is well advised to brace himself psychologically for the possibility that things will not turn out as he expected.

The appearance of a tiger in a dream is interpreted in another manner as well, and serves as a kind of warning dream that implies that someone the dreamer is going to meet in the near future will not be a good person. On the contrary, he will be the type who gets involved in conspiracies, and his intentions will be to harm the dreamer. The latter, therefore, must be very suspicious of every new person or contact during the forthcoming period of time. The dream says: "Be warned!"

Till

If a person dreams about money and jewelry in a till, he can look forward to success in love. A dream about an empty till promises nothing but disappointment.

Timber

If a person dreams about seeing timber, it is a symbol of peace and prosperity. If the timber has dried up and warped in the dream, disillusionment is around the corner.

Tin

A dream about tin is a warning that the dreamer is surrounded by two-faced people.

Tipsy

If a person dreams about being tipsy, it is a sign of a cheerful, carefree disposition that can ignore life's vicissitudes. If he dreams that other people are tipsy, he does not care about the behavior of people around him.

Toad

The appearance of a toad in a dream implies that the dreamer is disturbed by acts of corruption – actions that are not pure and clash with honesty and justice. The dreamer is not at peace with himself, and he knows that he has to make up for deeds he has done or take back declarations he has made – things that are liable to hurt others. It is possible that the dreamer has not yet done anything bad, but he has had evil thoughts that have not yet been put into practice. In such a case, the dreamer's conscience is using the dream to force him to think about his intentions once more and convince him to abandon them. Something is tempting the dreamer to stray from the straight and narrow path; this could be acts of corruption whose motive is money or other perks. The dream is patently a warning against this

A B C D E F G H I J K L M N O P Q R S T U V W X Y Z

temptation, and it encourages the dreamer to act in the proper way in order to achieve his goals.

Toast

A dream about toast is a sign of a successful and enjoyable family life.

Toaster

A dream about a toaster means that a wish will soon come true.

Tobacco

A dream about tobacco or any other form of smoking augurs well. If the dreamer smokes in the dream and blows smoke rings into the air, this reinforces the fact that the dreamer has a gentle nature and tends to compromise. The smoking figure also attests to the fact that he has a tendency toward harmony and a strong desire, accompanied by action when necessary, to maintain normal relations with the people around him. If the dreamer dreams about someone else smoking, it indicates that the problems he is struggling with and deliberating about at present will be solved satisfactorily. The dreamer will be satisfied with the resulting situation. To sum up, a dream about smoking and tobacco means that positive events are in the offing.

Tocsin

If a person dreams about the sound of a tocsin, it predicts a battle that the dreamer will win. If a woman hears a tocsin in a dream, it is a sign that she will leave her husband or lover.

Toddy

If a person dreams about drinking a toddy, it means that his lifestyle will be altered by fascinating events.

Toilet

A dream about a toilet, especially one that does not look clean, hints that an investment made by the dreamer is going down the drain. All the energy he expended on a particular project has been wasted, and has not brought the hoped-for results.

If a married woman dreams about a toilet, the dream serves as a kind of warning: false friends are causing her "to grow horns." Behind her back, in secret, things are being whispered about infidelities. The dreamer has no idea that she is the victim of these people. She is well advised to keep her finger on the pulse and look at the present reality – sooner rather than later. She has already become a laughing-stock in the eyes of the people around her.

Tomato

A dream about a tomato implies that the dreamer is now on the verge of beginning a particularly passionate affair. He will soon meet a person with whom he will not only share a common language and common interests, but also great love. The match that is on the threshold will be successful and promising.

Another interpretation of a tomato in a dream states that the dreamer has a desire and a need to fit into a new society and to blend into it. Whether out of necessity or out of a desire to make a change his immediate surroundings, the dreamer will find himself in new situations in which he will have to blend into a society with which he has not been familiar until now. He is happy to do so and is even looking forward to it.

A dream that features a perfect tomato – that is, a round, red, ripe and appetizing tomato – is a prophetic dream that implies that the dreamer will enjoy a good married life and a full and satisfying happy family life.

Tomb

If a person dreams about seeing tombs, it is a warning of unhappiness and letdowns in business. If the tombs in his dream are dilapidated and broken, it is a sign of serious illness and death. If he sees his own tomb in a dream, he will suffer from illness or disappointment. If he dreams about reading tombstones, it is a prediction of his illness.

Tongue

If a person dreams about his own tongue, his associates will view him with distaste. If he sees another person's tongue in the dream, he will be harmed by slander. If there is anything wrong with his tongue in the dream, it means that he will get himself into trouble if he speaks without thinking.

Toothless

If a person dreams about being toothless, it means that he is incapable of advancing, and is threatened by illness. If he dreams that other people are toothless, it means that his adversaries are attempting to slander him – but are not succeeding.

Toothpicks

If a person dreams about toothpicks, it means that he will be bothered by trifling worries and hassles. If he dreams about using a toothpick, it means that he will hurt a friend.

Topaz

If a person dreams about seeing a topaz, it implies wonderful luck and good friends. If a woman loses a topaz in a dream, she will be hurt by envious friends. If she receives a topaz in a dream, she will get involved in a fascinating love affair.

Tops — See Spinning tops

Torch

If a person dreams about seeing torches, it is a sign of enjoyment and good business. If he dreams that he is carrying a torch, it implies success in love and intrigues. A dream about an extinguished torch is a sign of worry and failure.

Tornado

If a person dreams about being in a tornado, it means that he will be devastated when his plans for becoming rich fail to materialize.

Torrent

If a person dreams about watching a swift torrent, it is a prediction of extraordinary hardship and problems.

A B C D E F G H I J K L M N O P Q R S T U V W X Y Z

Torture

A dream about torture of any kind attests to severe physical discomfort. The dreamer may not be in the best of health and may be suffering from pain that is causing him to have dreams of this kind.

Dreams about torture also express fear and anxiety about a secret the dreamer is trying to hide. Something he has concealed for many years is bothering his conscience and trying to burst out. He should examine the possibility of revealing the secret on condition that such an action does not cause irreparable damage. For instance, does the secret involve information that could cause the breakup of a family or prompt someone to commit suicide? If the secret does not involve something especially serious, revealing it could bring immediate relief.

Tourist

If a person dreams about being a tourist, it means that some enjoyable matter will divert him from his routine. If he dreams about seeing tourists, it is a prediction of problems in love and erratic business.

Tower

A dream about climbing a high tower can express expected success on the one hand and a feeling of danger stalking the dreamer on the other. The dreamer may well belong to the risk-taking type. Going up a tower resembles a financial deal involving shares or an investment in a developing country. The dreamer must consider his steps with great caution.

Toys

A dream about boxes and toys in colored packaging can express several things. First, it means that the dreamer feels a lack of attention and perhaps a lack of material things as well and yearns to receive gifts, just like a child. Second, it may refer to big economic success that will cause the dreamer to go on a generous shopping spree for all the members of his family and especially for the children among them. This is the time to buy a lottery ticket.

Trade

If a person dreams about trading, it is a sign of fair success. If, however, he dreams about failure in trade, he can expect hassles and anxieties.

Traffic circle

A dream that features a traffic circle attests to the fact that the dreamer feels that someone is leading him around in circles, preventing him from choosing his own preferred direction for advancement. A thorough examination is required in order to understand the sources of the feeling and enable the dreamer to make new decisions that will extricate him from the undesirable situation he is in right now.

Tragedy

If a person dreams about a tragedy, it means disillusionment and misunderstandings. If he dreams about being involved in a tragedy, it is a prediction of a catastrophe that will endanger him and cause him grief.

Trailer

If a person dreams about traveling in a trailer, it predicts a trip that is causing him anxiety. If he dreams about living in a trailer, it means bad luck.

Train

If a person dreams that he is in a smoothly-moving train that is not on tracks, his worries will be resolved to his advantage. A dream that features freight trains indicate positive changes. A dream about sleeping-cars signals that the dreamer's desire to attain wealth is motivated by lust and other immoral urges.

If a person dreams about sleeping on top of a sleeping-car, it means that he is wasting time and money on a disagreeable companion. If he is on the wrong train, it is a warning that he has chosen the wrong path in life and should correct his mistake.

Traitor

If a person dreams about seeing a traitor, it indicates that he is being threatened by enemies who seek his destruction. If he is accused of being a traitor, or considers himself one, he will not have much fun.

Transfiguration

If a person sees himself transfigured in a dream, he will enjoy the very high opinion of men of honor and esteem.

Trap

If a person dreams about falling into a trap, it means that he is a suspicious type, suspicious even of people who have done nothing to deserve it. If he himself laid the trap in the dream, it implies that he will soon lose a lawsuit and will employ underhand means to implement his plans. If he dreams about being caught in a trap, it means that his rivals will outsmart him.

If he catches animals in a trap, he will enjoy professional success. A dream that features an empty trap warns of an imminent mishap. A dream about a worn or non-functional trap is a sign of business setbacks and possible illness in the family.

Travel, trip

A dream that features a strange traveler arriving at the dreamer's home or workplace implies good news. If a dream features a person who is traveling to a distant place (it could be the dreamer himself), it is a bad sign. It could imply a personal or professional disappointment, especially if the trip is undertaken hastily and without preparation. The dreamer will be surprised by unexpected developments. The new situation will cause him confusion as well as financial losses. He will have to act quickly and muster every bit of creativity and resourcefulness he possesses. It is important for him not to become stressed out, but rather to act in a considered and rational way. Only in this way will be he able to extricate himself from the embroilment within a short time and without too much damage.

A B C D E F G H I J K L M N O P Q R S T U V W X Y Z

Tray

If a person dreams about seeing a tray, it indicates money that has been wasted idiotically and extremely unpleasant surprises. If a dream features trays containing valuable objects, it mean that he will have good surprises.

Treasure

If a person dreams about discovering treasure, it means that he will be assisted on his path to wealth by generous help from an unexpected quarter. If he dreams about losing treasure, it is an indication of bad business and disloyal friends.

Trees

Trees appear quite a lot in dreams, and the interpretations of their appearance differ in accordance with both the context and the manner in which they appear in the dream:

A tree (or trees) laden with fruit in a dream indicates the dreamer's many handsome achievements in almost every field. The dreamer will enjoy economic prosperity and an easy life in everything to do with the material aspect. He will not have to work hard to obtain money, but even if he is "set up for life" from the financial point of view, it does not ensure him a happy life.

A dream that features trees in bloom with fresh, green leaves is a good and promising sign for the future, especially in everything to do with love and marriage: all of the dreamer's wishes and dreams concerning love will be fulfilled, and he will probably be spared the frustration and heavy dramas that generally go hand in hand with sweeping love stories. The perfection in his relationship will also be expressed in the strong family ties he will build in the future, and his married life will be full and satisfying.

A dream that features trees with broken branches and no leaves is a warning dream that tells the dreamer that someone is trying to harm him and is even setting some kind of "ambush" or trap and waiting for the dreamer to fall into it. The scheming person is on the lookout for a good opportunity to trip the dreamer up, and the dreamer must be extremely cautious, be suspicious of people who deserve to be treated with suspicion, and watch his back.

A dream that features sick trees is a sign of family quarrels that will erupt in the near future. Differences of opinion within the immediate or extended family are liable to develop into unpleasant, full-blown, vociferous rows that will eventually lead to the breaking of ties among family members. The dream serves as an opening for dealing with the situation before it becomes irreparable. Prior knowledge of the approaching row may prevent things from deteriorating further.

If a dream features burned trees, it is a sign that the dreamer can expect a lack of luck in the field of marriage and will not get any joy out of it. Having said that, this lack of luck may affect the dreamer in fields other than love, such as money losses and material problems.

If the dreamer sees himself getting lost in the tangle of a forest and is surrounded by trees in all directions, the dream predicts that he will be successful in his ability to cope with problems and overcome obstacles in life. The dreamer can accomplish the goals he has dreamed about, and even if there are difficult things to tackle along the way, he will be able to cope with them and attain the goals he set for himself.

If a dream features trees that are beginning to wither and look yellow, it implies that danger or an illness is stalking the dreamer. He may not be aware of this, but the disease is incubating inside his body, and he should have a checkup so as to treat the illness at as early a stage as possible. If there are no signs of the disease yet, the dream warns of the emergence of some kind of disease that is usually liable to be caused by an incorrect and unhealthy lifestyle. If the dreamer suffers from great stress in his everyday life, smokes, does not engage in physical exercise, neglects himself and suffers from obesity – all of these can be factors that are liable to cause diseases. The dream serves to warn the dreamer that he is not doing anything about the situation and not taking steps to radically change his defective way of life.

If a person sees himself falling out of a tree in a dream, the dream attests to the fact that the person has suffered severe humiliation or some kind of abuse that has caused him psychological damage. The dream can also attest to losses he is suffering or is liable to suffer in the future, or to the loss of his job and income – in other words, his economic backing, without which he loses his self-confidence.

Trenches

If a person dreams about trenches, it is a warning of betrayal. He must take great care when embarking upon new endeavors or making new acquaintances. If the trenches in his dream have been filled, it means an accumulation of worries.

Triangle

The shape of the triangle, when it appears in a dream, is not coincidental, and in most cases is interpreted in mystical and mysterious contexts. The dreamer might be about to have mysterious or mystical experiences, or perhaps he had such experiences in the past, which influenced the present as well. He is struggling with things that he finds difficult to understand and explain, and feels threatened to some extent, since it is hard for him to comprehend them.

A dream about a triangle attests to the fact that the dreamer is deliberating about something, grappling with it and having a hard time deciding what is best for him. He is in a conflict that is difficult for him to deal with.

Some people interpret the internal struggle and conflict as stemming from the need to choose a life partner, or as connected to some other fateful decision whose consequences will affect the rest of the dreamer's life.

A dream about a triangle sometimes implies that the dreamer can expect to receive a surprising inheritance because of the loss of a person close to him who will die unexpectedly.

Tripe

If a dream features tripe, it is a portent of danger and illness. If a person dreams about eating tripe, he must brace himself for a bitter disappointment.

Triplets

If a person dreams about seeing triplets, it heralds

A B C D E F G H I J K L M N O P Q R S T U V W X Y Z

success in an enterprise that seemed doomed to failure. If a man dreams that his wife is giving birth to triplets, it signals a positive outcome to some complicated matter. If a person hears newborn triplets crying in a dream, an argument will be resolved quickly and satisfactorily. If a young woman dreams about having triplets, it means that she will be wealthy, but will not have luck in love.

Trophy

If a person dreams about seeing trophies, it means that someone that he barely knows will bring him luck or pleasure. If a woman dreams that she presents a trophy, the dream hints at unsavory pleasures and doubtful gains.

Trousers

A dream about trousers has many meanings. If a man dreams about elegant trousers he is purchasing or wearing, it means that he is very satisfied with his life at this moment. This person may have gotten married recently or become involved in a new relationship in which he feels good and influential. The dream hints at the blooming of his emotional life.

In contrast, if a woman (who is not married) dreams about wearing trousers, it implies problems with relationships or with her sexual identity. It is possible that this women feels the masculine facets of her personality more, and is wondering what this means. She must not be in a hurry to draw conclusions about lesbian tendencies, but there is no doubt that there is some kind of problem. This might be the result of a personal disappointment or crisis. In any case, she should seek professional help.

If a married woman dreams that she is wearing trousers, it indicates a severe crisis that is about to occur in her relationship with her husband. It is quite possible that there will be a separation or a divorce unless there is an immediate and drastic change in the situation. She may well be interpreting her sensitivity as weakness, and she may have genuine reasons for feeling that she is the one who "wears the trousers." This is liable to be reflected in the fact that her partner will lose his job and become dependent on his wife. This may already have happened, and only now is the woman allowing herself to express her emotions in a dream.

Trout

If a person dreams about trout, it is a symbol of prosperity. A dream about eating trout implies a comfortable life. A dream about catching a trout with a fishing-rod means joy and a good living. If the person dreams that the trout slips back into the water, this period of good living will not last long. A dream about catching trout with a net is a sign of an unparalleled financial boom. If the trout in the dream are swimming in murky water, the dreamer's triumph in love will turn bitter and mournful.

Trowel

If a person dreams about a trowel, it is a sign that he will succeed in overcoming hardship. A dream that features a rusty or broken trowel portends unavoidable bad luck.

A B C D E F G H I J K L M N O P Q R S **T** U V W X Y Z

A B C D E F G H I J K L M N O P Q R S T U V W X Y Z

Trumpet

A dream about a trumpet predicts nothing but good: a great opportunity is about to present itself. If a person hears a trumpet fanfare in his dream, a significant turning point is about to occur in his life.

This turning point will only be for the good, and the dreamer is facing a period during which his expectations, wishes and desires will be fulfilled. The recognition of his ability to make things happen will increase his self-confidence, and from then on, the sky's the limit.

If a person dreams that he himself is playing a trumpet fanfare, it means that problems that he has been struggling with until now are about to come to an end. Even if he is embroiled in problems for which he does not see a way out or a solution, the dream implies that they will all quickly disappear – as if by the wave of a magic wand. This will happen in a chain reaction, and the dreamer will get rid of them al at once. The forthcoming period of time holds nothing but good things in store for him.

Trunks

If a person dreams about trunks, it is a prediction of journeys as well as of bad luck. If he sees himself packing a trunk in a dream, it means that he will have an enjoyable trip. If he dreams that the contents of a trunk are scattered about, it means that there will be disputes and an unsatisfactory, hastily undertaken trip. A dream that features empty trunks indicates disappointment in love and marriage. If a young woman dreams about attempting unsuccessfully to open her trunk, it means that she will fail to win the heart of a wealthy man. If she dreams that she is unable to lock her trunk, she will not be able to go on a long-awaited journey.

Truss

A dream about a truss is a sign of bad luck and bad health.

Trusts

If a person dreams about trusts, it is a sign of middling success in the legal profession or in business. If he is a member of a trust, he will experience phenomenal success in an enterprise.

Tub

If a person dreams about a tub full of water, it is a sign of domestic harmony. An empty tub in a dream implies financial wealth along with distress. A dream that features a broken tub predicts domestic quarrels.

Tumble

If a person dreams about tumbling off anything, it warns that he is not as careful as he should be. He should be more meticulous in business. If he sees other people tumbling in his dream, he will profit from their carelessness.

Tumult – See Riot

Tune

A dream about a tune the dreamer hears has a

A B C D E F G H I J K L M N O P Q R S **T** U V W X Y Z

particularly profound meaning. The tune symbolizes the dreamer's emotions. Finally, the time has come for him to dedicate more space to his emotions in his life than he has up till now. A change may well occur in the dreamer's work or in his personal life. His considerations, which are generally rational, will change in character, and the dreamer will take a daring step based on a gut feeling. Success can be expected within a few months.

Tunnel

A dream about a tunnel indicates that the dreamer can expect a harrowing event. For a long period of time, the situation will not be clear. There could be a trip abroad – work-related or a private journey – that will last longer than planned,. A surprise encounter is liable to lead to a surprising consequence. A person who dreams of emerging from a tunnel can breathe freely. The dreamer, who has endured difficult times, finally finds the way out of the distress he was in. Things are about to clear up and from now on he will be successful in whatever he does.

Turf (race track)

A dream about turf means that the dreamer will lead a life of enjoyment and wealth, but his moral character will come under scrutiny by his closest friends. If he sees a green turf, something of interest will fascinate him.

Turkey

A dream about turkeys is a sign of thriving business and good crops. If a person sees turkeys being prepared for sale in a dream, it means better business. A dream about sick or dead turkeys is a sign of difficulties. A dream about eating turkey indicates that a happy event is in the offing. A dream that features flying turkeys implies a meteoric rise to fame. If a person dreams about shooting turkeys, it means that he will amass wealth by unscrupulous means.

Turkish bath

If a person dreams about taking a Turkish bath, it means that he will spend time far away from those dear to him, but will nevertheless have a great time. If he sees others in a Turkish bath in his dream, it means that he will enjoy congenial company.

Turnips

If a person dreams about turnips growing, it means an improvement in his chances in life – and this will make him very happy. A dream about eating turnips is a sign of illness, while a dream about uprooting them means better opportunities in life. If a person dreams about seeing turnip seed, the dream has a similar meaning. If a young woman dreams that she sows turnip seed, she will receive a good bequest and will find a good-looking husband.

Turpentine

If a person dreams about turpentine, it indicates that in the immediate future he will have futile and worthless appointments.

Turquoise

If a person dreams about a turquoise, it means that one of his wishes will come true, much to the joy of his family. If a woman dreams that she has a turquoise stolen, she will be thwarted in love. If she dreams that she comes by the turquoise dishonestly, she will pay dearly for making hasty decisions in love.

Turtle

The appearance of a turtle in a dream can be interpreted in different ways according to the context in which it appeared:

If the turtle appears without any particular "scenery" in the dream, it attests to a certain battle linked to matters of money or love in which the dreamer is involved. The struggle is passionate and involves fierce emotions, mainly of envy.

If the turtle appears in natural surroundings in the dream – in its natural habitat – the dream attests to the fact that the dreamer's deep desire will eventually be realized. This will not happen immediately; it will take time, but eventually the dreamer will reach "the promised land" and will accomplish his goal.

If a dream features a turtle lying upside down, it implies the opposite trend: the dreamer has reached a dead end, with no way out, and he will not see his wishes come true and his goals accomplished.

TV quiz show

If a person dreams about participating in a TV quiz

show, it means that he will soon have to answer unpleasant questions. If he wins, his reputation will remain intact. If he loses, it will be jeopardized.

Tweezers

If a person dreams about tweezers, it means that he will be harassed by unpleasant situations and the attacks of his friends.

Twine

If a person dreams about twine, the dream warns that his business is becoming embroiled in problems that will be difficult to solve.

Twins

When a person dreams about twins, the dream acquires a meaning only if they are seen together. In such a case, the dream attests to the fact that the dreamer has reached a crossroads. He has to choose the road that will set his business on the right track, but the dream hints at a lack of success in the economic realm, even if the dreamer does everything in his power to succeed.

A "correct" choice is not possible here, since whichever choice he makes will be unsuccessful. Luck is the name of the game here, and it makes no difference what the dreamer decides or which road he chooses – nothing he does in the economic realm will succeed. The situation is not identical for other realms.

A
B
C
D
E
F
G
H
I
J
K
L
M
N
O
P
Q
R
S
T
U
V
W
X
Y
Z

Typewriter

If a person dreams about using a typewriter, it means that he will soon be catching up with a long-lost friend.

Typing

If a person dreams about seeing typing in a dream, it predicts that he will have a disagreement with friends. If he dreams about typing without errors, is a sign of love and prosperity.

Typhoid

If a person dreams that he is ill with typhoid, he should take care of his health and be on the lookout for enemies. If there is a typhoid epidemic in his dream, business and health will drop to a low ebb.

U

Ugliness

A dream about ugliness does not bode well for the dreamer.

Ugly

If a person dreams about being ugly, it means problems in love and business. If a young woman considers herself ugly in her dream, she will treat her lover badly and no doubt cause a breakup. If a young person sees an ugly face in a dream, it is also a sign of problems in love. A dream that features an old-looking lover means a breakup.

Ulcer (stomach)

If a person dreams about an ulcer, it indicates bad business, the loss of friends and a breakup with someone he loves. If he dreams that he has an ulcer, it is an indication of his friends' dissatisfaction with his idiotic conduct.

Umbrella

A person who dreams that he finds himself under an umbrella on a rainy day is a resourceful and fortunate person. The future holds pleasant surprises for him. In contrast, a person who dreams that he has an umbrella but it does not open properly when it is raining feels that his plans are not being implemented as he would like them to be. The dreamer feels that he is unfortunate and does not have the strength to be hurt anymore. Recommendation: Plan every step carefully in advance.

Uncle

A dream that features an uncle is a sign of bad news in the near future.

Underground

If a person dreams about living underground, he must know that there is a threat of losing money and his good name. If he sees an underground railway in his dream, it means that he will become involved in a peculiar venture that will cause him worry and stress.

Undressing

If a person dreams about undressing, it is an indication of his involvement in a scandal. If a woman dreams about the ruler of her country being undressed, she will be saddened by threatened evil to those close to her. If a dream features other people undressed, it is a sign of immoral pleasures that will soon give way to sorrow.

Unfortunate

If a person dreams about being unfortunate, it is a sign of bad luck and trouble for him and other people.

A B C D E F G H I J K L M N O P Q R S T U V W X Y Z

Unicorn

If a person dreams about a unicorn, it is a sign of good luck and a comfortable life. A dream that features this mythical animal is connected to virginity and sexuality in the dreamer's life.

Uniform

A dream about a uniform (military, police, etc.) indicates that the dreamer does not receive recognition for his abilities or efforts. The dreamer is a person "who can do more" but he does not manage to fulfill his potential.

Another meaning is that a uniform predicts that the dreamer will win a lawsuit or a bureaucratic inquiry in which he or one of his associates is involved.

If the nature of the uniform can be positively identified – nurse's uniform, policeman's uniform, prisoner's uniform and so on – you should check the corresponding entry in this dictionary.

University

A dream about a university, whether it just appears in the dream or plays an actual part in it (for instance, if the dreamer is a university student), implies that the dreamer is soon going to extend his social circle and enjoy success.

A dream in which a university is seen, but nothing more, implies that the dreamer is an ambitious and achievement-oriented person who wants to accomplish as many objectives in his life as possible and achieve the goals he has set himself. The dreamer is a person who fights for his principles and does not give up, even if he has to overcome numerous obstacles in his path.

If the dreamer sees himself as a university student, he can expect a brilliant future in all areas: from a good marriage and establishing a supportive family to success in the financial realm. However, these things will only follow achievements that come from hard work, persistence, tenacity, and sticking to the goal. For the dreamer, achievements that stem from serious study are no less important than material achievements. He will be successful in all areas.

Unknown

If the dreamer sees himself meeting unknown people, it is a sign of good luck if the people are good-looking, or bad luck if they are ugly or deformed. If he feels that he is unknown, he will have bad luck as a result of peculiar events.

Unlucky – See Unfortunate

Urgent

If person dreams that he is championing some burning cause, it means that he will become involved in a matter that will require serious financial backing in order for it to succeed.

Urinal

If a dream features a urinal, it implies a chaotic home.

Urine

If person dreams about seeing urine, it means that he will be tetchy with his friends as a result of ill health. If he dreams about urinating, it is a sign of bad luck and failure in love.

Urn

If person dreams about an urn, it is a sign of a mixture of good and bad luck. A dream that features broken urns means sorrow.

US Mailbox

If a person dreams about a US mailbox, it means that he is about to get involved in deals that will allegedly be unlawful. If he drops a letter into a US mailbox, he will be held responsible for the misdemeanors of someone else.

Usurer

If a person dreams that he is a usurer, it means that his colleagues will treat him coldly, and he will suffer shocking setbacks in business. If he dreams that other people are usurers, he will drop a friend because of a betrayal.

Usurper

If a person dreams about being a usurper, it means that he will have a hard time establishing his right to an estate. If others try to usurp his rights in a dream, he will have a battle with his rivals, but in the end he will win. If a young woman dreams about usurpers, it means that she will be involved in a rivalry in which she will ultimately prevail.

A
B
C
D
E
F
G
H
I
J
K
L
M
N
O
P
Q
R
S
T
U
V
W
X
Y
Z

V

Vacation

A dream about vacation in general is a good dream that hints at positive things that are about to happen to the dreamer. It indicates that the near future will be filled with good and happy surprises and that the dreamer can expect tranquil, pleasant and enjoyable days. This kind of dream mainly refers to unexpected things that are about to happen to the dreamer – he did not plan them at all and never imagined that they would happen. The dream does not hint at anything specific. It could be the joyful visit of someone the dreamer has not seen for a long time from abroad or from a faraway place. It could be an unexpected sum of money or an excellent grade on a paper. It could be an impressive achievement that he or a member of his family notches up, much to the dreamer's surprise, and so on.

If a person dreams about planning a vacation, the dream implies that he can look forward to many happy days in the near future. Even if the situation appears impossible at the moment, fate is about to turn around, and the dreamer will enjoy great and unexpected happiness.

A dream about going on vacation prophesies that the dreamer can expect a special kind of entertainment that will provide a break in his routine and introduce something new into his life.

A dream about returning from a vacation is a sign that the dreamer can anticipate a period of prosperity, wealth, joy and happiness in his life – both from the emotional and mental point of view and from the material point of view. His life is getting onto a wonderful track of self-fulfillment and financial profit that will lead to a calm and quiet life. These things are especially true for a dream in which the feeling that accompanies the return from the vacation is one of elation, as in the case of someone who had a marvelous time. If the feeling is negative, as in the case of someone who is disappointed and reluctant to get back to the grind, the prosperity is limited and partial.

If a person dreams that other people are going on vacation, the dream implies that problems connected with money will be solved. He might win a large sum of money or become rich from other sources such as an inheritance or other legal sources of money.

Vaccinate

If a person dreams about being vaccinated, it means that his weakness for women will be unscrupulously exploited. If he dreams that other people are vaccinated, it means that he will fail in his quest for happiness and this will result in business losses. If a young woman dreams that she is vaccinated on her leg, she will suffer as a result of other people's treacherous behavior.

Vacuum cleaner

If a person dreams about a vacuum cleaner, it means that he will soon have to reach some snap decisions about personal or professional associations, at the risk of complications and embroilment.

A B C D E F G H I J K L M N O P Q R S T U **V** W X Y Z

Vagina — See Penis

Vagrancy

A dream about vagrancy implies many things regarding the way the dreamer relates to his life and how he fulfills the potential it contains. He feels that he wants to continue along a different path in life, but does not do so because fear prevents him from acting in the way he wants to. On the one hand, the dreamer does not want to lose everything he has built and created with his own two hands in his life so far, but on the other, he is crying out for a change, for something new that will excite him and sweep him along to new vistas. The fear of failure and of losing what he has already succeeded in building causes "delays."

In many cases, a dream about vagrancy indicates the dreamer's indecision concerning the social group to which he belongs. On the one hand, he likes to be in the company of interesting people who are not afraid to act according to the dictates of their conscience and methods, even if their steps do not always take society into consideration. On the other, he does not agree with their methods, so he sometimes finds himself surrounded by boring people who do not pose any threat of sweeping him away. He is vacillating between making friends with people who are considered "bad company" but who interest him greatly and staying away from them in favor of a stable life whose path is mapped out in advance.

If a person dreams that he has vagrant friends, the dream indicates that he will soon meet highly respectable people who will exert a good influence on his life.

Vagrant

If a person dreams about being a vagrant, it portends poverty and misery. If he sees vagrants in a dream, it is a sign of an epidemic in his surroundings. A dream about giving to a vagrant means that the dreamer's generosity will be acknowledged and approved of.

Valentines

If a person dreams about sending valentines, it implies that he will miss the opportunity of increasing his wealth. If a young woman dreams that she receives a valentine, she will go against the advice of other people and marry an ardent but weak lover.

Valley

If a person sees a silent valley in a dream, it is a sign that he is about to go through sad times. He must be psychologically prepared for this, but this phase will pass quickly.

A dream in which the dreamer is standing in a valley or walking through it hints at a move to a new home in the near future. A change of place is also a change of fortune, for better or for worse.

If a person sees a valley that is bustling with life in his dream, the dream implies that he is on the threshold of a good era of fulfillment, realizing his potential, and attaining mental peace and inner repose.

A dream in which there is a valley nearby indicates that the dreamer can expect a meeting with an old friend.

A dream in which the dreamer sees himself standing in

a high place like a mountain, looking down into the valley, implies that the dreamer suffers from a feeling of deep and heavy remorse for things he did in the past. These things are coming back at him like a boomerang, and he is finding it difficult to liberate himself from them.

Vampire

A vampire that appears in a dream is automatically linked to Dracula and to the myths of bloodsuckers. Therefore, bloodsucking is generally interpreted as greed – not for objects, but rather for the people of the opposite sex around the dreamer, and for the relationship he creates with them. The dream implies that the dreamer is very jealous of his partner and goes way over the top when expressing his jealousy. He does not respect his partner's freedom and "suffocates" him with love – or jealousy. Such a relationship is doomed to a bad end. The dream symbolizes a sick relationship with a partner, which can only end in scandal or even disaster. It is a kind of warning dream that tells the dreamer to exercise restraint in his conduct toward his partner. He should relate to this warning dream before it is too late. If he does not pay attention to the warning, the whole thing will come to a bitter end.

Varnishing

If a person dreams about varnishing something, it means that he will attempt to achieve fame by fraudulent methods. If he sees other people varnishing in a dream, it is a warning to him that his friends want to become rich at his expense.

Vase

When a vase appears in a dream, the meaning of the dream changes according to the way the vase appears. If it is an ordinary vase, without flowers, it implies that the dreamer is very self-involved, and it is now time he paid attention to those around him. His "egoism" causes him to consider his own interests only, without taking other people into account at all. The dream constitutes, therefore, a kind of mirror that forces the dreamer to look at himself so that he can change his ways and be more sensitive to those around him.

If the person who dreamed about a vase is single, the dream is prophetic, and implies that he will get married very soon. Not only will wedding bells chime, however, but a birth can be expected in the near future…

A dream in which the vase appears broken and smashed attests to the fact that the dreamer is facing times of sorrow and pain. He may soon be entering a phase in which he will wallow in depression. It will not be easy for him, but he will get by with the help and support of close friends or family members who care.

If a vase of flowers or a silver vase appears in a dream, it means that a romantic interlude is in the offing, bringing joy and happiness. The dreamer will soon get to enjoy the company of a beloved kindred spirit that is very dear to him. The immediate future is full of moments of happiness, spontaneous outpourings of nice gestures and a profound desire to give.

Vat

A dream about a vat is a negative sign, since it implies

that the dreamer will suffer at the hands of sadistic people who have gotten him in their clutches.

Vatican

If a person dreams about the Vatican, it means that he will receive unexpected perks. If he sees royal personages conversing with the Pope in a dream, he will become acquainted with high-ranking people.

Vault

If a person dreams about a vault, it is a sign of misfortune and death. If he sees a vault for valuables in a dream, it means that in spite of his modest lifestyle, people will be amazed at his actual worth. If the doors of a vault are open in the dream, trusted people will betray and abandon him.

Vegetables

A dream that features vegetables that are fresh attests to the fact that the person is a modest, humble person who makes do with little and knows how to enjoy simple, everyday things. His thinking is generally positive, and he is the kind of person who sees the full half rather than the empty half of the glass. Because of his nature, he is popular, and is usually surrounded by people who love and appreciate him.

If a dream features vegetables that are not fresh – that is, they are wilted and rotten – it is a sign that the dreamer is neglecting something and is suffering from problems as a result – either everyday problems or mental or emotional problems. He pays dearly for his neglect, since it causes one thing to lead to another, and ultimately he finds himself in a vicious circle that will be difficult to get out of in the future. He is well advised to take care of things quickly – sooner rather than later.

A dream in which the dreamer sees himself eating vegetables attests to the fact that he is a careful person who does not like to take risks. The dreamer is the type of person who thinks twenty times before taking a step that is liable to put anything at risk, or even before simply altering the situation he is in. In spite of his nature, which is not adventurous, he does not always manage to achieve his coveted goal, and in most cases he only gets "halfway." He is not a "winning" type; rather, he is hesitant – the type that does not take a step before examining every aspect and future implication thoroughly.

A dream in which the dreamer sees himself picking vegetables and gathering them in a basket is a sign of the material abundance that he will enjoy. He will soon enjoy a sound economic situation that will afford him a high standard of living and even a bit of extravagance.

Vegetables in a basket or a can in a dream: For a single person, it is an obvious sign that marriage is on the horizon. In the near future, the person will enter a relationship with commitments, even if it isn't marriage in the conventional sense. In any case, the dreamer will find himself in a committed relationship – out of his own free choice. If the dreamer is already married, the dream predicts an excellent marital relationship, the kind in which the spouses are very faithful to each other and do not let their eyes rove. Their commitment to each other is clear and understood, and they enjoy a stable and good married life. The dream predicts

A B C D E F G H I J K L M N O P Q R S T U **V** W X Y Z

that not only will this be the case in the future as well, but their relationship will become even stronger.

Pickled vegetables in a dream: This is a complex situation that implies the dreamer's many commitments that cause him to place things other than his family at the top of his list of priorities. This causes a great deal of tension in the family and can lead to disputes. The dream "shakes" the dreamer and reminds him of what really should be at the top of his list of priorities. He must not ignore the signs that appeared in the dream, since his subconscious is communicating with him, and his conscience is not clear with regard to the way he is leading his life. If he listens to himself, he will be able to prevent a lot of mental anguish in the future.

Vegetation

If a person dreams about green vegetation, it is a good omen: He can expect exciting surprises or good news.

Vehicle

If a person dreams about driving a vehicle, it is a sign of loss or ill health. If he dreams about being thrown from a vehicle, it implies sudden bad news. A dream that features a broken-down vehicle means failure in important undertakings. If he dreams about buying a vehicle, it means that he will recoup his losses. If he dreams about selling a vehicle, he will suffer a reversal in business.

Veil

If a person dreams about a veil, it means that he will not

be absolutely honest with his partner and will have to engage in little deceptions to keep him/her. If he sees other people wearing veils in a dream, it implies that he will be slandered and maligned by so-called friends. A dream that features an old or torn veil is a warning that the dreamer is surrounded by deceit. If a young woman dreams that she loses her veil, her deceit will be discovered by her lover, who will retaliate in kind.

If a person sees a bridal veil in a dream, it predicts an imminent, positive and joyful change in his life. If a young woman dreams that she wears a bridal veil, she will be very successful and prosperous in some endeavor. If the veil becomes loose in the dream, or something happens to it, she can expect pain and worries. A dream about discarding a veil means separation or shame. A dream that features mourning veils is a sign of sorrow and losses in business.

Vein

If a person dreams about his veins, and they look like veins are supposed to look, he is rendered immune to slander. If his veins are bleeding in a dream, unavoidable grief is in the offing for him. A dream about swollen veins means a rapid rise to honor and positions of responsibility.

Velvet

If a person dreams about touching velvet, it refers to hassles, arguments and domestic quarrels. A dream about velvet is a sign of success in business. A drean about wearing velvet means that the dreamer will achieve some measure of fame and honor. A dream that features old velvet means that his prosperity will decrease because of

A B C D E F G H I J K L M N O P Q R S T U **V** W X Y Z

his foolish pride. If a young woman dreams that she wears velvet, she will be accorded favors and honors, and will enjoy a selection of eligible lovers.

Veneer

If a person dreams about veneering, it means that he will deceive his friends routinely. His business undertakings will be unsavory.

Ventriloquist

If a person dreams about a ventriloquist, it means that he is going to be harmed by a dangerous matter of some kind. If he dreams that he is a ventriloquist, it means that his conduct toward people who trust him will not be above board. If a young woman dreams that she is confused by a ventriloquist's voice, it means that she will be tricked into an illicit affair.

Veranda

If a person dreams about being on a veranda, it means that an issue that is weighing on his mind will have turn out well. If a young woman dreams that she and her lover are sitting on a veranda, it predicts an early and happy marriage. A dream about an old veranda means decreasing hopes, as well as disillusionment in love and business.

Vermin

If a person sees vermin crawling in a dream, it is a sign of tremendous problems and illness. If he can get rid of them, he will enjoy average success, but if he cannot, death will threaten either him or a family member.

Vertigo

If a person dreams about vertigo, it means that his happiness at home will decline and his business prospects will look dim.

Vessels

If a person dreams about vessels, it is a sign of work and activity.

Vexed

If a person dreams about being vexed in a dream, it means that he will awake to many worries. If he thinks that someone is vexed with him, he will not succeed in settling a minor argument in the near future.

Vicar

If a person dreams about a vicar, it means that he is liable to act stupidly during a fit of jealousy. If a young woman dreams that she marries a vicar, she will suffer from unrequited love; either she will not marry, or she will make a marriage of convenience.

Vice

If a person dreams about indulging in vice, it means that he is giving in to temptation that will cost him his reputation. If he dreams that other people are giving in to a vice, one of the dreamer's relatives or acquaintances will have bad luck.

Victim

If a person dreams about being the victim of some plot, it means that the dreamer will be shattered by his enemies, and he will not enjoy domestic harmony. If he dreams that other people are victimized, it means that he will make money in an underhand manner and indulge in immoral affairs – much to the chagrin of the people close to him.

Victory

In most cases, a dream about victory serves as a warning sign to the dreamer. It implies that the dreamer must refrain from adopting a standpoint he is not at one with in a dispute. If he feels that the standpoint he is adopting is alien to him, and he is adopting it only in order to defend someone or in order to prove something, it would be preferable if he refrained from expressing it. It is liable to harm him.

If a person dreams of victory over a friend, the dream implies that the relations between him and his friend are not based on trust, and there will be no joy from them.

If a person dreams of victory over an enemy, it is a sign that he will soon enjoy wealth and honor. Life will smile upon him in everything to do with money, everything he sets out to do from the economic point of view will succeed, and he will be able to support the members of his family very well.

If a person dreams about a military achievement and victory in battle, he is aware of the fact that the people around him scoff at him. His image in their eyes is that of a "loser," and he will have to work very hard if he wants to change it.

Village

A dream that features a village (usually the kind of "picturesque" village we see in paintings or movies) hints at nostalgia or longing for a period of quiet and of forgetting about everything.

The dream does not provide a clear answer to the question of whether such a period will occur or whether it will simply remain a yearning. Some people claim that according to the amount of light, it is possible to answer this question: bright sunshine promises a period of tranquillity in the future, while dim or dull light means that the dream will not come true in the immediate future.

Vine

If a person dreams about a vine that contains grapes, it is an indication of hard work that will yield prosperity and great success. A dream about vines is a sign of success and joy. If a dream features flowering vines, it is a sign of good health. Dead vines in a dream warn of failure in an important undertaking. Poisonous vines in a dream imply that the dreamer will be taken in by a clever scheme, and his health will suffer.

Vinegar

Vinegar in a dream generally hints at the dreamer's state of health, and predicts that he is about to succumb to a disease. It is not a serious disease, but rather physical debility as a result of which the dreamer's state of health will deteriorate.

Sometimes vinegar in a dream also attests to the fact that

in the near future the dreamer is liable to get into conflicts with friends and become embroiled with colleagues in his workplace.

Vinegar in a dream also implies the dreamer's personality and character: he is a jealous person by nature. This trait explains why the relationships he has tried to build have frequently been destroyed, and why he often feels rejected, without being aware of the reason for it. The root of the problem lies in his lack of self-awareness regarding this trait. This places many obstacles in front of him in many areas of life, since he tends to attribute the problems to other things and not to the real issue that is tripping him up. His conduct causes the people around him to shy away from him. Rebuilding his shaky self-confidence, which causes him to behave in the way he does, will help him overcome these obstacles and become more accepted and well-liked.

Vineyard

A dream about a vineyard that yields a big harvest of grapes is a very good dream. It predicts success in business and in anything to do with money for the dreamer, but it also predicts success in general in anything to do with affairs of the heart: a great love, a positive response to a marriage proposal, and general success with his future partner. If the vineyard is overflowing with grapes and is green and full of leaves (in contrast to when the vines are naked and empty), it symbolizes abundance in almost every area of life.

If the dreamer is single, the dream predicts a successful family life with many children in the future.

A B C D E F G H I J K L M N O P Q R S T U V W X Y Z

Violence

Violence that is expressed in a dream when the dreamer acts violently toward someone else (but also if the dreamer sees another person in the dream acting violently) is a manifestation of the dreamer's lack of repose and tranquillity in his everyday life. Worries, fears, anxieties and a lack of confidence are all directed at the dreamer as a way of divesting themselves of their heavy loads. The dreamer, who does not dare to give free rein to his urges so crudely in reality, does it in an alternative way through the dream. There he gives vent to those urges and expresses anger, aggression and the other negative emotions and feelings that find release in this manner.

People who have dreams in which there are violent "scenes" get up with a feeling of relief, as if a heavy load had been lifted off them. The feeling of liberation is genuine, as if they had really undergone this experience.

Violets

Violets in a dream serve as a sign that the affair in which the dreamer is involved is gradually taking on a new reality of mutual commitment. The result of this affair will be serious and significant in the dreamer's life. Violets also symbolize various pleasures the dreamer will enjoy. These are linked to his love life. The physical relationship between the dreamer and his/her partner is excellent, and their lives will be filled with pleasures of this kind.

Violin

A dream about a violin augurs well. Playing a violin in a

A B C D E F G H I J K L M N O P Q R S T U **V** W X Y Z

way that is pleasant to the ear, especially when the dreamer sees himself playing, means that he is about to become more popular with the people around him. He can expect to advance toward prospective goals and enjoy greater social success than he has in the past.

If a string on the violin snaps, it does not imply a negative event. It refers to renewal from the physical or general point of view. The dreamer may become ill, but he will quickly recover from his illness. There may also be family disputes in which the dreamer intervenes and manages to convince those involved to effect a reconciliation.

Viper

A dream about a viper attests to one thing only: genuine difficulties in the sexual realm. The dreamer is not successful in establishing normal relations with the opposite sex and experiences both psychological and physical difficulties. This bothers him terribly and torments him relentlessly. The viper that appears at night spurs him to take action as soon as possible to deal with the situation.

Virgin

If a person dreams about a virgin, he can look forward to fairly good business dealings. If a married woman dreams that she is a virgin, she will agonize over her past and lose all hope in the future. If a young girl dreams that she is no longer a virgin, it is a warning dream: she is warned that if she behaves indiscreetly, she will lose her good reputation. If a man dreams about a wrongful, intimate relationship with a virgin, he will fail in some endeavor, and will be hounded by people's pleas for help. His hopes will be dashed as a result of keeping company with the wrong people.

Vision

If a person dreams about seeing a peculiar vision, it is a sign of ill health and bad luck in business. If he dreams about people appearing to him in visions, there will be rebellion and dissent in his country and family. If his friend is in a dissipated state in real life, the friend may appear suddenly in a vision, wearing white. Any type of vision in dreams portends unusual developments in business and changes in the dreamer's private life – often temporarily for the worse, but eventually improving.

Visit

A dream in which the dreamer is visited is different in meaning than a dream in which he visits other people.

If the dreamer sees other people coming to visit him, it is a sign that the dreamer is about to make serious mistakes as a result of his exaggerated conceit. Words of praise that are directed at the dreamer turn his head. The way he thinks of himself and his inflated ego are liable to cost him dearly. He is liable to act hastily and do things that he will have to pay for later on – and the price will not be low.

If a person dreams that he visits other people, it is a sign that good news is about to arrive – the kind of news that will be very significant for the dreamer. He will receive this news from someone who is very close to him – a soul mate or a close family member. The deliverer of the news is also very significant, since the way in which the words are delivered is very important.

A dream in which the visit was a happy one hints that in the near future, the dreamer will get to go on a long trip or journey during which he will undergo unique experiences. Instead of going on a trip, however, the dreamer may enjoy some other special entertainment that will leave its mark upon him for a long time.

If, in contrast, the visit made a sad impression, it is a sign that evil and malicious behavior will humiliate the dreamer. He is about to find himself at the center of an embarrassing situation that will cause him great shame, even though it is not his fault that he got into such an embarrassing situation. One of his associates will make him feel very uncomfortable, and this will lead him into a really humiliating situation.

Vitriol (sulfuric acid)

If a person dreams about vitriol, it means that he is reprimanding someone unjustifiably. If he dreams about throwing vitriol on people, it means that he is liable to behave ungratefully toward the people who want to help him. If a young woman dreams that a jealous rival throws vitriol in her face, it means that she will be the innocent victim of someone's hatred. For a businessman, a dream about vitriol signifies enemies and persecution.

Voices

If a person dreams about hearing voices (without seeing their source), it means that he will soon experience feelings of distress, sadness or depression. If he dreams about hearing calm, pleasant voices, it is a sign that he will make up quarrels peacefully. If the voices in the dream are shrill

A B C D E F G H I J K L M N O P Q R S T U **V** W X Y Z

and angry, it is a prediction of unpleasant and disappointing situations. The sound of weeping voices in a dream predicts that the dreamer will hurt a friend in a fit of anger. If he dreams about hearing the voice of God, it means that he will endeavor to adopt higher moral standards, and will be admired by worthy people. If a mother hears her child's voice in a dream, it is a sign of misery and agonizing doubts. A dream about hearing a voice of distress or warning hints at the dreamer's own bad luck or that of someone close. If he is able to identify the voice in the dream, it could indicate an illness or an accident.

Volcano

If a person sees fire erupting from a mountain peak, it is a sign that a disaster is about to befall an acquaintance or friend of his.

Climbing a volcano in a dream symbolizes problems on the personal level with one's mate, which come to the fore mainly in noisy rows and hurling terrible insults at each other.

If boiling lava is seen gushing out of a volcano, the dream attests to the fact that the dreamer is tortured by feelings of sorrow and wretchedness about something he did in the past, which he desperately regrets. Unfortunately, he cannot turn the clock back.

A dream about a volcano also serves as a kind of warning dream: The dreamer must curb his emotions, otherwise he will pay dearly. This is particularly true with regard to jealousy. If the dreamer suffers from jealousy, he must restrain himself, because if not, he could cause irrevocable damage that he will pay for all of his life.

A B C D E F G H I J K L M N O P Q R S T U **V** W X Y Z

Vomiting

A dream about vomiting of any kind always attests to detaching oneself. In most cases, it refers to the desire of the people around the dreamer to detach themselves from him, sometimes for no apparent reason. People will try to break their ties with the dreamer without him knowing why or wherefore or being able to check things out.

Vomiting in a dream, especially if it occurs during eating, also attests to the fact that the person's conscience is bothering him. The knowledge that he has done something wrong and that he has to mend his ways will not give him any peace, and he knows deep down that he has to take steps in order to get rid of these pangs of conscience. It irks him, and he feels a cloud of gloom looming over him wherever he goes.

Vote

A dream in which the dreamer sees himself taking part in a vote attests to his lack of self-importance – and even more so if the dreamer's vote is the deciding vote – one way or the other. The dream not only implies that the dreamer suffers from a lack of confidence and from low self-esteem, but also that he is a person who lacks initiative. Having said that, the dreamer recognizes his abilities, and knows that he can achieve much more in his life if he identifies the source of the problem that is causing him to suffer from low self-esteem.

Voting in the elections

A dream in which the dreamer sees himself going to the

polling booth and casting his ballot attests to the fact that he has a need to make a difference from the social point of view and that he is sensitive to social injustices. His sense of justice is highly developed, and he has a fierce desire to make a contribution to public life and to take an active part in the life of the society around him. This all stems from the fact that he knows that he can "move things" and has the talents and ability to effect change. The dreamer has charisma, powers of persuasion, the ability to stand in front of an audience, and excellent organizational capabilities. He is aware of these talents and is yearning to find a way to give them free rein. These things are innate, and whether he likes it or not, he will eventually find himself involved in public endeavors – possibly even in politics.

Voucher

If a person dreams about a voucher, it means that hard, constant work will prevent success being snatched away from him. If he signs a voucher in a dream, it means that the people around him place their trust in him, in spite of his enemies' endeavors to the contrary. If he dreams about losing a voucher, it implies that he will have to fight with his associates in order to ensure his rights.

Vow

If a person dreams about a vow, it is an indication of an improvement in business and in his financial situation. If he makes or hears vows in his dream, it means that he will be accused of underhand conduct in business or love. If he dreams about taking clerical vows, it means that he will display unflagging honesty throughout some difficult situation. If he dreams about breaking or ignoring a vow, it means that disaster will strike his business.

Voyage

If a person dreams about making a voyage, it means that he will receive an inheritance. A catastrophic voyage in a dream means false love and financial difficulties.

Vulture

A vulture in a dream (like other birds of prey such as buzzards, bearded vultures and so on) attests to the fact that the dreamer has a serious and ruthless adversary who is determined to hurt him. Deep inside, the dreamer knows who it is, even if in his everyday life he opts to ignore it and get on with his life as if this threat were non-existent.

The dream, which serves as a kind of warning dream, does not let him ignore the situation he is in and spurs him to take action. If he does not overcome his enemy, the latter, who does not shy away from any mode of action, will succeed in accomplishing his destructive objectives.

W

Wading

If a person dreams about wading in clear water, it is a sign of wonderful but transient pleasures. If he dreams about wading in murky water, it is a warning dream: it warns him of illness and sorrow. If he sees children wading in clear water in a dream, it is a sign of good luck in business. If a young woman dreams that she wades in clear, bubbly water, her dearest wish will soon come true.

Wafer

If a person dreams about seeing wafers, it is a sign of an imminent confrontation with enemies. If he dreams about eating wafers, it is a sign of a decrease in income. If a young woman dreams that she bakes wafers, it means that she is tortured by the fear of not marrying.

Wager

If a person dreams about making a wager, it means that he will use underhand means to promote his schemes. If he dreams that he loses a wager, he will be harmed by associating with people of a lower social standing. If he wins a wager in a dream, his fortune will be repaired. If he dreams that he is unable to put up a wager, it implies the

A B C D E F G H I J K L M N O P Q R S T U V **W** X Y Z

frustration and devastation he is liable to experience as a result of the blows dealt by fate.

Wages

Receiving wages for work in a dream means that the dreamer has an enemy or several enemies of whom he is completely unaware. They are plotting against him, undermining him and seeking to harm him without his realizing it. The dream serves to warn the dreamer against complacency and rouse him to action. His enemy or enemies are liable to cause him irreversible damage, and he must not ignore the dream, otherwise it will be too late. He is well advised to take this warning dream seriously and act immediately.

Wagon

A dream about a wagon means that the dreamer will have an unhappy marriage. Furthermore, he will be plagued by worries that will make him old before his time. If he dreams about driving a wagon down a hill, it is an indication of events that will cause anxiety and loss. If he dreams about driving a wagon uphill, it indicates an improvement in business.

A dream about driving a heavily loaded wagon means that the dreamer's sense of duty will keep him in check, although he longs to discard it. A dream about driving a wagon into muddy water is a dire prediction of worry and unhappiness. A dream about a covered wagon implies subtle treachery that will sabotage the dreamer's progress.

If a young woman dreams that she drives a wagon dangerously close to the edge of an embankment, she is liable to be forced into an illicit entanglement and will be petrified of being found out. If she dreams that she drives a wagon across clear water, she will have an enjoyable affair, with nothing reprehensible about it. A dream that features a dilapidated wagon is a symbol of failure and trouble.

Waif

A dream about a waif is a sign of troubles of a personal nature and particular bad luck in business.

Wail

If a person hears a wail in a dream, it portends terrible news of disasters and misery. If a young woman hears a wail in a dream, she will be abandoned in her hour of need, and possibly in her shame.

Waist

A dream that features a round, shapely waist means that the dreamer will receive a nice amount of money. A dream about a small, distorted waist implies failure and vindictive quarrels.

Waiter / Waitress

This kind of dream attests to the fact that the dreamer aspires to improve his situation and standing in life, but is finding it difficult to do so. The chances of improvement in the foreseeable future are small, especially if the dreamer sees himself as a waiter. It is reasonable to assume that behind the smile he is forced to wear, he feels miserable. He may feel pain in body and soul. He is doing the job only for the money, but this does nothing to improve his situation either.

If a person dreams that he is working as a waiter, it indicates that he can expect an unpleasant incident to occur. A large loss of money is liable to bring the dreamer to the point that he will lose his job and be compelled to make do with a simple job that entails serving others whose status is higher than his. If a person dreams about a waiter serving him in a restaurant or at some kind of function, he is about to receive surprising news from a distant quarter. It could well refer to a sum of money that will come to him as a result of an inheritance from a distant relative.

Wake

If a person dreams that he attends a wake, it means that he will forgo an important appointment in order to go to attend an unsavory meeting. If a young woman dreams that she sees her lover at a wake, it means that she will surrender to some man's impassioned pleas, thus losing her honor.

Waking up

A dream in which a person sees himself being woken up by a certain person hints that the latter will soon arrive for a visit. In general, the dream implies that a much-loved person from the past or someone who lives in a faraway place will arrive unexpectedly, without giving advance notice. The meeting with him will give the dreamer a lot of joy and happiness.

Walking

Walking in a dream is characterized according to both the features of the walking and its nature. If a person dreams that he is walking along confidently, it means that if fate has not favored him up till now, it is about to do so, and his future will be excellent. The change will be positive in several aspects, and the dreamer will experience new and unknown things that will do him nothing but good.

A dream about walking backward hints at the loss of money as well as the loss of other people's affection. The dreamer will lose things that are dear to him – either on the material or on the spiritual level.

Walking along a lengthy path implies that the dreamer is facing problems that he has to deal with and solve. Generally, the dream hints at finding successful solutions, at a good ability to cope and at the dreamer's special powers to withstand difficult situations.

A dream about walking at night implies that there is repressed anger in the dreamer's heart and only he knows at whom it is directed. He must try to get rid of this anger, release it and solve the problems that led to these bad feelings. If he does not, it is liable to manifest itself in health problems at a later stage.

A dream in which the dreamer sees himself walking particularly quickly implies that he is treating everyday matters with a heavy hand. He must lighter up and flow with things, and refrain from getting into conflicts that make matters worse.

A dream about walking slowly is a sign that the dreamer tends to take every bit of gossip he hears about himself to heart. He must view things in their correct proportion and not become upset about every crumb of gossip.

A B C D E F G H I J K L M N O P Q R S T U V **W** X Y Z

If a person sees himself limping in a dream, it is a sign that he will not be lucky in the forthcoming period of time.

Walking on burning coals is a sign that the person is about to experience enlightenment and alter his view of the world completely. A powerful spiritual event that could be accompanied by powerful and significant scenes may bring him to the point of losing his senses. His future path will be completely different than it is today.

If a person dreams that he is walking on burning things or on a boiling hot surface, it is a sign that he will lose money or property in the future.

Walking along a railway line in a dream is a sign that the person is about to embark on adventures and undergo new and exciting experiences that will exhilarate him and change his life. This dream also implies a significant change in the dreamer's way of life in the future.

Walking stick

If a person sees a walking stick in a dream, it means that he will clinch deals without giving them their due consideration, and this will cause him a lot of trouble. If he dreams that he uses a walking stick while walking, it means that he will depend on other people's counsel. If he admires beautiful walking sticks, it means that he will entrust his business concerns to others, and they will be loyal.

Wall

If a dream features a high wall or a high supporting wall that radiates strength and sturdiness, it is actually a warning dream that predicts that danger looms in the near future. There is definitely cause for concern, and the dreamer should pay close attention to his moves in the forthcoming period of time so that nothing bad happens to him or his family. The source of the evil may reside in people who are plotting to bring the dreamer down, and he should keep his eyes open and be alert to everything concerning his relations with thc people around him. The more threatening the wall seems – as if it is "closing in" on him – the greater the danger, and he must take extra precautions.

If, in contrast, the dream features a crumbling, ruined and falling wall, it is a sign that the dreamer can be calm and collected because it means that nothing bad will happen to him and his family. The dream implies that even if the situation all around is bad, and even if it looks as if everything is "collapsing," the dreamer himself is actually immune to danger and can lead his life without any hitches. There is no reason to worry, and he can bc absolutely sure that everything will work out well.

Wallet

If a person finds a wallet in a dream, it indicates prosperity and financial success. The loss of a wallet in a dream predicts disappointment and frustration. If he sees wallets in a dream, it predicts that he can expect duties of an agreeable nature. An old, dirty wallet in a dream means hard work that will yield poor results.

Walnut

If a person dreams about ripe walnuts, it is an excellent sign. If he sees walnuts in a dream, it means that he will marry a rich partner. A dream about eating walnuts implies that the dreamer is wasteful and extravagant. If he dreams

A B C D E F G H I J K L M N O P Q R S T U V **W** X Y Z

A B C D E F G H I J K L M N O P Q R S T U V **W** X Y Z

about cracking a rotten walnut, it means that his hopes will be brutally dashed. If a young woman dreams that her hands are stained with walnut juice, it means that her lover will leave her for someone else, and she will regret her former indiscretions.

Waltz

If a person dreams about watching people waltzing, it means a fun-filled friendship with a lively person. If a young woman dreams that she is waltzing with her lover, she will be greatly admired, but no one will want to marry her. If she sees her lover waltzing with a rival in a dream, she will use her wits to overcome obstacles. If she sees herself waltzing with another woman in a dream, she will be admired for her goodness and charm. If she sees a wild whirl of waltzing people in a dream, she will be so carried away with desire that she will not be able to resist any man who wants her.

Want

If a person dreams about being in want, it means that he has behaved foolishly, ignoring the harsh realities of life, and is now afflicted with grief and trouble. If he is satisfied with being in a state of want, he will be stoic in the face of adversity, and his troubles will gradually disappear. If he dreams about relieving want, it means that he will be admired for his generosity, but will derive no pleasure from doing good deeds.

War

A person who dreams that he is on a battlefield can expect to be injured in the near future. He should be careful on the roads. If a person dreams that he is killed in a war, the dream does not indicate a death. It implies that the dreamer is very worried and frustrated. He does not feel that his family members or friends value him sufficiently, and sometimes thinks that only after his death will they recognize his contribution and his uniqueness. This kind of dream hints at depression and hardship. Recommendation: Be careful in anything to do with traveling. Do not take unnecessary risks.

If a person dreams that he is taking part in a war that his side is winning, it means that he is going to succeed in a big project he has taken upon himself. That person invested a lot of time and energy, and now he is tired and feels that the time has come to quit. The waiting and effort will pay off. Success is just around the corner.

Wardrobe

If a person dreams about his wardrobe, it means that he will risk his fortune in order to appear better off than he actually is. If he has a limited wardrobe, he will take risks.

Warehouse

A person who dreams that he comes to an empty warehouse should be careful when choosing business partners. He may well fall into a trap that the others have set for him and find an empty place instead of a full place, as was promised him. A destroyed or burned warehouse, or one situated among some trees in an isolated place are all warning signs of a bad deal that the dreamer is liable to become involved in. However, a dream about a scrap warehouse is a positive sign. There is every chance that the dreamer will inherit a large sum of money unexpectedly.

Warrant

A dream about a warrant being served on the dreamer means that he will be involved in an undertaking of such magnitude that he worries about it. If a warrant is served on someone else in a dream, the dreamer runs the risk of his actions causing serious disputes or misunderstandings.

Warts

If a person dreams that he suffers from warts on his body, he will not be able to prevent attacks on his good name. If the warts disappear, he will overcome the obstacles on the way to fortune. If he dreams about seeing warts on other people, it refers to the presence of sworn enemies nearby. If he treats the warts, he will fight energetically to prevent danger to himself and his family.

Washboard

If a person sees a washboard in a dream, it is a sign of embarrassment. If he sees a woman using a washboard, it means that women will deplete the dreamer's fortune and energy. A dream that features a broken washboard signifies his downfall as a result of impure and decadent living.

Washbowl

If a person dreams about a washbowl, it is an indication of new careers that will interest him. If he washes his hands and face in a washbowl, it indicates that he will have a passionate and enduring relationship with someone for whom he had not always felt passion. If the washbowl in the dream is dirty or broken, he will regret for an illicit affair that gave him little pleasure and hurt others badly.

Washerwoman

If a person dreams about seeing a washerwoman, it symbolizes infidelity and a peculiar occurrence. A dream about a washerwoman is a sign of flourishing business for the businessman, and of abundant crops for the farmer. If a woman dreams that she is a washerwoman, she will throw discretion to the winds in her attempts to hold onto an illicit relationship.

Washing

If a person dreams about washing himself, it means that he is proud of the large number of affairs he is having.

Wasp

If a wasp appears in a dream, it means that the dreamer can expect trouble. In the near future, he may receive worrying news that will cause a temporary crisis in his life. He may have problems both in the employment field and in his family or marital life. Often, a dream like this indicates that an argument or friction with the dreamer's partner is possible. The problems that emerge between them will cause rows and even a cooling-off period or a separation. The crisis will only be temporary, and it will pass after some time.

A dream that features a wasp can also indicate the fact that soon the dreamer will receive a bequest from a highly respected person or from a wealthy family member. This is likely to happen as a result of a death or a trip to a distant place.

If the wasp in the dream is the secondary element while its sting is the main topic of the dream, it indicates someone in the dreamer's immediate surroundings who is envious and jealous of him will place obstacles in his path. He is liable to find himself in a situation of loss or of failure that he did not anticipate. The dreamer must be careful of people whose goals he is not completely sure of, and try to get to the bottom of their actions if they seem suspicious to him.

Waste

If a person dreams about wandering through wasteland, it is a sign of failure and uncertainty instead of sure success. If he wastes his fortune, it means that he will be burdened with domestic responsibilities against his will.

Watch

If a person dreams about a watch, it means that he dreamer will be successful as a result of well-planned business strategies. If he looks at a watch to see the time in a dream, it implies that rivals will get the better of him. If he dreams about breaking a watch, it portends a threat of loss and trouble. If the glass falls out of the watch in a dream, it is a sign of carelessness or disagreeable associates. If a woman dreams that she loses a watch, there will be domestic disharmony. A dream about stealing a watch foretells that a dangerous enemy will slander the dreamer. If he dreams about giving a watch as a gift, it means that he will neglect his main business in order to go after trivial and unworthy pastimes.

Water

Dreams about water have many meanings, all connected to the content of the dream. In principle, water is a sign of a blessing. Water in the house symbolizes abundance and an unexpected income, prosperity and plenty, health and success for the whole family. A dream about resting at the side of a flowing stream offers a hint of new possibilities that would reach the dreamer if he were just daring enough to take the first step. If a person dreams that he falls into a lake or river and drowns, he can expect to go through a difficult time after which he will have huge and surprising success. Sailing in a boat on a river or lake implies a possible romantic development.

Water carrier

If a person dreams about water carriers, it means good luck in love and business. If he himself is a water carrier in a dream, he will go up the ladder of advancement.

Waterfall

This type of dream symbolizes a process of purifying and cleansing the toxins that accumulate in both body and mind. The fall reflects the entry of new and renewing energies and a lot of optimism, a flow and a development toward new events. Water symbolizes a new beginning and happiness. There could be a win in a lottery or an unexpected inheritance.

Water lily

If a person dreams about a water lily, or about seeing them growing, it means that he will experience a combination of prosperity and grief.

Watermelon

If a person sees a watermelon in a dream, it implies that the dreamer is propelled through life by vague fears and anxieties. He is not stable: he is dominated by superstitions and allows his fate to be dictated by mystical things.

It seems that the dreamer's mind is not completely stable and firm, and he feels as if he is a leaf blowing in the wind. He is the type of person who seeks answers from scholars and wizards. It seems to him that his fate is predetermined and that he has neither the power nor the ability to change things. This is also the reason why he sometimes does not act in his own behalf, since he feels that no matter what he does, things are predetermined anyway. His inability to change things is liable to lead him to self-destruction, and he must be very careful of this.

This warning is even truer for a person who sees a watermelon with a knife lying next to it in a dream. In such a case, the dreamer must realize that his mental state is poor, and, since he finds it difficult to maintain a normal mental state by himself, that he must not be ashamed of seeking counseling and help. The help of professional person can be very effective.

Waves

If the waves are clear, it means that the dreamer understands exactly what he has to do in a complicated matter. If the waves are muddy or stormy, he will make a fatal error.

Wax

A dream about wax attests to the fact that the dreamer can expect success, even if it is not unqualified. He is blessed with all the necessary traits for success, and success will indeed shine on him, but with one serious reservation: He must avoid involving his emotions and he must exercise only cold reason, otherwise he will fail. His tendency to follow his emotions and intuition is inappropriate – and it is unjustified in this case. He must consult with professional people such as an accountant, an economist and so on in everything to do with business, and not just rely on himself.

Some people interpret a dream about wax as a warning dream. According to this interpretation, the dream warns against extravagance, wastefulness, an ostentatious lifestyle, hedonism, and heedless expenditures. If the dreamer restrains this tendency, and controls his expenditures, the danger will pass. He must be more responsible, thrifty, and calculating. This seems almost impossible to him, but if he does so, he will not get into difficulties and serious financial problems from which he will find it difficult to extricate himself later on.

Wax taper

If a person dreams about lighting wax tapers, it means that he will meet up with long-lost friends at a pleasant event. If he dreams about blowing wax tapers out, it is a sign of disappointment as well as of lost opportunities of meeting valued friends because of illness.

Way

If a person dreams that he loses his way, he can kiss successful deals goodbye unless he manages his business with the utmost care.

Wealth

If a person dreams that he is very wealthy, it means that he has the guts and determination to face and solve life's problems. If he dreams that others are wealthy, it means that his friends will bail him out of risky situations. If a young woman dreams that she belongs to a circle of wealthy people, she has lofty ambitions and will find someone who can help her realize them.

Weasel

If a person dreams that he sees a weasel out hunting, he should be very wary of making friends with former enemies, since they are just looking for an opportunity to destroy him. A dream about killing weasels is a sign of overcoming enemies.

Weather

If a person dreams about the weather, it is a sign of changes in fortune. Advancement will abruptly be replaced by difficulties. If he dreams about hearing or reading the weather report, it implies that he will move house after a great deal of deliberation. However, the move will be to his advantage.

Weaving

If a person dreams about weaving, it means that he will vigorously object to any attempt to prevent him from amassing wealth. If he sees others weaving, it means that his surroundings will be wholesome and comfortable.

Web

If a person dreams about a web, it is a warning dream: it warns him that underhand friends will try to hurt him. If the web in the dream is stiff, he will resist the attacks of jealous people who want to exploit him.

Wedding

There are many different interpretations for a wedding in a dream. In most cases, what determines the meaning of the dream is whether the dreamer is married or single. Sometimes the dreamer can see himself in a marital state that is different than his actual situation. A dream about a wedding expresses a "heart's desire."

If a single person dreams about his wedding, the dream implies that he can expect to receive unpleasant news. Some people interpret such a dream as an expression of a

A B C D E F G H I J K L M N O P Q R S T U V W X Y Z

fierce desire for a relationship, a yearning for marriage.

If a person dreams about the wedding of other people, the dream attests to the fact that joy and happiness will be the dreamer's lot in life.

If a married person dreams about the wedding of other people, it is a sign that the dreamer is deeply jealous of his partner.

If a single woman dreams that she is a bridesmaid, the dream foretells that others will find husbands and marry before her.

If a person dreams about a wedding and the emphasis is on the fact that the guests were particularly happy, the dream predicts a happy marriage for him.

Conversely, if the wedding guests look sad, the dream predicts that the marriage will not last long, and that the separation will be fast.

If a person dreams of receiving a wedding invitation, it is a sign that soon tumultuous and exciting news will reach a close friend. It could be a friend who lives overseas, or it could be a close friend of the dreamer who will be very successful.

If a single person dreams of the point in a wedding where the priest is blessing the couple, the dream implies that the person will find love through matchmaking, or that someone will help him find love. In most cases, this will happen by someone introducing him to his future partner.

If a person dreams of a wedding in which the ring is missing, it is a sign that before he gets married, he will go though a series of problems and misunderstandings with his intended partner. There will be quarrels and conflicts, but in the end, the couple will get married happily.

A dream in which a single woman finds her dress

missing at the altar is a warning that she must get rid of every silly obstacle before the wedding and not get involved in petty things.

A dream about the mother-in-law at a wedding implies that if the bride is rigid in her opinions and is not flexible and tolerant enough, this will harm the couple and even cause them to break up.

A dream about wedding gifts is a sign that material surprises are in the offing.

Wedding clothes

A dream about wedding clothes is a sign that the dreamer will participate in nice new things and make new friends. A dream that features dirty or crumpled wedding clothes implies that he will become alienated from a person for whom he has high regard.

Wedding ring

If a woman dreams that her wedding ring is bright and shiny, it means that she will not have to concern herself about worries and infidelity. If her ring gets lost or broken in her dream, she will suffer grief because of bereavement and incompatibility. If a person sees a wedding ring on someone else's finger, it means that he will not honor his vows and will pursue immoral pleasures.

Wedge

If a person dreams about a wedge, it means that he is liable to become involved in a business dispute that will lead to a severing of relations with relatives or even between lovers.

A B C D E F G H I J K L M N O P Q R S T U V W X Y Z

Wedlock

If a person dreams that he is trapped in miserable wedlock, it means that he will become embroiled in an unfortunate matter. If a young woman dreams that she is dissatisfied with wedlock, it predicts that she will become involved in scandalous affairs. If a married woman dreams about her wedding day, it is a warning that she should brace herself for grief, disillusionment, conflicts and jealousy. If a woman dreams that she is happily and safely married, it is a sign of good luck.

Weeding

If a person dreams about weeding, it means that he will encounter difficulties with an undertaking that ought to bring him honor. If he sees other people weeding in a dream, it means that he is afraid that his adversaries will ruin his plans.

Weeping

If a person dreams that he is weeping, it is a sign that there will be bad news in the family If he sees other people weeping in a dream, it means that there will be a joyous reunion after a period of separation. If a young woman dreams about weeping, it denotes lovers' quarrels that can only be resolved if she is prepared to make compromises.

Weevil

A dream about a weevil is a sign of bad business and deception in love.

Weighing

If a person dreams about weighing, it is a sign of an imminent period of prosperity. If he sets his mind to it, he will accumulate a tidy sum. If he dreams about weighing other people, it means that he will manipulate others into doing whatever he wants. If a young woman dreams that she weighs her lover, he will do her bidding at any time.

Welcome

If a person dreams about receiving a warm welcome into any society, it means that he will acquire distinction and strangers will treat him with respect. His fortune will grow to the desired dimensions. If he dreams that other people are welcomed, it means that his warm and cheerful character will be the key to his success and pleasure in life.

Well

If a person dreams about falling into a well, it is a sign of overwhelming despair. If his dream features a well caving in, his enemies will get the better of him. If he dreams about drawing water from a well, it means that his most urgent desires will be fulfilled. If the water from the well is not pure, there will be unhappy consequences.

If a person sees an empty well, it means that he will be mugged if he confides in strangers. If he sees a well with a pump in it, his prospects are likely to be advanced. If a person dreams about an artesian well, it means that his intelligence will allow him into the realms of knowledge and enjoyment. If he dreams about working in a well, it means that he will have troubles because he is not focused on the correct things.

A B C D E F G H I J K L M N O P Q R S T U V **W** X Y Z

Welsh rarebit

If a person dreams about preparing or eating Welsh rarebit, it means that his affairs will become complicated because he allows himself to be distracted by cunning women and superficial amusements.

Wet

If a person dreams about being wet, it means that a certain type of enjoyment might bring him nothing but loss and disease. It is a warning dream: he should beware of the temptations offered by apparently well-meaning people.

If a young woman dreams that she is soaking wet, she will fall into disgrace as a result of having an affair with a married man.

Wet nurse

If a person dreams about being a wet nurse, it means that he will either be widowed or will have to take care of elderly people or small children. If a woman dreams about being a wet nurse, it means that she will have to support herself.

Whale

Generally, a whale in a dream is interpreted according to the context in which it appears. In most cases, the whale is seen in the sea, in water, and is therefore interpreted as a danger that is liable to emerge from an unexpected quarter. The dreamer has no way of knowing in advance what the danger or its source is, but the dream is prophetic in that it prepares the dreamer for the unknown.

In certain cultures, the whale is interpreted as a symbol of the "cosmic" womb. In other words, dreaming about it can be interpreted as the dreamer's desire to return to the womb and be protected from the world, just as an infant is protected in its mother's womb. Simplistically, this dream can be seen as a kind of yearning of the individual for the love and the warmth that he is lacking in everyday life. He does not necessarily seek it from the "Big Mother," but from a woman he loves, from the "wife of his bosom" or from a lover.

Whalebone

A dream about seeing or working with whalebone is a prediction of a solid and beneficial alliance.

Wheat

Wheat symbolizes abundance, success and happiness, particularly if it appears in a dream in the form of a large, golden wheat field or in bundles of sheaves. However, even a single sheaf of wheat in a dream symbolizes plenty and success.

If wheat appears in a dream in an industrial context, that is, in the context of the beer or whisky that is produced from it, it attests to the fact that the dreamer will enjoy health and longevity, and will live a comfortable and pleasurable life.

Other interpretations link wheat to basic human needs such as bread, water, love and sex. According to this interpretation, the person who dreams about wheat is a modest person who makes do with little. He does not need much more than those basic things, and the minute he has this basis in life, he doesn't ask for the sun and the moon. He makes do with what he has, and is always happy with what he has.

Wheel of fortune

A dream about the wheel of fortune with its astrological symbols reflects the dreamer's feeling of having missed out. This can come to the fore in many areas. The feeling may derive from missing an opportunity to have a serious career in a field the dreamer loves or in a field at which he excels. It may stem from not taking advantage of opportunities to spend more time with the children or devote himself more to his home and family. In any event, the dream also predicts that the dreamer will be given a second chance.

The dream also hints that studying hard will bear fruit. The dreamer will enjoy prosperity and success in anything he turns his hand to, and his labor will yield good dividends.

Wheels

If a person sees wheels revolving quickly in a dream, it means that he will work hard and economically, and will enjoy a happy domestic life. A dream that features stationary or broken wheels is a sign of an absence or a death in his household.

Whetstone

If a person dreams about a whetstone, it informs him of pressing anxieties, and warns him to keep a close tabs on his business affairs if he wants to stay out of trouble. He may have to undertake an unpleasant journey.

Whip

If a person dreams about whipping an attacker, it means that he will earn respect and wealth by industriousness and bravery. A dream about a whip symbolizes unfortunate conflicts and unreliable alliances.

Whirlpool

If a person dreams about a whirlpool, it is a sign that there is great danger to his business on the horizon. He must take great care not to ruin his reputation in some sordid affair.

Whirlwind

If a person dreams that he is in the path of a whirlwind, it implies that he is facing a change that may be catastrophic for him. If a young woman dreams that she is caught in a whirlwind and cannot control her skirt from flying up, she will get involved in a clandestine affair that will become common knowledge and cause her to be ostracized.

Whisky

In most cases, a dream about whisky is a sign of disappointment. If the dream features whisky in bottles, it means that the dreamer will protect his interests carefully and they will increase in consequence. If he dreams about drinking whisky alone, it means that his egoism will drive his friends away. If a person dreams about destroying whisky, it is a sign of losing friends because of miserable behavior. If a person sees or drinks whisky in a dream, it means that he is attempting to accomplish an objective after many setbacks. If he only sees whisky in the dream, it means that he will never accomplish the objective.

Whispering

If a person dreams about whispering, it is a sign that he will be the subject of the malicious gossip of people in his vicinity. If he hears a whisper that is intended to warn him or give him advice, it means that he needs to seek counsel.

Whistling

A dream in which the dreamer sees himself whistling or hears a friend or a stranger whistling attests to the fact that someone is gossiping about him behind his back. It is possible that vicious and harmful rumors about him are being spread, and he is well advised to be on his guard in order to deal with them and refute them.

The dream implies that the gossipmongers have malicious motives and want to cause the dreamer's downfall. They loathe him and are doing everything in their power to get rid of him.

The dreamer should be on the alert, discover the identity of the people who are slandering him and destroy the gossip before it spreads and is much more difficult to deal with.

White lead

If a person dreams about white lead, it is a warning

dream: it warns him that he is endangering members of his family because of his carelessness. Prosperity is also not on solid ground right now.

Whitewash

If a person dreams about whitewashing, it signifies that he wants to win back his friends' approval by kicking disgusting habits and discarding objectionable companions. If a young woman dreams that she is whitewashing, it is a sign that she has devised a sophisticated strategy of deception to win back her lover.

Widow

If a person dreams about being widowed, he can be sure that his spouse will have a long life. A dream about being a widow/er predicts that malevolent people will cause the dreamer many hassles. If an unmarried person dreams about being widowed, he can expect to get married in the future. If a man dreams about marrying a widow, it means that a project that is important to him will collapse and fizzle out.

Widowhood

If a person dreams of being widowed, the dream implies the opposite – his/her spouse can expect a long life.

If a single person has this dream, it implies imminent marriage.

If a person dreams about the state of widowhood when he is not a widower, the dream implies that many plots are being devised behind the dreamer's back, and that someone

A B C D E F G H I J K L M N O P Q R S T U V W X Y Z

is trying to put obstacles in his way and complain about him. The person or people who want to harm him are in his immediate vicinity, and he must be suspicious and not trust anyone – not even people whom he believes could never wish to harm him.

Wife

If the dreamer sees his wife arriving for a visit, it is a sign of a quarrel and strife between the couple. The disputes that will be the couple's lot will not give them any peace. They must be more patient with each other, since if they are not, their relationship is liable to deteriorate to the point of divorce.

Wig

Wearing a wig in a dream is an indication of the dreamer's hesitancy and inability to act without deliberating. The dreamer cannot decide on anything in one fell swoop and be satisfied with his decision. He always feels that if he were to do things differently, perhaps it would be better.

Wearing a wig in a dream also indicates that problems are likely to crop up in the dreamer's love life. There will be a conflict involving the dreamer, who finds it difficult to make decisions in life under the best of circumstances. The dreamer is debating between two potential romantic partners.

If a wig gets lost in a dream, it is a sign that the people the dreamer thought to be his true friends are plotting their revenge on him.

If a person dreams that one of his friends is wearing a

wig, it is a sign that he will receive an anonymous letter bearing good news, or that he will come into a large inheritance quite unexpectedly.

Wild

If a person dreams about running around wildly, it portends that he will fall or have an accident. If he sees other people acting wildly in a dream, it means that setbacks will cause him to be anxious and agitated.

Wild man

If a person dreams about seeing a wild man, it means that his enemies will brazenly try to sabotage his endeavors. If he himself is a wild man in a dream, his plans will not go well.

Wildness / Raging

If a person dreams that he participates in a wild, unruly event that causes him to panic, it means that he is liable to face financial difficulties in the near future.

Will

If a person dreams about writing a will, it is actually a sign of a long and happy life. A dream about making a will is a portent of problems. If a person dreams that his wife or anyone else thinks that a will is disadvantageous to them, it means that soon there will be conflict and turmoil regarding some event. If a person fails to prove a will in a dream, it means that he will run the risk of being slandered. If he loses a will in a dream, it is a bad omen for business. If he

A B C D E F G H I J K L M N O P Q R S T U V W X Y Z

dreams about destroying a will, the dream warns him that he is about to be an accomplice in an act of treachery and fraud.

Willow tree

A dream about a willow tree attests to the fact that the dreamer is in some kind of dilemma concerning his immediate family. The situation with which he is struggling is not easy – in fact, it is almost impossible, and there does not seem to be any way out of it. The dreamer knows that it is almost impossible to improve or fix the family situation as it looks at the moment, and there is no doubt that the psychological pressure exerted on him for this reason is enormous. On the one hand, the dreamer does not want to break up the family unit, with everything that implies, and on the other, he does not see any other way out that will be satisfactory to him and will unite the family. The dilemma he is in is at its height, and only the attitude of the rest of the family can finally determine the direction in which the dreamer will ultimately operate.

Wind

Dreams about winds can serve as a warning sign to the dreamer and his family. A dream that features a gale that causes the house to collapse implies a serious economic downfall. One of the family members may also contract a disease. It is a good idea to undergo medical tests. Wind and rain are a better sign since they herald the winter. This is the time for the dreamer to find a cozy corner at home and think carefully about the steps that can be taken in the forthcoming period of time in order to consolidate his financial situation.

A B C D E F G H I J K L M N O P Q R S T U V **W** X Y Z

Windmill

If a person sees a windmill working in a dream, it means that he will be happy and wealthy. If a dream features a stationary or non-operational windmill, troubles will take him by surprise.

Window

A general dream that features a window is a sign that endless expanses are about to open up before the dreamer. This will cause him to make extreme changes in his life, just as he always wanted to do but didn't dare – or conversely, he will not be able to do so for various reasons. This is the right time to implement the changes he always wanted to make and to exploit the changing trends in his life positively, since they will enable him to implement all the things he dreamed about but did not succeed in bringing off.

If a person sees a closed and barred window in his dream, it implies that he is liable to become criminally involved. He must be careful, since opportunities he comes across are liable to lead him to act in negative ways. He should not listen to advice that may turn out to be bad advice later on, nor should he respond to far-reaching investment proposals or to offers of a partnership that is liable to yield rotten fruit. He must examine his potential actions carefully before doing anything.

A wide-open window in a dream is a hint that the dreamer must grab a bargain with two hands or take an opportunity that he can exploit right now, because it won't recur.

A broken window is a sign that an exceptional adventure

or affair in which the dreamer is involved is about to end. The affair or adventure is very unusual by nature – a kind of once-in-a-lifetime thing. This could be cheating on a spouse, embezzlement, a partnership in something specific (it could be some kind of crime), and so on.

If the dreamer sees himself looking out of a window, it is a sign that a quarrel in which he was involved with a person close to him will come to an end and be resolved satisfactorily. The dreamer will overcome the crisis, the friendship will become real again, and the dispute will end as if it had never happened.

If, in contrast, a person dreams that someone else is looking at him through the window, it is a warning dream. The dreamer must be careful of malicious gossip that is liable to cause him damage not just at the present time but also in the future. The dreamer must stay away from gossip-mongers who can slander him and cause him mental anguish, since the false accusations and defamation are liable to be his lot for a long time, and it will be difficult for him to get shake them off.

Wine

A person who dreams that wine causes him to be light-headed and act foolishly is a reasonable and logical person who allows himself to let go only when he is free of the burden of reason that weighs heavily on him.

A dream about wine-tasting in a wine-cellar attests to the possibility of an improvement in the dreamer's economic situation – not necessarily as a result of hard work or successful business initiatives. It could be a win in a lottery.

If a person dreams of breaking a bottle of wine, it

indicates a period of transition between success and failure. The dreamer may have succeeded in everything he has undertaken until now, but things are about to change for the worse without any prior warning.

A dream about barrels of wine overlooking the sea or stored securely in the belly of a large ship attests to financial security in the future. A dream in which the dreamer drinks wine that was poured for him from a barrel in a dark cellar indicates a successful business trip. A young girl or young woman who dreams about drinking wine is liable to find herself in a crisis with her boyfriend. There could also be unpleasant events such as the cancellation of an engagement or wedding.

Wine cellar

If a person dreams about a wine cellar, it means that he can look forward to wonderful times im.

Wineglass

If a person dreams about a wine glass, it signifies that he will be deeply wounded by a disappointment.

Wings

If a person dreams about having wings, it is a sign of his fear for the safety of someone who is traveling far away. If he sees the wings of birds or fowl in a dream, it signifies that he will eventually overcome all his problems and will achieve wealth and status.

A
B
C
D
E
F
G
H
I
J
K
L
M
N
O
P
Q
R
S
T
U
V
W
X
Y
Z

Winter

A dream in which the dreamer sees gloomy weather, dark rain clouds, heavy showers, cold, gray weather, snow, storms and strong winds hints at success. In most cases, the dream implies that the dreamer will reach enlightenment by means of which he will become known in certain fields. The dreamer can expect to experience elation and become able to reach a level of high consciousness and make use of it in his everyday life. As a result of such experiences, it will be easier for him to achieve success in life and make his wishes and desires come true. The goals in the dreamer's life are about to change, and he will feel more satisfied with his life even if he succeeds in realizing fewer of the goals he set himself in the past.

It is important to mention that a dream about winter can also reflect a "wintry" feeling only. The dreamer need not actually see one of the signs of winter in his dream in order to know that it is about winter. The feeling itself is sufficient, and it is individual for each person. The very fact that the dreamer is aware of winter, or that things happen in the middle of winter, is enough.

Wire

If a person dreams about wire, it means that he will make many short trips that will not be to his advantage. A dream that features old or rusty wire means that the dreamer is bad-tempered and makes the people around him miserable. If he sees a wire fence in a dream, it means that he will be cheated in a deal.

Wisdom

If a person possesses wisdom in a dream, it means that he will be courageous in difficult circumstances. He will overcome them and elevate himself to a higher plane of living. If he lacks wisdom in the dream, it means that he is not exploiting his talents at all.

Witch / Wizard

A dream about a visit to a witch or wizard is positive and attests to a mystical event that can be expected soon. The dreamer will be in a new place where he will meet somebody or experience something he has never experienced before. This event will influence his life. He may receive a job offer that will be compatible with his most secret wishes. Alternatively, the meeting may affect him in the romantic realm. In many cases, the dream implies an adventurous step that the dreamer would never have dared to think about if he had not gotten into a peculiar situation that enabled him to deviate from his everyday habits and strike out in a new and completely different direction.

Witness

If a person dreams about bearing witness against other people, it means that trivial incidents will cause him great distress. If other people bear witness against him in a dream, he will have no choice but to decline to help friends in order to preserve his own interests. If he dreams that he is a witness for someone who is guilty, it is a sign that he will be implicated in some shameful matter.

Wizard

If a person dreams about a wizard, it means that he will have a large family that will cause him displeasure and inconvenience. For young people, this dream is a prediction of loss and breakups.

Wolf

If a dream features of a wolf in any form, it signifies bad news. The news will be even more terrible if the dream is about a pack of wolves. If a person dreams about a wolf, it indicates that one of his employees is a thief and a traitor. If he dreams about killing a wolf, it means that he will outwit enemies who seek to discredit him. A dream about hearing a wolf's howl tells the dreamer that there is a plot to beat him in straightforward competition.

Woman

If a person sees a particularly old woman in a dream, it is a sign that he is facing spiritual or religious enlightenment. He will become increasingly interested in matters that are connected to mysticism, spirituality and lofty things, and will dabble in them more and more. The interest that these things arouse in him will cause him to relate to this field in a more serious way, and he will gradually change his lifestyle and his world-view.

An especially ugly woman who appears in a dream implies that the dreamer will not find repose. People around him will bother him and nag him, and will not leave him alone. This will undermine his mental state if he does not know how to take things in the correct proportion and relate to them lightly. He should even know how to laugh at thc whole thing and regard it with humor. This phase will be brief and will pass rapidly, so it is not worthwhile getting into a bad mood or letting emotion dominate reason.

If the dreamer sees more than one woman in a dream, the dream implies that he is about to embark on some kind of social affair that will engender a great deal of gossip that may be particularly malicious. It is possible that some social move made by the dreamer, such as friendship and contact with certain elements, is the cause of the gossip around him. In any case, this gossip will only die down and be forgotten if the dreamer knows how to keep a low profile and is not inordinately conspicuous in his actions.

Wooden shoe

If a person dreams about a wooden shoe, it is indicative of solitary wandering and poverty. In love, it is a sign of infidelity.

Woodpile

If a person dreams about a woodpile, it portends problems in business and love.

Woods

If a person dreams about the woods, it is a sign of changes in his affairs: if the woods are green, the change will be positive. If they are dry and brown, it will be disastrous. If they are on fire, his plans will reach fruition and bring lucrative results.

If a person dreams about dealing in fircwood, it mcans that his determined hard work will lead to wealth.

Wool

If a person dreams about wool, the dream predicts business expansion and prosperity. If the wool in the dream is dirty or stained, he will look for a job with people who despise his beliefs.

Work

If a person dreams about working hard, it means that he will be successful by means of focusing his will and energy on the desired goal. If he sees other people at work in his dream, it means that he is surrounded by an atmosphere of optimism. If he dreams about looking for work, it means that he will profit from some inexplicable event.

Workshop

A dream that features a workshop implies that the dreamer is on the correct path in life and is succeeding in achieving the goals he set himself. Not only will he achieve these goals, but he will ultimately realize other aspirations in life that he never dreamed he would realize.

If a tidy workshop appears in a dream, it means that a window has opened up in the dreamer's life, permitting him to accomplish other objectives in the professional arena. If the dreamer is involved in trade or marketing, his business will prosper and bloom.

If the workshop in the dream looks untidy and chaotic, the dreamer will indeed enjoy great social success and a wide circle of friends, but from the professional point of view, he will not succeed in notching up significant achievements. If the dreamer works with raw materials and depends on their regular delivery, he must prepare for a loss or a non-delivery of the raw materials, and this will harm his work and his revenues.

Worm

A dream about a worm is the same as a dream about a snake, except that the dreamer, while he is dreaming, minimizes the importance of the message of the dream, so it seems to him that he is dreaming about a worm. Thus, every dream about a worm should be interpreted like a dream about a snake, but less resolutely.

Wound

If a person dreams about being wounded, it is a sign of distress and problems in business. If he dreams that other people are wounded, he will be judged unfairly by his friends. If he dreams about dressing a wound, it implies that soon he will be lucky.

Wreath

If a person dreams about a wreath of fresh flowers, it means that soon he will have the chance to make a lot of money. A dream that features a dry wreath is a sign of sickness and problems in love. A dream about a bridal wreath means that things that are unclear will sort themselves out for the best.

Wreck

If a person dreams about seeing a wreck in a dream, it

means that he will be hounded by worries about poverty and failure in business. A dream about a railway wreck in which he is not involved means that someone close to him will be in an accident. It could also mean that the dreamer will have business problems.

Wrestling

A dream in which a person sees himself wrestling with someone attests to the fact that he is going through a period of disputes and strife. He is deeply troubled by serious differences of opinion with a person who is close to him or with someone at work. It is a serious dispute, not a minor passing crisis. The path to resolving the conflict is not easy and requires large resources of emotional strength on the part of the dreamer, because he is emotionally involved in the matter. His anger and fury are so great that he wants to solve everything by means of physical force rather than by talking and clarifying. He is well advised to find ways to calm down in order to think logically about a solution to the conflict. It may be a good idea for him to distance himself physically from the object of his anger for a "chilling out" period so that his peace of mind can be restored. Physical force will not solve problems – it will only worsen them. The dream constitutes a kind of mirror of the whole situation, enabling things to be seen from the correct perspective.

If a person sees himself attempting to prevent wrestling in a dream, the dream is positive, and implies that the dreamer can expect good health and a long life.

If a person sees himself wrestling with an animal in a dream, it implies that he can expect financial success and honor. The dreamer will become the center of things socially, people will cherish and respect him, and he will enjoy economic success.

If a dreamer sees himself wrestling with a person who is significantly stronger than he is, it is a sign of the debility from which the dreamer will suffer. This refers to a poor physical condition that is liable to cause serious diseases. It will be difficult for the dreamer to cope with these diseases by himself, and it is highly likely that he will require protracted medical treatment and even hospitalization in order to get back into shape.

Writing

A dream that features the action of writing (with a pen or pencil on paper), with the dreamer himself doing the writing, implies that the dreamer's future is somehow involved with something to do with acquiring an education: studies, higher education or acquiring a profession.

A dream in which the dreamer sees someone who is familiar to him writing hints that the dreamer will soon receive news or an announcement with positive contents.

A dream in which the dreamer sees an unfamiliar person writing indicates the feeling of loneliness that is bothering the dreamer.

X

X-ray

If a person dreams about an X-ray, it is an indication of fear of poor health or serious financial problems. A dream about being X-rayed means that some authority will try to disclose something that would be damaging to him and his family. The dreamer must find out what it is in order to protect himself.

Xylophone

If a person dreams about playing a xylophone, it predicts a delightfully happy occasion. A dream that features a broken xylophone means that he ignored advice and opportunities during times of trouble and is advised not to do so again.

Y

Yacht

If a person sees a yacht in a dream, it means that he will have a break from work and cares. If a yacht is grounded in a dream, it means that various plans for fun will not materialize.

Yankee

If a person dreams about a Yankee, it is a sign that he will remain loyal and dutiful; if he is not careful, however, he will be defrauded in some deal.

Yardstick

If a person dreams about a yardstick, it indicates that although his business will be unusually brisk, he will be overcome with worry.

Yarn

If a dream features yarn, it predicts success in business and an industrious partner at home. If a young woman dreams about working with yarn, it means that she will find an excellent husband who will be proud of her.

A
B
C
D
E
F
G
H
I
J
K
L
M
N
O
P
Q
R
S
T
U
V
W
X
Y
Z

Yawn

If a person sees himself yawning in a dream, it implies that he is not alert to the possibilities that are presenting themselves and to the events that are occurring around him. He is therefore in real danger, since there are people who are undermining him both at work and in the family with the aim of stripping him of his assets.

Yearning

If a person dreams about yearning for someone, it means that he will soon receive good news from faraway friends. If a young woman dreams that her lover is yearning for her, she will soon receive a longed-for proposal. If she dreams that she tells her lover that she is yearning for him, she will be abandoned.

Yeast

It almost goes without saying that a dream about yeast implies that the dreamer can anticipate prosperity and growth, and even if he does not feel this right now, in the future everything will prosper and grow for him. His financial and material situation will be good, and if he is cultivating a business, it will thrive. Having said that, he must not rest on his laurels, since if he does not plan his moves meticulously, he is liable to lose everything. He must be on the alert and not slack off for a moment, since the situation is liable to deteriorate if he does not make sure to keep his finger on the pulse.

Yellow bird

If a person sees a yellow bird darting around in a dream, it means that he will be petrified of the future as a result of some momentous event. If the yellow bird in the dream is sick or dead, it means that he will suffer for another person's stupidity.

Yew tree

If a person dreams about a yew tree, it is a sign of disease and disillusionment. If a dream features a dead and bare yew tree, it portends a tragic death in his family, for which no material possessions can compensate. If a young woman dreams that she sits under a yew tree, she will be tormented with doubts about her lover's fidelity. If she dreams that her lover is standing near a yew tree, she will hear that he is ill or unlucky. If she admires a yew tree in a dream, she will be ostracized by her family because of choosing the wrong man.

Yield

If the dreamer yields to the will of someone else, it is a sign that he will waste a wonderful opportunity of advancement because of pathetic vacillation. If he dreams that other people yield to him, he will be granted unique privileges and will be promoted above all his colleagues. If his hard work yields poorly, worries and anxiety are in the offing.

Yoke

If a person dreams about seeing a yoke, it means that he

will conform to the desires and customs of others against his will. A dream about yoking oxen means that the dreamer's subordinates will accept and obey whatever he suggests or says. If he dreams about failing to yoke oxen, it means that he will worry about a friend's bad conduct.

Yolk

An egg yolk in a dream usually foretells good and successful things for the dreamer. Just as the yolk is not self-standing, but generally appears in the egg, it is advisable to look at the entry for *Egg* and combine the interpretation of the yolk with that of the egg. If the yolk in the dream looks particularly conspicuous, the dream should be interpreted positively, since as we said before, a yolk expresses optimism, good news and glad tidings.

Young

If a person dreams about young people, it implies that he will make up family quarrels and make plans for new business endeavors. A dream about being young again means that he will try in vain to retrieve lost opportunities. If he dreams about seeing young people at school, it means that he will be prosperous.

Yule log

A dream about a yule log means that the dreamer will attend happy and festive events that he has been anticipating.

Z

Zebra

Without any doubt, this is a warning dream. The dream warns the dreamer of a fatal accident, of a very serious accident that may not be fatal, or of a serious disease. Whatever the case may be, the dreamer himself is involved; the dream does not refer to a member of his family or any other person who is close to him. As a result, he must pay attention to this warning. It is in his power to change this "fate": he must know how to conduct himself with extreme caution during the forthcoming period of time. This may refer to the way he drives his car or behaves as a pedestrian, or to the extent to which he is attuned to the organs in his body. Every signal from an organ in his body can hint at some kind of problem that needs to be examined. The name of the game is not to neglect anything. Ignoring any kind of pain, which is liable to signal the onset of a disease, will not help. The dreamer must deal with any problem quickly by consulting with a physician and not neglecting it. If he does this, he may be able to prevent the evil that is in store for him.

Zenith

If a person dreams about a zenith, it implies prosperity and the successful choice of a mate.

Zephyrs

If a person dreams about zephyrs, it means that he will give up wealth for love, and his love will be reciprocated. If a young woman dreams that she hears the gentle zephyr and feels sad, she will miss her lover, who was compelled to travel far from her.

Zinc

A dream about working with zinc or seeing it means good progress and brisk business. If a person dreams about zinc ore, it means that he will soon enjoy success.

Zipper

If a person dreams about a zipper, he can begin to plan the wedding of a member of his family. A zipper that does not appear in an article of clothing can also refer to a surprise of a large amount of money from somewhere. Dreams about a zipper are typical of a period during which the dreamer finds treasures or wins a lottery.

Zodiac

If a person dreams about the zodiac, it is a symbol of peace, prosperity and economic and social success following a lot of effort and hard work. A dream that features a peculiar zodiac means that he will have to fight off some impending sorrow. If he dreams that he is studying the zodiac, it means that he will become well-known because of his connection with strangers.

Zoo

A dream about a zoo implies that the dreamer can make his wishes come true. He can set his ideas in motion. He must know that his dreams can be realized.

If a person sees himself walking through a zoo on his own in a dream, it is a sign that someone will soon manage to irritate him and cause him great disappointment. In contrast, if he sees himself walking through a zoo with his family, the dream implies that his hopes will materialize, sometimes in ways that he cannot foresee at the moment.

A dream about a husband and wife visiting a zoo means that the dreamer is nurturing false expectations and will ultimately be very disappointed. As great as his expectations are, so his disappointments will be.

According to another version: A dream about a visit to a zoo bears glad tidings, mainly on two planes – the social and the domestic. The dreamer will be surrounded by friends and people who care about him and will never find himself alone. His family, too, whether it already exists or whether it will exist in the future, will be strong and supportive. The dream does not promise the dreamer success on the economic or professional planes, but implies that he will enjoy success and calmness in anything to do with his social life and basic security. The dream actually hints at the existence of basic security in the dreamer's life. This will enable him to push ahead in life – in other fields as well. The dreamer can be absolutely sure that he enjoys stable "backing" and the total support of the people around him. The feeling of inner tranquillity that will accompany him through life will give him the courage to try out new and fascinating experiences.

A B C D E F G H I J K L M N O P Q R S T U V W X Y **Z**

A FULL LIST OF ALL THE ENTRIES THAT APPEAR IN THIS GIANT ENCYCLOPEDIA

A

C

D

E

F

G

H

I

J

K

L

M

N

O

P

Q

U

V

W

X

Y

Z